For my good friend Mike,

thank you for

moving to Ponte Vedra!

You are a welcome

breathe of fresh

air and good fun!

Peace,
Bob

LIGHT IN THE GARDEN

THE IGNATIAN PATH TO FORGIVENESS, INCLUSION, AND LOVE

Five Years Later
A Second Time Through
Annotation 19
of the
Spiritual Exercises
of
Ignatius Loyola

September 18, 2016 to May 20, 2017

Robert C. Hart

LIGHT IN THE GARDEN

ISBN: 978-0-692-91697-1

Book design by Sarah E. Holroyd (http://sleepingcatbooks.com)
Cover photo of the meditation bench at Serendipity

For my wife, Sallie Ann,
and for our four children,
Rob, Will, Melissa, and Jennifer

LIST OF PHOTOGRAPHS

TABLE OF CONTENTS

ACKNOWLEDGEMENTS

MY DEEPEST appreciation goes to Sallie Ann Hart, my wife of thirty-five years, and counting. She has been traveling on this journey with me since long before I realized it was a spiritual journey. Of course, I knew that she was a Catholic, though I had no idea what it meant to her that we had to be married by a Presbyterian minister. I considered myself quite understanding when she excused herself to attend Mass every Sunday for twenty five years. She never pushed me to join her, or complained that I had no faith. However, from the moment ten years ago, when I first expressed an interest in exploring Catholicism, Sallie Ann has steadfastly supported my effort. We have traveled this spiritual road together, from the Jesuits at Georgetown, to RCIA in Houston, to Franciscan mysticism in Assisi, to the footsteps of Saint Paul in Turkey and Greece. She joined me in prayer and meditation each day for almost ten months when I went through the Spiritual Exercises of Ignatius five years ago. She has done so again during the past two-hundred and forty-four days. Without her, none of this would have happened.

Sister Joan Gabbin was my spiritual advisor when I first did the Ignatian Spiritual Exercises. There are no words sufficient to express my gratitude for her support and friendship during that extraordinary part of my journey. Since then, Sister Joan has been a co-conspirator in the Sister Parish Ministry and my efforts working for Justice and Peace in the Diocese of Saint Augustine. Her love has no boundaries.

My good friend Chris Dorment played a crucial role in my faith journey when he invited me to join the Arrupe Advisory Board of the Woodstock Theological Center at Georgetown University three

years before I became a Catholic. He continues to inspire me to be a better person, and a better Catholic. My close friend Peter Kaplan has inspired me at numerous points along the way, choosing to be baptized as an Episcopal at about the same time that I became Catholic.

My deep and active faith would not be possible without the love and support I have experienced from numerous members of the Catholic clergy. I owe an incalculable debt of gratitude to those listed here alphabetically, and to many more: Monsignor Keith Brennan, Sister Ilia Delio, Bishop Felipe Estevez, Father Juan Reyes Fabian, Jim Finley, Father Frank Iacona, Sister Kim Jordan, Father Gap LoBiondo, Father Tom Mailloux, Father Richard Rohr, Father John Robbins, Deacon Dan Scrone, the Carmelites at Futuro Vivo-Sister Eva, Sister Inez, Sister Kristina, and Father Mario Serrano. They may find some of my understandings and beliefs to be mildly heretical, for which I apologize in advance. The doctrinal errors are mine alone.

I owe a great deal to my Living School "Skype group"—Evan Miller, Matt Mumber, Nora Smith, and Claire Pamplin—along with the others in my small group, my cohort, and the staff and faculty. They have kept my faith alive and growing. All the leaders and missionaries in the Sister Parish Ministry at Our Lady Star of the Sea and in the Dominican Republic bring me closer every day to the true meaning of service in my faith.

This list is not exhaustive. Several stand out in particular, including Don Barnhorst, Bob Lopresti, Theresa Kenny, Katie Houser, Diane Foley, Dan Scheuble, and Kevin Bing. Not a day goes by that I do not encounter Christ in yet another person, growing from the experience.

I cannot end these acknowledgements without expressing my deepest gratitude for Maggie, our Texas black dog, my constant companion and closest friend.

Bob Hart
July 2017

PREFACE

A pupil once asked the Master, "Why does the Torah tell us to place God's Holy Words upon our hearts? Why does it not tell us to place them in our hearts?" The Master answers, "It is because as we are, our hearts are closed, and we cannot place the holy words in our hearts. So, we place them on top of our hearts. And there they stay until, one day, the heart breaks, and the words fall in."

WHAT FOLLOWS is a very personal book about my faith journey, the latest stage of which began ten years ago in the cardiac recovery room at Banner Good Samaritan Hospital in Phoenix, Arizona. I was there recovering from triple bypass surgery, following my third heart attack over a three-month period. Still in the fog of anesthesia, intubated and unable to speak, only vaguely aware of my whereabouts, I awakened with a powerful sense of urgency. For the first time in my life, I felt a desperate need to know who I was and why I was alive. My heart had indeed broken. Little did I know that God's Holy Words had fallen in.

The journey from the hospital bed in Phoenix to the meditation bench in my garden in Ponte Vedra Beach has not been straight, but it has been constant. Each time I think I have arrived, I realize I have only just begun. T.S. Eliot says it very well, *"What we call the beginning is often the end. And to make an end is to make a beginning. The end is where we start from."*

One of the lessons I have learned over and over again is that I am not unique, nor is my faith journey. Countless numbers of men and women have been asking life's deep questions since the very moment that humans realized they were humans. More than eight hundred years before Christ, great thinkers in China, India, Persia, and the Middle East came to surprisingly similar answers to the primary moral questions. The earliest teachers in every part of the world and in every age provided guidance for their students and followers, leaving behind road maps and instructions.

My earliest advice was to keep things simple, listen carefully, and go slow. Of course, I ignored that most of the time. Some of my journey, particularly what is called the Rite of Christian Initiation for Adults, followed a precise script and was carefully managed. As a general rule, however, I read everything I could find about spirituality and personal growth, following threads of thought wherever they led.

About six years ago, shortly after Sallie Ann and I moved to our new house from Houston, Texas, I learned about a book called *The Spiritual Exercises of Ignatius Loyola*. When I finally had a chance to read it, I realized it was essentially an instruction manual for spiritual discovery. Ignatius described his own path to conversion. He wrote his book to assist others, both in making their individual journeys, and, perhaps more important, in advising and guiding still others seeking spiritual conversion.

Ignatius Loyola

As described by *Ignatian Spirituality*, Saint Ignatius Loyola was born in 1491, one of 13 children of a family of minor nobility in northern Spain. As a young man, he was inflamed by the ideals of courtly love and knighthood and dreamed of doing great deeds. But in 1521, he was gravely wounded in a battle with the French. While recuperating, Ignatius experienced a conversion. Reading the lives of Jesus and the saints made him happy and aroused desires in him to do great things. He realized that these feelings were clues to God's direction for him. Over the years, he became expert in the art of **spiritual direction**. Over the period 1522 to 1524, he collected his insights, prayers, and suggestions in a book called *Spiritual Exercises*, intended primarily as a guide for spiritual directors leading someone through a conversion or discernment process. With a small group of friends, Ignatius founded the Society of Jesus, or the Jesuits. He conceived the Jesuits as "contemplatives in action."

He described the Exercises as follows:

> By the Spiritual Exercises is meant every way of examining one's conscience, of meditating, of contemplating, of praying vocally and mentally, and of performing other spiritual actions, as will be said later. For as strolling, walking and running are bodily Exercises, so every way of preparing and disposing the soul to rid itself of all the disordered tendencies, and, after it is rid, to seek and find the Divine Will as to the management of one's life for the salvation of the soul, is called a Spiritual Exercise.

Ignatius divided the Exercises into four parts:

First, the consideration and contemplation on the **sins**;
Second, the **life of Christ** our Lord up to Palm Sunday inclusively;
Third, the **Passion of Christ** our Lord; and,
Fourth, the **Resurrection and Ascension**, with the three Methods of Prayer.

For centuries, the Exercises were most commonly done as a "long retreat" of about thirty days in solitude and silence. In recent years, the most common way for lay people to do the Exercises is Annotation 19, a "retreat in daily life," which involves a program of daily prayer and meditations, lasting from eight to ten months. As with other forms of Ignatian retreat, Annotation 19 entails a commitment to keeping a journal. This is my journal.

The Annotation 19 Exercises begin with a Preparation Period, followed by the four Ignatian parts, referred to as Ignatian Weeks, each lasting for several calendar weeks. I have followed the Handbook for Annotation 19 written by Father Joseph Tetlow. The Handbook includes a prayer and a goal for most Calendar Weeks, and a scripture reading or thought piece for each day of the week. I have included the prayers, goals, and daily readings as "directions" at the beginning of each daily reflection. Directions are italicized. My reflections, in standard font, begin with several characters in bold font.

INTRODUCTION

FIVE YEARS ago, from September 4, 2011 to June 24, 2012, I did Annotation 19 of the Spiritual Exercises of Ignatius Loyola. Almost every day for more than two hundred and fifty days, I spent an hour or two (often longer, very seldom any shorter) praying, meditating, and writing down my reflections in a journal. Sister Joan Gabbin of Our Lady Star of the Sea Catholic Church provided spiritual direction, guiding me through the Exercises. We followed the Handbook for Annotation 19, the *Exercises in Daily Life*, written by Father Joseph Tetlow, the Director of the Montserrat Jesuit Retreat House in Lake Dallas, Texas. I published my journal in 2012, in a book entitled *One Man's Journey*.

On September 18, 2016, I will begin Annotation 19 for a second time. I will do the Exercises without a Spiritual Director. Maggie, thank God, will be with me each morning, again starting at 6:00 with prayer in the library, followed by reading each day's Scripture or thought piece, then reading it again. On most days, we hope to walk down to the bench in the meditation garden to meditate, both about the reading, and about whatever comes up. When we return to the library, I will sit in the leather chair to reflect and write in my journal. Maggie will curl up in her bed by the garden door. Most days, the process takes about three hours. Obviously, the process will change when I travel, which will be at least monthly when the mission schedule picks up again in January. My intention is to develop a suitable routine for the Exercises each morning in the Dominican Republic, or wherever I happen to be.

Why Annotation 19 again, and why now?

My personal journey in the five years since I finished the Exercises and published my journal has certainly not been quiet. Like everyone else on the planet, I am a new person every second of every day, sometimes changed to a noticeable extent. For me, the greatest change in who I am has been spiritual. My faith in God, and the small part I play in His great creation, have continued to grow stronger, even as they have changed and evolved. I am now more comfortable in my personal relationship with God, and, even more important, I have found a very rewarding place in two new *communities of encounter* (borrowing the phrase from Pope Francis): The first is the *Living School* community, which consists primarily of professors, lecturers, and students of the Living School at the Center for Action and Contemplation in Albuquerque, New Mexico. There are now more than 360 graduates of the two-year program, with another 500 students enrolled or accepted. Applications for the cohort of 2018–2020 will be accepted beginning in June, 2017. The second community consists of the more than 600 missionaries and the thousands of villagers and patients who have been touched by the *Sister Parish Ministry* of Our Lady Star of the Sea Catholic parish in Ponte Vedra Beach, Florida.

Among other things, these two communities, both gifts from God, participate with Him as He momently creates me, converts me, and increases my consciousness of the universe. The Living School is an experiential faith *learning* project that *feeds my head*. The Sister Parish Ministry is an experiential faith *service* project that *feeds my heart*.

My faith is different today, just as I am different and the world is different. I want to better know this new person I have become, and understand him in the context of the new world. Once again, I want to meet Christ each day in the quiet rhythm of Ignatius—*patiently, delicately,* and *deeply* **seeing** Him in my evolving faith. The Exercises provide a perfect environment and a sound program for this encounter.

The Living School

Father Richard Rohr launched the Living School at his Center for Action and Contemplation in Albuquerque, New Mexico, in 2013. Officially, the Living School is rather well described to applicants in this brief, but accurate, announcement.

> The Living School for Action and Contemplation offers a unique opportunity to a select group of students to deepen engagement with their truest selves and with the world. Discover your authentic identity and grow your capacity to embody this calling in the world. Through rigorous study and contemplative practice, awaken to the pattern of reality—God's loving presence with and in all things. Embrace a rich heritage of faith from the Christian mystical tradition. Learn from three of the greatest living contemplative teachers, Living School core faculty Father Rohr, Cynthia Bourgeault, and James Finley.
>
> The Living School welcomes applicants who are committed to both contemplation and action, who are willing to receive the lessons of darkness and suffering, and who are open to profound transformation and change of consciousness. The Living School is an "emergent" or para-school, on the edge of the inside; it is not affiliated with any church or institution of higher education. As such, formal degrees or certification are not offered. The reward is the experience itself—learning and practices that can support students' continued growth as fully human, God-indwelled beings.

It is said that the first pancake is always sacrificed to the pan. I joined 180 other students in the first cohort, the "pancake cohort," of the Living School in September, 2013. All of us were learning as we went, not just the students, but the professors and the staff as well. For me, the Living School was an intensely powerful experience, beginning on the first day of the application process, extending through every day of exhaustive reading for two years, and continuing into the present.

While there is a lot of teaching about contemplation, including a strong admonition that each student should develop and maintain a daily "practice," the Living School for me was an indescribably delightful deep dive into the rich tradition of Christian mysticism. Before my Living School experience, I had dismissively considered a mystic as someone involved in the "supernatural" or "paranormal." While all of the mystics certainly explored the big mysteries of life, death, and God, the best description of a mystic is simply someone who has lived through a transformative spiritual experience and then written about it. While most of the mystics were learned theologians and long-serving clergy in the church, others were ordinary men and women capable of describing an extraordinary event.

Father Rohr writes that "Christianity isn't primarily a moral matter; it's a mystical matter that only works when the mind and heart operate together with new eyes that *see* everything at depth." I knew virtually nothing about the Christian mystics when I entered the Living School. As I went through instruction to become a Catholic in 2008 and 2009, I was given a small taste of the rich tradition of Catholic theologians and saints, but only a taste. The two years of the Living School were a complete immersion in what Father Rohr calls the Perennial Tradition.

Starting with a lecture from Father Rohr that walked us through the long history of Christian mysticism, our cohort was assigned as many as four books a week, each seemingly longer and more filled with messages than anything I was accustomed to reading. The long list of great men and women includes many names I had never heard:

Philo (d. 50)
Plotinus (d. 270)
Anonymous author of the Cloud of Unknowing (500?)
Pseudo-Dionysius (d. 518–528?)
Hugh of St. Victor (d. 1141)
St Bernard of Clairvaux (d. 1153)
Hildegard of Bingen (d. 1179)
St. Clare (d. 1253)
Bonaventure (d. 1274)
Mechthild of Magdeburg (d. 1285)
John Duns Scotus (d. 1308)
Marguerite Porete (d. 1310)
John Tauler (d. 1361)
St. Catherine of Siena (d. 1380)
John of Ruusbroec (d. 1381)
Julian of Norwich (d. 1416)
Theresa of Avila (d. 1582)
Jacob Boehme (d. 1624)
Brother Lawrence (d. 1691)
Thérèse of Lisieux (d. 1897)
Raimondo Pannikar (d. 2010)

These were not just great thinkers whose works I had not read. I had literally never heard of them!

There were also many familiar names on the reading list. We read, or read again, Aristotle (d. 322 BCE) and Plato (d. 347 BCE), St. Augustine (d. 430), Dante (d. 1321), Immanuel Kant (d. 1804), William James (d. 1910), Karl Jaspers (d. 1969), and Martin Heidegger (d. 1976). The on-line lectures opened me to very different levels of understanding of these great thinkers. Reading them again in the Living School took me on research journeys that covered virtually all my university classes in philosophy, history, and Western Civilization.

We read the poets Rumi (d. 1273), Hafez (d. 1389), Gerard Manley Hopkins (d. 1889), Rainer Maria Rilke (d. 1926), T.S. Eliot (d. 1965), and Mary Oliver. I was frequently reminded of my lawyer and dear friend Rupert Simpson, who died tragically at age 43. We traveled and worked together in Poland extensively from 1990 to 1993. He would finish each day reading poetry, often only two or three lines. Then he would walk around the room repeating the lines, stopping occasionally to "wax eloquent" about life, death, and love.

We learned that it was Pseudo-Dionysius the Areopagite who said that knowledge of the truth "comes only by means of this sincere, spontaneous, and entire surrender of yourself and all things." And St. Jerome (d. 420) famously said that "Plato located the soul of man in the head; Christ located it in the heart." Julian of Norwich taught that "All shall be well, and all shall be well and all manner of thing shall be well." It was like drinking water from a fire hose, each new mystic reaching deeper and deeper into unexplored places in my mind and heart.

Some of the greatest mystics received special treatment, involving multiple lectures and lots of reading. We were introduced at depth to Francis of Assisi (d. 1226), Meister Eckhart (d. 1327), John of the Cross (d. 1591), Teilhard de Chardin (d. 1955), and, especially, Thomas Merton (d. 1968). I continue to read and study these great men today. What an incredible list!

All three of our primary professors—Father Rohr, Jim Finley, and Cynthia Bourgeault—qualify as contemporary mystics. Finley was a novice at the Trappist Monastery of Gethsemane, with Thomas Merton as his novice master. Ilia Delio, one of the most powerful guest lecturers and a Teilhard scholar, opened our minds to the connection between quantum physics, the Big Bang, Genesis, and the Prologue of John's Gospel.

After two years in the Living School, reading the assigned authors and many others who came up in the process, and more than a year after being "sent out," continuing to read the mystics, who are my favorites? Who are my "magnificent seven" teachers? While I learned, and continue to learn, from almost every one of these great men and women, there are three living teachers, and four from the past, whose work has particularly touched my heart, thereby entering my deepest faith place. Father Rohr, Jim Finley, and Ilia Delio are the three still alive. Eckhart, John of the Cross, Teilhard, and Merton are the four that have died.

I read and love **Father Rohr** every day because I receive his daily reflection in my email, and because it uniformly speaks to me where I am that day.

The love I feel for **Jim Finley** is inexplicable (perhaps ineffable?). I can go long periods without talking to him, or listening to his tapes, or reading his books, and then something brings us together and it is as though I never left him.

Ilio Delio is both an old friend (I worked with her at Woodstock), and an incredible speaker and theologian. I am embarrassed to admit how often I hardly noticed Ilia at the Woodstock meetings, considering her an incredibly bright, but very quiet theologian. I was never certain what it was she studied. Imagine how much more I might have learned!

Meister Eckhart speaks to me as much as anyone I have known all my life, both before and after my conversion event. He just makes complete and total sense, and he does so teaching and preaching in the early part of the fourteenth century, a century that would experience the Black Death, which killed as many as 200 million people on the planet, and the Hundred Years War.

John of the Cross fits rather nicely into my final four. Both of his two "big books"—*Ascent of Mount Carmel* and *Dark Night of the Soul*—make tremendous sense for the kind of conversion I am having. Even now, nearly ten years after my journey was finally launched, I find myself "climbing in the dark." However, it is his poem, the Spiritual Canticle, that takes me out of myself.

Teilhard de Chardin came late to my favorites, largely because I simply could not understand him. Ilio helped me, as did Father Denis Edwards. When I finally "got it," everything changed. Everything. My faith exploded into a beauty and certainty that I cannot adequately describe to this day.

Thomas Merton completes the list. I was introduced to the writings of Merton many years ago, when he was in the headlines for opposing the war in Vietnam. I do not remember reading anything serious or spiritual, only a handful of anti-war pieces. Since I agreed completely with what he said, I decided he was a good guy. More than forty years passed before I picked up *Seven Story Mountain*. The rest is a history similar to many, many others. When Jim Finley casually mentioned that Merton was his novice master at Gethsemane, I thought I had died and gone to Heaven. If the writing of the 13th and 14th century mystics begins to put me to sleep, I pick up *New Seeds of Contemplation* or *No Man is an Island* or *Thoughts in Solitude* and I am awake for the night.

These seven great teachers present a present an understanding of life, death, and the origin and destiny of the world that is radically different from anything I had ever known. They teach the importance of surrendering all that I am until nothing is left and God can enter. They teach the fundamental importance of putting my faith to work. Ignatius called it a contemplative in action. Of course, Father Rohr's home base is the Center for Action and Contemplation.

I could go on and on, still not adequately conveying the extraordinary breadth and depth of the Living School curriculum. To call it life changing would be an injustice. Father Rohr likes to use the fancy word **orthopraxy** when describing the Living School.

> In the study of religion, **orthopraxy** is *correct conduct*, both ethical and liturgical, as opposed to faith or grace etc. This contrasts with **orthodoxy**, which emphasizes *correct belief*, and ritualism, the use of rituals.

This focus on "what we do," rather than what we say or believe, has always resonated for me, long before I began this spiritual journey. Both my early career, building low-income housing, and the international electric power industry, to which I devoted the last thirty years of my working life, were based on making something happen, on *conduct* that "moved the needle." I wanted to see the results of my efforts in the form of bricks and mortar, boilers and turbines, and, ultimately, shelter and energy. God's first commandment is to love Him, and then to love our neighbors as ourselves. Jesus taught that *doing something*—serving the poor, healing the sick, feeding the hungry, and housing the homeless—all ways to actively love our neighbor—was more important than *being something*.

The Living School did not introduce me to the idea that God is a verb, not a noun, and that the verb is *love*. I had been saying that since I began my journey in 2007. However, the Living School did teach me what this meant. Among other things, I learned that the concept was as old as all the world's Wisdom Traditions, from Judaism and Christianity to Buddhism and Islam. My developing understanding of stages and states of consciousness came from the Living School. I came to love the Bible more, primarily because Father Rohr introduced me to what he calls the Jesus Hermeneutic, reading the scriptures the way Jesus used them in His ministry. The frequent references Jesus makes to the scriptures were consistently limited to those verses that focused on inclusion and mercy. I am now comfortable with the metaphoric quality of both the Hebrew scriptures and the New Testament.

Perhaps the most important and transforming faith message from the Living School has to do with upending the concept of "substitutionary atonement." That concept begins with the traditional doctrine that mankind was somehow begun as a great mistake, stained with "Original Sin," a mistake that required God to send His only Son to be brutally killed. Only that murder could atone for the "sins of all mankind," only that tragic death could cause God to forgive and love mankind.

The big idea of the Living School can be summed up in one concept.

> *Jesus did not come to change the mind of God about humanity.* It didn't need changing. God has organically, inherently loved what God created from the moment God created it. *Jesus came to change the mind of humanity about God.*

The power of that simple statement is huge. The long journey through the deep and wonderful tradition of great Catholic mystics showed me that this is not a new idea, somehow a "New Age" bit of relativistic flim-flam. This has been the core Gospel of Jesus Christ from the beginning. It is the theological basis for the Beatitudes.

It is important to note that I am completely aware that there were many Christian thinkers and writers down through the ages whose work was not on the reading list of the Living School. Many early Christians preached a perfectly odious form of anti-Semitism. Every form of tribal exclusion has been preached from the ambo in every age, all making "the Other" wrong, all consigning anyone different to Hell and Damnation forever. I suppose there could be an alternative to the Living School, one that selected only these hateful writings, using them as a basis for rejecting Christ (or, for the truly warped mind, using them to claim Christ in defense of racism, tyranny, and worse). Hate exists in every age, and it has always had articulate advocates. The Living School is a vibrant, exciting experience, boldly asserting that love does conquer hate.

The Living School was incredibly powerful. However, for me, it was not the vehicle that would allow me to put my faith into action, to act on the deep teaching of the mystical tradition and our contemporary mystical teachers. For that, I needed a new ministry. Incredibly, that ministry was born and would grow into maturity right alongside the Living School. Orthopraxy lies at the heart of the Sister Parish Ministry.

The Sister Parish Ministry

The Sister Parish Ministry of Our Lady Star of the Sea Catholic Parish is a mission program organized around a partnership between our parish in Florida and two poor parishes in the Dominican Republic. Together with a few men from a retreat program at my Parish, I started the Sister Parish Ministry in the late fall of 2012, not long after being accepted for the Living School. The idea arose in connection with one of the goals of CRHP (a parish retreat program, Christ Renews His Parish), which is to see the CRHP graduates put their new "faith fire" to work in a service capacity. Father Frank Iacona was then the clerical advisor to OLSS CRHP. He threw out the idea of a Sister Parish program, but did not describe what that was, or what it did. So, seven men, including Father Frank and, significantly, Don Barnhorst, a retired surgeon, gathered at my house every two weeks to discuss the concept. Terry Williams, Jim Moore, Javier Salinas, and Victor Gonzalez all shared the CRHP experience. They also had high interest in and energy for mission work.

After two months of these meetings, and with significant assistance from Catholic Relief Services, we contacted Father Mario Serrano of Jesuit Refugee Services in Santo Domingo, Dominican Republic. Don and I went down to the DR in January of 2013, and again, with others, several times over the next few months. The first full mission trip took place over the Labor Day weekend in September 2013, coincidentally the week before the first Living School conference in Albuquerque. Thirty-six men, women, and young children counseled pregnant women (and girls), built temporary housing units, and organized an impromptu medical clinic. It was, frankly, an outrageous and totally unexpected success. That nascent idea has since become a formidable ministry.

The Sister Parish Ministry was conceived as a program of faith in action (I had not yet heard the word "orthopraxy"!). We are what we do. One of our partner parishes, Domingo Savio, is located in Los Guandules, one of the poorest barrios of Santo Domingo. The other partner parish, San Antonio de Padua, serves the residents of a small town located east of the capital, as well as residents of a number of *bateyes* (villages that began as migrant labor camps for sugar cane workers brought in from Haiti over the last century), occupied primarily by Haitian families. These partnerships are active relationships, which involve hard work, connection, bonding, and service from all partners. They are not states of being, they are states of doing.

The residents of both the barrios and the bateyes of our partner parishes are truly the poorest of the world's poor. They generally occupy dirt-floored houses, most with leaking roofs, consisting of little more than a single room, with no electricity, running water, or sanitation facilities. Food, potable water, clothing, medicine, and employment opportunities are absent or in extraordinarily short supply.

The primary service purpose of the partnerships established by Sister Parish Ministry is to radically change this situation. Together with residents of the communities, and with volunteers from other organizations in the Dominican Republic, we are providing medical care, building houses and chapels, and working with local residents to develop their communities.

Despite the apparent disparity in resources, our Sister Parish Ministry is a "solidarity-based partnership," defined by Catholic Relief Services as one rooted in the belief that we all have much to give and to receive by being in a relationship with peoples and communities with a reality very different from our own. Our relationship offers everyone involved an opportunity to grow deeper in faith and solidarity with our sisters and brothers in a different culture and country.

The Ministry's activities include a number of missions each year to Santo Domingo and Guerra, some for medical treatment, some for family and motherhood education and support, some for housing and community improvements, and some for sustainable economic development. A major priority of every mission trip is to deepen the personal relationships between and among the missionaries from Florida and the residents of the communities in and surrounding Santo Domingo and Guerra. Another major priority of the Ministry is to build institutional relationships with various organizations in the Dominican Republic, including governmental entities, universities, foreign assistance organizations, religious groups, and businesses.

Meister Eckhart wrote:

> God's ground is my ground and my ground is God's ground. Here I live on my own as God lives on His own. All our world should work out of this innermost ground without a why or a wherefore. Then, God and the soul do one work together eternally and very fruitfully. Then, all that this person works God works. And Just as I can do almost nothing without God, so too God can accomplish nothing apart from me.

I am frequently asked to describe Sister Parish, and explain what we do and both why we do it, and why we do it in the communities where we work in the Dominican Republic. My answer has become the motto of the ministry: *Encounter in community though service*. Our Sister Parish partners in the Dominican Republic now say, *Encontra en Comunidad a traves Servicio*.

Encounter. First, and most important, the missions provide opportunities for **encounter**—*transformative personal experiences of the Divine*. These opportunities come up on the individual level for each person, on the family level, when several family members travel together, and on the group level. Pope Francis wrote that, "an encounter between God and one's self begins first and foremost by acknowledging that we are being encountered by our Creator who loves us infinitely." An encounter requires a dynamic back and forth between two entities. In his pastoral exhortation *Evangelii Gaudium*, Pope Francis urges the faithful to "a renewed personal encounter with Jesus Christ, or at least an openness to letting him encounter them." Christ is constantly reaching out to all persons, but the *event* of an encounter happens when that invitation is acknowledged and responded to by a human being. There is a divine vulnerability to reaching out, an eagerness, waiting in hope of a response. Pope Francis again, "We must go out to meet others, and with our faith we must create a 'culture of encounter,' a culture of friendship, a culture in which we find brothers and sisters, in which we can also speak with those who think differently, as well as those who hold other beliefs, who do not have the same faith."

Community. The encounter is more likely to occur in **community**—the *relationship between and among our missionaries, our counterpart volunteers and the individuals, groups, and communities that* *we serve.* Again, the stress is on the idea of intention. We try to go beyond the circumstantial or accidental relationships that result from working together. We *intentionally* focus on the sisterhood of our parish relationship, the partnership status of our joint volunteer relationships, and the unity of our relationships with everyone in Mamey, Guerra, and Domingo Savio. There is a growing sense of community among the pregnant women (and new mothers) in Mamey, the elderly receiving food, the students receiving aid, and the new homeowners. We do what we can do to support these groups *as groups.* And we do what we can to support the community of missionaries, now numbering more than six hundred, who have traveled to the Dominican Republic from Ponte Vedra Beach.

Service. Finally, the best opportunity for an encounter to occur in a community is through **service**—*doing work,* whether that is the obvious work of the medical teams in their clinics, or the efforts of other missions to clean, paint, construct, and build chapels, houses, or infrastructure projects. As everyone who has ever been involved in mission work repeatedly says, the house we build is not the point, rather, it is the spiritual experience and relationship value that is created. But that experience and value would not be possible, or, at least, as powerful, without the work project. Meister Eckhart again:

> The outward work will never be puny if the inward work is great. And the outward work can never be great or even good, if the inward one is puny or of little worth. The inward work invariably includes in itself all expansiveness, all breadth, all length, all depth. Such a work receives and draws all its being from nowhere else except from and in the heart of God.

Work projects require planning, organization, and substantial amounts of money—all prior to the arrival of the missionaries in country. Antonio Rodriguez has volunteered since July, 2013, to oversee material acquisition, contractor negotiation and supervision, and financial management for all construction work. Daniel Jose and Ezequiel Torres have both volunteered and worked full time for Sister Parish. Daniel is stepping into the role of Country Director.

Our former Country Director, Tanya Luciano, along with volunteers from Santisima Trinidad, parishioners from San Antonio de Padua, and students from the medical school at UNIBE all joined together in managing the logistics of the missions. Several young people in Mamey have been serving as Leaders since April, 2016.

The Sister Parish Ministry is now firmly established as a full-fledged community outreach program at Our Lady Star of the Sea. Several very experienced mission leaders—Katie Houser, Diane Foley, Catharine Savilla, Brian Ott, Andy Sears, Bob Lopresti, Don Barnhorst, and Tony Hartman—have each led as many as four missions. By the time I finish these exercises in May 2017, we will have built six chapels, a school, and thirty-five houses. We installed storm drainage, and built a park, a pig barn, and several new latrines in the village of Mamey. We field three medical missions each year, treating a patient database of more than five thousand people. Nine missions are now regularly scheduled each year.

Like the Living School, Sister Parish has literally transformed my life. All the cerebral, intellectually challenging, and mystical beauty of the Living School finds concrete expression in the people and projects that Sister Parish has made a fundamental part of my life. Sister Parish is a "hands-on" experience. I know the people in the villages. I know their children and their parents. The villages are places where everyone knows my name. In countless ways, Sister Parish feeds my heart, making it grow each time I am engaged, whether in Florida or in the Dominican Republic.

The combined impact of the Living School and the Sister Parish Ministry is the primary motivation for this second trip through the Exercises. More than anyone else in the ministry, I experience encounter in community through service. Meister Eckhart writes, "What we plant in the soil of contemplation, we shall reap in the harvest of action." Welcome to my garden.

Bob Hart
September 2016

PREPARATION PERIOD

CALENDAR WEEK ONE

September 18

John 4: 1 14, The Samaritan Woman at the Well

Now when Jesus learned that the Pharisees had heard, "Jesus is making and baptizing more disciples than John" [2]*—although it was not Jesus himself but his disciples who baptized—* [3] *he left Judea and started back to Galilee.* [4] *But he had to go through Samaria.* [5] *So he came to a Samaritan city called Sychar, near the plot of ground that Jacob had given to his son Joseph.* [6] *Jacob's well was there, and Jesus, tired out by his journey, was sitting by the well. It was about noon.*

[7] *A Samaritan woman came to draw water, and Jesus said to her, "Give me a drink."* [8] *(His disciples had gone to the city to buy food.)* [9] *The Samaritan woman said to him, "How is it that you, a Jew, ask a drink of me, a woman of Samaria?" (Jews do not share things in common with Samaritans.)* [10] *Jesus answered her, "If you knew the gift of God, and who it is that is saying to you, 'Give me a drink,' you would have asked him, and he would have given you living water."* [11] *The woman said to him, "Sir, you have no bucket, and the well is deep. Where do you get that living water?* [12] *Are you greater than our ancestor Jacob, who gave us the well, and with his sons and his flocks drank from it?"* [13] *Jesus said to her, "Everyone who drinks of this water will be thirsty again,* [14] *but those who drink of the water that I will give them will never be thirsty. The water that I will give will become in them a spring of water gushing up to eternal life."*

SALLIE ANN is in the hospital. She was taken by ambulance Thursday night after choir practice, following hours of nausea and vomiting, along with intense stomach pain. Friday was one of the worst days imaginable. Blood tests indicated that Sallie Ann has acute pancreatitis, something caused by gall stones, among other things. Ultrasound Friday morning showed that she had no gall stones, leaving us worried about other possible causes. A CT scan Saturday morning showed no signs of tumor, growth, or cancer. Thank God. I spent several hours Friday night, and early Saturday morning, contemplating life without Sallie Ann. My prayers since midnight Thursday have been filled with tears, probably of the most selfish nature. I cannot bear the thought of this house, my ministries, this parish, and any of the other things that make up my life, in her absence. Sallie Ann is barely conscious. Most of the time she is sleeping, or drugged to the point of not being able to speak. Her pain seems unbearable.

It feels a little strange to be turning to the Ignatian Exercises in this time of crisis. On the other hand, perhaps these Exercises are the best possible way to spend this frightening Sunday morning.

As I begin for the second time this long period of daily prayer, reflection, and contemplation, I am delighted to do so reading this wonderful passage from the Gospel according to John. Acceptance of the Other has long been a central component of whatever spirituality I claimed to have. Growing up a Mormon in southern Idaho, I must have been influenced by that faith's strong tradition of welcoming strangers and resisting oppression. The Mormons themselves were outcasts, persecuted everywhere they stopped along the long trek from upstate New York to Utah. From the very early days of the church, missionaries reached out to other countries, beginning a tradition of multiculturalism that extends to the present day. Multi-lingual understanding and acceptance are highly valued. Sadly, the

Mormon Church did not extend full membership to African Americans until 1978, a glaring exception to the generally inclusive practice of the church.

The story of Jesus and the Samaritan woman at Jacob's well is the classic example of accepting the Other, embracing difference, and ignoring tribal traditions of intolerance. Jesus not only drank water with the woman, he used the woman's bucket. He offered her His water, making it clear that it would be a radically different kind of water from any she had ever drunk before. As I reflect on this living water, it strikes me just how connected the new water is to the acceptance of the Other. When we move from a tribal level of consciousness to one that embraces difference, all of our senses begin to change. We begin to see, taste, hear, and feel a deeper, richer reality, one that transcends the narrow prejudices of the earlier stages of consciousness. Here, Jesus said, *taste* this. Accept its difference.

I am also struck by the implications of a "spring of water gushing up" within us. Meister Eckhart talked about *bullitio*, literally the "boiling" of the inner life of the Trinity, which becomes *ebullition*, the "boiling over" of God's love into the love of all creation. The notion of God's love boiling over and His living water gushing up within me come together in a powerful image.

After contemplating these images, I walked down to the garden with Maggie to pray, beginning again the practice that made these Exercises so wonderful five years ago. I am older now. I will be 72 when I finish the Exercises next May. I have finished the Living School. I have presided over the formation of Sister Parish, a service ministry in our parish that seems well-grounded. The final mission of 2016 returned from the Dominican Republic two weeks ago. Even as these two dominant activities come to an end, I am powerfully reminded of T. S. Eliot, "What we call the beginning is often the end. And to make an end is to make a beginning. The end is where we start from."

Our son Rob and I stayed at or close to the hospital, more or less around the clock. I could never have survived these past few days without him. I pray for Sallie Ann. I ask for wisdom and understanding as I begin this Ignatian journey again.

September 19

John 10: 1–21, The Good Shepherd and His Sheep

"Very truly, I tell you, anyone who does not enter the sheepfold by the gate but climbs in by another way is a thief and a bandit. ² The one who enters by the gate is the shepherd of the sheep. ³ The gatekeeper opens the gate for him, and the sheep hear his voice. He calls his own sheep by name and leads them out. ⁴ When he has brought out all his own, he goes ahead of them, and the sheep follow him because they know his voice. ⁵ They will not follow a stranger, but they will run from him because they do not know the voice of strangers." ⁶ Jesus used this figure of speech with them, but they did not understand what he was saying to them.

⁷ So again Jesus said to them, "Very truly, I tell you, I am the gate for the sheep. ⁸ All who came before me are thieves and bandits; but the sheep did not listen to them. ⁹ I am the gate. Whoever enters by me will be saved, and will come in and go out and find pasture. ¹⁰ The thief comes only to steal and kill and destroy. I came that they may have life, and have it abundantly.

¹¹ "I am the good shepherd. The good shepherd lays down his life for the sheep. ¹² The hired hand, who is not the shepherd and does not own the sheep, sees the wolf coming and leaves the sheep and runs away—and the wolf snatches them and scatters them. ¹³ The hired hand runs away because a hired hand does not care for the sheep. ¹⁴ I am the good shepherd. I know my own and my own know me, ¹⁵ just as the Father knows me and I know the Father. And I lay down my life for the sheep. ¹⁶ I have other sheep that do not belong to this fold. I must bring them also, and they will listen to my voice. So there will be one flock, one shepherd. ¹⁷ For this reason the Father loves me, be-

*cause I lay down my life in order to take it up again. * [18] *No one takes it from me, but I lay it down of my own accord. I have power to lay it down, and I have power to take it up again. I have received this command from my Father."*

[19] *Again the Jews were divided because of these words.* [20] *Many of them were saying, "He has a demon and is out of his mind. Why listen to him?"* [21] *Others were saying, "These are not the words of one who has a demon. Can a demon open the eyes of the blind?"*

SALLIE ANN remains in the hospital, still largely unable to talk due to morphine and Phenergen. I have a Sister Parish meeting tonight, where I want to say something about the hospital and the loneliness of this vigil. Frankly, I am afraid. Driving from the hospital early this morning, I called Deacon Dan Scrone, taking great comfort from his strength and support. I find it very difficult to focus on John's Gospel, and wolves and sheep.

There are parts of this passage that speak loudly and clearly to me. When I reflect on my friends who have died, I am invariably reminded of verse 11 ("You are the good shepherd…"). Each and every one of my friends was a good shepherd for me. My memory of them is overwhelmed by gratitude.

Other parts of the passage, especially verse 5, trouble me. "They will not follow a stranger…" sounds a little exclusionary. I choose not to believe that Jesus would call Moses, Buddha, or even Mohammed, strangers. I choose to believe that verse 16 ("I have other sheep that do not belong to this fold.") is another way of saying there are no strangers. I need to be careful about this practice of rejecting anything that comes close to saying that Christ is the only way, that Christians are the only ones to be saved, and that any other source of wisdom must be excluded. I believe that inclusivity and mercy are the most important elements of my faith, and I am convinced they are at the heart of Christianity and true Catholicism. But I cannot critically read every passage or listen to every homily, looking for the word or phrase that violates my purity code.

Maggie and I walked down to the bench in the garden to pray for Sallie Ann. I ask especially for openness and humility.

September 20

Luke 5: 27–32, Jesus Eats with Sinners
[27] *After this he went out and saw a tax collector named Levi, sitting at the tax booth; and he said to him, "Follow me."* [28] *And he got up, left everything, and followed him.*

[29] *Then Levi gave a great banquet for him in his house; and there was a large crowd of tax collectors and others sitting at the table with them. The Pharisees and their scribes were complaining to his disciples, saying, "Why do you eat and drink with tax collectors and sinners?"* [31] *Jesus answered, "Those who are well have no need of a physician, but those who are sick;* [32] *I have come to call not the righteous but sinners to repentance."*

YESTERDAY, I called Sallie Ann's son Will and her sister, Mary Lou, telling them it was time to come together. Mary Lou arrived after 11 p.m. last night from Connecticut. Will arrives tonight. Sallie Ann had two teenage sons when I married her, both of whom are very close friends of mine today. Rob lives here in Jacksonville, spending many nights a month at Serendipity, our house in Ponte Vedra. Will lives in Seattle, Washington. Mary Lou lives in Simsbury, Connecticut. As I await their arrival, I am once again trying to move my focus and attention from Sallie Ann to Luke's Gospel.

Like the story of the Samaritan woman at the well, this passage from Luke is all about the Other. Tax collectors were about as bad as it could get among the Jews of the first century, perhaps even worse than people from other tribes. Tax collectors were turn coats, betraying their fellow Jews for their own selfish interest. But Jesus spoke to Levi, and then joined him at a banquet where many more tax collectors were present. Jesus accepted them as worthy of receiving His message and, presumably, His forgiveness. I put myself at the table. To a limited extent, I was embarrassed to have become wealthy by collecting taxes from my friends and countrymen. I took comfort from the presence of my fellow tax collectors. Then this stranger, this rabbi, openly invited me to leave everything and follow Him. I looked around my library and started negotiating with myself about which things I could keep! Maggie and I prayed together about Sallie Ann, about gratitude, and about humility.

September 21

Mark 12: 1–12, The Parable of the Tenants
  Then he began to speak to them in parables. "A man planted a vineyard, put a fence around it, dug a pit for the wine press, and built a watchtower; then he leased it to tenants and went to another country. ² When the season came, he sent a slave to the tenants to collect from them his share of the produce of the vineyard. ³ But they seized him, and beat him, and sent him away empty-handed. ⁴ And again he sent another slave to them; this one they beat over the head and insulted. ⁵ Then he sent another, and that one they killed. And so it was with many others; some they beat, and others they killed. ⁶ He had still one other, a beloved son. Finally he sent him to them, saying, 'They will respect my son.' ⁷ But those tenants said to one another, 'This is the heir; come, let us kill him, and the inheritance will be ours.' ⁸ So they seized him, killed him, and threw him out of the vineyard. ⁹ What then will the owner of the vineyard do? He will come and destroy the tenants and give the vineyard to others. ¹⁰ Have you not read this scripture:

> *'The stone that the builders rejected*
>   *has become the cornerstone;*
> *¹¹ this was the Lord's doing,*
>   *and it is amazing in our eyes'?"*
  ¹² When they realized that he had told this parable against them, they wanted to arrest him, but they feared the crowd. So they left him and went away.

THIS PASSAGE from Mark's Gospel has so many messages and meanings, at least to me, that it is hard to understand. One key to understanding is the actual identity of the cast of characters: The owner of the vineyard is God, the vineyard is God's kingdom, the tenants are the people of Israel, the servants are the prophets of the Hebrew scriptures, and the son is Jesus Christ. I am very frustrated by the actions of the tenants. God gives His people the kingdom, but they reject Him. God sends the Prophets to remind the people of God's wishes. The people reject and kill them. Finally, God sends His son, Jesus, and the people reject Him as well. The stone the builders rejected is the Son of God, now the cornerstone of God's kingdom.

Where am I in this passage? First, I fantasized that I was one of the tenants, an ungrateful recipient of God's generosity. Like my fellow tenants, I rejected the prophets. With difficulty, I imagined rejecting Jesus as well, taking the role of one of those who shouted out from the crowd, "Kill Him." This was such an unpleasant experience that I fantasized again, this time taking the role of one of the prophets. I could not understand why the people would not accept what seemed to be such an obvious argument about the gift of a vineyard, and God's right to expect them to do what they were asked to do. I moved back and forth in my fantasies, taking the part of the prophet, then the ungrateful citizen of Israel. I consider how often I have sinned, knowing so clearly at the time that what I was about to do was a sin, but persisting anyway.

The rejected stone is one of my favorite images. It comes up in my prayer as both my role, having been rejected at times, and the role of others that I have rejected, only to see them later in leadership positions. The parable is powerful.

My prayer today is once again for Sallie Ann and humility. This time, I ask as well for judgment.

September 22

Mark 9: 14–21, A Boy is Healed

When they came to the disciples, they saw a great crowd around them, and some scribes arguing with them. [15] When the whole crowd saw him, they were immediately overcome with awe, and they ran forward to greet him. [16] He asked them, "What are you arguing about with them?" [17] Someone from the crowd answered him, "Teacher, I brought you my son; he has a spirit that makes him unable to speak; [18] and whenever it seizes him, it dashes him down; and he foams and grinds his teeth and becomes rigid; and I asked your disciples to cast it out, but they could not do so." [19] He answered them, "You faithless generation, how much longer must I be among you? How much longer must I put up with you? Bring him to me." [20] And they brought the boy to him. When the spirit saw him, immediately it convulsed the boy, and he fell on the ground and rolled about, foaming at the mouth. [21] Jesus asked the father, "How long has this been happening to him?" And he said, "From childhood."

MY THOUGHTS were so far away from the Gospel of Mark this morning. I spent the night repeatedly running through a nightmare about losing Sallie Ann. I know one of us will die before the other, and the first death could happen at any time. That heady knowledge, however, is very different from the stark reality that has forced itself into my consciousness this week. Everything in my life revolves around Sallie Ann, including particularly my faith journey. When I am able to create some space between my thoughts and the immediate requirement to be a semi-responsible caregiver, I know I must return to this issue. Some day. Right now, I need the Exercises to take my mind away from the stubborn fear of solitude.

When I first read this passage from Mark's Gospel, it seemed to be truncated. I know from reading ahead that Jesus goes on to heal the child, causing someone in the crowd to say, "I believe, help my unbelief!" But that is skipping ahead. In today's passage, the question as to what Jesus will do is left hanging. I have to join the assembled crowd wondering what will happen next. What do I believe about the power of God with respect to entering the daily lives of individuals and healing them or solving their particular problems? The sickness of the child is expressed in terms of possession by an evil spirit, which must have been a common belief early in the first century. Healing the sick and driving out demons were essentially the same thing. I fantasized being the parent of that child. I imagined believing in demons. I tried to imagine a world without modern medicine. Of course, my mind went straight to Baptist Beaches Hospital and the many conversations that dominated my weekend. My child's illness/ possession began with an inability to speak. What might my child have said about this Jesus? What did I say? What thoughts did I suppress?

I pray for Sallie Ann. I want to be strong, but feel little strength.

September 23

Matthew 14:13–21, Jesus Feeds the Five Thousand

[13] Now when Jesus heard this, he withdrew from there in a boat to a deserted place by himself. But when the crowds heard it, they followed him on foot from the towns. [14] When he went ashore, he saw a great crowd; and he had compassion for them and cured their sick. [15] When it was evening, the disciples came to him and said, "This is a deserted place, and the hour is now late; send the crowds away so that they may go into the villages and buy food for themselves." [16] Jesus said to them, "They need not go away; you give them something to eat." [17] They replied, "We have nothing here but five loaves and two fish." [18] And he said, "Bring them here to me." [19] Then he ordered the crowds to sit down on the grass. Taking the five loaves and the two fish, he looked up to heaven, and blessed and broke the loaves, and gave them to the disciples, and the disciples gave them to the crowds. [20] And all ate and were filled; and they took up what was left over of the broken pieces, twelve baskets full. [21] And those who ate were about five thousand men, besides women and children.

Sallie Ann came home from the hospital last night. While she is still very weak, there seems to be a consensus that hospitals in general are not very safe from a multitude of infections. It is comforting to have her here.

As usual, I read the passage from Matthew's Gospel last night. It is another of my favorite stories from the ministry of Jesus. I fantasized being one of the disciples, feeling frustrated with my inability to satisfy the needs of the crowd. I spent some time trying to get my head around a crowd of 5,000.

Political rallies are sometimes that large and larger, but I have never addressed a crowd larger than 1,000. That seemed to be an absolutely enormous gathering. I imagine Jesus speaking to this huge crowd outdoors, with no loudspeakers, no PowerPoint presentation, and most of the crowd sitting or standing uncomfortably. I imagine Him healing the sick and listening to complaints from one person after another.

When the teaching was over, the restless crowd wanted food, which meant it was my turn to perform. And I failed. There was no food, at least nothing sufficient for this large group. So Jesus simply commanded us to begin feeding, giving everyone as much bread and fish as they wanted. The miracle of ever-expanding quantities of bread and fish was not immediately apparent. Only after we were clearly feeding more people than our initial supplies could possibly have fed did we begin to wonder what was happening.

September 24

Luke 15:1–32, The Parables of the Lost Sheep, the Lost Coin, and the Prodigal Son

Now all the tax collectors and sinners were coming near to listen to him. [2] And the Pharisees and the scribes were grumbling and saying, "This fellow welcomes sinners and eats with them."

The Parable of the Lost Sheep

[3] So he told them this parable: [4] "Which one of you, having a hundred sheep and losing one of them, does not leave the ninety-nine in the wilderness and go after the one that is lost until he finds it? [5] When he has found it, he lays it on his shoulders and rejoices. [6] And when he comes home, he calls together his friends and neighbors, saying to them, 'Rejoice with me, for I have found my sheep that was lost.' [7] Just so, I tell you, there will be more joy in heaven over one sinner who repents than over ninety-nine righteous persons who need no repentance.

The Parable of the Lost Coin

⁸ *"Or what woman having ten silver coins, if she loses one of them, does not light a lamp, sweep the house, and search carefully until she finds it?* ⁹ *When she has found it, she calls together her friends and neighbors, saying, 'Rejoice with me, for I have found the coin that I had lost.'* ¹⁰ *Just so, I tell you, there is joy in the presence of the angels of God over one sinner who repents."*

The Parable of the Prodigal and His Brother

¹¹ *Then Jesus said, "There was a man who had two sons.* ¹² *The younger of them said to his father, 'Father, give me the share of the property that will belong to me.' So he divided his property between them.* ¹³ *A few days later the younger son gathered all he had and traveled to a distant country, and there he squandered his property in dissolute living.* ¹⁴ *When he had spent everything, a severe famine took place throughout that country, and he began to be in need.* ¹⁵ *So he went and hired himself out to one of the citizens of that country, who sent him to his fields to feed the pigs.* ¹⁶ *He would gladly have filled himself with the pods that the pigs were eating; and no one gave him anything.* ¹⁷ *But when he came to himself he said, 'How many of my father's hired hands have bread enough and to spare, but here I am dying of hunger!* ¹⁸ *I will get up and go to my father, and I will say to him, "Father, I have sinned against heaven and before you;* ¹⁹ *I am no longer worthy to be called your son; treat me like one of your hired hands."'* ²⁰ *So he set off and went to his father. But while he was still far off, his father saw him and was filled with compassion; he ran and put his arms around him and kissed him.* ²¹ *Then the son said to him, 'Father, I have sinned against heaven and before you; I am no longer worthy to be called your son.'* ²² *But the father said to his slaves, 'Quickly, bring out a robe—the best one—and put it on him; put a ring on his finger and sandals on his feet.* ²³ *And get the fatted calf and kill it, and let us eat and celebrate;* ²⁴ *for this son of mine was dead and is alive again; he was lost and is found!' And they began to celebrate.*

²⁵ *"Now his elder son was in the field; and when he came and approached the house, he heard music and dancing.* ²⁶ *He called one of the slaves and asked what was going on.* ²⁷ *He replied, 'Your brother has come, and your father has killed the fatted calf, because he has got him back safe and sound.'* ²⁸ *Then he became angry and refused to go in. His father came out and began to plead with him.* ²⁹ *But he answered his father, 'Listen! For all these years I have been working like a slave for you, and I have never disobeyed your command; yet you have never given me even a young goat so that I might celebrate with my friends.* ³⁰ *But when this son of yours came back, who has devoured your property with prostitutes, you killed the fatted calf for him!'* ³¹ *Then the father said to him, 'Son, you are always with me, and all that is mine is yours.* ³² *But we had to celebrate and rejoice, because this brother of yours was dead and has come to life; he was lost and has been found.'"*

WHEN I CAME in from my meditation, Sallie Ann was awake, showered, and sitting downstairs. She is clearly on the mend. Thank God for all the prayers.

My first week ends with two of my all-time favorite parables, the lost sheep and the prodigal son. I often puzzle over the simple clarity and beauty of the message in the parable of the lost sheep. This message flies in the face of all the social justice theory that so often gets back to finding the best solution for the highest percentage of the population. A system based on what is best for the most ignores the one lost soul from the outset. Jesus talked about a radically different system, one that elevates a minority of one into the decisive position. I am certain to return to this theme, soon and often.

The parable of the prodigal son is often called the parable of the loving father. Like the lost sheep for whom the shepherd went back out into the night to search, the prodigal son had lost his way. So when the father, like the shepherd, opens his arms to the returning son, forgiving all, the lesson is both clear and powerful. I have brothers, both of whom remained closer to my parents than did I. Like the father in this parable, my father never counted me out, never gave up, never held against me my decision to remain away. I disappointed my parents big time, especially with the ignoble end to my mission and my divorce. The mission fiasco had serious implications for them, ultimately forcing them to leave their home and community. Yet they loved me through both failures.

CALENDAR WEEK TWO

Oh, Lord my God,
You called me from the sleep of nothingness
merely because of Your tremendous love.
You want to make good and beautiful beings.
You have called me by name in my mother's womb.
You have given me breath and light and movement
and walked with me every moment of my existence.
I am amazed, Lord God of the universe,
that You attend to me and, more, cherish me
Create in me the faithfulness that moves You,
and I will trust You and yearn for You all my days.
Amen.

September 25

Luke 11: 1–13, The Lord's Prayer

He was praying in a certain place, and after he had finished, one of his disciples said to him, "Lord, teach us to pray, as John taught his disciples." [2] He said to them, "When you pray, say:

Father, hallowed be your name.

 Your kingdom come.

[3] Give us each day our daily bread.

[4] And forgive us our sins,

 for we ourselves forgive everyone indebted to us.

 And do not bring us to the time of trial."

[5] And he said to them, "Suppose one of you has a friend, and you go to him at midnight and say to him, 'Friend, lend me three loaves of bread; [6] for a friend of mine has arrived, and I have nothing to set before him.' [7] And he answers from within, 'Do not bother me; the door has already been locked, and my children are with me in bed; I cannot get up and give you anything.' [8] I tell you, even though he will not get up and give him anything because he is his friend, at least because of his persistence he will get up and give him whatever he needs.

[9] "So I say to you, Ask, and it will be given you; search, and you will find; knock, and the door will be opened for you. [10] For everyone who asks receives, and everyone who searches finds, and for everyone who knocks, the door will be opened. [11] Is there anyone among you who, if your child asks for a fish, will give a snake instead of a fish? [12] Or if the child asks for an egg, will give a scorpion? [13] If you then, who are evil, know how to give good gifts to your children, how much more will the heavenly Father give the Holy Spirit to those who ask him!"

THE PRAYER for the week includes the statement that God wants to "make good and beautiful beings." That is a powerful declaration. I repeated that part of the prayer over and over. He made me in my mother's womb to be a good and beautiful being. That is a lot to take in. Then the passage from Luke's Gospel, instructing us how to pray, then admonishing us to pray, and pray, and pray again. It was easy to fantasize about being that person going out at midnight looking for help for a friend. It seems like I have spent most of my life seeking, asking, and knocking on doors! To say that I dislike it is to seriously understate the case. I raised money for business projects and ideas from 1970 until 2007. Most of the time, I was able to base my request on the assertion that the person who said yes would be amply rewarded right here on earth and very soon. Since 2007, I have occasionally attempted to raise money for philanthropy, most often linked to my mission activity. There is certainly no monetary return on these philanthropic "investments." While it is difficult to measure, I have found that the spiritual returns from my philanthropic activity are incalculable.

September 26

Psalm 139, The Inescapable God
  ¹ O LORD, you have searched me and known me.
  ² You know when I sit down and when I rise up; you discern my thoughts from far away.
  ³ You search out my path and my lying down, and are acquainted with all my ways.
  ⁴ Even before a word is on my tongue, O LORD, you know it completely.
  ⁵ You hem me in, behind and before, and lay your hand upon me.
  ⁶ Such knowledge is too wonderful for me; it is so high that I cannot attain it.

  ⁷ Where can I go from your spirit? Or where can I flee from your presence?
  ⁸ If I ascend to heaven, you are there; if I make my bed in Sheol, you are there.
  ⁹ If I take the wings of the morning and settle at the farthest limits of the sea,
  ¹⁰ even there your hand shall lead me, and your right hand shall hold me fast.
  ¹¹ If I say, "Surely the darkness shall cover me, and the light around me become night,"
  ¹² even the darkness is not dark to you; the night is as bright as the day, for darkness is as light to you.

  ¹³ For it was you who formed my inward parts; you knit me together in my mother's womb.
  ¹⁴ I praise you, for I am fearfully and wonderfully made. Wonderful are your works; that I know very well.
  ¹⁵ My frame was not hidden from you, when I was being made in secret, intricately woven in the depths of the earth.
  ¹⁶ Your eyes beheld my unformed substance. In your book were written all the days that were formed for me, when none of them as yet existed.
  ¹⁷ How weighty to me are your thoughts, O God! How vast is the sum of them!
  ¹⁸ I try to count them—they are more than the sand; I come to the end—I am still with you.
  ¹⁹ O that you would kill the wicked, O God, and that the bloodthirsty would depart from me—
  ²⁰ those who speak of you maliciously, and lift themselves up against you for evil!
  ²¹ Do I not hate those who hate you, O LORD? And do I not loathe those who rise up against you?
  ²² I hate them with perfect hatred; I count them my enemies.
  ²³ Search me, O God, and know my heart; test me and know my thoughts.
  ²⁴ See if there is any wicked way in me, and lead me in the way everlasting.

PSALM 139 is so incredible. The very concept of an all-knowing God used to be difficult for me to accept. For most of my life, I ignored questions of faith. When I did believe (or profess to believe) I repeated the party line, falling back on the notion that faith requires believing in the absence of facts or clear understanding. My new teachers—Rohr, Delio, Teilhard—opened my eyes to the possibility that the Big Bang was consistent with God creating all of creation in a single instant, triggering an evolutionary process that is still underway. I was there 14 billion years ago, just as I will be here 14 billion years from now. God knew me then and knows me now. This evolutionary process is moving because He set it in motion, and it is moving in fits and starts in the direction of the unitive consciousness of God.

Today is the day of the first presidential debate between Clinton and Trump. I am deeply concerned for the future of everything I have ever believed in regarding politics and the public square. I pray for the country. I pray for ever greater clarity and understanding. I pray for acceptance of this unfolding mystery.

September 27

Prayer on My Dossier

In the notebook, I jot down all the vital statistics of my life. As I note each piece of data, I raise my mind to God my Maker, and praise and thank the Creator for this detail in my life history and in myself. Note: God chose that I should come to be in a particular place and time, of particular parents and race, and all the rest. Am I content with God's choices for me? So to begin, I write down my parents' full names, birthplaces, and birth dates. I note my own birthday, where I was born, and any significant medical details. I note my sex, race or ethnic group, hair and eye color, and my physical build. I also note my siblings—name, birthdays, significant details; and I note my extended family of uncles and aunts and cousins. I note the cities and addresses I lived at before I was seven. All this, God chose for me; for all this, I praise and thank God. Then I note down a half dozen personal characteristics and qualities that were bred into me before I had a choice. Self-assurance or anxiety, intelligence, the language or languages I speak, habits of study, activities I take pleasure in. I note at the same time a half dozen characteristics and qualities that I have inherited from my parents or my extended family, those that I like and perhaps some that I would just as soon not have. All this, too, God chose for me within the human family; for all this, I praise and thank God. I go on to note down five or six personal qualities in myself that I particularly like. Perhaps I am quiet, or outgoing, and I like that about myself. Perhaps I am thorough, or sensitive to others' feelings, or truthful. Perhaps I have lots of energy, or accomplish a great deal. I note down these qualities and acknowledge them as gifts from the One who makes me. For all this, too, God chose for me within the human family; for all this, I praise and thank God. Finally, I go on to note down five or six personal qualities in myself that I do not particularly like. Perhaps I am too tall or short, or cannot shake an ugly attitude. Perhaps I have a negative image of myself. Or find it too easy to dislike other people. Or am diabetic. I note down these qualities and acknowledge them as gifts from the One who makes me. For all this, too, God chose for me within the human family; for all this, I praise and thank God. Whenever my time is up, I recite Psalm 130. But I remember that God did not finish making me once, long ago, when I was conceived or born. I remember that **God continues making me** *and has hopes for me and desires that I keep growing in love until I love as completely as God does.*

I began my meditation this morning after playing tennis, a pattern I also followed in 2011 and 2012, when I first did these Exercises. Once again, as was the case then, the way I feel right now confirms the incredible value of physical exercise, particularly as I grow older. This was the first tennis I have played since Sallie Ann went into the hospital. I feel good about my health. I feel good about the community of men and women with whom I play tennis. I simply feel good about being alive. Importantly, Sallie Ann was stronger this morning than she has been since she entered the hospital twelve days ago. Prayer works.

Today's meditation text, *Prayer on My Dossier*, instructs me to write a dossier. Five years ago, I interpreted this to mean a life history. After more carefully reading the instructions, I now see it as more of a recitation of certain facts and memories limited to the circumstances of my birth and early life, up to the age of seven. The purpose of the dossier is to provide a basis for understanding the kind of person God made me to be, through nature, my genetic make-up, and nurture, my early environment.

> God chose that I should come to be in a particular place and time, of particular parents and race, and all the rest.

God knew me before I was born. He chose these parents at this time and in this place for me to become incarnate. I have struggled with these statements all my life. It simply made no sense to me that God, the maker of the universe, could care about one insignificant little person born into an insignificant family in an Idaho farm community.

In spite of my early religious education and my mission service, I essentially rejected the concept of a providential God; a God with a personal interest in me. During the early years of my Catholicism, from 2007 to 2011, I largely chose to avoid the implications of a providential God. At best, I was an uncomfortable believer. At worst, I continued to quietly reject the idea.

About five years ago, I discovered Teilhard, reading, with little comprehension, *The Divine Milieu* and *The Phenomenon of Man*. Sometime after that, I studied the works of Ilia Delio and Father Denis Edwards. I slowly came to understand how quantum physics, the Big Bang, and the science of evolution fit so well into Genesis and, especially, the Prologue of John's Gospel. I began to understand Teilhard.

I also began to slowly wrap my head around the implications of infinity. *A God capable of infinite love can love me completely, and, at the same time, love every one of the other 107 billion humans that have ever lived on earth just as completely.* This may be obvious to some, but it has been a consciousness-expanding realization for me.

Like all of God's other creatures, I came into existence at the very moment of the Big Bang. All of us were first cosmic energy, then cosmic dust, and finally, over more than 14 billion years, we became the individual parts of God's evolving universe that we are today. This is all very heady stuff. God starts the process. He is the Creator. He created the whole universe in the instant of the Big Bang, and He is continuously creating the universe through the amazing process of evolution.

God chose the process of evolution to govern the unfolding of His universe. All of the choices that go into *natural selection* based on *adaptation to the environment* are, therefore, God's choices.

The Big Bang occurred roughly 14.7 billion years ago. The first signs of life appeared 4 billion years ago. I am not clear how natural selection worked during the first 10 to 11 billion years, but I am content to let it remain a mystery. I do more or less understand how that first life form gradually reached the point, some 6 million years ago, when the very earliest primates began to exhibit human characteristics.

About 200,000 years ago, the natural selection process became infinitely more complicated by the emergence of sapient human beings, to whom God gave *free choice*. Since that time, God's processes have been susceptible to the high likelihood that humans would make a series of very poor choices.

I sat with all of this for a long time this morning. Consider the incredible period of time this universe existed before the arrival of humans. Carl Sagan, the great astronomer, once said that if the Cosmic Calendar were the size of a football field, then "all of human history would occupy an area the size of a person's hand."

As incredibly short as the human era is compared to the age of the universe, it is still long enough for 12,500 generations of human beings. Every one of the humans in each of those generations exercised some level of free choice. Every one of them would have played an important role in the dossiers of their offspring.

It would take humankind 195,000 years to evolve to the point of primitive forms of writing. It was then, roughly 3,000 years ago, that humans in several different locations began to explore the concepts of good and evil, along with an intense interest in the meaning of life.

Teilhard believed that the combination of natural selection and the collective action of all the free choices being made by all the humans on the planet would eventually evolve into greater levels of consciousness. Eventually, creation would evolve to the point of *unitive consciousness*, when God and all of His creation would be one and, more important, *be conscious of their oneness*. God's creative process is evolution. The goal of that process is unitive consciousness. The governing rules are natural selection and free choice.

I believe that God made me in that great burst of energy that started the process. In that energy was all the inert gas and all the inorganic matter that would make up the universe for 10 billion years. Also in that massive explosion of energy were all the life forms that would evolve over the next three billion nine hundred and ninety-six million years from the first eukaryote to the early primate that first displayed certain human characteristics.

As I reflect on this, I imagine all of the billions of minute selections that had to be made in the earliest simple life form for it to reach the complexity of a human being. I reflect on all of the billions of free choices that had to be made by these early men and women to reach the point when they could write in the very simplest form.

The pace of change is quickening. From first acquiring the ability to write, humankind has developed in a mere three thousand years to the point where we are governed by Moore's law, doubling the speed of our computers every two years!

I reflect on all of the free choices that were made in the life histories of the parents and siblings of each of my parents. Consider their dossiers. God put in place the system of natural selection and free choice that resulted in the extremely complex interaction of so many millions of creatures required to finally produce me. Yes, He created me. But it was not as simple as the words would lead one to believe.

MY DOSSIER

MY PARENTS, Glen Robert Hart and Gwendolyn Irene Hoopes Hart, were both born in Idaho on April 10, 1922, and May 10, 1921, respectively. Mom died September 10, 1997, in Indianapolis. Dad died August 8, 2008, in Bountiful, Utah. Sometime before they died, both of my parents wrote or dictated short life histories. I read those histories this morning for the first time.

Dad

Dad grew up in southeastern Idaho, in farming communities near Twin Falls. His father was a dairy farmer, proudly raising Milking Shorthorn cattle. Dad's parents, Charles and Ethel Currington Hart, moved to Idaho from Minnesota, along with most

of the rest of their family. Dad writes that his Currington grandparents were Methodist, while both his Hart grandparents and his parents were Presbyterian. Both sides of the family were "of English descent." His mother died in 1947. I only remember Grandpa's second wife Edith, a grandmother about whom I have fond memories. Dad's family was important throughout my life, although mostly very distantly. He had two brothers, Ralph and Warren, and two sisters, Belle and Miriam. His cousins were rodeo cowboys, both competing nationally and serving in leadership position in the Idaho Rodeo Cowboys Association and the Professional Rodeo Cowboys Association of America.

From Dad's history (he is writing about his childhood, and references to Dad are to his own father):

> It always helped our income to be able to sell registered bull calves. We kept the heifers to expand the herd. The sale of the bulls provided operating money. It really helped especially during the depression years to have a little extra.
>
> Dad was always kind of a leader in the community and raised good crops and kept up to date on everything. He was active in the Grange. He held many offices in Grange work and was Master of the Grange for some time. He was also on the school board. We were one of the first to get electricity in the area. We owned one of the first dishwashers ever made. We got electricity on the farm when I was 5 years old, which would have been 1927. From that time on we had an electric milker.
>
> Another thing that Dad did that was quite ingenious was to build pig pens right against the barn. He ran a pipe from the cream separator so that he could feed the skimmed milk to the pigs. That way they could have animal protein along with the ground grain that we fed. They really grew fast and we didn't have to carry the milk to them.
>
> I was proud of my attendance record [at school]. I went 7 of the 8 grades without either being absent or tardy. I started 4-H club when I was 10 years old. Dad was our community 4-H leader. I started FFA as a freshman in high school. I just had the heifers my freshman year. When I was a sophomore I bought four registered Black Poland pigs, 3 gilts and a boar.

I love Dad's reference to 4-H Club. Many years later, in 1954, Dad started a tractor maintenance 4-H club for the families around our farm. I remember taking apart and rebuilding a Case VAC tractor, probably the last time I did anything mechanical in my life. International 4-H is back in my life today. In the past few months, we have been talking about organizing a 4-H club in the Haitian communities that our Sister Parish Ministry works with in the Dominican Republic. The apple falls close to the tree.

Dad grew up and went through public schools in and around Buhl, Idaho. He went to the University of Idaho in 1941, entering the class of 1945. Like it did for people all over the world, the war prevented him from graduating with his class. His roommate was Charlie Wilson, who left school after the first semester to join the Navy. Charlie was killed early in 1942 by a Japanese plane strafing his ship. Oddly enough, I always thought my middle name came from Charlie Wilson, even though the obvious source was my grandfather. Dad was in ROTC at the University of Idaho, moving up to Advanced ROTC in the spring of 1942, which required him to join the Army.

Mom

My mother was the only daughter of John Clarke Hoopes and Ivy Bickmore, who lived and farmed in the area between Tetonia and Rexburg, Idaho. John Hoopes was the 12th child born to Daniel and

Katherine Clark Hoopes. Mom was born in Rexburg, Idaho, the third child in the family. Her brother Earl was born in 1924, and her brother Clint, in 1926. Mom had two older brothers, Dan and Clark. The family was among the early Mormon settlers in Weston, Idaho, near the Utah border. They moved to the Teton Valley shortly after the end of World War I. Mom wrote in her history:

> There we would live this camping life, yet mother cooked for hired men. There was no electricity so she had to cook on a coal range. No electricity meant no running water. We hauled our water in large tanks from a spring in the mountain and emptied it into a cistern. We would get all of our water by lowering a bucket on a rope and drawing up a bucket of water. They used to say that the hired men would see who could go the longest without asking for water, because if the bucket was empty they would have to draw a full one.

They were Democrats in a part of the world that became increasingly Republican. Being part of the Democratic party was important to them, something that has clearly been part of my own life. I remember political conversations from as early as the 1952 election of Dwight Eisenhower, and working in every campaign from as early as 1956, when I worked in the Frank Church senate campaign. Mom's brother Dan was head of the Idaho delegation to the 1968 Democratic Convention in Chicago, a position he used to name me sergeant-at-arms of the delegation.

Mom often claimed to have been treated as a princess when she was young, a status she achieved both because she was the only daughter and because her father insisted upon it, both for her and her mother. I remember her as proud, almost haughty at times, and very grand. Even though she constantly complained about it, Mom acted as though the tiny house we eventually lived in out in the desert was a palace. She certainly described her parents' house in Rexburg as one of the very best houses in the area, with every modern convenience available.

Mom started college at Ricks College, a junior college in Rexburg, then went up to Moscow to finish at the University of Idaho. She met Dad there. Mom wrote in her history that they met in November, 1942, were engaged in January, 1943, and were married on March 6, less than two months later. Dad had to leave college to return to Buhl to run the farm, a "vital industry" during the war. Nonetheless, he was soon called up, but given a deferment before having to report to duty. My older brother, Leonard, was born February 7, 1944, and I was born almost eleven months later, on December 28, 1944. Dad's deferment was up in November, so Mom moved back to Rexburg to stay with her parents. Dad was in basic training in San Diego when I was born.

Dad was mustered out of the Navy at the end of the war in the Pacific, returning to Buhl to farm for two years before using the GI Bill to return to the University of Idaho. He finished his degree in Vocational Agriculture in one year. I actually remember nothing from that year in Moscow. There is a picture of me holding an icicle, standing on a sidewalk between snow drifts that were over my head on both sides. For most of my life, I have felt certain I remember the heavy snow that year. The truth is, I only remember the picture.

After Dad's graduation, the family returned to Filer, where Dad taught school. My younger brother, Wayne, was born in nearby Twin Falls on November 5, 1950.

The Farm

In 1951, Dad bought a 400-acre parcel of land located about fifteen miles west of Blackfoot, Idaho. The first four years on the farm were disastrous. The first year, deep wells were not finished in time to water, and thus save the crops. Hail storms wiped out the crops in the second year. Wheat prices plummeted in 1954, the first time we actually had any wheat to sell.

All my adult life, I have been somewhat obsessed by the house I live in. The story of our family struggle to build a house on that farm in the Snake River desert offers a very plausible explanation. And my mother's grand visions clearly planted aspirational ideas in my young mind.

The first planting year, 1951, Dad rented an apartment in Blackfoot. Mom wrote, "We had one room at the farm. It was one we built at my parents' yard in Rexburg and hauled down on a truck." Mom would drive to and from the farm all day, picking up parts and supplies. After less than a month, she decided to move out to the farm to live. Dad purchased an army surplus tent, installed it on a wooden floor, and designated it the bedroom for Leonard and me, and for the hired men. Wayne, Dad, and Mom slept in the one room, which was also the kitchen and family room. Obviously, the bathroom was an outhouse. Mom cooked three meals a day for eight people over a campfire. Kerosene lanterns provided light. Only through considerable lobbying by Mom was the power company ultimately forced to run a single-phase power line to the farm. We spent that winter in California, where Dad worked at the GM automobile factory east of Los Angeles.

When we returned to the farm in the early spring of 1952, Dad built a second one-room structure, which would serve as the bedroom for Mom and Dad. The other room continued to serve as the kitchen and family room. The tent would be the bedroom for the "boys" for another three years. Finally, when Mom was pregnant with Connie in 1954, we expanded the house to four rooms and brought the plumbing inside. I was old enough to help with the construction of the addition. All I remember is digging the footers through the rocky soil.

The family was now under one roof, which covered a four-hundred square foot house (about the size of the new houses we are now building for families in Mamey). Connie, born in 1955, and Nancy, born in 1956, had their bedroom. The three boys had a bedroom. My parents had a bedroom. We continued to live, cook, and eat in the original one-room. We lived in that house until 1959, the year I started high school. Thanks to a good crop and high prices in 1958, Dad decided to make a major addition to the house. We added a bedroom (converting one of the older bedrooms into an office), another bathroom, and a master bedroom. The house, now complete, was still an ungainly, patched together, single-story ranch house. Somewhere in that decade, I must have developed an unrequited passion for architecture and design.

Mom hated the farm, and resented Dad for moving us there. I always found that odd since it was her brother who promoted the idea. She wrote in her history:

I kept thinking, both of us spent four years in college to prepare us for a good life and here we are, trying to eke a living from this sub-marginal land. Glen never agreed with me on my description of the land, but I am of the same opinion still. After one of the good years, our best, we again remodeled the house. It always made me very angry when salespeople would come out from town and exclaim about such a nice place *for farmers*. The prejudice was evident. We were second class citizens. Although I had never liked a farm or farm life, I knew my family members were well-educated people who enjoyed the better things in life.

Dad built migrant worker housing in 1954 as well. Navajo Indians came up from Arizona and New Mexico to work in the sugar beet fields of northern Utah and southeastern Idaho. The migrant housing that we built was not radically different from the housing we lived in—no electricity, outdoor plumbing, and many people in the same room. I note this in this review of my early life only because I am now working with migrant Haitians in the Dominican Republic. We are building houses for families that are not radically different from the housing Dad built sixty years ago, in Idaho. Amazing.

The year 1954 was significant for another reason. Dad and I were baptized together in the Mormon Church. Leonard had been baptized the year before. All the members of Mom's family were Mormon. Dad and Mom were married by a Mormon at the LDS Institute at the University of Idaho. Dad agreed that we children would be brought up as Mormons, but he resisted officially joining the church. The family story, now largely debunked, is that Dad needed to sell the potato crop in 1954, and joining the church would improve the price.

Ironically, 1959, the year we made the final addition to the house, was a difficult year financially on the farm. A late spring frost combined with an early fall frost to virtually destroy our crop. Dad was under pressure from the banks that provided his crop loans. The Farm Home Administration kept us in business. Nonetheless, Dad took a job teaching Vocational Agriculture the next year, which was another bad crop year.

I found this in Leonard's history:

> The start of school my senior year [1962] was a big day. Mom stood out on the lawn and watched as all five children got on the bus together for the first time—me as a senior, Bob a junior, Wayne in 7th grade, Connie in 2nd grade, and Nancy as a first grader. Later that year she started to substitute teach. The only game Mom ever got to see me play was my senior year at a home game. The coach sent in my brother Bob. He was injured and had to be carried off the field.

My memory of my high school years has always included Dad's presence at every sporting event. Both Leonard and Wayne remember things quite differently. I am reluctant to give up my version, if only because it is one of a very few fond memories I have of my early life.

Dad was painfully quiet, probably shy. I have warm recollections of walking along an irrigation ditch listening to Dad name the plants, even catching a floating seed and describing the plant from which it came. He knew everything there was to know about plants and animals. He knew how to do things, like build the house or layout the irrigation system for the whole farm, or breed and raise all kinds of animals. When he and my mother argued, I always took his side, though never out loud!

Dad and Mom were both teaching school in 1963 when I left to go to college. Farming had become increasingly difficult, complicated by the fact that Dad suffered from constant skin cancer caused by spending so much time outside. At some point in 1963 or 1964, the family moved into Moreland, seven miles from the farm. Not long thereafter, they sold the farm to one of our neighbors. In late 1965 or early 1966, notably the year of my excommunication from the Mormon Church, the family moved to Terre Haute, Indiana, where Dad accepted a job to work as Farm Manager of an experimental farm owned by Pfizer. He worked there until he retired in 1988.

My Siblings

Leonard

My only older sibling was born the same year I was born, only eleven months earlier, on February 7, 1944, in Wendell, Idaho. Siblings this close in age are notoriously either very close or constantly fighting. Sadly, Leonard and I have spent most of our lives at odds with each other. My earliest memories involve demanding that my parents give me whatever gift they gave him, denying him any age preference or status as the oldest son. I competed with him in school, albeit from the grade behind. Now I can see that being the second child gave me an inherent advantage. I followed him, but knew what mistakes to avoid and what avenues to pursue. I am not proud of my behavior.

Leonard was an early fan of computers and digital technology. Even at the University of Idaho, he worked in the computer center, twenty years before IBM came out with the IBM PC personal computer. His first full-time job after college was teaching at the University computer center. Sadly, he dropped out of law school to take that job after learning that his first wife, Kathy, was pregnant.

Leonard continued to work as both a teacher and manager in computing centers at different colleges for several years. By 1972, I had started a low-income housing development company with projects about to be completed in Kentucky and Mississippi. I asked Leonard to join the company as head of property management. From his history:

> I became disillusioned with the bureaucracy in education and when my brother Bob offered me a position managing his rental properties in the south. In 1972, I left teaching and moved to New Orleans. For the next five years I worked for five different companies (he kept merging or splitting up) in the south moving from New Orleans, LA, to Gulfport/ Biloxi, MS, and ending in Mobile, Alabama.

Leonard stayed in Mobile after I moved from real estate development to coal mining, and he lives there now. He ultimately joined Gulf Lumber Company, working there for seventeen years. Leonard has two sons and has been married four times. His present wife, Shirley, has been not only the right life partner, but also the best imaginable person to deal with Leonard's health problems.

Leonard's health is a serious problem. He has fought the debilitating side effects of adult diabetes for years. I think about him a great deal, especially as I do these Exercises. He is part of who I am. I have never properly shown him the love that I feel.

Wayne

My younger brother Wayne, born November 5, 1950, in Twin Falls, was frequently described by Mom as the brightest child in the family. He earned a Bachelor's degree in Biological Sciences at Indiana University, graduating in 1973. He went on to the University of Wisconsin for his Master's Degree in Biology. Oddly enough, Wayne started his energy career about the same time I started mine. He worked initially in the Office of Energy of Idaho Governor John Evans, a Democrat (no surprise). He then worked as the solar energy project manager, among other positions, at Bonneville Power Administration. He ultimately returned to Boise, Idaho, where he continues to earn an income as a consultant to the Idaho Public Utilities Commission.

I recently visited Wayne in Boise to be present for his double bypass surgery. While Wayne was still too anesthetized to talk, I had time to get to know his very nice wife, Theresa, and his daughter, Veronica. Theresa is Wayne's third wife. His first wife was a favorite in the family, but the marriage ultimately ended because of differences about having a family. Wayne, ever the idealist, believed in Zero Population Growth, choosing to have a vasectomy while he was still in college. He then married his second wife Teri, and, surprise of all surprises, she had his child, a daughter named Veronica. Wayne and Teri were divorced in 2008.

Veronica decided a few years ago that *she* wanted to be *he*, a decision Wayne has accepted with incredible grace. Veronica became Ronnie, then Hal, and is considering yet another name change, to Dio. The transgender issue is difficult for me, not because I reject transgender people, or question the validity of their decisions. I do think it is a terribly big decision, not one to be taken lightly. After hours of conversation with Wayne's child, I am certain that she or he is very unhappy, and is bitter about life in general. I am not persuaded that her sexual identity is the core problem. She seems to be moving from a very unhappy young woman to a very unhappy young man.

I love Wayne. He has lived a life of extraordinary loyalty to his ideals and to his family.

Connie

Connie was born on February 28, 1954, in Blackfoot. I left Idaho when Connie was only nine years old, so I have little memory of her as a child, and none as a teenager. The Connie I know and deeply admire was a grown woman when I came to absolutely adore her as a mother, a sister, and an anchor in our family. After first attending Purdue University for a couple of years, Connie was graduated from Brigham Young University in 1976, with a Bachelor of Science degree in Child Development.

She was a teacher throughout her working life, beginning with preschool and special needs children. While living in Canada, where she lived with her husband Kirt (she was married on August 18, 1977), she taught life skills to young adults on a reservation, and taught the parents of preschoolers. Even while staying at home with her children (she now has seven children), she operated a preschool in her house.

Connie would have been about ten years old when the family moved from the farm into Moreland, then, a year later, to Indiana. Connie wrote:

> I don't have very many memories of the farm years. I remember helping dad build barbed wire fences by handing him parts. I also remember being with him when he was changing the irrigation with the ditches. And helping a little with the potato harvest by sitting on the spuds in the truck and pushing them out. And I think a little of picking clods off the conveyor belt but mostly being told I was too young. And possibly pulling boards out of the truck, but mostly being told I was too young for that, too. I was occasionally able to help feed the cows in the new area by the house. And I remember picking raspberries and weeding in the garden.

I also remember climbing on the piles of wheat in the granary but I think that was just for fun. My favorite memories on the farm include riding horses, walking on the shoulders of my older brothers, racing on the front lawn and being amazed at how fast Dad was, playing in the old chicken coop and in a patch of trees and flat rocks by a small junk area, and all of the homemade donuts filling the kitchen at potato harvest. I also remember cuddling with the cats on a bed in the old bunkhouse—and digging a skunk out from under that house…

I have some not so favorite memories as well. One kind of funny one of being served pollywogs on saltine crackers topped with cake sprinkles and being told they were sardines. And other teasings and mean treatments by older brothers. I also remember Mom losing her temper with the brothers. I could never understand how mom got so mad on one Christmas riding home from grandparents—until I was a mom and realized how much stress and lack of sleep comes with the holidays! I am afraid I don't have a lot of positive memories of you and Leonard. And Wayne I remember being more of a pest when we were young, and not wanting him to play with me and Nancy. And then times when Wayne and I would gang up and tease Nancy.

And, of course. I cannot leave out the memories of heated discussions around the dinner table. Later I learned that Mom played the devil's advocate to encourage broader thinking, but to me it was just raised voices and arguing and very unpleasant. I always felt like politics was way more important in our home than religion.

While Connie became more religious when she moved out to Provo, Utah, to finish college at BYU, she recalls a prayer from her freshman year at Purdue.

After I had left for college and learned to pray regularly, I remember one prayer that involved the whole family. I didn't like how our family argued and fought so much and that holiday times were not always happy. So that year everyone was going to be home for Thanksgiving—a rare occasion. I didn't want it marred so I prayed really hard for a good, peaceful weekend. And was so grateful when that is what it was.

In the years toward the end of Dad's life, when he was living in a retirement home near Salt Lake City, Connie assumed a powerful leadership role in the family. Being in closest proximity to Dad, Connie was the source of information about his status. She was a strong presence throughout his final days, including his funeral.

Her daughter lived for some time in Asheville, North Carolina, where our daughter Jennifer now lives. Connie supported a friendship that grew up between the cousins, and helped soften the blow of that friendship ultimately ending.

Nancy
One year after Connie was born, Mom had the last of her children. Nancy was born in Blackfoot on May 21, 1955.
From Nancy:

We moved to Indiana in June of 1966—fifty years ago this year! I agree with Wayne that Mom and Dad were happier in Terre Haute than they were in Idaho. Our lives just got better, and Mom and Dad loved Terre Haute from the first day. They made close friends through Pfizer, at church, and in various organizations that Mom got involved in. Owning and operating The Canister [a specialty retail kitchen store] was quite rewarding for Mom. Connie and I were happy in Terre Haute, too, especially with our ward at church, where we made great friends and had youth leaders we loved and admired.

I first worked as a mother's helper for you and Phyllis in the summer of 1971, I believe, in your big house on Clermont Avenue. Jennifer had just been born. I could tell things were rocky between you and Phyllis. Then I went back again when it was just Phyllis and the girls in the summers of 1972 and 1974, and I think it was a smaller house also on Clermont. I remember rocking three-month old Jennifer and losing my heart to her. Your kids really felt like my kids those summers.

It saddens me to read that Nancy could tell things with Phyllis were not working out. My memory of how things ended with Phyllis has been significantly altered with the passing of time. I recall a perfectly friendly couple that simply decided marriage was not for them. Obviously, we both treated our marriage with a great deal more respect than that innocent gloss suggests.

Melissa and Jennifer, our daughters, have fond memories of Nancy as a nanny. Sadly, the necessities of life for single working mothers required them to live with nannies all their lives. Phyllis was as much a workaholic as I ever was, leaving home very early each morning and returning long after the girls came home from school.

More from Nancy:

I graduated from BYU in April, 1977; my major was Humanities with an emphasis in English. I loved BYU and my studies there. 1977 was a big year. Mom and Dad took Connie and me to Europe in May, Terry and I were married in June, and Connie and Kirt were married in August.

We had Ryan nine months later, in March of '78. (Nine and a half months later, I always used to say with a blush.) Emily was born in April 1980, Elizabeth in April 1983, Laura in August 1987, and Rebecca in July 1989.

We lived outside of St. Louis for the first nine months. Terry worked at McDonnell-Douglas Aircraft Company and I taught high school until Ryan was born. When Terry's dad died in February of 1978, we felt a need to live closer to his mom. So Terry got a job at Eli Lilly and Company, and he's been with the company for almost 39 years.

I stayed home with the kids for about 20 years, and I very much enjoyed mothering full-time. I gave occasional tours at the art museum in Terre Haute to keep learning and teaching. When Ryan started college, I began to feel a need to help out with expenses. I first got a job at Martinsville High School as a remediation aide, working two days a week the first year, and three days a week the second year. Those jobs helped me ease back into teaching. I got my full-time English teaching job there in 1998. I have loved teaching but have never liked how busy it makes my life, and I regret that Laura and Rebecca grew up with a much more harried mother than Ryan, Emily, and Beth did.

Like Connie, Nancy has grown into a solid rock in the family, her church community, and her teaching profession. Her children are diverse and interesting, each of them doing something that makes me proud as an uncle.

What extraordinary women Connie and Nancy have become! I am left to wonder how much differently I might have developed had their influence been greater in my life. Sadly, I left the family while they were so young.

Personality Traits

Those aspects of my person that were genetic are fairly obvious. I am a white male born in the United States near the beginning of one of the longest periods of economic expansion in the history of the world. Being white and male are not advantages of which I am proud. The world should not accord white males any greater status or head start in life than anybody else. The world I spent most of my life in—the second half of the 20th century in the United States—was certainly better for women and people of color than other eras and other parts of the world. But I pray for the day when being either white or male has no advantages. I have an athletic body, even though I was only successful in sports because my schools were so small. I was born with a reasonably good mind. My parents were alive, together, and caring throughout most of my life. Mom died when I was in my fifties. Dad died when I was in my mid-sixties.

Perhaps more important than anything else, both of my parents were college graduates. While that is true for around a third of the people alive in the United States today, it was much less common in 1944. Robert Putnam, author of *Our Kids*, argues that children of two college-graduate parents are upper class from birth. He compares the lives of those children with the lives of children born to two parents who only finish high school. The comparison is dramatic in terms of everything from health to lifetime earnings. All the reasons Putnam offers for these advantages were true in my case. My parents talked to us over meals, often several times each week. They strongly encouraged reading. They were both school teachers, and were both proud of never missing, or even being late for school when they were children. Compare my upbringing to that of children whose parents struggled with divorce, incarceration, addiction, and long periods of unemployment. We were poor, but we hardly lived in poverty. We went to school in simple clothes, not rags. We ate three healthy meals a day, even if dietary standards have changed some over the decades.

Mom's almost delusional pride certainly had an impact on my personality and ambition. The details of the grand life she envisioned were never clear to me, so my ambition was not to achieve a certain career, house, or lifestyle. Rather, I simply wanted more. Some might applaud the drive and ambition that resulted from my interaction with Mom. I am not sure. I don't admire social climbing, and I have clearly done a lot of it over the years. Further, the other side of the ambition coin is dissatisfaction with whatever I achieved, and a powerful drive to have more, do more, and be more.

Somewhere in the mix of those early years of hard luck and poverty, two other themes—hard work and politics—were very firmly implanted.

First, I developed the habit of working hard. In some respects, that was the most important trait for my long climb from obscure penury to whatever level of fame and fortune I have attained. I worked hard at everything I did, from school through every phase of my career.

The second was public service, and its close relative, politics. From my earliest memories of family dinners, whether they were Thanksgiving affairs with the extended family, or a dinner with the hired men in the little house on the farm, I remember people talking about politics and the public good. My mother's family was both very liberal and active in the Democratic Party, so gatherings that included Uncle Clint and Uncle Earl were guaranteed to be loud, fun, and up-to-the-minute in terms of the limited amount of political news available to us in southern Idaho. During all my years working throughout the world, these two themes—hard work and great interest in the public square—were both extremely valuable and surprisingly rare.

There were other gifts from those early years. I was then, and remain, intensely curious. I enjoy learning new things, visiting new places, meeting new people, and even mastering new software. My siblings and I learned to read early, and learned to love reading. Finally, we—the Hart children—were blessed with sufficient brain power to put all of these various gifts to work, both frequently and effectively.

Most people would argue with any suggestion that I am quiet, and few actually know about my frequent isolation. I seek isolation constantly, leaving meetings a little early or arriving a little late, all to avoid conversation with others. It seems credible that this is a personality trait I inherited, by nature or nurture, from Dad.

I have attempted to summarize the personality traits I believe I owe to my parents and early surroundings. Some of these are quite dominant all of the time, others seem to come and go. While it is possible that I developed a few of these later in life, the longer I contemplate all that my parents and siblings wrote and what I can remember, the more I can see the very early origins of most of these traits.

Positive	Negative
Hard working	Envious
Curious	Greedy
Creative	Easily bored
Success-oriented, driven	Climbing
Ambitious	Generally dissatisfied
Passionate	Aloof
Intelligent	Arrogant
Interested in public affairs and politics	Insecure
Adaptable	Image-conscious
Skeptical	Disobedient
Enthusiastic	Profligate
Rebellious, defiant	Ambitious
Charismatic	Insubordinate

Consider the gifts I have been given. Yes, I was born white, male, relatively intelligent, and living in one of the wealthiest parts of the only planet that we know can sustain life. Yes, my parents modeled certain behaviors, counseled other behaviors, and genetically passed on to me yet other behaviors, all of which go into making me the person that I am. They did this because of the choices they made within the rather narrow context of how and by whom they were raised, taught, and counseled. And to be precise, I have made choices with the inputs of all the influences of nature and nurture on my life. Friends, teachers, bosses, and parents all contributed something to the context within which I make choices, but I am responsible for those choices. I cannot "blame" any of my choices on anyone else, including God. He did not want me to make the many poor choices I have made. And just as I cannot blame Him for the poor choices, I cannot give Him all the credit for the good choices. So, how can I call myself a believer? How can I show gratitude to God for all the gifts I am not certain He gave me?

Bear with me on this comparison, but consider the remark of Saint Theresa of Avilla that "of course there is a hell, but there is no one there." I could say that no, God did not plan for me to be sitting in this library at this moment, typing on this computer while listening to this news channel at this particular time today. But He would not be surprised to find me here, doing what I am doing.

What I believe is that He is creating me right here, right now. What I am doing and where I am doing it are part of His continuing creation. In that sense, it is—I am—not an accident. I am a tiny part of an infinitely large universe, eternally being created according to a beautifully simple plan to ultimately achieve unitive consciousness. Every tiny part of the context within which I freely make choices is part of that infinitely large universe eternally being created.

So yes, I am grateful for every part of this context, every single element of which is a gift from God. In fact, every part of my context is the consequence of God's gifts given to the whole community of people, places, events, and things that make up my existence. The parts of that "creation community" that appear to be "bad," "sinful," or "evil" are not accidents, nor are they the result of mistakes or missteps in the evolutionary creation. Taken all together, the good and the bad, the righteous and the evil, and the promising and the futile, all are acting on all of creation to move it ever forward to greater consciousness. For all of what is wrong with the universe today, there is no question that it is a world at a higher level of consciousness than the world of yesterday. And tomorrow, the universe will be at a higher level of consciousness than it is today. We, the bit players in this enormous drama, will do what we do, quite unaware that collectively, inexorably the world is making progress. That is the plan!

September 28

Matthew 6: 25–34, Do Not Worry
  25 "Therefore I tell you, do not worry about your life, what you will eat or what you will drink, or about your body, what you will wear. Is not life more than food, and the body more than clothing? 26 Look at the birds of the air; they neither sow nor reap nor gather into barns, and yet your heavenly Father feeds them. Are you not of more value than they? 27 And can any of you by worrying add a single hour to your span of life? 28 And why do you worry about clothing? Consider the lilies of the field, how they grow; they neither toil nor spin, 29 yet I tell you, even Solomon in all his glory was not clothed like one of these. 30 But if God so clothes the grass of the field, which is alive today and tomorrow is thrown into the oven, will he not much more clothe you—you of little faith? 31 Therefore do not worry, saying, 'What will we eat?' or 'What will we drink?' or 'What will we wear?' 32 For it is the Gentiles who strive for all these things; and indeed your heavenly Father knows that you need all these things. 33 But strive first for the kingdom of God and his righteousness, and all these things will be given to you as well.

  34 "So do not worry about tomorrow, for tomorrow will bring worries of its own. Today's trouble is enough for today.

I **DID NOT** finish my dossier yesterday, and will be surprised if I finish it by the end of the month. I have decided to move on, returning to the dossier when I have time. I intend to read the daily reading each day, reflect on that reading, and write my thoughts in this journal. The advice not to worry about tomorrow is not advice I have heeded much in my life. Not surprisingly, given my personality, I have pretty much always had a plan, and worried about implementing that plan. Even when I was at my laziest and least responsible, I was promising myself that I would be and do better tomorrow!

As I work on my dossier, I consider the lilies of the field with a certain amount of envy. Yes, they seem to flourish and grow beautifully wherever they are, "neither toiling nor spinning." I have not been so fortunate. I have considered the places I have found myself to be starting places, each requiring effort—a lot of effort—to get to where I need to be. I know, this is not accepting life on life's terms, or being satisfied with what I have. It is a driven, compelled, and often out-of-control striving for more. Even now in my retirement, I want Sister Parish to be more and do more, never quite happy with what is.

John Caputo offers a fitting prayer.

> God is the passion of life, the passion of my life, the passion of my unknowing, my passion for the impossible.

I cherish my passion for the impossible. It has served me well.

September 29

Prayer of Consideration: The Lilies of the Field

Jesus called on His disciples to "consider" the lilies of the field, and we should do the same. The lily does not choose in which field it will stand. When it grows from seed or runner, it finds itself in this field, with this hard clay or soft loam. So do I find myself on a "field"—the twentieth century, America, a state, city, town, neighborhood? How much of my life world is my making; how much is God's? The lily has no control over what grows around it. When it shoots up, it might have to fight for its life with thorns or clumps of crabgrass. Or it might be outshone by great sunflowers. So have I very little control over what surrounds me. I live in corporate structures, in political processes. I am caught up in earning a living, buying insurance, preparing for illness and old age. I cannot change the stock market or banking practices or taxation. I cannot make the ghettos disappear, or dry up acid rain. How much of my life world is my making; how much is God's? The lily of the field has absolutely no control over the weather—rain or drought, it must simply stand and endure. So have I no control over nations warring on one another, or over international cartels poisoning the air with pollutants. I cannot control whether people around me drug themselves and fill the atmosphere of my life world with fear and violence. I cannot control people feeling prejudice toward me and my kind. I cannot make male chauvinism or strident feminism go away, or stop people from aborting babies or abusing their children. How much of my life world is my making; how much is God's? The lily came up a certain kind of lily of a certain color and shape, and its shapeliness and health depended on the spring and the summer, and whether grazing cattle let it grow. So did I come up a certain kind of person, of a certain color and shape. So were my psychic health and physical shape much influenced by the forces around me when I was coming up. And until now, all created things have let me live and even thrive, though many, many threatened and still threaten me. How much of my life growth is my making: how much is God's? For all that, not even Solomon dressed up in gold-embroidered brocade was any more lovely than that lily. So for all that has shaped and misshaped me, for all that has given me health and inflicted ill health on me—I am precious in the eyes of God, and honored, and God loves me as I am. Otherwise, I would not be as I am, though God would be glad were I to slough off my selfish sins. But they are trash compared to God's creating love in me, whose love will burn them away like flakes on the bark of a flaming pine log. How much of me is mine; how much can be God's?

THIS IS A powerful reading. I am precious to God as I am, where I am, and doing whatever I am doing. God loves me no more or no less. That is a HUGE concept! How could He love me in my worst moments? I know I hate myself. I know I disappoint people I love. The challenge is beautifully expressed in the serenity prayer. Give me the serenity to accept the things I cannot change, the courage to change the things I can, and the wisdom to know the difference. In all cases, either those I accept with serenity or those I courageously change, God loves me. His love will not increase when I choose correctly or decrease when I make poor choices. Nonetheless, my purpose for being is to love God, full stop. That purpose is not unlike the purpose of the lily to be beautiful. Neither my purpose nor that of the lily is dependent upon the soil, the weather, the grazing cattle, nor any other exterior condition.

September 30

Isaiah 43:1–7, Israel's Only Savior
¹ But now thus says the LORD, he who created you, O Jacob, he who formed you, O Israel:
Do not fear, for I have redeemed you; I have called you by name, you are mine.
² When you pass through the waters, I will be with you; and through the rivers, they shall not overwhelm you; when you walk through fire you shall not be burned, and the flame shall not consume you.
³ For I am the LORD your God, the Holy One of Israel, your Savior. I give Egypt as your ransom, Ethiopia and Seba in exchange for you.
⁴ Because you are precious in my sight, and honored, and I love you, I give people in return for you, nations in exchange for your life.
⁵ Do not fear, for I am with you; I will bring your offspring from the east, and from the west I will gather you;
⁶ I will say to the north, "Give them up," and to the south, "Do not withhold; bring my sons from far away and my daughters from the end of the earth—
⁷ everyone who is called by my name, whom I created for my glory, whom I formed and made."

"**FOR YOU ARE** precious in my sight, and honored, and I love you. Everyone who is called by my name, whom I created for my glory, whom I formed and made, I love you." This is such a beautiful passage. It is tempting even now to read this without reflection, to conclude that this is how God felt about the nation of Israel. At least that is what the Prophet Isaiah thought, an Israeli prophet. What else would he say to the Israelites? That interpretation is extremely exclusive, suggesting that anyone not "called by name" is not loved.

After reflection, however, I read it differently. Israel is only a metaphor for all of creation. God created, formed, and called by name all of creation and every creature in the universe. Infinite and eternal love is an overwhelming concept, not easy for any finite being, (particularly this one!) to understand. This inclusive, all-embracing understanding fits so well with the concept of a loving God, of a God who created all that is out of love, and continually creates this universe with and by love.

Early this morning, I learned that a little girl named Anabel returned very late last night to her home, a tiny house in Mamey. Her mother was told yesterday that Anabel's WILM's tumors had grown, and that she will die shortly. The doctors wanted to keep Anabel at the hospital to die in as much comfort as possible. Her mother could not accept that. I wanted to be angry with the mother for selfishly saying she wanted Anabel with her at home.

As I write this, I understand the mother. I love the very fact that she wants Anabel with her at all.

October 1

Repeat Psalm 139 (page 26)

ONCE AGAIN, I read through Psalm 139 humbled, both by the words and by my efforts each day this week to return to my dossier. I return in my thoughts to my growing understanding of cosmic divinity. As the psalmist says, I was "intricately woven in the depths of the earth," beheld by God in "my unformed substance." I continue to be troubled by efforts to fit whatever we think or believe into scripture, rather than letting scripture speak to us. Whichever way one looks at it, however, Psalm 139 resonates with me. After reading the simple histories of my parents, and reflecting on all the ways they formed me, the words "all the days that were formed for me [were written] when none of them as yet existed" are very powerful. So many of the personality traits that I have vainly taken credit for from time to time can be seen in the lives and stories of my parents. So many times and in so many ways I have thought of myself as so very different from my family, the lone sheep, the lost son, the Harvard success, and so much more. Yet all of me was there before. "I come to the end" and I am with you and you are with me. Even my differences have the fingerprints of my family all over them. This is not a bad thing, but it certainly speaks volumes about the obvious need for gratitude and humility.

CALENDAR WEEK THREE

Lord, Mighty God,

In power and wisdom You shape me and my world.

You chose my life world—my time, my city, my language.

You give me understanding and passions;

You fill me with desiring and with energies.

You give me voice to sing songs to You for all creation.

For all that has passed between us, I thank You.

To all that You are now doing in me, I say yes.

In the name of Him whom everything says yes,

Jesus my Lord and good brother, who lives and reigns with You,

forever and ever. Amen.

October 2

Luke 4: 16–30, The Rejection of Jesus at Nazareth

¹⁶ When he came to Nazareth, where he had been brought up, he went to the synagogue on the sabbath day, as was his custom. He stood up to read, ¹⁷ and the scroll of the prophet Isaiah was given to him. He unrolled the scroll and found the place where it was written:

¹⁸ "The Spirit of the Lord is upon me,

because he has anointed me

to bring good news to the poor.

He has sent me to proclaim release to the captives

and recovery of sight to the blind,

to let the oppressed go free,

¹⁹ to proclaim the year of the Lord's favor."

²⁰ And he rolled up the scroll, gave it back to the attendant, and sat down. The eyes of all in the synagogue were fixed on him. ²¹ Then he began to say to them, "Today this scripture has been fulfilled in your hearing." ²² All spoke well of him and were amazed at the gracious words that came from his mouth. They said, "Is not this Joseph's son?" ²³ He said to them, "Doubtless you will quote to me this proverb, 'Doctor, cure yourself!' And you will say, 'Do here also in your hometown the things that we have heard you did at Capernaum.'" ²⁴ And he said, "Truly I tell you, no prophet is accepted in the prophet's hometown. ²⁵ But the truth is, there were many widows in Israel in the time of Elijah, when the heaven was shut up three years and six months, and there was a severe famine over all the land; ²⁶ yet Elijah was sent to none of them except to a widow at Zarephath in Sidon. ²⁷ There were also many lepers in Israel in the time of the prophet Elisha, and none of them was cleansed except Naaman the Syrian." ²⁸ When they heard this, all in the synagogue were filled with rage. ²⁹ They got up, drove him out of the town, and led him to the brow of the hill on which their town was built, so that they might hurl him off the cliff. ³⁰ But he passed through the midst of them and went on his way.

THE PASSAGE Jesus read from Isaiah, slightly modified, is read each Sunday of this, another Jubilee Year. (Leviticus 25:10–11 calls for a Jubilee Year every fifty years.) Bring good news to the poor, release the captives, recover sight to the blind, and free the oppressed—these are the great goals of the Gospel. I think it very important to note that Jesus was not announcing something new to the people of Israel. He was reminding them of what their own prophets were saying 800 years earlier.

Karl Jaspers called the period from the eighth to the third centuries before Christ the *First Axial Age*. When I was initially taught about the First Axial Age only two years ago, I must admit it went largely over my head. Reading the passage today, it suddenly seems completely obvious. The larger message is about the cosmic evolution of consciousness. Everywhere on the planet, thinking people were reaching similar conclusions about morality, and man's relationship to man. I begin to appreciate the incredibly lengthy time frame of evolution when I consider that this level of consciousness was present throughout much of the human race nearly three thousand years ago, and it is still only aspirational. Three thousand years is not even a blink of the eye on the time scale of the universe. Most people in most parts of the world have been back sliding ever since that first great period. I know there are many good and decent people, and many great thinkers, who argue that we are entering or have entered a second axial age. If that is so, explain Wahhabism, the radically conservative strain of Islam, or the current global ascendance of anti-intellectual, anti-elite politics.

The second part of the passage from Luke's Gospel provides some defense for our Sister Parish Ministry efforts to deal with disease and poverty in a Haitian village in the Dominican Republic. Each time we travel to the DR, we drive by pockets of poverty in North Jacksonville, then fly over areas of poverty in the rest of Florida, the rest of the Caribbean, and the rest of the Dominican Republic. Going where we go does not preclude us from also working in other places, but I have to readily admit that we have finite gifts of time, talent, and treasure. Choosing one place to share those gifts is at the same time not choosing other places. I believe we can only hope that everyone does something somewhere. Perhaps the aggregate good will prevail over the aggregate bad.

October 3

Prayer of Consideration: The Way Things Are

Consider first that God the Lord creates all things at every moment. We tend to focus on "the Big Bang" at the very beginning, or on evolving life. But God continues to create at each moment. Even as we grow and mature, God continues creating me out of nothing, momently. His passionately creative love burns at the core of all my self, my Origin. God creates me in the concrete, not in general. God chose my time and place, my parents, my gifts. God keeps shaping my humanness and my personhood and my self. God creates "out of love," which means that God wants to share His love, to have others to love and to be loved by. I am intelligent and free so that I can love, as God my Maker loves. In calling me to live my special qualities and characteristics, God planted deep in my self an original purpose—the concrete expression of God's hopes in and for me. My life is to discover in myself that original purpose—what my concrete self "adds up to"—and to live it out. If I grow to be the person God has been hoping I would become, I manifest God's power at work, God's glory. For the glory of God is a human person fully alive. If I know who God is and who I am, and live out that knowledge, I will praise God in the morning and thank God in the night, and intend to fulfill God's hopes for myself and for my life world. All creatures have such an original purpose. I am also to live among created things as to reach my own, using or not using, enjoying or not enjoying others, depending on whether they help me express my original purpose. Yet even in this order and harmony, the Creator courteously leaves us with freedom. We are to choose whether to keep the rightness and justness and order. Where we choose not to, we wreak havoc on the earth. God surely knows this. But God's hope has always been that mankind would live out the recognition that He always comes first, and enact that recognition in creating our life together in order and in love. God's will is our peace. Not the peace of silence and death, but the quietly humming peace of a dynamic, wonderfully orderly love. This is what God hopes for on the earth.

THERE IS SO much to reflect upon in this meditation. I read it last night, hoping to ponder it during the night. It worked remarkably well. My mind was (and is) filled with a jumble of ideas and connections. So, when I came down to the library this morning, I prayed for clarity.

The idea of the importance of discovering our true purpose to determine what "our concrete self adds up to" is certainly not new. It is said of St. Francis that he prayed multiple times each day, "Who are you God? And who am I?" Meister Eckhart taught that the answers to both questions are essentially the same, that when I can finally reduce my*self* to nothingness—to what matters—I discover that all that is essential in me is God. Which brings me back to the Teilhard concept that each of us, along with the whole of the universe is inexorably evolving toward unity with God. Our great cry, "God, make us one!"

How do I apply this growing understanding that my purpose in life is to achieve wholeness, through which to find oneness with God? Henri Nouwen wrote that, "Spiritual maturity is not knowing what to do with your whole life, but just knowing what to do next." This makes total sense. It fits so well with the admonition to simply "do the next right thing." Nouwen also said, "Prayer is the best way to make our home in God." This is probably not bad advice. When in doubt, pray. Meister Eckhart said, "If the only prayer you ever say in life is thank you, it would be enough."

Beyond that for me, the next right thing has to begin with taking care of my family, starting of course with Sallie Ann, particularly at this time of her illness. It seems so long since I filled my days with Sister Parish. The last mission was the medical mission the first week of September, now a full month ago. The long fall hiatus in mission activity was one of the reasons I decided to do these Exercises at this time. I miss the high level of activity, concern, even drama of Sister Parish. The next right thing to do almost every day has been something either here or in the Dominican Republic connected with Sister Parish. The ministry has become my purpose. Which is not a bad thing. However, it leaves me wandering around the house quite a bit during the fall season without mission trips. I feel disconnected from them all.

October 4

Hosea 11: 1–4, God's Love for Israel
   When Israel was a child, I loved him, and out of Egypt I called my son.
   ² The more I called them, the more they went from me; they kept sacrificing to the Baals, and offering incense to idols.
   ³ Yet it was I who taught Ephraim to walk, I took them up in my arms; but they did not know that I healed them.
   ⁴ I led them with cords of human kindness, with bands of love. I was to them like those who lift infants to their cheeks. I bent down to them and fed them.

THE PASSAGE speaks to me about the relentless, but generally futile, efforts of our spiritual leaders, our parents, our families, and all our "better Angels" to exhort us to virtue, however one, from time to time, defines virtue. Today in his meditation, my Living School teacher, Father Rohr, talked about virtue as simplicity. Addiction to *more* is perhaps the greatest of all addictions. It is the core principle of capitalism. Choosing less, choosing to be satisfied with enough, these, for me, are the hardest challenges.

Today, I ask God for the strength to do what I know is the right thing to do, and for a deeper understanding of my weakness in this respect. Grant us Your grace of calm as we wait in the path of Hurricane Matthew, now hitting Haiti and causing heavy rain in Mamey and the other villages around Guerra.

October 5

Psalm 103, Bless the Lord
  ¹ Bless the LORD, O my soul, and all that is within me, bless his holy name
  ² Bless the LORD, O my soul, and do not forget all his benefits—
  ³ who forgives all your iniquity, who heals all your diseases,
  ⁴ who redeems your life from the Pit, who crowns you with steadfast love and mercy,
  ⁵ who satisfies you with good as long as you live so that your youth is renewed like the eagle's.
  ⁶ The LORD works vindication and justice for all who are oppressed.
  ⁷ He made known his ways to Moses, his acts to the people of Israel.
  ⁸ The LORD is merciful and gracious, slow to anger and abounding in steadfast love.
  ⁹ He will not always accuse, nor will he keep his anger forever.
  ¹⁰ He does not deal with us according to our sins, nor repay us according to our iniquities.
  ¹¹ For as the heavens are high above the earth, so great is his steadfast love toward those who fear him;
  ¹² as far as the east is from the west, so far he removes our transgressions from us.
  ¹³ As a father has compassion for his children, so the LORD has compassion for those who fear him.
  ¹⁴ For he knows how we were made; he remembers that we are dust.
  ¹⁵ As for mortals, their days are like grass; they flourish like a flower of the field;
  ¹⁶ for the wind passes over it, and it is gone, and its place knows it no more.
  ¹⁷ But the steadfast love of the LORD is from everlasting to everlasting on those who fear him, and his righteousness to children's children,
  ¹⁸ to those who keep his covenant and remember to do his commandments.
  ¹⁹ The LORD has established his throne in the heavens, and his kingdom rules over all.
  ²⁰ Bless the LORD, O you his angels, you mighty ones who do his bidding, obedient to his spoken word.
  ²¹ Bless the LORD, all his hosts, his ministers that do his will.
  ²² Bless the LORD, all his works, in all places of his dominion. Bless the LORD, O my soul.

HURRICANE Matthew entered our lives in a major way today. Storm watches and warnings were established for most of the east coast of Florida, including Ponte Vedra Beach. Our friends Jane Reis and Connie and Jay Shafran arrived from Charleston (the Shafrans were vacationing from Malibu). We made a sometimes-vacillating decision to wait out the storm at home.

The passage today is essentially all about gratitude. These are all the things God has done. Bless Him for doing them. Reflecting on the 14 billion years that have already passed in the eternal history of the universe, I have been thinking about how amazing it is that I am alive at this time. I know about right and wrong. I know about my reason for being, and I know about the possibility of unitive consciousness. *I know that I know about these things.*

Imagine being part of that first life, four billion years ago. Not only were these single cell beings unable to reason, there is every likelihood that they had no senses whatever. Or imagine if my place in the Universe were to be a different form of life, a plant or an insect. I would still be a form of the same cosmic dust from which all the universe originated, but I would certainly not be journaling about my prayers and meditations!

Yes, I have much for which to be grateful. For reasons that are beyond comprehension, I am able to sit in my library (a beautiful interior space that I designed), look out the circle-top double doors at a parterre garden (that I also designed) and relate both the interior and exterior spaces to long traditions of architecture and architects. I am surrounded by books written by authors from all around the world over the past two millennia.

Most of these books are commentaries on, or elaborations of, the Hebrew scriptures, and what we call the New Testament. The authors of these books were shaped by nature and nurture to not only have the ability to think these incredible thoughts, but also both the ability and the inclination to pass them on to posterity. Imagine the number of people, both great leaders and common learners, who have read these words. Imagine the circumstances in their lives that shaped them to have the desire and the ability to read and sometimes expand upon the thinking of the long line of men and women before them.

It is often said that a flock of birds or the smile of a small child are reminders of God's presence and His greatness. God is also abundantly present in the wisdom, tradition, and experience of all these authors in whose presence I sit each day.

October 6

Job 1:21, 38, 30, 40:1–5

²¹ He said, "Naked I came from my mother's womb, and naked shall I return there; the LORD gave, and the LORD has taken away; blessed be the name of the LORD."

Job 38

Then the LORD answered Job out of the whirlwind:

² "Who is this that darkens counsel by words without knowledge?

³ Gird up your loins like a man, I will question you, and you shall declare to me.

⁴ "Where were you when I laid the foundation of the earth? Tell me, if you have understanding.

⁵ Who determined its measurements—surely you know! Or who stretched the line upon it?

⁶ On what were its bases sunk, or who laid its cornerstone

⁷ when the morning stars sang together and all the heavenly beings shouted for joy?

⁸ "Or who shut in the sea with doors when it burst out from the womb?—

⁹ when I made the clouds its garment, and thick darkness its swaddling band,

¹⁰ and prescribed bounds for it, and set bars and doors,

¹¹ and said, 'Thus far shall you come, and no farther, and here shall your proud waves be stopped'?

¹² "Have you commanded the morning since your days began, and caused the dawn to know its place,

¹³ so that it might take hold of the skirts of the earth, and the wicked be shaken out of it?

¹⁴ It is changed like clay under the seal, and it is dyed like a garment.

¹⁵ Light is withheld from the wicked, and their uplifted arm is broken.

¹⁶ "Have you entered into the springs of the sea, or walked in the recesses of the deep?

¹⁷ Have the gates of death been revealed to you, or have you seen the gates of deep darkness?

¹⁸ Have you comprehended the expanse of the earth? Declare, if you know all this.

¹⁹ "Where is the way to the dwelling of light, and where is the place of darkness,

²⁰ that you may take it to its territory and that you may discern the paths to its home?

²¹ Surely you know, for you were born then, and the number of your days is great!

²² "Have you entered the storehouses of the snow, or have you seen the storehouses of the hail,

²³ which I have reserved for the time of trouble, for the day of battle and war?

²⁴ What is the way to the place where the light is distributed, or where the east wind is scattered upon the earth?

²⁵ "Who has cut a channel for the torrents of rain, and a way for the thunderbolt,

²⁶ to bring rain on a land where no one lives, on the desert, which is empty of human life,

²⁷ to satisfy the waste and desolate land, and to make the ground put forth grass?

²⁸ "Has the rain a father, or who has begotten the drops of dew?

²⁹ From whose womb did the ice come forth, and who has given birth to the hoarfrost of heaven?

³⁰ The waters become hard like stone, and the face of the deep is frozen.

³¹ "Can you bind the chains of the Pleiades, or loose the cords of Orion?

³² Can you lead forth the Mazzaroth in their season, or can you guide the Bear with its children?

³³ Do you know the ordinances of the heavens? Can you establish their rule on the earth?

³⁴ "Can you lift up your voice to the clouds, so that a flood of waters may cover you?

³⁵ Can you send forth lightnings, so that they may go and say to you, 'Here we are'?

³⁶ Who has put wisdom in the inward parts, or given understanding to the mind?

³⁷ Who has the wisdom to number the clouds? Or who can tilt the waterskins of the heavens,

³⁸ when the dust runs into a mass and the clods cling together?

³⁹ "Can you hunt the prey for the lion, or satisfy the appetite of the young lions,

⁴⁰ when they crouch in their dens, or lie in wait in their covert?

⁴¹ Who provides for the raven its prey, when its young ones cry to God, and wander about for lack of food?

Job 39

"Do you know when the mountain goats give birth? Do you observe the calving of the deer?

² Can you number the months that they fulfill, and do you know the time when they give birth,

³ when they crouch to give birth to their offspring, and are delivered of their young?

⁴ Their young ones become strong, they grow up in the open; they go forth, and do not return to them.

⁵ "Who has let the wild ass go free? Who has loosed the bonds of the swift ass,

⁶ to which I have given the steppe for its home, the salt land for its dwelling place?

⁷ It scorns the tumult of the city; it does not hear the shouts of the driver.

⁸ It ranges the mountains as its pasture, and it searches after every green thing.

⁹ "Is the wild ox willing to serve you? Will it spend the night at your crib?

¹⁰ Can you tie it in the furrow with ropes, or will it harrow the valleys after you?

¹¹ Will you depend on it because its strength is great, and will you hand over your labor to it?

¹² Do you have faith in it that it will return, and bring your grain to your threshing floor?

¹³ "The ostrich's wings flap wildly, though its pinions lack plumage.

¹⁴ For it leaves its eggs to the earth, and lets them be warmed on the ground,

¹⁵ forgetting that a foot may crush them, and that a wild animal may trample them.

¹⁶ It deals cruelly with its young, as if they were not its own; though its labor should be in vain, yet it has no fear;

¹⁷ because God has made it forget wisdom, and given it no share in understanding.

¹⁸ When it spreads its plumes aloft, it laughs at the horse and its rider.

¹⁹ "Do you give the horse its might? Do you clothe its neck with mane?

²⁰ Do you make it leap like the locust? Its majestic snorting is terrible.

²¹ It paws violently, exults mightily; it goes out to meet the weapons.

²² It laughs at fear, and is not dismayed; it does not turn back from the sword.

²³ Upon it rattle the quiver, the flashing spear, and the javelin.

²⁴ With fierceness and rage it swallows the ground; it cannot stand still at the sound of the trumpet.

²⁵ When the trumpet sounds, it says 'Aha!' From a distance it smells the battle, the thunder of the captains, and the shouting.

²⁶ "Is it by your wisdom that the hawk soars, and spreads its wings toward the south?

²⁷ Is it at your command that the eagle mounts up and makes its nest on high?

²⁸ It lives on the rock and makes its home in the fastness of the rocky crag.

²⁹ From there it spies the prey; its eyes see it from far away.

³⁰ Its young ones suck up blood; and where the slain are, there it is."

Job 40:1–5

And the LORD said to Job:² "Shall a faultfinder contend with the Almighty? Anyone who argues with God must respond."

Job's Response to God

³ Then Job answered the LORD:

⁴ "See, I am of small account; what shall I answer you? I lay my hand on my mouth.

⁵ I have spoken once, and I will not answer; twice, but will proceed no further."

NEWS OF HURRICANE Matthew is dire, with a forecast for a direct hit some time tomorrow along the east coast of Florida, including particularly Ponte Vedra Beach. Our house guests left this morning, going west and north to avoid the storm. Sallie Ann is very concerned, and I am uncomfortably stubborn. We will decide later today what to do, though each passing hour further limits our alternatives.

These passages from Job are simply beautiful. What a wonderful description of the universe and the amazing creations that fill it. The fundamental point is that this universe and all its wonder and majesty are vastly greater than me. I am infinitesimally small in the face of all of it, overwhelmed by its grandeur and glory. It is appropriate that this giant storm is bearing down on us now, representing as it does the awesome power of this universe. Sadly, the storm today stands in the way of further meditation on the conversation with Job.

The prominent Lutheran, Reverend Thomas Weitzel, offered this prayer for storms.

God of heaven and earth, God who carries our lives and the lives of our whole community in your hands, be with us in the peril of this day/night. Help us to release our anxieties and fears into those same caring hands, knowing in faith that your will for us is life and everlasting good. Send your holy angels to watch over us and guard us. May they spread their holy wings to give us shelter against the storm. For you alone, O God, are all good, all life, all love, and that love is for us; through Jesus Christ our Lord.

October 7

Isaiah 45: 7–13

⁷ I form light and create darkness, I make weal and create woe; I the LORD do all these things.

⁸ Shower, O heavens, from above, and let the skies rain down righteousness; let the earth open, that salvation may spring up, and let it cause righteousness to sprout up also; I the LORD have created it.

⁹ Woe to you who strive with your Maker, earthen vessels with the potter! Does the clay say to the one who fashions it, "What are you making"? or "Your work has no handles"?

¹⁰ Woe to anyone who says to a father, "What are you begetting?" or to a woman, "With what are you in labor?"

¹¹ Thus says the LORD, the Holy One of Israel, and its Maker: Will you question me about my children, or command me concerning the work of my hands?

¹² I made the earth, and created humankind upon it; it was my hands that stretched out the heavens, and I commanded all their host.

¹³ I have aroused Cyrus in righteousness, and I will make all his paths straight; he shall build my city and set my exiles free, not for price or reward, says the LORD of hosts.

HURRICANE Matthew arrives today sometime after 2 p.m. Watching the news about an approaching storm is maddening. A police chief in Melbourne, Florida, instructed his officers to be sure there were sufficient body bags for the impending mass fatalities. Governor Rick Scott is constantly warning us that this storm will kill anyone who does not evacuate. While I understand the need to urge evacuation, this kind of admonition is simply fear mongering.

When I designed Serendipity, our house, I went to great lengths to meet the maximum hurricane code in Florida, far exceeding what is required in our area. Doors and windows are all Luxbaum units, capable of sustaining missiles shot at a velocity of 150 MPH. Our generator will power the main house and both guest houses for 30 days. Walls are poured, steel reinforced concrete, sandwiched between Styrofoam forms. I added four feet of fill material, bringing the first-floor elevation to a level almost 20 feet above sea level. We did all of this for a house located a block from the ocean, with a street, two rows of houses, a golf course, and a lagoon separating us from any storm surge or high wave activity. This will be the first test of all this effort. While I have numerous ways to describe Serendipity, it is, more than anything else, a monument to the false gods of material success. I believe it is beautiful, fully expressing all that I have learned about classical design and exceptional construction.

It is "green," with photovoltaic electric power generation, geothermal heat and hot water, and as many other characteristics of environmentally sound design and construction as I could find. However, its very size belies this effort to be environmentally responsible.

Serendipity is a testament to my lifelong desire to design and build a "grand house," one that pulled together everything that I had learned from my study of architecture, especially the history of residential architecture. I wanted a classical manor house, symmetrically disposed against a strong central axis. I wanted high ceilings and tall doors and windows. I wanted each space to be rigorously symmetrical, just as these spaces were to be symmetrically arranged with respect to each other and to the site plan itself. I wanted garden views from each door and window, views that picked up an axis within the house and repeated it outside.

Achieving all of that requires either an extraordinarily gifted architect, or a great deal of space. My limited gifts as an architect required that I solve design problems with more space, much more space! Serendipity has more than 13,000 square feet of living space, two exterior pavilions, and four quite separate gardens. Ceilings are twelve feet high on both the first and second floor. Most exterior doors and windows are ten feet high, and all interior doors are eight feet high. As I said, Serendipity is a monument to excess, something that, while beautiful, goes against almost everything I am committed to in these twilight years.

The storm left the Bahamas as a Category 4, with winds as high as 135 MPH. It was downgraded early this morning to a Category 3 as it passed through Daytona Beach, 96 miles south of us. We are now expecting winds of 75 to 100 MPH, a seven- to nine-foot storm surge, and ten inches of rain. We have never been in a hurricane of this magnitude. I was out of the country when Sallie Ann evacuated Houston twice for storms. She is nervous, to say the least.

The one good thing about the storm is the absence of internet, television, and other electronic distractions. I have been able to read a little, engage in longer and deeper conversations, and even spend more time meditating.

Isaiah could not be a more apt reading for me this morning, as I await this awesome force of nature. The message is simple: I am not in control. God, Nature, or the vast Evolutionary Universe, call it what you will, acts as it acts. Who am I to question these acts, or the forces behind them?

Sallie Ann sent me a version of the Serenity Prayer: "God, grant me the serenity to accept the people I cannot change, the courage to change the one I can, and the wisdom to know it's me." This is perfect for a house full of people nervously awaiting a hurricane! Both this and the original also fit rather well with Isaiah.

I ask God today to grant me serenity, calm, and acceptance. I do not, cannot, and need not control this situation. Allow this proximity to the raw power of the universe to deepen my faith in, respect for, and acceptance of His presence in my life.

October 8

Repeat Luke 4: 16–30, The Rejection of Jesus at Nazareth

WE SURVIVED Matthew. I vowed last night never to stay in our house during a hurricane again. It is not the wind, or the rain, or the storm surge. Rather, it is the incredible level of Sallie Ann's anxiety!

The week ends with the reading from Luke's Gospel with which it began, in which Jesus reads from Isaiah. As I meditate about this passage, I am reminded of one of the central teachings of Father Rohr's book *Falling Upward*. He compares a person's life to a container, suggesting that the first half of our life is spent building the container, and the second half, filling the container.

Building the container begins with a foundation, which is put in place during the first six or seven years of our lives. Obviously, our parents, siblings, and other early sources of influence, including our long genetic history, all play crucial roles in building this foundation.

The next step in the process is the erection of the exterior walls that form the "picture" we want the world to see. Father Rohr described these walls as the false self—the person we think we are, rather than the person we truly are. Thomas Merton wrote often about the false self and the true self, suggesting that many of us wrap bandages around the false self to prevent people from seeing what it is of which we are so ashamed. Whether the exterior of our container consists of walls that project our superficial self, or bandages designed to hide our shame, the concept is essentially the same.

The halfway point in life, which almost never occurs midway chronologically, is the point when a decision is made about what to put into the container. I now understand this decision to be a form of *transforming spiritual experience*. The transforming event probably takes both the form of filling an empty container, and removing the bandages from our wounded sense of who we are. The decision point or transforming event is the place where we truly come face to face with the great issues of life. Father Rohr suggests transformative events require either great suffering or great love.

Personally, I like the image of the divine dance, used by many authors and poets down through the ages. In my mind, this dance is going on all around us all the time, but we often choose not to join it. T.S. Eliot writes:

> At the still point of the turning world. Neither flesh nor fleshless;
> Neither from nor towards; at the still point, there the dance is,
> But neither arrest nor movement. And do not call it fixity,
> Where past and future are gathered. Neither movement from nor towards,
> Neither ascent nor decline. Except for the point, the still point,
> There would be no dance, and there is only the dance.

Transformational change occurs at still points. Perhaps we have descended so far that we hit a bottom and movement stops. At that point of "neither ascent nor decline," we decide to join the dance. Or we are speechless in the face of a sudden act of great love or kindness. At that moment, perhaps only for that moment, we join the dance. Thomas Merton ends his wonderful book *New Seeds of Contemplation*, with this:

> The world and time are the dance of the Lord in emptiness. The silence of the spheres is the music of the wedding feast. The more we persist in misunderstanding the phenomena of life, the more we analyze them out into strange finalities and complex purposes of our own, the more we involve ourselves in sadness, absurdity, and despair.
>
> But it does not matter much, because no despair of ours can alter the reality of things, or stain the joy of the cosmic dance which is always there. Indeed, we are in the midst of it, and it is in the midst of us, for it beats in our very blood, whether we want it to or not. Yet the fact remains that we are invited to forget ourselves on purpose, cast our awful solemnity to the winds and join in the general dance.

Merton teaches that the primary distinction between the false and true selves is the distance from oneness with God. All the things we do that take us further from God encourage and build up the false self. Conversely, all the things we do to bring us closer to God encourage and build up the true self. This notion relies heavily on the idea that we entered this universe one with God, and that it is our purpose in life to retain, achieve, and maintain wholeness, and, through that, oneness. These concepts have become integral parts of my faith journey, and of my understanding of my own life.

The passage in Luke's Gospel positions Jesus in the synagogue in Nazareth, where he grew up. People there must have known Jesus as the son of Joseph the carpenter, as a young boy playing with other children, and as a teenager, becoming a man. He must have been many things to them, but certainly not a rabbi, a prophet, nor, least of all, the Messiah. The "outer garment" of the self they had come to know bore little relationship to the inner man Jesus was becoming. This might be stretching the concept of false self and true self quite a lot. Suggesting the Son of God had a false self might be approaching blasphemy. That is certainly not my intention.

Relating this passage to the beginning effort I have made on writing my dossier, I am struck with several observations.

First, what I have described in what I have written thus far says rather little about the container called Bob Hart, either as I came to present him, a "person" who changed from time to time over the years, or as the person I came to be after my "great conversion." I talk about my parents, my siblings, and the personality traits I may have developed or acquired being born in this particular family, in this place in the universe, and at this time in history. I do not describe the power, positions, and possessions that I would eventually gather around myself in an effort to convey a message, or many messages, to the world.

Second, the person formed by the circumstances of my birth might have been closer to the true person I would ultimately discover than I have always believed. I am not sure. I want to think about that a lot as I move forward in these Exercises. Is it possible that I set out to build a container that would hide certain basic facts, disguising that person as carefully as I could? We lived modestly, to say the least, something I was certainly not proud to have everyone know. While I have an image of my parents as being in love and openly showing that love, the fact is that they were probably very unhappy throughout most of my childhood, bickering about the farm and all that went with it. Dad was certainly a little quiet by nature, but much of what I saw was probably his resignation in the face of constant harping by Mom. There were other things about me at that time that I wanted to hide, despairing of ever changing them.

The question is whether there was a person there before I even knew what it meant to be poor, or how a happy home life differed from one filled with strife. Was the young boy on the farm my true self, unadorned by container walls or hidden by bandages? Or were even these images merely part of the life container I was building at that early age? Even now, as I reflect on my very dim memory of my early life, I cannot say with any certainty that I personally remember sleeping in the tent, or using an outhouse. While I can remember my parents fighting in the car, and vaguely remember being spanked, most of my life before my mission failure is a rather complete blur. It is as though that trauma erased everything that happened before it, including my early years on the farm, my school years, my early experiences with girls, and my friendships. Just writing this brings up flashes of hazy recollections, but nothing very solid.

I know with great clarity that I eventually spent many years building an empty life container. The persona that I would create certainly grew up poor on a farm west of Blackfoot, Idaho. He escaped that life by going to Harvard University, serving a Mormon mission, failing at that mission, and starting over again, more or less from scratch. The life that led up to the mission failure might have been, for all intents and purposes, a good story with which to begin a new and improved container. Or not.

Nancy provided an interesting opposing version of my characterization of my relationship with my parents. She wrote in her note to me about this:

First, I never thought Mom and Dad looked at you as the Black Sheep, but more as the Golden Child. Mom and Dad valued education so highly, and placed such an emphasis on intelligence, that you were the wunderkind. Extremely bright, goal-oriented, successful in high school, in debate, at Boys' Nation, as valedictorian [sic], and—to cap it all off, heading off to Harvard—I think they were over the moon about it all. I think Mom and Dad loved *brightness* in a child more than anything else—even more than *goodness* in a child. As younger siblings, we were excited about your success, too. It made you quite exotic to us. You and Leonard were never warm or cuddly with Connie and me; there was always a stand-off-ish-ness about you both, and we grew up thinking we were outside your realm of interest. But we were proud of you in our dorky, younger sister way.

I believe Mom and Dad were crushed when you decided to go on a mission. Again, I was very young. But I think they railed about you throwing your scholarship away. When you came home early, they may have been embarrassed, but I don't remember hearing a word of that. All I remember is that Mom got mad—*at the Church*. Neither Mom nor Dad ever seemed mad at you, but Mom was bitter and resentful *for years* at the way the Church handled it.

I wish we would have talked about it openly as a family. Your coming home early was the elephant in the room for a long, long time, and I don't think that did any of us any favors. You wouldn't be wondering now—more than fifty years later!—about how we all felt, if we had just talked about it, shared an explanation, some understanding, and acceptance.

I did some writing recently about my own growing up in the Church, and I realized that as a family, we were embarrassed to talk about spiritual things. Other families did that, but it seems it would have been too awkward for the Harts. It's like we went to church, but church didn't come home with us. Good values were clearly taught—honesty, service, kindness—but we definitely didn't talk about God, or prayer, or divine help. Add to that initial reluctance about spiritual subjects a disturbance in the natural flow, like you coming home early, and it's no wonder your mission was the un-talked-about subject for the rest of our lives.

I don't know much about what happened in Germany or how it was handled by the Church, either in your mission or back home in Idaho. Mom told me once that you and your companion took some girls on a tour of a castle, that you and one girl were off by yourselves for a time, yet that nothing happened. That's all I ever heard. Of the aftermath, she said you were told you had to stand up in church and apologize to the whole congregation. If that was the case, and if what you described in *One Man's Journey* was the case, I am so sorry. I want you to know that would never happen today. Missionaries come home early from missions every so often, and I've never known them to be treated with anything but love and acceptance. If they or their parents don't offer an explanation, no one asks.

Mom and Dad were proud of you finishing so well at Harvard, getting married and having a family, doing well in your various enterprises. It wasn't your divorce that caused them sadness so much as your pulling away from them. It seems like that was about when you began to distance yourself from the family. Even then you would reach out in generous ways, like when you treated Mom and Dad to a great trip somewhere—was it Haiti? I don't remember the details. You weren't particularly interested in the day-to-day business of their lives; I don't think they talked to you every Sunday night the way they did with the rest of the kids. You were still, in many ways, the Golden Child, but I'll have to say I think it was painful for them that you stayed out of touch for periods of time.

In 1984 Mom read an article called "The Trick of Children" in a magazine called *Current Contents*. It impacted them both quite a bit and Dad made copies at Pfizer and handed them out to several people. When he gave me my copy, he mentioned that it made them both think of you. I thought about it as I began writing tonight and actually found my old copy in my files. It's written by a woman raising a young son. He must have been a toddler at the time, and she spoke about how intimate their relationship was at the time, and how she knew it would not always be. She writes, "Between us there is no shame, no inhibition. He thinks me beautiful; he wants to grow to be like me. And I am bound to fail him, and bound to lose him. Daily the gap between us grows. He is not mindful of it—but I am. Oh, I am." She writes about treating her own mother with "an offhand and rather inattentive disregard," and wonders if her mom ever felt the fierce, protective love she felt for her son. She ends the article, "This frightful responsibility! I invited it, and I carry it out in a workaday way. But I quail secretly at the number of mistakes I'm bound to make, what I'll saddle him with, what the price for both of us would finally be. I'll give the world a son, heavy with the grief of giving him at all. Then and after, he'll drift in and out of my view, keeping secrets, neglecting me, while I watch from a distance, unrequited."

Their rereading and keeping the article, handing it around as a powerful read, telling me it made them think about you, sticks with me better than anything they said or did during those years. I can't remember the chronology of when you were more or less distant with them, but I do know the distance was hurtful to them. If you had been a black sheep, they probably could have written you off, somewhat. I think it's because you were so important to them that they wanted to be in closer touch. Also—I'll be honest—there were times when you were the proud young man, and they knew they seemed prosaic, un-hip, small-townish, to you.

It's how it ends that counts. Particularly after you and Sallie Ann married, they felt more connected to you. While you still didn't call and chat about everyday things, you had them as guests to your home, you came to the family reunions, and you were particularly involved at the last reunion with Mom at Hot Springs, Arkansas. I feel like she ended her life feeling good about all five of her kids and their situation in life. Mom and Dad would be SO PROUD of the good work you are doing now. In fact, I believe they are so proud, because they know.

Perhaps there was a fairly interesting person born in Rexburg and raised on a farm west of Blackfoot. Perhaps hard work, strong parental discipline, a ferocious ambition made even greater by my ambitious mother, and a keen mind sharpened by my parents encouraging me to read—perhaps these are the foundation blocks of my true self. Something to ponder.

Donald Trump, the GOP candidate for president, will debate Hillary Clinton tomorrow in the second presidential debate. A tape was released yesterday in which Trump graphically describes his sexual exploits, bringing a torrent of criticism from some of his staunchest supporters. There is talk that his running mate, Mike Pence, will withdraw from the ticket, resulting in chaos. Many are suggesting Trump quit the race. To say the least, these are interesting times.

CALENDAR WEEK FOUR

Almighty and ever-caring God, You are powerful to give life and to take it away. You order all things from end to end, beyond my comprehension, beyond my imagining. Your passionate hope is that every person be saved from selfishness and self-destruction. You want no one to perish, to live forever alone. Instead, You want a reign of love to rise from within our hearts and embrace each human person and everything on earth. I praise You and I thank You that You teach me these things through Christ our Lord.

Amen.

October 9

Ephesians 1: 3–14, Spiritual Blessings in Christ
³ Blessed be the God and Father of our Lord Jesus Christ, who has blessed us in Christ with every spiritual blessing in the heavenly places, ⁴ just as he chose us in Christ before the foundation of the world to be holy and blameless before him in love. ⁵ He destined us for adoption as his children through Jesus Christ, according to the good pleasure of his will, ⁶ to the praise of his glorious grace that he freely bestowed on us in the Beloved. ⁷ In him we have redemption through his blood, the forgiveness of our trespasses, according to the riches of his grace ⁸ that he lavished on us. With all wisdom and insight ⁹ he has made known to us the mystery of his will, according to his good pleasure that he set forth in Christ, ¹⁰ as a plan for the fullness of time, to gather up all things in him, things in heaven and things on earth. ¹¹ In Christ we have also obtained an inheritance, having been destined according to the purpose of him who accomplishes all things according to his counsel and will, ¹² so that we, who were the first to set our hope on Christ, might live for the praise of his glory. ¹³ In him you also, when you had heard the word of truth, the Gospel of your salvation, and had believed in him, were marked with the seal of the promised Holy Spirit; ¹⁴ this is the pledge of our inheritance toward redemption as God's own people, to the praise of his glory.

THE BEAUTY of this morning's clear sky, calm wind, and dry air is overwhelming. The beautiful weather actually appeared yesterday, literally hours after we felt the last vestiges of Hurricane Matthew. It is especially wonderful in the quiet of this morning, sitting outside on the meditation bench, hearing only the sounds of the waves and birds. Maggie is with me, as she has been every day since I began these Exercises again. We are both five years older, but she still looks like a puppy. I am certainly no longer a boy.

The passage from Paul's letter to the Ephesians builds on one of the themes I contemplated yesterday. God "chose us in Christ before the foundation of the world to be holy and blameless before Him in love." We entered this life in union with the love that is God. We have been one with the universe since it began. Our natural state is union, not separation.

The prayer for this week, suggested by Father Joseph Tetlow, the Jesuit author of the guide for these Exercises, contains some wonderful lines that speak to God's desire that we move beyond our false selves:

> Your passionate hope is that every person be saved from selfishness and self-destruction. You want no one to perish, to live forever alone. Instead, you want a reign of love to rise from within our hearts and embrace each human person and every thing on earth.

These words seem very obvious to me now, after five years of learning that God is love and that we are one in that love. Selfishness, self-destruction, and other forms of sin separate us from the oneness of God. There is a certain optimism inherent in Catholicism in general, and Jesuit Catholicism in particular. The sacrament of reconciliation, traditionally called confession and forgiveness, accepts as completely normal that we will sin in one way or another. We will think thoughts, say words, and commit deeds that separate us from God. However, by confessing these sins to a priest, we make it possible for the priest to forgive us in the name of God. We can then begin anew.

Jesuits call for a daily Examen, about which I learned during my first ten-month run through these Exercises. Each night, we examine our day's actions, noting the things we have done that separate us from God, and asking His forgiveness. Other faith traditions incorporate some form of daily review of thoughts, statements, and actions, followed by the appropriate making of amends and resolution not to continue along that path.

I am struck particularly in today's passage with the phrase "the forgiveness of our trespasses, according to the riches of his grace that he lavished on us." This grace is unearned, unwarranted, freely given, always available. Grace is such a huge concept that it is virtually impossible to comprehend. What gets through to my "pointy little head" is that God constantly, eternally invites us to do the right thing, giving us chance after chance after chance to say yes.

I pray that I will take up this invitation soon and often. I pray for clarity and understanding. I pray for humility. I pray for the grace of the practice of gratitude.

October 10

2 Corinthians 5: 14–18, Christ's Love Compels Us

14 For the love of Christ urges us on, because we are convinced that one has died for all; therefore all have died. 15 And he died for all, so that those who live might live no longer for themselves, but for him who died and was raised for them.

16 From now on, therefore, we regard no one from a human point of view; even though we once knew Christ from a human point of view, we know him no longer in that way. 17 So if anyone is in Christ, there is a new creation: everything old has passed away; see, everything has become new! 18 All this is from God, who reconciled us to himself through Christ, and has given us the ministry of reconciliation;

I BEGAN THIS morning reflecting on the tragic state that our political system is in, still running the debate last night over and over again in my mind. Trump promised that he would jail Hillary if he were elected, something I never thought I would hear in this democracy. All in all, the largely petty and petulant debate represented quite accurately this political year.

The passage from Corinthians has been one of my "go to" scriptures for at least the past five years, dating from my first CRHP weekend. "So if anyone is in Christ, there is a new creation; everything old has passed away; see, everything has become new!" I have touched on the topic of "my conversion" in several reflections.

I intentionally use the word *conversion* because it makes clear that change is still occurring. My search for God has not ended. Thomas Merton addresses this when talking about the true self: "If I find Him, I will find myself, and if I find my true self, I will find Him." In a very real sense, any progress I make in finding my innermost self is progress in my journey toward God. All of the things I have done since my conversion began, which range from intense intellectual study to equally intense missionary activity focused on poor Haitians in the Dominican Republic, have moved me slowly, but surely, closer to that common discovery: Of my true self and God.

This journey is neither alone, nor without enormous assistance. Father James Martin says it this way: "God desires for us to be the persons we were created to be; to *be* simply and purely, and in this state, to love God and to let ourselves be loved by God.... The desire for our true selves to be revealed, and for us to move nearer to God, is a desire planted within us by God." This is consistent with the notion that the constant change inherent in the evolutionary process has a clear goal, and is moving in a clear direction, which is unity with God. The minuscule changes in me, such an insignificant part of the universe, can hardly be compared to the infinite and eternal changes in all of creation, but the movement toward oneness with God is very much the same.

The passage from Paul's letter to the Corinthians begins with the line "one has died for all; therefore, all have died." Reflecting on this brings to my mind the concept of dying before I die. In the Gospel of Luke, the Evangelist says that "anyone who loses his life for me will save it." What has to die is our false self, our ego. Again, I go back to the still point, the bottom, from which further descent is not possible, in the moment before ascent has begun. At that point, if I am lucky, I experience a death that allows me to live.

On a somewhat lighter note, Maggie and I walked down to the bench in the garden this morning to sit. The sky was a brilliant blue behind floating clouds. There were herons and egrets along the edge of the garden and the banks of the lagoon. The ocean waves were loud, but peaceful. I tried to contemplate the death of my false self, but the beauty of the morning moved me into a place of such joy that any thoughts of death, even a death before rebirth, were impossible.

I read this beautiful little poem by Mary Oliver, "Poem of the One World."

> This morning
> the beautiful white heron
> was floating along above the waves
> and then into the sky of this
> the one world
> we all belong to
> where everything
> sooner or later
> is a part of everything else
> which thought made me feel
> for a little while
> quite beautiful myself.

I pray in silence, giving thanks for the morning, the sky, and my conversion. I know that I am in every instant a new creation. This morning, especially, I like what I am becoming.

October 11

Romans 8: 14–17, For Those Led by the Spirit
[14] For all who are led by the Spirit of God are children of God. [15] For you did not receive a spirit of slavery to fall back into fear, but you have received a spirit of adoption. When we cry, "Abba! Father!" [16] it is that very Spirit

bearing witness with our spirit that we are children of God, [17] and if children, then heirs, heirs of God and joint heirs with Christ—if, in fact, we suffer with him so that we may also be glorified with him.

Romans 8: 26–27

[26] *Likewise the Spirit helps us in our weakness; for we do not know how to pray as we ought, but that very Spirit intercedes with sighs too deep for words.* [27] *And God, who searches the heart, knows what is the mind of the Spirit, because the Spirit intercedes for the saints according to the will of God.*

THE THEME of these preparation weeks is the deep connection we have with God, even when we try to ignore it, or act in opposition to that which He teaches. Out of our suffering will emerge the glory of wholeness, through which we achieve oneness with God. We must die before we live again in order to die again. The rebirth occurs at the still points of deepest suffering or deepest love.

Paul is telling his readers in Rome that the "Spirit intercedes with sighs too deep for words," aiding them in prayer. I am reminded of the wonderful poem, "Footprints in the Sand."

> One night I dreamed a dream
> As I was walking along the beach with my Lord.
> Across the dark sky flashed scenes from my life.
> For each scene, I noticed two sets of
> Footprints in the sand,
> One belonging to me and one to my Lord.
> After the last scene of my life flashed before me,
> I looked back at the footprints in the sand,
> I noticed that at many times along the path
> Of my life,
> Especially at the very lowest and saddest times,
> There was only one set of footprints.
> This really troubled me, so I asked the Lord
> About it.
> "Lord, you said once I decided to follow you,
> You'd walk with me all the way.
> But I noticed that during the saddest and most
> Troublesome times of my life,
> There was only one set of footprints.
> I don't understand why, when I need You
> The most, You would leave me."
> He whispered, "My precious child, , I love you
> And will never leave you.
> Never, even during your trials and testings.
> When you saw only one set of footprints,
> It was then that I carried you.

The lifelong journey toward wholeness, toward the knowledge of true self and, through that, conscious oneness with God, would be impossible without help. Yet I have difficulty with this concept, again wondering how God could be troubled to intercede in the struggles of one unimportant being in the infinite and eternal expanse of the universe.

As I meditate on this problem, I am struck with the importance of a desire implanted in the deepest part of my soul to do the right thing. I believe that desire is present, even though I do not always respect it. Could it be that God's intercession in my life occurred at the initial point of creation, when the whole of the Universe came into being with unimaginable force, propelling it in a direction toward the ultimate goal of oneness? Or does He intercede in each instant that I am created anew? Whichever it is, the desire I feel, the desire to find my true self, is part of His creative energy.

Finding my true self is hard to put into action. I like the admonition to simply do the next right thing. Henri Nouwen spent the last several years of his life living in the L'Arche community near Toronto. He loved the simplicity of his work with disabled residents. They did not ask about theology or discuss the great issues. Rather, they said "Feed me, dress me, touch me, hold me.... Kiss me, speak with me."

I am reminded of a day I spent working with Stop Hunger Now, an ecumenical effort to package meals for hungry people around the world. I had just returned from the first mission trip of our Sister Parish Ministry, where my role was that of tour director, travel guide, construction superintendent, and overall leader. In stark contrast, my role at the Stop Hunger Now gathering was to pour various beans and grains from large bags into large boxes, from which others would package them into small bags. All day long for more than six hours, I simply opened the large bag, lifted it up to the boxes, and poured out the beans, oats, and rice. Loud music was playing. The day was quite warm. I danced, sang songs, perspired heavily, laughed, and opened, lifted, and poured over and over again. It was sheer joy not to be in charge of anything. I simply did the next right thing, and loved it.

Discussing the false self, Father Rohr wrote, "Once you learn to live as your true self, you can never be satisfied with this charade again; it feels silly and superficial."

Since dedicating most of my life to the mission work of the Sister Parish Ministry almost four years ago, I do feel "silly and superficial" doing almost anything else. I cannot imagine a vacation that does not involve service work. Nor do I want these Exercises to get in the way of my mission work.

I guess this is a version of the Mary and Martha dilemma.

Mary: Praying, meditating, contemplating, and journaling are wonderful ways to begin each day, and very clearly help me to understand what is happening, and to be grateful to God for the role He plays in my life.
Martha: But if they become excuses to avoid service, they take me away from my true self.

As Father Rohr would say, it is not *either/or*, it is *both/and*.

I pray for wisdom, and for the spiritual maturity to do the next right thing. I pray for the simplicity of service. I pray for balance in my life.

October 12

Repeat Luke 15: 11–32, Parable of the Prodigal Son (or the Righteous Father)

HE WHO WAS once lost is now found. This could so easily be my motto, and that of so many others. For me, it has been true over and over again. Just preceding the story of the prodigal son in Luke's Gospel are the stories of the shepherd going back out to find the one lost sheep among the one hundred, and the woman searching for the one lost coin among ten. The message in all three parables is essentially the same, and it is the essence of the "upside-down" Gospel. The poor will have the Kingdom, the mourning will find comfort, the meek will inherit the earth, the hungry and thirsty will be filled, the merciful will be shown mercy, the pure in heart will see God, the peacemakers will be called children of God, and blessed are the persecuted. The rich, educated, powerful, entitled rulers, soldiers, tax collectors, judges, and Pharisees who were once on top are suddenly at the bottom. What was up is now down. The lost are found.

As much as I love this message, I have devoted most of my life to accumulating power, prestige, and possessions. This is exactly the opposite course of action from that advocated by not only Jesus, but virtually every great spiritual leader in the long history of humanity. Winning the race, getting the highest grades, getting into the best schools, landing the best job, being the first promoted, and receiving the largest bonus—these are the goals and ambitions of all good people, right? Our parents, coaches, and mentors wanted this for us, just as we want this for our children. Oh, I can add that I was also admonished to be honest and play fair, but win, nonetheless.

The upside-down Gospel does not work well in a capitalist economic system, or in the social and political structures that support that system. Mormons try to celebrate material success as a part of the Gospel. Popular televangelists like Joel Osteen in Houston advise their listeners to pray for a higher bonus, a better job, and a newer car. But this is not the Gospel of Jesus Christ found in the New Testament.

My Catholic teachers work hard to teach the upside-down Gospel. They criticize profligacy and celebrate frugality. However, the need to raise capital for all manner of good causes forces them to seek out the most materially successful among their flock, praise them for their success, and honor them more than others. While I would like to flatter myself that it is my commitment to deepen my faith that has earned me a certain status in my parish, the simple truth is that it is my ability to support various causes financially that earns the most respect.

Reflecting on the message in this passage, I return to the quiet of my library, and the beauty of the meditation garden. Praying alone, meditating alone, and silently contemplating the meaning of this passage from Luke's Gospel, the essential message of the upside-down Gospel resonates deeply within me. I am enough. I have enough. The only way I can increase my joy is by giving it away to others. I was lost, and now am found.

Once again, I prayed this morning for oneness. Doing so reminded me of a discussion my Living School Skype group is having, in which they pray for wholeness. I do not have a clear understanding of how these two concepts differ, and how they are the same. Some definitions:

Wholeness is a condition in which we are identified with a central core (such as the Self or the soul) which is in an active, productive relationship with the various aspects of our life (internal and external).

Oneness is not based on a relationship among different parts; it is based on an awareness of a common essence, such as spirit or life-energy. A sense of oneness is a characteristic of the state of enlightenment. *The Buddha said that the individual no longer exists in this oneness; he or she is lost like a drop of rain falling into the sea.*

One of the powerful teachings of Father Rohr is the need to find wholeness in our lives, healing the dualism that, in a certain way, is a normal part of maturing. Part of growing into a higher level of consciousness is learning how to deal with contradiction, paradox, inconsistency, and mystery. The real world is not all black and white, right and wrong, my way or the highway. Wholeness involves putting together the splits and distinctions of life; seeing reality as both/and, not either/or.

We studied Julian of Norwich in the Living School, an extraordinary mystic of the late 14th century. Julian uses the word "oneing" to describe the Divine Union. In Julian's words, "The love of God creates in us such a oneing that when it is truly seen, no person can separate themselves from another person." In another passage, she writes that "the soul who contemplates is made like the one who is contemplated." This is very similar to Meister Eckhart, who wrote, "The eye through which I see God is the same eye through which God sees me."

Teilhard teaches that the whole of the universe began as one dramatic burst of energy, with everything that was or would ever be for all eternity one with everything else. We started as one and are moving inexorably toward re-uniting as one.

In fact, I need (and want) both oneness and wholeness. I pray for wholeness such that I can ultimately become one with God and His creation.

October 13

Luke 13: 10–17, Jesus Heals the Crippled Woman on the Sabbath
[10] Now he was teaching in one of the synagogues on the sabbath. [11] And just then there appeared a woman with a spirit that had crippled her for eighteen years. She was bent over and was quite unable to stand up straight. [12] When Jesus saw her, he called her over and said, "Woman, you are set free from your ailment." [13] When he laid his hands on her, immediately she stood up straight and began praising God. [14] But the leader of the synagogue, indignant because Jesus had cured on the sabbath, kept saying to the crowd, "There are six days on which work ought to be done; come on those days and be cured, and not on the sabbath day." [15] But the Lord answered him and said, "You hypocrites! Does not each of you on the sabbath untie his ox or his donkey from the manger, and lead it away to give it water? [16] And ought not this woman, a daughter of Abraham whom Satan bound for eighteen long years, be set free from this bondage on the sabbath day?" [17] When he said this, all his opponents were put to shame; and the entire crowd was rejoicing at all the wonderful things that he was doing.

NOT SEEING the forest for the trees. The leader of the synagogue was so focused on the day of the week that he could not see the crippled woman, or, incredibly, the miracle of Jesus' cure. As I reflect on this passage, I am struck with how often little pictures get in the way of big pictures, of how often we are blind to amazing truth due to arguments over syntax. In a way, my journal for several of the past few days has reflected a similar obsession with details, word meanings, and little things. The large message of silence has been lost. I talked right through my conversation with God.

Like the opponents of Jesus, I feel shame. I pray for the grace to listen in silence.

BUILDING MY CONTAINER

WHEN I WROTE my dossier two weeks ago, I stopped the story of my own life while I was still on the farm in Idaho. It was there that the foundation of my life container was created, both by nature and nurture. The next step in the process is the construction of the actual container, beginning with the exterior walls. Father Rohr called these walls the false self that we want to project to the world. Thomas Merton suggested that the exterior of the container actually consisted of bandages wrapped around the false self in shame.

Either way—walls that project our superficial self, or bandages designed to hide our shame—the concept is essentially the same. The hope, of course, is that someday we will fill our empty container with something true, something we come to love rather than seek to hide. Most of my life story is about building my container. I was sixty-two years old before I realized it was empty.

Harvard, the Mormon Mission, and Harvard Again

In the fall of 1963, I took a big step forward in the construction of an impressive container, one that would hide my fears and insecurities and, at the same time, project an image of material success. I left the high desert simplicity of Idaho for the sophisticated streets of Cambridge, Massachusetts, to enter Harvard University.

During my freshman year, I was surrounded by a handful of inspirational Mormons, all of whom had served missions for the Mormon Church. Largely in reaction to the shock of Harvard and Cambridge, compared to Snake River High School on a hill near Moreland, Idaho, I left college after that freshman year to answer a mission call to West Germany. After serving 19 months, I was falsely accused of violating my oath of celibacy, excommunicated from the church, and sent home from my mission. My faith life was essentially over.

For the next forty years, I would describe myself as a moral agnostic. I tried to do the right thing. I cared for those less fortunate, and generally worked toward improving their lives. This is certainly not to say that I was relatively free from sin. Far from it. But I knew that I was sinning. I simply had no religious affiliation, coupled with a strong distaste for institutional religion. I had no conviction with respect to God, other than what I would now describe as a rational world view that respected the amazing role of nature.

I returned to Harvard and applied myself to my studies, majoring in Government. With considerable help from my Junior Tutor, George Lodge, I did well in my classes, and researched *campesino* organization in the Dominican Republic in preparation for my honors thesis. Samuel Huntington was my thesis advisor. My closest friends were Richard Padgett, a graduate student from Utah, and Phylis Cox, a Radcliffe student from Massachusetts.

First Marriage

Phyllis and I were married in the summer of 1968, following several months of separation while I was working on the Gene McCarthy campaign for President. After a brief honeymoon in the Dominican Republic, where I was supposed to be writing a book based on my thesis, we moved to Boise, Idaho. I started my business career working for Boise Cascade, first in executive development, and then in the new housing and community development group. Phyllis took a job in the Boise Community Action Program, part of Lyndon Johnson's Great Society initiative. We bought a great little New England–style house, white clapboard with green shutters, on a very respectable street. Based on the math, Phyllis was pregnant with Melissa by sometime in November.

I started traveling within weeks of our arrival in Boise. The pattern for all new executive employees was to leave Boise on Monday morning and return late Friday afternoon. The big prize was to fly in one of the company planes, which also meant traveling with a senior officer of the corporation. I learned very early about the corporate ladder, and devoted myself to climbing higher and faster than any of the other young turks.

In spite of the travel and hard work, my memory of that first year of marriage is very positive. Boise is a great town to live in, and Boise Cascade was the best international company to work for in Boise at that time. Phyllis and I were both active in local Democratic politics, which was not at all divisive in those years. The Vietnam War was divisive, but not along party lines. The insidious polarization we know today only began in earnest during the Nixon Watergate years, and, even then, moderate Republicans far outnumbered the Goldwater conservatives.

We moved our small family from Boise to Atlanta to Santa Monica, each move part of the climb up the career ladder at Boise Cascade. The frequent moves, together with my constant travel, must have been hard for Phylis. Add to that my decision to leave the security of Boise Cascade to start my own company. I still traveled every week. And we moved the new company twice in the first six months, first from Santa Monica to Houston, then from Houston to Denver.

Phyllis decided to get her law degree from Denver University. Our marriage was a little rocky before we moved to Denver, but we decided to work things out. Phyllis was pregnant with Jennifer by the summer of 1970. We moved to a house on Lookout Mountain, a wonderful little community in the foothills of the Rocky Mountains above Denver. After Jennifer was born in March of 1971, we moved back down to Clermont Street in Park Hill.

We separated shortly after Thanksgiving, 1972. Melissa was three years old, Jennifer was only a year old. I have been an absentee father ever since then, obsessed by my pursuit of success at the expense of everything else in my life.

It is important that I describe my feelings during this difficult period. While I readily admit that I was fixated on my passionate effort to build a container of material success, I also wanted and valued the roles of husband and father. My memories of the first several years after I left Phyllis are consistently sad. I was painfully alone most of the time. I once saw a book titled *Sweet Sorrow, Bitter Joy.* That describes rather well how I felt when I saw my daughters.

Career

Quite by accident, project development became my life work. Housing projects, coal mines, and power plants all involve conceiving, developing, financing, and operating major physical assets. During my lifetime, the value and importance of assets has waxed and waned several times. Along the way, great fortunes have been made in "asset-light" commercial activity, trading financial and physical contracts rather than developing and owning hard assets. I have always preferred what I considered to be the "real thing," the buildings and equipment that I could touch, the structures that I would hopefully be able to see decades after I played my part in their existence.

The idea of building housing for low-income families actually arose during my Junior year at Harvard. A group of us were engaged in a campaign against slum lords in the Boston neighborhood of Roxbury, a crowded, poor urban area notorious for dilapidated housing. We organized rent strikes, seeking to force landlords to upgrade to the building codes or, if that failed, have the housing authorities condemn the buildings. One afternoon, following a "successful condemnation" of a building, one of the now former tenants asked the simple question, "Where am I supposed to sleep tonight?" I resolved then to one day build new housing for the poor.

I learned about Federal Housing Administration support for builders and owners of low-income housing at Boise Cascade. I was successful in developing four projects for the company in Texas and Louisiana, providing affordable apartments for more than three hundred families.

Low-Income Housing

In retrospect, my decision to strike out on my first entrepreneurial venture with three credit cards and the grand sum of $3,000 in capital looks insane. Nonetheless, before the end of my second year on a regular payroll, I left Boise Cascade to start Hart Associates, a low-income housing company in Houston, Texas.

I was soon joined by Thad Alston, another Harvard College graduate, who had gone on to Harvard Law School when I left academia for the business world. We changed the name of the company to Hart-Alston. We were the only black and white partnership in Houston. Hart-Alston developed three moderately large housing projects by the fall of 1971, which prompted us to move from racially-difficult Houston to Park Hill, a race-friendly neighborhood in Denver, Colorado. Shortly after we arrived in Denver, Thad decided to leave our little company to return to his home in Seattle to practice law.

I recruited another Boise Cascade "young Turk," and attacked the growth of Hart Associates with a vengeance. We traveled constantly, and worked extremely long hours when we were in Denver. I remember frequently returning to the office after dinner, certainly not something endearing to my young wife.

When Phyllis and I separated at the end of 1972, I moved to Beverly Hills, California, selling the project pipeline of Hart Associates to Transcontinental Realty, and becoming President of its low-income housing operations. After little more than a year, I left Transcontinental to become President of Whittaker Corporation's housing division, which had projects in several different states, Puerto Rico, and the US Virgin Islands. I moved the headquarters from Los Angeles to Denver.

My real estate career consisted of a year at Boise Cascade, a year at Hart-Alston, a year at Hart Associates, a year at Transcontinental Realty, two years at Whitaker, and, after a decade away in the energy business, two more years with Hart Associates in Washington, DC. In that short time, however, and in spite of all that moving around, I developed and built more than 7,500 dwelling units. Yes, my efforts in real estate created some important parts of my container, particularly projecting skill in making things happen. Yes, I acquired a certain amount of power, prestige, and possessions. But I also provided decent shelter for a very large number of low-income families.

It is often said that anyone can be a real estate developer. Buying and selling a house, or trading up a rented apartment are real estate activities that require little or no skill. While I certainly believe the process of conceiving, developing, and financing large income-generating real estate projects does require significant knowledge and ability, it is not the same commercial and engineering challenge as that posed by energy projects. It is still a puzzle to me that I was able to make international energy my career for more than thirty years. I am often reminded that it was just as much a puzzle to everyone who knew me!

Coal Mining

One day in the fall of 1973, I received a phone call from an acquaintance in Mesquite, Texas, from whom we had optioned a piece of property some time earlier. We never exercised the option, thus forfeiting the few hundred dollars we had paid for the option. My friend asked that I intercede in a partnership dispute involving a piece of property in Mingo County, West Virginia. There was an engineering report that confirmed the property contained a large amount of coal. I explained that I knew nothing about coal or mining or anything else involved in energy. He argued that I nonetheless knew about partnerships and deals.

I agreed to stop in Huntington, West Virginia, to meet his partners and argue on his behalf. When the partners denied me access to the meeting for lack of standing, I drove two hours down the Tug Fork of the Big Sandy River, past the town of Kermit, to a rope bridge over Marrowbone Creek. I will never forget walking across that rope bridge to meet with an old man named Blankenship, the owner of the coal property in dispute. I "optioned" the property for a few hundred dollars, giving me a legal interest in the discussion about its lease and exploitation. I returned to Huntington, used my "interest" in the property to negotiate a suitable arrangement for both my friend and myself, and became a coal miner.

Since I was recently divorced, living alone, unattached, and probably not very satisfied with my life, I moved from Biloxi, Mississippi, to Delbarton, West Virginia. I settled into my used trailer over a weekend. I purchased some books about coal mining, leased a bull dozer, and commenced to build the first of three deep mines.

Over the next six years, I purchased or leased equipment for deep mining, contracted with a local family to operate the equipment, and then designed and built a coal preparation facility, complete with railroad siding and tipple. I worked with brokers, sales representatives, and directly with buyers to sell my coal to utilities in the United States, and to steel companies from Japan to the Netherlands.

I fell in love with coal. While it was then and continues to be a perfectly dreadful business, with coal prices seldom sufficient to pay the costs of mining the coal, I learned to love and respect the families in the hollows, the equipment companies, the geologists and engineers, and the long chain of coal sales people, railroad representatives, port and shipping executives, and international coal traders. I love them still. Every year or so, the price of coal would spike to a level that allowed me to make some serious money for a few weeks, just enough to maintain my credit and my high expectations.

Eventually, I rented a house in Washington, DC. Every week, I flew to Charleston, either in a small plane or on US Air, then drove two hours across the state to the mine in Delbarton, a tiny town (just a store and a post office) on the banks of Hell's Creek, a tributary of the Tug Fork. I lived alone in that single-wide trailer, ate primarily steak and salad, read everything I could find about energy, and lived a strangely good life. Sadly, by the end of the 1970s, the periods during which the price of coal was far below the cost of mining it grew longer and longer. It is fair to say that I was insolvent for most of that period of my life. There was not even enough financial substance to seek bankruptcy protection!

Finally, in 1981, during one of the brief periods of high prices, I sold the coal mine for enough to pay all my creditors and make a significant distribution to all my investors. I used my share of the proceeds to start a small international coal trading operation, US Carbon, with my old friend Randy Phelps.

In the fall of 1982, I was recruited by a headhunter to head Agip Coal USA, the Italian national energy company's United States coal operations. I had monthly board meetings in Milan, Italy, which provided an opportunity for my new wife Sallie Ann (I will talk about Sallie Ann later) to join me on regular trips to Europe.

I spent the decade from 1973 to 1984 in the coal business. To say it changed my life would be a gross understatement. Operating the mine did not make me an engineer, and it certainly did not make me wealthy. But I did earn some credibility in the energy industry, both domestically and internationally. I established standing as a corporate CEO. I endured long periods of operational and financial difficulty, staying with it until I was able to pay all my debts and take care of all my employees. My container was looking pretty good.

Electric Power

The Congress of the United States passed the Public Utility Regulatory Policies Act in 1978, which, among other things, required electric utilities to purchase power from qualified independent producers. I learned about this during a coal sales call on a utility in Maine, when the coal buyer said that I could sell them electricity instead of coal. I said I knew nothing about generating electricity. He said, yes, but you know nothing about mining coal!

Together with my friend and partner, Randy Phelps, I formed US Energy Corporation in 1984, raising initial operating funds from Bill Koch, one of the Wichita, Kansas, Koch brothers that have been so prominently involved in conservative politics over the past several decades. US Energy developed a wood-fired power plant in Fort Fairfield, Maine, which was one of the very earliest fully project-financed energy projects in the world.

In 1986, I organized and headed Oxbow Geothermal, an independent power company owned by Bill Koch, focused on the development and construction of a geothermal resource field and power plant in Dixie Valley, Nevada.

I ultimately sold my interest in US Energy to Randy in 1988, fortunately retaining my interest in Fort Fairfield. As I mentioned, I took a two-year break from the energy business to go to architecture school and build more real estate.

In 1989, I organized an international electric power company focused exclusively on privatizing the electric power sectors of the eastern European countries emerging from the orbit of the Soviet Union. I traveled to Poland sixty-three times in the four years 1990 to 1993, primarily working on the privatization of the Krakow heat and power facilities. The World Bank had agreed to provide debt financing. Several international investors, including prominently IVO, the national electric power company of Finland, provided both the seed capital for the development effort, and the equity for the privatization.

In 1994, I was recruited by a headhunter to become Chief Executive Officer of the Coastal Corporation's independent electric power division. Over the next five years, I grew Coastal Power into a world-class power producer, with projects in operation or under construction in several countries, including El Salvador, Guatemala, Nicaragua, Pakistan, Bangladesh, and, significantly, the Dominican Republic.

In 1999, when I started what would become the last company I would organize and lead, I needed capital, just as I had always needed capital. This time, however, we were setting out to build and acquire power plants throughout Asia, Africa, and Latin America. We needed a great deal of capital, upwards of $700 million.

Even while trying to raise that capital, we were able to organize a successful effort to participate in and win the bidding for the privatization of the power generation sector of the Dominican Republic. We bid for and won major power generation assets being sold in Peru, Chile, and Argentina.

Throughout 2001, I engaged in a very unsuccessful six-month global tour of sovereign equity funds, private equity investors, and other sources of equity. All ninety-one (!) of the potential sources of funds that I visited said no, some quite forcefully.

Finally, the Commonwealth Development Corporation ("CDC"), a British government entity formed in 1947 to support development in the poorest countries in the world, said yes. They agreed to combine their existing electric power assets and a great deal of capital with my management team to form a new company. As its primary founder, I became CEO. We named the new company Globeleq, for Global Electric Equity, a name I never really liked.

Globeleq became the largest emerging market power generation company in the world. We focused all our efforts on bringing electric power to the poorest parts of the world, in many cases bringing electricity to people and places that had never had it before.

Stop for a moment to reflect on what my container looked like at that time. I was a successful international energy CEO. I had ownership interests in power generating assets in the Dominican Republic, Chile, Peru, and Argentina. I was the founder of what was rapidly becoming a serious player in the global power industry. I was happily married to a beautiful, sophisticated woman. We lived in a wonderful house that I had designed. We traveled extensively, always in style. From the outside, I have to say the image was not bad. No one could see the part of me I wanted to hide. In fact, I was quite oblivious to it as well. I spent far more time looking into a mirror than into my soul.

Shortly after forming the new company, CDC went through a reorganization, essentially dividing itself into a public part, which would continue to provide funds as a financial limited partner, and a private part, which would manage the funds as a private equity general partner. Since the investment in Globeleq preceded this reorganization, it was an anomaly, fitting somewhere between the two new parts.

Ultimately, however, the private equity management team took the lead role in managing the British investment in Globeleq. The first action on the part of the new managing director was to insist that Globeleq be relocated from Houston, Texas, to London, England. I refused to relocate, setting up a power struggle that, had I been completely honest, I knew I would eventually lose.

In the fall of 2005, I underwent a Cardiac CT, a non-invasive test for calcium build up in my cardiac arteries. I was driving on the freeway near our Houston office when the doctor called, advising me to pull off the road before being told the results of the test. This dramatic phone call turned out to be the beginning of the end of my career. The scan revealed extensive calcium build up in my cardiac arteries, causing my cardiologist (for the first time ever, I established a relationship with a cardiologist such that I would thereafter refer to him or her as "mine") to conduct an angioplasty. Two stents were placed in my cardiac arteries.

It is important to note that I had no pain, no shortness of breath, no discomfort in my arms, and no other indication of anything being wrong. Nonetheless, the experience caused some consternation with my overlords in London. The angioplasty gave the British a sufficient excuse to suggest I should no longer be the CEO of the company. My new title was Founding Partner of Globeleq. They left me financially secure, allowing me to retain my equity interest in the very generous profit sharing plan. This eventually led to my becoming financially independent for the first time in my life.

I want to be clear. I was sixty-one years old. The outside of my container had been built very well. After years of dedicated worship, I had finally achieved power, prestige, and possessions beyond my dreams. The false gods had delivered.

Power. While I was not a public celebrity by any means, I was well known in my profession. As I liked to say, the people that mattered knew me, the rest didn't count very much. Significantly, I was a corporate Chief Executive Officer. While I certainly had the important limitations of a Board of Directors and a Chairman, I had significant power over the resources and people that made up my organizations.

Prestige. It was often said that while I never had any significant money, I lived as though I were wealthy. For most of my working life, I earned a very good annual income, but spent all of it on a lifestyle that, while not lavish, was certainly beyond comfortable. I frequently spoke at industry meetings. My lifestyle was one of privilege. The problem was that I was the most ardent believer in the false message conveyed by my image. As my old boss, Oscar Wyatt, would say, I was drunk on my own whiskey.

Possessions. When my first power plant was sold in 1995, I was able to put some money in the bank, but left it there for less than a year. I designed and built a very nice house in Houston, using all the proceeds of that sale and a little more. We lived on Ella Lee Lane for almost fifteen years. I drove expensive German cars, always new every three years. We had all the "things" we needed, and virtually all that we wanted.

As I have said, in terms of spirituality, I was a moral agnostic. I simply did not have a position, one way or the other on the existence or presence of God. In that sense, I was agnostic. Not a believer, but not an unbeliever either. However, I believed in and practiced what I considered to be moral behavior, which, for me, meant doing good in the world. My moral code was based on helping the people at the margins of life. I talked about this at Board meetings, and at staff meetings. I talked about it when I visited the power plants we operated. I talked about it at industry meetings. And I practiced what I preached. We worked only in the poorest countries, providing essential energy to the poorest people.

Depression

At the height of my material and image success, I was removed from my position as CEO of the company I had founded. I considered the shift from CEO to Founding Partner to be the end of my career, which, for me, was essentially the end of my life. When I assumed that all three of the illusory gains of power, prestige, and possessions were threatened, I began to spiral into the deepest, darkest, most frightening despair imaginable. The identity that had served me so well was suddenly invalid.

The Chief Executive Officer was now Finding Pasture. All of the people I had so carefully recruited, trained, and inspired no longer worked for me. In my despair, I assumed they no longer respected me. I was embarrassed to be seen by them. My mental state was never diagnosed as clinical depression, but that was only because I refused to seek help. Most days began with a feeling that all I had ever worked for no longer existed, and went down from there. Suicide was a constant thought, followed by revulsion against myself for the cowardice of not following through.

What is now clear to me is that my physical and mental conditions were only symptoms of a much greater spiritual crisis. Each dark morning began with a desire for complete isolation, in which I did grapple with some of the big issues of life, death, love, and pain. But I avoided God. I accepted only those answers that offered "death and adversity." How could anyone love the miserable person behind my mask? I loathed that person.

My Heart Breaks, and the Holy Words Fall In

On October 17, 2007, I suffered the third heart attack in five months, this time while I was at a retreat center outside of Phoenix, Arizona. My memories of that cardiac infarction, as the doctors describe these events, are almost humorous.

It had begun almost a month before, when I had experienced incredible angina pain, writhing in anguish for hours before going to the hospital for a full round of tests. There was no increase in troponin, the enzyme that signals heart muscle damage. Assuming the cause of the pain might be gastrointestinal, the doctor ordered an endoscopy, which also turned up no evidence of a problem.

The angina pain continued in milder form for the next couple of weeks. Early in the evening of October 16, I started coughing uncontrollably. Of course, my chest hurt, but I associated it with the coughing. Walking to the dining pavilion that night, I remember throwing up several times, almost projectile vomiting. I was embarrassed, but amused as well. My worst memory is hearing someone complain about the mess on the sidewalk! I feigned ignorance. An hour or so later, someone found me unconscious on another sidewalk. An ambulance took me to the local hospital where elevated troponin levels confirmed a cardiac event.

I remember being asked two questions: Was there anyone to call? What was my religious preference? I gave them Sallie Ann's telephone number. I said Catholicism. At that time, nothing could have been further from the truth. While I was clearly no longer Mormon, I had not seriously considered any other form of religious affiliation. In fact, while I had occasionally allowed for the hypothetical existence of someone or something greater than myself, I abhorred institutional religion. While this must have been primarily the result of my own excommunication, I was also quite a typical product of a long and successful secular education. I remain an avid reader, moving from one obsessive interest to another with some frequency. Prior to 2007, spiritual writing was not one of those obsessions.

Spiritual Journey

As I emerged from the anesthesia in Banner Good Samaritan Hospital in Phoenix, where I had my bypass surgery, God's holy words fell into my "broken heart." This was my still point. This was the day I joined the Cosmic Dance.

I started talking about a spiritual journey. My sister Nancy's son, Ryan, lived in the area, so he came to visit. I talked so much about my desire to find God that he assumed I wanted to return to the Mormon faith. *Not so fast*, I remember thinking!

My very good and long-time friend, Buddy Tudor, sent me a book, *The Language of God*, by Francis Collins. It was based on *Mere Christianity*, a C.S. Lewis book that I had read during one of my intermittent obsessions. After the Collins book, I started reading Lewis again, which led to Reinhold Niebuhr and Thomas Merton, among others.

Sallie Ann, a cradle Catholic, had been attending Mass alone for years. As part of my new journey, I started going with her to St. Anne's Catholic Church, where Father John Robbins was Pastor. Slowly but surely, Father John became a truly close friend. He loved Sallie Ann, and came to like me, both because of Sallie Ann, and because he fully supported my spiritual journey. He did so without pushing Catholicism. When he talked about religion, it was in broad non-denominational terms, almost secular philosophy. I will never forget Father John telling me that the two most important words in Catholic, Christian, or simply a full life were *inclusivity* and *forgiveness*. I truly loved that.

One of my greatest criticisms of institutional religion is its tribal fixation on exclusiveness. "My way or the highway." "We, and only we, have the keys to the kingdom."

Father John was talking about something entirely different. The longer I walked on my new journey, the more I realized how important it was that I be *included*. While I was not able to express it clearly at that time, I was suffering in part from extreme isolation. It is still a problem.

Forgiveness resonated in large part because I was beginning to understand just how false the gods were that had been leading me astray. There had been many false gods. I had been quite a successful follower. I needed to be forgiven by numerous people I had deeply hurt, but, perhaps more than anyone else, by myself. The process started slowly and continues to this day.

Eventually, I suggested to Father John that I seriously investigate becoming Catholic. Neither he nor Sallie Ann pushed me, though they both offered quiet support. So I began the Rite of Christian Initiation of Adults ("RCIA"), a weekly course of instruction in what it means to be Catholic. Since I had only been baptized by the Mormons, a baptism not recognized by the Catholic Church, I was required to take two years of RCIA. I also had to obtain an annulment of my prior marriage. The annulment process, I was told, would take at least two years.

About the same time that I met Father John, Chris Dorment, another old and close friend, invited me to join the advisory board of the Arrupe Program, part of the Woodstock Theological Center at Georgetown University. I found it oddly amusing that I was asked to promote Catholic values in business *before* becoming a Catholic, and *after* retiring from business. Over the next five years, Arrupe, Woodstock, and the Jesuits would become central to my life and my conversion.

On April 3, 2010, at the Easter Vigil service at St. Anne's Catholic Church on Westheimer Road in Houston, Texas, I was baptized, confirmed, and had first communion. While my Catholic faith teaches me that my baptism included forgiveness of all my prior sins, I knew in my heart that I was still very much a sinner. I still felt isolated. I still followed the false gods. But I was well launched on the greatest journey of my life.

October 14

Repeat the Prayer of Consideration: The Way Things Are

I PRAYED ON my knees this morning. There can be no question that it is different from praying on the bench or sitting in my chair. The discomfort focuses my mind in a positive way. While I prayed for many things, I returned over and over again to the struggle I have with God's direct role in my personal life. Reading the meditation passage after I prayed, my focus was particularly drawn to these lines, which mention God's hope in and for me:

> God planted deep in my self an original purpose—the concrete expression of God's hopes in and for me. My life is to discover in myself that original purpose—what my concrete self "adds up to"—and to live it out.

While my logic might seem tortured at times, I have sorted out my own approach to how God acts in all of creation. It is certainly not original. Rather, it is based on and includes the teaching of the Jesuits, the Living School, RCIA, and all the great thinkers and theologians I have read and been taught about over these years.

Father Rohr writes,

> Foundational love gives us hope and allows us to trust 'what is' as the jumping-off point toward working together for 'what can be.' The life, death, and resurrection of Jesus shows us what's fully possible. God will always bring yet more life and wholeness out of seeming chaos and death.

God creates this universe, including me, momently through evolution, a process that has been moving inexorably toward the God-given goal of unitive consciousness since time began, now calculated to be more than 14 billion years ago. All of the universe began one with God, is still one with God, and will always be one with God. That includes me. I am a miniscule, totally unimportant part of the whole universe, but I am central to my universe. God planted deep in me the purpose of becoming a whole person, fully conscious of His presence in me, and of my complete and total unity with Him. If, when, and as I become increasingly whole—as I fully embrace what my concrete self "adds up to"—I know that I can only live out my purpose through service to others.

What then is my prayer? I ask God for various graces, which I believe are part of the totality of love with which God created me and which God imbued within me. These are not graces or gifts only given when I ask for them in the proper way, or earn them through proper behavior. God gave me these gifts at creation, gives them to me again at my birth, and gives them to me over and over again in every second of every minute of every hour, day, year, and decade of my life. What I am actually praying for is to be conscious of the particular grace, aware of it in my life. As Meister Eckhart wrote, "*If* the only prayer *you ever say in your entire life* is thank you, *it will be enough.*" I already have the grace, the gift, and the blessing. I need to thank Him, and I need to become conscious of all those graces in my life.

Psalm 139: "for I am fearfully and wonderfully made."

I pray with gratitude for these graces. I pray for awareness of all these blessings.

October 15

Repeat Luke 15: 11–32, Parable of the Prodigal Son

INTELLECTUALLY, I have considered God to be a verb, not a noun, for years. I say the words, God *is love*, and God is *in relationship* with Jesus Christ and the Holy Spirit. Quite honestly, however, I am not comfortable with my true ownership of these concepts. I understand the human need for substance over relationships, nouns over verbs. When I say God created the universe through the process of evolution, there is somewhere in my thought process a substantive being, acting to launch the creative process. It is difficult for me to accept that a "relationship" started the process. Likewise, praying to a relationship requires a change in my comprehension. I have struggled to describe in my journaling over the past month my faith in God as the source and the goal of the universe. God is the source and the goal of every creation in the universe, including me. He made me who I am, how I am, and what I live for. He did this, or, better, He *does this* through constantly and momently creating me through the evolutionary process, within which I have a certain amount of free choice. I cannot choose different parents, or different circumstances of my birth, or a different past. A large part of who I am today is the result of the free choices I made each day over all the days that I have been alive. And those choices were all made within the environment that formed me, both through nature and nurture.

When I became Catholic, I professed a belief in the Trinity, something I understood even then to be a relational Godhead that included God the Father, Jesus Christ the Son, and the Holy Spirit. But I was not at all clear what the concept of *relational* actually meant or means. Every time I attend Mass, I recite the Nicene Creed, expressing in considerable detail my belief in substantive members of the Trinity, each quite clearly nouns, not verbs. Yet every time I come to the line "seated at the right hand of the Father," I say to myself, *not really.*

As I prayed this morning, asking for understanding for my reflection on the story of the prodigal son, I struggled again with the simple question, *Who are you, God?* Like Saint Francis, "Who are you, God? And who am I?" Being in such good company provides me little help in finding clarity on this truly crucial question. Maybe it is sufficient to answer simply, "Not me." It is a good start to believe at the deepest level that God is something outside of me.

The parable of the Prodigal Son includes numerous messages about God and His relationship with me. The Righteous Father, obviously a metaphor for God, cares about the least among his children. He cares for the sinner who seeks forgiveness. He forgives and is inclusive, the two most important aspects of our faith. Father Rohr based the curriculum and the whole concept of the Living School on three pillars—Scripture, Tradition, and Experience. He urged us to read Scripture through the lenses of mercy and inclusion. The fancy word for an approach to reading and understanding Scripture is *hermeneutics*. Applying the hermeneutic of mercy and inclusion would elevate this parable (and the two that proceed it, the Lost Sheep and the Lost Coin) to a very high position. I sat on the meditation bench in silence for a long time this morning, reflecting on the messages of these parables. Whether God is one substantive person with three natures, or a three-part relationship of love, or whatever He is, He/She/It is merciful and inclusive. And the message of these passages is that we should be so as well. John of the Cross wrote, "God cannot be known. He can only be loved." I pray for greater understanding. I pray for patience to grow. I pray for wholeness. I pray for oneness.

CALENDAR WEEK FIVE

Almighty and ever-watchful God, You are beginning and end, alpha and omega. You start all things, and bring all things back to Yourself. For no living creature can make itself come to be; no living being wakes itself from nothingness. Nothing in me could have made You love me, or forced You to want me to be. Since before I came to be, You have loved me with an everlasting love, and now Your totally free love burns at the core of my life, at the core of myself. I acknowledge You Creator and Lord, once at the start of all things and always, all days, as the beginning of all things. You alone are Lord, living and reigning forever and ever. Amen.

October 16

Ephesians 2: 1–10

You were dead through the trespasses and sins² in which you once lived, following the course of this world, following the ruler of the power of the air, the spirit that is now at work among those who are disobedient. ³ All of us once lived among them in the passions of our flesh, following the desires of flesh and senses, and we were by nature children of wrath, like everyone else. ⁴ But God, who is rich in mercy, out of the great love with which he loved us ⁵ even when we were dead through our trespasses, made us alive together with Christ—by grace you have been saved— ⁶ and raised us up with him and seated us with him in the heavenly places in Christ Jesus, ⁷ so that in the ages to come he might show the immeasurable riches of his grace in kindness toward us in Christ Jesus. ⁸ For by grace you have been saved through faith, and this is not your own doing; it is the gift of God— ⁹ not the result of works, so that no one may boast. ¹⁰ For we are what he has made us, created in Christ Jesus for good works, which God prepared beforehand to be our way of life.

READING THROUGH this passage last night, I was struck with how totally true it is for me. Indeed, I was "dead through trespasses and sins." Reflecting on it again this morning, it occurs to me that my "death through sins" is not a simple issue of my past. I do not rise from the death of sin just once in my life, suddenly becoming alive in and through the grace of Christ's saving action. I die in sin and am reborn in His grace over and over and over again. That is the great dilemma of free choice. Knowing all that I know about right versus wrong, knowing as I do that I will not be truly happy doing the wrong thing, I persist in repeating the very behavior I have sworn not to repeat. The deeper message of divine grace is that there is literally nothing I can do that will cause God not to love me. Returning to the conundrum I struggle with repeatedly, "Who are you God? And who am I?" I understand God to be a relational "boiling over" of love. The universe came into existence through this outpouring of love. All of creation, including my sorry self, is newly created moment by moment through this outpouring of love. God's saving grace is simply another way of expressing the action of Love in the universe, and in my life. Whatever choice I make in any particular moment or event, God's Love is not changed. My life, on the other hand, is changed for the worse when I sin, and changed again for the better when I do the right thing. It is my choice—Heaven or Hell, selfish or selfless, surrender or resist, let go or hang on.

I pray for the strength of conviction required to do the right thing. I pray for open eyes and an open heart. I express gratitude for the graces of inclusion and forgiveness.

October 17

The Way Things Can Be

   My life world offers me a welter of wonderful things—careers, places to live, consumer goods, travel, various educations. After I have set my face against anything sinful, how will I decide which among them to go for?

   I could choose in several ways. First, I could simply follow fad and fashion. Hankering after the latest clothes and activities and trips, I could do what everyone else is doing right now.

   Or second, I could simply follow my own native tastes. If I grew up loving open country, I could choose to live in a suburb simply because I prefer it and for no other reason. If my natural preferences lead me to pursue some profession, I could simply follow that lead, figuring that God would not make me hanker for something that would do me harm.

   Or third, I could set some definite goal for myself, to bring me to transcend myself, reach fulfillment, and do some real good for others. For example, I could have the ambition of being a federal judge or having total financial security or making some important discovery in genetics. Then I could aim everything toward that goal.

   A fourth way would be more difficult. I could begin with the premise that I will never do anything to break my relationship with God, my Lord, but will choose only what my conscience freely allows. Then I will wait to find out what God hopes for in me.

   To achieve this mind-set, I have to believe that I can know what God hopes in me, and I have to hope that I can find that out.

   I will also have to hold tremendously careful balance among all the welter of wonderful things that my life world offers me. I will not let myself get so stuck on any of them that it will incline me to this or that decision. That would mean that I would not follow the first or second way of choosing—by doing what everyone is now doing, or by merely following my own native preferences—and not even the third—by setting my own life goal for myself without asking God what my Creator wants in me. To put that another way: I would not try to tell God what will make me happy (that judgeship or a heap of money or a brilliant scientific career). I will wait to find out what God has been hoping in me—and live confident that it will make me happy.

   Of course, I cannot sit back and expect God to strike me the way God struck Paul of Tarsus. I have to pray, to consider, and take counsel with trusted friends. I have to attend to what the whole Church now engages in and hopes for, and what the official teachers (bishops and theologians in their own ways) are teaching. I have to try this or that and see how it goes. but I will always be hoping to find God desiring me, God shaping my life world, God bringing the Reign to reality. I hope to find what God wants first, and then I will decide what I let myself want and what I will choose.

   *Holding this kind of **indifference** among God's almost infinite number of gifts makes a person a great force for good. What a power she is who does not much care where she lives as long as God's hopes are being realized! What a power he is who does not much care whether he lives wealthy or not, only as long as God's justice is being done! Such a person truly finds God in all things—God creating, God raising up justice and peace in all things, God working busily so that no one will be lost, but everyone brought to the Reign.*

Principle and Foundation

   Man is created to praise, reverence, and serve God our Lord, and by this means to save his soul.

   The other things on the face of the earth are created for man to help him in attaining the end for which he was created.

   Hence, a man is to make use of them in as far as they help him in the attainment of his end, and he must rid himself of them in as far as they prove a hindrance to him.

*Therefore, **we must make ourselves indifferent to all created things**, as far as we are allowed free choice and are not under any prohibition. Consequently, as far as we are concerned, we should not prefer health to sickness, riches to poverty, honor to dishonor, a long life to a short life. The same holds for all other things.*

Our one desire and choice should be what is more conducive to the end for which we are created.

Active Indifference

*When we say "indifferent," we do not mean apathy but rather Karl Rahner's definition of indifference as a kind of removal or distance away from things that make true vision possible and is required for proper decision. **This indifference** does not exist for its own sake but is the choice of what is most conducive to the end. It is **freedom for making a decision according to God's will**.*

The influence of previously held views keeps us from having this indifference and consequently from being able to make a free decision.

*It is the exact opposite of unconcern or apathy. St. Ignatius is not inculcating insensibility to natural desires. He is not aiming at a person without human loves, but one in whom all other loves are so informed by God's love that they cannot keep their hold on the heart if they are separated from it. So indifference means that I do not incline one way or the other in a decisive manner until I have discerned the will of God. **Discern first, decide later!***

This does not come about through good will alone, or by saying that I am indifferent nor is it the resolution not to let myself be carried along by the crowd: it demands rather the existential distance from things that frees the will to reject its own previous prejudices. It means that I dispose myself, seeding a poised freedom... "the eyes of the handmaid are on the hands of the master" kind of freedom.

Almighty and ever-caring God, You are powerful to give life and to take it away. You order all things from end to end, beyond my comprehension, beyond my imagining. Your passionate hope is that every person be saved from selfishness and self-destruction. You want no one to perish, to live forever alone. Instead, You want a reign of love to rise from within our hearts, and embrace each human person and every thing on the earth. I praise You and I thank You that You teach me these things through Christ our Lord. Amen

THE MEDITATION reading today is longer than most scriptures, and it contains several very valuable concepts. Three, in particular, speak to me.

The first is a fundamental element of any form of transformational journey. I think of it as essentially Ignatian in its simplicity. *Do those things that bring you closer to God. Avoid those thing that take you away from God.* This is not an admonition to be perfect or never sin. It is both easier than that, and far more realistic. I am reminded of the Merton prayer, part of which reads as follows:

> But I believe that the desire to please you does in fact please you. And I hope I have that desire in all that I am doing. I hope that I will never do anything apart from that desire.

This adds another element of simplicity. The desire to please God is already pleasing to Him, whatever we ultimately say or do. However, if that desire is genuine, it is highly likely that we will do the better thing, if not the best; and avoid the worse thing, much less the worst.

The second concept is *active indifference*, one that I have struggled with since I first went through these Exercises five years ago. The first several times that I saw the words and read through the explanation, I understood that I was being advised to be indifferent with respect to doing the right thing or the wrong thing. This is not the idea at all. The concept asks us to check our personal preferences at the door, even if for only a short time, before making virtually any decision. For just an instant, we are *indifferent* as to which way to decide a particular question. By doing so, by holding up for just a few minutes, we create time and space to ask and answer another question: What would please God? This is the *active* part of active indifference.

The third concept in this meditation is *discern before deciding*. In one sense, discernment is simply another way of saying *decide carefully*. In a more profound sense, however, it requires that I check with God before deciding. For me, this clearly does not mean that I pray that God will send me a clear sign, pointing me in the right direction. I like the words in the meditation:

> Discernment "demands . . . the existential distance from things that frees the will to reject its own previous prejudices."

Existential distance is that space that is created when I stop to ask what is the more merciful, more forgiving, more inclusive—simply, more loving choice. My existence is a function of God holding me in His loving embrace instant by instant by instant. In that moment when I discern, I am consulting the best part of who I am, perhaps the only real part.

I pray for as much existential distance in my life as I can possibly create. I pray that I will always pause to reflect on the presence of love in my life, making all my decisions from that reservoir of love.

October 18

Genesis 22: 1–19

After these things God tested Abraham. He said to him, "Abraham!" And he said, "Here I am." ² He said, "Take your son, your only son Isaac, whom you love, and go to the land of Moriah, and offer him there as a burnt offering on one of the mountains that I shall show you." ³ So Abraham rose early in the morning, saddled his donkey, and took two of his young men with him, and his son Isaac; he cut the wood for the burnt offering, and set out and went to the place in the distance that God had shown him. ⁴ On the third day Abraham looked up and saw the place far away. ⁵ Then Abraham said to his young men, "Stay here with the donkey; the boy and I will go over there; we will worship, and then we will come back to you." ⁶ Abraham took the wood of the burnt offering and laid it on his son Isaac, and he himself carried the fire and the knife. So the two of them walked on together. ⁷ Isaac said to his father Abraham, "Father!" And he said, "Here I am, my son." He said, "The fire and the wood are here, but where is the lamb for a burnt offering?" ⁸ Abraham said, "God himself will provide the lamb for a burnt offering, my son." So the two of them walked on together.

⁹ When they came to the place that God had shown him, Abraham built an altar there and laid the wood in order. He bound his son Isaac, and laid him on the altar, on top of the wood. ¹⁰ Then Abraham reached out his hand and took the knife to kill his son. ¹¹ But the angel of the LORD called to him from heaven, and said, "Abraham, Abraham!" And he said, "Here I am." ¹² He said, "Do not lay your hand on the boy or do anything to him; for now I know that you fear God, since you have not withheld your son, your only son, from me." ¹³ And Abraham looked up and saw a ram, caught in a thicket by its horns. Abraham went and took the ram and offered it up as a burnt offering instead of his son. ¹⁴ So Abraham called that place "The LORD will provide"; as it is said to this day, "On the mount of the LORD it shall be provided."

¹⁵ The angel of the LORD called to Abraham a second time from heaven, ¹⁶ and said, "By myself I have sworn, says the LORD: Because you have done this, and have not withheld your son, your only son, ¹⁷ I will indeed bless you, and I will make your offspring as numerous as the stars of heaven and as the sand that is on the seashore. And your offspring shall possess the gate of their enemies, ¹⁸ and by your offspring shall all the nations of the earth gain blessing for themselves, because you have obeyed my voice." [19] So Abraham returned to his young men, and they arose and went together to Beer-sheba; and Abraham lived at Beer-sheba.

THERE ARE many levels on which to reflect on this story about Abraham and Isaac. One level is the historical narrative, which traditionally held that Abraham lived during the second millennium before Christ (or before the common era, BCE). As an aside, I found it interesting to read that Abraham was born in the year 1948 *after creation*! This is historical dating based on the view that the age of the world is around 4,000 years, not the scientifically based age of 14.7 billion years. Somewhat more logical dating puts Abraham in the period I have described earlier as Jaspers' First Axial Age, somewhere between 800 and 300 BCE.

I am intrigued by a second level on which to understand the role of Abraham in world history, which is that as the father of the three "religions of the book"—Christianity, Islam, and Judaism. There is an annual Table of Abraham dinner here in Jacksonville, which is a dinner bringing together local leaders of the three religions for an evening of fellowship. I am a big fan of interfaith efforts, especially in this election year, when Muslims have come under such extraordinary criticism.

Then there is the rather uncomfortable level of God testing the faith of Abraham. How can a Trinitarian, "relational," loving God test a person's faith, particularly with the murder of a son? So I back away from the literal words as far as I can, hoping to find some metaphoric understanding that makes sense. The Hebrew scriptures were written to convey certain simple messages to the Israelites. In a rather crude and, to me, distasteful way, this story does suggest that God demands obedience, but He is also "kind" enough to back off at the last minute. It does not work for me.

Finally, this story could be viewed as the basis for the Atonement theory of Christ's mission. We have sinned. God loves us, so He sends His only Son for us to kill so that we can be forgiven for our sins. This certainly does not work for me.

What happened during my meditation today was a series of "thought trips" in some way connected to the theme of literal Atonement Theory versus the notion of "at-one-ment." The metaphor of God incarnate is God as man or God as me. God's love boiling over in love for His Son, Their love expressed as the Holy Spirit, and all of that love flowing out and flowing in, capturing all of creation in the flow. Abraham disappeared in the warm thoughts of my own body dancing with the Divine, incorporating the water from the lagoon and the ocean, the light in the morning sky, and the green in the grass and garden all around me. I began the morning with tennis and a work out in the gym, so I was both tired and happy to be alive.

As I sat in Mass last night, I felt surrounded by love. I saw a friend whose birthday was yesterday, to whom I had expressed best wishes, and who had warmly acknowledged my wishes. I saw several people who have traveled to the Dominican Republic to serve on missions for Sister Parish, including the Co-Founder of the Ministry. I saw friends from CRHP and Cursillo and the Lector Ministry. I saw friends from our granddaughters' school. The daughter of one of my closest friends was singing in the choir. The son of another close friend was an altar server. It warmed my soul to see them, and acknowledge them and be acknowledged by them. In short, I was surrounded by community, a community that is hugely important to me, a community that I love.

Yet virtually every one of the people I saw and spoke to last night was almost certainly in a different political party from me and had different preferences for the upcoming election. And I am certain that they hold their political views as strongly and sincerely as I hold mine, and have reasons for their positions that are as sound and logical to them as mine are to me.

And then I thought about the rancor and divisiveness of this important political campaign that is coming to such a sorrowful end. The news last night reported a firebombing of a Republican Party office in North Carolina, something that was very likely done by a radical group in the Democratic Party. Radical Republicans are telling news reporters to jail the Democratic nominee, or worse. There are questions about what will happen after the election, whether everyone will recognize the winner, or even whether some form of violence could erupt.

Well, I know what I will do after the election. Obviously, I want my candidates to win and will be sad if we lose. But I will continue to love my friends, every one of them. I will respect them, and I will honor their families, their faith, and their service. I will continue to be grateful for this community. God's infinite and eternal love knows no party distinctions, political differences, or voting preferences. I am deeply grateful for that.

October 19

When you repeat a passage, give more time to the ideas, desires, feelings that were particularly strong and good, and to those that seem to have been particularly problematic or obscure or vexing. Go back to those places where you felt discouragement, revulsion, anger, or simply nothing at all, places like the **black holes** *in our universe from which no light or warmth comes. Go back also to those places where you felt great encouragement, love for God, and enthusiasm to go on places like the* **volcanoes** *on our globe that throw up blazing rivers and that roar with energy. You will visit many of these black holes and volcanoes during the Ignatian Exercises.*

AS I READ through the passage about Abraham and Isaac again this morning, I was particularly struck with the deception of Abraham, both telling the two young men to wait with the donkeys, and telling Isaac that God would supply the lamb. At the time Abraham said those things, he was lying. On a literal level, the whole story discourages me. And I remain frustrated with the metaphoric value, which I assume is that we are to be obedient to this petty God, trusting in Him to right the wrong before it is too late. Not my favorite story on any level.

Consider this comment from Jim Finley, our Living School teacher.

> What do you do when you've tasted that without which life will remain forever incomplete? How can you be content to be living estranged from that completeness? That's really the thing. See, having tasted that, without which life remains forever incomplete, how can I be in collusion with the *ongoing indifference* that allows me to go along in continued estrangement from being grounded in that completeness?

For me, this "ongoing indifference" is easily confused with the "active indifference" advocated by Ignatius. If I am truly "tuned in" to that which pleases God, why would I need to be indifferent with respect to any decision I have to make? I am not speaking of the angry God teasing and testing Abraham, but of a relational God of overflowing love. Especially in my case, now that I am retired and comfortably independent, why would I ever hesitate to discern? Matt Mumber, my Living School classmate, who is still working as an oncological radiologist and supporting a young family, provides this answer:

> The ongoing indifference is a habit for me…it's what I do in the "real world" in order to support my family, bring home the bacon, etc. It's a way of viewing what I do in the real

world more than what I actually do...there are days when I remember that every step and every miss-step is filled with grace—bringing the unknown into the known...and then there are days when it all seems like an uphill battle that I struggle in alone and afraid. The unknown overwhelms me in those times and the known needs to be controlled and forced and not just enjoyed and allowed. Being grounded in completeness is a gift that cannot be lost or earned, and yet it must be noticed, nurtured and remembered This is the work of contemplative practice and this is the beauty we share together.

My Living School friends are impressive. Again, Finley asks, "what do you do when you've tasted that without which life will remain forever incomplete?" How can I join the divine dance, sitting on the bench in the early morning light, listening to the waves and the birds, feeling as light as the clouds, and then casually walk away and join in the commercial, egoistic pattern of everyday life? I want to answer this question honestly and realistically.

First, I am not convinced that I am capable of maintaining the spiritual *state* of high awareness for an extended period of time. I am not certain it would even be healthy. Hopefully, there is a gradual *stage shift*, when I move ever closer to a level of non-dual, inclusive consciousness. And in moments of great awareness—the "peak experiences"—of morning prayer, the combination of both higher *state* and higher *stage* of consciousness does indeed provide the "taste without which life will remain forever incomplete." Just knowing the joyous taste from time to time puts me in a better place than I have ever been in my life.

Second, and somewhat related to the first, it strikes me that having tasted the sublime joy does not mean there will never again be decisions to make, both mundane and ethereal. While I suppose part of the appeal of the hermit's life is the elimination of as many decisions as possible, even the most remote hermitage will involve some decision. The active indifference of Ignatius is a straightforward way to make any and all decisions. And it is not that complicated. Stop, reflect on the choices of action. Discern which option moves more in the direction of God (loving, inclusive, selfless, forgiving), and choose it. The mere necessity of making a practical choice requires coming down from the spiritual high.

Active indifference is the alternative to an instant and constant bias for self. It is the pause before action. I need to train my instincts and desires to "stop, look and listen." If I consistently choose the selfish option, knowing in my heart the joy of peak, loving, non-dual experience, that is ongoing indifference.

I pray this morning for this country. The final presidential debate is tonight, bringing us closer to the end of this truly awful political year. I am afraid there will be no winners. Mrs. Clinton will have to deal with such an angry and spiteful Congress that she will find it hard to get anything done. Mr. Trump will continue to build on the hate and fear of his followers, either preparing for another political move or simply using them to make money. I pray for the strength to avoid persistent, ongoing indifference.

October 20

Isaiah 6: 1–13

In the year that King Uzziah died, I saw the Lord sitting on a throne, high and lofty; and the hem of his robe filled the temple. ² Seraphs were in attendance above him; each had six wings: with two they covered their faces, and with two they covered their feet, and with two they flew. ³ And one called to another and said:

"Holy, holy, holy is the LORD of hosts;
   the whole earth is full of his glory."

[4] The pivots on the thresholds shook at the voices of those who called, and the house filled with smoke. [5] And I said: "Woe is me! I am lost, for I am a man of unclean lips, and I live among a people of unclean lips; yet my eyes have seen the King, the LORD of hosts!"

[6] Then one of the seraphs flew to me, holding a live coal that had been taken from the altar with a pair of tongs. [7] The seraph touched my mouth with it and said: "Now that this has touched your lips, your guilt has departed and your sin is blotted out." [8] Then I heard the voice of the Lord saying, "Whom shall I send, and who will go for us?" And I said, "Here am I; send me!" [9] And he said, "Go and say to this people:

   'Keep listening, but do not comprehend;
   keep looking, but do not understand.'
[10] Make the mind of this people dull,
   and stop their ears,
   and shut their eyes,
so that they may not look with their eyes,
   and listen with their ears,
and comprehend with their minds,
   and turn and be healed."
[11] Then I said, "How long, O Lord?" And he said:
"Until cities lie waste
   without inhabitant,
and houses without people,
   and the land is utterly desolate;
[12] until the LORD sends everyone far away,
   and vast is the emptiness in the midst of the land.
[13] Even if a tenth part remain in it,
   it will be burned again,
like a terebinth or an oak
   whose stump remains standing
   when it is felled."
The holy seed is its stump.

FOR THE FIRST time since moving to Florida six years ago, I have started going to the gym, only one block away! Today, following tennis, I went for the fifth time. I make no forecasts! But I can say without doubt that physical exercise helps my state of mind, especially my ability to meditate and reflect on the Exercises. Praying at the bench in the garden was magical this morning. A clear sky, dry air, temperature in the mid-seventies, and the "quiet" of the waves breaking on the beach and the bird cries over the lagoon—all of these make the effort to be acutely aware more achievable. I literally tingled with connection! "The whole earth was full of His glory!"

The words Isaiah spoke in response to the Lord's query, "who shall I send?" resonate over and over again in so many situations. "Here I am; send me." For all my moods of frustration and regret, this has been my response to virtually every call throughout the course of my life. At times, I ignored family and other commitments to accept any and every opportunity to take on the next thing. In retrospect, I am generally happy that I so quickly and dependably said yes to opportunities, even though I was clearly not quite prepared to do so. I subscribe to the advice that the best way to learn how to have a baby is to get pregnant. That was certainly the situation when I left Boise Cascade to start my first company in 1970, not even two years out of college. I bought a coal mine with neither sufficient capital nor the slightest idea how to mine coal. I started my first electric power company in the same situation—no capital, no experience, and only a hazy idea of what I wanted to do. Even after I retired, I worked to create the Sister Parish Ministry with little idea of what a parish partnership even involved.

Not everything I said yes to worked out. There were certainly instances when more careful discernment would have been hugely beneficial, both to my causes and, especially, to the people who joined me. On balance, though, I am an enthusiastic advocate of "Here I am; send me!"

In his teaching about mystics in his book *Following the Mystics*, Jim Finley touches on a similar theme.

> Now the one who embodies this fullness knows something. And what they know is that there's nothing in them that's not also completely in you. That's what they know. They also know that you would not believe them if they told you that. So spiritual teachers don't argue. They accept it as a temporary arrangement—your recognition of it in them because they know that's the closest you can bear to get to it. The fact that you are unexplainably boundary-less in the intimacy of your limitations—you're just not quite up to taking that one on. So they accept it temporarily so that mutuality slowly emerges in the dynamics of the exchange, and so on.

It is one thing to take an action without certainty as to the outcome. I think there is significantly greater risk in taking a leap of faith with respect to non-dualistic oneness with the universe. Letting go of my distinctiveness, accepting the boundary-less nature of my relationships with other people and all of the universe—these are very hard for me. After all, the answer Isaiah gave, and the answer that has characterized my life was always "Here **I** am, send **me**." This statement is centered squarely on the ego. Much better would be, Here we are; send us!

I pray for the humility to be one with others. I pray for the strength to continue saying yes.

October 21

Romans 8: 28–29
   We know that all things work together for good for those who love God, who are called according to his purpose. [29] *For those whom he foreknew he also predestined to be conformed to the image of his Son, in order that he might be the firstborn within a large family.*

WHAT A POWERFUL message of optimism, albeit limited to those who "love God." One of the lessons from Job is that a loving God is not a guarantee for good luck. And the worldly success of evil men raises questions about the infallibility of this quid pro quo system. Even as I write this, I check my implicit criticism of the exclusionary message of Paul.

What I believe is that there is an ultimate goal of evolution. All of the universe is moving inexorably toward that goal, becoming more complex, more aware, and, painfully slowly, more non-dual. All of the universe is "predestined" to join in this massive, infinite, and eternal progress. My part in this drama is infinitesimally small and unimportant when viewed from the perspective of the universe, but enormously large and critically important to me. I was born with a long list of blessings, starting with being a white male in the United States. There may one day be a world and time where and when these three accidents of birth—white, male, US-born—are not such unfair advantages, but it would be silly to ignore them during the seventy-two years I have been here.

Other personality traits that make up who I am are the result of nature and nurture in my life, and, importantly, in the lives of my parents, siblings, friends, and teachers. Is this predestination? My understanding of evolution leads me to think not.

Nonetheless, at those times when I fully embrace the relational love of a Trinitarian God, when I join the dance, it seems that all things work together for good. Even when I am not clearly aware of the good, when I continue to see pain, fear, and suffering in the world, fully engaging in the dance makes those bad things better.

I am grateful for the dance. I am grateful for those fleeting moments when I feel my whole body lifting off the bench to join in the rhythm of waves and birds and water and sky and incomprehensible love. I pray for the quiet that allows me to experience this joy. I pray for wisdom and understanding.

October 22

Repeat, **black** *holes and* **volcanoes**.

THE IGNATIAN Exercises are a form of *discursive meditation,* the simplest explanation of which is meditation where mind and imagination and other faculties are actively employed in an effort to understand a deeper level of consciousness. The Greek words for the two approaches to both meditation and theology are *kataphatic* (or cataphatic) and *apophatic.* I first learned about these concepts when I did the Exercises in 2011, and learned more in the Living School. Kataphatic theology seeks to *say something* about God, using words, images, and other forms of communication. Much of the Bible is kataphatic, as is most formal religious activity. The path of affirmation or *via positiva* ascribes to the divine the highest attribute that one can conceive. Thus, if love is the highest form of expression, the seeker finds meaning following the way of love as a spiritual path.

Apophatic theology, the *via negativa,* on the other hand, seeks God in *nothingness* or through denial (it stems from *apophēmi,* Ancient Greek for "to deny"). It is knowing through unknowing. It seeks to empty the mind of all thought, all images, and all sensation. *Via negativa* deconstructs the foundation of thought, and disrupts the mind's attempt to order reality. Meister Eckhart called this the "God beyond God." John of the Cross refers to it as *nada.* A fundamental teaching of Father Rohr, derived from apophatic meditation, is the ability to hold seemingly contradictory or paradoxical claims of truth; to think in terms of *both/and* rather than *either/or;* to *transcend and include.*

Kataphatic theology is the basis of discursive meditation. When I seek understanding of a particular passage by "populating" the story with real people, including especially myself, I am way over on the kataphatic side of the continuum between the two forms of theology. I talk to God, and listen to Him as He talks to me. I play with Jesus as a boy on the beach. I am in the room with Him when He performs miracles. Obviously, I know that I am fantasizing these experiences. However, the more I surrender myself to the fantasy, the more I allow the people, places, and actions to reach my senses—sight, sound, smell, and touch—the more deeply I experience the meditative effort.

Apophatic meditation is much more difficult for me, though I readily concede that it is a deeper and profoundly more spiritual experience. As I read the mystics down through the ages, the goal seems to be to progress through various forms of kataphatic knowing to a state of such oneness with the Divine and all of creation that nothing needs to be said, or even thought. The goal of kataphatic knowing is apophatic unknowing. It is pure union.

John of the Cross described the difference between kataphatic and apophatic like this: "The difference between these two conditions of the soul is like the difference between working, and enjoyment of the fruit of our work; between receiving a gift, and profiting by it; between the toil of travelling and the rest at our journey's end." I remember learning in college more than fifty years ago that it was virtually impossible to both enjoy a painting and describe it at the same time.

In fact, I believe that both forms of meditation are essential; at least they are for my spiritual journey. Discursive meditation requires serious effort. It requires that I engage my affections, my emotional commitment to the images and events in my fantasy. I can become weightless with exquisite joy. And I can become desolate, filled with shame and remorse. The more I give myself over to the reality of my fantasy, the more deeply I feel the impact of the experience. Oddly, both consolation and desolation leave me more peaceful. That is to say, whether the deep experience is joyful or sad, I feel better for having reached something deep within me.

These thoughts about meditation arose this morning when I sat in the darkness before tennis, then returned as I read over my reflections from this week. I am extremely pleased that I seem to be back

in the habit of sitting with these passages, reflecting on them, and journaling. I return to my musings often during the day. I am aware of moments of heightened consciousness hours after I have put down my journal. I notice the stimuli—the garden sounds or cloud patterns or the people in my life. Oddly, after completing the Exercises in the summer of 2012, I stopped meditating altogether. Or, at least, I stopped journaling.

Father Rohr loves an icon known as *The Trinity*, created by the Russian painter Andrei Rublev in the early 15th century. I ordered a copy about two weeks ago. It arrived the other day and I placed it in my library on the table next to where I kneel to pray each morning to begin the Exercises. Art historians say that *The Trinity* depicts three angels, presumably those who visited Abraham as described in Genesis 18:1–8. Father Rohr sees in it the Divine Dance, the *perichoresis* (circle dance) of Father, Son, and Holy Spirit. The original hangs in the Tretyakov Gallery in Moscow. There is a small rectangular shape below the chalice on the table in the picture. It is speculated that this once held a mirror, which would allow the viewer of the icon to see themselves in the circle. Father Rohr likes to use this to signify our individual participation in the relational nature of the Trinity. I have only prayed with this icon for three days, but I can say already that the fantasy of joining in a movement of faith with the Trinity is powerful.

I pray that I will be able to live with paradox, especially as this political season comes to an end. By its very nature, voting is dualistic. I cannot vote for or support *both* the Democrat *and* the Republican. There is a genuine paradox. I will not be able to vote as the hierarchy of the Catholic Church advises me to vote and, at the same time, vote as my conscience tells me to vote. Can I live with this paradox?

Calendar Week Six

Lord, mighty God, You offer me so much. You give me many days and years, so many strengths and abilities, so many rich things and splendid machines, and You surround me with so many whom I may love. Teach me this one thing above all Lord: How am I to choose? Then I hope to return to You as many wonders as You have poured out on me. Through Christ Jesus, My Lord and good brother. Amen.

October 23

Romans 7: 14–25

[14] For we know that the law is spiritual; but I am of the flesh, sold into slavery under sin. [15] I do not understand my own actions. For I do not do what I want, but I do the very thing I hate. [16] Now if I do what I do not want, I agree that the law is good. [17] But in fact it is no longer I that do it, but sin that dwells within me. [18] For I know that nothing good dwells within me, that is, in my flesh. I can will what is right, but I cannot do it. [19] For I do not do the good I want, but the evil I do not want is what I do. [20] Now if I do what I do not want, it is no longer I that do it, but sin that dwells within me.

[21] So I find it to be a law that when I want to do what is good, evil lies close at hand. [22] For I delight in the law of God in my inmost self, [23] but I see in my members another law at war with the law of my mind, making me captive to the law of sin that dwells in my members. [24] Wretched man that I am! Who will rescue me from this body of death? [25] Thanks be to God through Jesus Christ our Lord!

So then, with my mind I am a slave to the law of God, but with my flesh I am a slave to the law of sin.

The prayer for this week asks God to answer the question, "How am I to choose." It has been suggested that the primary purpose of the Exercises is to provide tools to help us make better decisions. Active indifference is one of those tools. Discerning what would be pleasing to God or most loving is one of those tools. Ignatius described major life decisions as "elections," writing that "a good election can be made when sufficient light and knowledge is received through experience of consolations and desolations, and through experience of the discernment of different spirits." He recommends that important decisions await a "tranquil time, when the soul is not disturbed by different spirits and can use her natural powers freely and calmly." These decision tools make sense to me today. Slow down, get comfortable with the simple concept of "enough already," then decide on the straightforward basis of what brings me closer to Love versus what takes me further away from Love.

Sitting with the passage from Romans was not comfortable. Paul makes two very clear dualistic distinctions. First, he distinguishes between the "law of God" and the "law of sin." As I understand the concept of Manichaeism, it is essentially this stark separation of everything in life into good and bad, light and dark, or right and wrong. It is precisely the opposite of embracing paradox, of finding both/and rather than either/or. Second, Paul distinguishes between flesh and spirit. Tragically, this distinction has led to centuries of "body hatred" and "body shaming."

As I sat with this passage this morning, I was reminded by Father Rohr of something Carl Jung once wrote: "In my case Pilgrim's Progress consisted in my having to climb down a thousand ladders until I could reach out my hand to the little clod of earth that I am." Sadly, I generally buy into the dualistic view of right and wrong; of body bad, spirit good. I am such a bad, shameful being that only at the bottom of a very long descent will I find the little "clod of earth that I am."

Deep down, I think these negative thoughts are simple cop outs. Rather than wallowing in my littleness, I know that I can humbly grow closer to God through service than through self-denigration. The "election" I need to make each day is to get out of self, and into the dance.

October 24

Repeat Romans 7: 14–25

FOR THE SECOND day in a row, I sit with this dualistic passage from Paul's letter to the Romans. In fact, I spent a good part of yesterday and last night thinking about how uncomfortable the stark, simplistic dichotomies make me feel. The Law of God or the Law of Sin, no gray area, no room to consider complex implications or circumstances, no mitigating factors. I am sure there are some very clear alternative courses of action, which make easy decisions possible. However, each time I think of an actual situation, I can find room to apply some judgement and reason.

Later today, Sallie Ann and I will go to the local library to cast our votes in the 2016 election, one of the ugliest elections in my memory. We are obviously voting early. This is my journal, so these are my opinions. I have already proudly described the importance of the Democratic Party in my family and early upbringing. In more than sixty years of political activity, I have never wavered in my support of Democrats. However, I have always counted Republicans among my closet friends. Generally, we have had rational discussions. As the expression goes, we have disagreed without being disagreeable. However, the extreme polarization in our country's politics, which is getting worse each year, has changed this. Most of the time, including particularly in my Catholic faith community, political issues are simply not discussed. Sadly, the term "political issues" includes virtually any conversation not related to the specific task at hand (mission work, dining, sports, and business) or the weather. Even in discussions of faith, we must carefully avoid the thornier issues of Catholic Social Teaching. Today, however, must be an exception, simply because voting requires that we make a choice. Avoidance is not an option.

In my opinion, Donald Trump, the Republican candidate for President, is the poorest candidate that party has nominated in my political lifetime. He is poorly informed, totally lacking in curiosity, narcissistic, dishonest, and mean. These are personal characteristics that should have disqualified him from even seeking the nomination. With certain important exceptions, he has generally supported the Republican Party position on economic, social, and political issues. Thus, his economic program calls for lower taxes, less regulation, a smaller government, less organized labor, and greater private participation in the provision of public goods and services. His social program is pro-life, pro-guns, anti-immigrant, and pro-Christian (or, at least, anti-Muslim). His political program includes voter suppression at home (in the name of preventing voting fraud) and a somewhat isolationist position internationally. Note that during my political lifetime, Republicans have been strongly internationalist, favoring free trade, strong international alliances, and a more interventionist military posture. Trump is clearly opposed to free trade, dismissive of virtually all international alliances and organizations, and simply confusing with respect to military intervention. He would bomb ISIS to Hell, but not intervene in the actions of despotic rulers like Assad (or, in retrospect, Saddam or Gaddafi).

Hillary Clinton is the most derided and distrusted Democratic nominee since, well, Obama. I say this somewhat with tongue in cheek. Hillary is truly hated by at least forty percent of the voting public. Hated. I can honestly never recall *hating* a political opponent. But Hillary hatred has been around since even before she and her husband left Arkansas. Her reaction to this hatred has consistently included secrecy and obsessive privacy, which only exacerbates the problem. She and her husband have been hugely successful in amassing a fortune on the strength of their celebrity, but they are hardly alone in that. I personally think a certain amount of corruption is always present when large amounts of money are involved, so I question the actions and motives of many of the people in Clinton World. I wish there were less focus on wealth and star power at the Clinton Global Initiative meetings. I am reminded of the worst days of the power industry, when Enron ultimately imploded, bringing down so many energy companies at the same time. Enron introduced massive amounts of money to the personal enrichment and compensation plans and desires of executives. All that money had to lead to bad things, and it certainly did.

But I believe both Hillary and Bill have been scrupulously honest. They have released tax returns for thirty years, showing, I think, an average federal tax of more than 30 percent over the years. They give ten percent or more of their annual income to charity. After all the investigations of all of the transactions throughout all of these decades, we have uncovered dumb things done by both of them, and the stupid sexual behavior of Bill, but none of the serious claims of self-aggrandizement ever proved true.

Hillary is incredibly bright, deeply committed to social justice and the plight of the less advantaged. She is a classic Democrat. On most economic, social, and political matters, I have been in virtual lock step with Democrats most of my life. Even though I spent my career in the private sector, generally working to make traditionally public activities private, I believe strongly in the need for strong regulation and a relatively large government footprint. I favor high taxes on the rich and a high minimum wage. I strongly favor an all-inclusive and robust economic safety net, which translates into support for better Social Security benefits, public health care, and extremely aggressive economic assistance for communities and individuals adversely affected by globalization, trade, and ecological changes. Socially, I subscribe to an inclusive, forgiving view on everything from religious belief to sexual orientation. I believe in contraception, sex education, women's rights, and poverty alleviation as the best methods to reduce unwanted pregnancy and, thus, abortions. Internationally, I favor far more free trade than most Democrats (certainly the unions), strong international alliances, and an active international peace keeping role for the United States. When I was in college, people said that I was "too liberal to be radical," meaning that I could always see something of value on the other side of an issue. I am not comfortable with the idea of "non-negotiable."

I like the political advice from the Catholic Church contained in the USCCB document *Forming Consciences for Faithful Citizenship*. I carefully read this summary earlier today, and intend to read it again before voting.

USCCB Forming Consciences for Faithful Citizenship

Pope Francis, in *Evangelii Gaudium*: "An authentic faith always involves a deep desire to change the world, to transmit values, to leave this earth somehow better than we found it." In this fight for justice, God gives us a special gift, hope, which Pope Benedict describes in *Caritas in Veritate* as "bursting into our lives as something not due to us, something that transcends every law of justice." Thus, we take up the task of serving the common good with joy and hope, confident that God, who "so loved the world that he gave his only Son," walks with us and strengthens us on the way.

God is love, and he desires that we help to build a "civilization of love," one in which all human beings have the freedom and opportunity to experience the love of God and live out that love by freely making a gift of themselves to one another.

There is the absolute priority of "going forth from ourselves toward our brothers and sisters" as one of the two great commandments which ground every moral norm and as the clearest sign for discerning spiritual growth in response to God's completely unconditional gift. Love compels us to go into all the world and proclaim the good news to the whole creation.

Some issues are considered by many Catholics, including the leadership, to be "non-negotiable." Clearly, both our faith and our Constitution are based on the right to life, which, it is argued, governs the issues of abortion, euthanasia, stem cell research, and human cloning. Just to be clear, this "non-negotiable" right to life also governs the death penalty and war, both of which are apparently negotiable.

For me, the most difficult aspect of the right to life issue is the determination of when protected life begins. Everything in the universe is imbued with the life force of the divine. All animals and all plants are alive. So, yes, both the sperm and the egg are alive, as are, obviously, the fertilized egg and the embryo. St. Francis argued that all life is precious, and deserves honor and respect. The question is not life, but rather protected life. When does the life form become protected under our Constitution, and under God's law that "thou shalt not kill"?

I struggle with this, ultimately concluding that the answer relates to the viability of the fetus. One textbook definition is: "*Fetal viability* is the potential of the fetus to survive outside the uterus after birth, natural or induced, when supported by up-to-date medicine." Science cannot be precise as to when the fetus is viable, and new medical procedures are making it earlier all the time. There is substantial agreement around 20 to 24 weeks as the earliest date for viability. Abortions any later than this, referred to as late-term abortions, require ending the life of a viable person. In fact, only one percent of the abortions in the United States are late-term, roughly one quarter of which are performed due to very serious health risks. That still leaves as many as 12,000 late-term abortions performed solely because the mother chooses not to take the child to term. These are the most troublesome abortions for me, leading to my own preference for laws against them.

Fetal viability is not the only nuance in this very difficult area. What if the life of the mother is legitimately at risk? What if there are twins, only one of which can be delivered alive?

While I do not want to see any unwanted pregnancy, thus eliminating all abortions of choice, I recognize the simple fact that many women get pregnant when they do not want to. Birth control gives couples a choice before pregnancy. Medical abortions (pills) and simple surgical abortions give them choice after pregnancy during the first 20 to 24 weeks. Thereafter, only a difficult and expensive surgery is possible. While I personally oppose abortion, particularly late-term abortion, I do not consider it to be my choice what someone else does.

Ultimately, whose choice is this? Is it the government? And, if so, what if the government is a despotic dictatorship that seeks to "purify" the gene pool by killing some people based on intelligence, race, or sexual orientation? We all agree that the government should not have the right to actively cause the death (which clearly applies to forced abortion, and should apply to the death penalty and war), but can the government prevent a mother or her family from making the decision, even with the best advice of the most knowledgeable doctor? Should the government prevent medical research limited to non-viable life forms? In most instances, I can reasonably see nuance; the paradox of sound reasoning from reasonable positions in conflict.

Voting is not as clear cut as our polarized world would have it be. In the end, I will still respect my friends who vote differently from me. I will not hate them. I will not consider them undeserving of

God's grace (as if my view on that were relevant). At the end of the day, I remain deeply committed to a faith that puts forgiveness and inclusivity at the top of the list of values. I have no interest in belonging to a smaller group of the truly pure. It is inconceivable to me that Jesus Christ would have felt otherwise.

October 25

Hebrews 2: 5–13
   ⁵ Now God did not subject the coming world, about which we are speaking, to angels. ⁶ But someone has testified somewhere,
   "What are human beings that you are mindful of them,
   or mortals, that you care for them?
   ⁷ You have made them for a little while lower than the angels;
   you have crowned them with glory and honor,
   ⁸ subjecting all things under their feet."
   Now in subjecting all things to them, God left nothing outside their control. As it is, we do not yet see everything in subjection to them, ⁹ but we do see Jesus, who for a little while was made lower than the angels, now crowned with glory and honor because of the suffering of death, so that by the grace of God he might taste death for everyone.
   ¹⁰ It was fitting that God, for whom and through whom all things exist, in bringing many children to glory, should make the pioneer of their salvation perfect through sufferings. ¹¹ For the one who sanctifies and those who are sanctified all have one Father. For this reason Jesus is not ashamed to call them brothers and sisters, ¹² saying,
   "I will proclaim your name to my brothers and sisters, in the midst of the congregation I will praise you."
   ¹³ And again, "I will put my trust in him."
   And again, "Here am I and the children whom God has given me."

SEVERAL THINGS came up for me as I sat with this passage this morning. Paul (or whoever the author of Hebrews was) includes a quotation from Psalm 8:4–8 at the beginning of this passage that troubles me, particularly the line "subjecting all things under their feet." Instinctively, I bristle at the notion that we humans have been given all the rest of creation to use for our glory. Some of my friends in the hydrocarbon industry use this as a reason to mine more coal and produce more oil and gas. I have never understood the leap from "subjecting" creation to "abusing" creation. The concept of stewardship comes up. We humans are here on earth for such a short time, borrowing the planet and all that is in, on, and over it with full knowledge that we are only temporary residents. Good stewards do not use, abuse, and discard.

My thoughts then turned to the concept of "perfection through sufferings," which has been so fundamental to my own conversion. I drove to Orlando yesterday for an Ability Housing open house, listening all the way down to Jim Finley's lectures on healing trauma through spirituality. Over and over again, "Uncle Finley" emphasized the crucial value of embracing suffering in order to find our innermost truth. He taught us about John of the Cross and the dark night of the soul, which Finley describes as "kind of the central operating process through which a person comes to mystical awakening."

Everything I have learned about spiritual transformation, deep conversion, and true healing convinces me that they are all forms of mystical awakening. Father Rohr likes to say that such a transformation can only result from deep suffering or deep love. At depth, there is a similar vulnerability involved in both deep suffering and deep love. To be "perfected by suffering" is to be made aware of the presence of goodness at the very core of ourselves. When I say "goodness," think God, true self, or unitive consciousness.

Finley says that "in the midst of this struggle [transformed people are] being strangely illumined in a depth of consciousness that they never knew before." Bizarrely, there is great illumination at the very darkest point in the dark night of the soul, an illumination that reveals the unity of God in us, and our deepest self in God. Finley describes this as the "axial moment," a moment when we suddenly, unexpectedly turn inward and downward into the deepest part of ourselves. To some extent, the goal of every morning meditation is to rediscover this axial moment, to move from the superficial level of "head space" to the vulnerable level of "heart space." I do not experience this every day, to say the least, but it happens more frequently all the time.

October 26

Repeat Hebrews 2: 5–13

The theme of ascent through descent has been in my meditations all week. My first Father Rohr book was *Falling Upward*, the very title of which suggests that we must fall in order to rise. I struggle with this, not so much in theory as in practice. Clearly, when I am at my lowest, I am most vulnerable. But when Jim Finley suggests that when "completely vulnerable [we] unexpectedly come upon within [ourselves] a depth of preciousness," I wonder.

Generally, in my utmost vulnerability, I am in abject misery. I have too often projected toughness, even arrogance, as a means to climb out of the deep hole, but it has never worked to end the misery. Of course, arrogance is not vulnerable. Just the opposite. Reflecting on this, I am struck with how easy it is to confuse wallowing in misery with honest vulnerability. Being miserable is intensely egocentric. It is all about self, even self-pity. To be truly vulnerable, one must get out of self.

Finley argues that at the point of complete vulnerability we say to ourselves, "I'm really here. I really count." Or, "My life is a gift." These are not selfless thoughts. No wonder Jim describes the transition from suffering to liberation as alchemy. "The depth of suffering opens out into the depths of pure liberation from suffering."

Janis Joplin sings, "Freedom is nothing more to lose." When we finally reach bottom, when there is no lower to go, then in that state of complete abject misery, we discover the light. John of the Cross teaches that *nada*, nothingness, is the route to transformation.

I sat with this in silence for almost an hour. The simplest way to describe my feelings is peaceful. It was a perfect morning for tennis; a perfect time to sit in the dry warmth of late fall. I was reminded this morning that the time change, falling forward, will occur on Sunday. It is hard to believe that Daylight Savings Time has passed again. Life involves such interesting rhythms.

October 27

John 1: 1–18

In the beginning was the Word, and the Word was with God, and the Word was God. [2] He was in the beginning with God. [3] All things came into being through him, and without him not one thing came into being. What has come into being [4] in him was life, and the life was the light of all people. [5] The light shines in the darkness, and the darkness did not overcome it.

⁶ There was a man sent from God, whose name was John. ⁷ He came as a witness to testify to the light, so that all might believe through him. ⁸ He himself was not the light, but he came to testify to the light. ⁹ The true light, which enlightens everyone, was coming into the world.

¹⁰ He was in the world, and the world came into being through him; yet the world did not know him. ¹¹ He came to what was his own, and his own people did not accept him. ¹² But to all who received him, who believed in his name, he gave power to become children of God, ¹³ who were born, not of blood or of the will of the flesh or of the will of man, but of God.

¹⁴ And the Word became flesh and lived among us, and we have seen his glory, the glory as of a father's only son, full of grace and truth. ¹⁵ (John testified to him and cried out, "This was he of whom I said, 'He who comes after me ranks ahead of me because he was before me.'") ¹⁶ From his fullness we have all received, grace upon grace. ¹⁷ The law indeed was given through Moses; grace and truth came through Jesus Christ. ¹⁸ No one has ever seen God. It is God the only Son, who is close to the Father's heart, who has made him known.

THIS MAY BE my favorite passage in the Bible. It has been since I first began my current spiritual journey in the fall of 2007. Writing these words causes me to reflect on the spiritual journey that began and ended more than fifty years ago. Did I love the prologue to John's Gospel then? I was clearly not thinking about a "new cosmology," about the Big Bang and quantum physics. Honestly, however, these concepts were not at the forefront of my thinking ten years ago either. Perhaps it was simply the poetry, which is marvelous.

I have been living with the Cosmic Christ for the past five years—significantly, four years after I first came to know Ilia Delio. It is painful for me to admit that I simply did not appreciate her magical genius for so long. I can now say that she is one of the pillars of my spiritual understanding. The teaching of Sister Ilia, Father Denis Edwards, and the great Teilhard de Chardin is all contained in, or at least introduced by John's prologue. In the beginning was the Trinitarian God, a relationship of love that was pure energy. The entirety of the universe, including all energy and all matter, existed at that first moment and will never cease to exist. Infinity and eternity—all space, all time, all substance and all non-substance—literally everything that I cannot begin to comprehend was there at the beginning.

I sat with these thoughts for a long time. In the beginning was everything, and all of it was sitting with me on that bench. What an incredible feeling! *The light shines in the darkness, and the darkness did not overcome it.* What a glorious time to be alive! Somewhere in the distance is a world torn asunder by all manner of divisions, a painful campaign painfully drawing to an ugly close, and complex problems, as insurmountable as they are insoluble. But right here, right now, in my library, the darkness does not overcome the light.

October 28

Deuteronomy 30: 15–20

See, I have set before you today life and prosperity, death and adversity. ¹⁶ If you obey the commandments of the LORD your God that I am commanding you today, by loving the LORD your God, walking in his ways, and observing his commandments, decrees, and ordinances, then you shall live and become numerous, and the LORD your God will bless you in the land that you are entering to possess. ¹⁷ But if your heart turns away and you do not hear, but are led astray to bow down to other gods and serve them, ¹⁸ I declare to you today that you shall perish; you shall not live long in the land that you are crossing the Jordan to enter and possess. ¹⁹ I call heaven and earth to witness against you today that I have set before you life and death, blessings and curses. Choose life so that you and your descendants may live, [20] loving the LORD your God, obeying him, and holding fast to him; for that means life to you and length of days, so that you may live in the land that the LORD swore to give to your ancestors, to Abraham, to Isaac, and to Jacob.

AFTER READING through this passage twice, I found myself drawn to one sentence:

> But if your heart turns away and you do not hear, but are led astray to bow down to other gods and serve them.

What are these "other gods"? Surely power, prestige, and possessions. Quite likely, drugs, sex, and rock and roll as well. I need to sit with this.

I have been on this planet in human form for more than seven decades. I have been led astray by all these "other Gods" and more. It is obviously late in the day to deny my life. Not long after celebrating my sixth decade, everything in my life changed. It was then that I recognized my life container was empty. It was then that I embarked upon a journey to find the meaning and purpose of my life.

October 29

Repeat black holes and volcanoes.

AS THE PASSAGE from Deuteronomy states at the outset: "I have set before you today life and prosperity, death and adversity." The "black holes" of death and adversity in my life were concentrated in the eighteen months that began in the spring of 2006 with my demotion from CEO of Globeleq, and ended with a triple bypass in October of 2007. These were periods when, indeed, no light or warmth entered my life. The good news was that when my heart broke, the words of God fell in.

Several "volcanoes"—blazing rivers that roar with energy—have occurred in the time since my journey began. Several continue today. Without doubt, the most important is my extraordinary relationship with Sallie Ann, my wife of thirty-four years. It can truly be described as volcanic. We were married on Valentine's Day in 1982, after an incredible courtship that lasted almost two years. Looking back on that amazing beginning, it is hard to believe we maintained such a high level of excitement for so long. Neither of us is capable of much superficiality and small talk. She sent me the Cooper Edens book *Remember the Night Rainbow* the day after our first date.

> If tomorrow morning the sky falls…have clouds for breakfast. If you have butterflies in your stomach…ask them into your heart.

Even though that day was my 35th birthday, this was an amazing thing to do. But what made it Sallie Ann was that she had torn the cover off and written, "Don't judge a book by its cover." She thought I tried too hard to be cool, in the process hiding a better person inside. Who does that kind of thing?

Sallie Ann had worked for several years for Lifespring, a human potential training program. She was not only a senior trainer, but also one of the most effective marketing executives in the organization. Because of her efforts, many of the people I met during our courtship had done the Lifespring training, and most of them remain close friends today.

Our wedding was simply awesome. Two "small" details will say all that needs to be said: Sallie Ann wore a wedding dress made especially for her by Oscar de la Renta. Morty Sills, the New York tailor mentioned by Gordon Gekko in the movie *Wall Street*, made my white tie, along with a black cape lined in bright red. A little over the top, but memorable!

Sallie Ann and I met on December 27, 1979. Ronald Reagan, the President-elect, was less than two months away from assuming office. Iran held fifty-two hostages, who were released the day of Reagan's inauguration. I lived at Ranleigh Manor, a great old mansion in McLean, Virginia, which had become a kind of "half-way" house for single and divorced people in transition. A group of us, including the wife of the Carter Treasury official then in Tehran negotiating the release of the hostages, decided to hold an "Anti-Inaugural Ball," providing an event and a venue for Democrats. I wanted Sallie Ann to be my date at our ball, but she had already accepted an invitation to attend the official Inaugural events with another guy.

As it happened, one of my partners in the coal business was a close friend of the lead singer of the band playing at one of the official balls, the Black Tie and Boots (a quadrennial inaugural party given by the Texas delegation). I agreed to escort his daughter, sitting at the band table. When Sallie Ann entered the room with her date, it was as though all music and conversation came to an end, and all the other guests faded to a dull shade of gray. Sallie Ann wore a simply stunning, floor-length scarlet gown. Breaking protocol, I asked her to dance. It is a memory so powerful that it intruded this morning on my space on the bench in the meditation garden 35 years later!

Our relationship began while I was still very much in the coal business. I spent most week days at the coal mine. Weekends, which became longer over time, were all Sallie Ann. She was not a great fan of the Ranleigh Manor crowd, so most of our time together was spent with her friends from Lifespring and the journalism community in Washington.

When I met her, and throughout our courtship, she lived with David and Susan Brinkley in Georgetown. David was a true celebrity, not only part of the pioneering Huntley Brinkley Evening News on NBC, but an insider in political Washington. Thus, the courtship included some of the biggest names in Washington and New York, from Henry Kissinger to Al Gore to Casey Ribicoff. We joined a wild group of close friends from Kentucky and New York on trips to the Brinkley country house in Culpepper, Virginia, and to the annual Lexington Ball and Bluegrass Stakes in Kentucky. This surreal lifestyle continued for more than twenty years, until after David died in Houston in 2003.

My career contributed to the impression that we were a jet-set couple. We circled the globe together in 1983, returning from a trip to market Agip coal to Japanese steel companies. We stopped at the Taj Mahal in India, the tomb of Tutankhamen in Egypt, the Yad Vashem Holocaust Memorial in Jerusalem, and, of course, the Alta Moda fashion shows in Milan and Paris. To say that it was a heady time does not do it justice. And all of this was before I entered the international electric power business!

While there were hundreds of amazing days and nights during the quarter century that we spent together before the dark days of 2006 and 2007, I spent far too much time away from Sallie Ann, traveling extensively and working obsessively. In the five Globeleq years, I was away three weeks out of four. In spite of all that, and, far worse, in spite of the way I treated her during the dark days, she has been there whenever I needed her. I vaguely remember waking up in the cardiac recovery room, seeing Sallie Ann through the fog of anesthesia. I was intubated and unable to talk, so I motioned for the nurse to give me a pen and piece of paper. Sallie Ann kept that piece of paper, on which I had scratched, "Forgive me. I love you with my all heart." In the nine years since then, my love has only grown.

When I started the Exercises in the fall of 2011, a little more than a year after my baptism, I considered myself well launched on a spiritually healthy path. As I said then, I did not begin the Exercises in a state of despair. In my own view of myself, I was strong in my new faith, clear in what I needed to do, and wanted only to get on with doing it. I was generally very happy with my life.

I wish I could say that all my choices since my baptism have been good, that I have consistently chosen those things that bring me closer to God, not take me further away. It has not been so. But, as the song says, "I'm still standing." The "preparatory period" of these Exercises is ending today. Week One begins tomorrow, as we dig deeper into sin. There will be many opportunities to return to the black holes and volcanoes in my life story.

I end the preparation period more humbled by this undertaking than I thought I would be. I have touched on vulnerability. I have experienced greater awareness of the immensity of God's creation and my tiny part in it. I have begun to dig more deeply into knowledge of myself. I pray that the process continues. I pray for greater vulnerability and humility. I pray for wisdom and understanding.

IGNATIAN WEEK ONE

CALENDAR WEEK SEVEN

I want to feel the power of sin in my human nature and to be confused that I have sinned and not suffered so much for it.

Almighty and all-merciful God, I see with my own eyes the shame and wretchedness we humans practice on ourselves and on one another. I feel afraid that one force could cause so much havoc and destruction. But I ask to know that force in all its power and complexity. I ask to feel in human affairs and all through my own life world how subtly and virulently sin flourishes. Grant me courage, most holy God, to see sin in all its ugliness.

October 30

Now, about the angels:

1. First, I recall that Jesus said He had seen Satan plunging down from heaven like lightning
Luke 10:18 :18 He said to them, "I watched Satan fall from heaven like a flash of lightning.
2. Then I think about this. Do I believe that God creates intelligent beings other than humans? Do all intelligent beings have to have bodies? St. Thomas says that because angels have enormously powerful intelligence, they know things amazingly swiftly and make up their minds with their whole being. Once an angel decides for or against serving God, that angel's whole self has moved to enact the decision. What do I think about this? Suppose one vastly powerful being managed all the forces of our galaxy—and that being determined to take things into its own hands instead of keeping the laws God had set. What kind of destruction would that be? Suppose once I made up my mind and chose, that would be the end of it, and that same kind of destruction would wrack my whole self.
3. Then I see how I feel about the times I have chosen to do what I wanted instead of what I knew was right. How can it be that the angels are now soaked in hatred, and I can still change?
At the end, I turn to Jesus Christ, hanging on His cross, and I talk with Him. I ask how can it be that the Lord and Creator should have come from the infinite reaches of eternity to this death here on earth, so that He could die for our sins. And then I reflect upon myself, and ask:
What have I done for Christ?
What am I doing for Christ?
What ought I do for Christ?
And I talk with him like a friend. I end with the Our Father.

THE MEDITATION reading today is powerful. I read it over last night, and again this morning several times. It is the same reflection for both today's and tomorrow's readings. This text reminds me in clear terms that sin is part of this world, and that I am complicit in this worldly sin. By action or inaction, I have contributed to all manner of pain and suffering in the world. This general reflection will begin my session each day this week.

It certainly creates the right mood to "feel the power of sin in my human nature" and to be "confused" at how little I have suffered for my sins. While I have chased after the false gods of power, prestige, and possessions for most of my life, reflecting on my sin takes me directly to the year and a half at the end of my career when I reached bottom. The shame I felt then and continue to feel even now, almost a decade later, whenever I think about that period, is beyond description.

The reading asks that I look at the world around me, considering all the many things that are wrong with that world and my complicit guilt. I can do that. As a coal miner and power plant operator, I certainly contributed more than my fair share to both environmental problems and global inequality. But the deep personal emotion, the shame of that indirect guilt is nothing compared to how I feel about my own direct sin. Compounding the situation is the extraordinarily "high bottom" that I experienced. I have friends whose sins caused them to lose their jobs, their homes, their families, and everything else in their lives. I experienced none of this.

The depression that began in early 2006 took me to such a depth of despair that I simply did not want my life to continue. I loathed myself and acted out that loathing in odious ways. However, other than Sallie Ann, virtually no one was even aware that I was suffering. During this period, I became wealthy beyond anything I could ever have imagined. All the outward signs of success and stability were firmly in place. While I disparaged the effort, the British decision to make me Founding Partner was viewed as a promotion by the handful of people in the world who cared. Each time I suffered even the slightest physical problem, my whole extended family gathered around me in support. I "doubled down" on the worldly signs of success, with better cars, new clothes, extensive travel, and even speaking engagements.

It was all sham. There was nothing behind the façade. I was not just empty, I was rotten. How could it possibly be fair that I suffered so little on the outside? How could my bottom be so high? Frankly, it confounds me still.

That part of the reading specific to today introduces devils and angels to the discussion of sin. I believe in the metaphoric value of superhuman images, not in their actual existence. If their value is respected, metaphors might just as easily be real. The point is that there is good and evil in the world. Generally, good takes me closer to the love of God and evil takes me further away.

Then the Christ questions, which I am deeply grateful to be answering now, not ten years ago:

> What have I done for Christ?
> What am I doing for Christ?
> What ought I do for Christ?
> And I talk with him like a friend.

This week we began the stewardship campaign in our parish. Cards will be passed out next week in which we are to commit our time, talent, and treasure for the coming year. Essentially, we are meant to answer the Christ questions in and through this campaign, ideally, by talking to Christ as a friend.

Over the past three years I have given much of my life to Christ through Sister Parish, Ability Housing, the World Affairs Council, Georgetown, and various parish activities. I do not work in a real job, nor have I ever taken much in the way of vacations. So, committing *time* has been both natural and quite easy.

Based on a lifetime of starting and managing new companies, I assume my greatest *talents* are conceiving, designing, promoting, and inspiring new ideas and companies. So, I have clearly put these talents to work in most of these activities, certainly those that involved the greatest commitment of my time.

As to *treasure*, there are several ways to measure giving, and, like time and talent, I have surpassed most of these measures. My "tithe" percentage has recently been over 70 percent of my gross income, which has required that we dip into principal to pay our living costs. It is a large absolute number.

Now, talking directly to you, Christ, I need to share a little more truth. I have committed a large amount of time to Your service, attempting to make a difference in the lives of the poor and marginal. Were I to better organize my time, however, there is clearly at least an equal amount of time wasted every day. I continue to isolate as much or more than I did at my low point. A small portion of that isolation time is spent in spiritual reading, meditation, and reflection. Most of it, unfortunately, is spent on one form of ego gratification or another. Or worse. Of course, You know that.

My talents have always been exaggerated, especially in my own mind. Increasingly, I apply those talents erratically, starting enthusiastically, then becoming bored or distracted. It has always been so, but is much worse now. Again, You know that.

Which brings us to treasure, where my impressive giving over the past three years should matter. Again, there are flaws in this argument as well. I travel to the missions in style. I sometimes spend as much on shopping for things for myself as I give to the various charities. There is very little sacrifice involved in giving to Christ while holding back enough to live profligately.

So, Christ, I pray that I will internalize the message of stewardship now. We need to talk a lot over the coming few weeks, as I am confident I will need a great deal of strength and courage.

> Christ is the radiant light of God's glory and the perfect copy of God's nature, sustaining the universe by God's powerful command.

I ended the morning expressing my deep gratitude for the miraculous journey I have taken since I left that dreadful place. I pray the Our Father, trembling when I say "forgive me my trespasses." Indeed, I have been delivered from evil.

October 31

Now, about Adam & Eve:

1. I recall what St. Paul said to the Romans: "Well then, sin entered the world through one man, and through sin death, and thus death has spread through the whole human race because everyone has sinned"

Romans 5:12: Therefore, just as sin came into the world through one man, and death came through sin, and so death spread to all because all have sinned.

1 Corinthians 15:23:21 For since death came through a human being, the resurrection of the dead has also come through a human being;

2. Then I think about this. Even though I may believe that God brought humankind onto the face of the earth through evolution, I have to believe that at some point in time and on some spot on the globe, the earliest humans came into life. They grew intellectually aware of right and wrong, and some among them (the Church has always believed it was the very first) chose to do evil. They abused what was given to them. They chose to use what was forbidden by their own consciences. They decided willfully to make their own value system instead of letting the Spirit of God instruct them. From that sin came others, more and more. From that sin came death. So, from this earliest sin came flooding down all the misery, wretchedness, evildoing, and death—dealing in the world today.

3. What they did (some ordinary human action) can it have been so enormously, overwhelmingly worse than what I have done, and perhaps do? Yet, what comes from my sin? Why does God deal so differently with me? So I consider how I feel about all this.

Finally, I make my colloquy with Jesus crucified. How did You come to this? And the questions form in me:

What have I done for Christ?
What am I doing for Christ?
What ought I do for Christ?

I talk this over with Him and, as always, I end with the Our Father.

THE REFLECTION for today begins again with a general reflection on sin in the world and my role in that sin. When I consider my sinful life, I focus on my specific deeds and omissions, not on my part in the larger drama of mankind's sin on the global level. The US election is one week from tomorrow, with decisions to be made that will have a global impact for decades. It is drawing to a dreadful close, and I feel absolutely helpless in the face of forces and events way outside of my control.

It is instructive that these two readings, yesterday and today, emphasize not only sin, but even more, the enormous inequality in the consequences of sin. I am ashamed of my sin, but perhaps even more ashamed that I have been treated so unfairly well. Not only did I survive my descent into Hell by bouncing up from an incredibly high bottom, but I lived a relatively robust life of sin before even beginning that steep descent, and suffered very little pain for that as well. Sure, I built an excellent life container, with a few glaring exceptions. My excommunication did little to burnish my image. Divorce is not high on the list of my achievements. I lived expensively, and always gave myself the title of CEO, but the fact is I muddled through my working career a notch or two below the true successes. The CEOs of major corporations have a different work ethic from mine, and enjoyed better fortune. (Yes, fortune—pure, dumb luck—plays a big part in business success. I know because even my second-tier success involved amazing amounts of good fortune. I prefer not to say that corporate success is the result of greater blessings from God. I think that takes one to weird places logically and spiritually.)

I do not wish to complain about the benefits of my container. The point is that my container hid, at best, an empty core, and, at worst, a core of sin. Yet the consequences of my emptiness were vastly superior to those of people who sinned less, and had more authentic substance in their lives.

I pray for the ability to see sin clearly. I pray for the strength to stop sinning, to get out of myself. More than that, I pray for the wisdom, courage, and strength to right the injustice of unfair consequences.

November 1

Repeat the Sin of Adam and Eve

TODAY, AGAIN, the general reflection on sin begins the reading. In no small part because I am a progressive Democrat with an international bias, I have made an extremely long list of wrongs and evils in the world. If I were less international, I could ignore the problems of the seven billion people on this planet who do not live in the United States. If I were less progressive, I could ignore the massive problem of income inequality. The teaching of Ayn Rand, the patron saint of far-right capitalism, is anathema to me, even though I am strongly in favor of well-regulated free markets. If I had not spent my life in the hydrocarbon industry, I could deny the science of climate change.

But I am a progressive, international liberal with a conscience. The sins of the world weigh heavily on me. I am indeed confounded that so many others suffer so much while I live such an incredible life. My inability to change the world frustrates me to no end. I feel like I have been tilting at windmills my whole life. The one thing that seems to work is an intense focus on the next right thing. While I am not moving the needle much, if at all, on global poverty, climate change, and the possibility of a world at peace, I do experience moments of joy when I touch just one other person. While working through Sister Parish with the poorest of the poor in the Dominican Republic brings me a great deal of that joy, it nonetheless reminds me even more of the great inequity in the world. I need to remember that while I cannot make much of a difference in the whole world, I can make a difference in one life. And while I cannot make much of a difference in the lifetime of another person, I can certainly make a difference in at least one moment in that lifetime.

My mind wandered to the concept that death is caused by sin. I do believe sin is choice.

> [The first humans] abused what was given to them. They chose to use what was forbidden by their own consciences. They decided willfully to make their own value system instead of letting the Spirit of God instruct them. From that sin came others, more and more. From that sin came death.

Some death results from sin, like an alcoholic drinking himself to death or a drug addict overdosing. But I do not accept the idea that sinful choices are the primary cause of death, or even a major cause of death. Death is a part of life. It is a certainty that comes with life. In fact, death is as much a part of our existence as life. We did not come from nothing; nor will we return to nothing. We were here from the first moment of creation. We have always been and are now part of the eternal infinite.

I sat this morning with something Matt Mumber, my Living School friend, reminded me about, something that Jim English wrote.

> The mystery that utterly transcends me is utterly emptying itself and giving itself away as the very reality of me, of others, and of all things.

The Mystery that is God, the Trinity, the "Great Other," the "One" constantly empties Himself, Herself, or Itself through love as reality, a reality that includes all the bad in the world as well as all the good. There is an inevitable unity to this concept of the Trinity emptying itself as all of creation. We are one with God and each other. Sallie Ann posted this morning a wonderful statement by St. John of Chrysostom:

> If we cannot see Christ in the beggar at the church door, we will not see Him in the Chalice.

Classic. Either God is in all, or God is in nothing. And if He is in anything, He is in everything. I pray for justice, peace, wisdom, and harmony.

November 2

The Sin of One Person.

1. I come into God's presence and offer myself to Him.

2 Then, I compose myself in my real world. I consider how I live surrounded by violence and anger, in a deteriorating environment steeped in self-deception, untruth, and error, and under genuine threat of nuclear holocaust. I have to make my way through all this.

3. And now I ask of God what I yearn for: I ask God to let me feel shame at my thoughtless sins and my deliberate sins; I want to feel confounded by the truth that others suffer such dire things because of sins, and I have suffered so little, although I know I have sinned and do sin.

Now, think about a person who died in alienation from God.

1. I recall that Jesus said in one of His stories that a rich man, "Dives," had despised his wretched neighbor and ended up in a place divided by a great chasm from the bosom of Abraham, forever thirsty

Luke 16:19–31 [19] *"There was a rich man who was dressed in purple and fine linen and who feasted sumptuously every day.* [20] *And at his gate lay a poor man named Lazarus, covered with sores,* [21] *who longed to satisfy his hunger with what fell from the rich man's table; even the dogs would come and lick his sores.* [22] *The poor man died and was carried away by the angels to be with Abraham. The rich man also died and was buried.* [23] *In Hades, where he was being tormented, he looked up and saw Abraham far away with Lazarus by his side.* [24] *He called out, 'Father Abraham, have mercy on me, and send Lazarus to dip the tip of his finger in water and cool my tongue; for I am in agony in these flames.'* [25] *But Abraham said, 'Child, remember that during your lifetime you received your good things, and Lazarus in like manner evil things; but now he is comforted here, and you are in agony.* [26] *Besides all this, between you and us a great chasm has been fixed, so that those who might want to pass from here to you cannot do so, and no one can cross from there to us.'* [27] *He said, 'Then, father, I beg you to send him to my father's house—* [28] *for I have five brothers—that he may warn them, so that they will not also come into this place of torment.'* [29] *Abraham replied, 'They have Moses and the prophets; they should listen to them.'* [30] *He said, 'No, father Abraham; but if someone goes to them from the dead, they will repent.'* [31] *He said to him, 'If they do not listen to Moses and the prophets, neither will they be convinced even if someone rises from the dead.'"*

Luke 12:20 *But God said to him, 'You fool! This very night your life is being demanded of you. And the things you have prepared, whose will they be?'*

2. I think about this. Jesus himself said very clearly that some people were on the way to living forever apart from God. The Church has consistently taught that some deeds and some ways of life lead to self-destruction, to a life after life that can only be called totally wretched. If a person has really loved only himself or herself, and wanted only that—he or she may get it, forever, and live deeply alone and without love except self-love.

3. I remember that some dictators in this century have murdered vast numbers of people, because of their lust for personal power over others. Where are they now? I remember that some rich people spend their entire lives amassing money, while doing nothing for the poor and suffering right under their noses. What happened to them when they died? Other people spent their whole brief life relentlessly enjoying themselves in sensuality, really recklessly hurting and harming others, whom they simply use for their own pleasure. What happens to them when they die? Where are they now?

4. I imagine a young man in Vietnam, gradually growing callous as he fires into huts. He actually kills some people. He gets a taste for this deadly occupation. He figures he cannot tell who are the enemy and who are not, so it doesn't much matter. One day, he faces an old man and some children, and kills them quite wantonly and deliberately. Then he is killed. What kind of life did he lead? Where is he now?

5. Then I think about myself. Have I pursued some thing, destroying myself as I did it? Why haven't my stupidities caused the wretchedness that others' have caused? Do I want to risk ending up all alone, forever alone, loving no one but myself?

6. Then I make my colloquy with Jesus on His cross, letting the three questions rise in me:

What have I done for Christ?
What am I doing for Christ?
What ought I do for Christ?

I talk this over with him and I end with the Our Father.

THIS IS A powerful meditation. I read through it tonight and sat with it in a troubled state. I am not a great believer in Heaven and Hell. I heard that Saint Theresa of Avila once said that "yes, there is a hell, but there is no one there." I do believe that "ending up all alone, forever alone, loving no-one but myself" is Hell. However, it is not "out there" or in a place other than this earth. Selfishness and ego-centered choices can create the isolation and solitude of Hell, right here and right now. I sat with this all night.

The reading is just as stark this morning. Heaven and Hell, permanent choices, no gray area or nuance. A great deal of my discomfort derives from the suggestion of the permanence of the state of Hell. While I am not as convinced as I should be regarding the sacrament of reconciliation, I do believe that forgiveness is real, and very powerful. Few choices are permanent, and most are nuanced.

Even the clearest commandment, "Thou shalt not kill," has been modified by the church with the concept of a just war. While I generally oppose war in all its forms, I can certainly understand the arguments for action to prevent genocide. Deep down, I can also understand the arguments in favor of assisting the quiet death of a person suffering great pain. I understand the views of a victim's family regarding the death penalty for a person who rapes and brutally kills. Likewise, when the life of the mother is truly at stake, I understand the arguments for a late-stage abortion. I am not saying that I accept those arguments, but the very fact that I understand them makes me uncomfortable with the notion of the state intervening to take the choice away from the family, the individual, and the doctor. I am wary of the power of the state, just as I am wary of unrelated persons making deeply personal, very painful decisions for others.

I sit with these thoughts. I am not comfortable with my conclusions, but I am equally uncomfortable when I try to sit with the alternative. Strict laws requiring heavy punishment for anyone engaged in or supporting any form of abortion or assisted suicide will never prevent all individuals from making those painful choices. Generally, those with money will continue to find relatively safe access to implement their choice, while those at the margin will do so at great risk. Death penalty advocates will never prevent the occasional execution of innocents. Here too, access to resources will be a primary factor in the application of the harshest punishment. Action-hungry generals will always find a way to characterize any war as just, and countries that are relatively less able to defend themselves will more often be the target.

All these thoughts take me back to the reading. Heaven and Hell, clear-cut right and wrong, and permanent states of grace or sin—these are all views better suited to the world two thousand years ago than the world today. Heaven and Hell are states of immediate existence. Right here, right now, I am making decisions and taking actions that determine my immediate existence. That determination is for now, not tomorrow and not yesterday. All the good I did yesterday will not ease the Hell I am in today for the actions I take today. Nor do these decisions permanently determine my state of grace tomorrow. What I do for Christ today is the only pertinent question. I will answer it with actions, not intentions.

I pray that I choose Heaven today. I pray that I have the wisdom, judgement, and strength to act on my choice.

November 3

Repeat the Sin of One Person

THE CONCEPT of individual sin, as opposed to the suggestion of collective sin resulting from the actions of the angels or Adam and Eve, causes me to meditate on those periods in my life when I made the worst choices; when I sinned, choosing, in those moments, Hell over Heaven. For better or worse, I have now been around a long time. Two or three extremely dark periods stand out. Otherwise, I have lived more than half a century making choices that, I believe, moved me more in the direction of the light than the darkness. Even during those long periods of relative "goodness," however, I sinned, loving no one as much as myself.

I remember sitting with a counselor once, attempting to make the case for the relative goodness of my life. He simply asked about my failed marriage, and the long periods when I had been an absentee father. The failed marriage occurred when I was not living in darkness, not struggling with any internal demons. Yet I was extremely self-centered, an ego out of control. My handful of fans would describe me as driven to succeed, focused on my company and my mission to change the world. Others would say I was personally ambitious, that I was unable to form relationships, that I seldom considered others. These are starkly different perceptions. I sit with that incongruity.

There are several approaches to meditation. As I have already noted, most mornings during these Exercises, I will meditate using the imagery of the scriptural passage as the focus of my meditation. I will be present in my fantasy. The objective of the fantasy is to involve me, to engage my ego, in the metaphor or message.

My teachers in the Living School encourage apophatic meditation, the goal of which is the absence of ego. As I sit with the two perceptions of my life, I realize that the primary difference between the two is my ego. A relatively positive view of who I was (or am) and of the life I led takes the position that my ego was somehow secondary to the larger objective of making the world a better place. My obsession with my work had a noble purpose. A less positive view, which I believe to be accurate, sees my ego at the center of all my decisions and actions. What might have appeared to be "other-centeredness" was only an image that I portrayed, sometimes with more success than others.

Why is this important? Egocentric, self-centered attitudes and behaviors are precisely what sin is all about. The argument that good results from the wrong motives somehow compensate for that sin do nothing about the state of grace of the sinner. By acting out of self-interest, I am, in that moment, choosing Hell over Heaven. I am choosing to "risk ending up all alone, forever alone, loving no one but myself." This brings me back to the question of forgiveness. Does the choice I make in this one moment condemn me to be forever alone? I think not.

Even now, almost a decade after the end of my ambitious career, four years into the leadership of an extraordinary philanthropic ministry, I am most often egocentric and self-interested. That is almost certainly my "normal" state. Now, however, I have glimpses of something else, of a purpose and presence outside of my ego. I struggle with apophatic meditation. It is extremely hard for me to escape my ego. Occasionally, however, I am struck with the overwhelming presence of the Other. These moments do not generally occur during my efforts to meditate. The sheer joy of losing myself in the work of Sister Parish, or truly laughing (or crying) with another person, these are the moments when my ego subsides.

I end the morning unsettled, disconsolate. I pray for forgiveness, not just for the periods when I clearly lost my way, but for all the "normal" days in my life when I thought only of myself. I pray for the strength to choose Heaven now, to do the next right thing.

November 4

Repeat the Sin of One Person

Luke 16:19–31 [19] *"There was a rich man who was dressed in purple and fine linen and who feasted sumptuously every day.* [20] *And at his gate lay a poor man named Lazarus, covered with sores,* [21] *who longed to satisfy his hunger with what fell from the rich man's table; even the dogs would come and lick his sores.* [22] *The poor man died and was carried away by the angels to be with Abraham. The rich man also died and was buried.* [23] *In Hades, where he was being tormented, he looked up and saw Abraham far away with Lazarus by his side.* [24] *He called out, 'Father Abraham, have mercy on me, and send Lazarus to dip the tip of his finger in water and cool my tongue; for I am in agony in these flames.'* [25] *But Abraham said, 'Child, remember that during your lifetime you received your good things, and Lazarus in like manner evil things; but now he is comforted here, and you are in agony.* [26] *Besides all this, between you and us a great chasm has been fixed, so that those who might want to pass from here to you cannot do so, and no one can cross from there to us.'* [27] *He said, 'Then, father, I beg you to send him to my father's house—* [28] *for I have five brothers—that he may warn them, so that they will not also come into this place of torment.'* [29] *Abraham replied, 'They have Moses and the prophets; they should listen to them.'* [30] *He said, 'No, father Abraham; but if someone goes to them from the dead, they will repent.'* [31] *He said to him, 'If they do not listen to Moses and the prophets, neither will they be convinced even if someone rises from the dead.'"*

Luke 12:20 *But God said to him, 'You fool! This very night your life is being demanded of you. And the things you have prepared, whose will they be?'*

IT IS NOT too much of a surprise that I chose to be Dives, the rich man, in the parable with Lazarus. I used a powerful image I remember from Mumbai, India, twenty years ago. We were invited to dinner with a very wealthy Indian industrialist, who had recently built a palatial mansion that jutted out into the bay of Mumbai. As our car pulled into the *porte cochere* in front of the main entry, we nearly drove over a beggar lying in the road. Only ten feet away, we were greeted by a liveried doorman who acted as though the beggar did not exist.

In my fantasy, the doorman worked for me, routinely ignoring Lazarus lying in the drive. I was vaguely aware that Lazarus was partially blocking our gate, something that annoyed me. Thus, I was not unhappy to learn that he had died. I was not aware that he had sores on his body, or that he had been begging for food from our kitchen. Not long thereafter, I died.

In my fantasy, I was aware that I was dead, and that my surroundings were unpleasant. I was hot, thirsty, and in pain from something burning under and around me. In the distance, I saw Lazarus, the beggar from my gate, standing next to Abraham in what looked to be a verdant garden, cooled by a fountain. Strangely, I was close enough to call out to Abraham, asking for help. "Send Lazarus," I said, "have him dip his finger in the fountain and wet my tongue with the cool water." Abraham not only said no, but he also described a great chasm between us, separating me from the cool garden, and both of them from the agonizing flames that surrounded me. I sat with that image for a few minutes.

Heaven and Hell are here and now. Likewise, the great chasm between the rich and the poor exists here and now. Crossing over that chasm is virtually impossible. Even communicating across the chasm is difficult, resulting in two very separate worlds. Is there also a great chasm between sinners and saints? Does the very fact that one person receives good things during his or her lifetime, and another does not, mean that the first is a sinner and the second a saint? Is that not the message of the Beatitudes? The first shall be last.

I returned to the fantasy, now asking Abraham to send Lazarus to warn my five brothers of my plight. I listened to Abraham tell me that my brothers could listen to the same teachers that I had ignored. When I explained that a person returning from the dead would be more persuasive, Abraham scolded me, saying that if the living teachers could not persuade my brothers, there was no reason to believe they could be convinced by Lazarus returning from the dead. I sat with this on the bench.

What does it take to cause me to act in the right way? My early life experiences clearly included instruction and support for doing the right thing. From a very early age, I was taught to do unto others as I wanted them to do unto me. I was taught all the things not to do from the Ten Commandments, and all the things to do from the Beatitudes.

My parents, all my teachers in school, and all the great men whose books I read told me to do the right thing. My goodness, I preached these things as a missionary in Germany! I have done the right thing, and felt wonderful when doing so. So why do I ever not do the right thing? Am I waiting for someone to return from the dead? Or hit me "up side the head"?

Jim Finley teaches that God is creating me through His infinite love every second that I exist. How can God be creating me as a sinner? How bizarre is it that in the very moment of my creation, I choose sin? Does He love me into existence as a sinner with the same infinite love that creates me as a saint? The answer must be that He creates me with free will, and wants me to exercise that free will to do the next right thing.

November 5

A Meditation on Hell

Close your eyes and place your feet flat on the floor. Feel the solid surface under your feet and look for that solid place deep within yourself. Feel the air going slowly in and out of you. Hold your breath for a moment and feel the life surge within your body. As you breathe in again, breathe in the name of Jesus by saying silently, "Jesus, Lord." As you let the air escape from you, silently pray, "have mercy on me." Keep repeating this for a short time until you have completely relaxed.

You have come into the presence of God and offer yourself to Him. Remind yourself of your real world. Consider how we live surrounded by violence and anger, in a deteriorating environment steeped in self-deception, untruth, and error, and under genuine threat of nuclear holocaust. Through all this, we ask God what we yearn for: I ask God to let me feel the bone-deep sense of loss and pain that a person suffers who has lost love forever, so if I ever face a test, I will cling to God's love tenaciously.

Thinking about Hell:

1. First, remember that Jesus told His disciples about the Last Judgement. The King of Glory will say to some, "Come, you whom my Father has blessed," and to others, "Go away from me, with your curse upon you" from Matthew 25.

2. Then think about what Hell means.

First, alienation. We have inside ourselves an orientation toward others, and toward God. In Hell, we are oriented only towards ourselves.

Second, loneliness. I miss others, but I cannot say who those others are.

Third, frustration. My whole self is meant to be an "alleluia" spoken in praise and thanksgiving; in Hell, I can only snarl, frustrated of being my true self.

Fourth, absurdity. God wrote into myself those values—loyalty, fidelity, truth telling, honesty, service to others—that, being kept, would make me happy; but during my life, I chose other values that I deemed would make me happy—perhaps the values of pleasure, having power over others, feeling totally secure, spending money, and so on. Now, I know that the values I chose are absurd, without root in my own true self. I live absurd—now forever and ever.

Then wonder what it would be like as a place. What are the sounds and sights of a place where people live totally for themselves? What does the atmosphere feel like, where everyone lives lonely, selfish, and frustrated?

Imaging yourself in that condition for a while. What kind of bitter anger would I feel at myself? Would I regret doing the things that got me here? Could I ever forgive myself?

Finally, we turn to Jesus Christ and say:

Lord Jesus Christ, You have kept me from death after death, from the final loneliness. You have not let any creature send me down into death and into the pit. Oh, Lord, You have saved me and cherished me, even when I was mindless of You, maybe even when I really did not care about You. I can hardly believe such love: I cannot understand it. Please, Lord, let me fear more than anything else that I might lose You and Your love. Let me name that loss Hell. You, Lord, keep me out of there.

Amen.

IT IS THE Saturday morning before the election on Tuesday. Donald J. Trump is running neck and neck in the polls against Hillary Clinton. It is very easy for me this morning to sit in compliance with the instructions, that is, in the presence of God, reflecting on our world "surrounded by violence and anger, in a deteriorating environment steeped in self-deception, untruth, and error, and under genuine threat of nuclear holocaust." Seriously.

I have never in my lifetime been so desolate about the state of the world. Not only has the election been one of the ugliest in my memory, with both candidates deeply disliked and completely distrusted, but the prospect of governmental gridlock is guaranteed, regardless of the outcome of the election.

I cannot even imagine a Trump presidency. It is simply that unthinkable. He has promised to undo every good thing Obama has done in eight years, including all the executive actions on immigration, environmental policy, and gun safety. Trump will sign a repeal of Obamacare, revoke US participation in the Paris Climate Accord, take drastic action on virtually all trade agreements, increase the role of money in politics, and exacerbate the problem of inequality by lowering taxes on the wealthy. A Trump Supreme Court will likely reverse *Roe vs. Wade*, strengthen *Citizens United*, allow continued voter suppression, and prevent any sensible gun safety measures. In other words, everything that troubles me about the world today will get worse if Trump wins in four days, for which there is at least an even chance.

If Clinton wins, on the other hand, there is serious talk of commencing impeachment proceedings before she is even sworn in. Several Senators have announced that they will not consent to a single Clinton justice appointment. The Republican House will not agree to any part of Clinton's policy program, making that part of the election moot. What is there about that picture to offer hope or joy?

This morning, therefore, it is easy to find pain in my meditation. The thought piece describes Hell as the condition of alienation, loneliness, frustration, and absurdity. If I allow myself to honestly contemplate the world around me, I am in Hell. My only consolation is to find a place away from the world, which might be a very private space where I can be alone with God, or a place where I can work through my pain in service to others.

I walked away from my reflections in an effort to forget the world, not focus on it. Maggie and I went to the beach. The house is decorated to host a wedding reception for good friends from the parish tomorrow. The garden has never looked so good. The air is cool and dry, a perfect fall morning. The world seems far away. Thank you, God, for this beauty and tranquility.

While walking, I listened to the first two chapters of *New Seeds of Contemplation*, Merton's wonderful discourse on being a contemplative. I am afraid Merton would have frowned on my Exercises, considering that they are all about me, an exercise in ego. The goal of contemplation, he argues, is to finally get beyond self. As Paul says in Galatians, "It is no longer I who live, but Christ who lives in me." The Exercises are meant to include contemplation, but it is a different form of contemplation than that about which Merton writes (and my Living School teachers teach).

In some ways, listening to Merton soothed my aching heart. While making it clear that a contemplative could not be obsessed with the world and its problems, he was equally clear than contemplation and action go hand in hand. Importantly, Father Rohr's institution is named the Center for Action and Contemplation. This faith, my new and deep faith, is a living faith, grounded in a powerfully energetic Christ. Teilhard wrote:

> [The cosmos] is **fundamentally and primarily** living. Christ, through his Incarnation, is interior to the world, rooted in the world even in the very heart of the tiniest atom. Nothing seems to me more vital, from the point of view of human energy, than the appearance and, eventually, the systematic cultivation of such a "cosmic sense."

I believe this, yet I sin. I consistently revert to behavior that alienates me from what I know to be my true self. Merton described Hell as perpetual alienation. In the midst of so much love and community, I am lonely. My inability to make a difference in this dreadful world is deeply frustrating. All these elements of Hell are underscored by the absolute absurdity of the world during this political season. It is not I who lives, but an expanded I in a world consumed by me for my sake. This Hell cannot endure. At least, I cannot long endure in this Hell.

Today is the wedding day for our good friends, Steve Lube and Cindi Lindstrom. We will host a reception here at Serendipity. Sallie Ann is anxious, as she usually is when we have guests, especially strangers, in the house. She has used her magic to make Serendipity even more beautiful than ever. Perhaps not surprisingly, I, as the architect, am very proud of this house and the garden. I love it when people see it for the first time. Sadly, much of what makes me so proud of the design involves history and precedent. Virtually no one notices that, which is a warning about the likely value of the house in a sale.

Our annual parish Ministry Fair kicks off tonight. The Sister Parish Ministry must host a table after each of the five Masses today and tomorrow. I had some photos of the last few missions blown up to poster size. Caleb Lawrence worked on the handout that we used for the Ministry Fair two years ago. Stewardship is all about time, talent, and treasure. Sadly, treasure is the one form of stewardship that is easiest to message, so the Ministry Fair has largely become a part of the annual fund-raising drive.

I point this out even as I sit in torment. While I may not be truly contemplative in my consideration of my sin, I have clearly been thinking of little else.

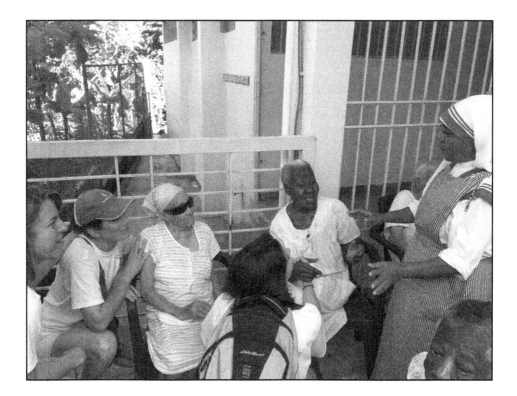

CALENDAR WEEK EIGHT

I want a sharp sense of how I have really sinned, and how much. I want the Lord to open me to a deep sorrow for and shame at what I have done. I wish I could weep like Simon Peter.

Almighty and all-merciful God, give me the strength of spirit to name my sins and the courage to feel shame for them. Let me feel confounded that my sins have not destroyed me as others' have. Teach me to weep for the hurt and harm I have sinfully inflicted on others. Please, Lord, I really want to live aware of how I have let this terrible evil root itself in my self and in my life world.

November 6

On my Sins, I **remember** *them.*

I will consider how the tendency to sin can ruin my life and rob me of eternal happiness. I discuss with the Lord the three questions:

1. What have I done for Christ in the past?

2. What am I doing for Christ in the present?

3. What would I like to do for Christ in the future?

As we experience God's tremendous love for us we also experience our own sinfulness. The following meditation is to experience personal sorrow. What I ask for here is the gift of contrition or sorrow which is the opposite of quiet feelings: Guilt focuses on the self and is always self-hatred and self-rejection, my own personal refusal to be forgiven. Sorrow is a true knowledge of my own sinfulness. It is seeing, what sin means in the light of God's love. It is a trusting sorrow.

The following meditations bring a healing forgiveness. It is important too, for myself to be aware that I am in God's love, that He lives in me and died for me.

Romans 7:13–25 *[13] Did what is good, then, bring death to me? By no means! It was sin, working death in me through what is good, in order that sin might be shown to be sin, and through the commandment might become sinful beyond measure.*

The Inner Conflict *[14] For we know that the law is spiritual; but I am of the flesh, sold into slavery under sin. [15] I do not understand my own actions. For I do not do what I want, but I do the very thing I hate. [16] Now if I do what I do not want, I agree that the law is good. [17] But in fact it is no longer I that do it, but sin that dwells within me. [18] For I know that nothing good dwells within me, that is, in my flesh. I can will what is right, but I cannot do it. [19] For I do not do the good I want, but the evil I do not want is what I do. [20] Now if I do what I do not want, it is no longer I that do it, but sin that dwells within me.*

[21] So I find it to be a law that when I want to do what is good, evil lies close at hand. [22] For I delight in the law of God in my inmost self, [23] but I see in my members another law at war with the law of my mind, making me captive to the law of sin that dwells in my members. [24] Wretched man that I am! Who will rescue me from this body of death? [25] Thanks be to God through Jesus Christ our Lord! So then, with my mind I am a slave to the law of God, but with my flesh I am a slave to the law of sin.

Luke 14:16–24 *[16] Then Jesus said to him, "Someone gave a great dinner and invited many. [17] At the time for the dinner he sent his slave to say to those who had been invited, 'Come; for everything is ready now.' [18] But they all alike began to make excuses. The first said to him, 'I have bought a piece of land, and I must go out and see it; please accept my regrets.' [19] Another said, 'I have bought five yoke of oxen, and I am going to try them out; please accept my regrets.' [20] Another said, 'I have just been married, and therefore I cannot come.' [21] So the slave returned and reported this to his master. Then the owner of the house became angry and said to his slave, 'Go out at once* *into the streets and lanes of the town and bring in the poor, the crippled, the blind, and the lame.'* [22] *And the slave said, 'Sir, what you ordered has been done, and there is still room.'* [23] *Then the master said to the slave, 'Go out into the roads and lanes, and compel people to come in, so that my house may be filled.* [24] *For I tell you, none of those who were invited will taste my dinner.'"*

Psalm 51:1–21 *Prayer for Cleansing and Pardon To the leader. A Psalm of David, when the prophet Nathan came to him, after he had gone in to Bathsheba.*

[1] *Have mercy on me, O God, according to your steadfast love; according to your abundant mercy blot out my transgressions.*
[2] *Wash me thoroughly from my iniquity, and cleanse me from my sin.*

[3] *For I know my transgressions, and my sin is ever before me.*
[4] *Against you, you alone, have I sinned, and done what is evil in your sight, so that you are justified in your sentence and blameless when you pass judgment.*
[5] *Indeed, I was born guilty, a sinner when my mother conceived me.*

[6] *You desire truth in the inward being; therefore teach me wisdom in my secret heart.*
[7] *Purge me with hyssop, and I shall be clean; wash me, and I shall be whiter than snow.*
[8] *Let me hear joy and gladness; let the bones that you have crushed rejoice.*
[9] *Hide your face from my sins, and blot out all my iniquities.*

[10] *Create in me a clean heart, O God, and put a new and right spirit within me.*
[11] *Do not cast me away from your presence, and do not take your holy spirit from me.*
[12] *Restore to me the joy of your salvation, and sustain in me a willing[] spirit.*
[13] *Then I will teach transgressors your ways, and sinners will return to you.*
[14] *Deliver me from bloodshed, O God, O God of my salvation, and my tongue will sing aloud of your deliverance.*

[15] *O Lord, open my lips, and my mouth will declare your praise.*
[16] *For you have no delight in sacrifice; if I were to give a burnt offering, you would not be pleased.*
[17] *The sacrifice acceptable to God] is a broken spirit; a broken and contrite heart, O God, you will not despise.*

[18] *Do good to Zion in your good pleasure; rebuild the walls of Jerusalem,*
[19] *then you will delight in right sacrifices, in burnt offerings and whole burnt offerings; then bulls will be offered on your altar.*

Galatians 5:13–22 [13] *For you were called to freedom, brothers and sisters; only do not use your freedom as an opportunity for self-indulgence, but through love become slaves to one another.* [14] *For the whole law is summed up in a single commandment, "You shall love your neighbor as yourself."* [15] *If, however, you bite and devour one another, take care that you are not consumed by one another.*

The Works of the Flesh [16] *Live by the Spirit, I say, and do not gratify the desires of the flesh.* [17] *For what the flesh desires is opposed to the Spirit, and what the Spirit desires is opposed to the flesh; for these are opposed to each other, to prevent you from doing what you want.* [18] *But if you are led by the Spirit, you are not subject to the law.* [19] *Now the works of the flesh are obvious: fornication, impurity, licentiousness,* [20] *idolatry, sorcery, enmities,* *strife, jealousy, anger, quarrels, dissensions, factions, ²¹ envy, drunkenness, carousing, and things like these. I am warning you, as I warned you before: those who do such things will not inherit the kingdom of God.*

The Fruit of the Spirit *²² By contrast, the fruit of the Spirit is love, joy, peace, patience, kindness, generosity, faithfulness,*

1 John 2:1–11 *Christ Our Advocate. ² My little children, I am writing these things to you so that you may not sin. But if anyone does sin, we have an advocate with the Father, Jesus Christ the righteous; ² and he is the atoning sacrifice for our sins, and not for ours only but also for the sins of the whole world.*

³ Now by this we may be sure that we know him, if we obey his commandments. ⁴ Whoever says, "I have come to know him," but does not obey his commandments, is a liar, and in such a person the truth does not exist; ⁵ but whoever obeys his word, truly in this person the love of God has reached perfection. By this we may be sure that we are in him: ⁶ whoever says, "I abide in him," ought to walk just as he walked.

A New Commandment *⁷ Beloved, I am writing you no new commandment, but an old commandment that you have had from the beginning; the old commandment is the word that you have heard. ⁸ Yet I am writing you a new commandment that is true in him and in you, because the darkness is passing away and the true light is already shining. ⁹ Whoever says, "I am in the light," while hating a brother or sister, is still in the darkness. ¹⁰ Whoever loves a brother or sister lives in the light, and in such a person there is no cause for stumbling. ¹¹ But whoever hates another believer is in the darkness, walks in the darkness, and does not know the way to go, because the darkness has brought on blindness.*

I go back to the places where I have lived and see what happened there. I recall the things I have done with others—work, friendships, projects, play. I think back to schooling and work places. When I recall an incident or an action, I carefully visit it in the presence of the Lord Jesus: what went on here? What's behind the words and gestures? What was my project then? What was in my heart?

It was impossible to exclude from the focus of my reflections the events of yesterday and last night. Our good friends were married at our church in the afternoon, then came, with all the wedding party, to our house for a fabulous reception. The Sacred Sound choir played and sang for both wedding and reception, and the musicians continued talking about both until the early hours of this morning. The whole experience was very special for several reasons.

First, I encountered *Christ in community* throughout the day. It was (is) a marriage of two adults, both of whom have children and, in one case, grandchildren. Both extended families were present, along with many fellow parishioners from OLSS. Prayers and blessings during the Mass continued at the reception. Table conversations, celebratory toasts, the choice of music for listening and dancing, and the interactions among the guests all included Christ. We talked about His presence in the room, and we could see Him in each other's tears during frequent emotional moments.

Second, it was a day filled with *layered family.* There were great-grandparents in their nineties, and flower girls not yet six years old. Brothers, sisters, cousins, aunts, uncles, parents, and children—layer after layer after layer. I am a sucker for family connections. In our mobile, fractured, polarized, and dispersed society, relationships between and among families across generations are precious and rare.

Third, it was a day to reflect on *my own marriage.* We sat with our granddaughters during Mass, competed in the toasts we offered to the newlyweds, danced together during the best songs, and reveled together in the joy of Serendipity. The house, the garden, and the people combined in harmony and beauty.

Finally, it was a day of very *special connections* to some of the most important people we have come to know in Florida. Father Frank, Deacon Dan and Peggy, Caleb and Katie, everyone in the band, and the friends from CRHP and Sister Parish and the Lector ministry—every one of these people have touched Sallie Ann and me often and deeply.

All morning long, I have tried to re-focus my thoughts on my life of sin, but with little success. As Julian of Norwich said repeatedly, "Love trumps sin." Love and sin wage continuing battle, but love always wins in the end.

The meditation piece today ends with the instruction to "go back to the places I have lived, recall the people, friendships, projects, and play," all for the essential purpose of examining my sin during each of these moments and at each of these places. I started the process, making a simple list of places, people, projects, and play.

November 7

Repeat On my Sins, I remember them.

John 21: 17 *He said to him the third time, "Simon son of John, do you love me?" Peter felt hurt because he said to him the third time, "Do you love me?" And he said to him, "Lord, you know everything; you know that I love you." Jesus said to him, "Feed my sheep."*

I go back to the places where I have lived and see what happened there. I recall the things I have done with others—work, friendships, projects, play. I think back to schooling and work places. When I recall an incident or an action, I carefully visit it in the presence of the Lord Jesus: what went on here? What's behind the words and gestures? What was my project then? What was in my heart?

SITTING ON the bench this morning, I reflected on the "places, people, projects, and play" in my life that contributed to my sin. Sin, as I understand it, is separation from God, including thoughts, words, and deeds that move me *away* from God, rather than *closer* to God. My short list of worldly goals—power, prestige, and possessions—all take me in the wrong direction. Most "achievements" result in greater power, prestige or possessions. In fact, it is hard to couple the concept of *achieving* with anything other than selfish goals.

That said, however, the goals I set for every Sister Parish mission—encounter, community, and service—all go in the right direction. We say, we cannot "achieve" them, or "make them happen"; we can only assume a position that offers the least resistance to their happening. We surrender to the grace of encounter and community. What we know is that we *can* serve others, and, in the process, lower our resistance to grace.

When I look at the last six years of my life, beginning with the move from Houston to Ponte Vedra Beach, I see a long list of activities and projects, each of which involves many people, some of whom have become friends. Being honest, it is hard not to conclude that most of this frenetic activity was aimed at *achieving*, not experiencing or encountering. Power and prestige were ever-present possibilities, and I am sure my keen instincts noticed that.

Perhaps the worst "sin" over this period was, or is, obsession, even compulsive addiction. I explain my obsessive behavior away by attempting to shift the focus from me and my objectives to the beneficiaries of the service. Residents of Mamey, the missionaries themselves, and parishioners of our Sister Parishes all benefitted from the mission. So much so, in fact, that whatever status I or other leaders might enjoy is totally lost in the margins. The homeless who are housed by Ability Housing couldn't care less about the prestige of the Board members. They, the formerly homeless, now live in a house!

Two thoughts about this "intention dilemma" occur to me. First, as Merton states it so well in the prayer at the end of *Thoughts in Solitude*:

> My Lord God, I have no idea where I am going. I do not see the road ahead of me. I cannot know for certain where it will end. Nor do I really know myself, and the fact that I think that I am following your will does not mean that I am actually doing so. But I believe that the desire to please you does in fact please you. And I hope I have that desire in all that I am doing. I hope that I will never do anything apart from that desire. And I know that if I do this you will lead me by the right road, though I may know nothing about it. Therefore will I trust you always, though I may seem to be lost and in the shadow of death. I will not fear, for you are ever with me, and you will never leave me to face my perils alone.

Yes, there is clearly some prestige and a little power involved in founding and running the Sister Parish Ministry, but my *desire* is to please God. That helps.

My second thought took me all the way back to a conversation I vaguely remember from Snake River High School. I forget now with whom I was speaking, but the gist of what was said was that I differed from other people because, through my energy and charisma, I "could make things happen." "Making things happen" is how I have defined myself throughout my life, including these twilight years. I have been guided by an ambition to make these words from John Caputo true: "[T]he bonds of the present are not nailed down by necessity but broken open by the possible, by the possibility of the impossible."

Other people work harder, other people are smarter, and other people are often better equipped with various personal skills and resources, but I can often make things happen faster, better, and more often. Some people say I follow the advice, "Ready, shoot, aim," and I know it is sometimes true. At the end of the day, however, I think it is generally true that good things have happened due to my leadership.

Reflecting on my sin brings me to another painful consideration. I am often quite lonely. I isolate, even in the midst of all the people I have somehow brought together and the activity I have caused to occur. Sallie Ann spends time before and after every event, talking to her many friends. In contrast, I arrive late and leave early, avoiding contact even with people around whom I am comfortable.

I am guilty of "situational friendship," very seldom establishing deep relationships with anyone outside of the particular project or activity that caused us to meet. The striking characteristic about my effort to list the places, people, projects, and play was the extent to which the people were almost exclusively work or project related. The only non-work relationships were established and are maintained by Sallie Ann. The fact that there are four exceptions after 72 years gives me absolutely no comfort.

November 8

Second, I weigh my sins:

I look steadily at the ugliness of my sins, how revolting these actions and words were. I see that my sins would be wretched things even were they not against God's commands or my own conscience.

Then I look steadily at myself. Who am I, who do these things? Am I the best and most important person around? Does my value outweigh the value of all the saints and angels ? that I should insist on having my own way over against God's hopes? Sometimes I seem to be a canning factory whose every tin is steeped in salmonella; everything I touch is tinged with selfishness.

Finally, I will turn to God my merciful Lord. I will say to God whatever occurs to me, pouring out my thoughts, and saying thanks that he has given me life through all this up to this moment. I determine to do none of this again, if God will help me. And I end with the Our Father.

FOCUSING ON my sin is indeed very painful. I have not journaled extensively about the darkest moments in my life, particularly the eighteen months that finally brought me to my bottom. I am not sure how helpful it would be to write a detailed reflection in this journal. I know what went on. I continue to think about that period, about the people I hurt, and the damage I did to relationships. In fact, I have thought about it every day for almost a decade. If nothing else, thinking about the worst days of my life reminds me to be thankful for the good days. It is an integral part of my effort to renew each day my commitment to maintain the state of my spiritual condition.

In some respects, the dark days mask the extent to which I lived in a state of sin for years. Compared to 2006, I am tempted to say, I was a saint most of my life! However, it is only fair to say that I was selfish and self-centered most of the time. I was frequently arrogant. I treated people as objects, seeing them solely as means to achieve my ends. It is deeply depressing to go through the people and places in my life and realize how few of the names I can even recall!

In fact, the exercise of making a chart showing people, places, projects, and play is not yet finished. It is incredible how much of my life is now only a blur. Yet I recall thinking that I was the center of the universe, and that whatever I was working on was the most important thing happening anywhere in the world! While I can now easily accept that I was not that critical to the continued existence of the universe, it is amazing that what I was doing turns out to be extremely forgettable.

It was often ugly. My associates would talk about my "purple face" moments, when my anger would spiral out of control. As I turn to God to express my gratitude, I begin with the unbelievable extent to which so many great people continued to work with and for me, year after year, company after company. I say thank you for the extraordinary run of success in the middle of such difficult circumstances. In retrospect, everything I did was beyond difficult. Virtually every project or company that I organized required large amounts of capital, yet I had none of my own, and little basis to ask others to invest. But I did ask, and time after time, they said yes. It is not a pretty story of vaulting from one success to another, but it is a string of blessings improbably running through a variety of seemingly impossible challenges.

November 9

Again, I weigh my sins
  Luke 9:25 *What does it profit them if they gain the whole world, but lose or forfeit themselves?*

THIS HAS BEEN one of the worst days of my recent memory, and it is not yet noon. It began in the wee hours as the election results came in, providing painful evidence that Donald J. Trump will be our next president. Even now, hours after I first heard the news, especially after listening to Hillary Clinton's concession speech, I am close to tears. For several years, the forces of fear and hatred have been ascendant in the world. Nonetheless, Barack Obama, here in the United States, and Pope Francis, as the head of the global Catholic Church, have been shining beacons of the just and the good and the dignified and the inclusive and the forgiving. Obama did so even as he has faced continuous, ugly opposition. Pope Francis is more accepted as a leader among non-Catholics and, particularly, non-Americans. For me, just their presence gave me something to believe in, regardless of the signs of doom both here and around the world. I could think about them when my local parish became too exclusive and reactionary. I could still breathe in the dense conservatism of north Florida's social, economic, and political smallness.

Now, however, the future looks bleak. Trump has promised to roll back or undo in his first one hundred days all the good things that Obama did over eight years. Frankly, I will not be personally touched by most of these actions by Trump. I am, after all, a retired, relatively wealthy white man. Trump's proposed tax changes, including eliminating the estate tax, will be favorable to me. Repeal of Obamacare, while it will affect Cesar and Rosa, will actually reduce the cost of their insurance, which we pay. As for the climate change measures, I suspect I will be long dead when most of the damage is noticeable to humans. Caring for "future generations" has never been the primary motivating factor in my life.

Sadly, however, much of my hope dies with these election prospects. I will be almost 76 when the first term of Donald Trump ends. Obamacare; Dodd Frank; the Paris Climate Accords; TPP; DACA and DAPA; a Supreme Court sensitive to voting suppression, *Citizens United*, gun safety, women's rights, and LGBT rights; and Presidential dignity will all be distant history by then. Social Security and Medicare, while not critical to our lifestyle, may be in serious jeopardy. Income inequality will almost certainly be worse than it is today. God only knows what the global situation will look like. But I will be an even older man than I am today. Why should I care about anything I can no longer hope for?

I sit with these sad thoughts. I sit with the importance of being inclusive in my own thinking. I return to the issue of my own sins.

How do I weigh my sins? I know they are heavy. I know that they have overtaken my total existence from time to time. But how do I compare the weight of my sins to the lightness of my joy? Many times over the past several months I have joined with others in saying "love conquers hate," or "love Trumps hate." I believe that. I have lived a life exemplifying the mottos of "love conquers fear," "hope wins," "stiff upper lip," and many more like that. This tells me something about the weight of sin in my life.

Yes, I *sin*. I have sinned throughout my life. I continue to sin. But I *believe* more than I *sin*. I *hope* more than I *fear*. I *love* more than I *hate*. I believe that my *drive* exceeds my sin and my fear and my hate. In truth, I actually believe my *drive* exceeds my *ambition*.

Many times throughout my life, I have been presented with a choice to maximize my personal earnings rather than my accomplishments or the success of my team or my dream. I push my personal remuneration to the background.

I sit with thoughts about my life choices. Is there anything I might have done differently? Of course there is. Given the chance to do it all over again, would I make the better choice? I am not sure.

November 10

First, I considered my sins, Second, I weighted my sins, Third, I look steadily at my God:

He creates me constantly, giving me good to do, shaping in me needs and purposes that will lead to my holiness and happiness, raising good desires in me for His love and for great love of my fellows and of my own self. God is gentle and courteous. God is wise and supremely patient. God gives all gifts and even His Self. And what do I do but trash my holy needs and purposes and ignore and despise many good desires, to go chasing after pleasure and power. How am I like God?

Fourth, I look at all God's creation:

When I look at the beautiful order in the universe and in the consciousness of animals and birds, I am astounded that they did not turn on me, each in its own way, as a serious blotch on the beauty. While I refused to be my true self, gravity held me and the sun refused to burn me to a crisp. When I did hideous things, flowers offered me their fragrances nonetheless and birds still sang when I walked around. Even though I was deeply alienated from God, the laws He printed into earth and sea and air sustained my air filled my lungs, food digested in my system, light entered my eyes. And I was totally out of sync! More than that: Why weren't holy people moved by the Spirit to end my evildoing, if not me myself? How could God's angels have kept protecting me, instead of cutting me down? Why didn't the earth swallow me up? Why wasn't I snatched off to the place where a lot of people just like me have gone?

JOHN CARR, the founder and chairman of the Georgetown Initiative on Catholic Social Thought and Public Life, is holding a conference today to discuss the implications of Donald Trump's victory on Tuesday. It is timely for me to be in Washington. I spent part of my morning reflecting on the election and the country, reading Father Thomas Berry's *The Dream of the Earth*. Berry died in 2009 after teaching and writing about environmental ethics for years. Father Rohr has said that Berry influenced him as much as Teilhard. When I read in the thought piece this morning that God "printed laws into earth and sea and air, which sustained the air that filled my lungs, provided the food digested in my system, and created the light that entered my eyes," it sounded like Berry.

God creates me constantly,

> …giving me good to do, shaping in me needs and purposes that will lead to my holiness and happiness, raising good desires in me for His love and for great love of my fellows and of my own self. God is gentle and courteous. God is wise and supremely patient. God gives all gifts and even His Self.

I sit with that, reflecting on the enormous implications of such a benign Creator. Once again, I ask myself, how could such a God possibly create me in this very moment as a sinning, shameful being? And why would He do so?

He does what He does, creating me with free will to make the choices I make. He does not intend for me to choose one way or the other. My choices are mine. His love is so immense (after all, it is eternal and infinite) that He will create me with and through His love in the next moment, and the moment after that, knowing that my choices may be for good or ill. I am saddened by my poor choices, as, I am certain, He is, but I alone am accountable for my actions.

I sit with the questions about the role of the angels. I understand angels to be metaphors for all the teachers and role models and friends I have known or read about throughout my life. The advice and counsel these people have given me is what it is. They have absolutely no responsibility for what I do with that advice. I know it is unfair that I am so much worse than others who do not even have access to all these "angels." Again, it is what it is.

Why are there other people who do exactly what I do, but suffer so much more than me? I put the question differently: Why has my bottom been consistently so high? Why have other sinners lost all that they own, all that they love, all that they even hope for, yet I sin and continue to be blessed?

November 11

Repeat the black holes and the volcanoes.

DEPRESSION has set in, worse than I can remember. I do not want to get out of bed, or read, or reflect. Journaling is painful. It is not as difficult as talking to other people, however. I am trying to understand why I feel so much worse after Trump's election than I have after the victory of other political opponents in life. It is not a deep mystery. Trump is unlike any other President we have ever contemplated. Returning to Jacksonville takes me further from the epicenter of the political disaster. I might be safer, but feel no better. John Caputo offers some sound advice:

> The name of God is the name of the chance for something absolutely new, for a new birth, for the expectation, the hope, the hope against hope (Rom. 4:18) in a transforming future. Without it we are left without hope and are absorbed by rational management techniques.

This morning, I feel completely left without hope. How in the name of God could this have happened?

November 12

Repeat a Meditation on Hell
Matthew 11:23 *And you, Capernaum, will you be exalted to heaven?*
No, you will be brought down to Hades.
For if the deeds of power done in you had been done in Sodom, it would have remained until this day.

IMAGINE A world where everyone lives lonely, selfish, frustrated, and absurd lives. Imagine that I am at the center of that absurd world. My first reaction to this imagined situation is that its primary flaw is having me at the center. A life focused on me, centered on and around me, and all about me is absurd. By its very selfishness, it is destined to be frustrating and lonely.

My depression worsened today. I slept more than twelve hours. That is not good.

There are other ways to deal with the election results. The simple fact is that I am a seventy-two-year-old, white Christian male. I have no debts, not even a mortgage. I am retired and I am fully engaged in a strong service ministry. There is little that the new government can do that will affect my life in the slightest. I keep repeating those words.

CALENDAR WEEK NINE

I ask God for a deepening and more intense sorrow for my sins. I ask to weep over them.

I call on you, Lady Mary, Mother of God, to gain this gift for me, to feel sin's horror in my heart; and in my spirit, sin's decay. I call on You, Lord Jesus, Redeemer, to share with me the dreadful freight you bore from all our sins. I call out to You, Father of all, to snatch me from blind oblivion and fill my spirit with light to know sin when I see it, to see sin where it works, to fight free of the sin I have engorged upon.

November 13

Repeat, about the angels:

The Triple Colloquy

If you remember, the colloquy is a conversation. It might help to picture yourself sitting with the one you are talking to, or walking along together, but deep in verbal (or written) communication.

The Triple Colloquy deals with a specific order of persons you are to talk with.

First, talk with Mary, the Mother of Jesus. Talk to her as you would your own m other, for she is the Mother of us all. Ask her for the graces you are praying for, that she might help you reach them through Her Son and the Father.

Then, with Mary, go to Jesus Christ and talk with Him. There, with the support of Mary, ask Jesus for the same graces and ask Him to accompany you, with Mary, as you finally approach the Father.

Come into God's presence and feel His love flowing through you. With Mary and Mother, and Jesus the Son, ask the Father for the same graces you have been praying for, that He, Himself, the eternal Lord of all, may give them to me.

End the colloquy as you always end your prayer time, with the Our Father.

ELECTIONS have consequences. There will certainly be policies implemented that will trouble me. Many of them, however, like the tax cuts and infrastructure investments, might very well boost the economy, temporarily at least. Since we are already at an unemployment rate less than five percent, stimulus is likely to increase worker incomes, a very positive development. Of course, there is also the problem that both the proposed tax cut and a deficit-funded infrastructure investment are totally inconsistent with intelligent counter-cyclical economic and fiscal policy. In this full-employment period of sustained growth, even if the growth is slower than we might want, a more intelligent strategy would be to pay down the debt. Or better, use the current low-cost capital to make truly massive infrastructure investments.

Obamacare is not my preferred approach to universal health care, so its complete repeal will probably open the way to a single payer system sometime in the future. In the meantime, though, a great number of patients and providers will be in a state of expensive and unhealthy confusion. Again, however, none of these policies will have a direct impact on my life.

I pray for Hillary and the people who worked so hard and so long in her campaign. I know they are in pain. Sadly, I expect that pain will last a long time.

It is generally somewhat difficult for me to truly understand the messages of the metaphors that make up the Bible. Satan plunging down from Heaven? At a time when the earth was flat, and the sun revolved around the earth, Heaven was up in the sky and Hell was down below the earth. Satan, the bad God, was presumably with the Father, the good God. The good God exiled the bad God to earth, thus creating the painfully difficult living conditions of early man. Adam and Eve, the first humans, lived in an idyllic garden free from worldly suffering. Then Satan, in the form of the snake, tempted Eve (of course the weak woman!) to sin, ending the good garden life. Only by resisting sin could we regain that state of bliss.

These myths existed throughout the world in the long period before and during the First Axial Age, which extended from about 800 BC to 300 BC. What are we to make of them today? I do not believe that death is the result of sin. We all die, sinners and saints alike. The degraded, lonely, alienated, frustrating life, which we call Hell, was possible for the first sapient human, just as it is for us today.

I do not believe there is a bad angel, Satan or one of his minions, sitting on my shoulder, tempting me to sin. My "bad angel" is my out-of-control ego. Virtually every choice I make in life focuses to a greater or lesser degree on pleasing my ego. Generally, the choices I make that are focused more on pleasing my ego are more likely to lead to alienation and absurdity than those focused more on others. Thus, they are sin.

Why am I able to enjoy such an incredible life given all the terrible choices I make? That is not just a mystery, it is also very unfair. Good people making great decisions live in pain at the very edge of life. This is the ultimate absurdity.

So, I have a three-part conversation, which includes Mary, Jesus, and the Father. The triple colloquy is a very Catholic concept. Mary, the mother of Jesus, is venerated as an intercessor, speaking and acting on our behalf with God. Oddly, Mariology, the tradition of venerating Mary, was not part of my study program when I became Catholic. I never once prayed the Rosary, something cradle Catholics find bizarre. Now, more than six years on, I understand but do not embrace the role of Mary. Thus, a triple colloquy for me would have been more logically a conversation involving the three persons of the Trinity—Father, Son, and Holy Spirit.

Nonetheless, I want to do these Exercises correctly. I sit quietly with the image of my own mother. We are talking about my behavior. There must have been a time when I asked my mother to intervene on my behalf with someone about something, but I can honestly not recall specific instances. Perhaps I said something like, "tell Leonard to stop teasing me." Generally, my recollection is that my mother was the disciplinarian, so I would have more likely asked for intervention from my father. But even contemplating that seems ridiculous. He would never have contravened her!

I sit now with a different image, that of Mary, the mother of Jesus. We are sitting in a very simple space, unadorned, but comfortable. She is not timid, nor difficult to approach. We talk about the Exercises, and about this period of focusing on my sins. Even as I reflect on this, I am acutely aware of the selfishness of the conversation. She is the mother of Jesus Christ, God incarnate, yet I ask her to listen to my story of sin! I stop and ask her about herself. What was it like teaching Jesus how to eat, dress, and take care of himself? What kind of child was he? Did she have other friends? We did not get to the hard topic of the Passion.

Mary stopped me and explained that she is very comfortable with requests for intercession. What graces was I seeking, and from whom? What was it that caused me to talk to her, instead of directly with Jesus and His Father? Were my sins of such substance that I would be embarrassed to discuss them directly? It was at her suggestion that we invited Jesus and His father into the conversation, making it a triple colloquy.

The four of us talked quietly. I was ashamed. I found it very difficult to discuss my deepest sins in the presence of Mary. I wept, not just in the imagined room with those imagined figures, but in my library, reflecting and journaling. After a long silence, I prayed the Our Father.

November 14

Repeat the Sin of One Person and the Triple Colloquy

SALLIE ANN had an early test at the hospital this morning, an endoscopic MRI. Dr. Jose Nieto, an acquaintance, summarized the results of the endoscopy, delivering the very welcome news that there is no cancer. She will almost certainly have her gall bladder removed in the next few weeks, but the procedure is both simple and safe. Hopefully, there will be no further occurrence of pancreatitis.

I began my reflections at the hospital, contemplating the deep funk I have been in since the election and what I could do to move on. Fortunately, I have these Exercises. I have resolved to watch, listen to, and read less news for the foreseeable future. I will read more fiction and spiritual books, listen to more music, focus more on my physical exercise regimen, and spend more time working on Sister Parish.

Reflecting on my life of sin has not done much to cheer me up! Repeatedly, I have interrupted my progress at achieving some goal or completing some project by sliding back into periods of selfishness. As I review my history, it is as if sometimes I question the validity of my goals. While I have been involved in business for more than forty years, I never put my personal financial wealth at the top of my agenda, nor my fame. I recall periods of rapid success being diverted by some complication, often a dispute with the source of the equity or the chairman of the board or simply my boss. It is as if I valued "my way" more than success.

Not surprisingly, these frequent disputes resulted in resentments, and the resentments resulted in loss of focus, drive, and energy. Throughout this sequence, I sinned. Pride, arrogance, and resisting authority are all ego-centered sins. In my resentment, I clearly spoke ill of whatever person of authority I blamed for interfering with my course of action. I gathered others around me in a chorus of resentment. Reflecting now on this repetitive behavior, I am ashamed.

I sit with the image of Mary, Jesus, and the Father. We are in a room with a fire pit, around which we are sitting. We can talk quietly and still be heard over the sound of the fire. They have asked me to recall for them the times when pride led to dispute, dispute to resentment, and resentment to sin. I tried to make my role sound as good as possible, but the pattern was impossible to hide, or to dress up in prettier words. What is the grace, I asked, that can undo my shame?

How can I fully make amends to the people who were counting on me to succeed? It was not so much that I hurt them by what I did (though there was plenty of that), but that I caused them to work toward a reward that was denied because of my pride and arrogance. They joined me in the effort because they were to share in the reward. My behavior cost me some measure of success, but it cost all of those who were working with me their share as well. This realization seems new to me today. I see the faces of my numerous associates and employees, and the faces of their families. I imagine what would have been the case had I maintained all those successful trajectories all the way to the final reward.

November 15

Repeat, I remember my Sins and the Triple Colloquy

THE WEATHER is finally turning colder. Tennis began this morning under clear skies with a temperature just above 50 degrees. Thank God for all the numerous blessings that go into my ability to play tennis at my age, including the luxury of living next to a racquet club now, and having access to tennis courts most of my adult life. While I do not play well now and never have, I am lucky to be able to move and run and hit balls, all blessings not available to everyone. I reflected on this for some time this morning. The very idea of tennis is not possible for most of the seven billion people on the planet. How amazing that it is among my blessings, especially given the sinful nature of my existence.

Thomas Merton says that God "utters us into existence as unfinished thoughts," leaving it to each of us to complete the thought for good or for ill. God never intends for us to choose poorly. He does not encourage us to make bad choices in order to learn, even though we do learn from our bad choices. Reflecting on the unfinished act of God's role in creation, I understand that I am the co-creator of my existence. By finishing God's sentence, I have to own the completed thought, for better or worse.

In my colloquy this morning I raised the issue of my role in my own creation. Would it not be a much better idea for God to complete the process, resulting in a more perfect creation? Why allow me so much free will, when I have demonstrated such poor ability to choose well? A better question is why there are so many others whose choices do not end in sin and separation.

November 16

Again, I weigh my Sins.

DANIEL JOSE is here in Ponte Vedra. He arrived yesterday and will stay until Friday. Sallie Ann is concerned that the relative luxury of our existence is a daily affront to Daniel, that this house and everything about it must speak volumes to him about my profligacy. While I agree, I also see no alternative but honesty and transparency. I am who I am, and this life is very different than life in the batey. I pray for forgiveness and understanding.

Daniel is the leader of our Sister Parish Ministry in the Dominican Republic. He is a Haitian whose family lived both in Haiti and Mamey. His family, the Jose clan, is one of the two "leading families" in Mamey. Much of his early education came from one of the better schools in Haiti. When he returned to the Dominican Republic to attend university, he married Raquel Torres, a member of the other "leading family" in Mamey. Daniel came to the United States a week ago to attend a Model United Nations meeting in Washington, DC.

Daniel and I worked on the plan and budget for Sister Parish for 2017. It is hard work, even without the language difficulty. Two hours of accounting left us both exhausted. I am now reflecting on my sins in the context of sitting in the luxury of our dining room talking to Daniel about building a chapel in the village of El Alto for a total cost less than the price of the dining table at which we were sitting. It is not fair. It is not just. The vast inequality helps me to focus on my sins.

Who am I who does these things, and has these blessings? Why me? How can I ever make the unfairness right? Sister Parish is certainly a start, but both Daniel and I know how little I have moved the needle of justice. I have no good answers this morning.

I pray for forgiveness and understanding. I pray for strength to continue doing whatever I can to address this injustice. I talked to Mary, Jesus, and the Father individually and as a group about my guilt. I need as much intercession as possible, not just to make my case, but to solicit help and support for my feeble efforts. At the end, it is only possible to do the next right thing. God help me to know what that is, and give me the strength to do it, over and over again.

November 17

My Own Death

As always, I come into God's presence, offering Him my whole self, and compose my sinful self in this sin-filled world.

Then I ask God that thinking about my own coming death might deepen my understanding of sin and move me further and further away from it.

First, using my fantasy, I imagine that I lie dying in a hospital. How am I connected? Am I clearheaded or filled with drugs? Have I left things in order, or scattered and unfinished? How old am I, and who of my friends and family are around? Then, I ask myself: What would I like to have done between now and that event? What will I be glad to have done or left undone? What attitudes or actions would make me fear on that bed? What will seem valuable to me lying there? What will appear in all its true slightness and foolishness?. I can do this other ways (do I expect to die in an accident? an atomic explosion?), or go on to other ways. For instance, I could imagine that I am Lazarus, waiting for Jesus who does not come, and lying stiff on the cold stone with all my frozen fears—and then feeling His voice fill me with warm life. Would Lazarus ever have feared death again? Would he have seen his life world and its values and concerns as he had before? What would it have taken to really trouble him then? Or again, I could count the number of ways I might very well die on the most ordinary of days. How does that change the way I think of "ordinary days" and my everyday world? Or, finally, I could write my own obituary or an article reporting my own death. How does that make me feel? What would I want to blot out of what I did? What would I wish with all my heart I could include? Then, I will consider whether there are some things I ought to put my mind to.

After considering that, I make the Triple Colloquy

MY DEATH. In my initial fantasy, I am in the hospital, Baptist Beaches, only a few miles from my home. Since it is our local hospital, and since we are such a small town, I am known by the nurses and other hospital staff. Visitors come to my room many times each day. Sallie Ann, there to console me, greets them and shares her grief with them. I feel incredibly connected to this community and the people who are coming in and out of my room. It is as if my death were happening to another person, one without sin. Most of the people on the visitor list have no knowledge of Bob Hart the sinner. They have only met the image of me that I wanted to project in the parish and the community.

In the midst of this joyous celebration of the life people thought I lived, one of my old acquaintances from Houston walks into my room. The new visitor knew me at my bottom. He smiles politely when he is introduced, not letting anyone see that he actually holds me in disdain. Eventually, we are alone. He smiles knowingly. He asks, "How have you fooled all of these people for so long? Do they not know? You have never been a true friend to anyone, never, not once in your miserable life. You used your friends to advance your interests, never caring about them or their problems. You treated people as objects, never subjects, never as equals in a relationship." I wept then, feeling the stinging shame of exposure. The longer he was in the room, the more inconsolable my misery became.

Reflecting on this fantasy, I consider the real likelihood that someone could enter my hospital room at the end of my life and destroy everything I have created in the past ten years. It is actually possible, though not likely. In truth, I doubt anyone cares enough to expose me for who I am. It takes a great deal of effort to travel all the way to Ponte Vedra Beach to out someone for actions more than a decade old.

I am saddened by this reflection. I resolve to never again treat people in a way that could be exposed as heartless and cruel. I resolve to make every effort to live only one life, with no hidden persona about whom I would be ashamed. I pray for forgiveness.

On a lighter note, I saw these clarifying comments from Woody Allen:

> The chief problem about death, incidentally, is the fear that there may be no afterlife—a depressing thought, particularly for those who have bothered to shave. Also, there is the fear that there is an afterlife but no one will know where it's being held.

November 18

Repeat My Own Death, Consider the black holes and volcanoes.

A NEW FANTASY this morning. I am dying again, this time alone in the car, having run off the road into a telephone pole. I was in great pain for several hours, then finally numb with grief, embarrassment, and depression. The overwhelming questions in my mind are whether anyone would either notice or care. Stages of my life passed in front of me like a bad home video. Most of the images are in black and white, with occasional bursts of color. The dominant sound is the rush of the wind around my car, but it comes across as the sound of time passing. Glimpses of conversation go in and out, sometimes associated with the images and other times seemingly unrelated to me, my death, or my life. The longer I stay in the fantasy, the more anxious I am for the death to be real, for the peace and solitude to be permanent, and for judgement to be final. I sit with this reflection for what seems to be a very long time. Slowly, the peace takes over my thoughts. I am quiet. The images and sounds of my death are no more. I am aware of the room around me, and the garden outside the door. I see the fountain, but cannot hear the water splashing in the rill. Time is standing still.

In this moment, I feel triumphant over sin. An Albinoni trumpet concerto is playing quietly in the background. I am where I am meant to be, doing what I am meant to be doing. I am flowing with the flow, letting it take me where it wants. The sins I have been contemplating are very distant, belonging to another person. I know him, but am not him. I sit with this for several minutes. Or a few seconds. It is not important.

I return to the two different fantasies of my death. Yesterday, my friends surrounded me in the warmth of an upgraded room at the neighborhood hospital. Yet my strongest emotion was fear, followed quickly by loneliness. My visitors were celebrating my image, the outer layers of my life container, which I have always endeavored to burnish with the polish of commercial success. I talked to them without speaking, looked at them without seeing, thanked them for coming to my death bed not caring and, worse, not caring that they could tell I did not care. Today, however, I am alone. There is no one to fool but myself. Now, I realize that I have been the only one listening to my story for much of my life, but most of the time, I would create a fictional audience enraptured by the sweet sounds of my voice. Sad.

Today, I am alone. There is no audience. There are neither supporters nor critics. It is a peaceful solitude. I can hear sounds of creation around me, offering me its presence. I surrender to it, and to the incomprehensible suggestions of infinity and eternity. I realize finally that I am not alone at all.

I reflect on the two different kinds of solitude, wondering what I can do to create as often as possible the second warm and comfortable solitude. It dawns on me that it is not what I can do, rather it is what I do not do, or even try to do. I let the solitude surround me with its love. My only words are yes, and thank you. In the first solitude, I am working full time, primarily to maintain my image, or make it look even better. The words I use are some form of "look at me," "remember me," or "love me."

I reflect on the question about how prepared I am to die. Oddly, in my second fantasy, dying in the car alone, I am at peace with what is done and what is left undone. It is not that I am prepared or have tidied up all the loose ends. Rather, I am detached from any "to do" list. I am beautifully unattached to the consequences.

On the other hand, lying in the bed at the hospital among my acquaintances, I am petrified that people will now "find out" who I really am. There is a box of books that I have hidden away. While they are not bad books, they do expose a part of my life that I have chosen to hide. Actually, the profligacy that is so evident in my closet embarrasses me. I would rather my family and friends find a few pieces of well-worn clothing than the racks of suits and pants and shirts and ties and socks and sweaters that no one person could ever wear in two lifetimes. My shopping addiction will be quite apparent to anyone going through the closet, the shop outside, or my libraries. It is odd that these concerns are so unimportant in the second fantasy.

Daniel Jose returns to the Dominican Republic today, after a very full visit to the Sister Parish community here in Ponte Vedra. Melissa and her family arrive from Denver this afternoon. They will be here through Thanksgiving, joined by Jennifer and her family next week. I pray for peace and understanding in this expanded family gathering.

November 19

Repeat a Meditation on Hell and Luke 16:19–31

[19] "There was a rich man who was dressed in purple and fine linen and who feasted sumptuously every day. [20] And at his gate lay a poor man named Lazarus, covered with sores, [21] who longed to satisfy his hunger with what fell from the rich man's table; even the dogs would come and lick his sores. [22] The poor man died and was carried away by the angels to be with Abraham. The rich man also died and was buried. [23] In Hades, where he was being tormented, he looked up and saw Abraham far away with Lazarus by his side. [24] He called out, 'Father Abraham, have mercy on me, and send Lazarus to dip the tip of his finger in water and cool my tongue; for I am in agony in these flames.' [25] But Abraham said, 'Child, remember that during your lifetime you received your good things, and Lazarus in like manner evil things; but now he is comforted here, and you are in agony. [26] Besides all this, between you and us a great chasm has been fixed, so that those who might want to pass from here to you cannot do so, and no one can cross from there to us.' [27] He said, 'Then, father, I beg you to send him to my father's house— [28] for I have five brothers—that he may warn them, so that they will not also come into this place of torment.' [29] Abraham replied, 'They have Moses and the prophets; they should listen to them.' [30] He said, 'No, father Abraham; but if someone goes to them from the dead, they will repent.' [31] He said to him, 'If they do not listen to Moses and the prophets, neither will they be convinced even if someone rises from the dead.'"

UNDERSTANDING the universe today is not easy for me. I mean the science of it all. For example, I can write the words "the Trinity is a relationship between and among the Father, Son, and Holy Spirit," but I have difficulty getting my head around the notion that there are no actual, substantive persons, only the energy field of love. The words are easy. True understanding is not.

So it is also with *Hell*. There is no physical place that is Hell, nor is there a physical place that is *Heaven*. These are *conditions*, not places. Just as *Hell* is not "space bound," that is, limited by any physical constraints like being here or there, *Hell* is not "time bound," constrained to exist only after death or on occasions of sin. The *condition* of *Hell* can be and is right here, right now, just as it is everywhere all the time. *Hell* is not constrained by any clear, Manichean dualism. In fact, I suspect that most of the time, the *condition* or *state* of *Hell* exists right alongside the *condition* or *state* of *Heaven*. *Hell* is separation from God. *Heaven* is union with God. My purpose in life, my life goal, is to achieve perfect union with God, a union so perfect that no part of my existence is apart from God.

I get into some semantic trouble here as well. Since the beginning of the universe, I have been in perfect union with God. I have never existed except as one with God. However, my ego awakens at some point in my very early life, asserting itself not just as a "self" separate from God and all Others, but as an extremely important Self. The simple fact that my ego considers itself apart from, and more important than, God does not alter the reality of my perfect oneness with God. My ego has free will. It can choose to accept the reality of what is, or it can deny it. Until my ego surrenders to the simple, beautiful, grace-filled oneness that is my relationship with God and all His creation, I will at least partly live in and fight with the condition called *Hell*.

Alienation, loneliness, frustration, and absurdity are not punishments awaiting me sometime in the future when judgement has been passed on my sorry life. They are simply descriptions of the condition called *Hell*. I have felt—I now feel—every one of those effects, even when I am reflecting on the heron walking along the bank of the lagoon.

My existence is not *either* Heaven *or* Hell, it is *both* Heaven *and* Hell. I am not *either* apart from *or* one with God. I am *both* apart from *and* one with God. Actually, the deck was stacked in my favor at the beginning, and it is stacked in my favor over and over and over again. The Relationship called *God* is an infinite and eternal overflowing of love in the universe. At any one moment, and in all moments, I am completely filled with that Divine Love. It is not present on a conditional, teasing basis. Divine Love is all in, all the time.

Surrendering to that glorious reality should not be difficult. Why would anyone buy ill-fitting clothes on the Internet rather than meditate in peace with the unity of the universe? Why would anyone ever choose alienation or loneliness, or frustration, or absurdity? Worse yet, why would anyone exert extra effort to make the choices that separate one from God? The prayer for today is appropriate:

I call out to You, Father of all, to snatch me from blind oblivion and fill my spirit with light to know sin when I see it, to see sin where it works, to fight free of the sin I have engorged upon.

CALENDAR WEEK TEN

I ask God to reveal to me the mystery of sin in myself, more and more fully, and to give me the gift of repentance and of weeping for my sins.

Holy God, I grieve for what I have done and left undone. Holy God, I grieve that I have made myself disordered and my life unfocused. Holy God, I grieve over sin's horror on the earth and the vanity and emptiness of human affairs. Holy God, draw me to Your Holy Self.

November 20

Reflect on the past three weeks. The Triple Colloquy.

IT IS HARD to believe three weeks could pass so quickly. On that Sunday after the wedding and reception for Steve and Cindi, the world—my little part of it anyway—looked troubled, but optimistic. Hillary was limping to a winning conclusion of the long effort to become our first woman President, the Senate was still in sight, and the difficulties of the future were all discussed in the context of making progress without the House and in the face of Senate filibusters. I did not even contemplate a worse scenario.

Now, two weeks into the new world of Trump, I can hardly remember what it was like to imagine a different ending to the election story. I am watching less news on TV. I have been better focused on these Exercises. But generally, the world is so dismal that I still awaken hoping that the election was a dream, and that the cabinet being assembled is not real.

I am almost amused when I read the prayer for this week: "Holy God, I grieve for what I have done and left undone. Holy God, I grieve that I have made myself disordered and my life unfocused. Holy God, I grieve over sin's horror on the earth and the vanity and emptiness of human affairs."

The vanity and emptiness of human affairs. Obviously, this prayer was written long before the election was held, and it was written without any reference to that election. Human affairs would have been vane and empty regardless of who was running and who won. There would have been grieving to be done.

Christopher Leverett, the son of our very good friends in Houston, died this week, apparently of an overdose. He had been in and out of recovery for almost twenty years. His daughter, Cassie, stayed with us last summer as a short-term nanny for our grandchildren. She is now a brilliant, beautiful student at Columbia, the Ivy League college her step-grandfather Mark attended. Sallie Ann and I will go to Houston tomorrow for the funeral. It is sad.

Why do I continue to sin? I have been traveling a path of spiritual discovery for almost a decade. Each time I experience the joy of Divine presence, I make a solemn oath to myself never to act again in a way that separates me from that presence. Yet over and over again, sometimes within minutes of the experience, I knowingly separate myself from the Dance. What is going on?

Forgiveness is possible for those who repent. I wonder if forgiveness should even be considered in the absence of sincere repentance. On the other hand, the surest way to never seek forgiveness again is to insist upon purity of motive. I pray for wisdom.

Among the many things about which I need to repent is my obsession with current affairs, particularly my quick slide into depression now that Trump is elected. So much of what has been put in place over the past eight years and longer will soon be gone. There was little I could do about it anyway. And

Hillary would have been deadlocked, along with investigated to the very gates of Hell. So the issue, always the issue, is my sin.

I know more about sin than most, which is not meant to be a boast. The simple fact is that having some level of material success makes sin somewhat easier. My experience with people in Mamey, living at the very edge of subsistence, is that some sins are beyond their imagination. Daniel could not covet most of what he saw around him, simply because he could not form the mental picture of these material things being part of his existence. It does not seem sinful to want a dessert after dinner, or to want a simple cup of coffee. Expensive Italian gelato and Starbucks espresso drinks, however, do seem sinful. I only wish ice cream and latte were my serious sins!

November 21

Again, reflect on the past three weeks. The Triple Colloquy.

It is a cold fall morning, with clear skies over a temperature of 43 degrees. Sitting on the bench was so uncomfortable that I raced through the grieving prayer and a quick Our Father, then hurried back to the library to reflect more on the depth of sin in my life.

I suspect that I have been more focused on my sin throughout my life than many "better adjusted" people. There have been sinning "high points" like the period prior to my excommunication by the Mormons, the long, wild decade of the 70s, and the eternity that seemed to pass between my retirement and my heart attacks. It would not be difficult to generate nearly unanimous agreement about those periods. Certainly, when I intentionally recall the sins in my life, these periods stand out. But the other periods, the long stretches in between "peak sin," these were not sin free.

Something in my psychological make-up seems to trigger both the sin and the acute awareness of the sin and the shame that goes with it. I know people who live comfortable lives, joking and acting out in ways that clearly separate them from God, yet not slipping into deep depression each time that occurs. They seem to have a good time sinning. They are seldom remorseful. I cannot do that. When I sin, I know that I am sinning, and I almost immediately feel shame and guilt. Whether the sin is arrogance, profligacy, or the objectification of other people, I experience deep remorse before any profound pleasure kicks in. When this happens in the company of others, it is described as a "downer," pouring cold water on the event. Of course, my solution to that problem is to sin in isolation, avoiding contact with others, especially people I know well.

Isolation is both a cause and an effect of egocentrism. Even the Exercises are isolating. During this long fall season without missions to the Dominican Republic, my contact with the wonderful missionaries, many of them close friends, is very limited. I do not go out of my way to call or contact them, or any other friends for that matter. In fact, without weekly Mass, I suspect I would go weeks without speaking to anyone I know (other than Sallie Ann).

Reading helps, primarily by establishing a connection with the author that takes me out of myself. But reading can also be a mechanism for isolation, allowing me to avoid conversation with people around me. Isolation is not in itself a sin. Thomas Merton sought the quiet of the hermitage at the monastery, finding even the silence of the other monks a distraction from his meditations. But I have come to know Merton through his writing. I consider him a friend. However, as Lloyd Bentsen might say, I am no Thomas Merton!

November 22

Repeat praying about my own Death

SINCE FIRST meditating on my own death a few days ago, I have returned to it many times. Of course, this was easy today. We are in Houston, attending the funeral of Christopher Leverett, dead at 42, after decades of painful struggle with addiction. I reflect on the numerous times in my life when my choices could easily have resulted in my death. This sounds so dramatic, a self-important exaggeration. But I have frequently had too much to drink before driving. As the saying goes, I have "played with the wrong friends in the wrong playgrounds." Death would have been a lucky outcome, compared with the other possible consequences. How have I been so fortunate? Not only did I not run into something or over someone, but I was never pulled over or arrested in an entirely justified raid. Why? Some of the answers are sadly obvious. I am an old white guy, generally dressed in jacket and tie, looking so out-of-place that most people had to conclude that what was right in front of them could simply not be true. I looked around the room at the reception after the funeral, thinking once again I had fooled all these people. How different I must have been compared to Christopher. Little did anyone know.

November 23

Reflect on the past four days.

MELISSA, KEVIN, and I had lunch at the Palm Valley Fish Camp, my favorite place to eat in Ponte Vedra Beach. The day was sunny and cool, perfect fall weather. I tried to explain a little about the Exercises, but am not certain they understood why I did it the first time, much less this repeat after five years. As I explained the new dimensions of my faith, I was reminded of Peter  denying Christ in the Garden. My description of a non-substantive, relational Trinity; an inclusive community of faith; and an evolutionary act of creation sounded very "new age" or relativist. So much was true that little was true. My faith is too liberal to be radical. Yet when I think of the alternative, some form of righteous certainty based on a literal reading of scripture, I am repelled by the thought. I sit with this reflection, wondering whether I am embarrassed to admit my belief to my brilliant daughter.

November 24

All serious human endeavor demands self-restraint and self-sacrifice. Scientists deny themselves leisure and even food to keep concentrated. Athletes submit themselves to an iron regimen, year after year. Musicians determinedly practice hours each day. In somewhat this same way, those who enter seriously onto a quest for spiritual integrity and for a mature knowledge of and love for God practice self-restraint and self-sacrifice.

The Church's tradition goes back to Jesus' own life and even beyond that into the life of the People of God. Fasting, keeping long silences, refraining from celebrating, attending to communal prayers, avoiding this or that food or drink—these all come down to us from the People's practice thousands of years ago, certified by Jesus in His own life.

Note about penances that some times and periods call for them and some make them inappropriate. We wisely keep a diet during Lent; we are up to something odd when we resolutely fast during Christmas dinner. During the Ignatian Exercises, most of us find penances very appropriate when we are praying over sin and disorder and suffering.

About penitential practices themselves: All things considered, we ought to do those things that truly reach into our ordinary way of acting and into our real desiring, so that we are truly enacting our neediness. Putting aside alcohol or caffeine for a time are true penances for the addicted. Getting in a daily fixed time of energetic walking is true penance for the lazy. We probably should suspect our motivation should we enter onto penances that do us physical harm, or that make us something of a spectacle. What goes on when a person eats like a bulimic? Or when a person crops head hair so that it looks like a punk? Better to keep moderation and privacy in our penances.

Keep in mind that positive practices, doing good things in place of less-good things, make excellent penance. Read an article instead of watching a soap opera. Take time to keep a desk visibly ordered. Make phone calls to friends instead of sitting still gazing into the middle distance.

Carefully interpret the demands made by ordinary life. We can reasonably see them as penances, as freely chosen self-restraint and self-denial. Parents, for example, practice these constantly in order to rear their children. Office workers have to deny themselves continually, giving their attention to the others who need it right now and patiently wading through paperwork and dull figures. We used to talk about "offering it up"; we can still interpret the demands of our life world as true penances.

We tend to think that we can give ourselves to penances for three reasons:

1. First, to make up in our whole selves for the disorders and affronts of our sins before God. This is doing penance for our sins.

2. Second, to take steps to put balance into our acting and desiring, so that we are not led around by mindless habit or culture-determined desire. This means self-restraint and self-discipline.

3. Third, we do penance as a way of praying and asking God for what we want with our whole self, not just with our mind or lips. This enacts our neediness and moves God to succor us.

Luke 17:27,30

²⁷ They were eating and drinking, and marrying and being given in marriage, until the day Noah entered the ark, and the flood came and destroyed all of them.

³⁰ —it will be like that on the day that the Son of Man is revealed.

IT STRIKES me as quite unusual for this reflection on penance to fall on Thanksgiving Day. Fasting during the typically exorbitant family meal, which we chose to hold at the Ponte Vedra Club, would have been "resolutely odd." Twelve family members gathered at the Club. It felt very good. Now I am home, sitting in the library with Maggie, feeling blessed. The goal this week is to weep with the full knowledge of my sin, and of the damage I have done in my life. That is tough to do sitting here surrounded by all the trappings of material success. And with Maggie to keep it real!

November 25

Reflect on the past six days. The Triple Colloquy.

THE FAMILY left this morning at seven. Sadly, Jennifer and her family could not join us because of illness. Otherwise, it has been quite a successful Thanksgiving. Every gathering of this family involves a risk of something blowing up. Simply getting through the visit in one piece is a success. When I begin to think we are a particularly dysfunctional family, I read in the newspaper about similar problems in every family. We are not alone in our dysfunction.

The first Meditation on Hell was November 19, six days ago. I reflected on my own mental effort to understand the condition of Hell, wondering why anyone would choose to act in a way that separates one from God. Of course, I make that choice routinely. Why do I ever choose Hell, especially now that I am so dedicated to this spiritual journey?

On November 20 and 21, I was meant to reflect on the past three weeks. Since that time frame included the election, I had been doing little else every day. Even today, the news is about Trump spending Thanksgiving choosing his cabinet and lobbying Carrier about moving a plant to Mexico. I have been depressed most of the time since the election. Following the news, which I vow each day not to do, exacerbates that depression.

The reflection for November 22 asked that I pray about my own death, which was easy due to Christopher Leverett's funeral. On the 23rd, I was instructed to reflect on the four days from November 19 to November 22, all devoted to sin, Hell, and my death. Finally, the six days ended with a long discussion of penance. "Eat, drink, and be merry until the flood comes and destroys us all."

Trying to go back to the beginning to figure out what went wrong in my life—what caused me to choose Hell so often—is like peeling an onion. There is always another layer, another mistake in the past or a painful memory that stands out, which then leads me back even further in time, and then even further, in search of the ultimate truth. It is a futile exercise. All that matters now is learning enough to avoid making the same mistakes again.

I sat with that thought in front of the Rublev icon. Instead of a Triple Colloquy with Mary, Jesus, and the Father, I joined the circle of Father, Son, and Holy Spirit. For me, there is enormous power in the image of a Divine Dance. The relationship among and between the three members of the Trinity is all about movement—love overflowing from one to another, constantly emptying, filling and overflowing. It seemed a little silly to interrupt the dance by talking, so I joined the Dance. Sin, Hell, my death, penance—all these terribly dreary topics floated away into non-space. The Dance filled me with so much joy and love that I began to float as well. I was not in non-space. I could still sense the room around me and the floor beneath my feet. But there was no room for depression, or for depressing thoughts.

I ended the morning with the Our Father, joyously proclaiming my faith. What a morning!

November 26

Repeat the Meditation on Hell.
   Luke 12:4,5
   ⁴ "I tell you, my friends, do not fear those who kill the body, and after that can do nothing more.
   ⁵ But I will warn you whom to fear: fear him who, after he has killed, has authority to cast into hell. Yes, I tell you, fear him!

PRAYING FOR peace in front of the Rublev icon is not an effective way to enter into a meditation on fear and Hell. The invitation to the Divine Dance is so powerful that it washes away all the desolation this whole month of the Exercises is designed to evoke. For several moments, I sit with this joy.

Ignatius walked this long walk to Hell for a reason. He was transformed by the experience, and, as a result, he changed the direction of his life. He asks us to do that as well, again for a very clear reason. The evolution of our individual consciousness through stages beginning with sheer survival and building toward integral, non-dual awareness requires some "dark nights of the soul." As I review this past month, the evolution of my understanding of sin in my life, my "dances with the Devil," and my brushes with death, I can understand why Ignatius puts this dismal month at the beginning of the Exercises. Teilhard says "you cannot raise up a mountain without digging a pit. Everything that *becomes* suffers or sins." Unless I truly reach a bottom, I cannot, or will not grow. In a sense, the depth of my bottom is the limit of my growth.

I return to my sin, my death, and Hell. I peel away at the layers of the onion that is my life. I imagine myself *becoming something* during each of the many efforts to ascend Mount Carmel. It might be just a little self-important to suggest that my frequent bouts of sin were really just mountain climbing! Three major sins, or periods of sin, stand out: The end of my mission in Germany, the decade of the seventies, and the first two years of my retirement.

Sin on my Mission

The longest journey into the darkness was the painful experience in Germany in 1965, and the resulting nightmare of excommunication. I believed then that a violation of my oath of celibacy caused separation from God. While the ultimate violation was "going all the way," I knew that thoughts of being with a woman, flirting with girls and women, and even seeking opportunities to talk privately with girls or women—all these things were violations. As missionaries, we protected ourselves from these sins with our "companions," the other missionary with whom we were meant to be joined at the hip. Literally, except for bathroom breaks, we were never to be without our companions at our side. That was normally sufficient in most cases. While celibacy violations were by no means unheard of, they were certainly rare. Excommunication for celibacy violations was and still is extremely rare.

So how was I able to manage this enormous sin? Today, fifty years later, I must confess that I have no clear recollection of ever being alone around anyone without my companion, much less alone often enough to seduce a young woman, to arrange for her to spend time with me, alone long enough to do the deed. But that was the charge.

The alleged crime took place in Wurzburg, a Bavarian city only 75 miles to the east of our mission headquarters in Frankfurt. I had been in several cities in the area around Frankfurt, beginning with Neustadt an der Weinstrasse, south of Frankfurt, and going as far as Giessen on the north. It was summer when I was transferred to Wurzburg, and I was the senior missionary in the city. I think there were only four of us, and I remember being somewhat surprised at the small size of the Mormon community in the city. Wurzburg is a great fortress city on the Main River, by far the prettiest city I served in while a missionary. It was a warm, sunny summer. We rode our bicycles around the city, stopping at each apartment building. We climbed four flights of stairs, then knocked on every door as we walked back down. We did this for a minimum of four hours every day except Sunday, when we organized English classes and took boat rides on the river.

Fellowshipping, which was a practice that included every conceivable form of getting close to and involved with the people in our community, was frowned upon by the mission authorities. As missionaries, we were there to briefly explain the Gospel, then teach that Gospel for six one-hour lessons, and then baptize the target. Any further time spent was regarded as a waste. I protested this policy from the first week of my mission.

First, I argued, we were also charged with important pastoral duties. We were the pastors of the local mission congregations, often the only ordained Mormons in the community. Obviously, in the towns and cities where missionaries had been successfully active for many years, there were Mormon communities called Wards, each with a local Bishopric fully capable of discharging all the various pastoral duties. In most of the towns in the West German Mission in 1964, however, the local communities were too small for local leadership. We, the missionaries, presided over meetings and "tended the flock," which included everything from marriage to birth to death. Fellowshipping, I argued, becoming friends with and caring about the people in the community, was an absolute necessity for these pastoral duties.

Second, not only was it imperative that we become friends with the people already baptized, but it was also only human to care about the people we were trying to convert to a new faith. In most cases, certainly every situation I encountered, conversion to Mormonism was a big deal. The idea that two perfect strangers could unemotionally deliver six lessons (while remaining strangers), and convince people to accept this new faith was ridiculous. The rebuttal, of course, was that we were only vehicles for God to deliver the message. Conversions resulted from actions of the Holy Spirit, not from sentimental friendships with charismatic missionaries.

I remember a picnic with our English class, sitting on the grassy slope below the fortress (*festung* in German), watching the river boats floating lazily by on the glassy surface of the river. My memory is not clear about whether I met Petra and her mother at that picnic, or at an English class some time earlier. I do remember the two of them being there that day. I played the guitar very poorly, and could certainly not sing well, but I distinctly remember that they liked my effort. A friendship began that day. I was the star. From that day on, I remember being proud of my leadership ability and my "magnetic charm." In retrospect, numerous warning signals were going up, but I was blinded by my amazing personality.

Petra and her mother escaped East Germany in the months following the end of the shooting war. Their story intrigued me. As I remember it now, Petra was conceived as a result of her mother having been abused by Russian soldiers, part of the occupying army in East Germany. I cannot recall any man in the family, but that was quite common throughout Germany at that time. Most of my early encounters with Petra were with both her and her mother. Obviously, my companion was always present. We clearly talked about much more than the Mormon story. I wanted to learn as much as possible about the war years, the flight from the east, and the early years of the Marshall Plan in West Germany. I wanted their friendship, and I wanted them to consider me a friend.

When the relationship had clearly moved from innocent friendship to something dangerous, I recall asking for a transfer from Wurzburg to Ludwigshafen, a community on the south side of Frankfurt. After a few weeks, I remember the evening at a large meeting in Ludwigshafen, when two missionaries approached me at the lectern on the altar. They did not refer to me as Elder Hart. I remember the basement room of the mission home, where I was to be held in custody three weeks until the trial could be arranged. Beyond that, I remember crying without stop. I cried during the "trial," the ride to the airport, and the flight back to Boston from Frankfurt. It was reported by the Dean of Students that I was crying when I stopped at Harvard to determine my student status so late in the school year.

Whatever happened that night at the fortress above Wurzburg, I was already guilty of excessive pride, powerful lust, and a clear violation of the admonition not to become personally involved with the people we were teaching about Mormonism. I felt guilt for the pride and lust. I felt shame for the relationship that was outside the bounds. The depth of those feelings is truly amazing to me. Here I sit in the library at Serendipity, fifty-one years and a whole lifetime later, and I still feel the shame burning my cheeks. I still want to cry.

Sin in the Seventies

With the rather enormous exception of my mission, I finished the sixties very much an innocent. I did not date at all for the first full year after my excommunication. Then I met Phyllis and developed a deep friendship (fellowshipping again?) long before we dated. I managed to finish college, work in a presidential campaign for a full year, and begin my work life at Boise Cascade Corporation, all without ever even trying marijuana. I was certainly not a "ladies' man."

Phyllis and I divorced just as the decade of the seventies began. I consider the whole period between my divorce from Phyllis and my marriage to Sallie Ann a long period of sin. Much of what I did and how I lived was consistent with the times, which by no means makes it right.

I succeeded in both real estate and coal mining, that is, if success is defined as getting out alive! I did a little better than that, but there will be no monuments erected to remember me. In fact, now, only 35 years later, many of the apartment buildings I developed have come down. I sold the coal mine and paid all my creditors, but limited partners contested the distribution twenty years later.

I closed bars and night clubs from Biloxi, Mississippi, to New York and San Francisco. I carried on an affair with a married woman for several years. I remember once in a bar in Hawaii, describing my situation to a perfect stranger. He explained to me how easy and terribly wrong it was to break up a family. He urged me to fly away and never contact the woman again. It was good advice, but I did not listen.

It was not a decade to be proud of, and I certainly was not. Looking back now, I can see that I was ashamed of my life most of the time.

Sin in Retirement

The final period of extremely shameful behavior began shortly after I firmly established a relationship with the Commonwealth Development Corporation. The head of that group retired shortly after their board approved the largest investment they had ever made, agreeing to fund the creation of Globeleq, the company I formed to acquire, build, own, and operate electric power plants in the emerging markets of Asia, Africa, and Latin America. His successor announced that I would have to move to London if I wanted to continue as CEO of my company. It was the spring of 2003. I fought him and his decision for the next two years, growing increasingly resentful and depressed.

After winning what I thought was the final battle in the fall of 2005, I was diagnosed with coronary artery disease, a condition that continues to this day. At first, I had no visible symptoms. There was no shortness of breath or chest pain or tingling arms. Not then anyway. A routine test simply showed that I needed stents. Within weeks of the angioplasty, the head of the British company announced that I would be removed as CEO, and "promoted" to Founding Partner. Less than a year later, I met for the last time with my board and my key executives. Weeks after that, all of the assets of Globeleq were sold. While I became financially independent for the first time in my life, my depression was so deep that I could hardly acknowledge the fact.

My depression took me to so many dark places that I find it too painful to think about. Suffice it to say that three heart attacks a month apart in the summer of 2007 were a blessing. I emerged from triple bypass surgery determined to change my life. I am now in the process of doing so. I suspect the effort will continue until I die.

I reflect now on the passage from the Gospel of Luke:

> They were eating and drinking, and marrying and being given in marriage, until the day
> Noah entered the ark, and the flood came and destroyed all of them.

Indeed, I ate and drank, and married and was given in marriage, then the flood came and destroyed me. Advent begins tomorrow. This Ignatian week that began on October 30 ends today. It has only been one month, but the desolation I feel seems to have been with me forever. In truth, I am never far away from the shame and guilt I feel for all the sins in my life. I know that the Sacrament of Reconciliation is meant to allow me to go on with my life without these deep and painful feelings. I have not succeeded in my effort to accept forgiveness. Only when I am actively working in service do I momentarily forget my shame.

The second reading tonight at Mass, from Matthew 13, seems to have been written expressly for me. It is time now to prepare for the approaching day, to "lay aside the deeds of darkness and put on the armor of light."

> The night is almost gone, and the day is near. Therefore, let us lay aside the deeds of darkness and put on the armor of light. Let us behave properly as in the day, not in carousing and drunkenness, not in sexual promiscuity and sensuality, not in strife and jealousy. But put on the Lord Jesus Christ, and make no provision for the flesh in regard to its lusts.

I am resolved to make this an Advent to remember.

IGNATIAN WEEK TWO

CALENDAR WEEK ELEVEN

I want to hear Jesus' call. I want to feel how great His project is, and how tremendous His desire for it. And I want to be right there, working with Him.

Eternal Lord of all things, I feel your gaze on me. I sense that your Mother stands near, watching and that with you are all the great beings of Heaven: Angels and powers and martyrs and saints. Lord Jesus, I think you have put a desire in me. If you will help me, please, I would like to make my offering. I want it to be my desire and my choice, provided that you want it, too, to live my life as you lived yours. I know that you lived an insignificant person in a little, despised town. I know that you rarely tasted luxury and never privilege, and that you resolutely refused to accept power.

I know that you suffered rejection by leaders, abandonment by friends, and failure. I know. I can hardly bear the thought of it all. But it seems a toweringly wonderful thing that you might call me to follow you and stand with you. I will labor to bring God's reign if you will give me the gift to do it.

From Father Frank: Humility

November 27

The Kingdom

   * After I have accepted God's loving gaze on me, I offer my whole self to Him.

   * Then I remember Jesus accepting God's loving gaze on Him, as He moved around His homeland. I let my imagination move me into the little towns He was in, the synagogues, the roads He walked.

   * Now I am ready to ask God for what I want: Here, I want to be the kind of person who will hear when Jesus Christ the King summons me, and not be shy or hang back, be quick and persevering in following His lead.

   The First Part is a fantasy.

Imagine a grand nation with a tremendous people. See how they have been troubled and tested. For their nation's affairs have gotten badly botched. They feel tense and worried. Now imagine that they get a new leader. This leader sounds solid. A person who seems to have been handpicked by God for this people. The leader has unsurpassed charisma, is a physically beautiful person, shows tremendous political adroitness, makes people believe that good times are definitely on the way. Imagine that the people grow very, very content.

Then imagine for yourself the program that this fresh, excellent leader proposes for the people. With care and resoluteness, the nation's enemies can be overcome or won over. The economy needs careful overhauling, but it will be painful. Civil rights have eroded. Education stumbles along in disarray. Any program that could possibly succeed will require a lot of belt-tightening, and many groups will have to work through some very tough questions together.

Then, imagine that the leader gathers a special group. To this group, the leader gives a personal invitation. He gathers you and stands before you. Imagine that you sit right in front, listening. "I am going to inaugurate this program. I am going to see that it succeeds. Anyone who wants to work with me on it will have to put up with what I will put up with—extravagantly long hours, pitilessly hard work, going without not just luxuries but even without basic comforts, getting battered by public opinion and the media, and actually running the risk of being assassinated. But I can tell anyone who listens: This program will succeed and make millions of people's lives vastly better.

Change the fantasy and imagine that everyone has left. You sit alone. You wonder, What kind of person could reject such an invitation? What kind of person could accept it? Would I accept that invitation? Would I want to work with that kind of leader? Suppose I left that special group and walked away from the charismatic leader? what would I feel about myself later on? And you imagine accepting the invitation. What do you do? After a while, gently end the fantasy.

The Second Part uses the imagination but remains rooted in the real. I just apply my fantasy to Jesus Christ.

If a charismatic secular leader could demand loyalty (and many less excellent ones get unquestioning loyalty from their friends), what about Jesus Christ, whom God has made eternal King?

I let my fancy roam. I imagine Jesus surrounded by 72 disciples. They sit on a hill. Jesus talks with them, saying something like this: "It is my will to win over the whole of humankind. No enemy can defeat me or finally interfere with my Kingdom. I will draw all to myself. I will stay with my friends and we will labor and struggle, watch and pray. No one will have to go through anything that I do not myself go through. Whoever works with me and suffers with me will also share the glory of the Kingdom with me. I assure you, I will see my project crowned with total success." After feeling how wonderfully attractive Jesus' invitation is, gently end the fantasy.

Then consider that anyone with any sense at all will follow Jesus Christ. Consider this: some might want to walk more closely with Jesus Christ in this enterprise, though they cannot explain their desiring. If you feel inclined to do so, formally say this prayer to Jesus Christ:

Wow! The initial fantasy today requires an extraordinary imagination. Donald J. Trump has just been elected President of the United States. Handpicked by God? I don't think so.

> The leader has unsurpassed charisma, is a physically beautiful person, shows tremendous political adroitness, makes people believe that good times are definitely on the way. Imagine that the people grow very, very content.

For me to fantasize this about Trump will require a desire I cannot muster, and truly fantastic skills!

Seriously, sitting at the feet of President Trump, in thrall to his angry charisma, excited by his misogyny and racism, and willing to work around the clock to make his program a success—these are all beyond my wildest imagination. I can easily fantasize about the two times Barack Obama became President. While I could so easily imagine myself completely dedicated to Obama's success (it was much more than a fantasy), I am also aware of how half of this country and more than half of our Representatives and Senators wanted nothing more than Obama's failure. Over the past six years, they successfully blocked most of the programs advanced by his administration. In this recent election, slightly more than half of the population voted against Trump, although a majority of the Electoral College votes were won by him. Trump will be President of all the people, but will never have the full support of more than a minority. Such is the state of the United States today.

Moving on to a reflection of Jesus Christ in the role of the charismatic leader, I mix fantasy with history. I know that it is a fantasy to believe that I would have been among the handful that actually followed Jesus. I can imagine being in the large crowds—the five thousand—who heard him speak, and ate the bread and drank the wine that he miraculously provided. Most of those who might have been with me on those hillsides had completely vanished by the night of the crucifixion. Fifty years after the death of Christ, Paul wrote letters to the followers of Christ in several Congregations, none of which consisted of more than thirty or forty people.

What was different about the small group of true disciples? What would cause me to be a disciple today? Something extremely powerful had to move the early men and women to give up all that they had and follow Christ. They left homes, jobs, and families. They traveled all over the known world. It was also enormously dangerous for these people, many, if not most, of whom were killed or incarcerated within a few years of the crucifixion. In my fantasy, I imagine both push and pull.

The push came from the circumstances of life in Roman provinces during the early first century, especially Israel, where an open revolt was underway. Frankly, there was little for which to stay home. Both Roman and turncoat Israeli leaders were constantly searching for the revolutionary followers of Jesus, even though His message was about something much bigger than politics. Jobs must have been insecure, at best. I cannot describe unacceptable conditions, simply because so many people—the clear majority—did accept them. Most people chose to stay home, suffer the injustices of the Roman and provincial powers, and plod through life as their ancestors had for generations. However, while Jesus was not "pushing against an open door," Neither was he speaking to a perfectly comfortable audience in love with their lives.

The pull was actually something the Hebrew prophets had foreseen centuries before. The Messiah was here! The promise was fulfilled! Even those who would ultimately not join the movement must have been moved. All my life, I have lived at the edge of the revolution. I have been a progressive liberal, anxious to follow inspiring leaders who called for radical change. Most of my heroes were relatively unpopular, at least at the time I began to support them. I was most enthusiastic about Gene McCarthy in 1967 and Barack Obama in 2007. I did leave my college classes to campaign for McCarthy, but there was very little real sacrifice and absolutely no physical danger. I supported Obama from the luxury of retirement, financially secure and, sadly, so involved in my own spiritual darkness that I would have been ineffective actually working for him.

At the end of the day, it is a bridge too far to believe I would have followed Christ in the first three centuries. By the time Constantine made it a requirement of citizenship, it was no longer a sacrifice. In fact, it would have been braver to resist the imperial edict. Now, two millennia later, again from the great comfort of financially secure retirement, living in what most would call a mansion, I can proudly say that I am ready to follow Christ. Give all that I own away? Leave this house I designed? I don't think so. I will continue to generously support Sister Parish and other causes, and I will continue to work toward a unitive, accepting, inclusive stage of consciousness. I need this prayer today.

> Lord Jesus, I think you have put a desire in me. If you will help me, please, I would like to make my offering. I want it to be my desire and my choice, provided that you want it, too, to live my life as you lived yours. I know that you lived an insignificant person in a little, despised town. I know that you rarely tasted luxury and never privilege, and that you resolutely refused to accept power.
>
> I know that you suffered rejection by leaders, abandonment by friends, and failure. I know. I can hardly bear the thought of it all. But it seems a toweringly wonderful thing that you might call me to follow you and stand with you. I will labor to bring God's reign if you will give me the gift to do it.

Teilhard conceives of "God's reign" as something rather different from the teaching of much of the traditional church. His "Divine Project" is a *united effort to bring all creation together into one mag-*

nificent conscious loving union. The Kingdom of God is something that we can bring into being right here on earth, right now. In one sense, the Divine Project begins within me. If I get my head space in conscious loving union with my heart space, I will be in a position to join others in a global effort to achieve the same conscious loving union of all of creation.

That is a massive order. And it often feels like the great majority of the earth's population is actively working to achieve just the opposite. Listening to the news is not an uplifting opportunity to witness progress.

However, God has definitely given me the gifts required to do more than I am doing. That must be my focus. What can I do with my time, talent, and treasure to move this great project forward? One of my talents is to lead, and I can lead others to join me in this work. Today, I choose to make it my Advent resolution to add just a little more to my efforts to serve Him each day.

November 28

Repeat the Kingdom

FATHER FRANK wrote in his blog yesterday that "…on this First Sunday of Advent we are put on notice that we are pregnant with God and with ourselves…As we give life to God, we give life to ourselves." Advent is a time of preparation, a time of pregnancy, of expectancy. It is a time to be born again as we give birth to Christ in our lives.

I returned to the fantasy about the new leader in our troubled nation. Very little about Trump motivates me. I see no charisma. But half of the people in this country, many more than half of the people in my parish and in the Sister Parish Ministry, do see the charisma. I assume in the fantasy that there are no other options; that Trump is the only hope for the country and the world. In my fantasy, I make that only choice and join the Trump movement. This brings up an interesting dilemma. Can I follow Trump *and* stay true to my beliefs? Can I become a voice for inclusion, acceptance, and non-dual thinking *inside the Trump movement*? Why not?

I imagine myself riding up in a gold-plated elevator to the penthouse of the Trump Tower, entering the dining room, now converted to the Trump inner circle meeting place. I see Bannon and Kellie Ann and the children sitting at the table. The topic is putting the coal miners back to work. I announce that I owned coal mines in the seventies, and that I built power plants over the next three decades, sometimes using coal to fuel the plants. I explain the difference between metallurgical coal and utility coal. More steel is made in the United States today than ever, but now using electric arc furnaces, not the blast furnaces of last century. Coal is not required. Utilities are trying to make power at the lowest possible cost, which today means natural gas found and produced using fracking. Natural gas is cleaner to find and burn than coal, and easier to move in pipelines than coal is in trucks and trains, and it is abundant throughout the regions of the country closest to the energy markets. In order to put the coal miners back to work, we would have to revert to antiquated methods of making steel or ask utilities to use more expensive, dirtier fuel. Both coal and natural gas are hydrocarbons, and both add to global warming. Gas is the better choice.

I explain all this, and believe Trump hears me. His advisors explain that logic does not vote, that unemployed coal miners (and unemployed workers in all the supporting industries around coal) do not care about the relative merits of gas and coal. Remove the regulations imposed through Executive Order on coal burning power plants and at least some mines will reopen, and some miners will once again have jobs. One plant and one mine shift will be enough for the headlines. I agree, but I point out that this will be a short-lived solution at best, and will not restore health to the coal industry. The problem will still exist, but efforts to solve it will stall because the pressure to do something will abate.

It is not a persuasive fantasy, but I can imagine it. How different it is to consider Jesus in the role of the new leader. In hindsight, there is simply no question as to whether to follow Him or not. My view yesterday was that I would not have had the courage to do so in the first few centuries following His call. Think about that. Centuries! And after it became state policy to be baptized, I strongly suspect I would have done everything possible to make only a superficial commitment. Sitting with that thought, however, I wonder how a rural farm boy, thousands of miles away from the seat of power, would ever have heard about Jesus or even Constantine. Communications in the early fourth century did not include the printed word, much less Twitter. On the other hand, someone of the right sex, ethnic background, and education (though certainly not living in Snake River!) would probably have been aware of the Emperor's decision. For most people, I suspect, conversion was not based on an interior transformation, or even a Sacrament of baptism. The flags and coins might have changed, but very few hearts.

Father Frank recommends that we begin Advent with a commitment to be ready for the big day, our birthday and God's birthday. The first step, he argues, is to articulate a vision.

> In creating your vision, I invite you to reflect on the following virtues consecutively during the four weeks of Advent and then Christmas: *Humility, mercy, joy, generosity*, and *gratitude.*

I like this suggestion. If possible, I will add each of these virtues to the next five weeks of my Exercises. The virtue today and for the rest of this week is humility.

Father Rohr began this Advent season with meditations that characterize mature religion as religion that helps individuals transcend themselves. Transcending self is a wonderful way to express humility. Referring to one of his (and my) favorites, Father Rohr wrote:

> Ken Wilber sees religion as having two primary functions. The first is to create "meaning for the separate self." The second and mature function of religion is to help individuals transcend that very self. Great religion seeks full awareness and expanded consciousness (often called "holiness") so that we can, in fact, both give and receive in equal measure.

I stop and reflect on this. God created *me*, not a person *like me*. This was neither an accident, nor an error. His creation included all of nature and nurture for me, but not just for me. It also included nature and nurture for all those who influenced me and shaped my life world.

> The second function and goal of religion, Wilber says, "does not fortify the separate self, but utterly shatters it." Mature spirituality offers "not consolation but devastation, not entrenchment but emptiness, not complacency but explosion, not comfort but revolution." Rather than bolster our habitual patterns of thinking, it radically transforms our consciousness and gives us what Paul calls "the mind of Christ."

I cannot transcend that of which I am not aware. In effect, I must live before I die. The first function of religion is to make me aware that I am alive, I am even the center of life. The second function of religion is to shatter that self-centered consciousness.

Humility can easily become self-loathing, which is simply another form of self-centeredness. The idea is not to hate ourselves, but rather to love others more than ourselves.

Sister Mary Margaret Funk writes that achieving humility requires four renunciations:

1. we must renounce our former way of life,
2. we must renounce the thoughts and desires of that former way of life,
3. we must renounce our self-made concept of God, and, finally,
4. we must renounce our self-made concept of self.

She wrote the little book, *Humility Matters*, for fellow nuns or other religious living in community, but believes these renunciations are possible for anyone seeking humility. The renunciation of our concept of ourselves reminds me of the admonition that we "die before we die," referring to the death of the false self. Matthew 10:39: "He who finds his life will lose it, and he who loses his life for My sake will find it."

I end this morning praying for the grace of humility. I want to see value in all others. I want to see how little I have done to earn the enormous blessing I have in my life. I pray for understanding.

November 29

Ephesians 1:3–14, Spiritual Blessings in Christ

³ Blessed be the God and Father of our Lord Jesus Christ, who has blessed us in Christ with every spiritual blessing in the heavenly places, ⁴ just as he chose us in Christ before the foundation of the world to be holy and blameless before him in love. ⁵ He destined us for adoption as his children through Jesus Christ, according to the good pleasure of his will, ⁶ to the praise of his glorious grace that he freely bestowed on us in the Beloved. ⁷ In him we have redemption through his blood, the forgiveness of our trespasses, according to the riches of his grace ⁸ that he lavished on us. With all wisdom and insight ⁹ he has made known to us the mystery of his will, according to his good pleasure that he set forth in Christ, ¹⁰ as a plan for the fullness of time, to gather up all things in him, things in heaven and things on earth. ¹¹ In Christ we have also obtained an inheritance, having been destined according to the purpose of him who accomplishes all things according to his counsel and will, ¹² so that we, who were the first to set our hope on Christ, might live for the praise of his glory. ¹³ In him you also, when you had heard the word of truth, the Gospel of your salvation, and had believed in him, were marked with the seal of the promised Holy Spirit; ¹⁴ this is the pledge of our inheritance toward redemption as God's own people, to the praise of his glory.

THIS PASSAGE from Ephesians is powerful. It would be easy to read it as exclusionary, proclaiming how certain people were chosen to receive His inheritance. Indeed, they "were marked with the seal of the promised Holy Spirit." Of course, whenever one group is chosen and marked, someone else must have been un-chosen and un-marked, thus excluded from the "inheritance toward redemption as God's own people."

I choose to read it differently. I believe all of creation was chosen before the foundation of the world. I believe the very act of creation was an act of love.

> …he chose us in Christ before the foundation of the world to be holy and blameless before him in love…he set forth in Christ, a plan for the fullness of time, to gather up all things in him, things in heaven and things on earth.

In the "fullness of time," which is eternity, "all things in Heaven and on earth," meaning infinity, will be gathered up. This is about as inclusive as it is possible to be.

The power of this Advent season lies in my growing appreciation of the enormous profundity of what my faith proclaims. God, acting with, in, and through love, set in motion the evolutionary creation of *everything*. It is simply beyond comprehension. Almost fifteen billion years ago, everything that now exists as both changing matter and expanding energy existed solely as energy, exploding with a Big Bang that eventually led to all that I know of as the world around me. All of history, all of the future, all of the smallest nano particles and the largest planets and solar systems—all of this, both space and time, were present then, are present now, and will be present forever. What we will celebrate in four weeks is the moment two thousand years ago, when this awesome power became incarnate. For less than three painfully short years, the incarnation of God's love walked on this earth, launching a revolution that is still being resisted. His teaching turned the world upside-down, putting the first last and the last first.

Humility is the only rational response in the face of this massive truth. Sister Mary Margaret uses the device of the interview to teach about humility. She imagines interviews with Teresa of Avila, Therese of Lisieux, and John Cassian. Cassian, who lived from about 360 CE to 430 CE, enumerates ten "signs of humility" in his writings, which have come down to us as the *Institutes*. The first sign is to put to death all desires, which is a somewhat negative way of saying that we should elevate our desire to know God above all others.

His second sign of humility resonates with me. We are to conceal none of our thoughts and deeds from our elder, which I understand to be some form of confessor. I think this is terribly important, and, for me, quite difficult. One of the principles of healing spirituality is complete honesty, especially with one's most intimate advisors. Throughout my whole life, I have confessed only some, specifically not most, of my thoughts and deeds. I sit with this for a few minutes. The simple fact is that I am so filled with shame about my secret self that I want no one to know about it. Perhaps I could find a non-English speaking priest and tell him all that I am so ashamed about, but that rather proves the point. Reflecting on this, I can see how fully confessing all my secrets is a form of humility. The very few times that I have come closest to full disclosure have been wrenching emotional experiences, leaving me in tears for hours. This feels very much like self-loathing, not humility, but I suspect the shame is something that must be deeply experienced in order to forget.

Cassian goes on to list strict obedience as his third and fourth signs of humility. This makes sense to me, but also heads the list of my greatest challenges. For reasons that must go all the way back to my early upbringing, I have always resisted authority. Much of my mission experience was based on resistance rather than obedience. I continue to chafe under the teachings of the Catholic Church, constantly rationalizing some way to disobey.

I end this morning with sadness. Humility headed Father Frank's list of virtues to be used in developing a vision for this Advent season. I have a long way to go.

November 30

Hebrews 2:5–13, Exaltation through Abasement
   ⁵ Now God did not subject the coming world, about which we are speaking, to angels. ⁶ But someone has testified somewhere,
      "What are human beings that you are mindful of them,
      or mortals, that you care for them?

⁷ You have made them for a little while lower than the angels;
you have crowned them with glory and honor,
⁸ subjecting all things under their feet."
Now in subjecting all things to them, God left nothing outside their control. As it is, we do not yet see everything in subjection to them, ⁹ but we do see Jesus, who for a little while was made lower than the angels, now crowned with glory and honor because of the suffering of death, so that by the grace of God he might taste death for everyone.

¹⁰ It was fitting that God, for whom and through whom all things exist, in bringing many children to glory, should make the pioneer of their salvation perfect through sufferings. ¹¹ For the one who sanctifies and those who are sanctified all have one Father. For this reason Jesus is not ashamed to call them brothers and sisters, ¹² saying,
"I will proclaim your name to my brothers and sisters, in the midst of the congregation I will praise you."
¹³ And again, "I will put my trust in him." And again, "Here am I and the children whom God has given me."

THE MESSAGE that the world has been left in the hands of man has been used for centuries to justify environmental abuse. After all, God made the world to serve man, right? Obviously, this line of thinking is appalling. While the one line, "subjecting all things under their feet," seems to say that, it is the ultimate form of "cherry picking" to read the whole passage that way.

Ascending by descending is the message. Father Rohr called it "Falling Upward." Over and over again, I have found strength at the bottom. Now, re-reading that statement reminds me that I have continued to slip to a new bottom each time I have made any progress climbing Mt. Carmel. The core message of the Cross is strength through suffering. I sit with that this morning.

Surrender to win. As I reflect on this, my thoughts return to the times I have finally admitted I was not in control; the times I gave up and asked for help. The first thing that occurs to me is the incredible level of resistance I put up to avoid admitting I needed help. Not surprisingly, the level of resistance was proportional to the level of resentment (or denial). From the end of 2005 until the fall of 2007, my selfish, infantile resentment of the leadership of Actis, the British group that controlled the ownership of Globeleq, grew completely out of control. Everywhere I went, I tried to gather support for my position of having been wronged. Even when the assets were sold for an extraordinary profit, benefiting everyone beyond our wildest expectations, I complained. When my former colleagues and associates resisted my efforts to bring them on side, I added them to my list of enemies. With the deep resentment came deeper depression and acting out. But did I ask for help? Hardly.

Finally, when it was clear that everything I was and everything I had were slipping away, Sallie Ann made it clear she had had enough. At the bottom of the bottom, I could not even recognize that the game was up. I needed help to ask for help.

Thus began my spiritual journey. Climbing this mountain through the darkness, to borrow from John of the Cross, has not been a steady ascent. All along the way, I have slipped, regressed, rationalized, and tried shortcuts. The good news is that God is generous with second chances. The whole theology of a relational God of love is based on an eternal, infinite outpouring of that love. Grace is always present, never earned and never withheld.

Humility has been foremost in my thoughts, just as I hoped it would be. Admitting defeat, surrendering—these are humbling acts. As I reflect on it, self-loathing is not the dominant feeling at the bottom. Yes, I had to reach a point where I deeply disliked who and what I had become. Wallowing in self-pity, however, is not resolving to seek help. It was self-pity that caused me to seek agreement from my colleagues that I had been wronged. When I finally gave up, I had to radically understand that it was not about me. Giving everything I had away must focus not on the giver or the gift, but on the recipient. I am most at peace when I am in service. Sister Parish, Ability Housing, and the Georgetown Initiative are sources of strength for the journey.

I pray that I will finally stop testing Love; stop flirting with descent. I pray for wisdom and understanding. I pray for strength to give more, serve more, and deeply see others more.

December 1

Repeat the Kingdom

GOD'S GAZE on me is an amazing concept. Again, I am reminded that Meister Eckhart said, "the eye through which I see God is the same eye through which God sees me." I stared at the Rublev icon for a long time this morning, "gazing" into the Divine Dance. I imagined myself caught up in the dance, swinging and jumping in harmony with the Father, the Son, the Holy Spirit, and all of creation. It is a very powerful image, freeing me to be joyful and alive. I thought about the little party the other night, listening to the Old School band, which primarily consists of members of Sallie Ann's choir. I sat through the music, stiffly avoiding the dancing. I was restless and self-conscious.

Reflecting on that this morning, I remember the amazing friendship I had with Buddy Tudor. For more than forty years, Buddy gave me permission to dance. At times, I would say that he acted so much the fool that no one would notice me. That was not what was happening. Buddy simply lived in joy, even in the darkest days of his fight with cancer. His joy was infectious. I laughed and lived in his presence. Even now, thinking about Buddy fills me with joy. I miss him.

> After I have accepted God's loving gaze on me, I offer my whole self to Him.

Dancing freely requires the "offering of my whole self." I cannot think about how I look, how I am dressed, or how I am moving with the music. I must let go, I must surrender. Dancing, truly dancing, is humble.

I imagined myself walking with Jesus in the hills of Nazareth. Even as we climbed these rocky slopes, my mind would slip into the selfish thought about what people must think of me, walking with the Messiah. How unfortunate! I concentrated on the man in front of me, completely at ease, filled with quiet joy. Intermittantly, Jesus would become Buddy in my fantasy. I realized that he was not thinking about how he looked when he walked and climbed. He simply did it. It was infectious. For at least some of the time, I walked *with* Jesus, unaware of others and, ever so slightly, unaware of myself.

Jesus walked as though He was dancing. He talked to His Father, but included the rest of us in the conversation. It was totally inclusive without effort or fanfare. Inclusion itself was the grace.

I pray with gratitude for the time I spent with Buddy today. My tears were tears of great joy and love.

December 2

Matthew 4:18–25, Jesus Calls the First Disciples

¹⁸ As he walked by the Sea of Galilee, he saw two brothers, Simon, who is called Peter, and Andrew his brother, casting a net into the sea—for they were fishermen. ¹⁹ And he said to them, "Follow me, and I will make you fish for people." ²⁰ Immediately they left their nets and followed him. ²¹ As he went from there, he saw two other brothers, James son of Zebedee and his brother John, in the boat with their father Zebedee, mending their nets, and he called them. ²² Immediately they left the boat and their father, and followed him.

Jesus Ministers to Crowds of People

²³ Jesus went throughout Galilee, teaching in their synagogues and proclaiming the good news of the kingdom and curing every disease and every sickness among the people. ²⁴ So his fame spread throughout all Syria, and they brought to him all the sick, those who were afflicted with various diseases and pains, demoniacs, epileptics, and paralytics, and he cured them. ²⁵ And great crowds followed him from Galilee, the Decapolis, Jerusalem, Judea, and from beyond the Jordan.

I WALKED DOWN to the beach this morning, intentionally trying to recreate the sensation of walking with Jesus by the Sea of Galilee. In my fantasy, I was a fisherman, casting my net a few feet from where Simon Peter and Andrew were casting theirs. I recall a similar fantasy five years ago, when I remember feeling very hurt not to be called by Jesus to follow Him. Strange how selfish and self-centered that feels today. Today, I am simply honored to watch the charismatic leader work His magic. What can make grown men, albeit young men, leave their nets, their boat, and their father to join a cause? What kind of charisma did Jesus have?

I suppose the Holy Spirit could simply cause this loyalty to happen, almost magically. That does not feel right. Clearly, Jesus was "pushing against an open door." I suspect these men were sympathetic with the need for reform, and they were willingly part of the resistance movement in Israel. It was a time of revolution among the Jews, who were anxious to throw off the yoke of Roman rule, and, perhaps even more so, to rid themselves of the Jewish Kings, puppets of Rome. It is not clear to me that these Disciples were terribly religious, or deeply learned in the Hebrew tradition. They were apparently not Pharisees or Sadducees, the elite Jews and priests of the Temple. They were, after all, simple fishermen. Perhaps not so simple.

Did they believe they had little to lose by throwing down their nets to follow a reformer? While that is possible, I am not convinced. Something was going on with this man Jesus. His manner of speaking must have been incredibly powerful. He would soon speak to thousands of people without any form of amplification. Imagine that strong voice only a few feet away, naming you, calling you out, selecting you, choosing you. There was no time for discernment or careful consideration. Jesus said *you, now.* That was enough.

Reflecting on this, I consider some of the other charismatic people I have listened to and chosen to follow. Barack Obama could call me out, choose me, and I would follow him. I have only met a few great men, but thinking about it, I believe I would have responded similarly to any of them. Or I would have before I became burdened with family and possessions and commitments. Those men on that seaside were presumably unencumbered. Watching it in my fantasy, I am deeply impressed, even envious of their freedom to respond. I envied them their belief in a cause, a belief sufficient to evoke such complete commitment. In my life, there have been so very few such causes. I have cared about war and peace, racism, poverty, and inequality. But I have never given up all that I had to do whatever I could about these issues.

I sit with the concept of sacrifice. Those times in my life when I took huge risks, committed enormous amounts of time and energy to a new deal or new company, clearly looked like sacrifice from the outside. After all, I traveled incessantly, was away from home and family, and completely untethered to stability. And I did it repeatedly. In retrospect, I do not recall those situations as periods of great sacrifice. The thrill and excitement of the chase, of something new, always outweighed any pain or suffering I endured. To be truthful, very early in my career, I began to travel in as pain-free a manner as possible. First-class seats on the plane, five-star hotels, and Michelin-starred restaurants could hardly be considered "roughing it." The ease with which I left family obligations is hardly a virtue. Besides, in almost all of these cases, I believed I would ultimately benefit financially. I was not making a sacrifice for a cause.

So, I consider again the question whether I would have answered the call from Jesus. I think I would have dropped my net, left my boat, and walked away from my family quite happily. Even at that early stage, His reform movement was, one could say, "edgy," clearly at the forefront of possibilities in a time of great unrest. What is not so clear to me is how long I would have endured the simple, hard life of the early disciples. It is easy to say that the danger would have been exciting, but I suspect I would have been able to figure out that the life expectancy of the first followers of Jesus was not long. Nor is it clear whether I would have joined the group, or stayed long with them, without careful consideration of the ultimate benefit for me.

My reflection on humility today borrows from one of my Living School classmates, Evan Miller, who reminded us of something Jim Finley said. Jim advises us to listen carefully in silence. "One learns to practice the experiential humility of refraining from commentary, stay in a stance of non-judgmental receptive openness to the flow of the beauty not yet thought about." As I sit with this advice, I can understand the lack of humility implicit in immediate response, especially if there is anything in the response that negates the thinking or understanding of the speaker. A silent pause implies respect for the comment, even if I ultimately do not agree.

This experiential humility feels a little like the Ignatian concept of active indifference. This statement is from the meditation piece for October 17.

> **Active Indifference**. When we say "indifferent," we do not mean apathy but rather Karl Rahner's definition of indifference as a kind of removal or distance away from things that makes true vision possible and is required for proper decision. *This indifference* does not exist for its own sake but is the choice of what is most conducive to the end. It *is freedom for making a decision according to God's will.*

Active indifference is allowing time for the will of God to influence our discernment. Listening in humility respects the speaker, allowing time for the beauty of the thought and sound to develop. More accurately, the silent time allows me to experience the beauty that was there all along, unheard only by me. Of course, the two concepts could be the same: The development of God's will during the silence allows me to experience the beauty of what has been said.

I pray for the ability to see the beauty in silence. I pray for the courage to make sacrifices for the things I believe in.

December 3

1 Corinthians 15:20–28

²⁰ But in fact Christ has been raised from the dead, the first fruits of those who have died. ²¹ For since death came through a human being, the resurrection of the dead has also come through a human being; ²² for as all die in Adam, so all will be made alive in Christ. ²³ But each in his own order: Christ the first fruits, then at his coming those who belong to Christ. ²⁴ Then comes the end, when he hands over the kingdom to God the Father, after he has destroyed every ruler and every authority and power. ²⁵ For he must reign until he has put all his enemies under his feet. ²⁶ The last enemy to be destroyed is death. ²⁷ For "God has put all things in subjection under his feet." But when it says, "All things are put in subjection," it is plain that this does not include the one who put all things in subjection under him. ²⁸ When all things are subjected to him, then the Son himself will also be subjected to the one who put all things in subjection under him, so that God may be all in all.

WHEN JASPERS coined the phrase First Axial Age, he described a global phenomenon that occurred during the period 800 BCE—300 BCE. Certain individuals in China, India, Persia, Egypt, and Israel were simultaneously asking questions about, among other things, the purpose of life, the source of life, and the reason for life and death. Like everyone else I know, as I grow older, I am increasingly intrigued by the prospect of my death. Paul addresses these questions of death in the passage today, from his letter to the Corinthians.

Some of the lines in the passage are routinely used to suggest that both the concept and the fact of resurrection were introduced by Jesus, though Paul refers to Christ, not Jesus or Jesus Christ. I reflected first on the notion that Jesus was the historical incarnation of God, who lived some 2,000 years ago. Consider the idea that He was the "first fruits of those who have died," or "all die in Adam so all will be made alive in Christ." It is at least implied that there was no resurrection before Jesus was resurrected, which leaves many millions of souls who lived prior to the time of Jesus in a state of limbo (not referring to the tradition of Purgatory, a place between Heaven and Hell).

However, reflecting on the same concept using "the Christ," referred to as "the Word" in the prologue of John's Gospel, leads to a different reading:

> In the beginning was the Word, and the Word was with God, and the Word was God. This one was in the beginning with God. All things came into being through him, and apart from him not one thing came into being that has come into being. In him was life, and the life was the light of humanity. And the light shines in the darkness, and the darkness did not overcome it.
>
> And the Word became flesh and took up residence among us, and we saw his glory, glory as of the one and only from the Father, full of grace and truth. John testified about him and cried out, saying, "This one was he about whom I said, 'The one who comes after me is ahead of me, because he existed before me.'"

In this sense, of course Christ was the first fruit. He preceded everything. And Adam, as a metaphor for the first human, did introduce human death. This struggle to fit the words of the scripture into the scientific reality, as I have come to understand it, is neither easy nor fruitful. It is also unnecessary. Everything in the Bible is metaphor, even that which approximates history, or can be tied to either scientific or historical evidence.

Those who "belong to Christ" will be resurrected (find new life) before those who do not belong (unless we start with the assumption that all belong, which makes the statement rather meaningless). For me, the metaphoric understanding means that surrendering to Christ (or any other holy name for God) brings new life now. The metaphoric understanding of "reign until He has put all His enemies under his feet" simply suggests that my surrender to a higher power cannot be occasional or selective. It must be complete and constant.

I sit with the concept of surrender. Over the past nine years, I have heard a thousand times or more that surrender is the key to recovery, to a conversion in the journey. The hardest part of surrender for me is that it never ends. I cannot surrender this morning, then reign supreme again this afternoon. Yet that is precisely what my ego wants to do.

Humility requires surrender. I thought about the old joke, "You don't have to run faster than the bear to get away. You just have to run faster than the guy next to you." Humility does not require that we be wallow in the self-pity of assuming we are the worst. It does require that we acknowledge the superiority of the guy next to us. I know it seems like I have the analogy backwards. Humility is seeing deeply the people around me, accepting them as superior to me simply because they are not me. In that acceptance is respect, and even love. I can be right in an argument over words or ideas, but I am not, therefore, better than the other person.

CALENDAR WEEK TWELVE

I want to know, to love, and to follow Jesus my Lord.

Welcome, Lord Jesus Christ, into our flesh, into the heart of humanness. I welcome Your godly holiness upon earth. I welcome Your complete humanness upon my life world. I welcome You, Yourself, into my life and self. I thank You that I may embrace humanity and find myself embracing You. For You remain in our flesh now and forever, among humankind whose eyes reflect Your eyes, whose use of words matches Your use of words, whose need of You matches Your willing need for us.

From Father Frank: Mercy

December 4

Reflection on Mary

I come to the moment of Jesus Christ's conception in my humanity. As always, I enter into God's presence and feel His gaze rest on me, and I offer to Him my whole self. Then I do three things:

First, I remember the "history" that I am praying about: The Holy Trinity knows the whole world of humankind and sees how we are ravaging the earth, making life terrible for one another, and turning many of ourselves into ruins. Out of God's infinite and eternal love, the Father sends the Son down to enter into all this, to save it. And then they send the announcement to our Lady Mary.

Second, I compose myself, as I have done before, in this real world. I am utterly embedded in humanity and in all that goes on. And after seeing the whole of earth, I bring myself to Nazareth in Galilee, where Mary stays.

Third, I ask for what I want. What I want right now is a deep intimate knowledge of Jesus. I want a strong love for Him. And I want to follow where He goes.

Then I cover these three points in some way or other by fantasy, meditation, or contemplation—and after I have worked through them, I consider what it all means to me, to my life world, and to the whole of the human race.

First, I look at all the people on the earth—races and ethnic groups; some at desks and some at wars; they laugh, play, weep, struggle; they are infants, grown, dying. I watch God watching all this, and I wonder what God feels. I see Mary staying in Nazareth.

Second, I listen to the riot of sounds—music and machines; friends chatting and enemies reviling; typewriters and hand grenades; mobs and riots. I listen to God's thoughts: "Let us save all these people… And I hear the announcement to Mary.

Third, I move into the frantic activities of earth speeding, constructing, fighting, playing, blowing up buildings, riding horses, flying jets, all too often destroying human life or the humanity in living persons. I see God working busily, initiating the Incarnation, laboring among humankind.

And I see the angel announce the message and Mary bow in acquiescence.

At the end, I will consider what I ought to say to God the Lord, or to Mary, or to Jesus, who now lives forever in my humanness. As I always do, I close with an Our Father.

YESTERDAY was the annual Parish Christmas Exposition, where, among other things, the Sister Parish Ministry offered for sale napkins embroidered by a group of twelve women in Mamey. They not only sold out, but have orders for many more. The sale earned more than $3,200, an amount that puts it far ahead of every other effort we have made in the past three years to find an income-generating project for the village. I am still in shock.

Today at Mass, our dear Father Santhosh, a priest from southern India, announced he would be leaving Ponte Vedra, returning for another assignment in his home state of Kerala, India. It was an emotional parting, making this Advent Mass especially meaningful. It was also the day the RCIA graduates were presented to the Parish as new Catechumens and Candidates. It brought back powerful memories of my own presentation to the parish community of St. Anne's in Houston in December, 2009.

I reflect on the first three concepts of today's assignment: Christ entered His own creation as an incarnate part of humanity; I am embedded in that same humanity; and I want to know Christ intimately. Any one of the three concepts is beyond the reach of a normal day of meditation. Christ incarnate? Wow! Human just like me? Not possible! Do I want to know this person? Absolutely.

To me, the overriding message of these connected ideas is that Christ entered His creation precisely for the twin objectives of first, proclaiming it, creation, a glorious product of the Divine, and second, making it clear that there is in each of us a spark of the Divine. Both concepts are, at the same time, revolutionary, and logically obvious. This amazing universe is the result of a Divine source, and is evolving in a Divine direction. As infinite, eternal elements of this creation, we too have a Divine source and a Divine direction.

I read a very critical review of Father Rohr's recent book, *The Divine Dance*, which took great exception to the very thought of any divinity in mankind. There were also digs at Father Rohr's suggestion of certain feminine qualities in the Trinity. Early stages of consciousness depend on dualism and separation to establish and maintain order in the universe. At magic and tribal levels of consciousness, God must be greater than Man and Mankind, and must always be. Similarly, God must be masculine, because being great requires being masculine. Sad.

This is a profoundly complex universe, spanning time and space beyond our human ability to comprehend. During our infinitesimally tiny moment on this insignificantly tiny planet, what, to us, is huge noise and frenetic activity must be cosmically unnoticeable. Yet from my egoistic perspective, there is enormous activity surrounding an incomprehensibly huge globe. Moreover, when I consider that Jesus was born on this earth more than two thousand years ago, and that during every one of those years all races and tribes were making loud noise and wild motions, the incomprehensibility increases.

I sit with the idea that in all of that space and time, noise and motion, mundane and sublime, I have only this moment, in this chair, in this quiet place. Just me, alone with my prayers and reflections. I allow Mary, just Mary, to enter my space, quietly, humbly, the way Mary would. I hear Mary say yes. I know, because I have lived here almost seventy-two years, that Mary's quiet "yes" will be heard around the world for the next two millennia.

The incessant noise and frenetic activity will continue, even get worse. Wars, disease, pestilence, and every manner of sin will continue. But the quiet *yes* can still be heard. In some small ways, it prevails. I pray in gratitude for that.

December 5

Repeat the Reflection on Mary

POPE FRANCIS says that a little bit of mercy makes the world less cold and more just. I like that, just as I like so much of what this wonderful Pope says and stands for. I find it very odd and quite troubling how many Catholics in my community dislike Pope Francis and long for the end of his leadership. Ideological dislike of peace and justice brings out the worst in everyone.

Today, again, I reflect on the humanness of Jesus Christ. On so many levels, this is a simply revolutionary thought. All of the great wisdom contained in the global awakening of the First Axial Age maintained a separation between the gods and man. Occasionally, the various gods became involved with humans, even fathered children. Most ancient kingdoms eventually claimed ordination by the gods. But Gods and men were separate, as were life and death and Heaven and Hell. Jesus shattered that tradition by becoming man. He was not a god pretending to be human to help in battle, or, much worse, a human pretending to be a god in order to garner support for power or position. Jesus became man as a humble carpenter in a poor community, in an outer and largely insignificant province of the Roman Empire.

It would be hard to imagine a more human existence. He did not claim power, prestige, or possessions as His birthright, nor did He seek to lead a "shooting revolution." His upside-down Gospel exalted the least among us, the sick, imprisoned, poor, and blind. The first shall be last and the last shall be first. What amazes me to this very moment is how extraordinary it is that this humble man with such a humble message could shape history. Sadly, most of history is a story of rejecting the teachings of Christ. However, throughout the past two thousand years, in the west, at least, the message of Christ has been celebrated in name, even though more honored in the breach than the observance.

On my individual, little human scale, the message has experienced something of the same battle. I have been influenced by Christianity for all my 72 years, but I have certainly not lived it continuously. The good news on the individual level is that those brief moments when Christ's message does get through seem to be prevailing for me. I reflect on the notion that a single moment of sincere right action can atone for much of a life pursuing the wrong things. Grace is always present. His mercy is always available. By their very definition, grace and mercy are not earned or deserved or justified or intended to balance any scales. They are simply, beautifully available.

I pray today for acceptance. I want to be merciful, just as the message from Christ and His church on earth is mercy. Advent is a season of mercy.

December 6

Luke 1:26–38

[26] In the sixth month the angel Gabriel was sent by God to a town in Galilee called Nazareth, [27] to a virgin engaged to a man whose name was Joseph, of the house of David. The virgin's name was Mary. [28] And he came to her and said, "Greetings, favored one! The Lord is with you." [29] But she was much perplexed by his words and pondered what sort of greeting this might be. [30] The angel said to her, "Do not be afraid, Mary, for you have found favor with God. [31] And now, you will conceive in your womb and bear a son, and you will name him Jesus. [32] He will be great, and will be called the Son of the Most High, and the Lord God will give to him the throne of his ancestor David. [33] He will reign over the house of Jacob forever, and of his kingdom there will be no end." [34] Mary said to the angel, "How can this be, since I am a virgin?" [35] The angel said to her, "The Holy Spirit will come upon you, and the power of the Most High will overshadow you; therefore the child to be born will be holy; he will be called Son of God. [36] And now, your relative Elizabeth in her old age has also conceived a son; and this is the sixth month for her who was said to be barren. [37] For nothing will be impossible with God." [38] Then Mary said, "Here am I, the servant of the Lord; let it be with me according to your word." Then the angel departed from her.

MARIOLOGY, the theology of Mary, was somehow left out of my RCIA instruction. Of course, we read the Gospel accounts about Gabriel calling Mary, and I knew there was a chapel devoted to Mary at the parish. But we Catechumens were not taught the Rosary, nor any of the numerous prayers and acts of contrition shown by all cradle Catholics to the Virgin Mary. Later, perhaps during my first heavy reading about Catholicism, I learned about the dogmas of Perpetual Virginity, Immaculate Conception, and Assumption. I must confess that I did not fully appreciate the importance of these dogmas. As one of my teachers is fond of saying, Christ was incarnate of Mary whether Mary was a virgin always, once, or never. And the doctrinal value of either St. Anne's virginity (or absence of the stain of Original Sin) or the form of Mary's reaching Heaven elude me. Nor am I a big fan of the various Marian shrines around the world.

However, the extraordinary humility and obedience shown by this child in Galilee, as reported in the Gospels of Matthew and Luke, is beyond amazing. The poetry of this passage from Luke's Gospel, "Greetings, favored one! …Do not be afraid, Mary, for you have favor with God." Imagine the enormous power of these words. Cut through all the dogma and reflect only on the profound idea that God became human! All those ages of dualism, separating God and Man and Heaven and Earth, were about to be torn asunder. God was about to be a baby! He would cry and pee and poop and hold His mother's finger, just like every other natural being.

I sit with that image early this morning as I wait at the airport, about to fly to the Dominican Republic for a very brief planning trip. I reflect on the babies that are born in the poorest houses of the poor village of Mamey. Jesus was born in just that much poverty, and would honor the poor more than any King before Him. The upside-down Kingdom had been announced to Mary, though she could not have known it at the time. I reflect on the love that she showed her Son throughout His too short life.

Jesus was even younger when He died, and did so in a publicly humiliating way. Mary could never have known what she was facing on that day the angel announced that she was favored by God. I love this song, written by Mark Lowry.

> Mary, did you know that your Baby Boy would one day walk on water?
> Mary, did you know that your Baby Boy would save our sons and daughters?
> Did you know that your Baby Boy has come to make you new?
> This Child that you delivered will soon deliver you.
>
> Mary, did you know that your Baby Boy will give sight to a blind man?
> Mary, did you know that your Baby Boy will calm the storm with His hand?
> Did you know that your Baby Boy has walked where angels trod?
> When you kiss your little Baby you kissed the face of God?
>
> Mary did you know..
> The blind will see. The deaf will hear. The dead will live again.
> The lame will leap. The dumb will speak the praises of The Lamb.
>
> Mary, did you know that your Baby Boy is Lord of all creation?
> Mary, did you know that your Baby Boy would one day rule the nations?
> Did you know that your Baby Boy is heaven's perfect Lamb?
> The sleeping Child you're holding is the great "I am"

I am now writing this on the plane, flying from Miami to Santo Domingo. The first plane left Jacksonville at 7:15 this morning, one of the earliest flights I have taken since Sister Parish began. I hate early flights! Getting up at 4 a.m. to drive to the airport in the dark is not my idea of a great way to start the day.

I reflected on how easily my meditation has been interrupted by my complaints about personal comfort! Here I am, traveling to the Caribbean to do good work for Sister Parish, reflecting on Mary hearing from an Angel that she was about to become the mother of the Messiah, yet allowing myself to be distracted by the inconvenience of travel.

I sat with images of Mary and Joseph traveling from Nazareth to Bethlehem. It is estimated that this eighty-mile journey probably took them about four days. They walked, Joseph leading a donkey, Mary astride the donkey (she must have been close to nine months pregnant). I am flying 1,104 miles this morning, and will be in Santo Domingo for lunch. Yet I complain!

December 7

Repeat Luke 1:26–38

THOUGHTS OF Mary have been with me since reading the passage from Luke's Gospel. I read it again just now and sat with the reflection of how much Mary was told, and how much she was not told. Yes, she would have a baby and He would turn the world upside-down, but He would be killed by a mob after being tried by the Chief Judge, the King, and the Roman Prefect. He would be mutilated, then crucified and left hanging on a cross. Mary knew nothing about this when she became pregnant with the Son of Man.

I toured Mamey yesterday, shortly after I arrived in the Dominican Republic. Heavy rain left the village muddy and difficult to negotiate. My first meeting was with the embroidery ladies, who expressed gratitude and excitement about their success. Their napkins sold out at the annual church expo last week, earning these women more than $500 net. Putting this in context is important. The first installment of profit for each woman will be 1,769 pesos, which amounts to more than a week's wages for able-bodied Haitian men. Women typically receive much less, *if they are employed at all.* The simple fact is that there is virtually no employment for men or women in the bateyes. In all four years that we have been working in Mamey, we have tried one "business" after another, from a computer center to a barber shop to an extensive pig farm. This is the first profitable activity! Kudos to the women of our Sister Parish Ministry—Katie, Coleen, Carmen, Molly, and all the others. Especially high praise for Odalis and the dozen women in Mamey who embroider what they call "Monique's Threads of Love."

Dinner last night was frustrating. The Mamey leaders joined me for a working dinner. We tried to go over the financial reports, a difficult subject even when language is not a problem. My Spanish is not up to financial reporting, nor is the beginning English of the leaders.

We have just returned from a long meeting with Father Juan, his parish council, Sister Eva and Sister Inez from Futuro Vivo, and the Mamey leaders. The headline from the meeting is simple: Two missions from Florida arrive early next year, expecting to work on two chapels and four houses. We must reach agreement on design for the chapels, negotiate contracts for the work to be done in advance of the missions, and complete that work before the missionaries arrive. The next three weeks, leading up to Christmas, are difficult in any part of the world, but especially in Guerra. Then we face the difficulty of working in the heavy rain of January in the Dominican Republic. And, of course, somebody has to pay for it all. It was a pressure-filled meeting.

December 8

John 1:1–18, the Prologue

¹ In the beginning was the Word, and the Word was with God, and the Word was God. ² He was in the beginning with God. ³ All things came into being through him, and without him not one thing came into being. What has come into being ⁴ in him was life, and the life was the light of all people. ⁵ The light shines in the darkness, and the darkness did not overcome it.

⁶ There was a man sent from God, whose name was John. ⁷ He came as a witness to testify to the light, so that all might believe through him. ⁸ He himself was not the light, but he came to testify to the light. ⁹ The true light, which enlightens everyone, was coming into the world.

¹⁰ He was in the world, and the world came into being through him; yet the world did not know him. ¹¹ He came to what was his own, and his own people did not accept him. ¹² But to all who received him, who believed in his name, he gave power to become children of God, ¹³ who were born, not of blood or of the will of the flesh or of the will of man, but of God.

¹⁴ And the Word became flesh and lived among us, and we have seen his glory, the glory as of a father's only son, full of grace and truth. ¹⁵ (John testified to him and cried out, "This was he of whom I said, 'He who comes after me ranks ahead of me because he was before me.'") ¹⁶ From his fullness we have all received, grace upon grace. ¹⁷ The law indeed was given through Moses; grace and truth came through Jesus Christ. ¹⁸ No one has ever seen God. It is God the only Son, who is close to the Father's heart, who has made him known.

REFLECTING on this passage, which includes some of my favorite verses in the Bible, takes me to some delightful places. Teilhard, Ilia Delio, and Denis Edwards used the Prologue of John's Gospel as the entry point into their wonderful theology. The statement that "All things came into being through him" makes the concept of creative evolution not just possible, but virtually inescapable.

Sitting with that statement for a few minutes brings up the role of Scripture in my faith. Father Rohr insists that Scripture is the first and, to a large extent, most important component of the three-legged stool—Scripture, Tradition, and Experience. That is not the case for me.

I love the long and deep tradition of the Church, especially the Catholic tradition, which includes so many great Doctors, Fathers, Saints, and mystics throughout the full two millennia. Many of these incredible thinkers were banned before being fully accepted. Some have still not been accepted by many conservative Catholics. But the richness of their thinking and the beauty of their writing are music for my soul.

Experience is a deeply personal thing. Sometimes I listen to the stories of the men and women in our CRHP community and wonder at how little they have experienced, or, at least, that they choose to share. My almost 72 years seems so rich in experience, which, in almost every case, resulted from sin and suffering. From the very early years of my life, which are now shrouded in the mysterious twilight of my feeble memory, all the way up to the meetings yesterday in Guerra and Mamey, I have been blessed with an awesome amount of experience. I have been filled with joy and crushed with depression. I have clearly found my spiritual core through my experiences of the Divine.

Scripture, however, has been a challenge. I suppose that has always been the case, though I think I have greater difficulty as the years go by. Even this wonderful prologue to John's Gospel requires a great deal of trimming, squeezing, and logical adjustment to fit into the theology and cosmology of creative evolution. I know there are legions of good Christians who will say I have it all backward; that the tailoring must be made in how I view the world, such that my world view fits the scripture, not the other way around. That does not work for me.

The texts of two thousand years ago were written when the world was flat, the sun revolved around the earth, and creation took place in six days, all key elements of the cosmology of the era. These writings should not be the touchstone for clarity and truth. The people involved—the Evangelists, scribes, translators, and curators, who created the body of work that was presented to the councils for canonization—were good and honest men (probably not many women in the early centuries!), who genuinely believed the documents with which they worked accurately described the events that occurred.

Let's stipulate that they *were* accurate accounts of the speeches and sayings of Holy men, and, in some cases, even *were* the actual writings of Holy men. But I do not believe that the "finger of God" wrote the words in those manuscripts and scrolls. I do not believe the writings of the Hebrew prophets and kings deserve any greater respect than the writings of Teilhard or Merton or Meister Eckhart.

Starting from the position that the Scriptures are Sacred Canon requires that we adjust both tradition and experience to fit the strained logic of these books and letters. I prefer just the opposite, which makes me a lousy man of faith. I do see great value in the Scriptures. I do love the reflections that result from reading and sitting with the Scriptures. As I read back through this reflection today, I feel some "heretic's guilt." I am sorry. It is not a great way to end the day's exercise.

December 9

Philippians 2:6–11
⁶ who, though he was in the form of God,
did not regard equality with God
as something to be exploited,
⁷ but emptied himself,
taking the form of a slave,
being born in human likeness.
And being found in human form,
⁸ he humbled himself
and became obedient to the point of death—
even death on a cross.
⁹ Therefore God also highly exalted him
and gave him the name
that is above every name,
¹⁰ so that at the name of Jesus
every knee should bend,
in heaven and on earth and under the earth,
¹¹ and every tongue should confess
that Jesus Christ is Lord,
to the glory of God the Father.

YESTERDAY ended sadly. Anabel, a little girl in Mamey, died. Dr. Laura Beverly, a permanent fixture in our Sister Parish Medical missions, first diagnosed Anabel with WILMS' tumor a year ago. Bishop Estevez blessed Anabel in March of this year, during the St. Joseph's Academy mission. Following that Mission, Sister Parish provided financial support for Anabel to travel to Santo Domingo for chemotherapy. Then in August, we learned that Anabel's mother was using the money for other purposes.

Anabel's tumors had grown to a frightening size. She was given only a few weeks to live. Miraculously, Anabel stopped complaining about pain, started eating regularly, and lived another three months.

I am struck with how sad Anabel's death made me last night and again today. The primary purpose of Sister Parish is *encounter*. From the very first exploratory trip with Don Barnhorst four years ago, we have stressed the relative unimportance of projects and patients. Yes, it is nice that a poor family in Mamey has a new house or students have a new school. And it is certainly good that children and elderly people are seen by a doctor. Those benefits notwithstanding, however, the great value of the mission experience is the *encounter* with God that results directly from an *encounter* with the Other, whether that Other is a child in Mamey, an older woman at Hogar San Jose, a fellow missionary from Ponte Vedra, or even the "other self" that each of us hides behind our projection of a self we want people to see. In my experience, encounters are very brief, often lasting only seconds, and are almost always totally unplanned. What can be planned, what we try to do in every aspect of Sister Parish, is to remove barriers to encounter, creating circumstances where encounter is possible.

It is also my experience that some encounters eventually result in relationships based on love. When the fleeting moment occurs multiple times with one person, or in one setting, I begin to care. Writing this causes me to stop and say "hello, of course you care"! The truth, however, is that generally, I don't care. Generally, people come into my life and go out again, leaving behind nice feelings, but no deep relationships. I am sorry to admit that. Reflecting on this, I run back through the years and places and people and projects and try to remember the caring relationships. They are few and far between.

Yet I am saddened by Anabel's death. My guess is that there have been many more "caring relationships" throughout the years, very few of which spanned much time or reached much depth. And that is ok. At the time, just like now with Anabel, my caring was genuine, and it was based on the encounter that occurs when two people truly see each other. There was little reciprocity in my encounter with Anabel. Even her mother barely notices me when I visit Mamey. But something happened several months ago that allowed Anabel into my heart space. Therein lies the key: Anabel fed my heart. She made me a better person. I was the primary recipient in that encounter, not Anabel.

Sitting with that, I realize that there have been untold numbers of "Anabels" in my life, people who have entered into my personal space to feed my heart. I remember virtually none of them. Again, that is probably ok. On occasion, I suspect, the feeding was reciprocal. I hope so.

Reflecting on mercy this morning, I ponder the difference between mercy and justice. I have often considered mercy something granted in the place of, or instead of, justice. Rather than justly punishing someone for doing wrong, I will magnanimously show mercy. That feels very selfish to me, putting me in the center of both the application of justice and the grant of mercy. I prefer to think about mercy in the same sense as forgiveness. When I have been wronged, or think I have been wronged, my choices are to strike back or to show mercy. Mature spirituality requires forgiveness and mercy. Innocent children can be excused for instinctively claiming "he hit me first." Not adults. I am reminded of the Twitter feed of a popular politician.

December 10

Reflect on everything this week.

SALLIE ANN learned last night that she will have her gall bladder removed. Surgery has not yet been scheduled. I know she is apprehensive.

Anabel's death, and my trip to the Dominican Republic, diverted my attention from the other two major stories of the week. First, yesterday was the feast of the Immaculate Conception, a Holy day of obligation, and one of the important Catholic holidays. Well, if I failed the Catholic test with my reflections on scripture at the beginning of this week, I am about to run into huge problems with my reaction to this feast day. Immaculate Conception. Really? Is it really dogma that Mary's mother was "without the stain of Original Sin," whatever that means? Did the Council of Trent really have so little to do that they had to endorse the doctrinal importance of two levels of virginity, thus removing the incarnation of Christ that much further from the beauty of the passage in Philippians?

Which brings me to the second major story of the week that was lost in the events, the incredible lines from the letter of Paul to the Philippians.

> [He] emptied himself, taking the form of a slave, being born in human likeness. And being found in human form, he humbled himself and became obedient to the point of death— even death on a cross.

The beauty of this passage for me is derived both from the poetry of the language, and from the powerful concept of Divine Humility; Divine Service; Divine Obedience. If Christ, the Son of God, could be born human, obedient to the point of death, then, quite obviously, every one of us can certainly do the same thing. Actually, we have little choice with respect to either our birth or our death, but the point is that we do have choice whether to humble ourselves, serve others, and obey commandments. There are other messages as well. Human likeness is not so bad. Even Christ became human. And Divinity is not so remote. At least one man was Divine. The dualistic gap between human and divine may not be so great as our *either/or* upbringing has led us to believe.

This is not meant to take anything away from the Divinity of God. He does not need to be less in order for us to be more. The power of the concept that there is a spark of the Divine in each of us is immense. It does fly in the face of all the efforts over the centuries to focus on the depravity of mankind. The doctrines of Original Sin, Immaculate Conception, the Virgin Birth, the Perpetual Virginity of Mary, and even her Assumption all strike me as part of the emphasis on "humanness" as bad.

I pray for humility, understanding, and wisdom. I am excited to be back in Advent mode.

CALENDAR WEEK THIRTEEN

I ask to enter into the mind of the One who chose to be born as I was born. I ask to love this little Infant so that my life will fall into His life's pattern.

Lord Jesus, right from the moment of Your birth, You lived with both the little and the great. You charmed and challenged and won them all. Lord, let me feel Your charismatic warmth, that tremendous welcoming grace that made the simple love You and their leaders seek You in the night. Teach me to rest easy where You are, easy as hairy shepherd and smooth-shaven savant, easy as the Lady Mary who bore You gently, easy as Joseph who held You, your abba! Accept the homage of my heart along with the shepherds' adoring gaze and the gifts of worshipful kings.

From Father Frank: Joy

December 11

I meditate and contemplate on the Birth of Jesus, His first moment of independent human life. As always, I enter into God's presence and feel His gaze rest on me, and I offer to Him my whole self. Then I do three things:

First, I recall for a moment that I am going to think about sacred history: A young girl, nearly nine months pregnant, came down from Nazareth because the Roman Emperor levied a tax on a population that we have records of. Joseph, her spouse, walked with her and they spent the night in a cave just down the hill from the little town of Bethlehem, overlooking broad historic fields.

Second, I compose myself in that cave, waiting for Messiah to be born.

Third, I ask for what I want: I want to know Jesus intimately, friend to friend. I want to share great love with Him. I want to go where He goes and do what He does.

Then I will enter into the event of Jesus' birth. I can do this in a number of ways.

Sometimes, I just watch the people: Mary and Joseph, and others. Or I catch something of what they say, and feel the emotion in it. Or I see what they are doing and everything that is going on. Whatever I contemplate, I let speak to me about my life world and myself.

In some prayer, I might just start in the middle of what is going on. Or I might move around in the event, just watching it happen around me.

Or thirdly, I might just stay with one or another person there, entering into their feelings and perception, while the events themselves go on their way.

At the end, I try to gather myself together and then tell the Lord what I have to tell, or perhaps talk with Mary or even with the Infant Jesus. As I always do, I close with the Our Father.

FOR THE FIRST several moments this morning, I imagined myself in the period two thousand years ago when Mary and Joseph walked from Nazareth down to Bethlehem. When we visited the Holy Land years ago, we drove up to Nazareth from Jerusalem, where we were staying. The wide highway ran about one hundred miles along the western side of the country, away from the Jordan River. The drive took less than two hours. Looking back now, I am sorry we did not take the longer route, driving east from Jerusalem to the river, then following it north toward Galilee.

When Joseph and Mary took the journey, their route took them down out of the Nazarene hills to the river, then followed the Jordan south, turning west again near Jericho to climb back up to Jerusalem and then to Bethlehem. The eighty-mile journey is estimated to have taken four days. There was obviously no highway. In my imagined journey, the "road" to the south was similar to the well-worn paths of the Camino de Santiago, from France down into Santiago de Campostela in Galicia.

In my fantasy, most of my fellow travelers were walking, their few belongings strapped to a donkey, which plodded alongside. We walked in small groups, finding safety in numbers. We had been warned against the risk of bandits, or skirmishes between the revolutionaries and the authorities.

We walked at a slow pace, partly due to Mary's pregnancy and partly due to the slow and steady pace of the foot traffic on the road. The way was crowded with people walking in both directions, traveling to their place of birth to pay the tax levied by the Roman Emperor. Even walking only two or three miles an hour, we had time to eat a long mid-day meal and to talk around the fire with fellow travelers in the evenings. I joined those conversations, curious about what Joseph and Mary were saying, and curious about the comments of others. My interest in politics and current events was present even then.

Joseph seemed proud of his young wife, and was happy about the baby due imminently. He seemed old to be having a first child, just as Mary seemed quite young. Joseph was a carpenter, fully capable of earning a sufficient living to support a small family. They were clearly poor, like all working-class people for most of history. The difference between their living conditions and those of the destitute was very thin. In fact, most of the truly poor were also handicapped in some way, typically a disease or deformity that would be quite easily cured or corrected today. Joseph was more comfortable talking about his work and family than about the political situation.

Other travelers wanted nothing more than to talk about the simmering revolution. While zealots were not well organized for another five or six years, the conditions that would ultimately lead to the First Jewish-Roman War in 66 CE already existed. Tax collectors were despised, just as the occasional, but increasingly frequent, assessments from Rome were resented. The Jewish hierarchy seemed to be totally in league with the Roman authorities. Puppet kings and Chief Judges, nominally Jewish, had been completely co-opted by the Emperor. Looking at history from the viewpoint of Rome, this cooptation has always been considered one of the brilliant aspects of their empire. Certainly, in the early decades, local religious traditions and, to a large extent, legal systems were allowed to continue. Over time, obviously, power corrupts, and the absolute power of the Roman Empire corrupted absolutely.

Most of the time, for most people, the sheer difficulty of daily life prevented much consideration and conversation about politics. We talked about sore feet and the chill in the air. We complained about the smell of the animals. We bemoaned the paucity of inns. We laughed about the antics of children and the haranguing of the wives. I liked the people on the road. I particularly liked Joseph. Like my own father, Joseph talked very little. I was naturally attracted to his competence and the way he made it easy for me to pitch in and help with the smallest of tasks. I was not happy to reach the fork in the road where Joseph and his family would go on to Bethlehem while I stayed in Jerusalem.

I sat on the bench in a sweater, chilly in the cool, but beautifully sunny, morning air. Maggie was happy. The egrets could not have been more elegant. I prayed in gratitude for what seem to be endless blessings.

December 12

Repeat the meditation on the birth of Jesus, and Luke 2:1–7
In those days a decree went out from Emperor Augustus that all the world should be registered. ² This was the first registration and was taken while Quirinius was governor of Syria. ³ All went to their own towns to be registered. ⁴ Joseph also went from the town of Nazareth in Galilee to Judea, to the city of David called Bethlehem,

because he was descended from the house and family of David. ⁵ He went to be registered with Mary, to whom he was engaged and who was expecting a child. ⁶ While they were there, the time came for her to deliver her child. ⁷ And she gave birth to her firstborn son and wrapped him in bands of cloth, and laid him in a manger, because there was no place for them in the inn.

EMPEROR AUGUSTUS was the first Caesar, and founder of the Roman Empire. One of my favorite memories is hearing the son of a friend of ours saying "*iacta alea est,*" which, he explained, is Latin for "the die is cast." Who knows that kind of thing?! Certainly not I.

I do love history, and have studied the history of Rome on several occasions over the years. My bouts of Roman history often begin with something only tangentially related to Roman history, most frequently architecture. The source book for most classical architecture, *De Architectura,* war written by Vitruvius in the first century BCE, shortly before Gaius Octavius (or Gaius Julius Caesar) famously crossed the Rubicon. Doing so, Caesar violated the sacred obligation never to invade Rome, saying as he did so "iacta alea est," "the die is cast," meaning he had taken an action he could not take back. The Roman Republic was essentially ended that day, replaced by a dictatorship that became an Empire and lasted in some form for fifteen centuries.

Christianity and Rome became inseparable when the Emperor Constantine declared Christianity the official faith of the empire in 313 CE. While this permanently launched the religion on the world stage, it was also the date that the new Gospel was very nearly destroyed. In fact, I am amazed at how persistently the Christian mystics and a very small handful of official leaders have preserved the core messages of Christ. It has been an ugly official history. Most of the leadership most of the time, has been corrupted by power, prestige, and possessions. The upside-down Gospel was turned upside-down, over and over again.

Yet the essence of the faith persisted. So, my journey with Mary and Joseph from Nazareth to Bethlehem gave me many opportunities to explore this early "dossier" of Jesus. Who were His parents? How did they live? How would their lives and values influence the Son of Man?

I was particularly intrigued by the strange reality of living in a far-flung province of an empire. While the United States is not an empire in the same sense as ancient Rome, in another very real sense, we are an imperial power. I have traveled all over the world all my life during a period when there was realistically no competing power to the United States. I have lived with the certain knowledge that no other passport meant as much as mine. (I am certain many of my British friends would challenge that statement!)

Joseph and Mary, however, walked that road in timid fear whenever Roman centurions were near. They stood aside for tax collectors and religious leaders. To be clear, they were not the lowest in the social order walking toward Jerusalem. There were beggars. There were sick people. I am sure that scoff-laws were hiding wherever they could along the way. Joseph and his young bride were working people, wealthy enough to be assessed a tax and be required to register.

I read that there were estimated to be about 300 million people on the earth at the time of Christ, compared to 7 billion today. There were about 50 million people in the Roman Empire, of whom only two million were Jews. Not all Jews lived in Palestine, and most that did were in the areas of Judea and Samaria, not Galilee where Jesus was born and lived most of his life. Nazareth had a population of fewer than 500 people! The point is that Jesus grew up in a humble family in a very small community in a remote province of the Roman Empire. And even at its largest, the Empire represented only twenty percent of the world's population. Yet Joseph was important enough among his 500 Nazarene neighbors and the 50 million Roman subjects to be required to register and pay taxes. In truth, that is significant.

However, it is simply inconceivable that these two people, walking quietly alongside me on that rocky path, were to be parents of the person that would change the world forever after His birth. What is even more inconceivable is that He would preach for only three years, ride into Jerusalem a hero, then be crucified on a cross at the demand of His own followers.

Father Frank's vision goal this week is *joy*. Yesterday was Gaudete Sunday, from the Latin *gaudete*, rejoice! Father Frank added this poem to his weekly blog. It was so powerful that I chose to add it to my journal. Quoting Father Frank, "Ten years ago, Rev. Andrea Ayvazian shared her Christmas wish."

> If we dug a huge grave miles wide, miles deep
> And buried every rifle, pistol, knife, bullet, bomb, bayonet…
> If every light-skinned man in a silk tie said
> To every dark-skinned man in a turban
> I vow not to kill your children
> And heard the same vow in return
> If every elected leader would stop lying
> If every child was fed as well as racehorses bred to win derbies
> If every person with a second home gave it to a person with no home
> If every mother buried her parents not her sons and daughters
> If every person who has enough said out loud I have enough
> If every person violent in the name of God were to find God
> We would grow silent, still for a moment, a lifetime
> We would hear infants nursing at the breast
> Hummingbirds hovering in flight-two lovers sigh across the ocean
> We would watch old wounds grow new flesh
> And jagged scars disappear…
> And we would once again give birth to God.

I ended the morning walking further down the beach than I have for a couple of years. Even though we live in a town named Ponte Vedra Beach, in a house only a block from that beach, I find it easy to forget just how beautiful and joyous that beach is every day. As I walked, the ocean in my fantasy was alternately the Sea of Galilee or the Aegean Sea. In both cases, I was in another age, walking with Disciples in Galilee or with the Apostle Paul along the shore near Philippi. I found it easy to feel joy. I have *enough*. I said it out loud again and again. Then I returned to the library in the big house surrounded by beautiful gardens, knelt before the icon of the Trinity, and thanked God for all that I have. Which is way more than enough.

December 13

Luke 2:8–20, The Shepherds and the Angels
    [8] *In that region there were shepherds living in the fields, keeping watch over their flock by night.* [9] *Then an angel of the Lord stood before them, and the glory of the Lord shone around them, and they were terrified.* [10] *But the angel said to them, "Do not be afraid; for see—I am bringing you good news of great joy for all the people:* [11] *to you is*

born this day in the city of David a Savior, who is the Messiah, the Lord. [12] This will be a sign for you: you will find a child wrapped in bands of cloth and lying in a manger." [13] And suddenly there was with the angel a multitude of the heavenly host, praising God and saying,

   [14] *"Glory to God in the highest heaven,*
   and on earth peace among those whom he favors!"

   [15] *When the angels had left them and gone into heaven, the shepherds said to one another, "Let us go now to Bethlehem and see this thing that has taken place, which the Lord has made known to us." [16] So they went with haste and found Mary and Joseph, and the child lying in the manger. [17] When they saw this, they made known what had been told them about this child; [18] and all who heard it were amazed at what the shepherds told them. [19] But Mary treasured all these words and pondered them in her heart. [20] The shepherds returned, glorifying and praising God for all they had heard and seen, as it had been told them.*

As Christmas approaches, the story of the shepherds and the birth in the manger should bring back memories of Christmas seasons past. For what seemed like a very long time, I attempted to conjure up images from some of these memories. Frankly, I was surprised at how few formed clearly in my mind. I remember no Christmas before my mission to Germany! There is a faint memory of a red rubber fire engine. Leonard was given one, and I demanded the same gift. The memory is so dim that I suspect I may remember being told about fighting Leonard for "gift equality."

There is a faint memory of Christmas with Phyllis and her family in Vermont. Mr. Cox read from the Bible (or maybe from the poem, "Twas the Night before Christmas"). I think the Cox tradition was to cut or buy a tree Christmas Eve, and decorate it that night.

There are some vague memories of good times at Canyon Ranch with Sallie Ann, but not specifically memories of Christmas Day or anything religious. I must have skied a few times over Christmas while I lived in Colorado. More recently, I can remember Sallie Ann's first husband at Christmas dinner, not really a religious experience!

Why does the story of the shepherds feel so ingrained in my psyche? My guess is that many inchoate memories exist in my disheveled memory bank, all of them very pleasant. The Bible stories, whether wise men or shepherds or frankincense and myrrh, all run together. I mentioned something to Monsignor Brennen on the first Sunday of Advent about this being the first Advent I can remember focusing on *as Advent*!

Intentional experience, like anything else intentional, is simply a different form of experience. For most of my life, most experiences came and went without intention. I was there, but I was not present. That cannot possibly be true! But it is. I sit with this sadness and frustration for some time.

Earlier today, after playing tennis, I worked with Sallie Ann, sending pies and cakes to various friends for Christmas. It was a truly wonderful experience. She always sets up a wrapping station, where she wraps gifts every day, beginning right after Thanksgiving and ending late on Christmas Eve. She listens to Christmas music. Colorful bags and packages line the walls all around the table, which holds paper, ribbon, scotch tape, labels, and everything else necessary for a commercial wrapping program. When I think about it, Sallie Ann's annual wrapping station *is* my abiding Christmas memory.

Mirabai Starr was quoted by Father Rohr in his meditation today:

   The all-powerful truth of the Trinity is the Father, who created us and keeps us within him.
   The deep wisdom of the Trinity is our Mother, in whom we all are enfolded. The exalted

goodness of the Trinity is our beloved Lord: We are held in him and he is held in us. We are enclosed in the Father, we are enclosed in the Son, and we are enclosed in the Holy Spirit. The Father, the Son, and the Holy Spirit are enclosed in us. All Power. All Goodness. All Wisdom. One God. One Love.

Reading this brings back such powerful memories of listening to her speak, both in New Mexico and on a CD I listened to during a recent walk. Mirabai is a poet, a modern mystic, and a joy to be around. I love the concept of being enclosed by the Trinity, just as each of us encloses the Trinity. It is a powerful image of non-dual consciousness.

I am occasionally struck with how seldom our lives are filled with laughter. It is not that we are sad or melancholic, just that we have limited occasions to giggle. Few of our friends here in Ponte Vedra Beach are particularly funny. Sallie Ann and I have not been overly filled with mirth during this fall dominated by health issues. Yesterday and today, however, we laughed long and hard as we ordered cakes and pies, ran errands, and visited with Father Frank. I wonder if we are alike or different from other couples our age. It is hard to know how often and how much people laugh. Of course, the worst way to cause laughter is to suggest that we laugh. I suspect one key to laughing more is surrender; to give up the self-conscious effort to "look cool." During this week of rejoicing, it also helps to focus on the source of joy. I am listening to a Christmas playlist including Pentatonix, the Mormon Tabernacle Choir and Handbell Ringers, and the Brooklyn Tabernacle Choir. This music does not produce laughter, but I am certainly filled with mellow joy.

I pray for consciousness. I pray for memory. I pray for presence. I pray in gratitude for joy.

December 14

Repeat Luke 2:8–20, the Shepherds and the Angels

SALLIE ANN learned Monday that her gall bladder surgery would be tomorrow, Thursday, December 15. Laparoscopic gall bladder surgery is a very common, and generally very safe, procedure. Dr. Thomas Austgen, the surgeon who repaired my double hernia last summer, will operate on her.

I am reminded of an amusing story involving gall bladders. In the summer of 1974, I ran an apartment management company in Biloxi, Mississippi. One of our projects was a large complex owned by a surgeon. The doctor and I met with the Prudential Insurance Company, which held the mortgage on the property, which was in default. Prudential proposed a revised loan schedule that would require payments far greater than what the apartments could generate. When the doctor agreed to the new schedule, I asked if he had lost his mind. He answered that there was nothing to worry about, the payments required him to remove only three more gall bladders a week!

Sallie Ann is certainly not laughing about her pancreas and gall bladder issues. She is now sixteen pounds down from her weight prior to the pancreatitis. She is too thin, and continues to eat very little, fearing that something will trigger another bout of the very painful pancreatitis she experienced three months ago.

We went to the Advent Penance service last night. The Sacrament of Reconciliation, as Confession is now known in the Catholic Church, is one of my favorites. While I am not totally convinced that the priest has any supernatural power to grant me absolution, I am persuaded that the act of vulnerably admitting to a sin in the presence of another person has great healing power. It is important that the person hearing the confession grant absolution, regardless of any authority or power. If nothing else, absolution is a recognition of the vulnerability of the confessor.

The Ignatian Examen is a similar daily program of inventory, confession, seeking help, and making amends. I am not familiar enough with other Wisdom Traditions such as Buddhism and Islam to know whether this element is present, but I would not be surprised to learn that it is.

These thoughts on penance took me far afield from the shepherds and the angels described in Luke's Gospel. Their role was to bear witness to the good news of the birth of the long-promised Messiah. No inventory. No confession.

There is an interesting connection, however, between, on one hand, willingness to be vulnerable, to see with clear and honest eyes our defects, and, on the other hand, the powerful reminder of the incarnate Christ of our intrinsic goodness. Father Rohr reminded me of that this morning in his meditation.

> What you do to the other, you do to yourself; how you love yourself is how you love your neighbor; how you love God is how you love yourself; how you love yourself is how you love God. *How you do anything is how you do everything.*
>
> Faith is not simply seeing things at their visible, surface level, but recognizing their deepest meaning. To be a person of faith means you see things—people, animals, plants, the earth—as inherently connected to God, connected to you, and therefore, most worthy of love and dignity. That's what Jesus is praying for: That you could see things in their unity, in their connectedness.

Behind, inside, and beneath my flawed container, there is an extraordinary creation. That creation is my true self. It is permanently connected to my Creator, and to all the rest of creation. Yes, my true self is worthy of love and dignity, just as are all the people and things I have treated with disrespect and unkindness. Every person and everything that I objectify; that I see as "I, it," demands that I recognize them as subjects, "I, Thou." The shepherds used different language, but they were announcing the Good News of I, thou!

I pray for the wisdom and understanding to truly, deeply, honestly see the Other as subject. I pray for forgiveness for the people, places, and things I have treated as objects.

December 15

Matthew 2:1–12, The Visit of the Wise Men

[1] In the time of King Herod, after Jesus was born in Bethlehem of Judea, wise men from the East came to Jerusalem, [2] asking, "Where is the child who has been born king of the Jews? For we observed his star at its rising, and have come to pay him homage." [3] When King Herod heard this, he was frightened, and all Jerusalem with him; [4] and calling together all the chief priests and scribes of the people, he inquired of them where the Messiah was to be born. [5] They told him, "In Bethlehem of Judea; for so it has been written by the prophet:

[6] 'And you, Bethlehem, in the land of Judah,
are by no means least among the rulers of Judah;
for from you shall come a ruler
who is to shepherd my people Israel.'"

⁷ Then Herod secretly called for the wise men and learned from them the exact time when the star had appeared. ⁸ Then he sent them to Bethlehem, saying, "Go and search diligently for the child; and when you have found him, bring me word so that I may also go and pay him homage." ⁹ When they had heard the king, they set out; and there, ahead of them, went the star that they had seen at its rising, until it stopped over the place where the child was. ¹⁰ When they saw that the star had stopped, they were overwhelmed with joy. ¹¹ On entering the house, they saw the child with Mary his mother; and they knelt down and paid him homage. Then, opening their treasure chests, they offered him gifts of gold, frankincense, and myrrh. ¹² And having been warned in a dream not to return to Herod, they left for their own country by another road.

I AM SITTING in the waiting room at Baptist Beaches this morning, waiting for Sallie Ann to be taken in for her gall bladder to be removed. While the venue does not lend itself to quiet reflection, the event contributes a solemnity to the morning that works quite well. Sallie Ann is very nervous, more so than a laparoscopic procedure would suggest. This whole business with the pancreatitis, the weight loss, and the constant testing has taken its toll.

All of the stories in the Bible about Herod make it quite clear that he was, to say the least, an unpleasant fellow. Even as I write this I am reminded that there were several Herods in the Jesus story. This Herod, called Herod the Great, died not long after the birth of Christ. His sons, Herod Antipas and Herod Archelaus, followed him in villainy.

Herod the Great's secret meeting with the wise men, hoping to learn from them exactly where and when Jesus would be born, anticipated one of the worst stories in the whole Bible, the killing of the young boys in and around Bethlehem. It is unfathomable to imagine that the greatest event in history could be accompanied by infanticide!

My reflection on the visit of the wise men gives me little joy this morning. On the one hand, the story evokes the happy image of a bright star guiding wise men from the East to the birthplace of the new king of the Jews. On the other hand, it is a story about an evil king, envious of a child that might fulfill a prophecy. How often are evil and good so close together? How often does an ostensibly innocent, even solicitous welcome, mask a murderous intent?

I am reminded again of the penance service last night. Good and evil are precariously close to each other in so much of what we do, and what we are tempted to do. Our moral task is to discern between that which takes us closer to God and that which takes us away from God. Infanticide is an obvious example of an action going in the wrong direction. So are the actions of Herod Antipas, killing John the Baptist, and condemning Jesus to death, putting the question to the mob.

While I could say that evil is always lurking nearby, I can also take the view that amazing goodness is ever present. Both statements are true. Which aspect of truth do I choose to see? Clearly, the choice I make from one moment to the next determines how I feel about my life and its purpose. It can be said that a major task of discernment is not just choosing the better course, but *seeing* the good option in all of life.

The news out of Syria this morning reminds me of the colossal failure of our modern, civilized world society. In this season when people all around the world are preparing to celebrate peace and love and the birth of a new Messiah, a few thousand homeless, devastated, war-shocked residents of Aleppo are trying to get out of the way of the civil war in Syria. In a now-classic photograph, it looks like every last one of the people fleeing the bombs is trapped in one block of one street, lined with the shells of buildings that seem to defy gravity. How could this be happening today? How could this kind of carnage coexist alongside conferences on peace and love and transcendental meditation? The picture was taken earlier this week, a week that at our parish, like many others, began with a breakfast with Santa for the children.

In this third week of Advent, I am struck with the bounteous opportunities to find joy in life. There is sadness as well. Antonio and Daniel reported this morning that Tomas, one of the elders in Mamey, died during the night. These deaths of the elders in Mamey will only increase in number as the years go by. We have been feeding twenty-seven men and women each day since September, 2013. When we began the feeding program, most of the elders were in their sixties, but not in great health. Now, coming on to the fifth year, death will be commonplace in the village. While it is sad, especially for family left behind, it is obviously expected. The truly difficult deaths are those of the young, like Anabel and Margarita's sister.

My own feelings about death remain as complicated today as they were when I reflected on my own death earlier this fall. Father Rohr touched on my deep conviction this morning:

> We are sons and daughters of heaven and earth—both at the same time. Much of the work of enlightenment is to allow these two identities to coexist, just as Jesus did. For [Father Rohr], it is the core of Christian faith.

Not only are we "sons and daughters of Heaven and earth—both at the same time," we are also, in a sense, experiencing both life and death at the same time. We exist now as part of creation, just as we have for almost 14 billion years, and just as we will for all of eternity. Death does not mean that we cease to exist, only that we exist in a different form.

It is entirely appropriate for me to consider Meister Eckhart and John of the Cross and Teilhard and Merton as my teachers *in the present tense* because they are here with me now. They have conveniently left evidence of their presence in the form of their wonderful writing, and the writing of so many others who, like me, have learned from them. The teaching, the teachers, the learning, and all those who have learned, exist together now and for all time, here and everywhere. That is the incomprehensible quality of infinity and eternity.

Understanding this will not make me less sad when my loved ones die, nor make me miss any less those of my close friends who have already died. Death separates us physically, however much we may be united in the deeper reality of the universe. When I feel closest to my friend Buddy Tudor, who died in 2010—when I am laughing and talking with him in my mind—I feel a twinge of sadness that I cannot hug him, or kiss his balding head. But he is no less real for that, nor does my melancholy shake the certainty of my understanding.

My only prayer today is one of gratitude that Sallie Ann is home and sleeping comfortably.

December 16

Repeat Matthew 2:1–12, the Visit of the Wise Men

THE SACRED Sound choir used our front hall for their weekly rehearsal last night. It was surreal. Sallie Ann was upstairs in bed. Maggie was impounded in Cesar and Rosa's house. Every room on the first floor was rocking out to the somewhat contradictory sounds of Catholic rock and roll.

After reading again the account of Herod the Great and the wise men, I tried to sort out the timing of Herod's infanticide. Doing so caused me to learn more about this troubled man, who successfully brought charges against three of his sons, then had them killed. Why is he called Great? While I am sure there are valid historical reasons for the title, my surmise is that his greatness was largely the result of the major construction projects he completed during his reign. This causes me to reflect on the greatness of other leaders, such as several of the Roman emperors, Napoleon, Lincoln, and more. Many great builders are remembered as great leaders, primarily because they leave behind permanent changes on the face of the planet, even though history has a way of destroying much that was once considered permanent.

Lincoln's greatness was not his building program, but rather the impact of his decisions to free the slaves and to wage war to preserve the unity of the country. Oddly, Ulysses Grant is not remembered for his actions to implement Lincoln's policies, which he did rather well. History seems to have forgotten Ulysses Grant and Andrew Johnson because of the actions of Rutherford Hayes, who engineered a compromise in 1877 that effectively ended Federal enforcement of civil rights in the South.

Why am I thinking about that today? I am very afraid that we are about to witness a massive reversal in policies in this country, policies that were put in place over a half century for the benefit of the poor, the sick, the young, the aging, the climate, and even for gun safety. As recently as 1970, a Republican President, Richard Nixon, presided over the creation of the EPA, approved price and wage controls, and strongly advanced the civil rights agenda of Lyndon Johnson. Since the ugly end of Nixon's second term as President, the right wing of the Republican Party has been patiently chipping away at the social safety net, income redistribution, and regulatory checks on capitalism that had finally been put in place. However, until the election last month, this relatively solid structure was held in place by a very slim majority of the voters in about twenty states. On November 9, 2016, we awakened to right wing Republican control of more than 30 state legislatures and governor's mansions, the House, the Senate, and the Presidency. With that control, the Supreme Court will have a right-wing majority within three months, when the seat of Antonin Scalia is filled.

The next four years could see a massive change in virtually every aspect of our society, economy, and political system. My fear is that this change will be like the reversal in policies that occurred in 1877, when everything accomplished by the bitter, tragic Civil War was turned on its head. In politics, voter suppression and the role of big money will grow, allowing for changes in other areas to become permanent. In the economy, taxes on the rich will go down, safety-net benefits to the old, poor, and ill will be pared back, and the global barriers that have come down over the past thirty years will once again be erected. Finally, in the social area, the rights of gays, Muslims, immigrants, and women will be eroded.

There is no doubt that slavery left the ugliest stain imaginable on the history of the United States, a stain that remains today. The Electoral College will select Trump as our 45th President, even after he lost the popular vote by more than two million votes. I have often argued that the Electoral College is simply a reflection of the relative weight of the rural population of the country in 1870, compared to the urban population. Sadly, slavery played a major part in the logic behind the Electoral College. The framers of the Constitution made several distasteful concessions to the slave states, including, significantly, the allocation of Congressional seats and Electoral College votes. Direct election by the people would have favored the states with the largest populations, which, even then, included the industrial states of the North. Thus, both Congress and a directly elected President would eventually oppose slavery.

> The Convention tied presidential electors to representation in Congress. By this time the Convention had already agreed to count slaves for representation under the three-fifths

compromise, counting five slaves as equal to three free people in order to increase the South's representation in Congress. Thus, in electing the president the political power southerners gained from owning slaves (although obviously not the votes of slaves) would be factored into the electoral votes of each state.

By the time the three-fifths rule was finally abolished, Jim Crow policies had effectively limited the power of the former slaves at the ballot box. How can anyone understand this history and nonetheless continue to support these vestiges of such a troubled time?

What does this have to do with the wise men? Well, really nothing. Consider this a rant, not a reflection. It is sincere. My fear is real. I pray that I am wrong.

Now that Sallie Ann has had a good night's rest, Maggie has been allowed back into the house. She has assumed her position next to me in meditation, both in the library and in the garden. I dressed warmly, but still shivered under a sunny sky as the cold wind blew up the lagoon. The statue of St. Francis, nestled in the bushes below the meditation bench, worked to calm my troubled soul. Maggie's search for lizards helped as well. The problems of the world have so little to do with this tiny this patch of earth, and this insignificant moment in time. Reflecting on that fills me with joy.

December 17

Review and reflect on the week.

WHAT A BIZARRE week this has been! I returned from tennis feeling on top of the world, feeling all the joy from "playing" with my friends on the playground, basking in the sun on a cool day with no moisture, and hitting the tennis ball uncommonly often and well! Pope Francis turned 80 today, celebrating, as he typically does, by inviting eight homeless people to join him for breakfast. There are not enough words to describe this Pope's importance to my faith.

I started my reflection this morning re-reading the prayer for this week. "You lived with both the little and the great." Pope Francis is truly living like Christ. Perhaps the best line in the prayer, however, is this:

Teach me to rest easy where You are.

This is simple, clear, and very challenging. Teach me to rest easy where You are. I repeated it again and again, both in the library and down at the bench. Then I read through my journal for the week, which does not reflect a great deal of "resting easy"!

I have meandered through Roman and US history, questioned my memory, and explored my death. Somehow, scriptural passages about the wise men, the shepherds, and various angels have triggered far-ranging thoughts and memories.

Now, just two weeks before Christmas, I want to walk again with Joseph and Mary along the banks of the Jordan River. I checked "the Google" for the weather in Jerusalem today, learning that it is similar to the weather we are enjoying in Ponte Vedra, sunny, but a little cooler. Accordingly, we were dressed lightly, knowing that as the sun climbed higher in the sky and we warmed our bodies by walking, the day would be hot. Joseph and I talked about his feelings when he learned that Mary was pregnant with the Messiah.

Full disclosure compels me to admit that Deacon Dan and I will present an interview between Joseph, played by Deacon Dan, and an interviewer, played by me, at all five Masses this weekend. So my conversation with Joseph along the river this morning followed the interview I would be reading tonight and tomorrow. Dan has written or found a realistic idea of what an interview would have involved. When asked how he felt to learn his betrothed was pregnant, Joseph answers the way most men would answer today, in angry shock. Mary was somewhere around fourteen years of age, only one year older than our twin granddaughters! It is inconceivable for me to conceive of Alexis or Alison being pregnant, or even thinking about boys! In my fantasy this morning, however, I had to consider my reaction if one of my granddaughters not only announced she was pregnant, but followed it with a story about an angel, and being "overtaken by the Holy Spirit." As a grandfather, I would be in shocked disbelief. As a betrothed, expecting to marry this young virgin when she came of age, I would have been bitter in my disbelief. What kind of old fool did she think me to be?

Talking to Joseph this morning, I tried to stay away from the topic of his young wife's pregnancy. We discussed his role as a carpenter, making things with his hands. We talked about his pride in this ability to create things and solve practical problems. I pushed him a little on how he felt about having to leave Nazareth and walk all the way to Bethlehem, only to register and pay taxes to support the Romans. He was not as interested in politics as I, no surprise!

I sat for a long time with the image of Joseph, Mary, and the donkey on the bank of the river. I prayed that I might be "easy where Christ was," that I might be comfortable in the knowledge of what was to come at the end of this Advent season. I thanked God for the joy that I feel at the end of this wonderful week. I thanked Him that Sallie Ann was healing.

CALENDAR WEEK FOURTEEN

I want to know, to love, and to follow Jesus Christ.

Lord Jesus Christ, How intimately You desired to know us, starting among us as an infant, leaving nothing out. Your love ties You to us—even when some among us drive You away into all kinds of exile. But You just keep coming back to Your saints and holy ones. Lord, I say yes to Your being here housed in our flesh.

From Father Frank: Generosity

December 18

Luke 2:22–38, Jesus Is Presented in the Temple

²² When the time came for their purification according to the law of Moses, they brought him up to Jerusalem to present him to the Lord ²³ (as it is written in the law of the Lord, "Every firstborn male shall be designated as holy to the Lord"), ²⁴ and they offered a sacrifice according to what is stated in the law of the Lord, "a pair of turtledoves or two young pigeons."

²⁵ Now there was a man in Jerusalem whose name was Simeon; this man was righteous and devout, looking forward to the consolation of Israel, and the Holy Spirit rested on him. ²⁶ It had been revealed to him by the Holy Spirit that he would not see death before he had seen the Lord's Messiah. ²⁷ Guided by the Spirit, Simeon came into the temple; and when the parents brought in the child Jesus, to do for him what was customary under the law, ²⁸ Simeon took him in his arms and praised God, saying,

²⁹ "Master, now you are dismissing your servant in peace,
*   according to your word;*
³⁰ for my eyes have seen your salvation,
³¹ which you have prepared in the presence of all peoples,
³² a light for revelation to the Gentiles
*   and for glory to your people Israel."*

³³ And the child's father and mother were amazed at what was being said about him. ³⁴ Then Simeon blessed them and said to his mother Mary, "This child is destined for the falling and the rising of many in Israel, and to be a sign that will be opposed ³⁵ so that the inner thoughts of many will be revealed—and a sword will pierce your own soul too."

³⁶ There was also a prophet, Anna the daughter of Phanuel, of the tribe of Asher. She was of a great age, having lived with her husband seven years after her marriage, ³⁷ then as a widow to the age of eighty-four. She never left the temple but worshiped there with fasting and prayer night and day. ³⁸ At that moment she came, and began to praise God and to speak about the child to all who were looking for the redemption of Jerusalem.

MY MORNING reflections were interrupted by attending Mass three times to join Deacon Dan in presenting the homily, which was a little skit about St. Joseph. We did it last night at Mass and will do it again this evening. The idea was to present information about the man whose young betrothed suddenly announces she is pregnant, then tells a long story about an angel giving her the news that she was to be "overtaken" by the Holy Spirit. In our account, Joseph was understandably angry and hurt about the pregnancy and completely disbelieving regarding Mary's story of its cause. As the interviewer, I raised skeptical questions about all the angels, those appearing to Mary and Elizabeth, and, especially, the angels appearing in Joseph's dreams telling him to accept the whole thing: Mary, her story, and the child. It was fun, and also enlightening for me. Among other things, I was not aware that the last time Joseph is seen or heard of in the Bible is the day when Jesus is presented at the temple. He must have died sometime during the next fifteen or twenty years, otherwise he would certainly have been present, like Mary, during the ministry of Jesus.

After the third morning Mass, the parish presented a bit of a lunch for Father Santhosh, who is leaving Ponte Vedra to return to his native India. He is the genuine article, humble, funny, and easy to love. He will leave on January 5, flying to Cochin, in Kerala State. I visited there when I worked for Coastal. We were considering a power plant at the Cochin Refinery, at that time one of the largest in India.

I read from a little book called *On Suffering*, a collection of short sections of various writings of Teilhard. He writes with greater power than anyone else I read. The translations of his sentences are invariably long, but the poetry comes through nonetheless.

> Every individual life, if lived loyally, is strewn with the outer shells discarded by our successive metamorphoses—and the entire universe leaves behind it a long series of states in which It might well have been pleased to linger with delight, but from which it has continually been torn away by the inexorable necessity to grow greater. This ascent in a continually sloughing off of the old is indeed the way of the cross.

I think of those "metamorphoses" in my life in which I "might well have been pleased to linger." Doing so reminds me of the many unfinished tasks along the way. What might I have accomplished had I remained a coal miner in West Virginia? Or a free market pioneer focused solely on the former Soviet republics? Or a loyal corporate CEO at Coastal? I could go on and on. Discarding each of those "shells" forced me to grow. Perhaps I was only devising new facades to hide the inner me and project a new image to the world. As the song goes, "regrets I have a few."

After reading the passage from Luke's Gospel a second time, I walked down to the bench with Maggie. It was a balmy 67 degrees on this fourth Sunday of Advent, one week before Christmas. There seem to be more birds than usual. I sat with two strong images: Simeon and Anna. What had the child Jesus done to alert the two of them that he was the promised Messiah? Was there some kind of aura, even at that early age, that caused these two people of faith to see the future of Jesus' life? Or, and this made sense to me, was there something about the faith of these two people that allowed them to see what others could not see? The account says nothing about Jesus reading scripture better or differently than other young children being presented that day. He performed no miracles. The spiritual event occurred not in the child, but in Simeon and Anna. They performed the miracles of seeing and prophesizing.

Father Frank asks us to consider generosity this week, obviously, a good thing to do in the days leading up to Christmas. I am struck once again at how impressive Sallie Ann's wrapping table is, and how extraordinarily generous she is every year. Presents, each one carefully chosen and beautifully wrapped, have gone out to more than a hundred people. As usual, I have not begun. I take some solace in the fact that Sallie Ann gives from both of us to all family members, and all our mutual friends. That still leaves Sallie Ann for me. If this year follows the normal course of things, I will ask her what she wants later in the week!

December 19

Repeat Luke 2:22–38, Jesus Presented in the Temple

IT WAS VERY dark this morning when I went down to the bench. Maggie wasted no time searching the bushes for lizards. I spread a towel on the bench to cover the dew, which nonetheless soaked through to my pants. This garden is simply spectacular in the morning darkness. The overcast sky lightens almost magically (I see no sun). The sound of the ocean waves breaking against the beach are louder than I remember them to be. Otherwise, the still point. I cannot stop myself from dancing. I do not want to. Joy overtakes my soul, filling me with an amazing appreciation of all the abundant good in my life right now. The longer I sit with this joy, the more difficult it is not to simply burst open, inviting all around me in as I cast aside this new shell.

Teilhard wrote:

> The only true death, the only good death, is a culminating outburst of life: It is the fruit of a desperate effort made by the living to become more pure, more stripped and bare, more taut as they force their way out of the zone in which they were imprisoned.

This captures so beautifully how I feel this morning. The energy of the darkness becoming light and the roar of the ocean silence are indeed an "outburst of life." The restraints of whatever outer container I have occupied until this very moment are loosened. I die and am reborn in the joy of this glorious day.

It seemed like an hour had passed before I walked back along the rill to the library. And it is only Monday.

December 20

Matthew 2:13–18, The Escape to Egypt and Massacre of the Infants
¹³ Now after they had left, an angel of the Lord appeared to Joseph in a dream and said, "Get up, take the child and his mother, and flee to Egypt, and remain there until I tell you; for Herod is about to search for the child, to destroy him." ¹⁴ Then Joseph got up, took the child and his mother by night, and went to Egypt, ¹⁵ and remained there until the death of Herod. This was to fulfill what had been spoken by the Lord through the prophet, "Out of Egypt I have called my son."

¹⁶ When Herod saw that he had been tricked by the wise men, he was infuriated, and he sent and killed all the children in and around Bethlehem who were two years old or under, according to the time that he had learned from the wise men. ¹⁷ Then was fulfilled what had been spoken through the prophet Jeremiah:

¹⁸ "A voice was heard in Ramah, wailing and loud lamentation,
Rachel weeping for her children; she refused to be consoled, because they are no more."

TENNIS IN December and January at the Ponte Vedra Racquet Club is simply one of the greatest joys of my retirement. It is frankly something I would never have predicted, nor would anyone who played tennis with me for the first twenty years that I attempted to play the game. It is tempting to say that I play a much better game than ever, which is probably true. But it is not the whole story. I was asked to join this particular group of tennis players eight years ago, when Serendipity was under construction. They asked me to play not because of my skill, but because I was about a decade younger than the average age of the group! Now, at seventy-two, I am still younger than the average, which is about eighty, even though a few have finally retired. I look good next to some of these players, especially those having great difficulty walking!

I play tennis most Tuesdays, Thursdays, and Saturdays from 7:30 until 9:00 in the morning. When I return to the library and bench after tennis, I am invigorated and happy, both of which contribute to the quality of my meditation. Once, when I was speaking at an energy conference in Belgium, one of the other panelists excused himself for a run between the end of the day's meetings and the cocktail party. He arrived at the party less than an hour later, looking fantastic and filled with energy. As impressed as I was at the time, I never followed his example. I think about that on tennis days now, realizing, a little late, how closely related our physical, mental, and spiritual conditions are. Today was bitterly cold and humid, with a biting wind coming out of the north. However, we were all dressed for the weather, and the joy of playing far exceeded any discomfort caused by the cold wind.

There are two stories in the passage from Matthew's Gospel today, the flight to Egypt and the infanticide of Herod. I have already reflected on the extraordinary evil of Herod the Great. His infanticide, on learning that a "King of the Jews" had been born in the Bethlehem area, is simply beyond comprehension.

Of course, there are two stories in Exodus about infanticide. In the first chapter of Exodus, Pharaoh orders the killing all of the male babies born to Hebrews. That story ends much better than it begins, with apparently no killing actually taking place.

> The king of Egypt said to the Hebrew midwives, one of whom was named Shiphrah and the other Puah, "When you act as midwives to the Hebrew women, and see them on the birthstool, if it is a boy, kill him; but if it is a girl, she shall live." But the midwives feared God; they did not do as the king of Egypt commanded them, but they let the boys live. So the king of Egypt summoned the midwives and said to them, "Why have you done this, and allowed the boys to live?" The midwives said to Pharaoh, "Because the Hebrew women are not like the Egyptian women; for they are vigorous and give birth before the midwife comes to them." So God dealt well with the midwives; and the people multiplied and became very strong.

The second story appears in the eleventh chapter. Inexplicably, to me, God Himself is the perpetrator. Frankly, I think the story is ghastly. Its metaphoric value is lost on me.

> Moses said, "Thus says the LORD: About midnight I will go out through Egypt. Every firstborn in the land of Egypt shall die, from the firstborn of Pharaoh who sits on his throne to the firstborn of the female slave who is behind the handmill, and all the firstborn of the livestock."

To the best of my knowledge, there are virtually no historical examples of mass infanticide. Obviously, whenever genocide occurs, children are killed along with adults. The Holocaust is an obvious modern example, along with the genocidal wars in Africa that continue today. Aleppo and other cities in Syria and Iraq are tragic examples of brutal genocide, where bombs and bullets do not distinguish between combatants and non-combatants or adults and children. But these are not the odious intentional killing of newborn boys ordered by Herod. This is a crime without equal in the history of mankind.

How can history accord Herod the title of Great? Herod killed three of his sons, but other despots, including Renaissance Popes, have been accused of killing their children. I am not saying this to suggest in any way that filicide, the killing of one's children, is permissible. Among the great evils of hereditary power is the temptation to influence the order of succession with murder.

I put myself in Bethlehem, father to a one-year-old boy. My wife and I were so proud of our son, who was getting closer each day to walking and talking and blabbering in the way that all young children do. As a practicing Jew, I knew about the prophesies in Isaiah and Micah. In fact, this child born to Mary was not the first to be announced as the Messiah. I suppose what gave it greatest credibility this time was the order by Herod to kill the little boys.

We were desperate to get our boy out of Bethlehem, but Herod had spies throughout the community. Worse, every household in town with a son was attempting to do the same thing we were doing. It seemed as though the soldiers were moving up the street as fast as the rumors. Two of Herod's men literally broke our door down, swooping into our one room, shouting as they knocked our table over. They took our son. As we watched, along with other parents up and down our street, the soldiers brutally beheaded the boys. There are simply no words to describe the horror. Even in my fantasy this morning, I wept.

Rachel weeping for her children; she refused to be consoled, because they are no more.

"Because they are no more." I sat with that, wondering how any human being could ever do anything so evil. Herod was an old man. He would be dead within only a few years of this awful night. Why would he order such a horrendous crime? Then I am repelled by my own effort to find some reason behind Herod's actions. I weep with Rachel, because the children are no more.

I pray for peace. I pray for the people fleeing Aleppo today, and for the children of Syria, Iraq, Rwanda, Burundi, and the Congo. I pray for the truly awful soul of Herod.

December 21

Repeat Matthew 2:13–18, the Escape to Egypt and the Massacre of the Infants

GENEROSITY comes naturally to Sallie Ann. While her wrapping table is a signature tradition of the Christmas season, her wrap room was a design requirement for Serendipity. In addition to counter space for the actual wrapping, the wrap room has racks for rolls of wrapping paper, drawers for all the ribbons and paraphernalia, and a separate closet with shelves for gifts. She is constantly giving something to someone. It is an endearing trait. She sometimes complains that gift giving sets up a circular guilt, which obligates exchanges of gifts with near strangers. Scarcely has she uttered the complaint, however, than she is off to the wrap room for something creative.

I, on the other hand, do not participate in the process. David Brinkley was famous for the way he wrapped gifts. Perfect corners and no mess. I wrap essentially the same way I shuffle cards, which is so poorly coordinated as to defeat the effort. I am generous about some things. I tip well. I remember the service people in our lives, those who regularly wait on us in stores or park our cars or send our packages. In the years since I retired, I have been generous to a fault in respect of charities we support.

Sincere generosity needs to be anonymous, something that our world of instant communication makes difficult. I am always impressed when the stranger in the car in front of me at Starbucks pays my bill, a practice that noticeably increases during the Christmas season.

I am again reminded of my favorite line from Meister Eckhart:

The eye through which I see God is the same eye through which God sees me.

True generosity begins with *seeing* the Other in a different way, perhaps seeing with that spark of the divine inside each one of us. John of the Cross said something similar to this in *Ascent of Mount Carmel*:

The soul that desires God to surrender himself to it entirely must surrender itself entirely to him without keeping anything for itself.

I want God's presence each morning during meditation. I want Him to see me, to give Himself to me just for this moment. To be seen by God, I must see God. To receive God's surrender to me, I must surrender myself entirely to Him. I sit with these thoughts for a long time before returning to the passage from Matthew's Gospel.

While I am still deeply troubled by Herod, I want to enter into a fantasy about the flight of the Holy Family to Egypt. There are two reasons I find this fantasy relatively easy.

First, on several occasions during my life (but definitely not now!), I have been quite unencumbered by things. That is, I owned little more than I could rather easily fit into the trunk of my car. As I mentioned earlier, when I entered the coal business in 1974, I was able to move from Biloxi, Mississippi, to a trailer in Delbarton, West Virginia, over a weekend. My daughters lived with their mother in Denver. I was living alone in an apartment in Biloxi. I had few friends, no commitments, and measured my future plans in days, or even hours. Like the Holy Family, I could simply get up and go. Something like this freedom existed when I left Denver for Beverly Hills in 1972, the difference being that I left my home, my wife, and my family. (Reflecting on this makes me very sad. It had been the complete opposite of generosity, seeing and thinking about only myself in a moment of total self-interest.

Sidi Krir, a power plant that we owned outside of Alexandria, Egypt, is the second reason it is easy for me to fantasize the flight to Egypt. I remember the desert simply ending at the edge of the sea. Even in 2003, with a certain amount of industrial development, the land seemed barren and desolate. I can imagine the Holy Family feeling safe in this place.

Herod the Great died in 4 BC, suggesting that the Egyptian exile lasted at least four years. In my fantasy, there was an active Jewish community in Alexandria, allowing Joseph and Mary to participate in all the traditional ceremonies. The Jewish Quarter in Alexandria, several miles to the east of the area where Joseph settled, had flourished for more than three hundred years, and become a center of ancient scholarship. I allowed my love of libraries to put Joseph in a group of carpenters working on bookshelves for the famous Alexandria library. The young Jesus would occasionally accompany his father at work, thus gaining exposure to scrolls and manuscripts from a very early age. Since it was my fantasy, I allowed the boy to learn through osmosis!

On one of my visits to our power plant at Sidi Krir, I learned of the flourishing, distasteful, and phony tourist trade surrounding the tradition of the Holy Family stay in Egypt. How can anyone believe that any of the sites shown on the tourist map were actually visited by the Holy Family during the four or five years they were in exile? In fact, the Egyptian exile is only reported in Matthew's Gospel. In Luke's Gospel, they return from Bethlehem directly to Nazareth. Even if the account in Matthew's Gospel is the correct version of history, it is highly unlikely that the infant Jesus performed any of the miracles claimed by the tour guides. This commercialism is a sad reality for most of the historic sites all around the world, particularly when true believers have the opportunity to virtually canonize a place or relic.

What is fact is the mass emigration of Jews, presumably including the handful who were attracted to the "Christian sect," from Israel to Egypt in the years following the sack of Jerusalem in 70 CE at the end of the Roman war. However, it is a virtual certainty that most Christians who were "out" in the period prior to 313 CE, when Constantine made Christianity the official religion of the Empire, spent most of their time in hiding. About that time, near the end of second century CE, early Christian monks went out into the Scetis desert south of Alexandria. One of the three earliest monasteries is still in use. These are delightful places to visit, in part because they make no fantastic claims. Some of the early writings of the Desert Fathers are wonderful introductions to Christian mysticism.

After allowing my mind to wander a bit through ancient Egypt, I returned to my reflections on the story in Matthew. However comfortable the Holy Family might have been in Egypt, it was not home. Mary missed her cousin Elizabeth, and longed to return to Israel. The temporary nature of their Egyptian home only added to their fear of being discovered by Herod's spies.

I sat with the image of the difficult life Joseph and Mary had. While the world has celebrated the birth of Jesus for two thousand years, the circumstances of Mary's pregnancy and the difficulty of the trip to Bethlehem and birth of the child in a manger were hardly happy events at the time. On top of all that, the sudden flight to Egypt, living in fear for years, and trying to adjust to a community in exile must have been extremely hard, particularly for a new mother barely fourteen years old.

Angels were a big part of the story before the birth of Jesus. I wonder if there were any angelic comforts extended to the family during the long years of hardship. I pray in gratitude for all the luxury in my life, even in the worst times. I am grateful for the opportunities I have had to travel to the Holy Land, Jordan, and Egypt. In fact, I miss my career. I not only visited the world's most interesting places, I was actually there to do something with and for the local communities. All in all, it has been a great life!

December 22

Matthew 2:19–23, The Return from Egypt

[19] When Herod died, an angel of the Lord suddenly appeared in a dream to Joseph in Egypt and said, [20] "Get up, take the child and his mother, and go to the land of Israel, for those who were seeking the child's life are dead." [21] Then Joseph got up, took the child and his mother, and went to the land of Israel. [22] But when he heard that Archelaus was ruling over Judea in place of his father Herod, he was afraid to go there. And after being warned in a dream, he went away to the district of Galilee. [23] There he made his home in a town called Nazareth, so that what had been spoken through the prophets might be fulfilled, "He will be called a Nazorean."

YESTERDAY was the Winter Solstice, the darkest day of the year. The darkness has made this a perfect week to be reading John of the Cross. In the early, very dark hours before I left the library for tennis, I reflected more on generosity, which led me to the journey into the dark night described four hundred and fifty years ago by this wonderful Spanish mystic.

> Our journey toward God must proceed through the negation of all. One should remain in emptiness and darkness regarding all creatures. He should base his love and joy on what he neither sees nor feels—that is, upon God who is incomprehensible and transcendent....

The less they understand the further they penetrate into the night of the spirit. They must pass through this night to a union with God beyond all knowing.

God: Incomprehensible and transcendent. Moreover, John of the Cross urges the *negation of all* so that God becomes even less understandable. When we have reached *nada*—nothing—we finally penetrate the darkness and have a chance to achieve union with God.

Will Robbins is here for Christmas. As he has in years past, he played with us this morning, to the delight of my tennis crowd. It was dark, cold, and great fun. At one point in the morning, we realized that four liberal Democrats were on the court at the same time! This is virtually impossible in Ponte Vedra. In the first place, there may not even be four Democrats, and, if there were, they would never be found in the same place. It would cause the Governor to call out the National Guard! Maggie was waiting impatiently to join me in the library to resume our meditation.

Matthew's account of the return of the Holy Family from Egypt opens the messy box of Herod family politics. When Herod the Great died in about 4 BC, he was succeeded by his two sons, Archelaus and Antipas. Archelaus initially claimed to be the ruler of all Palestine. Antipas challenged the will. After some time, Caesar divided the kingdom, giving Archelaus the larger southern area, and Antipas, Galilee in the north. Of course, in that role, Antipas would later kill John the Baptist and preside over the crucifixion of Christ. It is hard to imagine a worse world into which Christ could have been born!

In my fantasy, I returned from Egypt with the Holy Family. We initially planned to return to Bethlehem in Judea, but were warned to stay away until the dynastic in-fighting was resolved. There was a certain amount of angelic confusion. Angels play an enormous role in the early life of Jesus. Not only did an angel tell Mary that she was to become the mother of the Messiah, and tell her cousin Elizabeth that she would be the mother of John the Baptist, but an angel told Joseph to be cool with the whole arrangement. Now, an angel brings the news that it is safe to return to Judea. What puzzled me is that the angel apparently had it wrong! Joseph was warned by friends that Judea was not safe.

Thus, we traveled north to the Galilee, settling in the little town of Nazareth. Frankly, while all of the land on both banks of the Jordan River was arid and rocky, I liked the cooler weather and quiet of Galilee. Nazareth was a tiny community. Everyone wanted to know about our travels in Egypt. I did not tell them any tall tales about the infant Jesus performing miracles!

I prayed with gratitude for this time in my life, when I can devote my mornings to reflection, meditation, exercise, and tennis with friends. I am grateful for the parish community and the opportunities Sallie Ann and I have to serve in so many ways. As I reflect on all of this, I am aware of this wonderful ball of black hair curled up at my feet. I am deeply grateful for Maggie, who has made every day of the past eight years better through her loyalty and dedication.

December 23

Repeat Matthew 2:19–23, the Return from Egypt and Massacre of the Infants

THE MORNING at the bench was once again cold and dark. The ocean was loud as waves angrily broke on the beach. It was truly a reflection in the dark about the Dark Night of the Soul, seeking that "negation of all" that leads to union with God. Strangely, I was overcome by joy.

Reflecting on the return of the Holy Family from Egypt, I considered a young boy, probably about five years old when his father was told by the angel to return to Israel. While I am a total failure with respect to any memories of my own youth, I know people, including Sallie Ann, who have quite clear pre-school memories. Jesus was old enough to remember growing up in a distant land, probably listening to Coptic Arabic in the streets. Greek was still commonly spoken in Alexandria, and schools in the Jewish quarter used Hebrew. Alexandria was the second largest city in the Western world at that time, behind only Rome. It had the largest Jewish population outside of Israel.

The boy Jesus returned to Nazareth, a tiny community of only 500 souls, where Aramaic was the language in the streets, and Hebrew the language in school. Alexandria must have been a real shock to the child bride Mary, who presumably never left her home before the journey down to Bethlehem, then the flight to Egypt. I sit with questions about the impact on a small child of these significant relocations during the first five years of his life. Was he too young for it to matter, or would the disruption have been even greater? And if his mother suffered from the journeys and the relocation, what kind of impact would that have had on the young Jesus? I assume that disruption and relocation are events that have the capacity to either build character or create disorder. The man Jesus would become certainly showed no signs of childhood distress!

I am excited about Christmas. These Exercises are an excellent way to prepare for the spiritual impact of this otherwise painfully commercial time of year.

December 24

Repeat and reflect upon the week.

SAINT JOHN of the Cross fills my meditation space, as he has every day of this dark week. I reflected more this morning on the impact he has had on my developing faith. When the Living School put both his *Dark Night of the Soul* and *Ascent of Mount Carmel* on the reading list, I read a little of the sometimes-thick prose, then put the books down. I simply did not understand. A Jesuit friend recommended that I start with *The Impact of God* by Iain Matthew. Matthew's book was literally transformative for me. I have been reading it again this week. He writes:

> The Gospel has eyes—"the eyes I long for so," John calls them—and the point comes on the journey where the bride meets those eyes which had long been looking on: "It seems to her that he is now always gazing upon her." It is a moment of exposure, as she finds herself a factor in another's life and heart… *It has been said that "a person is enlightened," not "when they get an idea," but "when someone looks at them."* A person is enlightened when another loves them. The eyes are windows on to the heart; they search the person out and have power to elicit life… Christianity is an effect, the effect of a God who is constantly gazing at us, whose eyes anticipate, radiate, penetrate and elicit beauty.

I love the idea that we become enlightened when someone looks at us. It is something I often see in Sister Parish, both in the missionaries and in the villagers. Matthew makes the repeated struggles of John of the Cross into special graces from God. Over time, I returned to John of the Cross, whose writings began to resonate with me. I think this was so because my own history has been one of repeated ascents out of dark nights, each time struggling with the challenge of surrender. John of the Cross writes:

> This dark night is an inflowing of God into the soul… The fire begins to take hold of the soul in this night of painful contemplation…. The understanding is in darkness…. The soul enters the night of spirit in order to journey to God in pure faith, which is the means whereby the soul is united to God.

The growth of my faith over these past five years has been amazing, even though not perfectly pure from a doctrinal perspective. My goal, by now I hope quite obviously, is to become and remain "united to God" so completely that I can lose myself in God. My darkness is only occasionally lit by the fire of pure faith, but I am increasingly in the faint light of a spiritual dawn or dusk, sensing His proximity.

The role of the Exercises becomes clear when I read and reflect on what John of the Cross says about contemplation.

> The first and principal benefit caused by the arid and dark night of contemplation: The knowledge of oneself and of one's misery…. Faith is a dark night for man, but in this very way it gives him light.

I sit with the words, "faith is a dark night for man, but in this very way, it gives light." This is true for me. Part of the darkness of my faith is the daily battle I wage against it. Skepticism and disbelief are my companions. Five years ago, I fought against the traditional doctrines—the virgin birth, the miracles, the angels, Heaven and Hell, and virtually every story in the Bible.

That battle continues today, but is, to some extent, complicated by my "new understanding" of God. Or perhaps the battle is made irrelevant. He exists only in and as a relational activity (a verb), joining in the Divine Dance as an outpouring of love. I love this beautiful understanding. I can get my head around most of it, most of the time.

Then I start to question the "rule of three," the need to add Christ and the Holy Spirit to the Dance. That feels forced to me, as though we are trying to fit the Biblical Trinity into a quantum physics concept. I struggle with efforts to read the Scriptures as actual history. I resist the whole concept of Canonization. I fight authority.

However, when I am down at the bench, a flight of pelicans will often swoop down over the lagoon in perfect unison. My disbelief evaporates in the beauty and precision of creation in that moment.

As I concluded my prayer this Christmas Eve morning, I listened to the news from Aleppo, Syria. It is a story of extraordinary sadness, one that provides lessons for all sides of several different arguments.

Maggie and I walked down to the beach, allowing me to reflect on Aleppo, refugees, Syria, Muslims, and the whole range of issues that come up when I see pictures of the tragedy underway this "holiday season." My thinking remains as conflicted today as it was so many years ago, when President Obama drew a solid red line in the sand.

Some years earlier, I humorously embarrassed myself with my ignorance of the situation in the Middle East. Several of our older Jewish friends had the idea that I was well-read on the subject of the Middle East generally, and on the dictators in the region particularly. Much later, we saw many of these friends at the wedding of the daughter of another good friend. They asked me over to their table and put the question, "What should be done about these terrible despots in the region?" I answered rather arrogantly, "I don't worry much about them. After all, they are rather long in the tooth. Look at Hafez Asad, who must be close to 80 years old." One of the men at the table said quietly, "Bob, Hafez

Asad died five years ago. His son has been in power since 2000." I have not been asked to comment on Middle Eastern affairs since then.

After that unhappy night, I visited the region several times during my years as CEO of Globeleq. We unsuccessfully bid on the privatization of the Jordanian national power generation company in 2005, and looked at new power plant opportunities in Saudi Arabia and Iraq. The Islamic Infrastructure Development Fund, whose office was in Bahrain, invested in our Bangladesh power company, requiring me to meet with them in Bahrain several times. By the time of the self-immolation of Tunisian street vendor Mohamed Bouazizi in December, 2010, I had once again immersed myself deeply in the current affairs of the area.

Robin Wright, a journalist and scholar with a long history in the Middle East, came to Jacksonville to speak to the World Affairs Council in 2012, shortly after publishing her book *Rock the Casbah*. My introduction of Robin at the University of North Florida remains one of my favorite (and shortest) speeches. I opened with a quote from the Persian mystic Rumi: "Out beyond ideas of wrong doing and right doing, there is a field. I will meet you there." Then I said, "Robin Wright has spent much of her life reporting from that field, talking often and with respect to all sides of every question. She invites us to meet her there this evening, to listen openly and without judgement."

I was personally excited and optimistic about the Arab Spring. There were several tragic consequences of that spring of hope, including the complete failure of all the nascent revolutionary efforts to achieve positive change. Many of us miss the real news of thwarted reform movements and ugly military actions. Our news has been filled with the politics of a Benghazi witch hunt, and the ostensibly poor decisions of Hillary Clinton in Libya. It is easy to say today that Libya would have been better off with Gadhafi, but many well-informed and wise people agreed at the time that the coalition effort to depose him was the right decision. I was a reluctant supporter. Obama clearly had mixed feelings, but was finally persuaded by a broad coalition that included our NATO allies and the Arab nations.

However, the greatest casualty of the Arab Spring is Syria. Bashar Asad used his government troops to resist the protesters, who rapidly became armed rebels. Like every other conflict in the region, the Sunni/Shia split among the Muslims had a major impact on the evolution of the skirmishes of 2011 into a full civil war in 2012. That civil war continues to this day. Asad is Alawite Shia, supported by Iran and its puppet militia, Hezbollah. The rebels are primarily Sunni, supported financially and with weapons by Saudi Arabia and other Sunni neighbors.

Obama generally took the side of the rebels, partly because Asad was a despotic ruler, and partly because there is a strong US bias against Iran and Iranian-backed efforts. However, the two strongest and most prominent terrorist organizations in the world, Al Qaeda and ISIS, are Sunni. By 2012, Al Qaeda was largely defeated, its few remaining leaders forced into hiding in Pakistan. ISIS had not yet emerged as a power, though the remnants of Saddam's Sunni military officers in Iraq had fled to Syria and were already organizing. Our failure to take action in Syria would benefit both Al Qaeda and ISIS.

When reports came out that Asad was using chemical weapons, Obama made his tragic declaration that proof of chemical weapons would mean a "red line" had been crossed. Something bad would happen to Asad if that happened. It was generally believed that the rebel groups were not yet under the control, or even significant influence, of the terrorists. Many smart people argued that the US should arm and otherwise support these "moderate rebels," and that some kind of decisive military action should result from Asad crossing the red line.

Obama chose to do nothing. He regards the situation in Syria as the greatest foreign policy failure of his term as President. I was opposed to military action at that time. I thought both Iraq and Libya had been stupid mistakes, and that any form of military engagement in the Middle East was foolhardy. Broader public opinion, however, was, at best, divided on the issue. Obama's failure to enforce the red line became a very easy target for his political opponents.

Over the four years since then, more than 400,000 people have died as a result of the Syrian civil war. Millions of refugees have fled to Turkey, Iraq, and throughout Europe. Both Al Qaeda and ISIS have become active participants in the fighting in Syria. Russia and Iran have entered the conflict. In other words, it is now a complete mess. Stronger words could be used.

Aleppo is the poster child of everything that went wrong in Syria and the broader Middle East. The news this morning is that Asad's forces are fully in control of the city, a city without citizens or infrastructure. There is no way to adequately describe the hopelessness of the situation. Trump threatens on one hand to cancel the Iran nuclear agreement and engage them militarily wherever they are active, which certainly includes Syria. On the other hand, however, Trump is playing footsy with Russia, and has strongly opposed the "regime change" efforts of both Bush and Obama. So where do we go from here? Sadly, I suspect Syria, like other parts of the world, will join the general slide into (or reversion back to) totalitarian rule. The battle between Sunni and Shia states will continue. The poor, the sick, the aged, and the children will all continue to lose on a scale that the world has not seen for decades. This is a spiritual crisis as much as a global power struggle. I read the news and weep.

John of the Cross teaches us to empty ourselves completely, making space for God's love, which He is pouring out to us. Creating that space requires that we achieve *nada*, nothing.

> To come to savour all
> Seek to find savour in nothing;
> To come to possess all,
> Seek possession in nothing,
> To come to be all,
> Seek in all to be nothing....
> To come to what you know not
> You must go by way where you know not
> To come to what you are not
> You must go by a way where you are not.

To John of the Cross, God is an approaching God. Our main job in life is not so much to *achieve* as it is to create a place to *receive* the constant outpouring of His love.

Advent comes to an end today. Tomorrow we enter Holy Week. In spite of the election in this country and the events in Syria and elsewhere in the world, it has been a memorable Advent, truly pregnant with anticipation. I pray for peace.

CALENDAR WEEK FIFTEEN

I want to know about how Jesus lived, thought, and acted. I want to stand under His standard, and to live out of His value system.

Lord Jesus Christ, You came to do the most important work anyone will ever do on this earth. When You got here, You just waited for long years patiently obeying parents and clients. You lived a family life in an ordinary town, You labored and prayed and rejoiced among friends. You seemed to do nothing important at all. Lord, teach me to see things as you see them. Teach me to value things as You value things, and myself, and my friends, and God above all.

From Father Frank: Gratitude

December 25

Luke 2:39–40,51–52, The Return to Nazareth
[39] When they had finished everything required by the law of the Lord, they returned to Galilee, to their own town of Nazareth. [40] The child grew and became strong, filled with wisdom; and the favor of God was upon him.
[51] Then he went down with them and came to Nazareth, and was obedient to them. His mother treasured all these things in her heart.
[52] And Jesus increased in wisdom and in years, and in divine and human favor.

JOHN OF THE Cross is still with me today. A line in his *Living Flame* reminded me powerfully of Christmas. I walked down to the bench and silently repeated this again and again in the beautiful early morning air.

> The Father spoke one word, who was his Son, and this word he *is always speaking* in eternal silence. It is in silence that the soul must hear it.

God has always spoken Christ, is speaking Him now, and will forever speak Him. The Word, the Son, Christ, and God Himself are all love. It is an eternal love, best listened to in silence. This is a powerful concept today.

I sat in *silence* as I reflected on Luke's account of the Holy Family returning directly to Nazareth from Bethlehem, not going to Egypt as reported in Matthew's Gospel. Like all of the other inconsistencies and otherwise difficult passages in the Bible, whether the Holy Family visited Egypt or not will not influence my faith. "Otherwise difficult" passages are not simply those that are inconvenient to me, though I clearly find it extremely "inconvenient" to believe in anything exclusionary or unforgiving. I believe quite a lot of the belief system of "literal Christians" (or literal Muslims or Jews) consists of inconsequential noise, events, and statements that, whether true or not, do not change the core principals of their personal faith. I also believe much of the noise is simply tribal nonsense designed solely to exclude others.

I believe in the universal, infinite, and eternal presence of God as Divine Love, in a universe moving inexorably, but painfully slowly, toward union in and with that Divine Love. I believe in the value of making choices every day that bring me personally closer to that union, eschewing choices that take me further away. I experience encounters with God on a regular basis, each of which fills me with indescribable joy. I love the community of God's creation, and experience joy whenever I truly, intentionally, see and relate to His creatures, whether my fellow man or my beloved Maggie. I am enlightened when others see me. Frankly, that is a lot more than I have ever believed in my life!

I have been reading the year-end reviews of the news and events of 2016, the extraordinary year that cannot end soon enough for me. When I studied architectural history, and later, when I had the opportunity, I tried to visit the places where that history was created. I wanted to visit Syria, both for Palmyra and Baalbek. Sadly, it never happened. The ancient city of Palmyra was on my list of "must see" sites, both for the truly ancient ruins of the Temple of Bel, and for the more recent additions of the Romans under Hadrian. In 2016, ISIS fighters took great delight in destroying the historical monuments in Palmyra. ISIS retook control of the city on December 11, which is why it was again in the news. But the damage was done over the past two years. It can never be undone. Sad.

While the differing account of the early travels of the Holy Family are a little disconcerting, I do value the description of Jesus and His relationship with His mother.

> [He] was obedient to them. His mother treasured all these things in her heart. And Jesus increased in wisdom and in years, and in divine and human favor.

Obedient and increasing in wisdom. That is high praise for any young person (or even those of us in our seventies!). I doubt there have been many periods in my life when this could be said about me. Obedience is not the first thing anyone would think about when my name is mentioned!

I sit with the conclusion of verse 52, "increased…in divine and human favor." People seemed to like this young man more and more over the years. That must have been true. Consider the swift reaction of the men He called to be with Him as disciples, or the size of the crowds that gathered to hear Him speak. Everything we read about Jesus suggests that He was a humble, quiet, steady person. He cared for people in the margins—the poor, sick, and sinning. He enlightened people by seeing them. Of course, He "increased in favor" in the eyes of His Father, and in those of the people around him.

I pray for peace this morning, in the world and in my life. I pray for forgiveness.

December 26

Repeat Luke 2:39–40,51–52, The Return to Nazareth

GENERALLY, we are told by psychologists and sociologists, the Christmas season is not a happy time of year. Expectations are sky high. Perfectionism afflicts those hosting guests, young and old. Broken families come together for the holidays, inevitably bringing with them reminders of why they are broken. I realized last night that my depression this year goes much deeper than the normal Christmas anxiety. The polarization in the world, this country, and my small community is very troubling, and very powerful. Events in the Middle East are seriously disturbing, with my old friend Bibi Netanyahu threatening to join the new Trump team and officially end any hope for long-term peace. The transition to a new government is seriously not funny. Policies and values that I had assumed were by now deeply ingrained in this country will be gone, simply gone, before I end the Exercises in May.

It is important that I be clear that I do not hate or despise the right wing of the Republican Party, or Likud and the extreme right wing in Israel, or Austria, France, the Philippines, and elsewhere in this global sea change. Especially here in Ponte Vedra, people who enthusiastically support positions one hundred and eighty degrees away from mine are my truest, closest friends. I am not just making noise when I say that I love them.

However, when the full agenda of the ideological far right is fully in place, everything that I have believed in, worked for, and respected for my entire life will be in the trash pile. Much of the program of the Diocesan Justice and Peace Commission, which I chaired, will be history. High quality public education, from pre-kindergarten through college, will only be available to those who can afford it. Medicare, which provides excellent health care for old people, rich and poor alike, will be weakened. Social Security, which provides the only financial support millions of Americans live on in old age, will be weakened. Voting rights will be suppressed without risk of Supreme Court correction. Efforts to address climate change will be stopped, and likely reversed. Gun safety will be redefined as universal weapon possession. The global barriers to the movement of ideas, people, capital, and goods, which have been coming down for decades, will once again be erected. Rights of minorities, whether religious, ethnic, sexual, or whatever, will suffer. Worse, due to gerrymandering, money in politics, and voter suppression, the very process of government will make these changes permanent.

Many of my conservative friends, especially in my church community, care about these things. They sincerely believe that robust economic growth, which they believe lower taxes and less regulation will achieve, will increase the size of the pie such that all lives everywhere will be better. Government action to redistribute wealth will be unnecessary because the lives of the poor, the aging, the mentally ill, the addicted, and everyone else in the margins will benefit from the trickle down of all this new wealth. Education and health care will be better when the government role is reduced.

Could I have been wrong all along? Have my efforts been futile, or worse, have they made lives poorer? There are no good answers to these questions. If, on one hand, I was making progress, it will have been in vain. If, on the other hand, I have been wrong all along, I have simply wasted much of my life. Again, this morning, I sit in despair.

Last night, Sallie Ann and I watched the 1946 movie, "It's a Wonderful Life," with James Stewart. Stewart's character lives a plodding life in a small town, struggling to make a modest living by helping his community. The Great Depression, World War II, and the villainy of the town's most wealthy man combine to bring the hero down, leading him to attempt suicide. An "angel second class" (no wings!) is sent by God to save our hero. We were both weeping at the end.

Christmas Day began well and got better by the hour. I dressed in bright red pants to read at the 11 a.m. Mass, then met a woman so anxious for the opportunity to read that I stepped aside, allowing her to read in my place. Sallie Ann and I then went to what has become a traditional Christmas Day Open House at the home of our good friends, Chip and Alison Keller.

Why do I fill my journal with this mundane news? As I reflect on the value of Christ in my life, the two concepts of *encounter* and *community* emerge as absolutely fundamental. For the four hours that we were in the company of the young children, the beautifully mature young adults, the incredible forty-year-old parents, and, finally, the other grandparents like us, we were enfolded in an encounter of community. Mind you, we were the only Democrats in the room! But labels did not matter in a house full of love, laughter, and generational joy. The impact is still with me.

One of my Christmas gifts was *Jesus*, a little book written by Hans Urs von Balthasar. Balthasar, who died before the ceremony that would make him a Cardinal in 1988, devoted the first twenty pages of this book to a full-throated defense of Scripture as the essential core of faith in Christ. He made sense, which, of course, completely upsets my long resistance to the central role of scripture. I read the chapters again this morning before turning to the inconsistency of Luke and Matthew's Gospel regarding the travel schedules of the Holy Family. I have to acknowledge that Father Rohr also regards Scripture as a critical leg in a three-legged stool of faith.

While I intend to read Scripture with a more open mind, I do want to point out that both Father Rohr and Balthasar cite Scripture as the key defense of Scripture. The circularity of this logic is not lost on me.

Once again, the important part of this passage from Luke is not the account of the trip directly to Nazareth (as opposed to a flight to Egypt), but rather the final verse, describing the growth of the boy Jesus into a man.

> [He] was obedient to them. His mother treasured all these things in her heart. And Jesus increased in wisdom and in years, and in divine and human favor.

Obedience, wisdom, and maturity lead to divine and human favor. I prayed with these thoughts forefront in my mind. Surrender, acceptance, and obedience are all goals for the new year. One of my Living School friends posted this beautiful poem by the Chaplain of Girton College, Ayodeji Malcolm Guite. It is one of his daily prayers for Advent, published in 2015 in the book *Waiting on the Word*.

O Sapientia

I cannot think unless I have been thought
Nor can I speak unless I have been spoken
I cannot teach except as I am taught
Or break the bread except as I am broken.
O Mind behind the mind through which I seek,
O Light within the light by which I see,
O Word beneath the words with which I speak
O founding, unfound Wisdom, finding me
O sounding Song whose depth is sounding me
O Memory of time, reminding me
My Ground of Being, always grounding me
My Maker's Bounding Line, defining me
Come, hidden Wisdom, come with all you bring
Come to me now, disguised as everything.

This is marvelous. It speaks to me this morning after Christmas. I pray for the wisdom to surrender to "the light that is within the light by which I see."

December 27

Luke 2:41–50, The Boy Jesus in the Temple
⁴¹ Now every year his parents went to Jerusalem for the festival of the Passover. ⁴² And when he was twelve years old, they went up as usual for the festival. ⁴³ When the festival was ended and they started to return, the boy Jesus stayed behind in Jerusalem, but his parents did not know it. ⁴⁴ Assuming that he was in the group of travelers, they went a day's journey. Then they started to look for him among their relatives and friends. ⁴⁵ When they did not

find him, they returned to Jerusalem to search for him. [46] After three days they found him in the temple, sitting among the teachers, listening to them and asking them questions. [47] And all who heard him were amazed at his understanding and his answers. [48] When his parents saw him they were astonished; and his mother said to him, "Child, why have you treated us like this? Look, your father and I have been searching for you in great anxiety." [49] He said to them, "Why were you searching for me? Did you not know that I must be in my Father's house?" [50] But they did not understand what he said to them.

I WENT DOWN to the library to meditate this morning after playing tennis in the foggy, misty cold. Fog brings out the quiet in silence. It wraps me closely, but in a chilly blanket.

I read and reread the verses from Luke, trying to put myself in the place of a twelve-year-old boy going to the big city for a festival. I wondered whether I would notice, or care, if my parents left without me. Would my interaction with the teachers have been so intense that I would be oblivious to the absence of my family for three days?

Interestingly, my initial reaction to this passage was a memory from my "coming of age" as a Mormon in Idaho. Mormons ordain young men into the Aaronic priesthood at the age of twelve, the same age Luke tells us Jesus had obtained when He entered the temple. There must certainly be a connection between the Mormon practice and this story about Jesus.

Jews celebrate Bar and Bat Mitzvahs at this age, but this ceremony did not exist at the time of Christ. However, many cultures and religions do have a "coming of age" ceremony. I read that Inuit boys go out into the wilderness with their fathers at age twelve, young Apache girls and boys became adult in elaborate ceremonies, and young Maasai in Kenya and Tanzania join the "warrior class" around this age. The point is simply that our bodies transition through the physical process of puberty at about this age, so it is entirely logical for there to be a cultural, ceremonial recognition of the change. Frankly, traditional cultures probably managed this much better than we do today. Odd how easily I can chase my thoughts down rabbit holes!

My ordination as a priest in the Aaronic priesthood meant, among other things, that I could serve the bread and water at the weekly Sacrament service. My memory of this is very warm and positive. I took great pains to wear a clean shirt and properly tied necktie. My recollection is that I was more fastidious about this than others, or, at least, that any effort to encourage me to dress well was pushing against an open door. It is no wonder that sixty years later, I am pleased to serve as a Lector, and that I am careful to dress well. I suspect there are many other ways the man could be seen in the boy.

The question Jesus puts to His parents is interesting. "Did you not know that I must be in my Father's house?" Why did Jesus seem to know about His ultimate ministry at age twelve, then withdraw for another eighteen years before beginning that ministry? He returned to the temple in Jerusalem with His parents every year, all the while "growing in wisdom" and "growing in favor." It seems odd that this is the only mention of Jesus distinguishing Himself at the annual Passover festival.

What an extraordinary young adult Jesus must have been as an older teen or a young man in his twenties. I reflect on the many young men and women I have interviewed, hired, and trained over the years. They all had such fresh curiosity and enormous energy. Just working with them was like a youth serum or a shot of Human Growth Hormone! When I consider how much I fed off of the youthful excitement of my young associates, I wonder what people working around the young Jesus must have seen. Was He given greater and greater responsibility in His father's carpentry shop? Did He ultimately "make the sale" for a new house or piece of furniture? Was His charisma growing during His twenties, preparing Him to simply "say the word and my soul shall be healed"? If we knew more about Him then, would we be surprised that the disciples dropped their nets and left their lives to follow Him? I think not.

I ended the morning in a very long silence, then prayed the Our Father.

December 28

Repeat Luke 2:41–50, The Boy Jesus in the Temple

TODAY IS MY seventy-second birthday. Almost three-quarters of a century! Many days, especially during these early morning periods of contemplation, it feels like I have been around a very, very long time. One of the great Willie Nelson songs ends with a line:

> Excuse me for living and being forgiven, just go on if you wanna be free
> But the last thing I needed first thing this morning was to have you walk out on me.

Amazingly, for all the damage I have done in life, and how little gratitude I have shown, no one, but especially God, ever walked out on me. In fact, my life has never been better. My line each day is "excuse me for living so well, and being forgiven nonetheless!" In the words of the great theologian, Frank Sinatra: "Regrets, I've had a few, but, then again, too few to mention."

President Obama, reminiscing on his two terms as President yesterday, said something like, "It takes so little time to live a life." I think that is true. On birthdays over the last few years, I often focus on how much time has passed. In fact, however, what I mostly feel is how little time has passed, and how quickly it happened. Only yesterday used to be only yesterday.

Thinking about the relationship of a twelve-year old child with family and friends brings up images of the young people we know here at OLSS. I am struck with how much love seems to exist in the families that we see, all of whom are active in Sister Parish. Father Rohr wrote about love yesterday.

> But who of us can say we have really loved yet? We're all beginners. We're all starting anew every day, and we're failing anew every day. Loving as imperfect, egoic human beings keeps us in utter reliance upon the mercy, compassion, and grace of God. We can never fully succeed by ourselves.

The concept of starting anew each day is fundamental in most teaching. Progress is never measured in increments longer than twenty-four hours. We humans start each day with a fresh page on which to write a maximum of twenty-four hours of life. I would prefer to put a little credit in the time bank, maybe live today for the next week, then rest. Life does not work that way.

Father Rohr goes on to elaborate on the last sentence, "We can never fully succeed by ourselves."

> It seems God gave us a commandment that we could not obey. Perhaps this is so we would have to depend upon the Holy Spirit. This is the greatness, the goodness, the wonder, the impossibility of the Gospel, that it asks of all of us something we—alone, apart, separate—cannot do! Only by living in love, in communion—God in us and we in God—do we find, every once in a while, a love flowing through us and toward us and from us that is bigger than our own. And we surely know it's not "we" who are doing it!

Today I feel connected to the community of encounter that Pope Francis teaches us to create. The Medical Mission leaves for Santo Domingo two weeks from tomorrow, so work has already begun on preparations, both here in Ponte Vedra, and in the Dominican Republic. I never cease to be amazed at the joy I experience through this ministry. What a gift to receive in this phase of my life, and to recognize so clearly on my birthday.

Maggie and I walked for a long time on the beach in 74-degree sunshine! Good Lord, how I love this dog! She is something very profound, and deeply meaningful in my life. I talk to her as though she understands everything, and generally agrees with me as well! She fills me with joy.

I pray in gratitude for all of the gifts that a long life has lavished on me. I began anew this morning to be open to, and aware of the love that surrounds and fills me. Even if I only glimpse it for a moment, today will have been a day worth living.

December 29

The Standards and Norms of Jesus Christ

Jesus Christ's norms for action and values for judgment differ so starkly from all others that those others seem all the same when compared with His. So you put yourself to work, with God's help, asking what values move the world around you, what standards does it judge by, and what values and standards does Jesus use.

I come into God's presence and feel His loving gaze, and then I offer myself completely to God.

First, I recall for a second that I am going to think about sacred history. Here I just recall that St. John's Gospel keeps repeating how darkness fights against light, the Liar against Truth, and death against life. More important, Jesus Himself plainly talks about two kingdoms, fighting to the death. His teaching is that there are two titanic forces at work in the world, both driven from within to dominate.

Second, I compose myself in this embattled world. I could imagine Jesus Christ and His followers on a splendid green plain, with wonderfully colored pavilions and bright flags billowing in gentle breezes. And then I could imagine the Liar with his followers in a deep ravine, all greys and shadows with the air dead still. But I must not let this imaginary geography obscure the real geography. That shapes the heights and deeps of my own heart, where dark and light, evil and good, still battle.

Third, I ask God to give me the courage to see clearly the face of good and the face of evil. I ask Him to teach me to understand intimately the way the Mind of Christ works, and also the way people who have chosen only this life make their decision and value things.

FIRST PART

First, fantasize something that novels and films have portrayed: Here is a person totally depraved. Inside a roiling anger, keen desire to destroy, vicious hatred for life. Now, imagine that interior comes to the exterior: What will the person look like? How will the face change? the hands? the eyes and mouth? Well, that's what the Liar looks like, if you really see him.

Second, consider how the Spirit of Evil wishes to clasp every one to itself. Evil wants to elicit evil; it's like radioactivity: whatever it touches, it radio-activates and poisons. It's like the plague caused by a highly contagious virus; open yourself to living contact with a victim, and you have contracted the plague. Whether you believe in a personal Prince of Evil (as Jesus surely did) or not, you know that evil spreads itself.

But third, how about those who want to serve God and keep good? How does evil touch them? Consider this: Time is money, and with money you can buy anyone's time. Money means privilege, and the privileged can always get money. Money means power because you can simply buy what you want done, and the powerful are without exception rich and getting richer. The monied can buy the best health care, and indeed absolutely demand it. They require attention whenever they want it. They acquire authority whether they have inner worth or not. You have to recognize that the mechanisms of disorder among people are lubricated by wealth.

Well, the Prince of Darkness—who always works by deception and in the dark—gets at the good person through that reality. First, you acquire something and you say to yourself, "Look at what I have." Then you grow convinced that you are someone special because of what you have, and you start talking to yourself in these terms: "Look at me with all this stuff!" You have shifted your focus from all the stuff (for which you might at first have been grateful to God) to your own self. In time, you grow convinced that what you have, you have by right—you have in and of your own self the right to all this stuff and to a lot more. You now think of yourself this way: "Look at ME!" You have begun to grow into pride, which is the conviction that you can decide what will make you happy and what values you ought to serve. In the end you say, "Look at me! Listen to me! I have a right!" Up to this very point, you may have done nothing sinful, but you have utterly forgotten how all comes to you as a gift (Not came, but comes), and have grown convinced that you are the origin and source of your own values. Once the Prince of Darkness has led you to that position, you have no defense against any opportunity to sin, even deadly sin.

You may find it difficult to think about all this, but beg God the Lord to teach you how an evil spirit can get hold of good people.

SECOND PART

This requires less space and time.

First, imagine Jesus leading His friends. How does He command? Does He tell them the Truth? What gestures does He use when sending a friend on a mission? what tone of voice? He claimed to be a king—what kind of king?

Second, notice that He explicitly and publicly told His disciples that they were to go throughout the whole world announcing Good News. They are to help, always, the outcast, the poor, the imprisoned. They are to heal and to feed, to clothe and to house. They are to speak openly and to invite all to believe and repent.

Third, Jesus also has His program: First, invite each person to live as though all were gift and they owned nothing of themselves. Even when they are rich, invite them to live so as to show that all they have is gift. Then next, help them to treat privileges, honors, and fame as the smoke that they are. Help them to see that the only legitimate power is that exercised for the sake of serving those over whom it is wielded. Help them to see that a life of frugality and powerlessness, freely embraced, brings tremendous safety and gives great authority. Then, finally, they will come most securely to know that they are totally created, momently, from nothing, by God the Lord. They will live convinced that God sets their values for them and decides what will make them happy. So, they will have grown humble. Once humble, no temptation will throw them and they will live the Mind of Christ Jesus.

AT THE END

First ask our Lady to beg Jesus for these gifts for you: to be received under His standard, and to have the courage to buy into Jesus' value system wholeheartedly. Ask, if you can, that if God the Lord wants it, you will live a poor and obscure life, the way Jesus did, thought little of by the rich and powerful as He was thought little of. (In all this, of course, you would yourself want to do nothing to offend God, and you would want no one else to do anything that would offend God.) End with the Hail Mary.

Then ask Jesus Himself for the privilege of standing with Him under His standard. End by repeating the Jesus Prayer for a while.

Finally, turn to the Father and ask for these gifts. End with an Our Father.

WHEN I READ through this reflection last night, I tried without success to absorb it all as one piece. Reading it again this morning, I came up with several different themes, each of which could take a week or more to think through, reflect on, and note in this journal. As always, I find myself taking issue with elements of the reading that are probably accepted doctrine of the official church.

My initial "opposition" involves the very first major theme: All of creation is caught up in the dualistic battle between good and bad, light and dark, and right and wrong. Dualism, by its very nature, requires a choice of *either, or*, leaving no room for *both, and*. There must certainly be some issues that are completely cut and dried, with no doubt about which course to take, and no opportunity to compromise. In my experience, however, the list of these issues is much shorter than this passage would have us believe.

"Thou shalt not kill," for example. That seems very clear cut. But killing, perhaps the greatest sin, involves several shades of gray, including a just war, self-defense, and taking a life in order to save another. These nuances are debatable in virtually every case. St. Augustine's famous dictum has been used in some form to justify virtually all forms of "official violence."

> They who have waged war in obedience to the divine command, or in conformity with His laws, have represented in their persons the public justice or the wisdom of government, and in this capacity, have put to death wicked men; such persons have by no means violated the commandment, "Thou shalt not kill."

Of course, the definitions of *public justice, wisdom of government*, or *wicked men* are the Achilles feet of this argument. One man's public justice is another man's public injustice. Evil and wicked governors are incapable of governmental wisdom. All too easily, a wicked man is simply someone with whom I disagree. Nonetheless, there are clear atrocities committed by both individuals and governments. No nuanced theory of justice could ever validate Herod's infanticide.

As I argued earlier, another nuance in the admonition "thou shalt not kill" is the definition of life. Restating the commandment to say "thou shalt not kill a *viable human being*" would address my concerns with judging birth control and very early stage abortion in the same way as abortion after viability. Limiting the commandment to human beings might bother some Hindus who regard cows too precious to kill, but would be regarded by most people as an acceptable modification. Arguments about when a fetus is viable will continue, but most of the polarized bitterness of the abortion issue would disappear if the requirement of viability were accepted.

Augustine seems to be asking for a commandment that reads "thou shalt not kill viable human beings unless the government tells you to do so or the human being in question is wicked." Personally, I truly believe the death penalty should be off the table. Life in prison is sufficient punishment for any and all crimes. The Catholic Church opposes the death penalty. However, a very large number of Catholics, especially here in North Florida, are strong advocates of the death penalty.

I am generally opposed to all war. Retributive violence has been spectacularly unsuccessful throughout history. Again, however, the end of war is not likely anytime soon. The "just war" exception has been expanded to include "preventive war." In addition to traditional notions of war only between nation states, we now have a perennial "war on terror," which is used to justify drone strikes and commando raids against non-state actors. I oppose all of these organized methods of killing simply because they do not solve the problem. Drone strikes recruit terrorists more than they kill them.

Killing in order to save a life, say in the case of conjoined twins or a similar medical crisis, makes sense when all other options have been exhausted. Likewise, I can understand and accept circumstances where killing in self-defense is justifiable. However, I think every effort must be made to defend without killing.

The point of all this today is that dualistic thinking is thinking at a very low level of nuance and consciousness. Nuance applies to most other (and lesser) sins as much as it does to killing. There are circumstances that can at least partially justify lying, stealing, and most property crimes. It is much harder for me to see nuance in sins like pride, arrogance, and the objectification of others.

There is a deeper level to the argument about the powers of good and evil, one that originated in Persia in the third century CE called Manichaeism. The official Catholic position seems to be a rejection of the so-called heresy of Manichaeism. However, the wording of today's reflection is totally Manichean. Austin Cline writes:

> Manichaeism is an extreme form of dualistic gnosticism. It is gnostic because it promises salvation through the attainment of special knowledge of spiritual truths. It is dualistic because it argues that the foundation of the universe is the opposition of two principles, good and evil, each equal in relative power.

Fundamental Christians, including conservative Catholics, continue to live in and preach from a dualistic universe. Frankly, life is easier without nuance and paradox, where choices, events, and people all simply fall into one of two categories. In that universe, there is little need to study, discern, reflect on, or contemplate.

The Living School teaches that learning to live with paradox is a critical part of a maturing spirituality. It is important to recognize and hold on to the truth and value in both sides of arguments and issues. Of course, this requires that we recognize and acknowledge that there is, in fact, truth and value on both sides. This political season has required a great deal of soul searching on my part. Seeing the "truth and value" in many of the Trump positions is difficult, particularly when his positions change so often.

Even though Jesus references the Prince of Darkness, it seems to me that He saw both sides of many situations. The stories of the Samaritan woman at the well, dining with the tax collector, and healing the son of the Roman soldier are all examples of His willingness and ability to see "truth and value" in everyone. Yet the thought piece today suggests just the opposite:

> Jesus Himself plainly talks about two kingdoms, fighting to the death. His teaching is that there are two titanic forces at work in the world, both driven from within to dominate.

Can there ever be any truth or value in the positions of the "titanic force" fighting against the light, in favor of darkness? Is this not something so clearly evil that dualism is the only right way to think? When we use terms like "the Prince of Darkness," or the "titanic force of evil," the subtlety of nuance and paradox seem like relativistic cowardice. We have painted a universe of black and white, with no shades of gray. The temptation in such a world is to say that anyone with whom I disagree is part of that titanic force, serving under the Prince of Darkness. And that is precisely what we see in our present polarized world. Peace and justice require a much greater mental and spiritual effort. Quite simply, they require that we love our enemies.

I pray for clarity and understanding. I pray for the courage to make choices that bring me closer to God, and avoid those that take me away from Him.

December 30

Repeat the Standards and Norms of Jesus Christ

IT HAS TURNED bitterly cold (for Florida that is) overnight. Maggie and I walked down to the bench, but quickly returned to the library. I reflected on another part of the thought piece.

> Money means privilege, and the privileged can always get money. Money means power because you can simply buy what you want done, and the powerful are without exception rich and getting richer. The monied can buy the best health care, and indeed absolutely demand it. They require attention whenever they want it. They acquire authority whether they have inner worth or not. You have to recognize that the mechanisms of disorder among people are lubricated by wealth.

I am considering this passage in the warm comfort of a luxurious library, sitting just inside an extraordinary garden. My life has been richly blessed with all manner of experiences and relationships, but I have also become wealthy. Frankly, I have to agree completely with the final sentence: "[T]he mechanisms of disorder among people are lubricated by wealth."

Does wealth make it impossible to become one with God and to achieve unitive consciousness with all of creation? Is it just harder to get into Heaven, or is it impossible? I know, there is nothing wrong with having money as long as we use our wealth to benefit others. Or, as any good leader of a parish, school, or mission program will say, as long as we support those good causes. In fact, the worst thing that could ever happen to a church community would be for all of its members to be poor! In truth, I can only speak for myself. Having money has never been necessary for me to live as though I had money. In other words, I have always lived extremely well. I have never saved money, even though I have never had a credit card, overdraft, or debt problem. I have been fortunate enough to remain healthy and stay marginally ahead in the rat race, thus having enough "flash cash" to pay my bills and appear wealthy. To be sure, I am clearly still a piker in today's world of the super-rich, with multiple residences, planes, and yachts. I have only one residence, and have never "wanted" a second home or vacation house. I have never taken regular summer vacations, or established a holiday routine. My hobbies are reading and tennis, neither of which requires great wealth. Most of my travel has been related to business.

However, the wealth that I do have has allowed me to "buy what I want done," to have excellent health care, a warm bed, good food, nice clothes, and to "demand attention." In other words, it has been sufficient to separate me from much of the reality of life experienced by more than ninety-nine percent of the world's population. Again, though, I return to the question raised by the reflection piece, has the wealth been the source or cause of my sins? Has my wealth prevented me from growing close to God?

For me, the answer is clearly no, money has neither caused me to sin nor prevented me from encounters with the Divine. In fact, having a comfortable level of wealth has allowed me to support numerous causes and activities that have directly contributed to my connection with God. Sister Parish and the Living School are only the most recent examples of the value to which money can be put. Doing the right thing does require making some right decisions. Many, actually most, of the people I know with comparable or greater financial wealth have made very different decisions.

As I reflect on this, I am reminded of my dossier, the description of my early formation as a person, and of my parents and siblings. The decisions I have made as an adult result in no small part from the factors, both nature and nurture, that formed me. Just as I believe there is a "spark of the Divine" in each of us, I believe that our instincts to do good, and to value justice were planted deep within us at a very early age.

What are the essential standards and norms of Jesus Christ? I believe they are pretty clearly set forth in the Beatitudes, which are essentially only elaborations of the commandments to love God and our neighbor. Wealth and status are gifts from God, whether inherited from our families or acquired during our lives. In both cases, we play a very small role in the process. So, having or not having wealth and status is not the important issue. What is important is what we do with these gifts.

December 31

Repeat and reflect upon the week.

As has been the case all my life, these past seven days have included Christmas week, my birthday, and New Year's Eve. I cannot remember when this week last began on a Sunday and ended on a Saturday. The goal set out at the beginning of this week was to know how Jesus lived, thought, and acted. I wanted to "stand under His standard, and to live out of His value system."

One of the strange mysteries to me is the very little we know about how Jesus lived, thought, and acted in the long period between His visit to the temple and the beginning of His ministry, close to twenty years later. I have read that most young Jewish men during the time of Christ married and began a family when they reached the age of 18 to 20. In fact, the Hebrew scriptures are quite firm about this. Yet we hear nothing about the marriage and family life of Jesus. Paul mentions in 1 Corinthians 9:5 that most of the other Apostles, including Peter, and the brothers of Jesus were married. I know that the doctrine of the perpetual virginity of Mary precludes Jesus from having brothers and sisters, but it would have had no effect on the Apostles or the "cousins" of Jesus. I would not be surprised to learn that Jesus had a very normal life, including a wife and children. All of this seems appropriate to His full incarnation. Likewise, it seems quite possible that Joseph would have reached the age where he would have been counting on his son to carry on in a leadership position in the family carpentry business.

What kind of spouse, parent, child, and citizen was Jesus? These are four of the most important questions any of us needs to ask about ourselves. Living a full, meaningful, and righteous life requires solid effort in these four roles. The value system of Jesus must have included norms appropriate to these roles. It seems entirely sensible to apply the standard that has evolved out of the Exercises, which is to do that which takes us closer to God. I do not read this to mean that not being a parent is a sin, or that choosing not to marry takes one further from God. Frankly, both roles, parent and spouse, carry with them many opportunities to sin, which would be avoided for a single person with no children.

The "Jesus standard" would be that a person making the choice to marry, or making the choice to become a parent, should do so doing "the next right thing," which is to choose in the direction of God, not away from God. Of course, none of us can avoid the obligation to be a good son or daughter. Even in a situation of abandonment or the early death of one or both of our parents, there is usually someone who plays that role in our lives. The admonition to do the next right thing applies in all cases. I wish we did know more about this from the stories of Jesus and the Apostles. The older I become, the more I consider these family roles to be important. A life well-lived except for the way in which I acted as husband, father, and son is simply not a life well-lived. Most of the items on my "do over" list relate to these roles. Most of the amends I have had to make in my life are here as well.

The two great commandments of loving God and our neighbor apply to our families. Further, if we are only to apply the messages in the Beatitudes to these family roles, a standard of behavior becomes clear. Nonetheless, in a time when the family is under so much pressure, literally falling apart in much of the world due to violence and poverty, I would think it would be nice to have an excess of information about how to perform these crucial roles.

I sat with this for a long time this morning. My meditation slowly shifted into an "attitude of gratitude." More accurately, I thought about Father Frank. The weeks to contemplate the five words for the Advent season are now ending. It has been a very different Advent and Christmas, more faith-focused each day, if only because of the hour or so that I sit in prayer each morning. As I prayed this morning, I reflected on the amazing journey I have been on. This has been my sixth Christmas week as a Catholic!

Calendar Week Sixteen

I want to know what ideas and images filled Jesus' mind in the desert and in Jordan. I want to love the One who entertained them. I would then follow Him.

Lord Jesus Christ, You left behind You all power and security to embrace the terrible risks of loving God in all and loving all in God. You walked through every valley of darkness. You faced the full force of evil, so that You would know a way to lead us out of sin and death. No desert could dry out Your love for God. No selfishness could dry out Your love for us. Lord, show me Your way.

January 1

Matthew 3:13–17, The Baptism of Jesus

¹³ Then Jesus came from Galilee to John at the Jordan, to be baptized by him. ¹⁴ John would have prevented him, saying, "I need to be baptized by you, and do you come to me?" ¹⁵ But Jesus answered him, "Let it be so now; for it is proper for us in this way to fulfill all righteousness." Then he consented. ¹⁶ And when Jesus had been baptized, just as he came up from the water, suddenly the heavens were opened to him and he saw the Spirit of God descending like a dove and alighting on him. ¹⁷ And a voice from heaven said, "This is my Son, the Beloved, with whom I am well pleased."

ONLY YESTERDAY I reflected on my own baptism, six and a half years ago in Houston. While there was no voice from Heaven, I have this image of people in amazement all around the world! No one who knew me in 2006 could ever have guessed that I would begin a spiritual journey a year later, and be baptized by 2010. I would have been the last to predict it.

I have returned to the library after lunch to write these reflections, and am happy I did so. Today was one of those very Catholic Sundays that I knew nothing about most of my life. Reading that makes me quickly add that there was nothing exclusively "Catholic" about today. It was a warm, loving day, filled with family and community. Our being Catholic was the least important of all that we shared. Sallie Ann and I joined a young family with four children, and an unrelated grandmother, for lunch at Palm Valley Fish Camp. This is my favorite local eatery, with great food, fantastic service, and way too much noise for old men!

We sat at a long table with four stair-step children, aged ten down to less than two, all clean, all attractive, and all with nearly perfect manners. As impressed as I was with the children, I was even more amazed at how effortlessly the parents managed to simultaneously engage in spirited conversation, and deal with the normal requests of young children. The family has recently returned to Ponte Vedra from Japan, where he was stationed with the Navy. He and I talked at length about the US military, and about the US role in Afghanistan and Iraq, where he had served. The table and the day were filled with joy.

Maggie and I walked down to the bench after lunch. Today was one of those days that makes Florida a favorite place to live in the winter. The weather was perfect: Sunny, temperature in the mid-seventies, and no humidity. I am grateful to be alive.

January 2

Repeat Matthew 3:13–17, The Baptism of Jesus

AGAIN TODAY, the weather defies both description, and the concept of seasons. The sun came up over the ocean at 7:30, in cloudless skies, a mid-sixties temperature, and the unbelievably beautiful sound of waves breaking on the beach. Maggie and I sat in the dark for the first hour, listening to the sounds of birds and waves, which eventually became the "sounds of silence." Time went by so quietly that it took the rising sun to interrupt my reverie. Another day in paradise!

Baptism is a wonderful experience. Even the word evokes a sense of excitement, of a new beginning. I love to reflect on the idea that Advent was a time of pregnancy, followed by a birth, and then a baptism. My own baptism as a Catholic in 2010 followed an incredibly long pregnancy! In truth, my understanding of my life history involves many beginnings, each preceded by some kind of pregnant anticipation. There was, in each of these distinct phases, a "life cycle," in which the birth was followed by growth, life, a twilight period, and, finally, death. In my memory, most of the baptisms involved some form of shock or pain, a dose of very cold water introducing me to each new life. It is an interesting stretch to view my life as one long, single event, with but one beginning.

Sadly, the partisan polarization in this country did not come to a discernable pause with the election. President-elect Trump has selected a particularly feisty Press Secretary, whose daily rants are already truly tiresome, and the inauguration is still three weeks away. Again, these Exercises are vital to my sanity, as well as my experience of joy.

I pray for wisdom, judgement, joy, and peace.

January 3

Matthew 4:1–11, The Temptation of Jesus
¹ Then Jesus was led up by the Spirit into the wilderness to be tempted by the devil. ² He fasted forty days and forty nights, and afterwards he was famished. ³ The tempter came and said to him, "If you are the Son of God, command these stones to become loaves of bread." ⁴ But he answered, "It is written, 'One does not live by bread alone, but by every word that comes from the mouth of God.'" ⁵ Then the devil took him to the holy city and placed him on the pinnacle of the temple, ⁶ saying to him, "If you are the Son of God, throw yourself down; for it is written, 'He will command his angels concerning you,' and 'On their hands they will bear you up, so that you will not dash your foot against a stone.'" ⁷ Jesus said to him, "Again it is written, 'Do not put the Lord your God to the test.'" ⁸ Again, the devil took him to a very high mountain and showed him all the kingdoms of the world and their splendor; ⁹ and he said to him, "All these I will give you, if you will fall down and worship me." ¹⁰ Jesus said to him, "Away with you, Satan! for it is written, 'Worship the Lord your God, and serve only him.'" ¹¹ Then the devil left him, and suddenly angels came and waited on him.

HEAVY RAIN and lightning greeted us this morning as we prepared to go over to the tennis courts. Maggie braved the wet for her business, but the bench was out for meditation. We endured the "discomfort" of the library, one of my favorite rooms in the world! I read the passage from Matthew's Gospel last night, and again this morning.

Forty days and forty nights of fasting would indeed famish a person! Forty is an important number in Scripture. I read that it is mentioned 146 times! (And I read that on the internet, so it must be true!) Moses famously lived forty years in Egypt, and another forty years in the desert before God selected him to lead his people out of slavery. Oddly, it was about forty years from the date of my excommunication by the Mormon Church to the date that I began my spiritual journey toward Catholicism.

I tried to put myself with Jesus in the desert, fasting for forty days and nights. As a mere human, not on the verge of being called to assume my ministry as a Messiah, I had enough sustenance to maintain life, but the bare minimum. I was delusional by the end of the second week. However, the point of this scripture is not the difficulty of the desert. This is a powerful message about temptation, about how even the Son of Man can be tempted.

Deacon Dan, from our Parish, and I performed a skit together for one of the homilies last year. He recited the Lord's Prayer, while I, hiding behind the organ, was the voice of God, talking to Dan about what he was saying, and why. One of my favorite lines in my part of the skit was "God's" response to the line, "Lead me not into temptation." "God" said that the line always amused "Him," since it was "His" experience that humans needed no leading as far as temptation goes. We find it very well without any help, thank you! It was funny, but also very true.

I know that I have a keen nose for temptation. I can find it anywhere, and I usually do. In the Our Father, the next line is "Deliver me from evil," which attempts to put the burden of resisting temptation back on God. Again, I know where the burden lies. I have mentioned before my new favorite version of the Serenity Prayer, but it bears repeating. "God, grant me the serenity to accept the people I cannot change, the courage to change the one I can, and the wisdom to know that it is I."

My struggle to be optimistic and hopeful in this New Year continues. Thankfully, the mission schedule picks up next week. I will not have much time to complain about politics or worry about what others are doing. While the election is over, I do intend to continue "speaking my piece" when asked. Jesuit James Martin commented on speaking out last week.

> Catholics should oppose, vocally, forcefully and actively, those aspects of [Trump's] political designs that would seek to marginalize or exclude people. Catholic social teaching asks us to stand in solidarity with the poor. And Catholic tradition has been filled with saints who stood up against repressive political systems: Dorothy Day, Daniel Berrigan, Oscar Romero, in modern times; as well as Joan of Arc, Thomas of Becket and Thomas More in the past. The Catholic has an absolute moral duty to dissent. To be "pro voice."

I am definitely "pro-voice," even though I have to be careful about that here in North Florida!

Satan represents entropy, a primary force in nature. Simply stated, the law of entropy states that each progressive stage of existence must be less than the previous stage by the amount of energy required to make the stage change. The Universe is on a downward cycle that will inevitably end in nothing. Christ answers Satan with a dynamic new law, one that is based on increasing energy, resulting from the compassion and love of God.

The temptations in the desert were all based on the power of domination. The rich, the powerful, the privileged dominate the world, and Satan, metaphorically, offered this domination to Christ. In His refusal, Christ put the poor, the ill, the enslaved, and the weak ahead of all those conventionally able to dominate. The upside-down Gospel defied the law of entropy, positing that the world would be better, greater, and, ultimately one with God. This teaching was so new at the time of Christ that virtually no one could understand it. When Constantine made Christianity the official religion of the dominant state, he inadvertently turned the message of Christ upside-down.

I sat with this understanding, saddened by the role of power and domination in the world, and, especially, in the church, throughout history. The brave, defiant, brilliant mystics spoke out against this, beginning at about the same time that Constantine made his fateful decision. I pray for the strength to resist temptation.

January 4

Repeat Matthew 4:1–11, The Temptation of Jesus

ALL THREE of the Synoptic Gospels include the story of Jesus going out into the Judaean desert after his baptism. The Judean desert is not a place I would want to spend a night in, much less forty nights. The metaphoric value of this stark, barren, forbidding wilderness is huge. When I was much younger, I briefly considered a survival experience with an outback adventure group.

A few lines from the description of one of their survival courses offers an interesting insight into what Jesus might have experienced in the desert.

> Instructors demonstrate techniques associated with the six essential concepts of wilderness survival: [S]helter, firecraft, food finding, water purification, off-trail navigation and rescue signaling. This fun 2-day course gives students the option of sleeping overnight in their own hand-made shelters and reviews important survival gear and equipment.

I wonder how "fun" the first couple of days were for Jesus, or what options He considered for sleeping overnight. Two thousand years ago, I imagine there were very few paths and walkways. There were wild animals, especially up in the hills, away from the river. It was probably just as dry and forbidding then as it is now. Wadis cut through the mountains, following the flow of pre-historic streams.

While the deserts on both sides of the Jordan River truly qualify for the name, they were not without human settlements. The Judaean desert lies on the west bank of the Jordan, between the Sea of Galilee and Jerusalem, a distance of less than two hundred kilometers. Israelis had been traveling back and forth along the river for centuries.

The Nabateans, a nomadic tribe of Arabs, had settled three centuries earlier in the desert along the eastern side of the Jordan, where they established the incredible city of Petra. When I visited Petra many years ago, I walked along the deep Bab al-siq wadi for several hundred yards before reaching the beautiful Treasury.

It is easy this morning to fantasize Jesus walking along a similar wadi in the Judaean. In my fantasy, we walked together, our voices echoing against the steep, high walls on either side of the sandy, dry stream bottom. I wanted to know whether He was even slightly tempted by offers of power, prestige, or possessions. Reading the passage from Matthew's Gospel, it seems as though Jesus did not hesitate for even a second to consider His need for bread in the desert.

By then, we were both hungry. In my fantasy, Jesus answered in a very quiet, thoughtful voice, making His point without fanfare or drama. "There are forms of hunger much more important than lacking bread. I want to feed that deeper hunger."

I asked Him about the offer of the whole world falling down to worship Him. Again, in that quiet voice, almost a whisper, "How can I take pleasure in you or anyone else violating your faith? You have come so far, and are finally only now comfortable about doing what it is that God wants you to do. Why would you break any of His commandments, especially now?"

When is enough, enough? The author, Frank Huyler, wrote about someone, "tired of throwing still more experiences onto the bonfire of his own confusion." Having too much, continuing to acquire, is like that; simply adding more stuff, including experiences, onto life's confusion.

It strikes me that the answer to the temptation of more is to be active in the effort to make a difference in the world. Especially now, I have little hope that anything I do will "bend the arc of history," but active efforts to address the tragic consequences of a world order dominated by power and greed will at least change me. That is a start.

January 5

Repeat the Standards and Norms of Jesus Christ

READING BACK through the thought piece on the standards and norms of Jesus Christ (read it in full in the December 29 reflection), several key words jumped out at me. I continue to struggle with the Manichean view of the world. The thought piece asks us to consider "the face of good and the face of evil," and the fact that "darkness fights against light, the Liar against Truth, and death against life."

It is not that I cannot see right and wrong, or that I deny the existence of both good choices and bad. Most of the relatively easy issues in life fall into these simple, dualistic categories. It requires little thinking or discernment to choose the obvious right and good, and to reject the obvious wrong and bad. Now, by saying this, I am not claiming to have always made the right choice, regardless of how easy it would have been! In fact, most of my wrong choices also fall under the category of stupid. I knew they were wrong on numerous levels, yet made them anyway.

Jesus introduced a radically different way to view the world, one that requires discernment, judgement, and moral intelligence. Ivy League degrees are not necessary to discern right from wrong, but "doing the next right thing" is not always obvious. Non-dualism is not "without values." It requires the kind of deep seeing that makes both sides of a situation visible. It allows the good to be seen alongside the bad, encouraging us to make "both/and" decisions, not "either/or" decisions.

There can never be too many statements and re-statements of this fundamental truth. Jesus turned the world of power, prestige, and possessions upside-down. Chapter 5 of Matthew's Gospel contains much more than the Beatitudes. Consider verses 43–48, on loving our neighbors.

> "You have heard that it was said, 'Love your neighbor and hate your enemy.' But I tell you, love your enemies and pray for those who persecute you, that you may be children of your Father in heaven. *He causes his sun to rise on the evil and the good, and sends rain on the righteous and the unrighteous.* If you love those who love you, what reward will you get? Are not even the tax collectors doing that? And if you greet only your own people, what are you doing more than others? Do not even pagans do that? Be perfect, therefore, as your heavenly Father is perfect"

The sun rises on the evil and the good. Rain falls on the righteous and unrighteous. There is very often both good and bad in the choices we are called to make, and in the gifts we receive. Money corrupts, power corrupts, rank corrupts, but there are good men and women with money, power, and rank. Discernment is the key, and it starts with the admonition, don't be stupid.

Louis Savary wrote a guide for doing the Ignatian Exercises from the perspective of Teilhard de Chardin. He argues that Teilhard thought in terms of "activities" and "passivities," rather than rights and wrongs. Being passive in the face of a society organized around the concept of domination and power (I think in terms of power, prestige, and possessions) is, to Teilhard, the greatest sin. Whatever we do to *resist*, matters. The standard of Jesus Christ is to actively assert the rights of the marginal against the power of the dominant class.

Our good friend Sister Kim Jordan was a very close friend of Father John Robbins, the Catholic priest who counseled me into the Catholic Church. She sent me a copy of Father John's homily on the Beatitudes. As Sister Kim says, Father John died in 2009, but his words live on.

> Today's Gospel is from the beginning of "The Sermon on the Mount; The Great Sermon"— The Beatitudes. The Beatitudes contains many of the lines and sayings of Jesus that are most familiar and loved, and least observed.
>
> The importance of these sayings, and especially those in today's readings, cannot be overstated. The Beatitudes are to the Christian Scriptures as the Ten Commandments are to the Hebrew Scriptures. I am not in favor of religious quotes and symbols in public buildings, but if I were I'd much rather have the Beatitudes in the lobby of a courthouse than the Ten Commandments.
>
> In this one brief list, Jesus completely reverses the values of the world of his day, and since nothing has really changed, of our day, too. You all know the term "Movers and Shakers," the people who matter. They are the rich, the beautiful, the happy, the well connected, and the powerful. Blessed are they.
>
> But Jesus says no. He gives us a new list of the Movers and Shakers, the people who matter. He says they are the poor and the sad, the hungry and the merciful, the clean of heart and the peacemakers, the insulted and the persecuted. Blessed are they.
>
> In fact, he offers each such person a reward. If you are poor and persecuted, you get heaven. If you are sad, you get comforted. If you are gentle, you inherit the earth. If you hunger for justice, you'll get it. If you are merciful, you'll receive mercy. If you make peace, you'll be God's own child. All of these types get a great reward.
>
> Imagine—it is the ones with no status who matter, whom God prefers! This is all pretty shocking because they sure don't matter to anyone else. And even worse, most of us aren't even on this list. So the kingdom of God belongs to these people, not to us.
>
> Even more shocking, the kingdom doesn't belong to the poor if they shape up, stop stealing, get a job. But it belongs to them simply because they are poor, just as they are.
>
> Which, of course, was a scandal to all the non-poor people who had jobs and did not steal and were morally good and even gave alms to the poor. We aren't left out; it's just that we don't have the free pass the poor have.
>
> This is what is called "the fundamental option for the poor" which runs through the whole Gospel. I don't know what to do about it any more than you do and it bothers me just as much as it bothers you. If we aren't blessed by being born poor; if we aren't meek or persecuted or gentle or especially merciful, what about us?
>
> Well, I guess we just have to stand by the poor and hope God has a "Plan B." Maybe it's that narrow door Jesus mentioned.

January 6

Repeat the Standards and Norms of Jesus Christ

THIS MORNING began in the glow of an incredible lecture at the Cultural Center of our parish last night by Dr. Stephan Esser. He once helped pick me up from the floor of the church when severe angina caused me to pass out. It was thus a little ironic for me to listen to him eloquently state the case for diet and exercise to prevent or reverse chronic killer diseases, particularly coronary artery disease. I prayed for the strength of commitment to stay with my current health regime, which seems to be making modest gains.

Once again, I read the thought piece for today, which is a repeat of the Standards and Norms of Christ introduced on December 29. One paragraph stood out in this reading:

> ... [C]onsider how the Spirit of Evil wishes to clasp every one to itself. Evil wants to elicit evil; it's like radioactivity: [W]hatever it touches, it radio-activates and poisons. It's like the plague caused by a highly contagious virus; open yourself to living contact with a victim, and you have contracted the plague. Whether you believe in a personal Prince of Evil (as Jesus surely did) or not, you know that evil spreads itself.

Is sin contagious? Do I "catch" sin from the people around me, or "spread" sin to others by my actions? My first reaction was to resist any similarity between physical, germ-spread disease on one hand, and moral failings on the other. On reflection, I considered how tempted I have been by the apparent "happiness" I have seen in some of the famous people I have most admired. Power, prestige, and possessions certainly looked good from a distance, particularly when I was making several critical life decisions. Certainly, my own actions have occasionally been an inducement to people around me to join me in whatever transitional pleasure I was experiencing.

What if my early models had been Thomas Merton or Father Rohr? What if I had never bought into the myth of "have more, be happier"? The simple truth is that my early adult years were surrounded by superb role models, and their example was contagious. I chose to start my working life developing low-income housing. Phyllis, my wife at the time, worked as a Community Organizer in the Great Society programs of President Lyndon Johnson. No, my gradual shift from seeking to "change the world" to focusing on "creating personal wealth" was something I did *in spite* of my role models, not because of them. It is certainly true that moving from Denver to Beverly Hills in 1972 was not a move designed to strengthen my commitment to frugality! The good news is that the seeds planted in my youth never completely died from lack of attention. The choices I made while "building personal wealth" all included significant elements of helping the less fortunate. I will hang on to that thought as long as I can!

What were the standards of Jesus Christ? Over the last five years, I have had the opportunity to internalize the upside-down nature of His Gospel. Both my work as Chairman of the Justice and Peace Commission of our Diocese and as Co-founder and Chairman of Sister Parish fit into what is sometimes called a "bias for the poor," or "bias from the bottom." That does not mean that I have lived and acted only within these norms. But I simply cannot advance ignorance as a defense.

Father Rohr speaks to this in his daily meditation today.

> Let's be honest, our culture places the most value on fame, power, and money. Even people who call themselves Christians are much more fascinated by celebrities and so-called suc-

cess than they are by the downward path of Jesus. Once you can see that God is in the ordinary and that you don't have to climb upward or be more pure or perfect to find God, you start honoring God in what Jesus calls "the least of the brothers and sisters" (Mathew 25:40) and in the very common earth beneath our feet. Thus God said to Moses, "Take off your sandals, for this is holy ground" (Exodus 3:5).

Reflecting on this simplifies the discussion about the Standards and Norms of Jesus Christ. I end the day with a quiet resolve never to forget the "Jesus bias." Each time I kneel to pray, I am reminded of my role in this drama, "Thy will, not mine, be done."

January 7

Repeat and reflect on the week.

RAIN DURING the night left the bench too wet to sit on for meditation. Maggie and I came down together, but hurried back to the library for prayer, reading, and long reflection on the Standards and Norms of Jesus Christ.

I read an article during the night that adds an interesting dimension to this discussion of Christian standards, particularly in this historically fascinating period approaching the Presidential Inaugural. Describing the typical rural, white Trump voter, the article by *New York Times* reporter Robert Leonard said:

> They are conservative, believe in hard work, family, the military and cops, and they know that abortion and socialism are evil, that Jesus Christ is our savior, and that Donald J. Trump will be good for America. They are part of a growing movement in rural America that immerses many young people in a culture—not just conservative news outlets but also home and church environments—that emphasizes contemporary conservative values. It views liberals as loathsome, misinformed and weak, even dangerous.
>
> The difference between Republicans and Democrats is that Republicans believe people are fundamentally bad, while Democrats see people as fundamentally good," said Mr. J. C. Watts, who was in the area to campaign for Senator Rand Paul. "We are born bad," he said and added that children did not need to be taught to behave badly—they are born knowing how to do that. He continued: "Democrats believe that we are born good, that we create God, not that he created us. If we are our own God, as the Democrats say, then we need to look at something else to blame when things go wrong—not us. We live in different philosophical worlds, with different foundational principles."

Watts, a former Congressman (and great quarterback) from Oklahoma is currently serving as President of Feed the Children. He is a Baptist Minister. His distinction between a Republican who believes people are "born bad," and a Democrat who believes people are "born good" is fascinating. I like to think this is a distinction, not between Republicans and Democrats, but rather between enlightened and unenlightened people of faith.

It has become central to my personal faith that the entire universe was created in love and for love. It was created by a positive, loving Creator, who launched this amazing universe with a powerful force driving us ever onward toward unitive consciousness. His two primary commandments are that we love Him back, and that we love each other. The idea that an innocent child is born bad appalls me. Worse, though, is the exclusionary concept that this evil baby can only be made good by a second birth, which can only occur when the grown child accepts Jesus Christ! What about the five billion people on the planet who are not Christian? Do they just stay bad? Absurd.

I like Watts. We have radically different political views, but he has always impressed me as a thinking conservative, quite capable of articulating a coherent alternative to liberal policies. He reminds me of former Congressman Jack Kemp. I believe they both genuinely care about the people in the margins of life. It is partly for this reason that I am troubled by the comment that we Democrats believe "that we create God, not that He created us." Could this actually be the prevailing view that religious conservatives have of what Father Rohr and the Living School are teaching? I know that I did not create God, but I do believe that I have always been a part of His creation. I also believe that a primary message of the incarnation was to end the dualistic distinction between human and Divine. I am not God, but there is in my soul a spark of the Divine.

Father Rohr quoted extensively from Brian McClaren yesterday. I love this, perhaps providing additional proof that I am a liberal Democrat (as though any more proof is needed!):

> Growing numbers of us are acknowledging with grief that many forms of supremacy—Christian, white, male, heterosexual, and human—are deeply embedded not just in Christian history, but also in Christian theology. We are coming to see that in hallowed words like almighty, sovereignty, kingdom, dominion, supreme, elect, chosen, clean, remnant, sacrifice, lord, and even God, dangerous vices often lie hidden. . . . We are coming to see in the life and teaching of Christ, and especially in the cross and resurrection of Christ, a radical rejection of dominating supremacy in all its forms. The theological term for [this] is *kenosis*, which means self-emptying. . . . Rather than seizing, hoarding, and exercising power in the domineering ways of typical kings, conquistadors, and religious leaders, Jesus was consistently empowering others. He descended the ladders and pyramids of influence instead of climbing them upwards, released power instead of grasping at it, and served instead of dominating. He ultimately overturned all conventional understandings of . . . power by purging [it] of violence—to the point where he himself chose to be killed rather than kill.

This is extremely powerful teaching. Christ descended, He released, and He served. Rather than seizing power, Jesus empowered others. He asks of us that we empty ourselves, that we make space for His love so that we can pour it out to others. This does not feel like new age apostasy to me.

My prayer this morning is for wisdom and judgement. I pray for the strength to remain firm in my conviction that the standards of Jesus Christ are first and foremost to serve others and to love my enemies. *Forgiveness* and *inclusion* remain the two most important words in my faith.

CALENDAR WEEK SEVENTEEN

I want to know what kind of friend Jesus was, and how He thought and felt about His friends, and about His mission. I want to love Him more, and to follow Him in His way.

Lord Jesus, from the start You invite ordinary people to come to where You live. When they come, You welcome them and call them to labor and rejoice with You. You are the most beautiful among all men, and I hardly believe You want me for Your friend. You are powerful, Lord. Draw me more and more into Your friendship and lead me along the way You took with friends.

January 8

John 1:35–42, The First Disciples of Jesus

³⁵ The next day John again was standing with two of his disciples, ³⁶ and as he watched Jesus walk by, he exclaimed, "Look, here is the Lamb of God!" ³⁷ The two disciples heard him say this, and they followed Jesus. ³⁸ When Jesus turned and saw them following, he said to them, "What are you looking for?" They said to him, "Rabbi" (which translated means Teacher), "where are you staying?" ³⁹ He said to them, "Come and see." They came and saw where he was staying, and they remained with him that day. It was about four o'clock in the afternoon. ⁴⁰ One of the two who heard John speak and followed him was Andrew, Simon Peter's brother. ⁴¹ He first found his brother Simon and said to him, "We have found the Messiah" (which is translated Anointed). ⁴² He brought Simon to Jesus, who looked at him and said, "You are Simon son of John. You are to be called Cephas" (which is translated Peter).

AS I READ through this familiar passage from John's Gospel last night, I realized for the first time that Andrew, the brother of Peter, was a disciple of John the Baptist before joining Jesus. According to John's Gospel, Peter became a disciple only after his brother introduced him to Jesus.

While not questioning Andrew's relationship with John the Baptist, Matthew 4:18–22 provides a different account of the call to discipleship, one that is, not surprisingly, consistent with the other Synoptic Gospels (after all, they are "Synoptic"):

> As Jesus was walking beside the Sea of Galilee, he saw two brothers, Simon called Peter and his brother Andrew. They were casting a net into the lake, for they were fishermen. "Come, follow me," Jesus said, "and I will send you out to fish for people." At once they left their nets and followed him.

Whether the charisma of Jesus worked, simply as He passed by John and John's followers, or when he saw two brothers fishing, the point is that Jesus had huge appeal. The prayer for this week begins by noting about Jesus that he "invites ordinary people to come to where [He] lives." I ask that He "draw me more and more into [His] friendship and lead me along the way [He] took with friends."

I have known a few people whose charismatic appeal is so great that they attract new friends almost magically. Words like "comfortable in his own skin" or "easy to be around" are often used. However, I think the attraction is more dynamic than the words *easy* or *comfortable* convey. It is a vigorous appeal, filled with potential. It is contagious joy.

It is very different from the allure of power, prestige, and possessions. These clearly attract, but the affect is not lasting joy. Rather, it is momentary elation, followed by envy or greed, a feeling of emptiness, not fullness. The message is "you need more." Achieving these things does not bring deep satisfaction. My experience is that the more *power*, *prestige*, and *possessions* I have, the more I want.

The message of Jesus is just the opposite. "You are enough. Even more than that, you have all you need and something more to share." The more I empty myself of love, the more love I have to give. Bonaventure wrote about the "fecund power" and fullness of God, about His "effluent dynamism." These are powerful concepts, literally bursting with energy, life, love, and joy.

Father Rohr introduced Sallie Ann and me to the Franciscan tradition in the spring of 2012 at a conference in Assisi, Italy. There we learned that John Dun Scotus followed Bonaventure in the rich tradition of Franciscan theologians of the late thirteenth century. The one word I associate with Dun Scotus is *univocity*, a doctrine which rests in part on the claim that "[t]he difference between God and creatures, at least with regard to God's possession of the pure perfections, is ultimately one of degree." Bonaventure presents us with a fecund God bursting with life, and Dun Scotus argues that there is some of that fecundity in each of us.

Returning to the reading today, thinking as a thirteenth century Franciscan, Jesus, the incarnate Christ, had a magnetic appeal that arose in no small part from His fecundity and fullness. He could attract friends and followers simply by walking on a road next to them. As creatures in His awesome creation, we have, somewhere in us, a spark of that divine power. Christ is that spark!

January 9

Repeat John 1:35–42, The First Disciples of Jesus

IT WAS COLD this morning. The wind chill was close to freezing, rare for us in North Florida, but nothing like the deep freeze that hit the rest of the country this weekend. Maggie and I walked to the beach in the cold wind. I looked a little strange, dressed as I was like a Florida Inuit, but I found the whole experience of sand, wind, and sea in the bright sun and bitter cold incredibly uplifting. There was not another soul on the beach. The library has never seemed so warm and welcoming.

Again, I prayed that Jesus would "draw me more and more into [His] friendship." I reflected on how few close friends I have had during much of my life. It is an awesome thought that Jesus could be a friend as close as Buddy Tudor! As I sat with these thoughts of friendship, it occurred to me how different my life is today than it has been over the years. I am surrounded by good friends almost every day, whether on the tennis court or at the Parish or in the Dominican Republic. My life is truly a life "in community." All of my friendships are positive, wholesome, joy-filled, and uplifting.

Meister Eckhart wrote,

> There exists only the present instant… a *Now* which always and without end is itself new. There is no yesterday nor any tomorrow, but only Now, as it was a thousand years ago and as it will be a thousand years hence.

I have spent a significant part of my life thinking about a yesterday when my friendships were limited by my ambition and selfishness. There is no yesterday! There is only Now, and in this always new present, I am loved and supported by strong communities of incredible friends. I am enough. I have enough. I have an abundant excess that only grows when I give it away.

This morning I offer a prayer of gratitude for the profusion of goodness in my life. I pray for humility. I pray for the strength to fully embrace this goodness, to feed it with the love that surrounds me, and to pour it out whenever and however possible.

January 10

Mark 1:16–20, Jesus Calls the First Disciples

¹⁶ As Jesus passed along the Sea of Galilee, he saw Simon and his brother Andrew casting a net into the sea—for they were fishermen. ¹⁷ And Jesus said to them, "Follow me and I will make you fish for people." ¹⁸ And immediately they left their nets and followed him. ¹⁹ As he went a little farther, he saw James son of Zebedee and his brother John, who were in their boat mending the nets. ²⁰ Immediately he called them; and they left their father Zebedee in the boat with the hired men, and followed him.

MARK'S ACCOUNT of Jesus calling His first Disciples is virtually the same as the account in Matthew's Gospels. Both differ considerably from the accounts in John's Gospel and Luke's Gospel. Whether the "miracle" is two brothers dropping their nets and following this apparent stranger, or Andrew rushing to his brother's house to suggest they follow a man neither of them had met, the message is essentially the same. A person of amazing charisma has somehow entered into the routine of their lives, interrupting the probably tedious pattern with a life-changing opportunity.

What would I do? I read the passage from Mark last night before going to bed, and again this morning before playing tennis. I have returned to the question of what I would do, over and over again. My life today is comfortable—exceedingly so, in fact. I follow an almost identical routine each day, each week, and, especially now in the "mission season," each month. What would it take for me to interrupt my regular schedule, drop all my commitments, abandon my family, and follow someone new?

It is relatively easy for me to imagine myself as a fisherman in the little community of Capernaum on the shore of the Galilee. While it was meant to have a population of about 1,500, three times the size of tiny Nazareth, it was still a village, all of the residents of which could fit into a small symphony hall. Not much was going on in the community. In my imagined life, I had few commitments, and what few there were, were of little importance. I am tempted to say that the disciples had nothing to lose. They left an empty, boring life, filled with bland people and tiresome family.

This is as unfair as it is untrue. I have to remember the fact that Andrew and Peter were just as involved in their lives then as I am in my life today. The question of what I would do is only meaningful when I apply it to my actual life in this house, among my loving family and friends, doing what I truly enjoy. Asked that way, I come up with a much different answer, or, at least, I struggle a great deal coming up with any answer at all.

The fact is that all of us live in a relatively complex environment that involves relationships, plans, and commitments. Of course, there are times in our lives that are less complicated than others. I often refer to my entry into the coal business as a choice I made when my life was relatively uncomplicated. When I was presented with the opportunity to move to a trailer in West Virginia to build and operate a coal mine, I was recently divorced, living alone, unattached, and probably not very satisfied with my life.

But here is the sad truth about that decision. I took my commitments and obligations less seriously than I should have. I did have two daughters, about whom I was clearly not thinking when I accepted life in a single-wide trailer. Viewed from the perspective of my parental obligations, my decision was reckless and irresponsible. The choice to jump into the coal business was more an exception that proved the rule. There were countless other opportunities that I passed over due to inconvenience or competing commitments.

There was also power behind the charisma of Jesus. His "suggestions" were sometimes unforgiving commands. Both Matthew's Gospel and Luke's Gospel report one potential disciple saying, "Lord, let me first go and bury my father." And Jesus said to him, "Follow me, and leave the dead to bury their own dead."

January 11

Repeat Mark 1:16–20, Jesus Calls the First Disciples

My plane for Miami departs Jacksonville in an hour and a half, giving me time to read Mark's version of the call of the first disciples again, meditate about it, and now reflect on my reactions. I have never been a great fan of "travel days," but find that my enthusiasm is less today than ever. Sleep eludes me on most flights, regardless of where I sit on the plane. Conversation with the person in the seat next to me is something I stopped more than a quarter of a century ago. I have almost certainly missed many fascinating people, not to mention potentially beneficial opportunities. Nonetheless, I am generally thankful not to be disturbed, and suspect the overwhelming majority of my seat mates were just as grateful not to meet another stranger. After waking up at 5 a.m. and meandering out to the airport, then flying and sitting all day, I will arrive in Santo Domingo at close to 4 p.m. this afternoon. I will be tired, a little grumpy, and pretty poor company for anyone I see this evening. However, this is the joy available from exotic foreign travel!

Mechtild of Magdeburg (d. 1280) once said, "The day of my spiritual awakening was the day I saw—and knew I saw—all things in God and God in all things." This speaks to me today, even as I sit at the airport. Teilhard called this awakening the day we accept that we live and move, and have our being in the *divine milieu*. We literally exist in an ocean of God's love, One of my favorite songs is "The Deer's Cry," also called "St. Patrick's Breastplate," written sometime between the 5th and 8th centuries. I can imagine the *divine milieu* in verse after verse, as Christ is described inside, outside, above, below, and to the sides of me.

> I arise today
> through the strength of heaven
> Light of sun, radiance of moon
> Splendor of fire, speed of lightning
> Swiftness of wind, depth of the sea
> Stability of earth, firmness of rock
> I arise today through God's strength to pilot me
> God's eye to look before me
> God's wisdom to guide me
> God's way to lie before me
> God's shield to protect me
> From all who shall wish me ill
> Afar and a-near

Alone and in a multitude
Against every cruel, merciless power
That may oppose my body and soul
Christ with me, Christ before me
Christ behind me, Christ in me
Christ beneath me, Christ above me
Christ on my right, Christ on my left
Christ when I lie down, Christ when I sit down
Christ when I arise, Christ to shield me
Christ in the heart of everyone who thinks of me
Christ in the mouth of everyone who speaks of me
I arise today.

If the physical presence of Christ on the shore of Galilee conveyed even a tiny part of the *divine milieu*, then it is no wonder the disciples dropped everything to follow Him.

Teilhard taught that we humans are not here on earth for the primary purpose of getting a good enough grade that we will be admitted into Heaven. Our purpose is not a personal salvation purpose. We are here for a great collective effort, joining with the Universal Being to consciously cooperate in total union with all of creation in love. That is a huge challenge, an awesome undertaking. Maybe those first disciples knew instantly that following in the footsteps of Jesus meant they would not be alone in the Divine Project.

I pray I will survive this day intact, more committed than ever to deeply knowing that I do live, move, and have my being in Him.

January 12

Three Couples

  * First, I recall this little fantasy:

Three good and deeply faith-filled couples happen to pull off a business deal that nets each of them a million dollars. Now, these three couples are good people, with strong consciences, and they did nothing wrong in the business deal. After a few weeks, at one of their regular get-togethers, they rather shyly begin to mention a feeling that they have each noticed. They do not feel entirely comfortable about having that money. This is a spiritual matter, for their consciences remain clear and firm. But they notice changes in their spirits. They are no longer eager for Sunday Mass (and the homilies vex them as never before). They feel differently about the bishops' pastoral on the American economy and the Pope's letter about communism and capitalism. They no longer feel in harmony with the Church, somehow. They admit feeling exultant that they made the deal and got the million dollars. They like having the money and are doing great things with it. Still … maybe they want it too much or something? It seems to be tainting their lives.

  * Second, at this juncture I set this fantasy aside and turn to God. I go and stand before the Blessed Trinity, with our Lady there, and the apostles, and in fact, I stand before the whole heavenly court.

There, I ask the Lord God Almighty for what I want: Lord, I ask to want, to desire, whatever will show in me Your holiness, Your power at work in the world and in me whatever will make me more certainly Yours.

  * Then I take up each couple as they go back and live out their way of dealing with this spiritual disquiet they feel, and I reflect on myself to see whether I would be with any one of the three couples.

First, this couple really wants to get rid of the disquiet. They talk a lot about it, at least in the beginning. But years later when they die—still rich they have done nothing at all about it.

Second, the next couple can't sit still in the disquiet. They want to keep the money and can't figure why they ought to get rid of it. Still, they do not want to live with uneasy spirits, a little tentative with God. So they take some steps. Systematically, they give money to the poor and the dispossessed and the underprivileged, mostly through the Church. In this way, they try to bargain with God: "If we give this to the poor, You ought to give us peace." When they come to die, they have done good things, but they have not reached solid inner peace.

Third, the final couple considered keeping the money and they also considered just giving the money away. But they had to admit that they did not really know whether either one would solve their uneasiness. Why would they keep it? Why would they give it away? So this is how they acted: They decided that they would not determine definitely to keep the money or definitely to get rid of it. They would wait to see what this disquiet really signified. Then when they knew, they would act. In this way, they generously said to God: "Either way. Show us and we'll do it. "

At the end, having reflected on yourself, use the triple colloquy, ending with the Our Father.

THIS MORNING was very different from most of the mornings since I began the Exercises. I awakened in my room at the Quality Hotel in the Dominican Republic, beginning the mission season again with the medical team this weekend. Aside from a brief exploratory trip in December, this is my first trip since the September medical mission. I have enjoyed the relatively long period of waking up at home, going down to the library and garden with Maggie, and spending a great deal of quality time with Sallie Ann.

I walked outside to the garden behind the hotel to pray. As it happens, prayer works rather well wherever I do it. This morning my prayer included a conversation with God about Teilhard's approach to these Ignatian Exercises. I have been reading more of Louis Savary's book *The New Spiritual Exercises*. Savary argues that Teilhard calls for a change of focus from "individual salvation and getting to heaven" to the communal *Divine Project*. This Divine Project rests on two foundations:

> 1) We humans are not separate from this planet nor from anyone or anything else on it or in it; and 2) we need to uplift everyone and everything on it or in it.

The Divine Project is a global effort to implement the teaching of Jesus Christ best described in Matthew's Gospel, both in the Beatitudes and in other passages. Today's reading, the Ignatian reflection on three couples, provides an excellent opportunity to examine this concept.

Three couples, each consisting of two good and decent people, come into a considerable sum of money. None of them want to use their newfound wealth for clearly sinful purposes. However, all of them feel a certain discomfort with all of that money. I attempted to put myself in the position of each couple. At the suggestion of Mr. Savary, I began my meditation with a prayer for the grace of freedom and objectivity.

The First Couple. As I imagined myself part of the first couple, I suddenly felt a powerful sensation that I had been here before. When Globeleq was sold in 2006, my share of the profit was more money than I had ever dreamt of having in my life. It came at a very bad time, when I was aggressively resentful of the British for removing me from the position of CEO of the company I had founded. I was depressed, angry, and self-destructive. In truth, I was in such bad shape that I gave little thought to either the idea that I was suddenly quite wealthy, or any honest consideration of what I would do with the money. Sallie Ann and I did not talk about it in any meaningful way.

When we did finally talk, we did virtually everything the first couple did in the reflection. We agreed to an annual gift to each of our children, essentially choosing a method of passing as much money as possible on to our children without estate taxes. We bought land in Florida and built a house, Serendipity. We put most of the money in the hands of a financial advisor, certainly not thinking about any charitable or spiritual uses for the money. We went to a conference in Assisi, Italy, that would turn out to be life changing, but that was certainly not intentional.

At about that time in my reflection, I allowed my fantasy to take over, thinking not about the reality of our lives, but rather about the first couple. We grew old and died, finally dying rich and unhappy.

The Second Couple. The primary difference in the story of the first and second couple has to do with the charitable uses to which the second couple put much of their newfound wealth. Putting myself in their place, I thought more than anything about the common practice among wealthy people, which is to write a check rather than getting truly involved. Most of the people I know with any substantial wealth fall into this category. Some simply write a few more checks, for a larger amount, to schools and charitable causes. They attend the charity balls and banquets. They open their house to dinners and events in support of the opera, ballet, symphony, and, less often, to groups working with the poor. They become important in the community. The fact is that these people are essential to the very existence of our culture, and much more in most communities. Thank God for charities and the people who support them. They probably spend very little time talking to God about what they are doing with their wealth, but the choices they make are vital. In my view, their giving clearly puts them ahead of people who die with their money in the bank. I am not clear about whether people in the charity circuit view their money as a gift from God.

The Third Couple. The third couple in the reflection begins their new life with money by doing nothing. Rather, they stop, they pray, and they wait for God to tell them what to do. To them, this money is not theirs, it is God's. He gave it to them as a loan with which to do good things, to participate in the Divine Project.

Ultimately, I believe Sallie Ann and I arrived at this place several years after we came into what money we have. Of course, by that time, much of the wealth was gone! Serendipity was finished, and we were comfortably using our wonderful house for ourselves and our family. We had traveled a bit, and were driving new cars. In my mind, I had worked extremely hard my entire life, had been badly treated by the British, and totally deserved the wealth that I had earned.

While I was not intentionally listening for God to tell me what to do next, somehow it happened. Sister Parish was not conceived to be the monthly mission program that it now is. I thought one or two missions a year for a year or two at most. That was about all any of us expected. Sallie Ann and I had no idea how deeply involved in its work we would become. While we are now the primary sponsors of the ministry, it is vastly more than a cause to which we write checks. It is the most important activity in my life, especially during the "mission season" of January to September. When she is not in the Dominican Republic with me, Sallie Ann is working on other aspects of the ministry.

My prayer today is that I will continue to listen to God about what my role in His Divine Project should be. I pray that He will continue to give me the graces of strength, judgement, and wisdom. I pray for the wonderful people who arrived today to work in the medical clinics for the next three days. I pray for the patients that will be served in this good work.

January 13

John 2:1–11, The Wedding at Cana

¹ On the third day there was a wedding in Cana of Galilee, and the mother of Jesus was there. ² Jesus and his disciples had also been invited to the wedding. ³ When the wine gave out, the mother of Jesus said to him, "They have no wine." ⁴ And Jesus said to her, "Woman, what concern is that to you and to me? My hour has not yet come." ⁵ His mother said to the servants, "Do whatever he tells you." ⁶ Now standing there were six stone water jars for the Jewish rites of purification, each holding twenty or thirty gallons. ⁷ Jesus said to them, "Fill the jars with water." And they filled them up to the brim. ⁸ He said to them, "Now draw some out, and take it to the chief steward." So they took it. ⁹ When the steward tasted the water that had become wine, and did not know where it came from (though the servants who had drawn the water knew), the steward called the bridegroom ¹⁰ and said to him, "Everyone serves the good wine first, and then the inferior wine after the guests have become drunk. But you have kept the good wine until now." ¹¹ Jesus did this, the first of his signs, in Cana of Galilee, and revealed his glory; and his disciples believed in him.

REFLECTING on this passage this morning, I smiled as I remembered proudly telling my guests that they should savor the first wine I served, knowing full well that I would go "$10 down" on each bottle served thereafter. I thought it showed my good sense. In fact, recently, long after I stopped drinking wine, I ordered wine for my dinner guests without telling the wine steward of my rule. When I paid the check at the end of the meal, I was shocked at the cost of the wine, which I am convinced my guests could not taste by halfway through the meal! I will risk continued violation of the "Cana Rule."

I attended Mass this morning with the medical mission at the wonderful chapel at Futuro Vivo. The Santissima Trinidad volunteers, UNIBE students, and San Antonio de Padua volunteers filled the small chapel and lined the walkway. It was cold and raining, very "not Dominican weather"! Nonetheless, standing in the chilly morning air, I was brought to tears looking from one person to the next, considering the miracle of this Sister Parish Ministry. When this started, I hoped for three things: Encounter, community, and service. Ideally, these would result for our missionaries from Florida, for the volunteers here in the Dominican Republic, and for the people we serve. Fundamentally, however, I hope for these outcomes for me. Again today, my expectation was fulfilled. I experienced a deep encounter with God during and after Mass, and did so in community with all of those people. Reflecting on this powerful experience, it was overwhelmingly obvious that both the encounter and the community result from the simple fact that we are together in service. This ministry works in my heart. I cannot be sure that everyone else (or anyone else), experiences the same phenomenon, but it really doesn't matter. As Thomas Merton said in his famous prayer, "I believe that the desire to please you does in fact please you."

This effort to bring "all creation together into one magnificent conscious loving union" is indeed a Divine Project. Consider that there are more than one hundred people engaged just today, just in this one medical clinic in this small community! Then imagine this happening in countless similar efforts in communities all over the world. It is a power for good that cannot be defeated! I pray in gratitude.

January 14

Repeat and reflect on the week

AGAIN, THIS morning, I prayed in the garden behind the hotel. The missionaries will depart soon for Santo Domingo, where we will hold a free medical clinic at Domingo Savio. I feel incredibly complete today. Yesterday included not only the clinic at Futuro Vivo, but also lunch with Father Mario Serrano, the Jesuit inspiration for Sister Parish. We talked about a new mission program in Jimani, a town due west of Santo Domingo on the Haitian border. Father Frank, the source of the very idea of a Sister Parish Ministry, served in Jimani many years ago, with the Claretian order of priests. I promised Father Mario that I would talk to our construction team.

Before praying this morning, I read the goal set for us this week: *"I want to know what kind of friend Jesus was, and how He thought and felt about His friends, and about His mission. I want to love Him more, and to follow Him in His way."* This is a very lofty goal.

I focused my energy on the nature of His friendship during His short public ministry. I believe the idea of a *divine milieu* began to emerge in the very early days, when Jesus started performing miracles for the express purpose of making it clear that His new Gospel was aimed at the bottom. The parables about the miracles elevated the poor, the ill, the incarcerated, the tax collectors, and the Roman centurions to the top of the social ranking. That message was like the Deer's Cry, coming from behind, in front, above, below, and from all sides. Being a friend of Jesus meant buying into His Project with all of one's life and energy. I suspect that being in His physical presence made it relatively easy to fully commit, floating on the cloud of His love.

In my fantasy, I put myself in the small group of early disciples, following Jesus as His ministry unfolded. Jesus was that rare kind of friend, who was consistent in His behavior. That is, He was the same kind of friend when we were alone as He was when we were in public, in a large group. He was the same kind of friend when things were going well, and when we faced challenges. He was the same kind of friend to the very poor and the outcast as He was to me and the other disciples.

The black Gospel singer, Tramaine Hawkins, sings a classic song about the friendship of Jesus.

> If you ever need a friend that sticks
> closer than any brother,
> I recommend Jesus, Jesus;
> because He's that kind of friend.
>
> He will never forsake you, even though
> He knows everything there is to know about you;
> I recommend Jesus, Jesus;
> because He's that kind of friend.
>
> He'll walk right in front of you
> to always protect you,
> so the devil can't do you no harm.
> He's faithful everyday
> to help you along the way;
> He's that kind of friend.

He'll walk right in front of you
to always protect you,
(so the devil can't do you no harm).
If within your heart you take Him in,
New life will begin, (He's) that kind of friend.

The concept of all creation evolving moment by moment, in the direction and with the ultimate goal of a unitive consciousness of love, mandates this kind of friendship. The commandment to love our enemies leaves little to the imagination. It is as simple as it is impossibly difficult.

As I sit with these thoughts, waiting for the bus to leave for Domingo Savio, I return to the notion that God is active, that His love is on the offensive at all times. He is not waiting for us to come to Him. He is moving toward us, waiting patiently for us to make even the tiniest amount of room for Him to enter into our hearts. There is no measured discussion of meeting halfway, or balancing the scales, or mutuality. God's starting position is *yes*. He *always loves us*. You would think that, with these odds, the whole world would make room for that love. Looking around me, I see something else. I pray that God will open my eyes to see His love in the world, to see the good, to join the chorus of yes. I pray in gratitude for this incredible group of medical missionaries and the amazing work they do. What a blessing for me to be here.

CALENDAR WEEK EIGHTEEN

I want to know Jesus of Nazareth, and to love Him, and to follow Him in His way.

Lord Jesus, You humbled Yourself by sharing with friends what You thought and felt and desired. Lord, as You gave them the gift of knowing You and feeling Your great love for them, let me come to know You, too, even so far away in another country and another time. If only I could feel Your love for me, I would love You then, and in my whole heart would resonate with what You think and feel and desire. That is what I want, if it please You, Lord.

January 15

Luke 4:14–22, The Beginning of the Galilean Ministry

[14] Then Jesus, filled with the power of the Spirit, returned to Galilee, and a report about him spread through all the surrounding country. [15] He began to teach in their synagogues and was praised by everyone.

The Rejection of Jesus at Nazareth

[16] When he came to Nazareth, where he had been brought up, he went to the synagogue on the sabbath day, as was his custom. He stood up to read, [17] and the scroll of the prophet Isaiah was given to him. He unrolled the scroll and found the place where it was written:

[18] "The Spirit of the Lord is upon me,
because he has anointed me
to bring good news to the poor.
He has sent me to proclaim release to the captives
and recovery of sight to the blind,
to let the oppressed go free,
[19] to proclaim the year of the Lord's favor."

[20] And he rolled up the scroll, gave it back to the attendant, and sat down. The eyes of all in the synagogue were fixed on him. [21] Then he began to say to them, "Today this scripture has been fulfilled in your hearing." [22] All spoke well of him and were amazed at the gracious words that came from his mouth. They said, "Is not this Joseph's son?"

THE IDEA THAT Jesus ran into resistance when He began His ministry should come as no surprise to anyone. His whole message was to turn the order of things upside-down, putting the first last and the last first. In one way or another, however, all of the Evangelists suggested something different in the rejection of Jesus. How could this mere carpenter's son teach and preach from the Holy Scriptures? Even though there seems to be pretty good evidence that Jesus was well taught in the Jewish tradition, He was clearly not part of the hierarchy. Mark's Gospel makes the case more clearly.

Prophets are not without honour, except in their hometown, and among their own kin, and in their own house.

Reflecting on this, two thoughts arise. First, it was not His proximity to His home community that raised questions about His teaching, or his "honor." It was the essence of His message. Love the poor, the imprisoned, the ill, the outcast. These are strong words. Even more alarming, however, must have been the admonition that we are to love our enemies.

Second, resisting the authority of a "local boy" might explain a lack of interest in attending meetings or listening to speeches. It is not something that should ever have led to such a brutal form of murder as a crucifixion. The mob's reaction to Jesus and His message was inspired by those at the top of the triple pyramid (of power, prestige, and possessions) feeling threatened.

Jesus quotes from Isaiah 61, reminding me of what Father Rohr calls the "Jesus Hermeneutic." Jesus uses scripture fairly often during His ministry, each time "cherry picking" His references using the filters of mercy and inclusion. Isaiah 61 certainly fits the criteria. It is so completely clear that the Gospel of Jesus Christ, the "New Covenant," was aimed at the bottom—the poor, the captives, the blind, and the oppressed. Rather than excluding these easily ignored groups, Christ exalted them. I can only express my utter disbelief and dismay that we are now two thousand years on from the time Jesus proclaimed this great Gospel, and still live in a largely Christian country where the central themes of that Gospel are ignored.

I am writing this in my hotel room at the Quality Hotel, following an incredible mission day in Mamey. It was a day filled with deep sadness, as I held a weeping Antes in my arms. She was mourning the death of her ten-year-old grandson earlier this week. But the day also contained the joy of hundreds of patients laughing with the doctors and nurses in the village. This is the eleventh medical mission since we started this ministry! The friendships are palpable.

January 16

Repeat Luke 4:14–22, The Beginning of the Galilean Ministry

It is early morning in Santo Domingo. The past four days have left me, at the same time, spiritually drained and spiritually fulfilled. Reflecting on this first mission of 2017, I am particularly moved by the shared mourning with Antes, whose house is SPM 1 (Sister Parish Ministry 1, the first house built by the ministry). Antes speaks virtually no Spanish, only Creole. As a result, my communication with her is mostly through touch. She moved into the house in the spring of 2015 with her daughter and three grandchildren. HIV and AIDS are still forbidden subjects in Mamey, whispered about in shame and seldom treated. The daughter of Antes has the disease, and has presumably passed it on to her children. Last week her ten-year-old son died from complications associated with HIV/AIDS. He loved to dance. I watched a video of his dancing, showing off for both his family and for our missionaries. He was a very good dancer!

For the second time, I experienced the deeply moving funeral practice of "*el novenario,*" a nine-day mourning ceremony that takes place in a different house each day. My first *novenario* experience was for a young mother whose infected arm led almost immediately to her death. I was with her when she told the doctor that she would not allow him to take her arm under any circumstances. She said she had to work to support her three young children. The children now live with an aunt and three cousins in Mamey.

No one, in any culture anywhere, wants to bury their young. Death should happen at the end of life, not the beginning. In my experience, grief and suffering are much better managed by the simply innocent people, existing at the margins of life, than by most of society. There are no filters for their pain. Antes held nothing back. She simply, openly, humanly, and intimately brought me into her pain, asking inoffensively for my compassion. I had no choice but to give it, and to deeply feel her agony. Holding her in my arms while she sobbed and wept and shook with grief defined this mission trip for me. My heart space opened. The better parts of me were fed with shared love.

I pray for even the smallest bit of help in making this tiny part of creation better, or, at least, less oppressive. I pray that my friends in Mamey will know that I am trying, that my intentions are genuine. I pray that I will find reasons to hope.

January 17

Matthew 4:23–5:12, Jesus Ministers to Crowds of People
²³ Jesus went throughout Galilee, teaching in their synagogues and proclaiming the good news of the kingdom and curing every disease and every sickness among the people. ²⁴ So his fame spread throughout all Syria, and they brought to him all the sick, those who were afflicted with various diseases and pains, demoniacs, epileptics, and paralytics, and he cured them. ²⁵ And great crowds followed him from Galilee, the Decapolis, Jerusalem, Judea, and from beyond the Jordan.
The Beatitudes
¹ When Jesus saw the crowds, he went up the mountain; and after he sat down, his disciples came to him. ² Then he began to speak, and taught them, saying:
³ "Blessed are the poor in spirit, for theirs is the kingdom of heaven.
⁴ "Blessed are those who mourn, for they will be comforted.
⁵ "Blessed are the meek, for they will inherit the earth.
⁶ "Blessed are those who hunger and thirst for righteousness, for they will be filled.
⁷ "Blessed are the merciful, for they will receive mercy.
⁸ "Blessed are the pure in heart, for they will see God.
⁹ "Blessed are the peacemakers, for they will be called children of God.
¹⁰ "Blessed are those who are persecuted for righteousness' sake, for theirs is the kingdom of heaven.
¹¹ "Blessed are you when people revile you and persecute you and utter all kinds of evil against you falsely on my account. ¹² Rejoice and be glad, for your reward is great in heaven, for in the same way they persecuted the prophets who were before you.

MOST OF THE time I forget my dreams. I will have some vague awareness that I had been in the middle of something, but can never quite put it together. Last night was different. The dream was so powerful that I wrote notes immediately upon waking, both during the night, and again this morning. Before turning to some reflections on the Beatitudes, I want to write something about this dream.

There were two distinct parts of the dream, the first involved Serendipity, our house in Ponte Vedra. We were in the process of selling the house, presumably having reached a time when we no longer needed so much space. In truth, we reached that point several years ago, before building Serendipity. It is not a house designed around our needs, or even our genuine "wants." The two of us need a house with perhaps 2,000 square feet of living space. We, especially Sallie Ann, wanted something a little larger, but definitely not more than 5,000 square feet.

In the dream, Serendipity had been sold, and we were looking at something else. Our "new house" was actually an upstairs wing of a house even grander than Serendipity. It must have been somewhere in Europe, a country house in England or an estate in the Italian countryside. We were considering three rooms, each so large that they would require considerable construction to become useful. The dream involved my effort to design the renovation of these rooms. What slowly became apparent was that I had lost my ability to design, to reflect on paper the ideas that Sallie Ann and I discussed. I reacted with anger, crumpling up each day's futile work product. At one point, I lit the drafting paper and table on fire. Then I woke up.

The second part of the dream took place on a body of water, I think perhaps a lake in Italy. Sallie Ann and I had hired a boat to take us to dinner. For most of my life I have considered myself quite the world traveler, an expert on great places to stay and eat. The driver of the boat was intent on taking us in a direction different from the one I insisted we take. The problem was that I could not remember any of the names of the restaurants or even the towns where I wanted him to go. We argued and I became angry. I eventually jumped off the boat into the water. Then I woke up.

Both parts of the dream involved my mental incapacity and loss of memory. I was deeply frightened by this loss of control. Even worse than my inability to recall and control "facts," I could not control my angry outbursts. The dream feels extremely real to me, unsettling me even as I recount it. My whole life has been about having knowledge and appearing intelligent. Losing my thinking ability scares me to death. I know other people who become belligerent and angry when they are confused, or cannot remember things. I fervently hope I am decades away from that situation.

Matthew's Gospel verses today are the very heart of the Divine Project, bringing all creation together in unitive consciousness and love. I am on the plane now, flying from Santo Domingo to Miami. Most of the other missionaries from the medical mission are on this plane. I look at them now, and see fellow soldiers in the army of the Divine Project. They healed the sick and afflicted, brought sight to the blind, carried laughter and joy to the tired and sad, and touched the hearts of everyone around them. All of this love and joy is with us now on the plane, and will be with us tonight at our All Hands meeting. If that is all there is, if the magic disappears by tomorrow, it will have been worth it. Little by little, step by step, heart by heart, we are changing ourselves and each other. It is yet another good beginning.

January 18

Repeat Matthew 4:23–5:12, Jesus Ministers to Crowds of People and the Beatitudes

JESUS COVERED a lot of ground during his relatively short ministry. Matthew writes that people throughout a large part of what we call the Middle East today knew about Jesus, and traveled substantial distances to hear Him teach. I think the area "throughout all Syria, the Galilee, Jerusalem, Judea, and even beyond the Jordan" was once called Greater Palestine, and included modern day Syria, Jordan, Israel, Lebanon, Palestine, and parts of Iraq and Egypt. The vast, thinly populated deserts of the Saudi Peninsula were crisscrossed with Bedouin trade routes, undoubtedly allowing word of this new Gospel to spread even further.

It is intriguing to read about all of the "diseases and pains" that were cured by Jesus, especially after this past weekend, when we worked to heal the sick in the barrios and bateyes of the Dominican Republic. I love and admire the doctors and nurses who make these mission trips. They seem to know that their very touch brings relief! I believe the first step in healing is simply *seeing* the Other, if possible saying their name. I watched several of our first-time missionaries do that this week in the "registration rooms." Normally Chris Goodell is in charge of this part of each day's clinic, but Joyce Moore did it in Chris's absence this trip. It ran like clockwork.

Each OLSS Sister Parish registrar, typically non-Spanish or Creole speaking, sits with a volunteer from either Santissima Trinidad or UNIBE. There is both a card for new patients and a computer printout of existing patients (our database now has more than 3,000 names). As soon as a patient sits down, the Sister Parish volunteer looks at the patient and extends his or her hand in greeting. There is a certain amount of fumbling and mumbling as the name is sorted out, all of which "humanizes" the experience for both sides.

From that point on through four more stations, the patient is addressed by name, "seen," and touched. I have been watching this process over four years and hundreds of patients, yet I am still amazed at what happens. The patient, typically Haitian and not accustomed to being seen, touched, and named by anyone, especially a white person from the US, is shy at first, then sits up a little or stands a little taller, finally breaks into a smile and continues to smile through vital signs, blood pressure, the doctor, and, finally, the pharmacist. I will never tire of watching this transformation.

It happens to our volunteers as well. At first a little reticent, probably more concerned with the rubber gloves and hand sanitizer than anything else, the volunteer slowly blossoms into a warm, happy healing presence. This is the magic of the Divine Project! It takes us into itself, immersing us in so much love that we are born again.

I pray that this ministry is only just beginning its life. I pray with enormous gratitude for all of the volunteers from Ponte Vedra, Santo Domingo, Guerra, Mamey, UNIBE, and, in our own simple way, from "beyond the Jordan."

January 19

The Three Phases of Humility

Three "degrees" of humility once raised in people's minds the image of three dynamic ways of living under God. "Phases" raises in our minds the changes that a living being passes through, more or less permanent, epigenetic (they build on one another), and always moving toward some kind of fulfillment and completion.

Humility is not a quality or a status, like eye color or height. Rather, it is the ongoing, appropriate enacting of a relationship, first of all of a relationship with God. Humility is like health (a complex set of relationships); it goes up and down, is more or less intense, good or bad.

The humble person positively, gladly, and creatively accepts creature hood. They affirm their limitedness in concrete particulars. They embrace having to depend entirely, in all, on God and actually delight in that. They do not demand to control everything in life, but deal with life as with a surprising series of gifts.

The humble person accepts creature hood as they find it. They include in this humankind's sinful condition, and that sinfulness in themselves. This acquiescence in the way things are I do not mean connivance, and I do not mean passivity flows from the decision to see things as they are and not to retreat into the subtle rejection of God's creating and governing by refusing to see things as they really are.

The first sign of the mere presence of humility comes when a person knows himself and their life world, with some clarity and objectivity. This is what the old dictum means: "Humility is truth."

But as Scripture says, "we are to do the truth lovingly." This means that humility must be enacted. It is not merely an attitude, and it is much less merely a feeling.

THE FIRST PHASE

I see the world as it is. I see myself, first of all, desiring certain things. I might, for example, want a certain job or to live in a certain city. However, I understand that I do not determine which of my desires lead to my authentic life and to my deep happiness; I depend on God for that. God the Creator and Lord has created certain values for and in me, so when I evaluate any thing or any action, I cannot make up the rules on my own. So, if I value very highly writing a certain letter in order to get the job I want, and then realize that writing this letter would violate my own conscience very gravely—then I do not write the letter. God sets my values. To use language we once used: I want and value certain things very highly, but I would not under any circumstances choose to place a desire or a value that I have in front of the desires and values that God writes into my own conscience. I depend on God for my conscience. I am gifted by God with a conscience—this concrete conscience, with its own dictates. I acquiesce in the concrete dictates of the conscience, I am glad to depend on God and to acquiesce.

To put it succinctly: I live to obey God who speaks in my spirit. For I know this: God has placed deepest in me a desire for Himself and I have chosen to enact my desire to belong to God before I enact any other desire, and I will enact no desire that would separate me from God. This is the first phase of humility.

THE SECOND PHASE

I begin to find in myself the desire to find God and to grow to love God. I do not spend my time "avoiding sin"; rather, I spend my time finding God. In this mind-set, I would not go against my own conscience deliberately even in relatively unimportant things. It is not so much that I want to keep from offending God and violating my own honesty and integrity. I have changed in this, that I have chosen to love God, and not just to obey God. Of course, I still want career, and job, and very much else, and in the pursuit of these things I often discover that I can attain a very important objective by just the mildest violation of my own conscience. I generally manage not to do that. I fear God, of course, and I dread acting unauthenticated. One thing helps a good deal: I see how vain and empty much of the world is. I see how futilely I would live, for example, were I to give myself entirely to the job I love. I would be a fool to count on earthly things to give me lasting happiness—they don't last. So, I see and perceive from within my own creature hood. I have happily accepted the wisdom of the prophets and the wise of old: The Lord's is the earth and all that is in it. But the fact is that I would find it impossible to follow my conscience so carefully except that a great love is growing in my life.

THE THIRD PHASE

In this phase, I come to see the earth and all that is in it through other eyes: the human eyes of Jesus of Nazareth. Jesus came into a culture utterly unlike my own except in certain essentials: people then wanted wealth, power, fame, and pleasure just as people today want them. Jesus went against culture and human inclinations, by choosing to be born poor and to live poor, by electing to join the powerless and the outcast. I do not find it so easy to go against culture. I take my culture into myself and then contribute to it in my turn; and following that culture, I want to know a lot and to be known as wise, to have many skills and to be known as an accomplished person, to have wealth and to be known as a solid citizen. But along comes my Lord Jesus Christ. I am seized by His Spirit, and filled with His love. I come to love Him to this extent, that I really want to see as He saw, evaluate as He evaluated, appreciate as He appreciated, and simply to live the way He lived. He so humbled Himself that He poured Himself out, living like the lower classes, making the simplest and most outcast welcome in His company, always serving. He kept on His course even when the choices He made under the Spirit led to great suffering and to a cruel death. I find to my astonishment that I want very much to follow along after Him in all that. I deliberately suppress any desire to be famous, powerful, wealthy, and known to be wise. I want to live as He lived. However, I do not demand that specific kind of life from God my Creator. I accept with my whole heart that the choice does not finally rest with me; and humility means precisely that I acquiesce in what God our Lord creates in me.

In this phase of humility, some find themselves in this state of mind: I know that I am a sinful person, and I find it astonishing that I feel summoned to intimate friendship with Jesus Christ. I know that His way leads to dying to the self. I know His way leads to the crown. While I do not feel impelled to go looking for suffering or invited to inflict suffering on myself, I do feel perfectly ready to take whatever suffering comes along, and I will accept it as from the hand of God because then I will be following Jesus.

Some find themselves in the following state of mind: I have come to love Jesus Christ with my whole self, and even if I am a sinful person, I want to be really poor so I can be like Him. I want to be misunderstood and looked down on. I truly desire to experience these hard things with Jesus, as long as no one who inflicts them on me insults God or offends his or her own conscience. For Jesus chose to live this way. He lived a quiet and hidden life, for a long time. He was let down and disappointed. I truly want all that, because I will be following Him more closely.

These are three phases or degrees of humility. They are three ways of loving God. They are also three ways of acknowledging my own creature hood, and three ways of entering into what it means to let God shape my values. The first is the way of the commandments. The second is the way of creative, active indifference. The third is the way of imitating Christ.

If I can let my own desires rise, I can take them first to the Lady Mary and ask that she ask Jesus to call me where He wants me. Then I ask Jesus to grant me to live authentically, and to give me the courage to live as His Spirit leads me. Finally, I turn full-hearted to the Father.

THREE PHASES of humility: 1. Follow the commandments, 2. Creative, active indifference, and 3. Imitate Christ. These are phases of humility, not arrogance or defiance or rejection of God. These are all good places to be.

The first phase of humility is essentially passive acceptance of God's laws. James Martin describes this as, "The first level is when one does nothing morally wrong. In other words, one leads a good life." In my dark periods, I clearly was not in this phase. Even in the high moments, I resisted the first rule of simple obedience.

My problem stems from my questioning of God's laws, particularly when they are determined solely by what can be found in the Scriptures, as interpreted by the Church, whether that Church is Mormon or Catholic. As I understand the reading, there is no third step of personal experience, no evaluation of the "official position" using judgement and discernment.

My immediate reaction to this understanding of humility is decidedly not humble! I object, I resist, I challenge, I ask for another opinion. Some of this reaction is most assuredly my stubborn ego, reluctant to give up control. My whole spiritual journey has been filled with the teaching, advice, and counsel of great men and women down through the ages, who have emphasized the "humanness" of creation. Humans make mistakes, all of us.

Jesus spoke Aramaic, as, presumably, did virtually all of rural Palestine, which includes all of Israel outside of Jerusalem. Based on stories of His visits to the temple, He must have been able to read and speak some Hebrew. While I have read some arguments to the contrary, most of what I have read and been taught quite clearly suggests that Jesus spoke virtually no Greek. And, of course, Jesus did not write his speeches and sermons in any language. They existed only as oral tradition for years.

When, by whom, and in what language the earliest written materials about Jesus first appeared still seems to be somewhat speculative. The earliest source documents were probably written about ten years after the crucifixion, and were probably written in Koine Greek. These early source documents were available to and used by the authors of the Gospels more than twenty years later, in the period 65 to 95 CE. Paul wrote his letters in Antioch, Corinth, Ephesus, and elsewhere, mostly in what is now southern Turkey, between 50 and 60 CE, also probably in Koine Greek.

The point is that the New Testament was written long after the death of Jesus Christ, and written in a language not spoken by Christ. Considering all of the scribes, translators, and medieval monks involved in writing down the stories, translating them, and copying them over and over again, how can we possibly insist that these few words must be the primary source of our religious principles and doctrines? To accept "God's word" taken from Holy Scripture as the basis for understanding the universe, and who we are in that universe, strikes me as a bridge too far. Add to that, however, the qualifying clause that doctrinal guidance must be limited to that Holy Scripture *as interpreted by the Catholic Church* (or, for my early life, by the Mormon Church) does not help much. For much of its history, the Catholic Church has been led by extremely questionable Bishops, Cardinals, and Popes. The great theologians and mystics I have come to know and love over the past few years were frequently banned while they were alive. The primary thrust of their teaching, that we and all of creation are one in Christ, and have been throughout our nearly fourteen-billion-year history, is still questioned by many conservative Catholics.

Passive acceptance of "the Bible and the Church" has never been possible for me. Even now, almost six years after my baptism, I am, if anything, even further away from passivity. It is important that I point out that these views on Holy Scripture and Church doctrine should not lead anyone to think that I will not continue to read and reflect on these Scriptures soon and often. In spite of my protests, on the whole, I believe, accept, and live by the fundamental elements of the Gospel.

The second level of humility is described by James Martin as "when a person who, when presented with the choice of riches or poverty, honor or disgrace, is free of the need for either. In other words, the person is free to accept whatever God desires, not being 'attached' to one state or the other." This state of creative, active indifference requires a shift from a "sin-avoidance" value system, to a "God-finding" value system. Sin avoidance seems to me to be the traditional "sin and redemption" approach to our very purpose for being. Life is a personal salvation system, designed to keep me out of Hell. The Teilhard alternative to this is focused on all of creation, not just on the individual. It demands of me that I get out of myself and join with all of creation, both temporally (eternity, from the Big Bang for all of time) and spatially (infinity, from here to everywhere). Moreover, salvation, avoiding Hell, and getting into Heaven, are not the objectives. Our collective purpose is to create Heaven right here, and right now, which, of course, is everywhere and always. We do this together with everyone of like mind in the world, and we do it with love. This certainly appeals to me. I will use my time, talent, and treasure for this honorable purpose.

The third phase of humility is significantly different. "I deliberately suppress any desire to be famous, powerful, wealthy, and known to be wise. I want to live as He lived." It strikes me that this third form of humility, while noble, would leave me much less capable, less able to participate in the collective effort to make the world better. In a sense, this third stage of humility requires that I fall back on the first stage, taking a course of action that might improve my *personal holiness*, but weakening the concerted action of the whole Body of Christ. I pray for the wisdom and judgement to understand humility, and for the strength to act wisely.

January 20

Repeat The Three Phases of Humility

MAGGIE AND I came down early this morning. The contemplation yesterday left me unsettled. Many mornings, I read Bruce Sanguin's blog on *Home for Evolving Mystics*. This morning, Sanguin quoted from two great mystical poets, one, Rumi, who wrote in the twelfth century, and the other, Christian Wiman, who presently teaches at Yale.

Rumi's verses could easily have been written by Teilhard.

I died as mineral and became a plant,
I died as plant and rose to animal,
I died as animal and I was human,
Why should I fear? When was I less by dying?
Yet once more I shall die human,
To soar with angels blessed above.
And when I sacrifice my angel soul
I shall become what no mind ever conceived.
As a human, I will die once more,
Reborn, I will with the angels soar.
And when I let my angel body go,
I shall be more than mortal mind can know.

This line from Christian Wiman reminds me of my resistance to "churchy religion":

…faith itself sometimes needs to be stripped of its social and historical encrustations and returned to its first, churchless incarnation in the human heart.

How should I be humble? When I returned to the library from the garden bench, the only possible answer seemed to be that I should strive to be humble in all of the three manners or stages described in the reading.

My resistance to the literal reading of Scripture, and to the sometimes difficult (for me) interpretations provided by Church authorities, need not be the overriding position. In fact, it is not. Most of the time, for most things, I am perfectly content to "transcend and include" both the literal and the metaphorical. Most of the time, again, for most things, I can "transcend and include" the occasionally frustrating edicts from the seat of ecclesiastical power.

I concluded yesterday that the third stage of humility, giving away everything in service and obedience, would leave me unable to participate as fully in the Divine Project as if I kept my "power, prestige, and possessions." This, itself, is "either/or," dualistic thinking. Things are never this black and white. The sensible, "both/and" route is to moderate spending on myself, both to leave more for the collective effort and, importantly, to experience the humility of frugality.

Today is the day of Donald J. Trump's inauguration. I am deeply depressed. I will end this morning's reflection by quoting in full from John Pavlovitz.

Let the record show that I did not consent to this.

Let it show that I did not vote for this man, that he did not represent me, that I did not believe he was deserving of being here, that I grieved his ascension.

Let History record my objection to him, to the ways he humiliated women and vilified Muslims and threatened protestors and disregarded people of color.

Let it record my repulsion at his tremendous cruelty, his lack of compassion, his contempt for dissension, his absence of simple decency.

Let witnesses mark down my disgust at the way he boasted of infidelity, at how he ridiculed a disabled reporter, at the way he attacked female opponents for their appearance, at the way he marginalized immigrants.

Let it be remembered that I did not look the other way when women accused him of assault, when the reality of his Russian alliances came to light, when he refused to share his tax records—though large portions of the American media and its people chose to.

Let it be remembered that I did not buy into the fear that he perpetuated of those with brown skin or hijabs or foreign birthplaces.

Let the record show that I looked on with disbelief as he spent countless early morning and middle-of-the-night hours following the election on social media, broadcasting a steady stream of petulant, insecure, incoherent messages instead of preparing to do a job he was ill-equipped for and seemingly not all that interested in.

Let the record show that I watched him assemble a Cabinet of billionaires and bigots, of people woefully unqualified to steward our children, our safety, our healthcare, our financial stability—and that I was horrified by it all.

Let it be remembered that my faith would not allow me to fall in line behind this man while so many professed religious people did; that I saw nothing resembling Jesus in him, and that to declare him Christian would have been to toss aside everything I grew up believing faith in Christ manifested in a life.

Let History record my grieving at the racism and bigotry and homophobia that characterized his campaign, marked his supporters, and is evident in his assembling Administration.

Let it be known that I was one of the more than 65 million people who voted for Hillary Clinton; who understood that though flawed, she was an intelligent, experienced, passionate public servant with the temperament, commitment, and qualifications to lead and lead well.

Let the record show that I greatly lamented the day of his inauguration, and that I promised to join together with other good people to loudly resist and oppose every unscrupulous, dangerous, unjust and dishonest act this new Administration engages in.

History has been littered with horrible people who did terrible things with power, because too many good people remained silent. And since my fear is that we are surely entering one of those periods in our story, I wanted to make sure that I was recorded for posterity:

I do not believe this man is normal.

I do not believe he is emotionally stable.

I do not believe he cares about the full, beautiful diversity of America.

I do not believe he respects women.

I do not believe he is pro-life other than his own.

I do not believe the sick and the poor and the hurting matter to him in the slightest.

I do not believe he is a man of faith or integrity or nobility.

I do not believe his concern is for anything outside his reflection in the mirror.

I believe he is a danger to our children.

I believe he is a threat to our safety.

I believe he is careless with our people.

I believe he is reckless with his power.

I believe America will be less secure, less diverse, less compassionate, and less decent under his leadership.

And if I prove to be wrong, it will be one of the most joyful errors of my life. I will own these words and if necessary, willingly and gladly admit my misjudgment because it will mean that America is a better and stronger nation, and the world a more peaceful place.

But right now, I don't see that happening.

Right now, I am worried for my country, concerned for our planet, scared for the future of my children, and greatly saddened that 62 million Americans seem okay with all of this.

I will watch some of the inauguration with friends today. It will be a sad day.

January 21

Repeat and reflect on the week.

READING AGAIN my reflections from yesterday, I sadly stand behind my decision to quote the Pavlovitz statement in full. This journal will exist long after the inauguration and presidency of Donald Trump. I hope with all my heart that I will have reason to revisit my feelings and the entry on January 20, 2017. For the good of the country, the planet, our Church, and my family, I hope to be proven wrong. But the dark, divisive, and xenophobic inaugural speech of our new president gives me little hope.

As I mentioned, Father Rohr introduced Sallie Ann and me to the Franciscan contemplative tradition in a conference in Assisi, Italy, in 2012. It was our first "in-person" introduction to Father Rohr. Little did I know how important this tradition would become in my life. Father Rohr wrote:

We know the contemplative tradition, or nondual consciousness, was systematically taught in the West as late as the 11th and 12th centuries in some Carthusian and Cistercian monasteries. The early Franciscans were the "accidental" beneficiaries of this more ancient understanding through the lay genius of Francis himself; the Rhineland Dominicans beautifully exemplify it; and the Carmelites gather much of it from their ancient history in Palestine at Mount Carmel. Its final flower, even supernova of expression, is of course in the 16th century mystics, Teresa of Ávila and John of the Cross. At great personal cost, Teresa and John reintroduced contemplation to the Carmelites. Other bright spots are Pseudo-Dionysius in the fifth century and The Cloud of Unknowing in the fourteenth century.

I would add Teilhard, Merton, Jim Finley, Ilia Delio, Pope Francis, and Father Rohr himself to this panoply of contemplative greatness. In this week, ending as it does with a reflection on humility, it is fitting that I humbly acknowledge with deep appreciation all that they have taught me, and continue to teach me. Working with the wonderful nuns at Futuro Vivo, the Carmelite school in Guerra, Dominican Republic, reminds me, each time again, of the powerful tradition of the Carmelites, as Father Rohr wrote, the "supernova of expression."

It is in this grand tradition that I am once again doing these Exercises. After five years of relatively continuous study, countless books and numerous lectures, I am struck most by how much more I have to learn, of how much I learn each day.

It is fitting that this week for me began in the Dominican Republic, serving with the medical mission, and ends with a reflection on humility. Nothing can humble a person more than these missions. I truly believe they are part of the Christ Project envisioned by Teilhard, part of a global, collective effort to make the world a better place.

Reflecting on it this morning, it occurs to me that mission work involves all three stages of humility. Clearly, our Church interprets the Holy Scriptures to say that we are meant to serve the poor, heal the sick, and otherwise care for those in the margins of life. This is the first stage of humility. Mission work also requires the most of our time, talent, and treasure, and the greater our time, talent, and treasure, the more we can accomplish in our mission efforts. This is the second stage of humility. Finally, mission work is humbling, making it clear that all the time, talent, and treasure in the world will never be enough to alleviate all the world's pain. This, the third stage of humility, is not only about giving away all that we have to serve the Lord. It is the realization that all that we have is not enough.

One of my "outside readings" this week has been Matthew Fox's *Illuminations of Hildegard of Bingen*, a fascinating study of this incredible twelfth century woman. She described her first vision as an extraordinary "white light" experience:

> When I was forty-two years and seven months old, a burning light of tremendous brightness coming from heaven poured into my entire mind. Like a flame that does not burn but enkindles, it inflamed my entire heart and my entire breast, just like the sun that warms an object with its rays.

Reflecting on that, I considered how mundane my own transformation has been. Just reading Hildegard's account of her first experience brought more heat and light into my personal contemplative space than anything that has ever happened to me. This is the power of the rich tradition of mystics and writers down through the centuries. They are teachers today, capable of feeding my faith, and making my heart grow. Audaciously, and somewhat presumptuously, I claim them as friends.

My goal for this week was to know Jesus of Nazareth, to love Him, and to follow Him in His way. In my quiet conversations with Jesus in the library and in the garden, I did come to know Him more each day. Talking to Him from the plane flying to and from Santo Domingo, and in the hotel or at the clinics, I came to know Him better. The combination of these Exercises and the work of Sister Parish is powerful. I pray in gratitude for this extraordinary opportunity. I pray for strength and wisdom.

CALENDAR WEEK NINETEEN

I want to know Jesus better, to love Him more, and to follow Him wholeheartedly.

January 22

Mark 10:46–52, The Healing of Blind Bartimaeus
⁴⁶ They came to Jericho. As he and his disciples and a large crowd were leaving Jericho, Bartimaeus son of Timaeus, a blind beggar, was sitting by the roadside. ⁴⁷ When he heard that it was Jesus of Nazareth, he began to shout out and say, "Jesus, Son of David, have mercy on me!" ⁴⁸ Many sternly ordered him to be quiet, but he cried out even more loudly, "Son of David, have mercy on me!" ⁴⁹ Jesus stood still and said, "Call him here." And they called the blind man, saying to him, "Take heart; get up, he is calling you." ⁵⁰ So throwing off his cloak, he sprang up and came to Jesus. ⁵¹ Then Jesus said to him, "What do you want me to do for you?" The blind man said to him, "My teacher, let me see again." ⁵² Jesus said to him, "Go; your faith has made you well." Immediately he regained his sight and followed him on the way.

THE LAST FEW days have been incredible on several levels. First came the inauguration of President Trump, complete with an inaugural speech so dark and divisive that even some conservatives called it the worst inaugural speech in US history. The non-stop hearings for the new cabinet officers made it very clear just how radical the policy changes are likely to be. Most of what Obama accomplished in the last eight years is in jeopardy, though I personally believe the damage from undoing all of the good things will become clear before irreparable harm is done. There is more hope in that sentence than conviction.

Then came the resistance marches on Saturday. All of the women in my family marched, along with more than three million women worldwide, in a show of peaceful, joy filled, but powerful resistance to the new President. Many of my friends, men and women, joined the festivity. I felt intimately involved while watching the numerous marches on television all day, reading the Facebook posts of family and friends, and talking on the phone several times. As dark as the inaugural speech was, as deeply concerned as I am about the direction of the country, and as depressed as I have been since November 8, this one day of global resistance filled me with delight. The connection with what seemed to be the whole world was palpable.

Maggie and I sat on the bench in the garden on this unseasonably warm winter day. The reading today from Mark evokes a strong sense of wonder at the simple faith of the blind Bartimaeus. "Let me see again!" These are words I have often wanted to say. When my faith journey began almost a decade ago, the desire to see through the miasma of despair was powerful. Bottoms do that to people. To my eyes, there was no path out of the mess I was in. I hated the Brits. I hated the doctors. I hated my body. I hated my soul.

John of the Cross encountered his dark night of the soul while ascending Mount Carmel. But he was *ascending*! I was neither ascending, nor descending. Rather I was spiritually motionless, stuck in a self-destructive pattern of behavior, making no effort to change. "Let me see again!" The only thing that could get me out of the mental and spiritual pit I was in was a major heart attack. No, that is not quite true. I needed three heart attacks to get the message!

The spiritual transformation that began in the fall of 2007 continues to this day. The Greek term *metanoia*, "putting on a new mind-set" describes this process well. Everything about my life has slowly changed, or, better said, is slowly changing. I am, finally, quite well physically. Even the occasional bouts of angina have been absent for close to a year. While I have been unhappy with the political situation in the past year, there is simply no comparison to the suicidal despair I felt in 2006. I laugh every day. I feel joy every day. I love my reading, my work with Sister Parish, my connection with the Living School, and the community of good friends that surround me.

Sometimes the fog of information from reading so much obscures my vision more than it elucidates. I read, then re-read, then read again. I read commentaries on the original sources. I listen to lectures and tapes. "Let me see again!" As much as I recognize the confusion of data overload, I remain convinced that there will soon be light enough to unravel the web of concepts, terms, dates, names, and facts. Then this will all make sense.

I pray for clarity. I pray for strength to continue the journey, to read more, to learn more, and to persevere.

January 23

Repeat Mark 10:46–52, The Healing of Blind Bartimaeus

THIS MONDAY morning in America begins with the extraordinary hangover of a disastrous, dark, and divisive Inauguration Friday, followed by an inspiring, delightful, and globally uniting Women's March Saturday. I find it unusually hard to get out of this "public space," and softly enter the private, internal space where I can quietly talk to God. Even though the temperature is unseasonably warm, close to 70 degrees, it was chilly on the bench. Listening to the ocean, the birds, and Maggie in the bushes slowly brought me into the moment.

"Let me see again!" The strength of this request, and the simple faith of Bartimaeus that Jesus would make it happen, are moving. I sat with this, meditating on the concepts of spiritual and moral blindness.

Back in the warmth of the library, I sat in front of the Rublev icon, thinking about the power of faith. Images of lighting candles ran through my mind: Special Advent services, candle ceremonies at various retreats, lighting the Menorah at Hanukkah. Each of these mental pictures represented the power of faith to bring light to a dark place, to make truth visible. John 9:25 is right on point.

> He answered, "I do not know whether he is a sinner. One thing I do know, that though I was blind, now I see."

In my broken, thankfully inaudible voice, I intoned the words from Amazing Grace, bringing up the image of President Obama after the Charleston shooting.

> Amazing grace how sweet the sound
> That saved a wretch like me.
> I once was lost but now I'm found.
> *Was blind but now I see.*

I love this song. It is the universal choice of broken people transformed by faith. The point is that, like Bartimaeus, I see through God's grace. I only have to surrender to His gift. Father Rohr frequently teaches about the extraordinary difficulty we humans have in accepting God's grace. "The free flow of unearned love, what we call grace, is almost a punishment for most people. They fiercely resist it."

I ended the morning with this thought from Hildegard of Bingen, "God has arranged all things in the world in consideration of everything else."

January 24

Luke 8:26–39, Jesus Heals the Gerasene Demoniac
²⁶ Then they arrived at the country of the Gerasenes, which is opposite Galilee. ²⁷ As he stepped out on land, a man of the city who had demons met him. For a long time he had worn no clothes, and he did not live in a house but in the tombs. ²⁸ When he saw Jesus, he fell down before him and shouted at the top of his voice, "What have you to do with me, Jesus, Son of the Most High God? I beg you, do not torment me"— ²⁹ for Jesus had commanded the unclean spirit to come out of the man. (For many times it had seized him; he was kept under guard and bound with chains and shackles, but he would break the bonds and be driven by the demon into the wilds.) ³⁰ Jesus then asked him, "What is your name?" He said, "Legion"; for many demons had entered him. ³¹ They begged him not to order them to go back into the abyss.

³² Now there on the hillside a large herd of swine was feeding; and the demons begged Jesus to let them enter these. So he gave them permission. ³³ Then the demons came out of the man and entered the swine, and the herd rushed down the steep bank into the lake and was drowned.

³⁴ When the swineherds saw what had happened, they ran off and told it in the city and in the country. ³⁵ Then people came out to see what had happened, and when they came to Jesus, they found the man from whom the demons had gone sitting at the feet of Jesus, clothed and in his right mind. And they were afraid. ³⁶ Those who had seen it told them how the one who had been possessed by demons had been healed. ³⁷ Then all the people of the surrounding country of the Gerasenes asked Jesus to leave them; for they were seized with great fear. So he got into the boat and returned. ³⁸ The man from whom the demons had gone begged that he might be with him; but Jesus sent him away, saying, ³⁹ "Return to your home, and declare how much God has done for you." So he went away, proclaiming throughout the city how much Jesus had done for him.

THE MOON WAS a bright white crescent in the cold black sky. All the stars were out. The ocean was quiet. We sat for only a few minutes before the cold was too much for me, though I suspect Maggie, already deeply involved in a lizard search, would have been fine. Walking back along the rill, I felt the strongly unpleasant feelings of dizziness and nausea. I prayed for a long time in front of the Rublev icon.

Last night, I read the passage from Luke about the exorcism of the Gerasene demoniac several times. In addition to meditating about what came up for me each time I read it, I tried to learn a little about Gerasenes, demons, and pigs. I know something about pigs. As I have reported elsewhere in this journal, I am a frustrated pig farmer in the Dominican Republic. By that I mean I have owned several pigs in partnership with men in Mamey. I have yet to make a single peso from my pigs!

Gerasenes were the people living in or near Gadara or Gerasa, both ancient cities on the eastern side of the Galilee, across the lake from Nazareth and Capernaum. This story of the demoniac is preceded by an account of Jesus crossing the Galilee with His disciples. Jesus calms a fierce storm, "rebuking the wind and raging waves."

Demons or evil spirits have been part of the official doctrine of the Church since the time of Christ. The Catechism of the Catholic Church states, "When the Church asks publicly and authoritatively in the name of Jesus Christ that a person or object be protected against the power of the Evil One and withdrawn from his dominion, it is called exorcism." I am agnostic on the subject of evil spirits, tilting heavily towards disbelief. Whether there are supernatural beings or not will not change my belief in creation spirituality.

There is, of course, powerful metaphoric value in the parables about exorcising demons and evil spirits. I heard a lecture once that emphasized three common characteristics in the demons encountered by Jesus. First, the demons cause self-destructive behavior in their victims. Second, the victims feel trapped. Finally, as a result of their "possession," the victims are separated from their families and normal lives. This sounds very much like addiction, whether to substances or patterns of behavior. Addictive drinkers and addictive gamblers complain about being trapped in downward spirals of self-destructive behavior. Addicts are ashamed of their behavior, characteristically avoiding friends and family, or, worse, pushing them away when they try to help.

The addiction metaphor continues in the descriptions of how Jesus heals the victims and exorcises the demons. Jesus asks the victim to believe in Him, and urges the victim to return to his family or community. Healing begins with surrender, with "letting go and letting Him." Most forms of healing require belief that a Higher Power, together with the community of others seeking a cure, are the only sources of healing.

Reflecting on the issue of addiction this morning, I am reminded of the extraordinary increase in both drug addiction and death from drug overdose in the past few years. The scale of the problem is described very well by the Department of Health and Human Safety.

> Our nation is in the midst of an unprecedented opioid epidemic. More people died from drug overdoses in 2014 than in any year on record, and the majority of drug overdose deaths (more than six out of ten) involved an opioid. Since 1999, the rate of overdose deaths involving opioids—including prescription opioid pain relievers and heroin—nearly quadrupled, and over 165,000 people have died from prescription opioid overdoses. Prescription pain medication deaths remain far too high, and in 2014, the most recent year on record, there was a sharp increase in heroin-involved deaths and an increase in deaths involving synthetic opioids such as fentanyl.

Incredibly, the death rate of drug overdose deaths is more than four times the death rate of gun homicides in the United States. Drug overdose deaths exceed deaths from automobile accidents. This is a terribly big deal, a tragic fact of life in our country today.

Whether drug addiction is possession by a modern-day demon or not, it is an issue that demands our attention. West Virginia, my home state while I was in the coal mining business, is "ground zero" for the opioid epidemic. A single pharmacy in Kermit, West Virginia, a tiny town with only 392 inhabitants, located only fourteen miles from my coal mine, received nine million hydrocodone pills in a two-year period!

Why are states like West Virginia, Kentucky, New Hampshire, and New Mexico such centers of drug use? The experts point to economic despair, widespread unemployment, inadequate mental health facilities, and a sense of isolation in small communities. I once knew the people living in Kermit, Delbarton, and many other small coal towns in Mingo County. Based on my experience, the experts are right.

What does this have to do with Jesus and the Gerasene demoniac? I think dealing with these modern evil spirits will require an even more powerful spiritual transformation than what occurred on the eastern shore of Galilee so long ago. I am not optimistic about any governmental program having much success in bringing about such a spiritual transformation, regardless of which party is in charge.

Our mission work in the Dominican Republic is important work. We deal with some of the poorest of the world's poor. But, thank God, we do not see much addiction. That is a good thing, because the format of our mission work is decidedly not suitable for addiction recovery. Our groups of untrained people work over long weekends, once or twice a year at most.

The drug epidemic needs dedicated, well-trained, full-time professionals working for several years in each of the afflicted communities. Perhaps a massive Peace Corps Twelve-Step program, one that recruits and trains large numbers of young college graduates to act as Twelve-Step group leaders and patient advocates, could help. These volunteers would work in their assigned communities for two years, giving them enough time to assist addicted individuals through the most difficult months of recovery.

I pray for wisdom. I pray for addicted people wherever they are, knowing that isolation and despair can exist in the middle of a large city just as easily as in a rural hamlet. I end my morning reflecting on Hildegard of Bingen,

> I [the Creator] have exalted humankind with the vocation of creation. Humankind alone is called to co-create.

January 25

Repeat Luke 8:26–39, Jesus Heals the Gerasene Demoniac

WE SAT IN the garden under another starry sky, clear and cold, the sound of the fountains murmuring in the morning air. It was as perfect as a North Florida winter morning could be. I prayed for my mind to be as clear as the sky, and to remain that way just a few years more. I prayed with gratitude that my physical health continues to be robust.

As we walked along the rill coming up from the garden, I smiled with quiet joy, thinking about how much I love the landscape we have created here at Serendipity. Every time someone sees the rill for the first time, I explain that rills are simply small streams. In Islamic "Paradise" garden architecture, rills represent ribbons of water that take us to Heaven. The rill in our garden is a replica of one that I drew more than thirty years ago, when I first visited the Alhambra in Grenada, Spain. That rill runs from the famous Lion Fountain to one circular pool, then to another, between rows of columns. In my garden, the columns are palm trees, the Lion Fountain is an antique garden fountain from Bordeaux. Instead of two circular pools, I end the rill in a single circular pool at the base of the pavilion. Especially on mornings like this, after meditating on the bench, I am deeply moved by the religious significance of the rill. I allow myself a moment in Paradise.

Reflecting on the reading from Luke again, I am reminded of C. S. Lewis, who wrote:

> There are two equal and opposite errors into which our race can fall about the devils. One is to disbelieve in their existence. The other is to believe and to feel an excessive and unhealthy interest in them. They themselves are equally pleased by both errors, and hail a materialist or a magician with the same delight.

As I said yesterday, I am agnostic regarding "devils." There is certainly no question that obsessions and addictions are as destructive and evil today as any demon ever was in the time of Christ. One reason I react as I do to the notion of another person, whether natural or supernatural, being responsible for my bad habits, is my concern about personal accountability.

Bad things are not generally a result of other people. We either have a genetic or physical condition, or we make a choice. Two very important caveats are required. First, in the presence of disease or a medical condition, the idea of blaming evil spirits or demons disappeared with the advent of modern medical science. Cancer and heart disease are no longer "evil spirits," and are not treated as such. There is a disease called addiction, which, like cancer, should not be treated as possession by an evil spirit.

Second, and in many ways more important, free choice is virtually never free. As a white male born in the United States in 1944, I have a vastly different level of free choice than a very long list of others. Anyone black, female, born in almost any other country, or born long before or, oddly, long after 1944, has fewer choices than I. Some of these restrictions on choice have lessened over the years, others worsened. The point is that free choice is not as simple in life as it is to say.

Reflecting on this, I wonder in awe at the power of the evolutionary mandate, which is to adapt to the environment. A black female born in Kenya in 1840 is highly likely to be enslaved by an American or British slaver. It is somewhat miraculous for that woman to even survive, much less succeed. Many did not survive, and most did not succeed. The relatively few who did, however, are powerful statements about making good choices in order to adapt to and thrive in a particular environment. From an evolutionary perspective, that woman is a far more promising member of our species than a white man born into a plantation family in Alabama in 1840. There is no question in my mind as to which of the two contributed more value to the global gene pool.

This is not an argument for adversity, for putting barriers in the way of choice to promote stronger decision makers. I fervently believe in a level playing field. Every possible effort should be made to achieve equality of opportunity for women, people of all ethnic and racial backgrounds, sexual orientation, and places and circumstances of birth. Equal outcomes will never exist, if for no other reason than our freedom to choose what to do with the hand we are dealt. But I have never seen any reason to limit opportunity for anyone, anywhere.

My mind eventually wandered to the pigs in the story. As a somewhat proud pig farmer, I can attest to the fact that pigs get a raw deal. As maligned as they may be in a village like Mamey for the way they smell, the way they eat, and the way they wallow in the mud, what Jesus did to those poor Gerasene pigs is harsh. Bible thumpers sometimes use this parable to justify killing animals. The story of a curse withering the fig tree is similarly used to argue that plants are also "below" humans.

Both Thomas Aquinas and St. Augustine used these stories to make the point that God's purpose was primarily for the good of men's souls, not for the well-being of their animals and plants. These "lesser" forms of creation are here solely for humankind's use. Thankfully, St. Francis provided an excellent role model for another viewpoint. My personal views on this issue are informed far more by Maggie than by my Mamey pigs.

The co-founder of Sister Parish and my good friend, Don Barnhorst, sent me a quote from George Eliot.

> My own experience and development deepen every day my conviction that our moral progress may be measured by the degree in which we sympathize with individual suffering and individual joy.

Don goes way beyond sympathizing with suffering. He takes some action every day to limit or reduce whatever suffering he sees. He is a good role model for reflection.

I pray this morning for strength and clarity in my convictions and in my actions. I pray in gratitude for this amazing universe, and for the astounding bounty that surrounds me, and makes the quality of my life so beyond belief.

January 26

Luke 19:1–10, Jesus and Zacchaeus
¹ He entered Jericho and was passing through it. ² A man was there named Zacchaeus; he was a chief tax collector and was rich. ³ He was trying to see who Jesus was, but on account of the crowd he could not, because he was short in stature. ⁴ So he ran ahead and climbed a sycamore tree to see him, because he was going to pass that way. ⁵ When Jesus came to the place, he looked up and said to him, "Zacchaeus, hurry and come down; for I must stay at your house today." ⁶ So he hurried down and was happy to welcome him. ⁷ All who saw it began to grumble and said, "He has gone to be the guest of one who is a sinner." ⁸ Zacchaeus stood there and said to the Lord, "Look, half of my possessions, Lord, I will give to the poor; and if I have defrauded anyone of anything, I will pay back four times as much." ⁹ Then Jesus said to him, "Today salvation has come to this house, because he too is a son of Abraham. ¹⁰ For the Son of Man came to seek out and to save the lost."

WHEN I READ through this passage from Luke about Zacchaeus last night, I was reminded of a recent homily from Father David Keegan at our parish. He pointed out that Zacchaeus was a man "short in stature," suggesting the *double entendre* of being both short in height and of lesser moral stature. Zacchaeus, a tax collector, was certainly considered to be of "lesser moral stature" than the good Jews in the community.

I am depressed again today, resulting, as usual, from political and social events. Elections have consequences, and the consequences of President Trump becoming president include new policies on immigration. Of course, we knew they were coming, and I, along with many others, have been troubled by the prospect of these policies since he first started talking about them during the campaign. The ban on Muslims has morphed, first, into a ban on immigrants from "areas where terrorists are active," then, to the ban announced yesterday against immigrants from Syria, Iraq, Libya, Somalia, the Sudan, Iran, and Yemen. Aleppo, an international symbol for the horror of the civil war in Syria, is now in total ruin. Yet the men, women, and children who once lived in Aleppo's bombed-out shells, and are now fleeing the true carnage of war, are not welcome here. How sad! Fr. James Martin said it all very well this morning:

> These measures, which mean the rejection of the stranger, the rejection of the person in need, the rejection of those who suffer, are manifestly unchristian and utterly contrary to the Gospel. Indeed, last year, Pope Francis said, "A person who thinks only about building walls, wherever they may be, and not building bridges, is not Christian. This is not the Gospel."
>
> Jesus himself is speaking to you from the Gospels. It is Christ whom we turn away when we build walls. It is Christ whom we reject when we slash quotas for refugees. It is Christ whom we are killing, by letting them die in poverty and war rather than opening our doors.
>
> "Today," St. John Paul II said, "the illegal migrant comes before us like that 'stranger' in whom Jesus asks to be recognized. To welcome him and to show him solidarity is a duty of hospitality and fidelity to Christian identity itself."

Sitting on the bench this morning, I thought about having Jesus spend the night at Serendipity. What an awesome thought! Like Zacchaeus, there are those who could easily say, "How could Jesus be a guest of the Harts? Such sinners!" In my fantasy, I joined with Zacchaeus, offering to give half of everything we have to the poor, and doing even more for anyone I might have hurt or defrauded over the years.

The operative line in the reading is the last: "For the Son of Man came to seek out and to save the lost." Indeed, in so many ways, all of us, so richly blessed in this hallowed enclave of Ponte Vedra Beach, are lost. True frugality, honest humility of possessions, and even poverty of spirit, all are simply impossible in this "land of milk and honey." Does that mean Jesus would stop here first? I think not. I suspect He can find plenty of lost souls in those places where He can also minister to the poor, sick, enslaved, and imprisoned.

I pray for understanding. I pray for this country. I pray for humility, and poverty of spirit. I want to feel the experience of Christ deep in my heart.

January 27

Repeat Luke 19:1–10, Jesus and Zacchaeus

A PACKAGE arrived last night from my sister, Nancy Metheny. In it were letters I had written to my parents from Germany during the period of my Mormon mission in 1964 and 1965. I read them all in one sitting, on the verge of tears the whole time. There was a lot in the letters that moved me, but more poignant than that were feelings generated by the messages I sent to my parents about how much I loved them, and about what was going on for me as a missionary.

Some of the letters were written during the first six weeks I was in Germany. I rode my bicycle through the streets of Neustadt an der Weinstrasse, a "junior companion," walking behind my senior companion, up and down the stairs of five-story apartment blocks. I spoke so little German I had to remain silent. My whole body ached. I was depressed about my inability to communicate, about my relationship with my companion, and about our complete failure to make progress cajoling the Germans into becoming Mormons. There is no question that my present distaste for "proselytizing missionaries"—whether Mormons, Jehovah's Witnesses, Catholics, or any other faith or cause—developed during those long weeks. In one early letter, I wrote, in quotes, "reality exists apart from man. I can experience it, but cannot change it." I think it is from Sartre, and it suggests that I was spending some of my first six weeks in Germany trying to impress my fellow missionaries with my erudition. Sad.

In the same letter, I quoted from Elia Kazan's *America, America.* "Only members of minority groups wear the eternal smile. Look around at the happy people—they have either made it, or given up the fight." Apparently, my fellow missionaries had been complaining that I took things too seriously. They thought I smiled too little. So little has changed in fifty years!

As it happened, I made faster progress mastering German and "climbing" the mission hierarchy than I had expected. A particularly touching letter was written on December 16, 1964, just before what would be my first Christmas ever away from my family (I had hitch-hiked home from Cambridge for the Christmas of 1963). In the letter, I lamented having met some atheists during the previous week. That set up an opportunity for me to "bear my testimony" to my parents.

I am proud of my Christian upbringing. Christ in the home, Christ in Church, Christ in school, not a convenient tool of the state or a story for the rich to oppress the poor, rather the living, tangible son of the living, tangible God.

I advised my young sisters to read the New Testament and the Book of Mormon. In my advice to my brother Wayne, I wrote,

As I look back on the mistakes that I made five years ago, I see they are the same mistakes I am making now. "A boy becomes a man when he considers himself to be a man." Carry yourself like a man, Wayne, dress like a man; act like a man, and you will be treated like a man.

The letter ends with my strong profession of love for everyone in the family.

The beauty of the Gospel; the beauty of prayer and a discussion with the Lord—these things defy description. This time of the year emphasizes these emotions and strengthens the bonds of love that unite a family—the bonds of love that make communication with the Lord a tangible reality.

Reflecting on these words today, fifty years and many lifetimes later, I am somewhat at a loss for how to react. It strikes me that I must have changed my life container a few times along the way, projecting radically different images to the world each time. It is possible that I was filling my container with goodness and faith while I was in Germany. I think not. I suspect this loving, faith-filled young missionary was only a superficial facade I was projecting to the Germans, the mission hierarchy, and my family. I say that in large part because I was such a different person less than a year after I wrote those letters.

Now, I could be wrong about this. It may have been the case that I had begun to put some good things in my life container, only to come to a dead stop when I was excommunicated. The "goodness" remained somewhere near the bottom of the barrel during all the years that I focused almost solely on building out the façade with power, prestige, and possessions. If this is true, then when I hit bottom ten years ago, there was something there with which God could work. I like this theory, even though the harsher view may be closer to the truth.

The last letters in the packet sent by Nancy were written in September, 1965, two months before my trial and excommunication. By then, I was one of the two or three most senior missionaries in the West German Mission, one of the leaders of the Mission, and a veteran of many baptisms, achieved in half a dozen towns throughout the mission field. I had recently met Petra and her mother. One of the letters, the last one written from Wurzburg, described both Petra and her mother, without names. It was a fairly detailed description, including a lengthy history of their difficulties in East Germany, and their flight to the West.

The final letter among those Nancy sent was written a week or two after I was transferred out of Wurzburg. My whole life was weeks away from going over an unbelievable cliff. Oddly, I was not yet aware that there were any problems ahead of me, much less a Bishop's court. I talked about finally knowing the love of Jesus Christ, and the importance of achieving oneness in that love! These words support the theory that at least some of my faith was real. It seems extraordinary that I had reached the core of my present understanding of belief more than half a century ago, before I had ever heard of any of the Christian mystics, or Father Rohr, or Pope Francis. Of course, the excommunication and disgrace three weeks later caused me to walk away from all of it, remaining for the next forty years in a spiritual desert.

Back in the library, I reflected on a passage from Thomas Merton's *No Man Is An Island*, which I have next to my bed. I awakened during the night to read his thoughts on the meaning of life.

> Our purpose in life is to discover this meaning, and live according to it. We have, therefore, something to live for. The process of living, of growing up, and becoming a person, is precisely the gradually increasing awareness of what that something is.

The letters from the mission field were part of my early effort to discover the meaning in my own life. I wish I had more of them. Leaving aside for a moment the possibility that everything in these letters was merely an act, two things stand out as I ponder where I was in this discovery process fifty years ago—first, my faith, even then, was much more about love than doctrine, and second, I had already discovered the fundamental importance of my "family of origin."

In the brief span of about six months, from late summer 1964 to the beginning of 1965, my faith evolved from one based on rote passages, taken largely from Mormon teaching and tradition, to a love-centered faith that anticipated much of what I feel today. While I am not totally clear about the sequence and duration of my movements during that period, the letters suggest that I began as a struggling "junior companion" in Neustadt an der Weinstrasse, moved, still a junior companion, to Giessen, and then, with a promotion to senior companion, moved to Idar Oberstein (I think the pattern was to stay about three months in each location). Obviously, during the late summer in Neustadt, I was busily learning both the German language and the "lessons," the basics of Mormon faith that I was meant to be teaching potential converts. There was little time for deep thoughts about ultimate meaning.

I recall being instructed not to venture even the slightest bit from the text of the lessons, something probably related as much to doubts about what I might inadvertently say in my poor German as a concern for doctrinal purity. The letters to my parents from Giessen reflect both far greater comfort in my German, and a growing desire to become closer to the people we were trying to convert, along with the recent converts. The instructions from the mission leadership were clear: Do not "waste" time becoming friends with these people, especially if that involves anything enjoyable. Our duty was to tell as many people as possible about the Gospel, giving them the minimum required for them to reach the decision to convert. Anything beyond that on our part would be a waste of time that should be spent giving the same opportunity to someone else.

In Giessen, I was frustrated that my senior companion would not allow me to read anything outside of the lesson plans, the Book of Mormon, and the New Testament. Frankly, the letters reflect an insubordinate, haughty, impatient underling, wanting control much more than seeking a better way to preach the Gospel. By then, my German had progressed much faster and further than was generally the case for new missionaries. I wanted to teach, but I especially wanted to have some success with the constant hard work. I was convinced that genuine friendship with both potential and existing converts was essential to that success.

In my first days as a senior companion in Idar Oberstein, I introduced all manner of "extracurricular" activities and lesson "enhancements." Love, never discussed in the letters from Neustadt and Giessen, had become the central focus. I had forgotten all of this, and am happy to realize it now.

Equally gratifying is the discovery that I recognized and acknowledged the importance of my parents and siblings in my life. I so easily accept the notion that I have always been so self-centered that I rejected or, at least, discounted, their role. What the letters show is that I have not always been so blind.

> It takes very little reflection to see that I didn't put myself in the various positions I am so happy with today. My political ideas and philosophic logic, really impressive to a lot of people, come straight from the dinner table. My genetic make-up (call it ½) and my domestic environment (another ½) have both been a shade or so better than average. I want to make it very clear to you how thankful I am and how much I love you."

Sadly, I largely abandoned my effort to express my love to my family shortly after my excommunication. The letters show that humility and self-knowledge do not reach a certain level, never again to regress. This is also true for faith, maturity, and judgement. My forty years of wandering in the desert began only a few days (hours?) after the trial, which is almost certainly the last time I checked in with God. The wandering can begin again just as easily today.

I ended the morning with another reflection on something Merton said in *No Man*:

> One of the moral diseases we communicate to one another in society comes from huddling together in the pale light of an insufficient answer to a question we are afraid to ask.

I pray for clarity. I pray for the strength to renew my faith each day.

January 28

Repeat and reflect on the week.

THE FIRST full week of life under President Donald J. Trump ended yesterday with yet another kerfuffle, this time over the cancellation of a meeting with the President of Mexico. Trump's wall is an embarrassment, one having the potential for serious damage to the relationship with Mexico and to the economy. For me, it is not as ominous as the executive actions the new President took in the area of refugees and immigration. While most Americans will never notice a four-month freeze on accepting refugees (and a potentially permanent halt on refugees from the war-stricken areas of the Middle East), just imagine what it means to a family that has been going through the two-year process for the past twenty months. Conditions in the refugee camp, the anguish at having to wait so long, and the uncertainty regarding the end result—all of these suddenly reaching the breaking point when the announcement is made that the system is frozen. What must that family think? How do they face today?

The wild statements, bizarre tweets, and extreme policy decisions of President Trump have a real-world impact on human beings. Lives are adversely effected, which is a gentle way to say ruined. He seems to be totally impervious to the damage his actions will cause. While I have been advised to simply turn off the news, that does not work well for me. Especially now, with "push" notifications coming from numerous sources, I cannot escape current events in the world. Frankly, I do not want to.

The outside temperature of 45 degrees was meant to feel like 37 degrees given the high humidity. We all looked like snowmen this morning on the tennis court, slightly overdressed for the cold air. Tennis was nonetheless exhilarating, a perfect prelude to prayer and reflection. Maggie, not bothered by the cold, was particularly vigorous in her pursuit of lizard playmates.

My meditation was consumed by gratitude, largely due to a wonderful dinner last night with Donna and Aviv Goldsmith, old friends and business associates (Aviv and I have worked together in three or four of my business incarnations). Donna described the Women's March on Washington in such glowing terms that Sallie Ann and I could talk of nothing else for an hour after dinner. More than half a million women and a few men on the Mall in Washington, and not a single arrest! That is awesome! What to do now with all of that energy and momentum is the topic of conversation all over the country.

Father Marie-Dominique Chenu, a progressive Dominican priest, wrote, "For even before people contemplate it, the sacramental universe is filled with God." I sat with that this morning, reflecting as well on the warmth of our dinner last night and the hope that still exists in this country. God is present before we are conscious of His presence, and He remains present, even when we become distracted.

Descartes famously declared, "Cogito ergo sum," I think, therefore I am. The existentialists took the opposite view, existence precedes essence. Sartre says it simply, "We mean that man first of all exists, encounters himself, surges up in the world—and defines himself afterwards." While I am certain that a great many very intelligent people have spent countless hours contemplating this logical quandary, I am content this morning to go with the non-dual proposition—I both think and exist. Which preceded which is not high on my list of concerns.

This has been a week of stark contrasts. The world outside is dominated by the tragic chaos of Trump. Economic disaster, inhumane treatment of the poor and disadvantaged, denial of climate science, an embrace of torture, and a reversal of efforts to make health care work—these are the elements of that outside bedlam. On the bench and in the library, however, the week has been about demons in pigs and tax collectors climbing trees, reminders of my life and faith half a century ago, and an evening of joy-filled reminiscence.

I am filled with immense gratitude for this life. I want to deepen my connection to Christ, His universe, and all the love and joy that surround and infuse me.

CALENDAR WEEK TWENTY

I want to know Jesus better, to love Him more, and to follow Him wholeheartedly.

January 29

John 6:1–15, Feeding the Five Thousand
  ¹ After this Jesus went to the other side of the Sea of Galilee, also called the Sea of Tiberias. ² A large crowd kept following him, because they saw the signs that he was doing for the sick. ³ Jesus went up the mountain and sat down there with his disciples. ⁴ Now the Passover, the festival of the Jews, was near. ⁵ When he looked up and saw a large crowd coming toward him, Jesus said to Philip, "Where are we to buy bread for these people to eat?" ⁶ He said this to test him, for he himself knew what he was going to do. ⁷ Philip answered him, "Six months' wages would not buy enough bread for each of them to get a little." ⁸ One of his disciples, Andrew, Simon Peter's brother, said to him, ⁹ "There is a boy here who has five barley loaves and two fish. But what are they among so many people?" ¹⁰ Jesus said, "Make the people sit down." Now there was a great deal of grass in the place; so they sat down, about five thousand in all. ¹¹ Then Jesus took the loaves, and when he had given thanks, he distributed them to those who were seated; so also the fish, as much as they wanted. ¹² When they were satisfied, he told his disciples, "Gather up the fragments left over, so that nothing may be lost." ¹³ So they gathered them up, and from the fragments of the five barley loaves, left by those who had eaten, they filled twelve baskets. ¹⁴ When the people saw the sign that he had done, they began to say, "This is indeed the prophet who is to come into the world."
  ¹⁵ When Jesus realized that they were about to come and take him by force to make him king, he withdrew again to the mountain by himself.

THE MORNING started early with a blunder. I watched the news before going downstairs and out to the bench. Any hope for quiet meditation was replaced with an urgent need to vent. Yesterday, President Trump issued an Executive Order banning refugees from Syria indefinitely, and immigrants from six other Muslim countries in the Middle East and Africa for at least four months. Passengers arriving last night on flights from these countries were detained pending deportation. Many of these passengers were legal residents, with valid green cards or student visas. Late in the evening, a Federal judge ordered a stay on the enforcement of the President's Executive Order. The whole mess depresses me. It is simply inconceivable that our country will close its borders to refugees, even to those who have been working as interpreters and support staff for our military in Iraq. Banning refugees from Syria, after watching for weeks the collapse of Aleppo, is beyond inhumane.

I found some solace in a prayer written by Jim Finley in June 2009.

> May each of us be so fortunate as to be overtaken by God in the midst of little things. May we each be so blessed as to be finished off by God, swooping down from above or welling up from beneath, to extinguish the illusion of separateness that perpetuates our fears. May we, in having our illusory, separate self slain by God, be born into a new and true awareness of who we are: [O]ne with God forever. May we continue on in this true awareness, seeing in each and every little thing we see, the fullness of God's presence in our lives. May we also be someone in whose presence others are better able to recognize God's presence in their lives, so that they, too, might know the freedom of the children of God.

I sat with this, tasting each sentence again and again, like a cow chewing its cud. The "illusion of separateness" seems more than an illusion when I consider all that has happened in the first eight days of the new administration. How can rejection of the stranger be one with God? How can the silly Trump wall be the act of a person in whose life God is present?

Then the first line of Jim's prayer takes control: May we be "overtaken by God in the midst of little things." The "little things" all around me in this early morning darkness, sitting in a beautiful library, looking out at the fountain, listening to Maggie mumble something in her sleep. Here there is no anger, rejection, deportation, shaming, or demeaning. Here there is only love. Here I am overtaken by God. I prayed the Jesus prayer.

The account in John's Gospel of Jesus feeding the five thousand, like similar accounts in the Synoptic Gospels, is considered to be of great importance, if for no other reason than it is found in all four Gospels. Each time I read it I am reminded of one of the teachers in my RCIA class telling the story of Noah's ark. Genesis tells us that Noah was 480 years old when God told him to build an ark containing 101,000 square feet of space. It took Noah 120 years to build the ark. When our RCIA teacher asked if this story seemed a little incredible to us, the catechumens, we said, "yes, of course." He then said, all you need to know is that God asked an old man to build a big boat and it took a long time! I loved that.

The feeding of the five thousand took place in the village of Bethsaida, which is believed to have been located very near to Capernaum, on the northern end of Galilee. Scholars believe Capernaum had a population of around 1,500, so Bethsaida must have been considerably smaller. A crowd of 5,000 people would have emptied most of the towns and villages on that end of the lake, something highly unlikely. I go back to my RCIA teacher, concluding that the 5,000 simply means "a very large crowd." I recently talked to our good friend Josephine Hoskins, an ordained Episcopal minister, about this story. She explained that the tradition in the time of Jesus was for anyone leaving their home for any length of time to carry small amounts of food in their pockets. Certainly, she said, the people following Jesus from place to place did so. So the story of feeding the 5,000 should be read as a metaphor about Jesus showing hospitality to a large group of people, sharing what He had with them to augment whatever food they had.

The message, then, would not be about miraculously making five loaves and two fish into the truly enormous quantities required to feed five thousand people. It would be a message about hospitality, welcoming the stranger, and bringing everyone into community. For me, this is a better message than the ostensible message of Jesus performing miracles.

For obvious reasons, my interpretation of the story is important for me, especially today. Jesus was consistently inclusive and forgiving in all of His actions and admonitions. He taught us to open our arms to the poor, the sick, the disadvantaged, and the stranger. He would be very unhappy with a ban on refugees!

I sit with this tendency I have to make everything fit my viewpoint, whether it is passage from Scripture, a meditation written by Ignatius five hundred years ago, or a prayer written recently by Finley. Am I forcing things? Is the whole effort to see faith in terms of creation spirituality, rather than sin and redemption, a new age gloss on tradition? Simply put, am I trying to make Jesus into a liberal Democrat?

It should come as no surprise that I do not think I am trying to fit a "square" Gospel into the "round hole" of my understanding. In fact, I can see no way in which any rational reading of any part of the Gospel of Jesus Christ can be interpreted as right-wing conservatism. Later, when these teachings are converted from wisdom to religion, and especially when that religion is made the official state religion, the tribal necessities of dualism and exclusivity take over. However, the great Christian mystics have been calling the Church out on this for most of its two-thousand-year history.

I join Finley in a prayer that I might "continue on in this true awareness, seeing in each and every little thing [I] see, the fullness of God's presence in [my life]." I pray for humility, patience, and understanding. I pray for strength to stand by my deep-felt beliefs. I want to know Christ, and to follow Him wholeheartedly.

January 30

Repeat John 6:1–15, Feeding the Five Thousand

THE REFUGEE and Muslim immigrant problems did not go away. In fact, the Trump White House doubled down, determined to fight the court-imposed stay. Protests erupted across the United States and throughout Europe. Father James Martin wrote some helpful advice, part of which reads as follows:

> How do I deal with these intense, sometimes overwhelming, feelings of frustration and anger? What do I do with them? Where is God in all this?
>
> Of course, righteous anger needs to be distinguished from plain old anger. That's where discernment comes in: Why am I feeling this? What is the real reason for my anger? To my mind, if the anger is on behalf of another person—that is, if you're angry because you see another person or group being unfairly treated—it's almost always righteous anger. If it's because you are being mistreated, it still may be righteous, but it may need to be more carefully discerned, to distinguish it from wounded pride. Again discernment is key.
>
> Jesus got angry fairly frequently in the Gospels: [W]hen he overturns the tables of the money-changers in the Temple precincts in Jerusalem; when he calls the disciples a "perverse and faithless generation;" when the fig tree does not bear fruit, and so on. Jesus also feels things deeply—very deeply. His heart is often "moved with pity" when he sees someone suffering. The Greek New Testament often uses the wonderful evocative word "*splagchnizomai*": [H]is bowels were moved—in other words, he felt it in his guts. Jesus's feelings move him to action on behalf of the other, or others.
>
> So if you feel a surge of indignation or anger about an unjust situation in the real world, don't ignore it. Or if you weep at the mistreatment of a group of people, don't think yourself foolish. This may be God moving your heart, with pity. But discern. Pray. And then, as you are able, like Jesus, act.

The hardest thing for me today is the feeling of hopeless despair. At my age, living in deeply red North Florida, I am absolutely powerless, part of a large and growing national resistance movement that is thus far also powerless.

We are now a very red nation. Trump is President. He will appoint a young, hard-right conservative Justice to the Supreme Court in the next few days. The Senate and the House are Republican. Thirty-three states have Republican governors. Thirty-two state legislatures are controlled by large Republican majorities.

The Democratic leadership is old, and tired. Voter suppression has significantly reduced the possibility of Democratic victories in some of the key swing states, significantly including North Carolina, Ohio, Virginia, and Wisconsin. Given the structure of the Electoral College and the Senate, the sparsely populated states between the coasts, the "flyover states," will prevail over the populous states on the coasts, where a clear majority of the country's population lives. This is not a picture that inspires hope.

At 72 years of age, I am not about to move to a swing state and run for office. Frankly, I am not prepared to reduce my annual giving to Sister Parish and Ability Housing in order to donate more to the Democrats. And with four grandchildren in middle school and one grandchild in need of special education, I am looking at a minimum of another ten years of heavy education costs. So what am I to do?

On the other hand, dinner with Donna Goldsmith, listening to her describe the immense power of that crowd of women, 3.3 million of them, did encourage hope. I was heartened watching the demonstrators protesting the immigration policy yesterday. If the Resistance can transform itself from a huge crowd marching in the streets to an election-winning political machine, the situation can change. I am reminded that the Tea Party did not exist on January 20, 2009, the day President Obama was sworn in. By August of that year, the Tea Party was present at virtually every House member town hall. They won the off-year elections of 2010 and 2014, and were the heart and soul of Trump's victory in 2016. If the Tea Party could do it, then the Resistance can do it. And if I can expose another few hundred young people here in Ponte Vedra to the transformational power of Sister Parish, or provide financial assistance to my grandchildren that helps them prepare for leadership, I will have done my bit.

Reflecting on the feeding of the five thousand today, I am even more inclined to discount the miraculous message, in favor of the hospitality message. I can certainly understand the reasoning of the Evangelists, writing thirty to sixty years after the crucifixion, to emphasize His paranormal powers. But Jesus was not about showing off, or proving himself as a supernatural being. His message was "lowercase," quiet, and humble. Helping the poor and welcoming the stranger does not require miraculous super power. Jesus consistently showed us the way that we, as humans, could and should love our neighbor. No super hero feats of courage and strength are required. Just love.

I read part of a poem from John O'Donohue. I made it part of my prayer as I ended the morning.

> I would love to live
> Like a river flows.
> Carried by the surprise
> Of its own unfolding.

I pray for the quiet conversion of my anger and frustration into love and acceptance. I pray for the strength to do what I can do, and do it well. Jesus faced far worse odds two thousand years ago, and He changed the world.

January 31

Mark 8:27–30, Peter's Declaration about Jesus
    [27] *Jesus went on with his disciples to the villages of Caesarea Philippi; and on the way he asked his disciples, "Who do people say that I am?"* [28] *And they answered him, "John the Baptist; and others, Elijah; and still others, one of the prophets."* [29] *He asked them, "But who do you say that I am?" Peter answered him, "You are the Messiah."* [30] *And he sternly ordered them not to tell anyone about him.*

VERY EARLY this morning, I stared up into the sky until I became dizzy, both physically and mentally. The stars in the dark sky seem so much brighter in these cold winter mornings than in the summer. Why? I actually asked "the Google."

It's partly because—on December, January, and February evenings—the part of Earth you're standing on is facing into the spiral arm of the galaxy to which our sun belongs.

Who knew?

The sky was immense this morning. I wondered about why Montana is called the Big Sky state, whether the sky there is larger than it is here. This morning, as I sat under the Big Sky of Ponte Vedra, I marveled at the obvious fact that it was the same sky under which I would sit in Montana or Santo Domingo. It is not similar to that sky, or a sky that generates the same awe and wonder. It is the same sky, viewed from what is actually a fairly small shift in angle of sight. The universe, God's creation, is *here*, with me, inside me, but also *out there*, beyond me, beyond even that vast sky.

Returning to the passage from Mark, I put myself in the shoes of one of the disciples, walking alongside Jesus as He introduced His message to one community after another. The village of Caesarea Philippi is twenty-five miles northeast of Galilee, in the foothills of Mt. Hermon and what we now call the Golan Heights. The Evangelist writes simply that "Jesus went on with his disciples to the villages of Caesarea Philippi," as though those villages were just up the block. Walking that distance on a relatively flat road would take most pilgrims on the Camino St. Jacques, all seasoned hikers, a good ten hours. My guess is that Jesus and His disciples made the journey in two days, which would have given them lots of time to discuss the identity of Jesus, and for Him to teach the disciples about His death and resurrection.

"Who do they say I am?" This seems like such an ordinary question for any person, perhaps more common for leaders and teachers. In part, it is a reasonable check on the effect of our life container. After spending so much time and energy building the best container possible, carefully selecting the facades that portray our most treasured images of ourselves, it is only natural to wonder how well we have done. "Who do they say I am?" Do they see what I want them to see? Can they see the cracks in my shell, see through to the secret parts about which I wanted no one to know? I sat with this for a very long time.

Jesus had other reasons for asking the question. His "secret" was massive by any standard. Yet he performed miracles, asserted spiritual authority, made extraordinary, upside-down claims. He was not hiding His Messianic self very well! Reflecting on this, it is truly extraordinary that His closest disciples could not only get it wrong, but could repeatedly deny it. Is it that hard to accept good news?

Obviously, it is. Two thousand years of history clearly show that I am not alone in resisting the implications of faith. Even the great mystics wrote beautifully and honestly about their doubts. More often, however, they persisted in writing and teaching the truth as they had come to know it. What they said endures precisely because they admitted uncertainty. I am also struck with how well history filters out the noise. Consider all of the words written over these two thousand years by little men and women, words of division and exclusion, words of tribal insecurity, words about an angry, vindictive God, words that totally rejected our growing knowledge about creation. Yet the words that survive, the teaching that continues to light the dark spaces and gently touch our hearts, these are the answers to the question Jesus asked his disciples. "Who do they say that I am?" I think the great Wisdom Tradition gets it right. I am grateful for the little fragment of that tradition that I am beginning to understand.

I ended the morning with this prayer of gratitude from *The Cloud of Unknowing*.

> That which I am and the way that I am,
> with all my gifts of nature and grace,
> you have given to me, O Lord, and you are
> all this. I offer it all to you, to praise you
> and to serve all creation,
> according to thy will.
> Amen.

February 1

Repeat Mark 8:27–30, Peter's Declaration about Jesus

MY DAUGHTER Melissa was on CNN last night, providing a personal reference for Judge Neil Gorsuch, President Trump's nominee to fill the Supreme Court seat left by the death of Justice Scalia more than a year ago. Melissa knows Judge Gorsuch well and considers him to be very bright, with high integrity and fundamental decency. I respect her view.

I remain deeply troubled by the new administration. While I consider President Trump to be intellectually and temperamentally disastrous, I worry even more about the cadre of zealots working for him under the tutelage of Steve Bannon. As he often does, Tom Friedman, a welcome voice in this wilderness of blind praise or kneejerk opposition, offered smart, positive advice.

> The way we lift American workers is not by building higher walls, but rather stronger communities—where business, philanthropies, the local school system and local government forge adaptive coalitions to enable every worker to engage in lifelong learning and every company to access global markets and every town to attract the smart risk-takers who start companies.

This is sound advice, but I wonder whether the dying towns in our rural heartland will ever stem the tide of young people leaving the farm for the big city. This would not be such a big deal if our political system were truly democratic, with political power following people, not tied forever to arbitrary geographic boundaries established centuries ago.

As I walked from the garden back to the library this morning, I reflected on how much impact my unquenchable thirst for more information about the history of Catholicism had on my first experience of these Exercises. I allowed that curiosity to interrupt virtually every morning's meditation. Now, five years later, the cataclysmic political changes going on here in the United States and around the world, intrude even more powerfully on my contemplation. As I mentioned at the outset, I seriously considered making a thirty-day silent retreat before (or instead of) embarking on this second round of Annotation 19. I wonder whether that would have been more effective in terms of removing me from the world, allowing my focus to remain solely on the inner growth of my relationship with Christ. On the other hand, Christ came into the world, in part to teach us to be like Him in this world, with all its messy political and social reality.

"Who do they say I am?" How many thousands of times have I silently wondered about this? I asked it when I was at my best as a leader, and, even more, when I was at my worst. Is "what they say" truly important? Why am I, are we, so anxious to know whether our projections of the person we want others to see are working? The answer is obvious, at least for me. I care about what others think about me, too much, I am sure. I allow positive reviews to inflate my ego, and, more often, I allow negative feedback to send me into a downward spiral of depression. Oddly, I find that my careful attention to public opinion is significantly lessened by prayer. It is not impossible to think of myself during prayer, but it is harder to do so than when I am fully alert to any attention I might attract from others.

In my effort to learn more about some of the mystics that were not the focus of the Living School, I have been reading the Rhineland mystics, including Mechthild of Magdeburg (d. 1282/1294). This mystical poet devoted essentially her whole life to writing *The Flowing Light of Divinity*. Like Marguerite Porete (d. 1310), Mechthild was a beguine, living a life of chastity, poverty, and service, essentially following the rule of an order of nuns, but without actually joining an order. I sat with her description of prayer at the end of my meditation this morning.

> Prayer is naught else but a yearning of soul … it draws down the great God into the little heart; it drives the hungry soul up to the plenitude of God; it brings together these two lovers, God and the soul, in a wondrous place where they speak much of love.

I pray to join God in that "wondrous place." I pray for clarity and humility. My deep desire is to know Christ, not to be distracted by what others think of me.

February 2

Mark 8:31–33, Jesus Foretells His Death and Resurrection
[31] *Then he began to teach them that the Son of Man must undergo great suffering, and be rejected by the elders, the chief priests, and the scribes, and be killed, and after three days rise again. [32] He said all this quite openly. And Peter took him aside and began to rebuke him. [33] But turning and looking at his disciples, he rebuked Peter and said, "Get behind me, Satan! For you are setting your mind not on divine things but on human things."*

HADEWJICH of Antwerp, perhaps the most famous of the beguines, wrote often about love. Maggie and I went down to the bench this morning, meditating about this beautiful bit of wisdom from Hadewjich.

> For this is love's truth; she joins two in one being, makes sweet sour, strangers neighbors, and the lowly noble.

I love her use of language, just as I am astounded at how much these thirteenth century women so completely anticipated our present understanding of faith. My faith does "make sweet sour," it joins me in one being with the community of belief that is the Body of Christ.

In today's passage from Mark, the Evangelist continues the story of Jesus talking to His disciples, introducing the powerful role of suffering, both in the Gospel, and in spiritual transformation. Descent is the path to ascent. For me, suffering has been the necessary condition for spiritual growth.

Both Father Rohr, in his lectures and his writing, and Thomas Merton, in *No Man is an Island*, teach the fundamental importance of suffering.

Moments of great love and great suffering are often the first experiences of nondual thinking. Practices of prayer largely maintain what many people first experience in deep love and suffering.

It is not at all surprising that the Apostle Peter would react the way he did when Jesus described the suffering that was coming. Who among us can casually accept suffering? Consider the suffering of mankind through periods of war, disease, drought, and upheaval. Consider close friends and family who have suffered through long periods of illness, only to die in pain. In every case, had we known in advance about the suffering, we would have exhausted every possible measure to avoid it.

When I reflect on suffering, I somewhat egoistically turn first to my own long history of descending into painful periods of misery. There have been many periods of suffering, and suffering in many forms. My earliest memory of suffering involves my painful experience as a late bed wetter. Not only was it a bitter embarrassment for me personally, but the measures used in the 1950s to deal with the issue were close to medieval. My parents only acted in what they genuinely believed to be my best interest, but among the methods they used to "cure" me were actions they hoped would shame me into stopping. My worst memory was being left outside for an entire night without my clothes. Even now, I cringe. I can recall no ascent resulting from that suffering.

I suffered during the trial in Germany, and descended from that low level to such a serious depression that my advisor at Harvard insisted I see a psychiatrist. After describing the Bishop's trial and my excommunication, the doctor said that he would have been worried if I had not been depressed! I suppose the vigor with which I pursued my career might be described as a blessing that resulted from my devastating excommunication. I "fell upward." I am not convinced.

There were certainly some miserable periods throughout the long forty years that I devoted most of my effort to power, prestige, and possessions. However, I believe my life from 1966 to 2006 was basically free of any real suffering. The events that caused the greatest pain in the lives of others are now only distant memories for me. In other words, the shame and guilt that I felt at the time were not lasting.

The years 2006 and 2007 were clearly different stories. I suffered, and I caused others to suffer with me. In this case, I have no doubt whatsoever that the depth of my misery led directly to my spiritual transformation. Ten years later, I am still rebounding from the hard impact of my bottom.

Has any of my suffering come even remotely close to what Jesus was about to experience? Absolutely not. It is hard for me to fathom His suffering, and to imagine that He knew in advance about the rejection, pain, and brutal death that was to come. I ended my meditation with this passage from Father Rohr on suffering.

There will be suffering and death along with love, joy, and resurrection. Most of us are so resistant to accepting suffering that Jesus walked through it himself and said, "Follow me." He showed us that on the other side of suffering is transformation. Love is stronger than death. The full, vibrant life that Jesus offers is big enough to include even its opposite: [D]eath. Unless a religion directly faces the issues of suffering and death, it is rather useless religion. Jesus holds these big questions front and center.

This morning I pray for humility in the face of the suffering of Christ. I want to know His level of acceptance and surrender. I want to experience His suffering so that I can know His love. I want to consider the big questions every day of my life.

February 3

Repeat Mark 8:31–33, Jesus Foretells His Death and Resurrection

THE OUTSIDE world continues to rudely enter my personal space. I listened to a debate last night about the plight of the unemployed working class in the industrial Midwest. The President would ostensibly help these people by ending immigration and forcing foreign companies to pay tariffs on goods they sell here in the United States.

Most of the job loss in the "fly over states" is the result of technology, not immigrants and not jobs going abroad. My whole life has been devoted to globalization, to lowering barriers, not raising them. The simple fact is that the success I had in the international electric power industry created more manufacturing jobs in the United States and Europe than it ever will in the developing countries of Asia, Africa, and Latin America. Closing our borders will bring about a global depression. It was madness in the 1920s. It is madness today. Michael Gerson, a generally conservative pundit, made the point clear in his editorial today.

> Our political system has been negligent in helping millions of Americans adapt during a period of rapid economic change. But those on the left and right who promise to reverse the process of globalization are economic charlatans. Their main policy response—tariffs and other forms of protectionism—is a proven path to trade wars and global recession, which hurt the vulnerable most.

Returning to the passage from Mark, I reflect on the fact that Jesus introduced His disciples to the idea of death and resurrection. In stating simply that He would "be killed, and after three days rise again," Jesus presented the concept of bodily resurrection, a concept largely unknown in the Hebrew scriptures. While some kind of existence after death *for the soul* is part of the ancient faith, it could hardly have been well understood by the disciples. This must have been a shocking thing for the disciples to hear; witness the reaction of Peter.

Putting myself in that conversation, I cannot imagine remaining silent. I would certainly have stayed out of the way, allowing Peter to take Jesus's rebuke. Later, however, I would have insisted upon discussing this radical new idea with the others. What could it mean that Jesus would rise again after three days? What happened to "dust to dust, ashes to ashes"?

What does it mean to me today? I long ago rejected the idea of bodily resurrection. I remember debating with my fellow Mormon missionaries whether we could pick the bodies we would have after death, choosing our thin, healthy, whole young bodies rather than the ones run over by a car or fully deteriorated at the end of a long illness. And resurrected to go where? The idea of a Heaven "up there" or "out there" does not work well with what we now know about the universe.

What I have come to deeply believe is that we will exist forever, joining Christ in both infinity and eternity. We exist now, just as we have always existed and will always exist, one with God and one with all of His creation. When we die, we will change form, but will not disappear. I believe that our consciousness, both personally and universally, is increasing. Does that mean I will have greater consciousness of the universe around me after I die? I clearly do not know. And that is ok.

For now, I am challenged by the task of becoming fully conscious of who I am, how I fit into this world, and, especially, how I relate to God. I pray that I will meet that challenge. I pray for greater consciousness, greater clarity, and greater strength to use my life for good.

Thomas Merton wrote a poem in honor of his brother, which was later turned into a song by Joan Baez called "The Bells of Gethsemane." These few verses spoke to me this morning.

> Come, in my labor find a resting place
> And in my sorrows lay your head,
> Or rather take my life and blood
> And buy yourself a better bed –
> Or take my breath and take my death
> And buy yourself a better rest

"Take my life and blood to buy yourself a better bed." This touches me deeply. I pray for humility. I pray for the strength to answer Christ's question with my actions.

February 4

Repeat and reflect on the week.

THIS HAS BEEN a very good week. For one thing, our daughter Melissa has been on national television twice, and has written an incredibly reasoned and thoughtful editorial for the *Washington Post*. She continues to support the nomination of her good friend, Judge Neil Gorsuch, for the Supreme Court. Melissa has taken the principled position that we should support the nomination of this obviously qualified man, regardless of our politics. Sallie Ann and I are very proud of her. I have supported Melissa in her position, earning in the process the ire of some of my liberal friends. Many Democrats are convinced that complete and total obstruction are the only proper courses of action in this time of tumult.

Last night, a Federal judge in the state of Washington struck down the President's ban on refugees. While I am certain a way will be found to get around the Constitution and re-impose the ban, I can savor this joyous interlude for the weekend.

I have loved the Exercises this week. Among other things, I am going through a very healthy period physically, carefully eating only healthy meals and working out in some way each day. As a result, I sleep very well, feel strong all day, and have lost twenty pounds. I am certain that my spiritual condition is connected to my physical and mental condition. Tomorrow I fly out to Albuquerque for a Living School retreat, then begin a very busy mission schedule, with four weeks in a row in the Dominican Republic. I am a little apprehensive about maintaining my daily regimen of spiritual and physical exercise over the next five weeks.

Reflecting on the periods in my life when I have suffered the most, I am reminded of a classic Yogi Berra quotation, "I made too many wrong mistakes." It is incredible how often Berra gets things right! I made a lot of mistakes in my life, both in the long, forty-year period when I was climbing the ladder of superficial success, and, especially, in the two years that I crawled along the bottom. Perhaps it was in that appalling period that most of my mistakes were wrong!

Spending much time dwelling on the bad times in my life has never seemed like a good way to grow stronger. While I never want to forget the lessons, I know that I only make progress primarily by facing forward, taking one step at a time into a better future. I made (and make!) most of my mistakes when I allow my false self to govern my actions. Merton's answer to the false self is finding the true self in God.

Every one of us is shadowed by an illusory person: [A] false self. This is the man that I want myself to be but who cannot exist, because God does not know anything about him. … My false and private self is the one who wants to exist outside the reach of God's will and God's love—outside of reality and outside of life. And such a life cannot help but be an illusion. … The secret of my identity is hidden in the love and mercy of God. … *Therefore I cannot hope to find myself anywhere except in him.* … Therefore there is only one problem on which all my existence, my peace and my happiness depend: [T]o discover myself in discovering God. *If I find Him, I will find myself, and if I find my true self I will find him.*

"Who do they say I am?" Unfortunately, merely asking the question suggests a pre-occupation with my image, the self I project to the world. Nonetheless, it is something about which I do worry. I like to think that I am not working in Sister Parish, or making these Exercises, only to make people think better of me. However, I would certainly prefer that people think good things about me than that they view my actions with righteous disdain.

Just saying that makes me think about my political views, which do cause some of my neighbors and fellow parishioners to view me "with righteous disdain." I am not much troubled by this, even though it does make me uncomfortable in some situations. Sallie Ann is convinced that it is a reason we are seldom invited to dinner by our friends. Possibly so. My hope is that "they say" I am a man of principle, proudly holding some unpopular views, but acting consistently and with integrity. Merton touches on this when he urges us to accept what he calls the seeds of our reality, planted by God.

The seeds that are planted in my liberty at every moment, by God's will, are the seeds of my own identity, my own reality, my own happiness, my own sanctity. To refuse them is to refuse everything; it is the refusal of my own existence and being: [O]f my identity, my very self. Our vocation is not simply to be, but to work together with God in the creation of our own life, our own identity, our own destiny.

I pray this morning for clarity with respect to true humility. I want to be respected for my thoughts and actions, but I do not want the desire for respect to be the driving force behind those thoughts and actions.

The Daily Examen is an important part of the Exercises. It is a practice I began five years ago while going through Annotation 19 the first time, and have continued, more or less consistently, ever since. While reading about Johannes Tauler (d. 1361), a student of Meister Eckhart, I came across another version of daily prayer, which is similar to the Examen. Tauler taught and preached during the painful years before, during, and after the Black Death in Strassburg. The prayer is meant to have originated with the Friends of God, a spiritual movement that was particularly active in the first half of the 14th century in Germany. Tauler taught and preached to the Friends of God for more than thirty years.

All those in whom the love of God, or the terror brought about by the dreadful calamities of the present, wakens a wish to begin a new and spiritual life, will discover great advantage in withdrawing into themselves every morning when they waken, in order to consider what they will do during the day. Should they find any evil thought in themselves, any purpose which is contrary to the divine will, let them give it up and cast it aside, to the glory of God. In the evening, upon going to bed, let them consider how they have spent the day. Let them recall what deeds they have done, and in what spirit they have performed them. If they discover that they have done any good, let them thank God, and give Him the glory. If they discover they have done evil, let them take the blame for it themselves, and lay the fault on nobody else, and let them deeply repent before God, saying to Him, 'O Lord, I sincerely repent and I firmly intend from now on with Thy help, to avoid sinning.'

The "terror brought about by the dreadful calamities of the present" obviously referred, among other things, to the Black Death. The "dreadful calamites" of 2017 are far away from my library and garden here in Ponte Vedra Beach. Nonetheless, my heart goes out to the victims of war and violence throughout the world. I pray especially for the more than sixty-five million refugees forced from their homes, uncertain about where they and their families will sleep tonight.

CALENDAR WEEK TWENTY-ONE

I want to know Jesus better, to love Him more, and to follow Him wholeheartedly.

February 5

Matthew 8:23–27, Jesus Stills the Storm

²³ And when he got into the boat, his disciples followed him. ²⁴ A windstorm arose on the sea, so great that the boat was being swamped by the waves; but he was asleep. ²⁵ And they went and woke him up, saying, "Lord, save us! We are perishing!" ²⁶ And he said to them, "Why are you afraid, you of little faith?" Then he got up and rebuked the winds and the sea; and there was a dead calm. ²⁷ They were amazed, saying, "What sort of man is this, that even the winds and the sea obey him?"

MY PLANE FOR Chicago left Jacksonville at 7 a.m., giving me the opportunity to once again swear never to take such an early flight! The problem is not the flight. Rather, it is the two and a half hours before the flight that I have to get up, get ready, and then drive to the airport. I am simply too old for this! The good news is that I am on my way to Albuquerque for a Living School Reunion Retreat. I will be with good friends in a good place, one ideally suited for the Exercises. I am writing this on the first leg of the trip, changing planes in Chicago for a three-hour flight. I hope it will allow me to take a nap.

"Why are you afraid, you of little faith?" It is said that "fear not," "be not afraid," and similar phrases, appear in the Bible 365 times, one for each day of the year. I have never counted, but can certainly attest to the fact that Jesus said something like this often. Fear is such a tragic instinct, even though it must have immense evolutionary value.

Despotic politicians appeal to our fear, particularly those, like Trump, who espouse the exclusionary policies of racism and nativism. An article in Atlantic magazine, clearly written before the election, is devoted to the power of fear in the Trump campaign.

> Fear pervades Americans' lives—and American politics. Trump is a master of fear, invoking it in concrete and abstract ways, summoning and validating it. More than most politicians, he grasps and channels the fear coursing through the electorate. And if Trump still stands a chance to win in November, fear could be the key.

There are alternatives, though they do not have the same visceral power of fear. I believe they have endured precisely because they eschewed fear. Abraham Lincoln's first inaugural address appealed to "the better angels of our nature." Martin Luther King said "the arc of the moral universe is long, but it bends toward justice." President Obama, borrows from both of these themes in one of the greatest lines from his victory speech in 2008.

> "[Hope is] the answer that led those who have been told for so long by so many to be cynical, and fearful, and doubtful of what we can achieve *to put their hands on the arc of history and bend it once more toward the hope of a better day.*"

These great men were all asking us to not be afraid, not be of little faith. Hope Trumps Hate! This is extremely important today, but, unhappily, I am not filled with much hope. For reasons that I am simply not able to understand, the whole tide of global politics seems to be moving backwards, away from inclusion and trust. There are more than 65 million refugees in the world today! How can we turn away from them now, when the need is so great? How can eighty percent of white Catholics in the United States vote for Trump? It cannot all be about abortion. There is something else going on. I believe it is the pervasiveness of fear. I believe the politics of fear is a very small politics, but one that has huge appeal today, not just here, but throughout the world.

Pope Francis has repeatedly added his voice to more than a century of Catholic social teaching that exhorts us to the virtue of welcoming the stranger. Tauler wrote in the 14th century, "Never trust a virtue that has not been put into practice." Based on our current attitude toward refugees, our present collective virtue of hospitality is not to be trusted.

I sat a long time, thinking about Tauler living and teaching in Strassburg for those miserable three years of the bubonic plague. What must it have been like to watch more than half of Europe's population die from the plague? Worse than that would have been close friends, students, parishioners, and the babies of parishioners. Half a century ago, as a freshman in college, I read *The Plague* by Albert Camus. I was obviously too young then, and too inexperienced, to grasp the deep meaning of suffering. My copy of the book still sits on a bookshelf in my library, gathering dust. It has probably not been opened in fifty years! I read through it this morning, noting some of my underlined passages.

> Still, if things had gone thus far and no farther, force of habit would doubtless have gained the day, as usual. But other members of our community, *not all menials or poor people*, were to follow the path down which M. Michel had led the way. *And it was then that fear, and with fear serious reflection, began.*
>
> He had examined the old man and now was sitting in the middle of the dingy little dining-room. Yes, despite what he had said, he was afraid. He knew that in this suburb alone eight or ten unhappy people, cowering over their buboes, would be awaiting his visit the next morning.
>
> For who would dare to assert that eternal happiness can compensate for a single moment of human suffering?

As troubled as I am about the problems in the world today, it is not as bad as that. Then again, I do not live in a crowded refugee camp in Turkey, desperately awaiting the final approval of my case, filled with hope for resettlement in the United States.

I pray for a better world. I pray that we will connect with our better angels. I pray for the strength to once again put my hand on that arc of history.

February 6

Repeat Matthew 8:23–27, Jesus Stills the Storm

ABOUT THIRTY graduates of the Living School are gathered at the Bosque Retreat Center in Albuquerque, New Mexico, for a reunion retreat. I arrived yesterday afternoon, took a long walk along the Rio Grande River, and then watched the Super Bowl on my iPad in my room. My body clock is still on Florida time, so I am awake in the pre-dawn dark. The retreat begins officially at 7:30 this morning.

My good friend, Sister Ilia Delio, recently wrote a note of sobering advice to her many followers, most of whom are worried about the state of the country and the world.

> Teilhard de Chardin had some keen insights on the power of *thinking* to evolve us. To think, he said, is to unify; thinking enables us to be artisans of the future. How we think and what we are thinking about shapes our lives and the future of our world…It is important to keep the thinking dimension of the Omega vision in mind because our world is currently in emotional overdrive. The new political regime in the U.S. has provoked a number of protests, and resistance is high. We are in a new age of anxiety and uncertainty. The barometer of distrust is increasing and the future seems dark and ominous at times. If one watches the nightly news and primetime television, then it is apparent we are strangely entertained by the dark side of humanity; we seem to be lured by the absence of light. But we do not have to watch the television to realize our world has become extremely fragile. Our planet is like a delicate piece of china that could be smashed to pieces at any moment. The plight of the poor, the devastation of the earth, and the ongoing tragedies of the oppressed in Syria, Africa and other parts of the world are heart-breaking.

As I sit with this message from Sister Ilia, it is obvious that she, and Teilhard, are referring to *thinking* in a radically different way. The dictionary definition of thinking is "the process of using one's mind to consider or reason about something." Generally, the normal thinking process utilizes inputs only from our physical senses. When Teilhard says that "to think is to unify," he is going deeper than the superficial level of sensory perception. The *thinking* he is talking about is something like what the late-Medieval mystics, particularly Meister Eckhart, described as a new way of *seeing* or *knowing*. For example, Eckhart wrote,

> Some people want to look upon God with their eyes, as they look upon a cow, and want to love God as they love a cow. Thus they love God for the sake of external riches and of internal solace; but these people do not love God aright… Foolish people deem that they should look upon God as though He stood there and they here. It is not thus. *God and I are one in the act of knowing.*

Eckhart distinguished between using the physical senses to perceive reality at a basic, rather limited level, on one hand, and using the deeper spiritual power to see a radically different reality, on the other.

> We are to be united with God *essentially*; we are to be united with God as one; we are to be united with God altogether. How are we to be united with God *essentially*? This is to be accomplished by a *seeing and not by a being.*

This echoes the Apostle Paul writing to the Galatians.

> I have been crucified with Christ. It is no longer I who live, but Christ who lives in me. And the life I now live in the flesh I live by faith in the Son of God, who loved me and gave himself for me.

Thinking with the interior spiritual sense does not require more effort. Rather, it requires surrender. Comprehending reality in this spiritual way was described by Spinoza as a higher level of cognition.

> The highest virtue of the soul is to apprehend God, or to comprehend things in the third— the highest—kind of cognition. This virtue becomes the greater the more the soul comprehends things in this way of cognition; therefore the one who grasps things in this way of cognition attains the highest human perfection and consequently becomes filled with the highest joy, accompanied by the conceptions of himself and of virtue. Hence from this kind of cognition springs the highest possible peace of the soul

Making these Exercises has the potential to awaken in me this higher level of cognition. Surrendering to the existence of a deeper, grander, and, ultimately, a more fulfilling truth requires letting go of the shallow reality of my daily life. This is not easy for me. I feel very uncomfortable with the concepts articulated by the mystics. I lose my mental balance. Just when I almost understand how it all fits together, I reach back for the handrails of small vision and humble cognition.

I can imagine Jesus saying, "What are you afraid of, you of little faith?" He would urge me to simply jump into the deep water of true self knowledge, of non-dual contemplation and oneness with God. He would ask that I *think*.

The morning ends uneasily for me. I prayed the Serenity Prayer, seeking the grace to accept the things I cannot change, the courage to change the things I can, and the wisdom to know the difference. After praying the Our Father, I joined my classmates for the first day of the retreat.

The first day of our reunion retreat has just come to an end. It feels like we have been together for a week! We met in small groups this afternoon, where we were asked, among other things, to answer the question why we had come to this retreat. Everyone in my small group had essentially the same answer: We came to feed from the table of Living School unity, theology, contemplation, and encounter. We came to be with each other! I want to record some of my thoughts from today, knowing as I do that these reunions will be very infrequent.

I left these reflections at around 7 a.m., after more than two hours of praying, meditating, and writing. The group gathered in a circle to begin the day with a "sit," a group guided meditation and prayer service. Sitting in that close community of "sent out" Living School veterans was magical. It was as though the spiritual energy impacted each of us in somewhat the same way, developing a rhythm as we moved effortlessly from silence to prayer and chanting. For me, I was home. I looked around the circle at one friend after another, smiling inwardly at the warmth and beauty of my love for each of them. To be clear, in our two years of Living School instruction, we did not spend weeks together in the same room. Our class met three times as a group of 180 students, and once in a smaller group of 20 students. While the "small group intensive" did allow relationships to develop, the other meetings were too large for much deep connection.

Yet we listened to the same lectures, both in person and online. We read the same assignments, and I would venture to guess that most of us chased our assigned reading along similar paths of additional sources. Somehow, deep connections were formed over the two years of the Living School, sometimes without even knowing each other's names.

Half of us chose a morning program of expressive art, focused on each of us making a mandala, a circular art form using, in the exercise this morning, photographs cut from various magazines. One of the women sitting next to me wept as she made her mandala, recognizing in the randomly chosen photographs elements of her life story.

My mandala was organized around a photo of Pope Francis, with brightly colored animals and birds around one side, a Reaper drone on the other side, and two small children walking away from the drone into the woods. Quite unintentionally, I created a story about God's infinitely variable creation, about man's ability to destroy life, and about the life and death struggle that traps children and animals in its tragic reach. Without aiming to do so, I found myself weeping as well.

We "sat" again before lunch, and a third time before dinner. There are insufficient words to express my gratitude for the Living School. Father Rohr triggered a deep transformation in my faith life, which, mind you, had just experienced a radical transformation. All of the spiritual energy and love contained in the two years of the Living School, the year of studying Franciscan mysticism before the Living School, and the year and a half of Ignatian and Sister Parish spiritualty since then, came together on this one day, the first of only three that we will be together. I am drained in that way that results from drinking from a firehose of love and joy. The only way to recover from my joyous exhaustion is to get right back into the experience at 7 a.m. tomorrow morning.

February 7

Luke 5:17–26, Jesus Heals a Paralytic

[17] One day, while he was teaching, Pharisees and teachers of the law were sitting near by (they had come from every village of Galilee and Judea and from Jerusalem); and the power of the Lord was with him to heal. [18] Just then some men came, carrying a paralyzed man on a bed. They were trying to bring him in and lay him before Jesus; [19] but finding no way to bring him in because of the crowd, they went up on the roof and let him down with his bed through the tiles into the middle of the crowd in front of Jesus. [20] When he saw their faith, he said, "Friend, your sins are forgiven you." [21] Then the scribes and the Pharisees began to question, "Who is this who is speaking blasphemies? Who can forgive sins but God alone?" [22] When Jesus perceived their questionings, he answered them, "Why do you raise such questions in your hearts? [23] Which is easier, to say, 'Your sins are forgiven you,' or to say, 'Stand up and walk'? [24] But so that you may know that the Son of Man has authority on earth to forgive sins"—he said to the one who was paralyzed—"I say to you, stand up and take your bed and go to your home." [25] Immediately he stood up before them, took what he had been lying on, and went to his home, glorifying God. [26] Amazement seized all of them, and they glorified God and were filled with awe, saying, "We have seen strange things today."

IT IS DARK and cold here in New Mexico. I walked down to the Rio Grande at 5:30, stopping often to look up at the stars. There are no words to adequately describe the fullness of the joy I feel this morning. I am surrounded by God's glorious creation, all quietly giving witness to the vastness of the universe. There are no restraints of time or space. This moment, on this trail, contains all moments on all trails. All of God's creatures are present in this moment and at this place. I am in the "here and now," realizing that my overflowing joy is a testimony to the fact that I am in all space and all time. I am connected to all of God's creatures. We have been one with God since the beginning of time, and will be until the end of time. I am deliriously happy to be alive.

It has always been my intention to read each day's passage the night before. I often forget to do so when I am home. Alone in my room here at the retreat center, with no television, I not only read it once before falling asleep, but read it twice more when I woke up during the night.

"Friend, your sins are forgiven you." Healing by forgiving. In one sense, I am as troubled by this as the scribes and Pharisees were in Luke's account of the event. Their concern was tribal and exclusionary. Only God can forgive sins, or, I am sure they would also have said, someone to whom God has giv-

en the healing certificate. Healing without proper authority! How blasphemous! Loving a person from the other tribe, caring for the outcast, accepting the refugee—all of these require "extreme vetting"!

These were not my concerns. The idea of healing by forgiving implies that the illness or condition involved a sin, an action that required forgiveness. Paralysis may have been considered such a condition two thousand years ago, I certainly don't know. Today, however, there are very few physical illnesses or conditions that fall under the category of sin. Addiction stands out, despite decades of insistence that it is an illness, not a sin.

Sitting with this, I begin to see exceptions to the idea that forgiveness is not healing. Loneliness, isolation, and the depression that goes with them, are conditions that might be healed by forgiveness. The person that must ultimately do the forgiving, however, is the lonely person himself or herself. It may certainly be the case that being forgiven by another makes it possible, or more likely, that I can forgive myself. Being broken, carrying shame or guilt around for any length of time—these require an acceptance of oneself as someone worth loving. The final healing of such a condition ultimately requires self-forgiveness. As long as I continue to hate myself, no amount of love and forgiveness from others can heal my wounds.

February 8

Repeat Luke 5:17–26, Jesus Heals a Paralytic

"WE HAVE SEEN strange things today." What a perfect description of this Living School reunion retreat! "Who are these people?," I asked, repeatedly. The second day ended last night with a discussion about what we can do about our political situation. While I am convinced that there were at least a couple of Trump voters in the group, they had the good sense to remain silent. The overwhelming sentiment in the group was grief. After an evening of drums and chants, most of us stayed in the Gathering Room to talk about what can be done by way of resistance. Some people wept when talking about DREAMers they were counseling. Some wept because the primary purpose of their lives went down in the election on November 8. It was not just that Hillary lost. The greater loss was the work that all of us had been part of, work to create a better world through education reform, health care reform, environmental reform, prison reform, a "soft power" approach to foreign policy, and more. The list is long. Many of us worked on this far-reaching program, in one way or another, all of our lives.

We lost because 77,000 people in three states voted for Trump, pushing the Electoral College over the required number. When all the votes were counted for the whole country, Hillary won a majority of more than three million votes. The Electoral College, however, had already been decided. Trump is the President, full stop. As hard as it is to believe, he prevailed over fifteen Republican opponents in winning the nomination, then he won a majority of the Electoral College votes. Accepting that simple fact is very hard to do. "We have seen strange things today."

Reflecting on the passage from Luke, I wonder about the men who carried the paralytic up to the roof, and lowered him down at the feet of Jesus. What kind of faith did they have to believe their friend would be healed? How could they have known that they were lowering their friend safely, and that Jesus would even be aware that they had done so? These miracles of Jesus had many purposes, of which the healing of the sick was perhaps least important.

As in most of the other miracle accounts, Jesus was making a point to the scribes and Pharisees. He wanted them to fully acknowledge His authority as the Son of Man. Jesus could not only heal, He could also forgive, and He could do both on the Sabbath. I would go much further today. Anyone can heal, forgive, and show love, and they can do it anytime. Modern medicine is capable of truly extraordinary feats of healing and fixing, yet I personally know of no doctor who won't acknowledge the frequent presence of someone else in the operating room. Cases of lay people healing through prayer are reported every week.

In fairness, there appears to be no scientific, peer-reviewed study that confirms the role of prayer in healing. In fact, in a March 31, 2006 article, the *New York Times* reported the results of a broad study suggesting the opposite.

> Prayers offered by strangers had no effect on the recovery of people who were undergoing heart surgery, a large and long-awaited study has found. And patients who knew they were being prayed for had a higher rate of post-operative complications like abnormal heart rhythms, perhaps because of the expectations the prayers created, the researchers suggested.

My personal experience, which is by no means scientific, includes numerous instances when I believed prayer worked. I prayed with the parents of a very sick child in Germany, fifty years ago, and watched the child recover. I have more recently been blessed and prayed for by priests. I felt immediately better, and I believe my hospital stay was shortened as a direct result of those prayers.

One important aspect of the power of prayer is the way it works on those who are praying. In my grief over the death of a young girl from Mamey, my prayer helped me move past the suffering. I have watched parents leave hospital rooms after prayer, significantly changed. This is no small matter.

Reflecting again on Luke's words, why would Jesus have been concerned that the scribes and Pharisees consider Him capable of miracles and great works? In a sense, it is like efforts to convert the ideologues on both sides of today's political spectrum. They live in a different fact universe, with firmly established conclusions that are not subject to persuasion. There is no point in trying to "convert" the other side. Perhaps Jesus, or, more likely, the Evangelists, wanted subsequent readers to be awed by Jesus's powers to perform miraculous feats. I am not persuaded.

I am writing this at the end of a nearly perfect day in the company of my wonderful classmates from the Living School. As we have for the past two days, our small group, the Pinyon, met in a circle at the end of the dining room. We had been given a list of questions to consider, one of which was about our brokenness. The sharing was remarkable, both for the vulnerability of each one of us, and also for the sensitivity that others in the group showed for the person sharing deep pain. Each of us had experienced brokenness. Each of us expressed gratitude for the role the Living School has played, and continues to play, in the healing process. Jason, Sara, Nancy, Jan, and Claire, all now intimate friends. I wonder now whether and where I will see any of them again. That question notwithstanding, I cherish the time we have had together this week.

The retreat officially ended with a Eucharist service tonight. Like all things Living School, this was an inclusive, loving, participatory experience. We prayed to Father God, Mother God, God of the Universe. We prayed for belonging, accepting, and loving. We greeted each other in silence, following the directions to look deeply at each other, joining our open palms in peaceful acceptance. At the end of the service, we offered peace to each other in joyous, powerful embrace.

All of the teaching of the Living School builds powerfully on the deep tradition of mysticism that I have been reading for the past few weeks. In a moment of quiet today, I read Johannes Tauler's comment on becoming one with God through the death of the will.

If man is truly to become one with God, all the faculties of the inner man must die and be silent. The will must be turned away from even the good and from all willing, and must become *will-less*.

He argued that our limited sensory faculties must undergo a form of death in order for us to be born again with spiritual sight. Goethe wrote, "And as long you do not have [the secret, primordial understanding of life], this *Die and Become*, you are only a dreary guest on the dark earth."

My prayer tonight is full of gratitude for Father Rohr, the Living School, my small group from this retreat, my small group from the Intensive Week, and all those who held my hand during my spiritual journey. Sallie Ann is foremost in my mind as I pray in gratitude for all that she did before and during the early years of my journey, and the wonderful role she plays each day now as my loving partner.

February 9

Matthew 14:22–28, Jesus Walks on the Water
[22] Immediately he made the disciples get into the boat and go on ahead to the other side, while he dismissed the crowds. [23] And after he had dismissed the crowds, he went up the mountain by himself to pray. When evening came, he was there alone, [24] but by this time the boat, battered by the waves, was far from the land, for the wind was against them. [25] And early in the morning he came walking toward them on the sea. [26] But when the disciples saw him walking on the sea, they were terrified, saying, "It is a ghost!" And they cried out in fear. [27] But immediately Jesus spoke to them and said, "Take heart, it is I; do not be afraid." [28] Peter answered him, "Lord, if it is you, command me to come to you on the water."

WAITING FOR the airplane this morning, I sat with one of my Living School classmates, who was also flying through Dallas. She lost one of her three children eight years ago, when he was killed in a helmet to helmet collision in high school football. I was not prepared for this. I felt at once sharp pain and profound compassion. Once again, I was moved by how much depth lies behind the façade of casual relationships. Sharing *at depth* is what distinguishes my Living School friendships from so many others.

Sallie Ann sent me something from Henri Nouwen this morning.

For most of my life I have struggled to find God, to know God, to love God. I have tried hard to follow the guidelines of the spiritual life—pray always, work for others, read the Scriptures—and to avoid the many temptations to dissipate myself. I have failed many times but always tried again, even when I was close to despair.

Now, I wonder whether I have sufficiently realized that during all this time God has been trying to find me, to know me, and to love me. The question is not, "How am I to find God?" but "How am I to let myself be found by Him?" The question is not "How am I to know God?" but "How am I to let myself be known by God?" And finally, the question is not "How am I to love God?" but "How am I to let myself be loved by God?" God is looking into the distance for me, trying to find me, and longing to bring me home.

God is aggressively reaching out to me, constantly looking for an access point into my broken, resistant, pride-filled soul. This is an extremely difficult concept for me to grasp. It is at the heart of surrender to win.

February 10

Matthew 14:22–28, Jesus Walks on the Water

Tauler wrote,

> Understanding requires the mental and spiritual movement from the "I" to the "all-I," becoming one with God and all creation.

The "all-I" is, as the Apostle Paul said, "Christ in me." Standing in the way of God's efforts is my enormous ego, "protecting" me from my better self, and from God's love. How crazy is that?

"Take heart, it is I; do not be afraid." Once again, Jesus admonishes His disciples not to be afraid. Reflecting on this, I wondered at how many miracles these disciples had already seen. Yet they were still not convinced that Jesus was the Messiah. Peter, acting as though he is the one disciple who believes, puts the question to Jesus in the form of a doubt. *"If* it is you, command me to come to you on the water." One has to ask how are we meant to believe today, two thousand years later, with no personal experience witnessing these miracles first hand?

God, allow me to see and live in the greater reality of the "all-I." Help me surrender to the death of my false self. I want to be re-born, fully involved in the second half of my life, filling my life container to the point of overflowing.

I recently watched a very good TED talk on the subject of addiction, which made one central point.

> The opposite of addiction is not sobriety, it is connection.

Maggie and I went down to the bench, where the beauty of sky, ocean, and garden were almost enough to offset the cold. After quickly praying the Our Father, we returned to the library.

February 11

Repeat and reflect on the week.

The 9th Circuit Court decided against Trump's position on the refugee ban. Sadly, the victory is likely to be very short lived. The President will simply write a new Executive Order, taking an approach that avoids the issues that caused him to lose these first two rounds. Someone sent me these passages from the Hebrew scriptures. We had been talking about the way Palestinians are treated in Israel today. Interesting reading from that perspective, particularly the first two readings, both of which reference the time when the Israelites were foreigners in Egypt.

> When a foreigner resides among you in your land, do not mistreat them. The foreigner residing among you must be treated as your native-born. Love them as yourself, for you were foreigners in Egypt. (Leviticus 19:33–34)
>
> *Do not oppress a foreigner*; you yourselves know how it feels to be foreigners, because you were foreigners in Egypt. (Exodus 23:9)

Catholic Charities is one of the largest and most active agencies responsible for refugee resettlement here in the United States. Some of our Sister Parish missionaries regularly assist in setting up the new housing for refugees coming into the Jacksonville area. These passages speak to that good work.

When you reap the harvest of your land, do not reap to the very edges of your field or gather the gleanings of your harvest. Do not go over your vineyard a second time or pick up the grapes that have fallen. *Leave them for the poor and the foreigner.* (Leviticus 19:9–10)

He defends the cause of the fatherless and the widow, and *loves the foreigner residing among you,* giving them food and clothing. And you are to love those who are foreigners, for you yourselves were foreigners in Egypt. (Deuteronomy 10:18–19)

"So I will come to put you on trial. I will be quick to testify against sorcerers, adulterers and perjurers, against those who defraud laborers of their wages, who oppress the widows and the fatherless, and *deprive the foreigners among you of justice*, but do not fear me," says the Lord Almighty. (Malachi 3:5)

"As for the foreigner who does not belong to your people Israel but has come from a distant land because of your name—for they will hear of your great name and your mighty hand and your outstretched arm—when they come and pray toward this temple, then hear from [H]eaven, your dwelling place. *Do whatever the foreigner asks of you*, so that all the peoples of the earth may know your name and fear you, as do your own people Israel, and may know that this house I have built bears your Name. (1 Kings 8:41–44)

It is painful to consider that so many Christians, particularly white Christians, supported President Trump, not just despite his refugee policies, but precisely because of them. Jewish voters have traditionally voted Democratic, and continued to do so in this election, voting only 24 percent for Trump. Trump won 58 percent of white Christians overall, 60 percent of white Catholics, 81 percent of white Evangelicals, and even 61 percent of Mormons! The New Testament is just as clear on this subject as the Hebrew scriptures.

For I was hungry and you gave me something to eat, I was thirsty and you gave me something to drink, *I was a stranger and you invited me in*, I needed clothes and you clothed me, I was sick and you looked after me, I was in prison and you came to visit me. (Matthew 25:25–36)

I will read from First Corinthians 2:6–10 at Mass tonight. Reading it through this morning, I reflected on the reference Paul makes to what "scripture says."

What no eye has seen and no ear has heard, what the mind of man cannot visualize; all that God has prepared for those who love him;

For most of this past week in New Mexico, our teaching on contemplation was about loving God. When we contemplate great music, a wonderful painting, a good friend, or the beauty of nature, we see "what no eye has seen," hear "what no ear has heard," and, more than anything else, become acutely aware of "what the mind of man cannot visualize."

CALENDAR WEEK TWENTY-TWO

I want to know Jesus better, to love Him more, and to follow Him wholeheartedly.

February 12

Matthew 10:1–16, The Twelve Apostles
¹ Then Jesus summoned his twelve disciples and gave them authority over unclean spirits, to cast them out, and to cure every disease and every sickness. ² These are the names of the twelve apostles: first, Simon, also known as Peter, and his brother Andrew; James son of Zebedee, and his brother John; ³ Philip and Bartholomew; Thomas and Matthew the tax collector; James son of Alphaeus, and Thaddaeus; ⁴ Simon the Cananaean, and Judas Iscariot, the one who betrayed him.
The Mission of the Twelve
⁵ These twelve Jesus sent out with the following instructions: "Go nowhere among the Gentiles, and enter no town of the Samaritans, ⁶ but go rather to the lost sheep of the house of Israel. ⁷ As you go, proclaim the good news, 'The kingdom of heaven has come near.' ⁸ Cure the sick, raise the dead, cleanse the lepers, cast out demons. You received without payment; give without payment. ⁹ Take no gold, or silver, or copper in your belts, ¹⁰ no bag for your journey, or two tunics, or sandals, or a staff; for laborers deserve their food. ¹¹ Whatever town or village you enter, find out who in it is worthy, and stay there until you leave. ¹² As you enter the house, greet it. ¹³ If the house is worthy, let your peace come upon it; but if it is not worthy, let your peace return to you. ¹⁴ If anyone will not welcome you or listen to your words, shake off the dust from your feet as you leave that house or town. ¹⁵ Truly I tell you, it will be more tolerable for the land of Sodom and Gomorrah on the day of judgment than for that town.
Coming Persecutions
¹⁶ "See, I am sending you out like sheep into the midst of wolves; so be wise as serpents and innocent as doves.

As THIS NEW week begins, I read through the instructions from Jesus to His twelve apostles several times. Verses 14 and 15 brought me back to the subject of refugees.

> If anyone will not welcome you or listen to your words, shake off the dust from your feet as you leave that house or town. Truly I tell you, it will be more tolerable for the land of Sodom and Gomorrah on the day of judgment than for that town.

Are we not inviting the families from all the violent parts of the world who seek refuge here in the United States to "shake off the dust" from their feet as they leave our immigration offices? It is hard for me to see our "extreme vetting" as anything other than a recruiting tool for radical Islamists.

Fifty-two years ago (!), as a missionary for the Mormons, we frequently read the passage from Matthew's Gospel as direct advice to us in proselytizing to the Germans. I vaguely remember joking that the only way we could get into a house would be to alternate between "being devious" and "playing dumb." Over the years, I have understood the phrase in verse 16 ("wise as serpents and innocent as doves") to mean sneaky, not wise, like a snake, and naïve, not innocent, like a dove.

In many ways, I do prefer the idea of preaching only to Jews (as opposed to Jews and Gentiles), which suggests only a different view or attitude about one's birth religion, not a radical change away from one's family and birth religion. I like it that the primary purpose of "evangelization" for Catholics is to bring fallen-away Catholics back into the church. This was decidedly not the primary purpose of our Mormon missions, which were specifically focused on converting people of different faith traditions. My conversion to Catholicism began inside me, and was based primarily upon conversations I had with God in my own time and in my own way.

The challenge to the twelve Apostles two thousand years ago was preaching and teaching about reforming the traditional religion of Judaism. The scriptural references were to the Hebrew scriptures. For most early converts, I suspect it was something like pushing against an open door. The persecution of early Christians came not from the fallen away Jews, but from the Romans and other Gentiles.

February 13

Repeat Matthew 10:1–16, The Twelve Apostles

CONTEMPLATIVE prayer is difficult for me under the best of circumstances. As my journal has clearly reflected over the past five months, public affairs and political news distract me a great deal.

For the past month, our weekly goal has been the same:

> I want to know Jesus better, to love Him more, and to follow Him wholeheartedly.

In these final two weeks before Lent, the passages from scripture will track Jesus as he enters Jerusalem several times, teaching, healing, and preaching His new Gospel, continuing to turn the social order upside-down. It is a time to savor these stories, growing closer to an understanding and deep friendship with Jesus.

Matthew's account of the instructions Jesus gave to His twelve Apostles is a "sending out," heralding the message they will hear at the Pentecost. I put myself in the place of one of the Apostles, listening carefully to the instructions of Jesus.

> "If anyone will not welcome you or listen to your words, shake off the dust from your feet as you leave that house or town."

These words resonated in my mind, reminding me of similar instructions given to me as a new missionary in Germany, fifty-two years ago: "Do not waste time 'fellowshipping'. Give the lessons, only the lessons, and only one time. If the potential convert does not agree to baptism, move on, shaking the dust from your feet." I resented those words then, even though I understand why the Mormon authorities would instruct us that way, just as I understand why Jesus instructed His Apostles with these same words.

Nonetheless, I resist the notion that there should be any limit on our efforts to preach the Gospel by our actions. I have made it clear that I have little time for hard proselytizing. Far be it from me to tell others how to live their lives. However, "turning the other cheek" makes infinitely more sense to me than putting limits on showing my love, or forgiving, or granting second and third chances. This seems to me to be at the heart of Jesus' message.

February 14: We have been married 35 years today.

John 2:13–22, Jesus Cleanses the Temple

¹³ The Passover of the Jews was near, and Jesus went up to Jerusalem. ¹⁴ In the temple he found people selling cattle, sheep, and doves, and the money changers seated at their tables. ¹⁵ Making a whip of cords, he drove all of them out of the temple, both the sheep and the cattle. He also poured out the coins of the money changers and overturned their tables. ¹⁶ He told those who were selling the doves, "Take these things out of here! Stop making my Father's house a marketplace!" ¹⁷ His disciples remembered that it was written, "Zeal for your house will consume me." ¹⁸ The Jews then said to him, "What sign can you show us for doing this?" ¹⁹ Jesus answered them, "Destroy this temple, and in three days I will raise it up." ²⁰ The Jews then said, "This temple has been under construction for forty-six years, and will you raise it up in three days?" ²¹ But he was speaking of the temple of his body. ²² After he was raised from the dead, his disciples remembered that he had said this; and they believed the scripture and the word that Jesus had spoken.

I WALKED DOWN to the bench with Maggie when I came home from tennis, reflecting on the reading from John's Gospel. As I reflected on the efforts of Jesus to cleanse the temple of its commercial activity, I could not help but consider the impact of market forces on bad behavior throughout history, but particularly today. *Demand* creates its own supply. The money changers and livestock dealers in the temple were there because animal sacrifice required it. Drug dealers prosper because addicts need them. Pornography flourishes because it is, by far, the most demanded service on the internet. We have been trying to "cleanse the temple" of drug supply for decades. All the efforts to interdict supply have come to naught, and will continue to do so as long as the demand for drugs exists.

The success of Jesus in cleansing the temple was not complete until the practice of animal sacrifice ended. As I understand the history, the small community of Christian Jews got the message while Christ was still alive (possibly when he stormed through the temple). For the rest of Judaism, the destruction of the temple by the Romans in 70 CE effectively ended the "Old Covenant" of animal sacrifice. Obviously, when there was no longer any need for sacrificial animals, the livestock dealers and money changers disappeared.

I was disturbed last night at a CRHP meeting to learn that many of my friends in the parish continue to believe in the need for indulgences, and for prayers and Masses to be purchased for the souls in Purgatory. For some reason, I have always assumed that Luther brought an end to the sale of indulgences. It only occurred to me after the meeting that this was the case for those protesting, not for the Catholics, against whom the protest was made. The Church did outlaw the purchase of indulgences in 1567, but with "contributions and other good acts" (with a limit of one indulgence per sinner per day), indulgences are still to be had. Objecting to this practice and belief will remain a very quiet part of my resistance!

February 15

Repeat John 2:13–22, Jesus Cleanses the Temple

AFTER A VERY restless night, I drove to the Jacksonville airport at 6 a.m., flew all day, and am now sitting, exhausted, in my room at the Quality Hotel. Travel is taking a much greater toll on me as I grow older. Making matters worse, my stomach ached all day. For the first time since I began the Exercises, I am too tired to make any sense out of my meditation. I am going to sleep.

February 16

Luke 6:6–11, The Man with a Withered Hand

⁶ On another sabbath he entered the synagogue and taught, and there was a man there whose right hand was withered. ⁷ The scribes and the Pharisees watched him to see whether he would cure on the sabbath, so that they might find an accusation against him. ⁸ Even though he knew what they were thinking, he said to the man who had the withered hand, "Come and stand here." He got up and stood there. ⁹ Then Jesus said to them, "I ask you, is it lawful to do good or to do harm on the sabbath, to save life or to destroy it?" ¹⁰ After looking around at all of them, he said to him, "Stretch out your hand." He did so, and his hand was restored. ¹¹ But they were filled with fury and discussed with one another what they might do to Jesus.

ONE OF MY new friends at the Living School sent me this poem by the Santa Rosa calligrapher and poet, Sherrie Lovler, yesterday. Called *The Sacred Life*, it deals with facing life's challenges.

There comes a time
when you want to run.
Run as far away as you can.

Run from your life.
Run from the task
that is so large
it cannot be done.
But your feet don't move.

And slowly
life opens up
and help appears.
Not in the form you expect
but in secrets
and winding roads
and gateways into
the world you long for
but don't know how to reach.

And the task
doesn't get easier
but life gets more beautiful
with a richness
you couldn't imagine
and a warmth
you had never felt

As you directly face
the immensity

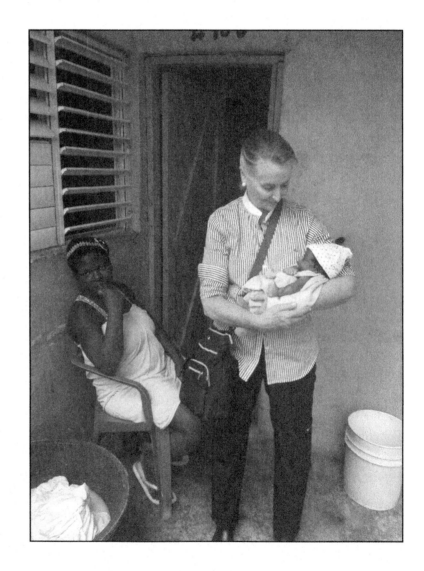

of what you are
called to do.

After meeting in the hotel lobby this morning, Antonio, Luke, and I drove to Caoba to see the construction project. Progress is spectacular. We will be ready for the mission to hit the job tomorrow morning. However, we did agree to demolish two old houses blocking the entrance to the chapel. We will build a "duplex" for the two elderly people living in the existing houses. Antonio and Daniel are a good team. The ministry clearly has a future!

I meditated in the beautiful garden here at CEFIJUFA, reflecting on Luke's story of the Man with the Withered Hand. The opposition to Jesus is now fully engaged, treating each new miracle as another reason to cast doubt and suspicion on His ministry. The message of this story today is not about withered hands, but rather about the battle between common sense and bureaucratic rules. Good should be done every day, and to all people. Exclusion is out, inclusion is in. Stringent rules that exist to perpetuate the power of the privileged are out, doing the next right thing is in.

The upside-down Gospel challenged the privilege, power, and possessions of the upper class and the few. This challenge continues to this day, two thousand years later. While I can argue that I worked hard to get to my position of privilege, it is still a grossly unequal system, with more barriers than ever to upward mobility.

February 17

Repeat Luke 6:6–11, The Man with a Withered Hand

MY STOMACH was a mess when I awoke this morning. I led the missionaries to the project site in Caoba then returned to CEFIJUFA to embrace the ceramic throne for most of the day. I have had a lot of time to meditate.

Reflecting on the story of the Withered Hand, along with several other accounts of miracles during the last weeks of Jesus's ministry, the message seems to shift from the specific problem (a withered hand) to the power structure that allowed the problem to exist or continue (the bureaucratic nonsense of the elite). This is a powerful message, one that rings very true here on the mission. For more than four years, we have been engaged in a sincere effort to partner with the poor residents of Mamey and Los Guandules. I believe we have been charitable on a level of shared strengths. We, the missionaries from Florida, have benefited enormously from what we have done, and we have frequently and loudly proclaimed that. The Dominicans and Haitians have benefited in numerous ways as well, including better health care, education, housing, places of worship, and places for leisure.

What we have not yet done is challenge the power structure that puts our partners in such great and continuing need. Why is it necessary that we build houses in 2017 with outdoor plumbing? Why are the roads in and out of Mamey virtually impassable most seasons of the year, making employment and small business opportunities merely day dreams? Why do the handful of Haitian men and women with college degrees make roughly half the annual salaries as their Dominican counterparts in the public schools and hospitals?

Christ's message in His final weeks on earth was clear. Do good work. Heal the sick and feed the hungry. But also clean the temples! Challenge the authority structures! Upset the apple carts!

One reason we are so timid regarding this next step is the strong prevalence of conservatism in our Church and our community. Challenging the power structures sounds too much like liberation theology, the teaching that briefly swept through some parts of the Catholic Church in the period surrounding and after Vatican II. The movement was banned when the powerful government officials joined hands with their close friends and relatives, the powerful church officials, to demand that it be banned. Challenge our authority, said the government officials, and we will strip you of your tax preferences and liberal property rights.

While resting my stomach today at the retreat center, I read from Hafiz, the other great 13th century Persian poet and mystic (other than Rumi!).

> What is the difference between your experience of Existence and that of a saint?
> The saint knows that the spiritual path is a sublime chess game with God
> And that the Beloved has just made such a Fantastic Move
> That the saint is now continually tripping over Joy and Bursting out in Laughter
> And saying, "I Surrender!"
>
> Whereas, my dear, I am afraid you still think you have a thousand serious moves.

I love that. Hafiz tells us that the Beloved's nature is pure Joy. The closer we come to Him, the more we are able to hear and feel God's laughter. The rhythm of His laughter is the music of the dance of life. That music is the essence of Love and it is the radiant core of every song of Hafiz.

The Catholic ministry for the newly engaged is having a weekend celebration here at the retreat center this weekend. Apparently, the weekend begins with loud singing, drums, horns, and repetitive jolly toasts. The peace of this place vanished! We can only hope they will find a more meditative approach to their vows tomorrow.

February 18

Repeat and reflect on the week.

THE MORNING began shortly after 5 a.m. with renewed rounds of diarrhea and nausea. By 7:30, it was clear that the judicious course of action would be to return home, which led to a harried and hassled, but successful, effort to get on a plane to Jacksonville. I am in Miami now, after making quite a scene on the flight from Santo Domingo, erupting frequently from both ends. This must end soon.

In my reflection, the first night of the mission, I talked about the important possibility that each missionary might experience multiple encounters during these five days, with themselves, with their fellow missionaries, with the villagers from the Dominican Republic, and, most important, with Christ. In every case, including an encounter with Christ, the counterparty to the encounter is already present, or soon will be. However, the encounter will not occur until and unless each of us lowers our resistance to the experience, becoming present to the presence.

Jim Finley taught me more about encounter and presence than any of my teachers. I love the way he uses words.

In the quietness of the sustained attentive gaze, we recognize a preciousness—an immediate worth or value for which no words can do justice. And we sense this is so because the worth or value is God's presence pouring itself out and giving itself away in and as the gift and miracle in whatever it is that may have captured our attention. Furthermore, we recognize ourselves to be one with this intimately realized experience of God pouring itself out in and as the gift and miracle of our life.

Sitting with the missionaries in the circle beneath the cross at the retreat center Wednesday night, I could not remember these wonderful words. Actually, I am not sure that the 14-year old missionaries would have grasped the concept of "God's presence pouring itself out in and as the gift and miracle of life." My words did come very close to Finleyesque when I talked about the need to lower our resistance to the encounter. Here is Jim's classic formulation.

I cannot make moments of nondual consciousness happen. I can only assume the inner stance that offers the least resistance to be overtaken by the grace of nondual consciousness. My spiritual practice is to sit each day in childlike sincerity with an inner stance that offers the least resistance to being overtaken by the God-given, godly nature of myself just the way I am.

Several times during the past few days, I have been confronted with a kind of spirituality and faith that is very different from mine. The CRHP team I am supporting for a presentation next weekend, our Lectio Divina group, and the seminarian accompanying us on this mission, are all deeply committed to a literal understanding of scripture. They believe in intense veneration of the Virgin Mary. They not only use words like Heaven, Hell, and Purgatory, they actually believe these are physical places where we will go after our death. All of the old issues that I grappled with and debated when I was a Mormon missionary in Germany more than fifty years ago continue to be issues for these friends. When we are resurrected, what body will we have? Our young, healthy body, or our old, tired, and run down body? Will we be reunited with our first wife, or second, or third? (Of course, absent the sin of divorce, this last is not an issue!)

I do not make them wrong for this different understanding. Lord knows, I am in no position to argue that I am right in the areas where we do not agree. However, I must acknowledge the intellectual and spiritual comfort that surrounds me in the Living School community. While we are of many different faith backgrounds, come from all over the world, and span more than six decades of age, we have come together around a handful of profound, but simple concepts. In addition to the relatively small group of Living School students—over 700 graduated or in school—there are the countless thousands who have read Meister Eckhart, John of the Cross, Teilhard, and Thomas Merton over the decades.

What are the elements of this "enlightened faith"? I suspect Living School graduates would give about 700 different answers. That faith is a deeply personal matter might be the lead article of enlightenment. Any suggestion that we are to swear allegiance to any "Living School dogma" would be rejected out of hand.

Nonetheless, there are some common themes.

- The ideas of *infinity* and *eternity* are very real, and they include the *here* and *now*, which is a very big deal for me. God created the universe about 14 billion years ago with the "Big Bang," a massive burst of energy that included all energy and all matter that ever were and ever will be. He is continuing this creation through the process of evolution, a process that is designed to increase our individual and collective stage of consciousness. This is big! This means that we were there at the beginning, that we are part of infinity and exist in eternity!

- God is an integral part of infinity and eternity. God has always been, and will always be. God is present, right here and right now.
- God is not a thing or a person, but rather a "relation." The verb *relate* is a better description of God than the noun relationship. I personally believe that God the Father, Jesus Christ, and the Holy Spirit are integrally involved in, and active components of this flowing Trinitarian relationship of love. God invites us to join with all of creation in this flowing love relationship, to dance in the Divine Dance.
- God is creating us momently, through a loving process of evolution. God has created man with free will, the freedom to choose whether, and how to participate in the divine relationship.
- God, Christ, the Holy Spirit, Elohim, Jehovah, the Supreme Being, Allah, Krishna, the Trinity, and many other names are Holy, all referring to the Divine. All deserve respect and honor.
- God loves us. God's love is unconditional. God does not love us because of what we do. God loves us because of who God is.
- God is not Santa Claus. He is not keeping a list of who is naughty and nice, rewarding at some point those on one list and punishing those on the other.
- Heaven and hell are relative states of being. Each of us can and does choose by our actions which state we are in from time to time.
- Encountering God is an incredible experience, one that is available to all of us at any time. For most of us, particularly any of us with some material success, this is an encounter we seldom experience. God is aggressive, in that He wants a relationship with each of His creations at all times. It is up to us to lower our resistance to His presence, to remove the barriers that prevent the encounter. Meditation, community, and service all have the capacity to lower barriers.
- Healing the sick, feeding the poor, housing the homeless, employing the jobless, and in every other way possible, we are meant to serve the people living at the margins of existence. These are fundamental articles of faith, not political statements.

There are probably more "articles of faith" that would find their way into a "creed of enlightened faith."

I pray today for relief from my intestinal distress. I pray for the missionaries I left behind in the Dominican Republic and for all the people we serve there.

CALENDAR WEEK TWENTY-THREE

I want to know Jesus better, to love Him more, and to follow Him wholeheartedly.

Lord Jesus, you groaned in grief with those bereaved. You were amazed at others' faith and trust. You glowed with consolation when the Father confirmed all Your choices. Lord, You know the deserts and the gardens of my human heart. Lead me Yourself through my mazes until I, too, glow with the confirmation of God.

February 19

John 11:1–44, The Death of Lazarus

¹ Now a certain man was ill, Lazarus of Bethany, the village of Mary and her sister Martha. ² Mary was the one who anointed the Lord with perfume and wiped his feet with her hair; her brother Lazarus was ill. ³ So the sisters sent a message to Jesus, "Lord, he whom you love is ill." ⁴ But when Jesus heard it, he said, "This illness does not lead to death; rather it is for God's glory, so that the Son of God may be glorified through it." ⁵ Accordingly, though Jesus loved Martha and her sister and Lazarus, ⁶ after having heard that Lazarus was ill, he stayed two days longer in the place where he was.

⁷ Then after this he said to the disciples, "Let us go to Judea again." ⁸ The disciples said to him, "Rabbi, the Jews were just now trying to stone you, and are you going there again?" ⁹ Jesus answered, "Are there not twelve hours of daylight? Those who walk during the day do not stumble, because they see the light of this world. ¹⁰ But those who walk at night stumble, because the light is not in them." ¹¹ After saying this, he told them, "Our friend Lazarus has fallen asleep, but I am going there to awaken him." ¹² The disciples said to him, "Lord, if he has fallen asleep, he will be all right." ¹³ Jesus, however, had been speaking about his death, but they thought that he was referring merely to sleep. ¹⁴ Then Jesus told them plainly, "Lazarus is dead. ¹⁵ For your sake I am glad I was not there, so that you may believe. But let us go to him." ¹⁶ Thomas, who was called the Twin, said to his fellow disciples, "Let us also go, that we may die with him."

Jesus the Resurrection and the Life

¹⁷ When Jesus arrived, he found that Lazarus had already been in the tomb four days. ¹⁸ Now Bethany was near Jerusalem, some two miles away, ¹⁹ and many of the Jews had come to Martha and Mary to console them about their brother. ²⁰ When Martha heard that Jesus was coming, she went and met him, while Mary stayed at home. ²¹ Martha said to Jesus, "Lord, if you had been here, my brother would not have died. ²² But even now I know that God will give you whatever you ask of him." ²³ Jesus said to her, "Your brother will rise again." ²⁴ Martha said to him, "I know that he will rise again in the resurrection on the last day." ²⁵ Jesus said to her, "I am the resurrection and the life. Those who believe in me, even though they die, will live, ²⁶ and everyone who lives and believes in me will never die. Do you believe this?" ²⁷ She said to him, "Yes, Lord, I believe that you are the Messiah, the Son of God, the one coming into the world."

Jesus Weeps

²⁸ When she had said this, she went back and called her sister Mary, and told her privately, "The Teacher is here and is calling for you." ²⁹ And when she heard it, she got up quickly and went to him. ³⁰ Now Jesus had not yet come to the village, but was still at the place where Martha had met him. ³¹ The Jews who were with her in the house, consoling her, saw Mary get up quickly and go out. They followed her because they thought that she was going to the tomb to weep there. ³² When Mary came where Jesus was and saw him, she knelt at his feet and said to him, "Lord, if you had been here, my brother would not have died." ³³ When Jesus saw her weeping, and the Jews who came with her also weeping, he was greatly disturbed in spirit and deeply moved. ³⁴ He said, "Where have you laid

him?" They said to him, "Lord, come and see." ³⁵ Jesus began to weep. ³⁶ So the Jews said, "See how he loved him!"
³⁷ But some of them said, "Could not he who opened the eyes of the blind man have kept this man from dying?"
    Jesus Raises Lazarus to Life
    ³⁸ Then Jesus, again greatly disturbed, came to the tomb. It was a cave, and a stone was lying against it. ³⁹ Je-
sus said, "Take away the stone." Martha, the sister of the dead man, said to him, "Lord, already there is a stench
because he has been dead four days." ⁴⁰ Jesus said to her, "Did I not tell you that if you believed, you would see the
glory of God?" ⁴¹ So they took away the stone. And Jesus looked upward and said, "Father, I thank you for having
heard me. ⁴² I knew that you always hear me, but I have said this for the sake of the crowd standing here, so that
they may believe that you sent me." ⁴³ When he had said this, he cried with a loud voice, "Lazarus, come out!" ⁴⁴
The dead man came out, his hands and feet bound with strips of cloth, and his face wrapped in a cloth. Jesus said
to them, "Unbind him, and let him go."

HAVING SLEPT so much during the past several days, albeit intermittently and with many unpleasant interruptions, I awakened early. Maggie was only too excited to rush downstairs with me, first to the library and then to the garden bench. It is a glorious morning! Cool, not cold; a quarter-moon, brightly lighting the sky; stars covering the Heavens; and the cascading waves, making their way up from the south. I was dizzy with awe, feeling vulnerable and inconsequential in this immense universe.

My stomach bruised, but never fully destroyed, the "pink cloud" of the mission. Diane, Daniel, and Antonio regularly sent pictures and updated progress reports. The combination of deep joy from the mission and the overpowering grandeur of the morning meditation left me susceptible to encounter. When I first read through the lengthy passage from John's Gospel last night, I was struck by how many messages were contained in this famous raising of Lazarus from death. In my blissful state this morning, I went straight for verses 25 and 26, sitting with them for a long time:

> I am the resurrection and the life. Those who believe in me, even though they die, will live, and everyone who lives and believes in me will never die.

He is the resurrection and the life. Believing in Him should be as simple as believing in night and day, or air, or the sky! Surrender to the gift of love. Accept the joy. Lower resistance to His presence. *He is always present! He always has been and always will be—eternally and infinitely!*

Allowing the scales to drop from our eyes is hard, solely because of our egoistical desire to retain control. I believe that all the thoughts, words, and deeds that take us further away from God's commandments make it harder to see Him. Doing no harm can get us to some kind of neutral state, but the greatest commandments—loving God and loving our neighbor—require that we go way beyond neutrality. The sweat pouring down our faces as we serve others acts like a glass cleaner on our eyes.

My prayer this morning is clarity of vision. I want to see God, to know Christ, to be present to His presence.

February 20

Repeat John 11:1–44, The Death of Lazarus

THE MORNING beauty today was even greater than yesterday. Maggie and I sat very still for almost half an hour. While I tried to empty my mind, I kept returning to the passage from John's Gospel.

As Jesus clearly states, the purpose for raising Lazarus from death was not to give him more time in his material body. Rather, it was to further establish the reputation of Jesus in these final days of His ministry.

This illness does not lead to death; rather it is for God's glory, so that the Son of God may be glorified through it.

Obviously, it becomes a little confusing when the person who is saying, "Not for my glory, but for the glory of God," is God.

Once we were settled back in the library, my thoughts returned to the verses I focused on yesterday.

I am the resurrection and the life. Those who believe in me, even though they die, will live, and everyone who lives and believes in me will never die.

John 3:16, Mark 16:16, and Romans 10:11 all say something similar. There is some very powerful exclusion in these statements. Yes, those who believe in Jesus will live, but what happens to the rest? What about the millions of people who lived before Christ was born? Or those born on the other side of the world?

I am intrigued by the concept of a Perennial Tradition, a single great river of knowledge and understanding that feeds many tributaries over time and space. Thus, it is possible for Karl Jaspers to describe an Axial Age, when the wisdom traditions of the Middle East, India, China, and the Americas were simultaneously reaching very similar conclusions about the meaning and purpose of life.

The statement, "those who believe in me, even though they die, will live," would be only slightly altered: "Those who believe in the Perennial Wisdom of loving their God, and their neighbor, shall live abundant lives here on earth and shall never die." Does this make religion too relativistic, too "loosy-goosy"? Or does it still leave the person who does not love God (however God is defined), and neighbor in trouble? Of course, it does.

However, I believe that all of creation has eternal life. And I believe that Heaven and Hell are states of being, not places for reward and punishment. The modification to the statement in John's Gospel should go like this: "Those who believe in the Perennial Wisdom of loving their God, and their neighbor, shall live abundant lives forever." That abundance can begin today. Heaven can be right here, right now. But our state is not permanent. We can slip (or sin, if you prefer). When we do, we will have difficulty sensing the presence of God. We will have erected barriers between ourselves and God (and others).

Stating this in Sister Parish terms, the goal is eternal *encounter* with God and all creation. That will only be possible if we build and maintain *community* with God and all creation. One essential ingredient in sustained encounter and healthy community is *service*, particularly service to the poor and marginalized in our world.

I pray for greater wisdom every day. I pray for wellness and strength.

February 21

Luke 7:1–10, Jesus Heals a Centurion's Servant
¹ After Jesus had finished all his sayings in the hearing of the people, he entered Capernaum. ² A centurion there had a slave whom he valued highly, and who was ill and close to death. ³ When he heard about Jesus, he sent

some Jewish elders to him, asking him to come and heal his slave. ⁴ When they came to Jesus, they appealed to him earnestly, saying, "He is worthy of having you do this for him, ⁵ for he loves our people, and it is he who built our synagogue for us." ⁶ And Jesus went with them, but when he was not far from the house, the centurion sent friends to say to him, "Lord, do not trouble yourself, for I am not worthy to have you come under my roof; ⁷ therefore I did not presume to come to you. But only speak the word, and let my servant be healed. ⁸ For I also am a man set under authority, with soldiers under me; and I say to one, 'Go,' and he goes, and to another, 'Come,' and he comes, and to my slave, 'Do this,' and the slave does it." ⁹ When Jesus heard this he was amazed at him, and turning to the crowd that followed him, he said, "I tell you, not even in Israel have I found such faith." ¹⁰ When those who had been sent returned to the house, they found the slave in good health.

THE MORNING began with tennis, followed by an Ability Housing Governance Committee meeting. As I sat with Maggie on the garden bench afterwards, I realized just how filled with joy my "twilight years" have become. I have good friends in both my tennis group and on the Ability board. Tennis leaves me feeling invigorated physically. Ability challenges me intellectually and, at the same time, feeds my heart.

The passage from Luke has been one of my favorite New Testament stories since I began this journey of faith. Though nothing will get me past my aversion to slavery, I like it that a Roman centurion has an ostensibly respectful relationship with his slave. I like it that this particular centurion was presumably a charitable person, having donated in some way to the construction of the local synagogue.

Jesus has always surprised us by reaching out to people at the margins; the poor, the sick, the sinners, and the prisoners. In this passage, Jesus surprises us by reaching out to a wealthy and powerful Gentile, who was also an officer in the occupying army. That is extraordinary!

Of course, the part of the story that comes down to us two thousand years later in every Mass is the humility and deep faith of the centurion. "Lord, I am not worthy that you should enter under my roof, but only say the word and my soul will be healed."

I concluded my contemplation by repeating that statement over and over again.

February 22

Repeat Luke 7:1–10, Jesus Heals a Centurion's Servant

THE GLOW FROM the Palmer Academy mission continues this morning. Sitting outside with Maggie, I continued to run through the experience in my mind, returning to the group sitting in a circle under the cross at the retreat center. I literally left my bed for one hour, pretended to eat some dinner, sat in the circle, then retreated to bed for two days before returning home. In that one hour, however, I was able to share my deep belief that Christ was aggressively present in our circle, on this mission, in each of the people we would meet, and in each of us. This is truly extraordinary! For many of the people sitting under the cross that night, it probably sounded like the same words they have heard all their lives. I am sure only a handful understood what I was saying. Some heard heresy. Some heard what I said, but assumed I meant to say something else. But even if only one person allowed the words to resonate, slept with them, repeated them, or included them in their prayers, and, as a result, removed enough resistance to allow Christ to "enter through their wounds," I would gladly return to that circle again and again.

Meister Eckhart considered the unity of God's creation to be the most important element of his faith.

All are sent or no one is sent, into all or into nothing. For in the kingdom of heaven all is in all. All is one and all is ours and in the kingdom of heaven everything is in everything else. All is one and all is ours. We are all in all as God is all in all.

When I finally, fully and unreservedly recognize that I am one with God, how can I then not love myself? This first step, seeing the Christ in ourselves, is both the most difficult and the most important step in the journey toward unity with God and His creation. Eckhart again:

God expects but one thing of you, and that is that you should come out of yourself in so far as you are a created being made and let God be God in you.

Seeing Christ in the person next to us or in front of us is virtually impossible if we cannot see Christ in ourselves. My all-time favorite statement from Eckhart is one I have repeated many times, simply because it resonates so strongly for me.

The eye with which I see God is the same eye with which God sees me.

Logically, if Christ is in me *and in you*, then *Namaste*, the Yogic greeting, makes complete sense.

The God in me greets the God in you
The Spirit in me meets the same Spirit in you

God certainly knew what He was doing when He established Himself as the aggressor in the divine love affair. He is eternally and infinitely present, including right now and right here. More than that, He is flowing into me, flowing around me, seeking a crack in my egoistic armor through which He can consume me.

It is simply mind boggling that my defenses are so great that He can only prevail rarely and briefly. The joy is so pure when I allow myself to experience His presence. Why do I fight it so? Why does it take great suffering to bring me to a place I want to be? Why is the great love kindled by a baby's smile or a flight of birds necessary to remind me that the experience of God is sublime?

I end the morning thinking about the joy of Sister Parish. More than anything else, this ministry reminds me that God is present, and that He is pushing His love into me, all the missionaries, and everyone we meet.

February 23

Matthew 17:1–9, The Transfiguration

[1] Six days later, Jesus took with him Peter and James and his brother John and led them up a high mountain, by themselves. [2] And he was transfigured before them, and his face shone like the sun, and his clothes became dazzling white. [3] Suddenly there appeared to them Moses and Elijah, talking with him. [4] Then Peter said to Jesus, "Lord, it is good for us to be here; if you wish, I will make three dwellings here, one for you, one for Moses, and one for Elijah." [5] While he was still speaking, suddenly a bright cloud overshadowed them, and from the cloud a voice said, "This is my Son, the Beloved; with him I am well pleased; listen to him!" [6] When the disciples heard this, they fell to the ground and were overcome by fear. [7] But Jesus came and touched them, saying, "Get up and do not be afraid." [8] And when they looked up, they saw no one except Jesus himself alone.

⁹ As they were coming down the mountain, Jesus ordered them, "Tell no one about the vision until after the Son of Man has been raised from the dead."

NAMASTE! The God in me greets the God in you. This stayed with me all night; walked with me in the breezy morning down to the bench, and sat quietly with me in the dark. A concept this easy to say should not be so monumental, so profoundly transforming. But it is. The God in me is deeply grateful for, and humbled by the thought.

I fell asleep last night reading Meister Eckhart. One implication of his central theme of *unity with God* is the fundamental importance of *equality*.

> Love will never be anywhere except where *equality* and *unity* are.
>
> All paths lead to God for God is on them *all evenly* for the person who knows with transformed knowledge.

Reflecting on this, it strikes me that it could be no other way. Inequality in the world is usually measured relative to power, prestige, and possessions. It is hard to imagine oneness in a situation such as ours, where the gap is so vast between the one percent with the greatest power, highest privilege, and most possessions, and the rest. And it is not a case of the one percent living "over there" while the rest of us "over here" share evenly what is left of the three Ps. The gap between any two groups or individuals, from the top all the way down to the last two people on earth, is sufficient enough to be divisive. Something in our culture emphasizes difference, not sameness. We constantly compare, then make foolish judgements about the relative worth or value of God's creatures.

One solution to this problem would be constant redistribution of every measurable aspect of our existence. I do favor a certain amount of redistribution, particularly in our modern capitalist economy, with its obscene level of inequality. There should certainly be no abject poverty in a society as wealthy as ours. All of life's basic requirements should be available to everyone, regardless of income. And, just to be clear, health care, education, and gainful employment are basic needs. Wealth should be redistributed sufficiently to establish a very strong safety net.

Generally, however, I believe material inequality, including power and privilege, will always exist. The ultimate unity Eckhart and Teilhard describe can nonetheless be achieved. On the level of the individual person and God, oneness requires the complete surrender of *self*, not of stuff. *Attachment to power, prestige, and possessions* must end, not their existence. This oneness is available right here and right now, at least fleetingly, to everyone.

On the much larger level of the universe and all of God's creation, there must be at least a sufficient reduction in inequality that the opportunity for oneness is realistically available to everyone. Even as I write this, I struggle with the fact that the best examples of *oneness* have been desert hermits who have reduced their ownership of the three Ps to absolutely nothing. However, the complete abandonment of the three Ps may have been the *result* of oneness, not its cause. I cannot imagine a hardened criminal, abused as a child and left with no life skills, becoming enlightened to the point of oneness. Then again, I can no more imagine a narcissistic billionaire, spoiled as a child and never wanting for anything (I don't need to say anything about having orange hair), becoming enlightened to the point of oneness.

Returning to the scriptural passage for today, I have heard a few homilies based on the story in Matthew's Gospel about the Transfiguration. The one that stands out in my memory focused on Peter. In the face of this amazing apparition—the Son of God with two of the greatest figures from the

Hebrew scriptures, Moses and Elijah—there are two basic choices, often expressed as "don't just stand there, do something." Peter quickly decided that he should busy himself with gathering the materials necessary to build three structures, one for each of the three "transfigured" persons. God interrupted Peter in mid-sentence, declaring in what I assume was a loud voice, "This is my beloved Son, in whom I am well pleased." In a sense, God was saying, "don't just do something, stand there (or get on your knees!)."

Meister Eckhart wrote:

> As long as we perform our works in order to go to heaven, we are simply on the wrong track. And until we learn to work without a why or wherefore, we have not learned to work, or to live, or why.

February 24

Repeat Matthew 17:1–9, The Transfiguration

In *The Phenomenon of Man*, Teilhard wrote this rather dense description of universal unity.

> Mankind, the spirit of the earth, the synthesis of individuals and peoples, the paradoxical conciliation of the element with the whole, and of unity with the multitude—all these are called Utopian and yet they are biologically necessary. And for them to be incarnated in the world all we may well need is to imagine our *power of loving developing until it embraces the total of men and of the earth.*

Reconciling "the element with the whole," requires that we accept something Teilhard describes as "a deep accord between two realities which seek each other, the severed particle that trembles with the approach of 'the rest'."

How often have I felt like a "severed particle," wanting desperately to be united with the wholeness hiding in the mystery of infinity and eternity? There are moments of exquisite joy when I sense the "approach of the rest." At these moments, I experience the oneness with God that is the core teaching of Meister Eckhart.

This morning I am experiencing one of those rare breakthroughs, when a light shines at the end of the tunnel of my constant reading. I fell asleep last night with my dog-eared copy of Teilhard, my glasses, and my pen resting in confusion on my pillow. Or, to be accurate, I awakened at midnight, still confused, to find them there! This morning, I could suddenly see Teilhard's *"power of loving developing until it embraces the total of men and of the earth"* as Eckhart's *"All is in all, all is one, and all is ours."* Even knowing that the confusion will probably return after a few moments of rest, I am filled with joy!

Is this the metaphor of the Transfiguration? Are there moments of brilliant clarity, when we can see beyond space-time limitations? At these moments, Christ is again telling us not to be afraid. Christ tells us to get up and go back to work. Eckhart says it this way:

> How wonderful it is to be so spiritually mature that one exists both outside and inside, one seizes and is seized, one sees and is seen, one holds and is held—that is the goal where the spirit remains at rest united to eternity. There, our work and activity in time are just as

noble and as full of joy as Mary Magdalene's retreat in the desert. Remember Martha with in her spiritual maturity was so real that her works did not hinder her.

Being at one with the universe is not being the same as everyone in the universe. In fact, Teilhard teaches that *"unity differentiates."*

February 25

Repeat and reflect on the week.

It is very early on this Saturday morning. The CRHP retreat starts in an hour with a Mass for the presenting team. I will not leave the retreat until tomorrow afternoon. I suspect this will be my last CRHP retreat. I have participated in five retreats on the presenting team, and, of course, my own receiving weekend. That is enough for me. Younger men should take over. At some time in the relatively near future, the same will be said about Sister Parish. Today is Don Barnhorst's eightieth birthday, and I am sure he will pull back from three missions a year. Even though I am younger, I cannot continue at my present pace of ten to twelve trips a year. But what would I do if I were to stop? At least for now, I do not need to add that to my worry list.

It has been an interesting week, which began while I was still in the hospital after four very sick days in the Dominican Republic. I read a lot while staying in bed Sunday and Monday, especially Meister Eckhart. What a treasure he is! Almost seven hundred years ago, this great teacher and preacher recognized the profound connection between the natural world, which science was only beginning to discover, and the world of enlightened spirituality.

Humanity in the poorest and most despised human being is just as complete as in the Pope.

We are all human, Pope and pauper. I am not enough of a Papal student to be able to enumerate the Popes whose humanity showed the most. Certainly, the popes associated with Vatican II are celebrated for its historical opening of the Church to the world. But Popes John XXIII and Paul VII were certainly not social liberals. Pope Leo XIII, famous among the Justice and Peace Catholics I have worked with, issued *Rerum novarum,* still regarded as the high-water mark of Catholic support for the rights of workers. Our current Pope is considered by both liberals and conservatives to be the most liberal Pope in history. While I have no idea whether that is true or not, I do believe Pope Francis would totally agree with Eckhart's statement. Pope Francis wants us to be a "poor Church for the poor." Compare that to Eckhart:

To live the "wayless" way, free and yet bound, learn to live among things but not in things. All God's friends live this way—among cares but not within cares.

Detachment is living among things, not in them, and among cares, not within them. More than any other thing, Eckhart teaches us to lose our attachments, even the desire to know God.

The hidden darkness of the eternal light of the eternal Godhead is unknown and shall never be known.

Eckhart uses a word that I remember very well from my experience as a missionary in Germany, *dasein*, roughly translated as "isness." Where Thomas Aquinas famously said that *"God is existence,"* Eckhart reverses the formula, stating that *"existence is God."* Everything that is—all the universe that ever was, is now, or ever will be—is God.

Teilhard unites modern science and faith in God using very similar language in his description of the Big Bang. The energy released at that moment contained all energy and all matter that would ever exist in and as the universe. For both Eckhart and Teilhard, *we were all there at the beginning, have always been present in this universe with God, and always will be*. Eckhart's *dasein*, "isness" combines well with Teilhard's infinite and eternal existence. Our challenge is to remove all the artificial barriers we erect between ourselves and our existence.

"Isness," the stark experience of my own and God's presence, requires freedom from all attachments. It is being present to the Presence. It is the experience I have when I lose myself working in Sister Parish, or serving in a Saturday morning soup kitchen, or even spending a weekend in a CRHP retreat.

My goal for this, my twenty-third week of these Exercises, was to *"know Jesus better, to love Him more, and to follow Him wholeheartedly."* The readings this week included the death of Lazarus, the healing of the Centurion's servant, and the Transfiguration.

One theme running through the week is the proximity of what will occur soon in Jerusalem. Jesus is nearing the end of His ministry. Much of His work involves making it clear to those at the top of the power system that things must change. The world is about to be turned upside-down. Neither raising Lazarus from death, nor healing the servant of the Centurion, were important solely in order to give the family of Lazarus a little more time, or restore the Centurion's servant to full service. Jesus wanted the Jews, especially those in power, to fully appreciate His message. I know Him better by knowing that. I love Him more because of that.

A second theme this week, both in the Exercise readings and in my outside reading of Eckhart and Teilhard, has been the continued emphasis on unity with Christ in all that I am, all that I do, and all that I love. Reading back through the first reading of the week, from the first chapter of the Gospel according to John, I was powerfully struck by this one little verse.

Jesus began to weep

How could I have missed this? Here is the Son of God, the Messiah, the King of the Jews *weeping for the death of His friend Lazarus.* The humanity of Christ is humbling. Reflecting on that is a great way to end the week, and end the morning to join my brothers at OLSS for the CRHP retreat.

CALENDAR WEEK TWENTY-FOUR

Lord Jesus, You tried with all Your might to help people understand the Spirit's teaching. You grieved that they wanted You, or someone, to take away their responsibility for their lives. When they extolled You, You did not rely on that. You went Your way, anointed by the love of faithful friends, anointed for Your death.

February 26

Luke 21:1–4, The Widow's Offering
¹ He looked up and saw rich people putting their gifts into the treasury; ² he also saw a poor widow put in two small copper coins. ³ He said, "Truly I tell you, this poor widow has put in more than all of them; ⁴ for all of them have contributed out of their abundance, but she out of her poverty has put in all she had to live on."

IT IS NOW Sunday evening. The CRHP weekend ended with the concluding banquet late this afternoon. I am home alone with Maggie, meditating on the retreat and its importance. CRHP is indeed a powerful program for parish renewal. There were seventeen men in the receiving team, several of whom are new to Our Lady Star of the Sea. A group of roughly twenty-five men served on the presenting team, along with another twenty men serving in the kitchen and as many as fifty men and women participating on Saturday night. Instead of spending yet another weekend attending perhaps one Mass, sitting and talking only with their families for an hour, then returning home, these seventeen men had the opportunity to meet with, talk to, and spend considerable time with almost one hundred parishioners. Moreover, every one of these one hundred serving parishioners considered it their primary purpose to warmly welcome each one of these men in a joyously friendly embrace.

Once again, I saw the magic of the CRHP formula at work. Along with seven other men, I "told my story," talking for about thirty minutes about my life and my faith journey. Like the others, I shared a fair amount of bad news along with the good, in fact, talking about my failures and challenges more than my success. In short, I was vulnerable. Each of us gave "witness talks" with a particular theme, ranging from spirituality to "Father's loving care." After each talk, the seventeen men, sitting at tables of six men, half receiving and half presenting, participated in "silly" table Exercises that included writing a prayer, composing a song, presenting a skit, creating a recipe, making a poster, and writing a poem—all around the theme of the eight witness talks.

This was my fifth CRHP retreat, including my own receiving retreat in 2011, two presenting retreats at OLSS, and two traveling retreats. The magic of telling and listening to life stories has worked every time. I am absolutely convinced that the only way to break through the barriers we all erect to prevent connection with others is story telling. The keys are vulnerability on the telling side, and intentionality on the listening side. While I am consistently both attracted to and amazed by people who ask questions, I virtually never experience it outside of the Living School and programs like CRHP. In the absence of asking life questions sincerely and answering them vulnerably, my experience is that most conversation is limited to weather, sports, and political posturing. I should add talk about children and grandchildren to the list, topics that can be discussed with total strangers without risk.

What happens after these weekend retreats is that the seventeen men become members of a growing community of "CRHPers," composed of men and women who will greet them with hugs and warm smiles at every Mass, on the streets, and in the local shops for years to come. They will participate in other Parish ministries, including Sister Parish, which is a special treat for me. I end the day with a prayer of deep gratitude for the experience, the new friends, and the joy of community.

February 27

Repeat Luke 21:1–4, The Widow's Offering

I AM SITTING with Maggie in the library on an incredibly beautiful late-February day filled with sunshine and joy. The reading from yesterday and today is another one of my favorite readings from scripture. From time to time, I wonder whether my giving to Sister Parish and other causes has reached the level of addiction. While I am less concerned about it than Sallie Ann, we cannot continue to give at this pace if we have any intention of leaving anything substantial for our children and grandchildren. This is particularly true if we continue to enjoy relatively good health.

Then I think about the widow and her "two small copper coins." We are giving only a trifle compared to that! Some years ago, a lawyer talked to me about a potential legal claim, noting that the amount in question would cause no change in the lifestyle of either party. I think about that often. The amounts that Sallie Ann and I have been blessed enough to give over the past few years have not changed our lifestyle in the least. We continue to live extremely comfortable lives, even flying in the front of the airplane on our "missions of mercy."

I met with the villagers of Mamey last summer to talk, yet again, about gratitude. Some of them were complaining about not receiving a new house or repairs to their existing houses, challenging us on our selection process. There were moments of loud shouting and embarrassing anger. As I left the meeting, Antes, the owner of SPM 1, the first house Sister Parish built in Mamey, came out to my car with a live chicken. She speaks only Creole, but her intention was beautifully clear. She wanted me to have the chicken as her expression of gratitude that we had built a house for her. I wept. I weep even now thinking about how important that chicken was to Antes. Two copper coins.

February 28

Mark 11:1–11, Jesus' Triumphal Entry into Jerusalem
¹ When they were approaching Jerusalem, at Bethphage and Bethany, near the Mount of Olives, he sent two of his disciples ² and said to them, "Go into the village ahead of you, and immediately as you enter it, you will find tied there a colt that has never been ridden; untie it and bring it. ³ If anyone says to you, 'Why are you doing this?' just say this, 'The Lord needs it and will send it back here immediately.'" ⁴ They went away and found a colt tied near a door, outside in the street. As they were untying it, ⁵ some of the bystanders said to them, "What are you doing, untying the colt?" ⁶ They told them what Jesus had said; and they allowed them to take it. ⁷ Then they brought the colt to Jesus and threw their cloaks on it; and he sat on it. ⁸ Many people spread their cloaks on the road, and others spread leafy branches that they had cut in the fields. ⁹ Then those who went ahead and those who followed were shouting,
  "Hosanna!
   Blessed is the one who comes in the name of the Lord!
  ¹⁰ Blessed is the coming kingdom of our ancestor David!
   Hosanna in the highest heaven!"
  ¹¹ Then he entered Jerusalem and went into the temple; and when he had looked around at everything, as it was already late, he went out to Bethany with the twelve.

THE LAST DAY of February this year falls on Shrove Tuesday, *Mardi Gras*, the day before Lent. The word *shrove* is derived from shrive, an old English word meaning *confess*. That feels appropriate in several ways. The CRHP retreat weekend included an opportunity to experience the Sacrament of Reconciliation, as confession is now called in the Catholic Church. I availed myself of that opportunity and can honestly say that it had a remarkably calming, but, at the same time, moving impact on me. Father David Keegan helped me to reach a new level of understanding of one of my persistent frustrations (my word for sins).

Reading the passage from Mark's Gospel about the colt Jesus rode on in this, his most glorious entry into Jerusalem, reminded me powerfully of my trip to Petra more than ten years ago. I had been in Amman, Jordan, for a meeting regarding the privatization of the Jordanian power system, and had a late afternoon flight the following day. So I arranged a flight down to Aqaba, which arrived near midnight. I slept for a few hours in the Edom Hotel before walking over to the entrance to the Bab al-siq wadi, arriving shortly after 5 a.m.. After walking more than three hours, I finally arrived at the base of the last hill that would take me to the Monastery. I was simply too tired to make the climb, so I hired a little donkey colt to take me the last few hundred yards. My feet both touched the ground! Recalling that now makes me laugh again, both because of how I looked, an aging white-haired American on this little donkey, and because of the laughter of the young boys pushing the donkey from behind. It was an amusing interval in an otherwise overwhelming experience. Petra is clearly my favorite ancient site in the world. Not even a year later, I would no longer be CEO of Globeleq, but I had not the slightest idea that was in my future.

I walked down to the bench, fantasizing myself walking alongside Jesus entering Jerusalem. The cheering crowds (perhaps the Jordanian boys laughing at me on the donkey!) gave our arrival a triumphant quality. Of course, Jesus knew what was about to take place, though I am not at all certain he was aware of the manner in which he would die. We arrived at the temple too late to do anything but look around, then returned to Bethany for the night. Over the next several days, we would often be walking back and forth between Bethany and Jerusalem, a distance said to be less than two miles.

What an amazing feeling of accomplishment and success! Crowds along the road shouting,

> Hosanna! Blessed is the one who comes in the name of the Lord! Blessed is the coming kingdom of our ancestor David! Hosanna in the highest heaven!

What had begun so quietly only a few months before had grown into a powerful, awe-inspiring movement, involving people from up and down the Jordan River, from the Dead Sea to north of the Sea of Galilee. This was Israel at one of its strongest points in history, the end of the Second Temple Period. And throughout all this land of growing foment and revolution, the Jesus movement was growing, proclaiming peace and brotherly love. It is simply unfathomable to imagine that these shouts of "Hosanna" from the crowds today would become "kill him" from the mob in such a short time. How could this happen?

I sat with this question for some time. Crowds are strange beasts. While fear has a strong impact on each of us as individuals, that impact is increased many times over in a crowd. I believe that is what happened to the crowds in Israel two thousand years ago. Both the Romans and their Jewish puppets used fear to turn the cheering crowds into jeering mobs. Fear of what? It seems to me today as though the messages of peace and love have suffered throughout history from fear-mongering despots using threats of force and hatred.

The early stages of consciousness, from egocentric through ethnocentric, are especially vulnerable to appeals of hate and fear. *Staying alive* is the primary focus of the earliest stages of consciousness, followed by the protective exclusion of tribe and cause. Crowds must have very low levels of consciousness. Or, better said, people in crowds must sink to very low levels of consciousness. Yelling fire in a crowded theatre is dangerous precisely because even the most enlightened people become instantly self-protective in the movement and mood of the crowd.

I played almost four hours of tennis today. My legs and feet are cramping, but it was a great experience. Our CRHP presenting team meets tonight with the receiving team for the last time. I am reminded again that CRHP truly renews the parish, allowing people to tell their stories to other people who will listen intentionally. The process is simple, but profoundly effective.

My prayer today is for the strength to maintain my Lenten goals of no Facebook and no news. Note that these are goals, not commitments. Facebook will be comparatively easy, since I am a relatively new user. News about current events, however, is another story entirely. I have been addicted to news in the background for most of the past half century. This will be a challenge!

March 1, Ash Wednesday, Lent begins

Repeat Mark 11:1–11, Jesus' Triumphal Entry into Jerusalem

MAGGIE AND I went out to the garden very early this morning. I have a plane to catch, traveling to Atlanta for the Council on Foreign Relations. That will be an interesting meeting, especially now that I have given up news for Lent!

I sat for a long time reflecting on the CRHP meeting last night. Each of us shared our experience of the weekend retreat. I suggested that the "secret" to CRHP is story telling with Christ. Story telling—telling one's own story and listening to the life stories of others—is a powerful method, perhaps the only real method, of forming bonds. It can move the participants past the level of superficiality, dependent almost completely on the level of vulnerability. I believe this is true in virtually all situations—work environment, trauma counseling, family relationships, and, especially, among men.

What makes CRHP special is the focus on Christ. I believe Christ is present in all of us, though most of us, most of the time, maintain very effective barriers to His presence. When we discipline ourselves to listen with intention, we remove, ever so slightly, the barriers to hearing Christ speak to us from the depths of the person speaking. Intentional listening requires that we stop taking inventory, stop looking at the way a person looks or is dressed, stop listening to the accent or grammar. It is surprising to me how different focused, intentional listening can be. Among other things, I remember so much more of what is being said. Importantly, glimpses of the Christ in the other person come into view, at times so powerfully that we weep.

Just as important is speaking vulnerably. At these moment, I believe the Christ in us becomes visible to the other person. Namaste, "The Christ within me salutes the Christ in you." Or, as Paul said in Galatians, "I live no longer, but Christ lives in me."

I believe accepting Christ in me requires that I first accept me in me. To "love my neighbor as myself" requires that I first love myself. This means forgiving myself, even for just a few moments. It requires that I enter my heart space, and speak from there.

Moreover, when I speak vulnerably, honestly, and from the depths of my heart, at least some of what I say is touched by the divine spark of Christ in me. Listeners will notice a change in my voice or cadence or affect. My vulnerability will have a contagious effect on the listener. *Emotional contagion* is actually a defined term, meaning the "phenomenon of having one person's emotions and related behaviors directly trigger similar emotions and behaviors in other people." At moments of deep sincerity, I believe the Christ in me calls to the Christ in the other person.

John Caputo wrote,

> A world without love is a world governed by rigid contracts and inexorable duties, a world in which—God forbid!—the lawyers run everything. The mark of really loving someone or something is un-conditionality and excess, engagement and commitment, fire and passion.

A world without Christ is a world without love.

March 2

Matthew 26:6–13, The Anointing at Bethany
⁶ Now while Jesus was at Bethany in the house of Simon the leper, ⁷ a woman came to him with an alabaster jar of very costly ointment, and she poured it on his head as he sat at the table. ⁸ But when the disciples saw it, they were angry and said, "Why this waste? ⁹ For this ointment could have been sold for a large sum, and the money given to the poor." ¹⁰ But Jesus, aware of this, said to them, "Why do you trouble the woman? She has performed a good service for me. ¹¹ For you always have the poor with you, but you will not always have me. ¹² By pouring this ointment on my body she has prepared me for burial. ¹³ Truly I tell you, wherever this good news is proclaimed in the whole world, what she has done will be told in remembrance of her."

MOST OF THE day today was spent traveling, albeit only from Atlanta to Jacksonville. It is odd how even an easy trip like that can exhaust me now. It was not always so. My stories of "walking a mile in the deep snow" are about flying all night from the United States to Europe, then going straight into an all-day meeting. I did that on dozens of occasions, when I worked for the Italian national energy company and also when I first started working with the British. Somewhere along the way, I realized I was not as present in those meetings as I appeared to be. Thereafter, I simply refused to accept meetings until after a long nap, if not a night's sleep.

Maggie met me when I came in the garage door, jumping and kissing and otherwise making it clear that she was happy to see me. I melt every time she does that, which is at least once every day! We walked down to the garden. It was very different in the late afternoon, with the sun dropping in the western sky behind the house. The quality of the air was different, not unpleasant, just different.

The line from the reading that stayed with me while we sat on the bench was sobering. "By pouring this ointment on my body she has prepared me for burial." Jesus may not have known there was to be a crucifixion, but He certainly knew His death was imminent. I fantasized that I was one of the disciples in the room in Bethany.

I had been part of the cheering crowd, welcoming Jesus into Jerusalem only days earlier. Our mood was joyous and triumphant, filled with laughter and great hope. That mood was no more. None of us enjoyed being scolded by Jesus. We all wanted so to please Him. As bad as it was to be admonished not to trouble the woman, hearing the thirty-year-old Jesus talk about His pending burial was much worse.

I was sad as we walked back up to the library. I am sad now. I pray for my brother, Leonard, whose battle with diabetes is not going well. I pray for the world. I pray for my soul.

March 3

Repeat Matthew 26:6–13, The Anointing at Bethany

CLEAR SKIES and cool temperatures greeted us as we walked down to the bench in the semi-darkness of dawn. The groundskeepers were working on the second green of the golf course. The beauty of silence returned when they moved on. I talked to Maggie about the anointing of Jesus.

The line that captured my thoughts this morning was the response of Jesus to His disciples for questioning the use of the expensive anointing oil. "For you always have the poor with you…"

One of my favorite authors is William Easterly, a World Bank economist and dedicated warrior in the long battle against global poverty. His book *The Elusive Quest for Growth*, published in 2001, tells the extremely sad and frustrating story of the half century of effort by the best people, with the best intentions, and with billions of dollars, to create economic growth, thus ending poverty. When World War II ended, the leading nations of the world met in Bretton Woods, New Hampshire, to formulate a plan for a World Bank and an International Monetary Fund. These "Bretton Woods Institutions," along with the new United Nations, would work together for the next fifty years to create global economic stability and stimulate poverty-ending growth in the poor countries of Africa, Asia, and Latin America. Easterly makes the point that all this effort has largely failed. The poor "will always be with us."

All my life I have worked at least tangentially in this "elusive quest." Low-income housing, power for poor countries, and now, Sister Parish, all are designed primarily to address poverty and the plight of people at the margins. My personal record is no better than that of the global community. In none of the countries and counties where I worked has a significant dent been made in poverty.

Oddly, over the past twenty years, largely since Easterly wrote his book, more than a billion people, mostly in China and, to a lesser extent, India, have moved out of abject poverty into the working middle class. This reduction in poverty has been accomplished by growth in these economies, precisely the goal which the global "anti-poverty" industry failed to achieve in the half century between Bretton Woods and the new millennium. Perversely, profligate consumerism in the developed countries, especially the United States, was the principle driver in the growth of China and other countries with low costs of production.

Returning to the reading, I am a little unsettled by what Jesus said, or, at least, how He said it.

For you always have the poor with you, but you will not always have me.

This does not sound like the Jesus who delivered the Sermon on the Mount! Even in His last days on earth, I am surprised at these rather self-serving words. Or, should I say, especially now, in the last days of His life on earth, Jesus was especially incarnate. He became Man, and in that capacity, He experienced some very human emotions, especially in the face of His imminent death.

My goal for this Ignatian Week Two has been to know Jesus better, to love Him more, and to follow Him wholeheartedly. Lent and Easter comprise the Third Ignatian Week, after which these Exercises seem to race to conclusion. There is no doubt in my mind that I have achieved my goals for the second week. I have come to look forward with excitement to each day that I spend with Jesus—reading, reflecting, writing, and contemplating for as long as three hours a day! Thank God for retirement!

While I could never have done this during my working life, neither could I do it in the first half of my life, when I was so devoted to building my life container. There are many choices with respect to how I spend my time in these retirement years. Sister Parish, the Living School, and these Exercises would certainly not have been in anyone's forecast for how I would spend my twilight years, especially not my prediction. These are second half activities. I believe a spiritual transformation occurred during the first two years following my heart attacks. I believe I not only understood the concept of first and second half of life, and the need to put something in my empty life container, but I actively set about making the filling of my container the primary purpose of my life.

Moreover, I believe it finally became clear to me that only by emptying my container in service to others could I ever realize the fullness of God's presence in my life. The "extended" Living School (I still read the mystics on a very regular basis) and these Exercises fill me with a vastly higher quality of understanding and joy than I have ever experienced before in my life. Sister Parish, Ability Housing, the St. Francis Soup Kitchen, and my somewhat greater effort to be a better husband, parent, and sibling are opportunities to empty that joy. I still sin, and I am still quite ego-centered, but, all things considered, I am in the best place I have ever been in my life.

I pray in gratitude for that. I pray that I can be present to the Presence in me, next to me, and in front of me every day.

March 4

Repeat and reflect on the week.

IT IS A WONDERFUL mid-winter Saturday, one that included tennis early in the morning, followed by the St. Francis Soup Kitchen, errands for Sister Parish, and a long nap! In short, it has been a perfect day. I will go to the 5:30 Mass soon, where I will lector and listen to Sallie Ann in the choir.

We have read from all three of the Synoptic Gospels, beginning with the Widow's Offering from Luke, then the Triumphal Entry into Jerusalem from Mark, and, finally, the Anointing in Bethany from Matthew. These three readings, each repeated the following day, were preceded with this prayer for the week.

> Lord Jesus, You tried with all Your might to help people understand the Spirit's teaching. You grieved that they wanted You, or someone, to take away their responsibility for their lives. When they extolled You, You did not rely on that. You went Your way, anointed by the love of faithful friends, anointed for Your death.

Each of the three readings informed us more about the life and person of Jesus Christ, and also contained an important moral lesson.

The Widow's Mite echoes the lesson from Pope John Paul II, "Nobody is so poor that he has nothing to give, and *nobody is so rich that he has nothing to receive.*" This is the primary basis for the Sister Parish Ministry. For all of us blessed to be born with all the advantages of sex, race, and ethnic origin that white, male Americans are blessed with, the widow's offering is a humbling lesson. What makes it so powerful, however, is that we receive so much more than we give, particularly when we are seeking no gift whatsoever.

My experience of Jesus entering Jerusalem to the cheers of the same crowd that would condemn Him to death so soon thereafter is marked by sadness. The mercurial mood of the crowd makes meaningless the adoration, and deepens the pain of the denunciation. Crowd noise and celebrity status seem to go hand in hand. Both are pretty empty. Now, I say that never having addressed a screaming crowd of thousands. As sure as I am writing this, I would be over the top with self-pride if ever I had the chance!

Finally, I am still troubled at the attitude of Jesus when He rebuked His disciples for their concern about the cost of the ointment. I like to believe that He would have enjoyed the anointing with the least expensive of ointments, and would have been pleased at anything the family of Simon would have done for the poor with the savings. The lesson I take from the passage in Matthew's Gospel is, therefore, conflicted, at best. Jesus was human. That is the message, and like all humans, He was occasionally proud, and could not have been very happy at the prospect of not being around for much longer to be anointed by anyone. I can relate to that.

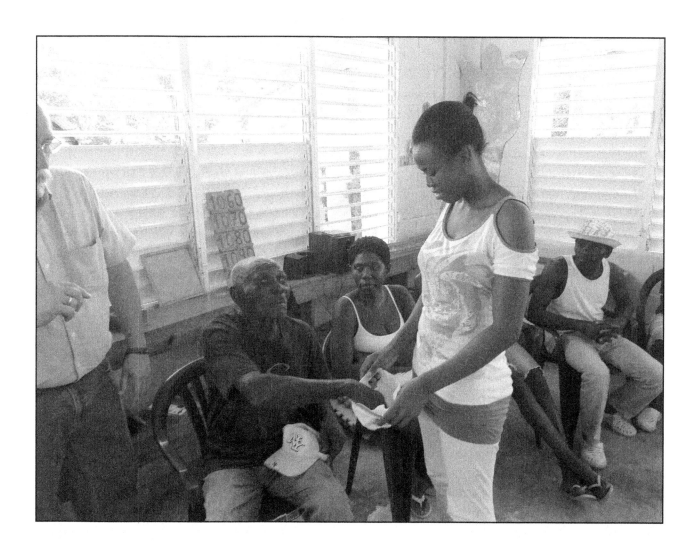

Ignatian Week Three

Calendar Week Twenty-Five

I want to feel sorrow at the wreckage, compassion with Jesus, and shame that He suffers because of our sins.

God our Creator and Lord, I beg of You that I may truly be a friend to Your Son and enter into His sufferings that He embraced for all the people You bring to life and for me

March 5

Luke 22:1–13, The Plot to Kill Jesus
¹ Now the festival of Unleavened Bread, which is called the Passover, was near. ² The chief priests and the scribes were looking for a way to put Jesus to death, for they were afraid of the people.

³ Then Satan entered into Judas called Iscariot, who was one of the twelve; ⁴ he went away and conferred with the chief priests and officers of the temple police about how he might betray him to them. ⁵ They were greatly pleased and agreed to give him money. ⁶ So he consented and began to look for an opportunity to betray him to them when no crowd was present.

The Preparation of the Passover
⁷ Then came the day of Unleavened Bread, on which the Passover lamb had to be sacrificed. ⁸ So Jesus sent Peter and John, saying, "Go and prepare the Passover meal for us that we may eat it." ⁹ They asked him, "Where do you want us to make preparations for it?" ¹⁰ "Listen," he said to them, "when you have entered the city, a man carrying a jar of water will meet you; follow him into the house he enters ¹¹ and say to the owner of the house, 'The teacher asks you, "Where is the guest room, where I may eat the Passover with my disciples?"' ¹² He will show you a large room upstairs, already furnished. Make preparations for us there." ¹³ So they went and found everything as he had told them; and they prepared the Passover meal.

SALLIE ANN and I have agreed to give up television news and Facebook for Lent. It has been my habit for close to forty years to have the television news on in the background wherever I am. CNN was launched in 1980, offering 24-hour news coverage throughout the United States, and in all the countries to which I traveled in those years. I turned the television on when I entered any hotel room, and continue the habit to this day. I began installing televisions in my office as early as the Watergate Hearings in May, 1973, which were broadcast by C-SPAN.

Not until last Thursday did I realize how quiet a room could be without television! We do listen to classical music in the background, but at very low volume. It actually is "background," not something that occasionally captures my attention. In addition to the silence, however, there is considerable peace in the absence of constantly Breaking News, whether any serious news is actually just breaking or not. Most of the time, the cable channels compete with each other by making the smallest event in the most remote part of the planet a crisis that must be reported immediately, over and over again!

I will admit to an addiction to political news. While it may be a little stronger with President Trump in office, I have been hooked since Vietnam, Watergate, Reagan's big move to the right, Clinton's new

Democratic Party and his impeachment, the hanging chad of the Bush/Gore election, the stupid tragedy of Iraq, the glorious hope and change of Obama, and then this still unbelievable presidential campaign and election. It is time for a break. I am not convinced that limiting myself to reading both the
New York Times and the *Washington Post* each morning qualifies as withdrawal, but it seems better
than the competitive hyping of the television.

This morning arrived quietly, with no television in the bedroom. Maggie and I walked down to the
quiet library, then out to the garden, which was alive with the sounds of creation. There was apparently
nothing of "breaking importance" to the birds, or in the ocean swell. We are back in the quiet library,
listening, without intention, to quiet baroque music.

The reading from Luke's Gospel begins with the account of Judas Iscariot deciding to turn traitor.

> Then Satan entered into Judas called Iscariot, who was one of the twelve

What strange madness is the level of greed that is so great it deserves to be referred to as "Satan
entering into" a person! In his weekly blog, which I read this morning, Father Frank suggests that sin
begins with a lack of gratitude.

> Or in other words, like Adam and Eve, we are simply ungrateful for what God gives us.
> Ingratitude is the genesis of all our sins. Our fall was and is that we aren't satisfied in what
> we have, and who we are. We want more. We want to be in total control.

What was Judas thinking? He had been with Jesus throughout His ministry, presumably walking,
eating, and listening to Jesus every day. He watched Jesus perform miracles. He heard the Father speak
from the sky. Judas knew how select he was to be one of only twelve apostles. But he wanted more. He
wanted total control.

In his daily meditation, Father Rohr quoted from his recent book, *The Divine Dance*. I liked the suggestion that resisting temptation can be a forward movement into the flow of the Divine, not simply a
negative reaction to an opportunity to sin.

> Once you have allowed yourself to be vulnerable and received infinite grace, you will find
> ways to *let the love flow through you, serving others*. People filled with the flow will always
> move away from any need to protect their own power. They will be drawn to the powerless,
> the edge, the bottom, the plain, and the simple. They have all the power they need; it always
> overflows, and like water seeks the lowest crevices to fill.
>
> When all three of those divine qualities start drawing you into the flow and when you're
> at home with *Infinity, Immanence, and Intimacy*—all Three—you're finally living inside a
> Trinitarian spirituality.

Avoiding, resisting, saying no—these are all negative actions, appropriately designed to move away
from, or push away, the temptation to seek more power, prestige, and possessions. While saying no to
the bad is certainly right, saying yes to the good is perhaps better. I like the idea of joining the flow,
serving the poor, dancing with God in the joy of His love.

Infinity, immanence, and intimacy are wonderful concepts, each conveying, in its own way, the
Higher Power, the presence greater than me that makes my faith journey both essential and rewarding.

March 6

Repeat Luke 22:1–13, The Plot to Kill Jesus

The sea was angry this morning. A cold wind, blowing up from the south, had whipped up waves, even on the lagoon. We sat in the dark, listening to the awakening universe, reflecting on this first week of Lent.

After introducing the traitorous role of Judas, the passage from Luke moves on to instructions from Jesus to His disciples regarding preparations for Passover. It reads like a mystery novel or, more accurately, like a revolutionary plot.

> …a man carrying a jar of water will meet you; follow him into the house he enters…. He will show you a large room upstairs, already furnished. Make preparations for us there…

One could read these instructions as supernatural knowledge from a God figure, who knows all things and can see into the future. Or, my preference, the instructions could reflect a carefully prepared meeting of conspirators seeking to avoid detection by the now suspicious scribes and Pharisees.

Reza Aslan, a prominent Iranian-American author I first met at the Council on Foreign Relations a few years ago, wrote *Zealot* in 2013, a compelling book about Jesus, set in the context of first-century Palestine. Describing the land and the time, Aslan writes:

> Scores of Jewish prophets, preachers, and would-be messiahs wandered through the Holy Land, bearing messages from God. This was the age of zealotry—a fervent nationalism that made resistance to the Roman occupation a sacred duty incumbent on all Jews. And few figures better exemplified this principle than the charismatic Galilean who defied both the imperial authorities and their allies in the Jewish religious hierarchy.

Ultimately, I break company with Aslan on the simple basis of faith in the divinity of Jesus. While Alsan has gone on to ever-increasing prominence, now as a producer of a television series called *Believer*, and would certainly not remember me, I consider him a friend and have great respect for his thinking.

Palestine in the time of Jesus was as actively revolutionary as the American colonies in the 1770s, or France in the 1780s. Plots, counter-plots, and complex webs of soldiers, spies, and counter-spies could be found everywhere, but particularly in Jerusalem, or Paris, or Boston and Philadelphia. Aslan makes a strong case for Jesus being very much a zealous revolutionary, not "just" the son of God!

What seems clear from this passage from Luke (repeated in similar language in both Mark and Matthew) is that Jesus was hiding the movements and whereabouts of His closest disciples during these final days of His life. He had secretly arranged the preparation of the upper room where the Last Supper would be held. Co-conspirators, with instructions for disguise and signals, were stationed to direct the disciples to the house.

It is likely that three different groups were concerned about the actions and followers of Jesus. First, He had clearly alarmed the Jewish religious establishment, challenging the priests, Sadducees, and Pharisees for commercializing and otherwise dishonoring the Temple. Second, the crowds that were drawn to Jesus must have been causing uneasiness for the Jewish political authorities, themselves puppets of the occupying Romans. Finally, but to a much lesser extent, the Romans were concerned about "disturbances" that must have been reported to them.

Two things continue to trouble me. First, how could the adoring crowd so suddenly become an angry mob? How could scores of people, who had witnessed numerous miracles and signs, shift in one week from passionate belief to livid scorn? My only answer is that there were two very separate groups of people. The seekers who walked long distances to hear this new prophet, who heard the Sermon on the Mount and witnessed the feeding of the five thousand, were very different people from the bloodthirsty groups who were fascinated with watching the crucifixions on Calgary. Religious seekers did not attend executions. And the morbid people who did attend executions were not that interested in learning about a new Gospel.

Second, I am troubled by the traditional teaching of the Church that Jesus was essentially a man of peace, not a political revolutionary. That does not seem credible to me. While "brotherly love" and "turning the other cheek" were different from a harsher, more judgmental religious teaching, who really cared? After all, "loving your neighbor as yourself" was not a concept originated by Jesus. Deuteronomy 6:5 was written more than 1,400 years before Jesus was born. It is hard for me to accept that the upside-down Gospel was enough to produce the condemnation and crucifixion of Jesus.

Jesus must have been feared more by the political authorities than by the religious authorities. While the story of Herod calling for infanticide when learning about the birth of Jesus strikes me as farfetched, Herod's fear of the Messiah was a political fear, not a religious fear. Whether intentionally or not, Jesus must have been perceived by the authorities to be a political revolutionary, capable of putting their power, prestige, and possessions at risk.

I believe that there is a powerful political and social message in the Gospel of Jesus Christ. Now, I also believe that this message is present in the Hebrew scriptures, and is present in the teachings of all the Wisdom Masters, from Buddha to Zarathustra. While it is not unique to Christianity, it is clearly present.

Catholic Social Teaching is as important to me as the Eucharist. In fact, the two are inseparable. Allowing a social and political order that marginalizes the poor, the old, the sick, and the sinner to continue unchallenged betrays the very Christ we remember at Mass. To believe is to be revolutionary. To be present to the Presence in this amazing universe requires that we act on our faith. The sad thing about the Church for all these centuries is that it has been so quiescent in the face of a social order and political power structure that are so contrary to its core teaching.

Jesus was crucified because some of the people who listened to Him teach actually heard what He said. Jesus did not challenge the pagan Gods. Jesus challenged the social and political apathy of everyone who heard him teach and preach.

March 7

Luke 22:14–20, The Institution of the Lord's Supper
    [14] When the hour came, he took his place at the table, and the apostles with him. [15] He said to them, "I have eagerly desired to eat this Passover with you before I suffer; [16] for I tell you, I will not eat it until it is fulfilled in the kingdom of God." [17] Then he took a cup, and after giving thanks he said, "Take this and divide it among yourselves; [18] for I tell you that from now on I will not drink of the fruit of the vine until the kingdom of God comes." [19] Then he took a loaf of bread, and when he had given thanks, he broke it and gave it to them, saying, "This is my body, which is given for you. Do this in remembrance of me." [20] And he did the same with the cup after supper, saying, "This cup that is poured out for you is the new covenant in my blood.

CATHOLICS spend a great deal of time and energy emphasizing the actual presence of the body and blood of Jesus Christ in the Eucharist. Through the mystery of transubstantiation, the bread and wine become human tissue and human blood, literally different substances. This is an exclusive teaching of the Catholic Church.

It is extremely important to most Catholics to distinguish themselves from other Christians, not to mention non-Christians. In varying degrees, Lutherans, Methodists, Anglicans, and Eastern Orthodox Christians all come close, but stop short of the literal change in substances. At Eucharistic celebrations, Catholics repeat stories of various scientific tests that confirm that what was once bread and wine is now human tissue and human blood dating back to the time of Christ.

I react very negatively to anything exclusive. The idea that the bread and wine used to celebrate the Last Supper in virtually every Christian Church is not real, while the Catholic host is real, strikes me as simply a tribal distinction, designed to make our tribe better than all the others. Personally, I believe Christ is present in all of creation, including the bread and wine offered at Mass as the Eucharist. When I say "all of creation," however, I include the bread and wine served in every other Christian Church. And, I do not consider non-Christians to be any less filled with Christ than the hardest praying Catholic who attends Mass every day.

Inclusion and forgiveness, these are the two words that Father John used to describe the core of the faith he invited me to share. I love those concepts as much today as I did ten years ago. Christ excludes no one from His grace. The worst sinner, the non-believer, and, yes, the most pious Catholic bigot—all are included in Christ's love.

Claire Hartman, the daughter of my good friend Tony Hartman, delivered one of the witness talks at the recent CRHP retreat. She was as polished and credible as any speaker I have listened to in a very long time. The subject of her witness was the Eucharist. She talked about the calming, even transformative effect of the Eucharist, but went on to emphasize the community of Catholics created by this common experience. At the Catholic Youth Congress in Poland last summer, Claire, and several other young people from our parish, joined a crowd of three million young Catholics, from all over the world, to celebrate Mass with Pope Francis. In a powerful way, Claire talked about *the body of Christ in the body of Christ*. Each one of those young people had just eaten a piece of the body of Christ, thereby becoming bound into a very special community of faith, itself the body of Christ.

While I loved the image of each of these young Catholics becoming one, I wanted to whisper in Claire's ear, "What about the young Catholics in the crowd who, for whatever reason, did not take communion? Were they not in the body of Christ? What about the other Christians, who gathered in Poland to be near the Pope? Or the non-Christians in the Polish countryside around the site of the Youth Congress?" I could go on and on. The point is obvious to me.

Reflecting on that this morning, I fantasized being an integral part of a whole collection of Russian wooden dolls—each successively larger doll enveloping the smaller dolls. I recalled the conversation at the Living School about *holons*, whole entities that formed a part of a larger whole entity. My whole person is a part of the whole community of Ponte Vedra Beach, which is a part of the whole county of St. John's, which is a part of the whole state of Florida, which is a part of the whole country of the United States, which is a part of the whole continent of North America, which is a part of the whole planet that is Earth, and so on and so on, infinitely into infinity. We are all whole, yet we are, at the same time, just smaller parts of yet larger wholes.

I pray for acceptance of tradition. I pray for the grace to include all those around me, even those who exclude others.

March 8

Repeat Luke 22:14–20, The Institution of the Lord's Supper

INCREDIBLY, I have developed something of a pattern in my life, albeit only when I am not traveling. Tuesday, Thursday, and Saturday are tennis. Monday, Wednesday, and Friday are gym and a short walk. Sunday is a long walk. For a host of reasons, I believe patterns are very important in life. Sadly, most of my life has been without pattern, caused in large part by my desire to focus on the next new thing. While this focus was extremely useful in my efforts to grow my various activities, it led to more isolation than was healthy. There are no "mulligans" in life, so I cannot do anything about how I lived and interacted with people over the half century of my active life. I finished the game with a lot of toys, but not as many warm relationships as I could have had, and would have liked.

After my core exercise with Nicole, my "trainer" (it seems both odd and a little silly to refer to someone as "my" trainer or coach or advisor) at the Ponte Vedra Gym, I sat on the bench, meditating about the Lord's Supper in the warm sun of mid-winter Florida. Jesus had been talking about his imminent death for several days. The secrecy surrounding the time and place of this last dinner together must have heightened the fears of all the disciples. I can imagine a very nervous group of men (and women?), perhaps whispering lest they be heard by nosy neighbors.

Leonardo da Vinci has shaped the memory that most of us have of the Last Supper. Painting 1,500 years after the event, with very little historical information to support his notion of what the dinner would be like, da Vinci made a painting said to capture the moment when Jesus announced that Judas would betray Him. Judas is in the group of three figures to the left of Jesus in the painting (on Jesus's right). The other two figures in that grouping are meant to be Peter and John, but the figure of John looks so feminine that many believe it to be Mary Magdalene. To my eye, the figure of Jesus is as feminine as that of John.

My reaction to this final dinner with Jesus is shaped much more by da Vinci's painting than by the words in any of the Gospels. Jesus, flanked by John, the Beloved Disciple, on His right, and doubting Thomas on His left, is pointing to the bread. This might have been the moment when He uttered the words,

> This is my body, which is given for you. Do this in remembrance of me.

My reaction includes both shock, at the betrayal of Judas, and awe, at the offering of a simple piece of bread by which to remember Jesus.

The dinner feels like a closing ceremony, celebrating what has been done, but also launching another phase. We disciples have bonded as a group over the past several months, sharing both the joyous excitement of the Gospel, and the anxious fear of reprisal by the authorities. It is extremely hard to wrap my head around the whirlwind of emotions. Judas, a traitor? How could that be? Our little band of brothers, bound together by joy and fear, was obviously reaching some kind of milestone in the journey we began when this incredible man asked us to follow him. We were whispering our joy to avoid detection by spies and agents of the Romans and their Jewish puppets. We worked to hide our anguish that our Master would leave us so soon. We were simply baffled as to what to do about the betrayal.

> I want to feel sorrow at the wreckage, compassion with Jesus, and shame that He suffers because of our sins.

This is my goal for this week. I cannot think about wreckage while I am so close to this man, sitting at this table, sharing His bread and wine. Yet, He talks about death and betrayal. I love Him and cannot imagine He will die. I can feel His pain. I know how much He has loved the transformation that has occurred in all of us, as individuals and as a tightly bound group. His love makes the betrayal that much more painful.

Praying on my knees in front of the Rublev icon, I sense the deep pain the Creator God must feel as He watches His creatures do so many stupid and hateful things, separating themselves from Him. Shock and awe. How could we do all the shocking things that we do? How can He persist in extending His awesome love?

March 9

John 13:1–20, Jesus Washes the Disciples' Feet

¹ Now before the festival of the Passover, Jesus knew that his hour had come to depart from this world and go to the Father. Having loved his own who were in the world, he loved them to the end. ² The devil had already put it into the heart of Judas son of Simon Iscariot to betray him. And during supper ³ Jesus, knowing that the Father had given all things into his hands, and that he had come from God and was going to God, ⁴ got up from the table, took off his outer robe, and tied a towel around himself. ⁵ Then he poured water into a basin and began to wash the disciples' feet and to wipe them with the towel that was tied around him. ⁶ He came to Simon Peter, who said to him, "Lord, are you going to wash my feet?" ⁷ Jesus answered, "You do not know now what I am doing, but later you will understand." ⁸ Peter said to him, "You will never wash my feet." Jesus answered, "Unless I wash you, you have no share with me." ⁹ Simon Peter said to him, "Lord, not my feet only but also my hands and my head!" ¹⁰ Jesus said to him, "One who has bathed does not need to wash, except for the feet, but is entirely clean. And you are clean, though not all of you." ¹¹ For he knew who was to betray him; for this reason he said, "Not all of you are clean."

¹² After he had washed their feet, had put on his robe, and had returned to the table, he said to them, "Do you know what I have done to you? ¹³ You call me Teacher and Lord—and you are right, for that is what I am. ¹⁴ So if I, your Lord and Teacher, have washed your feet, you also ought to wash one another's feet. ¹⁵ For I have set you an example, that you also should do as I have done to you. ¹⁶ Very truly, I tell you, servants are not greater than their master, nor are messengers greater than the one who sent them. ¹⁷ If you know these things, you are blessed if you do them. ¹⁸ I am not speaking of all of you; I know whom I have chosen. But it is to fulfill the scripture, 'The one who ate my bread has lifted his heel against me.' ¹⁹ I tell you this now, before it occurs, so that when it does occur, you may believe that I am he. ²⁰ Very truly, I tell you, whoever receives one whom I send receives me; and whoever receives me receives him who sent me."

THE WASHING of the feet remains one of the most powerful experiences I have ever been a part of, both washing the feet of others, and having someone wash my feet. Just reading the story from John's Gospel humbles me, reminding me of the deep level of vulnerability required from all of the participants.

Proskynesis, is the four-syllable Greek word used to describe the Persian act of bowing or prostrating oneself before a person of higher social rank. I intend to use the word at one of our Lectio Divina meetings with Deacon Dan, along with *koinonia, apophatic,* and *kataphatic*. Big Greek words do wonders for my image of mature humility (!). Seriously, this ancient Persian tradition was picked up by the Hebrews, where the practice of kissing the feet of the senior person was added. While I am not certain whether Jesus was the first great man to reverse the roles, bowing down to the person of lower rank, washing their often tired and sore feet, and concluding with the act of greatest vulnerability and respect, kissing one or both feet, it would certainly fit with His upside-down Gospel.

In that upper room that night, after a dinner filled with statements by Jesus about His imminent death, after the introduction of the rite of the Last Supper, and after extraordinary measures were taken to hide the time and place of the event itself, emotions must have been precariously on edge. While a knock on the door could signal that they had been found out, or a phalanx of soldiers could simply break the door down and rush up the stairs, Jesus had also just announced that there was a traitor among the twelve! It is hard to imagine a situation more fraught with fear and anxiety. What a perfect time and place for Jesus to "get up from the table, take off his outer robe, and tie a towel around himself."

Pope Francis washes the feet of Muslim refugees, migrants from all over the world, prisoners from the local prison, and *women*! In every instant, the Pope is sending a powerful message of inclusion, equality, and vulnerability. It is an extremely influential message, heard all around the world.

March 10

Repeat John 13:1–20, Jesus Washes the Disciples' Feet

As I reflected again this morning about the washing of the feet, I was particularly struck by how impactful it is, both to wash another person's feet, and, even more, to have someone wash my feet. Last year, the San Anastasia family mission coincided with Easter week. While everyone advised against the conflicts that would arise, it turned out to be one of the best missions ever.

The crowning event was the washing of the feet in Mamey. A young missionary from Florida was was in line to wash the gnarled, scabby, and dirty feet of one of the elderly Haitians from Mamey.

It was transforming. The boy started to weep as he watched the old man remove his shoes and socks. When he poured the water over the old man's foot, I noticed that the old man had started to weep as well. After he kissed the foot, he held it for several seconds. The old man reached out to touch the boy, who took his hand and held it while both of them wept. By now, most of the villagers and all the missionaries had stopped what they were doing, and were very quietly watching this incredible scene, some of them beginning to weep as well.

The boy helped the old man put his sock on, then turned to find his father in the group of missionaries. He got up from his knees, embraced his father, and allowed his weeping to become sobbing. While I am sure they held each other for only a few seconds, it seemed much longer. Importantly, it was long enough to allow most of us in the crowd to experience a deeply meaningful encounter. Christ was as present in the little chapel in Mamey that day as He was during the foot washing described in John's Gospel.

March 11

Repeat and reflect on the week.

Sallie Ann left early this morning to serve on the Presenting Team of Women's CRHP Team 23. I left at the same time to play tennis. I am now back in the library, after sitting with Maggie down in the garden for almost an hour after returning from tennis. It has been quite a week. We started with the plot to kill Jesus, which reached an important point when Judas took part of his money early on the day the disciples secretly met with Jesus for dinner. After reading Luke's account of the Last Supper, we turned to John's Gospel for an account of the foot washing. By any measure, this was an extraordinary week when it actually occurred, two thousand years ago. It has been an important week for me, this second week of Lent in 2017.

The goal suggested for me in the guidance is that I feel "sorrow at the wreckage, compassion with Jesus, and shame that He suffers because of our sins." I do feel sorrow for the inconceivable level of wreckage that occurred at the end of the ministry of Jesus. Part of what shocks me in that wreckage is how suddenly the mood seems to have shifted from adulation to persecution. I have speculated that it is due to the difference in the two groups of people, one that gathered to hear from an exciting new teacher, and a different one that routinely attended gruesome executions. However, the story clearly evokes sorrow.

The dictionary definition of compassion is, "a feeling of deep sympathy and sorrow for another who is stricken by misfortune, *accompanied* by a strong desire to alleviate the suffering." I do feel sorrow in connection with the "wreckage" of that last week in His ministry. My compassion arises as a result of my desire to alleviate the suffering, to do something about it, even now, two millennia after the event. I would add only that I feel powerless to do so.

As I consider the final goal, that I feel shame that Jesus suffers because of our sins, I want to distinguish what I feel from what I think many religious teachers have taught for centuries. I am not comfortable with the concept that Jesus died to make amends for the sins of Mankind. Nonetheless, I believe that Christ *today* suffers when we sin *today*. In other words, I believe that Christ is here now, with us now, suffering now when we sin, just as he rejoices when we serve Him by serving others.

CALENDAR WEEK TWENTY-SIX

I ask God to feel sorrow because of what Jesus went through, even anguish and tears. And shame at what Jesus endures for me.

Lord Jesus Christ, Did I know how, I would break my heart with grief for You. Of all the people in the world, You should have suffered least. I am ashamed of what we did to You while You broke Your heart with grief for me.

March 12

Matthew 26:30–56

[30] *When they had sung the hymn, they went out to the Mount of Olives.*

Peter's Denial Foretold

[31] *Then Jesus said to them, "You will all become deserters because of me this night; for it is written,*

'I will strike the shepherd,

and the sheep of the flock will be scattered.'

[32] *But after I am raised up, I will go ahead of you to Galilee."* [33] *Peter said to him, "Though all become deserters because of you, I will never desert you."* [34] *Jesus said to him, "Truly I tell you, this very night, before the cock crows, you will deny me three times."* [35] *Peter said to him, "Even though I must die with you, I will not deny you." And so said all the disciples.*

Jesus Prays in Gethsemane

[36] *Then Jesus went with them to a place called Gethsemane; and he said to his disciples, "Sit here while I go over there and pray."* [37] *He took with him Peter and the two sons of Zebedee, and began to be grieved and agitated.* [38] *Then he said to them, "I am deeply grieved, even to death; remain here, and stay awake with me."* [39] *And going a little farther, he threw himself on the ground and prayed, "My Father, if it is possible, let this cup pass from me; yet not what I want but what you want."* [40] *Then he came to the disciples and found them sleeping; and he said to Peter, "So, could you not stay awake with me one hour?* [41] *Stay awake and pray that you may not come into the time of trial; the spirit indeed is willing, but the flesh is weak."* [42] *Again he went away for the second time and prayed, "My Father, if this cannot pass unless I drink it, your will be done."* [43] *Again he came and found them sleeping, for their eyes were heavy.* [44] *So leaving them again, he went away and prayed for the third time, saying the same words.* [45] *Then he came to the disciples and said to them, "Are you still sleeping and taking your rest? See, the hour is at hand, and the Son of Man is betrayed into the hands of sinners.* [46] *Get up, let us be going. See, my betrayer is at hand."*

The Betrayal and Arrest of Jesus

[47] *While he was still speaking, Judas, one of the twelve, arrived; with him was a large crowd with swords and clubs, from the chief priests and the elders of the people.* [48] *Now the betrayer had given them a sign, saying, "The one I will kiss is the man; arrest him."* [49] *At once he came up to Jesus and said, "Greetings, Rabbi!" and kissed him.* [50] *Jesus said to him, "Friend, do what you are here to do." Then they came and laid hands on Jesus and arrested him.* [51] *Suddenly, one of those with Jesus put his hand on his sword, drew it, and struck the slave of the high priest, cutting off his ear.* [52] *Then Jesus said to him, "Put your sword back into its place; for all who take the sword will perish by the sword.* [53] *Do you think that I cannot appeal to my Father, and he will at once send me more than twelve legions of angels?* [54] *But how then would the scriptures be fulfilled, which say it must happen in this way?"* [55] *At that hour Jesus said to the crowds, "Have you come out with swords and clubs to arrest me as though I were a bandit? Day after day I sat in the temple teaching, and you did not arrest me.* [56] *But all this has taken place, so that the scriptures of the prophets may be fulfilled." Then all the disciples deserted him and fled.*

THE PLANE for Miami departed Jacksonville at 7:20 this morning. I am now on the plane flying from Miami to Santo Domingo. My heart is full today, even as I feel sadness at leaving Sallie Ann. While it was still dark early this morning, I walked in the garden with Maggie, overwhelmed by the magnitude of beauty and serenity that surrounded me. I recalled that brief walk several times on the early flight this morning. How could all of this have happened to me? How could someone as patently unworthy as I am, have been so incredibly blessed? It makes no sense. Today, however, I accept it with joy. I know I am doing the right thing in my efforts to give back, to "empty myself" of the love and joy that regularly reaches the overflow level in my heart.

Reading the passage from Matthew's Gospel, I reflected on the final verses, which strongly state that the trial and execution of Jesus had to happen because they were foretold by the prophets. I recently told a good friend, Jay Sengstacke, that Jesus must have been politically active, working for the overthrow of Roman occupation and the rule of the puppet kings. Otherwise, I argued, there would never have been such a brutal response. There were many religious figures in the early first century, all of them teaching new doctrines contrary to the official teaching of the Jewish leadership. Almost all of them were simply ignored. John the Baptist and Jesus were the two significant exceptions. Why? I contended that it was their political stance, not their religious teaching, that led to their execution. Other revolutionaries were routinely executed, many of them crucified. My friend answered me that none of that mattered. Jesus had to be crucified because it was an essential part of God's plan.

This is the principal message in verses 53–56 of Chapter 26 of Matthew. As clear as that message is, not just in Matthew's Gospel, but throughout the Gospels and the epistles of Paul, I am not comfortable accepting it. It makes no sense to me that God would insist upon the brutal sacrifice of His son for any reason. I am especially troubled by the argument that God's love was conditioned on that crucifixion.

I am about to join my good friends, Daniel Jose and Ezequiel Torres, the leaders of the Mamey leadership team, for dinner. I will end my uncomfortable reflections in the joyous anticipation of that dinner.

March 13

Repeat Matthew 26:30–56

I AM BACK at the hotel after a long day with the missionaries. The high point of the day, perhaps the high point of many days and weeks, was a meeting with the Mamey community in the chapel. I asked two of the young missionaries from St. Joseph's Academy, one from Spain and the other from Peru, to assist me by translating. I warned them that most meetings with the community were difficult, generally consisting of complaints. The surprise was so great that it is hard, even now, to describe what happened.

One young woman came to the front of the large group that had assembled in the chapel, looking very stern. I leaned over to one of the translators and cautioned her to expect the worst. To my extraordinary surprise, the woman thanked me and Sister Parish for her new house. Then Estella presented me with a beautiful plaque engraved with my name and some incredible words of gratitude. I wept as I attempted a response. Just writing this brings back those tears of joy.

It has been four years since Don Barnhorst and I first visited Mamey. What an extraordinary four years! The first mission in 2013, surprised all of us with its success. Then came the community center in 2014, with the school, the chapel, the water treatment facility. Then the houses in 2015 and 2016, including a park and drainage and latrines and the pigs! And now, in 2017, watching the volunteers and leaders from Mamey build houses and chapels in Caoba, El Fao, and, today, in El Alto. What an amazing four years! I am tired and happy and just a little overwhelmed. I pray a simple thank you.

March 14

John 18:12–27, Jesus before the High Priest

¹² So the soldiers, their officer, and the Jewish police arrested Jesus and bound him. ¹³ First they took him to Annas, who was the father-in-law of Caiaphas, the high priest that year. ¹⁴ Caiaphas was the one who had advised the Jews that it was better to have one person die for the people.

Peter Denies Jesus

¹⁵ Simon Peter and another disciple followed Jesus. Since that disciple was known to the high priest, he went with Jesus into the courtyard of the high priest, ¹⁶ but Peter was standing outside at the gate. So the other disciple, who was known to the high priest, went out, spoke to the woman who guarded the gate, and brought Peter in. ¹⁷ The woman said to Peter, "You are not also one of this man's disciples, are you?" He said, "I am not." ¹⁸ Now the slaves and the police had made a charcoal fire because it was cold, and they were standing around it and warming themselves. Peter also was standing with them and warming himself.

The High Priest Questions Jesus

¹⁹ Then the high priest questioned Jesus about his disciples and about his teaching. ²⁰ Jesus answered, "I have spoken openly to the world; I have always taught in synagogues and in the temple, where all the Jews come together. I have said nothing in secret. ²¹ Why do you ask me? Ask those who heard what I said to them; they know what I said." ²² When he had said this, one of the police standing nearby struck Jesus on the face, saying, "Is that how you answer the high priest?" ²³ Jesus answered, "If I have spoken wrongly, testify to the wrong. But if I have spoken rightly, why do you strike me?" ²⁴ Then Annas sent him bound to Caiaphas the high priest.

Peter Denies Jesus Again

²⁵ Now Simon Peter was standing and warming himself. They asked him, "You are not also one of his disciples, are you?" He denied it and said, "I am not." ²⁶ One of the slaves of the high priest, a relative of the man whose ear Peter had cut off, asked, "Did I not see you in the garden with him?" ²⁷ Again Peter denied it, and at that moment the cock crowed.

ONCE AGAIN this year, I will play the role of Caiaphas in the Live Stations of the Cross at Our Lady Star of the Sea. This will be the third year that our little group, with only a few changes, has gathered together on Good Friday in costume dress, to re-enact the events of the trial and execution of Jesus. It is a nice tradition.

I prayed this morning in the garden behind the Quality Hotel near the Santo Domingo airport. I awakened still overwhelmed by the community meeting last night in Mamey. I am not comfortable receiving this kind of public recognition and gratitude. I wonder what I will do when I go back to Mamey!

Caiaphas argued that it was better that one man dies than all the people. Caiaphas was talking about a political revolution, not a spiritual movement. The Romans and their puppets would seek to destroy all of the Jewish population to quell a rebellion, not a sect. In fact, that is exactly what the Romans did less than four decades after the death of Jesus.

Otherwise, what would cause such a statement? Again, I cannot believe it was just a teacher saying that we should love our neighbor, serve the poor, speak to the Samaritans and do good things on the

Sabbath. Good deeds like this could hardly have come to the attention of the national leaders and Roman occupiers, much less provoked them to such a brutal execution.

So, what difference does it make that Jesus was also a political revolutionary? He also taught a wonderful new Gospel. That is clear, and it is the essence of what has persisted down through the centuries. Rome remained in power for another five hundred years. The Jewish puppet leadership remained essentially intact, even after the sack of Jerusalem in 70 CE, until Agrippa, the final king in the Herodian dynasty, died. The Jewish political revolution was completely wiped out by the Romans. My point is that any political activity on the part of Jesus and the other first-century revolutionaries ended without success. It was the religious message that lasted.

That message is alive today. Yet it still remains elusive for most of the Christians in the world, much less the global population. I find it very sad that the truly revolutionary message of Jesus, the upside-down Gospel, inspires so little energy, either in its favor or in opposition. Only when one group seeks to take the power, prestige, or possessions of another group will the alarm bells ring and people take to the streets. The abject poverty of more than half of the global population is never a compelling issue because these people have so little. It only becomes a subject of controversy when efforts are suggested to take some of the wealth away from the well-to-do, the top ten percent of the population, to give to the world's poor.

A small group of missionaries were talking about some of this during a break this morning. I was delighted to learn that they were all fervently supportive of government efforts in the United States and around the world to welcome refugees, serve the poor, and redress the inequality that is growing worse each year. I asked if it was this mission experience that caused this view. To my pleasant surprise, their answer was that Sister Parish only confirmed their views regarding the essential need for government to do more for the poor, taking higher taxes from the wealthy to do so. The St. Joseph's students on the Sister Parish mission are generally seniors, and, as they say, this is not their first rodeo.

March 15

Repeat John 18:12–27, Jesus before the High Priest

THE CONVOLUTED trial of Jesus is a classic story of "passing the buck." The case against Jesus is passed from Annas, to Caiaphas, to Pilate, to Herod, back to Pilate, and then to the angry mob. The primary message in this passage from John's Gospel is really not about the trial. Rather, it is about Peter's denial of Jesus. A great deal is made of the fact that Jesus predicted this three-fold denial during the last supper.

As I reflected on the denial story, I was struck by two powerful thoughts. First, how painful it must have been for Jesus the man, not the Son of Man, but the incarnate human being, to be right in His prediction. Simply as a person, would it not have been a wonderful time to be wrong, to learn that your very dear friend could not bring himself to deny you? And for Peter, what extraordinary shame he must have felt for betraying his dear friend and teacher. Peter gave up his life for this Nazarene, leaving everything behind to follow Him. How awful he must have felt to have been so weak at the last moment.

In the great historical drama that seems mandated by destiny, these two human dramas may seem like small beer. But when I put myself in the position of either man, Jesus or Peter, I feel their pain. When Jesus later proclaims, "Forgive them Father, for they know not what they do," it is generally assumed that He is referring to the angry mob or to the Jewish leaders. Perhaps the person He is truly thinking about is His dear friend and cherished follower, Peter. I have only a very small group of friends, most of them former employees, that I would trust with my life. Yes, I would expect them to twist the truth to protect me, but that is not the case here. Peter had to lie to betray Jesus!

For whom would I give my life? Seriously. It is easy to speculate that I would give my life for a member of my family. I like to think so, but it is something so much easier said than done. Beyond family, however, which is what we are talking about in the case of the disciples and Jesus, I would not be honest to say that I would give my life, twist the truth, risk serious censure, or otherwise make much of a sacrifice for anyone that comes easily to mind. Would I work hard? Give significant financial support? Write a recommendation? These are all easy, and none carries much risk for me.

It is my sense of the relationship between Peter and Jesus that both would have answered that their relationship was such that true sacrifice was on offer by each for the other. This was not a casual friendship, nor an insignificant commitment between two people. Consider the multiple occasions when Jesus asked His close followers about their relationship, and about the understanding they had as to His role in the world and in their lives. So I believe Peter's shame was real, and Jesus felt real pain at being betrayed.

I am in the pink cloud of the mission, filled with energy and faith, all my emotions close to the surface. If it were possible, I would bottle this feeling. I know from experience that the more of it I give away, the more I will have to give!

March 16

Mark 14:53–72, Jesus before the Council

53 They took Jesus to the high priest; and all the chief priests, the elders, and the scribes were assembled. 54 Peter had followed him at a distance, right into the courtyard of the high priest; and he was sitting with the guards, warming himself at the fire. 55 Now the chief priests and the whole council were looking for testimony against Jesus to put him to death; but they found none. 56 For many gave false testimony against him, and their testimony did not agree. 57 Some stood up and gave false testimony against him, saying, 58 "We heard him say, 'I will destroy this temple that is made with hands, and in three days I will build another, not made with hands.'" 59 But even on this point their testimony did not agree. 60 Then the high priest stood up before them and asked Jesus, "Have you no answer? What is it that they testify against you?" 61 But he was silent and did not answer. Again the high priest asked him, "Are you the Messiah, the Son of the Blessed One?" 62 Jesus said, "I am; and

'you will see the Son of Man
seated at the right hand of the Power,'
and 'coming with the clouds of heaven.'"

63 Then the high priest tore his clothes and said, "Why do we still need witnesses? 64 You have heard his blasphemy! What is your decision?" All of them condemned him as deserving death. 65 Some began to spit on him, to blindfold him, and to strike him, saying to him, "Prophesy!" The guards also took him over and beat him.

Peter Denies Jesus

66 While Peter was below in the courtyard, one of the servant-girls of the high priest came by. 67 When she saw Peter warming himself, she stared at him and said, "You also were with Jesus, the man from Nazareth." 68 But he denied it, saying, "I do not know or understand what you are talking about." And he went out into the forecourt. Then the cock crowed. 69 And the servant-girl, on seeing him, began again to say to the bystanders, "This man is one of them." 70 But again he denied it. Then after a little while the bystanders again said to Peter, "Certainly you are one of them; for you are a Galilean." 71 But he began to curse, and he swore an oath, "I do not know this man you are talking about." [72] At that moment the cock crowed for the second time. Then Peter remembered that Jesus had said to him, "Before the cock crows twice, you will deny me three times." And he broke down and wept.

THE ACCOUNT of the trial in Mark evokes in me the same strong feeling as that I experienced when reading the other Gospel accounts:: The high priests were alarmed about more than what could have been passed off as a crazy person claiming the impossible. Again, strongly believing that the people in the crowds attending the trial and execution were very different from those who had come to hear Jesus teach and preach, it is not surprising that the high priests could arouse them to demand execution, to "spit on him, to blindfold him, and to strike him." Was Jesus persuasive as a zealous revolutionary? Were any of his followers part of the growing Jewish rebellion?

Or was the atmosphere in Jerusalem so filled with fear that both crowds and high priests could react with such violent hatred in the face of a Gospel of love? I know fear can do that, especially when that fear is spread through and among an occupied population, whose leadership has become puppet to the occupiers. When fear is used to motivate the mob, irrational results occur.

Whatever the circumstances, a ridiculous trial led to a gruesome execution. The treatment of the prisoner by guards, onlookers, and authorities, both Jew and Roman, was inexplicably horrible. At no point did Jesus pose a threat of either retaliation or escape. These horrific acts were ultimately the acts of a mob crazed by fear and hatred. Jesus did nothing in His ministry to arouse either fear or hatred. It was as though each of the persecuting groups or actors had a different grievance against someone or something other than Jesus. Nonetheless, they took it out on Jesus.

Late last night, I was the last to speak to the missionaries. They had gone around the reflection circle, each exclaiming the beauty and joy that they found in the faces and lives of the people in the villages. I somewhat vigorously objected. Poverty sucks, I said, over and over again. Do not be confused or deluded by the smiles on their faces or the authenticity of their love. They sleep, eat, play, and work in conditions dangerous to their health and well-being. Their education is often a very unfunny joke. Opportunities to improve their own lives, or the lives of their children are essentially non-existent. Poverty sucks!

A very important learning from this mission experience, a message to take home and ruminate on in the coming weeks and months, is that this does not have to be. God does not want massive inequality and abject poverty. God does not want social, economic, and political structures that systemically disadvantage one group over another. God calls us to seek justice, to correct the systemic flaws, to turn this world upside-down. We constantly hear the adage, "don't just give them fish, teach them to fish." There is another way to say that. "Don't just give them charity, work with them to change the system that creates such massive need for charity." Oddly, we do not hear the issue put this way very often today.

March 17

Repeat Mark 14:53–72, Jesus before the Council

THE NEWS WAS on in my hotel room this morning. I listened to a lengthy discussion about the "budget blueprint" issued by the Trump administration yesterday. It was surreal on several counts. Three stand out.

First, the budget reflects the shift in thinking from "soft power" to "hard power." For many years, really, all my life, US military power has been overwhelming, outpacing by every measure the military power of any other country. In fact, we spend more on our military than the next eight countries combined! For most of my life, every thoughtful person involved in either military or diplomatic leadership has argued that this intense focus on "hard power," the ability to project our military might, was totally unsuited to the post-Cold War world. We focus too little on "soft power," our diplomatic corps and the power of our values, and need to both develop and use that soft power more in every way. Military victories in Vietnam, Iraq, Afghanistan, and in various proxy wars throughout the developing world have proved to be futile in the absence of any significant success in re-building broken states, or repairing economies in ruins.

Trump initially talked a great deal about the abject failure of the war in Iraq, a needless war, wrongly targeted at Saddam on the basis of faulty intelligence. He argued, correctly in my view, that far too little was spent in the months and years after the "hard power" victory in efforts to make the country work again. So it came as a surprise for me to hear the description of the Trump budget yesterday as a "hard power" budget. More than $54 billion in additional military spending is proposed, with reductions of 25–30 percent in spending on the State Department, Foreign Aid, and international organizations. While I knew that this was the direction the new government was about to take, the stark reality of this budget proposal forced me to finally and fully focus on what it all means. Even PEPFAR, the highly successful anti-AIDS program introduced by George W. Bush, will be abandoned, along with every other program with any hint of "caring for the less fortunate," either at home or abroad.

Second, Mick Mulvaney, the budget director, explained that any money spent on climate science was "totally wasted." Thus, the EPA budget would be slashed, along with the federal funds devoted to research in the areas of oceanographic change or an understanding of long-term weather patterns. Ninety-seven percent of the world's scientists conclude that man-made increases in carbon in the atmosphere are causing irreparable harm to the environment. Yet the far-right fringe of the Republican Party denies this science. Once again, the stark reality of the new budget demonstrates just how consequential elections are. Trump is making it clear that these were not just campaign slogans. This country will now take an aggressively anti-science position. If possible, and to the extent possible, we will withdraw from the Paris Climate Accords. Trump is about to announce an end to regulations requiring improved fuel mileage in our automobiles. Regulations intended to reduce our use of dirty coal will be relaxed. Research will end.

Finally, one of the final vestiges of the Lyndon Johnson era War on Poverty, the Community Development Block Grant program, will be abandoned. One immediate casualty of this decision is a program called Meals on Wheels, a program providing food for the hungry, particularly those elderly people unable to leave their homes to go to food markets and restaurants. Mulvaney explained why this program would no longer be funded with this: "Research has shown that Meals on Wheels has not achieved any long-term benefits." I thought about that for a long time. Did he mean to say that the people who depended on this program for food died anyway? Or was the argument that the organizations that carried out the Meals on Wheels program were not profitable?

Ninety-two percent of the members of Congress are Christian. Thirty percent are Catholic. How do these men and women explain their support for this budget and the policies it represents? I suppose some people argue that the Old Testament message (they refuse to say Hebrew Scriptures) is one of hard justice, of might makes right. So "hard power" is simply an expression of Old Testament values, which are necessary for the "soft power," love thy neighbor values of the New Testament to properly function. As crazy as this sounds, I have heard it from members of my parish. I would think, however, that taking the name "Christian" implies a bias for the teaching of the New Testament, the new Gospel, the upside-down message of Jesus Christ.

I know that many conservative Catholics consider Pope Francis to be a temporary aberration. His teaching is a throw-back to the liberation theology so popular among Latin American Catholics prior to the papacy of John Paul II. As I hope I have made clear in this journal, it is this theology that attracted me to Catholicism, and, more fundamentally, to Christianity. Nonetheless, how do the Catholic Senators and Congress people so casually reject climate science? Pope Francis is not alone in his support of *Laudato Si.*

The concepts of serving the poor, healing the sick, freeing the prisoners, and housing the homeless are universally, timelessly true and good. How can anyone, Christian or otherwise, take a different view? It is an irony that the eight percent of Congress that is not Christian supports these concepts.

So I am sad as I begin my reflections today. I am slowly, painfully beginning to realize that the anguish I felt during the elections last fall was justified. The next several years (I can only pray that it will be limited to four) will be difficult. Everything that can be done to prevent the Trump policies from becoming permanent must be done. The damage must be limited. I am not very hopeful. I will be seventy-six years old when the next President is sworn in. At best, this President will have to undo considerable damage. At worst, the new President will face continued Congressional opposition. Actually, at worst the new President will be Trump!

I am at the end of the time I allocated for my reflections this morning, and must now organize myself to get to the airport in time to fly back to Jacksonville. It has been a wonderful mission. I cherish the little bit of resistance to the rightward drift of global political sentiment these mission trips provide. I may not change the world, but I hope to change at least a few days in the lives of a few people. The most important change is in my own troubled heart. I have a long life for which to atone.

March 18

Repeat and reflect on the week.

AFTER A WEEK in the Dominican Republic, the mid-winter temperatures in Jacksonville were way too cold for a long sit in the garden. Maggie and I are in the library, warmer, but in awe of the beauty of this very comfortable place. Comparisons of Ponte Vedra Beach and the communities surrounding Guerra are simply not fair. By any standard, the inequity between living conditions in the two places is shocking. This week ended with two different accounts of the trial of Jesus. Next week begins tomorrow with yet another account.

Reading what the Gospels have to say about the final weeks of the ministry of Jesus powerfully reminds me that these Exercises are nearing the final weeks as well. Oddly, I have followed the instructions much more closely during this second effort doing the Exercises. I have prayed and reflected every single day since I began, writing primarily about what comes up for me on that day. My reflections often wander some distance from the scriptural passage, but they do so only because events of the day weigh sufficiently heavy on my mind to take my thoughts in various directions. I think it would be less than honest not to follow that wandering path.

The candor with which I have recorded my reflections over these seven months raises some serious questions as to what I will do with this journal. While true, much of what I have written will unnecessarily offend many of the politically conservative members of my parish. I am under no illusion with respect to changing anyone's political views, especially in the polarized environment of these times.

At times, I may have allowed my regrets about various behavior to inform descriptions containing too much openness. We often tell the new CRHP brothers and sisters to be rather discreet in telling their stories. CRHP witnesses, like Ignatian journals, are not intended as acts of reconciliation. This journal is not the appropriate place for my confession.

A short prayer was recommended at the beginning of this week, one intended as part of the preparation for each day's meditation.

> Lord Jesus Christ, Did I know how, I would break my heart with grief for You. Of all the people in the world, You should have suffered least. I am ashamed of what we did to You while You broke Your heart with grief for me.

Reading this through several times this morning, I could not help but remember the story of the Rabbi and young student discussing the nature of the human heart.

> God's Holy Words are placed on top of the heart, and there they stay until, one day, the heart breaks, and the words fall in.

During these final days in the life and ministry of Jesus Christ, He must have been torn inside out in painful turbulence. On one hand, He had come to know human love. He had friends throughout Israel. He knew how deeply some of them loved Him. On the other hand, He was the Son of God, clearly knowing that this earthly mission was about to end, even knowing why. I imagine moving stealthily through the streets of Jerusalem with Jesus, to a quiet dinner with His Apostles, to the home of good friends, where His head is anointed with beautiful ointment and a great deal of love. All this time, I know that He knew. It is presumptuous to suggest that "I felt His pain!" No, I felt only my pain, feeling sorry for myself as I contemplated His absence, and fear for myself as I considered the search that was certain to be mounted for anyone who knew Him. To the pain and fear, then, I added shame for my weakness and self-centeredness. I knelt in silence for several minutes before praying the Our Father.

CALENDAR WEEK TWENTY-SEVEN

I ask God for sorrow with Jesus sorrowing, anguish with Jesus in anguish, tears and deep grief because of the great affliction Jesus endures for me.

March 19

Matthew 27:1–2, 11–14
  Jesus Brought before Pilate
  ¹ When morning came, all the chief priests and the elders of the people conferred together against Jesus in order to bring about his death. ² They bound him, led him away, and handed him over to Pilate the governor.
  Pilate Questions Jesus
  ¹¹ Now Jesus stood before the governor; and the governor asked him, "Are you the King of the Jews?" Jesus said, "You say so." ¹² But when he was accused by the chief priests and elders, he did not answer. ¹³ Then Pilate said to him, "Do you not hear how many accusations they make against you?" ¹⁴ But he gave him no answer, not even to a single charge, so that the governor was greatly amazed.

EACH WEEK at Mass, we follow the homily by reciting, in unison with the Celebrant, the Nicene Creed.

> For our sake, he was crucified under Pontius Pilate,
> He suffered death and was buried.

As the Roman prefect, Pilate's responsibilities clearly included presiding over the trial of Jesus, and ordering the punishment. However, all four Gospels portray Pilate as very reluctant to convict Jesus for what seemed to be doctrinal disputes among the Jews, not "crimes against humanity." Pilate would not have crucified Jesus for His statements. Yet because Pilate offered so little resistance to the chief priests and elders, ultimately following custom by putting the question of death to the mob, he will be remembered forever in history for one thing, the crucifixion of Jesus Christ.

I fantasized being in the role of Pilate, attempting to conjure up some feelings of understanding and forgiveness. All that came up was disgust at Pilate's vacillating weakness, his effort to pretend the matter was really in the hands of others—the Jewish leaders, the screaming mob, even Jesus Himself. "My hands are tied" said Pilate, each time a modicum of courage could have righted the great injustice.

Reflecting on this, I considered the infinite number of daily decisions I have made on the basis of comfort, or least hassle. Doing the right thing has never exposed me to the possibility of real harm or danger, but it has often required that I exert a little effort, that I "suit up and show up." I have made a few right calls, and have been extraordinarily fortunate that there were so few consequences for my doing nothing or actually doing the wrong thing.

Lent is drawing to its inevitable end. In less than a month, the Third Ignatian Week will end with the crucifixion. Over these next almost four weeks, we will read and reflect about the tragic pretense of a trial that preceded the handing over of Jesus to the mob. What are the lessons from this painful story? On how many levels was the mission and ministry of Christ distorted and corrupted during these short weeks?

March 20

Repeat Matthew 27:1–2,11–14, Jesus Brought before Pilate

READING MATTHEW'S Gospel again this morning, I am struck with the curtness of the initial reply to Pilate, then His silence in response to the chief priests and elders. Eight verses, 3 through 10, at the beginning of Matthew 27 were omitted from the sequence assigned for today. Assuming that these verses described some of the beatings endured by Jesus throughout the so-called trial, I looked them up in my Bible. The omitted verses describe the suicide of Judas, including the use of the thirty pieces of silver to purchase a potter's field, a "place to bury foreigners."

While the self-hanging of Judas offers no clue as to why Jesus was sullen and silent in the face of His inquisitors, it did lead to a long reflection on the organization and style of much of the New Testament writing. Great importance was attached to events that fulfilled prophecies from the early Hebrew scriptures. "For it is written" is a very common phrase. Each time I read it, I immediately suspect that the events described in the New Testament that were vaguely similar to the earlier prediction were altered just a little (or possibly a great deal!) to fit that prophecy. While I understand the importance of "scriptural verification" to the early authors of the various books of the New Testament, it is virtually meaningless to me. That is to say, the fact that something occurring today was foretold at an earlier time does not make it more or less true. If it is true, it is true, whether foretold or not. So, it is probably a good thing that these verses are omitted from today's reading.

Why was Jesus so abrupt with Pilate? Why say or do anything to annoy the Roman governor? Thus far in the story, it is the Jewish religious and secular leadership that have been the target of Jesus's criticism. The only Roman we have met is the Centurion, who was actually quite likable. Unless, as I have surmised, Jesus was more active in the Jewish revolution than we are led to believe in the New Testament. There could be many very good reasons why His political resistance to the Roman occupation was minimized.

By the time Paul wrote his letters, and the Evangelists wrote the Gospels, the Jewish revolution was building to what would be a tragic ending. John's Gospel was written a generation after the temple was destroyed and the Jews were sent out of Israel by the Romans. During the decades prior to the outbreak of open revolt in 66 CE, Rome was led by three of its worst emperors, Caligula, Claudius, and Nero. Zealots had been active since the beginning of the Common Era; the year Jesus was born. In the years that the Synoptic Gospels were written, civil war was fomenting among Zealot factions, and between the Zealots and the Jews who supported the Roman occupation.

My point is simply that it was a dangerous time to live in Israel. The danger was greatest among those who were critical of the Jewish leadership. Whether Jesus was a Zealot or not, His activities certainly aroused suspicion. His large following must have been particularly alarming. When recording the events of Jesus's life, therefore, the Evangelists, writing from 50 to 70 CE, would have minimized any political activity. Paul wrote all of his letters in this same period, beginning with Thessalonians in 50 CE, and ending with 2 Timothy in 67 CE. While Paul wrote all of his letters from places far away from the civil war and revolution in Jerusalem and the Galilee, he would still have wanted to avoid attracting any additional anger from the Roman authorities. Reflecting on this, it seems logical to me that this would have especially been the case for Paul, who considered the Gentiles to be his primary audience.

March 21

Luke 23:5–12

⁵ But they were insistent and said, "He stirs up the people by teaching throughout all Judea, from Galilee where he began even to this place."

Jesus before Herod

⁶ When Pilate heard this, he asked whether the man was a Galilean. ⁷ And when he learned that he was under Herod's jurisdiction, he sent him off to Herod, who was himself in Jerusalem at that time. ⁸ When Herod saw Jesus, he was very glad, for he had been wanting to see him for a long time, because he had heard about him and was hoping to see him perform some sign. ⁹ He questioned him at some length, but Jesus gave him no answer. ¹⁰ The chief priests and the scribes stood by, vehemently accusing him. ¹¹ Even Herod with his soldiers treated him with contempt and mocked him; then he put an elegant robe on him, and sent him back to Pilate. ¹² That same day Herod and Pilate became friends with each other; before this they had been enemies.

WE DROVE FROM Jacksonville to Savannah yesterday to celebrate Sallie Ann's birthday with our friends. Good food, good company, good conversation, and much laughter! We both needed the break.

I read the passage from Luke, still pondering the strange events during the last week of Jesus's life. What an odd footnote to history that Pilate and Herod became friends the day that Jesus was passed back and forth like a hot potato! As the story unfolds in Luke, the political leadership, both Roman and Jewish, seems to enter the scene only at the very end. And then only because the chief priests and scribes brought Jesus to them, complaining that His religious message was a threat to the political establishment. As I understand the history, the Zealots had been active for two or three decades, increasing their resistance as the Roman need for greater tax revenue was spreading throughout the empire. Tiberius, the emperor from 14 to 37 CE, began his reign as a relatively benign despot, strengthening the empire militarily and financially. However, Tiberius left Rome in 27 CE for Capri, and never returned. During the last decade of his life, which overlapped the active ministry of Jesus Christ, Tiberius ruled the empire from self-imposed exile in Capri, becoming increasingly cruel and disordered.

What has this to do with Pilate, or Roman rule in Israel? The year that Jesus began His ministry, Caligula was a teenage boy, whose family had been destroyed by Emperor Tiberius. Nonetheless, Tiberius invited Caligula to live with him in Capri, where the mad Tiberius, referring to Caligula, "nursed a viper for the people of Rome." Pilate was made prefect of Judaea by Tiberius in 26 CE, serving most of his prefecture while Tiberius and Caligula, described by historians as an "insane pervert," lived together in Capri. Who knows how the empire reflected the descent of Tiberius into his mental incapacity, or the growing power of the already mad Caligula as the heir apparent. Was Judaea so far removed from Rome that the imperial cruelty never reached the military and political forces governing Jesus and His followers?

The historian Tacitus described the period from 30 to 33 CE as a deflationary period in Rome, building slowly to a complete financial panic in 33 CE. Oddly, a significant part of the problem was a dwindling money supply. The imperial treasury was growing, even though taxes were low. In the absence of any financial stimulus, real estate lost value, putting real estate borrowing into default.

I can imagine this collapse of the credit system reaching far out into the empire, certainly to Israel. Tax collectors under the *publican* system were allowed to collect more in tax revenue than they were required to remit to Rome. Many tax collectors were also money lenders, particularly as they became increasingly wealthy through this "tax royalty." The history of the Zealots in Israel suggests that resentment of the Roman system of tax collection was a major reason for the revolution. Could there have been events associated with the Financial Panic of 33 CE that put pressure on Pilate, which in some way effected the trial and execution of Jesus? If this was the case, it has not become a part of the accepted history of the period. My own sense is that the Jewish Revolt and the role of the Zealots had more to do with pressure on the Evangelists than on the actual events in the life and ministry of Jesus Christ.

I ended my reflection today feeling as though I have been chasing a rabbit down and through a variety of strange rabbit holes. Jesus lived, taught, and preached His Gospel during a difficult period in the history of the Roman world. Israel was a particularly grim part of the empire due to the growing power of the Zealots, leading eventually to the Jewish Revolt and its disastrous failure in 70 CE. It is especially remarkable that the upside-down Gospel of Jesus Christ could survive these troubled times. It did survive, however, and, more than that, changed the world.

March 22

Repeat Luke 23:5–12

THE WEATHER turned cold and wet overnight, ending a wonderful spring-like period. The bench and garden were not inviting. I sat in the library and focused on how Jesus must be feeling during this bizarre trial. Our faith teaches us that Jesus was both human and divine. His divine self knew that the trial and crucifixion would be awful, but that He would rise again in glory. In a sense, I suppose He was smiling at His executioners.

His human self must have been in great misery. Not only was the treatment from His enemies indescribably vicious and painful, but He suffered the deeper pain of abandonment and denial by His friends and disciples. All that His divine self could say to His human self was, "Trust me, be not afraid, have faith."

As I reflect on that this morning, it occurs to me how much each of us is like Christ. We are human, but have in us the spark of the divine. When we listen to the quiet whispering of that divine spark, we are told to trust, have faith, and not be afraid. Our human selves struggle with this advice. Most of the time, when we think about the insignificance of our lives, the plight of the world, and the prospect of growing old and dying, we are afraid! We have little trust in the ultimate victory of God in His constant battle with sin and despair. Faith eludes us.

Like Christ, we are left with a simple set of tools, and few instructions. Love God, love each other, pray, and serve. Get out of self. Surrender to win.

This week has thus far been a blur. I returned from the Dominican Republic on Friday, very much in the pink cloud of mission service, tired enough to want to sleep for days. Tennis and a St. Patrick's celebration in the cultural center on Saturday. Dan and Jill Scheuble brought their adopted son Christopher to the church to be baptized on Sunday, after which we joined our regular group for Lectio Divina. Monday brought an Ability Housing meeting and the All Hands Meeting of Sister Parish. Then Savannah for Sallie Ann's birthday. I am still in the blur this morning. I pray for peace, clarity, and judgement.

March 23

Matthew 27:15–26, Barabbas or Jesus?

¹⁵ Now at the festival the governor was accustomed to release a prisoner for the crowd, anyone whom they wanted. ¹⁶ At that time they had a notorious prisoner, called Jesus Barabbas. ¹⁷ So after they had gathered, Pilate said to them, "Whom do you want me to release for you, Jesus Barabbas or Jesus who is called the Messiah?" ¹⁸ For he realized that it was out of jealousy that they had handed him over. ¹⁹ While he was sitting on the judgment seat, his wife sent word to him, "Have nothing to do with that innocent man, for today I have suffered a great deal because of a dream about him." ²⁰ Now the chief priests and the elders persuaded the crowds to ask for Barabbas and to have Jesus killed. ²¹ The governor again said to them, "Which of the two do you want me to release for you?" And they said, "Barabbas." ²² Pilate said to them, "Then what should I do with Jesus who is called the Messiah?" All of them said, "Let him be crucified!" ²³ Then he asked, "Why, what evil has he done?" But they shouted all the more, "Let him be crucified!"

Pilate Hands Jesus over to Be Crucified

²⁴ So when Pilate saw that he could do nothing, but rather that a riot was beginning, he took some water and washed his hands before the crowd, saying, "I am innocent of this man's blood; see to it yourselves." ²⁵ Then the people as a whole answered, "His blood be on us and on our children!" ²⁶ So he released Barabbas for them; and after flogging Jesus, he handed him over to be crucified.

Several days ago, I wondered how the Jerusalem crowd could turn so quickly from love to hate, from adulation to condemnation. It then occurred to me that there must have been two quite separate crowds, the "seekers," who traveled to hear and worship Jesus, and the "ruffians," who regularly followed the executions. Reading Matthew's account of the crowd choosing Barabbas deepens my conviction that the crowd Pilate was addressing was not the same crowd that listened to the great sermons and saw the miracles and signs. This crowd delighted in the perversity of choosing to kill an itinerant preacher, rather than a "notorious prisoner."

I am also struck by the casual gesture of washing one's hands of an obvious injustice. I think of this concept as one used when the person "washing his hands" of an action is not in a position to change the outcome. It means "I am not in control," not just, "I will not be blamed." Pilate could easily have ignored the crowd. The troops were his troops. He has no choice but to accept the blame.

March 24

Repeat Matthew 27:15–26, Barabbas or Jesus?

Our good friends, the Kaplan family, are house guests this weekend. Serendipity feels like a resort hotel, with some guests golfing, some going to the pool at the club, and others reading in the pavilion. It is a nice feeling. I spent the day reading what I have written in this journal for the past two months. The US House of Representatives considered the repeal of Obamacare, finally pulling the bill due to a lack of a majority of Republicans in support. It was a major defeat for Trump and Ryan, and a major defeat of my Lenten commitment to avoid all television news!

March 25

Repeat and reflect on the week

This has been a good week for the Exercises. The week began with Pilate saying his hands were tied, then ended when he washed his hands, attempting to rid himself of all complicity in the trial and death of Jesus. The second did not work because the first was not true. Pilate's hands could not have been tied by anyone in Judaea. He reported directly, and only, to Rome. His soldiers exercised total and complete control over Judaea. Twenty-five years later, after losing some initial skirmishes in the Galilee and Jerusalem, the Roman armies destroyed the temple and drove the Jews out of Israel.

I wasted a day this week, exploring the goings on in Rome at the time of the trial, in an effort to determine what, if any, impact they might have on Pilate's actions. By the time of the trial, Tiberius had sunk into a deep depression, isolating himself in Capri and largely ignoring the empire. Caligula, his adopted son and a future emperor, was living with him in Capri, beginning his own descent into a form of madness. From what I could learn, the prefects throughout the empire were left pretty much to their own devices, particularly regarding local conflicts.

The Jews were not under the threat of increasing taxes during the ministry of Jesus. Tiberius created a deflationary economy by not allowing the money supply to grow with the needs of the Empire, leading to a Financial Panic in 33 CE. However, there is no evidence that the fiscal difficulties in Rome had any effect out in the far reaches of the Empire.

The historical pressure experienced by Jesus and His movement was the discontent among the Jews under the occupation by the Romans. The Zealots, a dissident group advocating open rebellion, came into existence about the time of the birth of Jesus, and slowly grew in power over the next half century. There were certainly revolutionary stirrings in Jerusalem and along the Jordan River valley all the way up to the area north of the Galilee. I do believe some of the opposition to Jesus was His identification with the Zealots and their cause. It continues to be difficult for me to accept that the chief priests, scribes, and Roman political authorities would have been that bothered by a purely religious movement.

Nonetheless, the leaders were annoyed to the point of bribing Judas to betray Jesus, arresting Jesus for treason, bringing him before the Jewish courts and, ultimately, before the Romans. I have felt sorrow as I contemplate how Jesus must have felt, how alone He was during the trials, and how painful it had to be to see His closest disciples abandon Him.

What must Barabbas have thought? He was a revolutionary, a convicted rebel. He was not the kind of person who would have walked to Mount Hermon to listen to Jesus teach. He must have known that one day he would be captured and killed for his violent protests of the occupation. Even the crowd knew Barabbas. How shocked he must have been to hear them shout his name when Pilate asked who should be released.

I sat with these questions about Barabbas this morning, then walked outside in the warmth of an unseasonably nice day. What would I have felt if, obviously guilty, I was suddenly acquitted by a raucous crowd for what appeared to be no reason at all? Afterward, would I have learned more about this man who was crucified in my place? Would I have become a follower?

Probably not. I would probably have returned to my small group of rebellious Zealots, continuing to fight the Jewish puppets and their Roman puppeteers. Still, somewhere in the back of my mind, I would wonder about, and be grateful to, this teacher Jesus Christ.

CALENDAR WEEK TWENTY-EIGHT

I ask God for sorrow with Jesus sorrowing, anguish with Jesus in anguish, tears and deep grief because of the great affliction Jesus endures for me.

Lord Jesus Christ, Did I know how, I would break my heart with grief for You. Of all the people in the world, You should have suffered least. I am ashamed of what we did to You while You broke Your heart with grief for me.

March 26

Matthew 27:26–32
   ²⁶ So he released Barabbas for them; and after flogging Jesus, he handed him over to be crucified.
   The Soldiers Mock Jesus
   ²⁷ Then the soldiers of the governor took Jesus into the governor's headquarters, and they gathered the whole cohort around him. ²⁸ They stripped him and put a scarlet robe on him, ²⁹ and after twisting some thorns into a crown, they put it on his head. They put a reed in his right hand and knelt before him and mocked him, saying, "Hail, King of the Jews!" ³⁰ They spat on him, and took the reed and struck him on the head. ³¹ After mocking him, they stripped him of the robe and put his own clothes on him. Then they led him away to crucify him.
   The Crucifixion of Jesus
   ³² As they went out, they came upon a man from Cyrene named Simon; they compelled this man to carry his cross.

I WENT TO the early Mass (7:30) this morning. It has become an incredibly beautiful day, with clear skies, moderate temperature, and an extraordinary amount of God's creation parading in the air and the lagoon in celebration. Maggie and I joined them for several hours.

Reading through the passage from Matthew's Gospel, I am struck by the first line, which states that Pilate flogged Jesus before handing Him over to be crucified. How can Pilate "wash his hands" of this crime, then flog the man he presumably considers innocent? Then Pilate's soldiers stripped Jesus, put a crown of thorns on His head, and mocked Him. The whole saga of the arrest and trial would make me a revolutionary, even if I had only been a religious seeker.

Simon of Cyrene had an interesting role in history, forced to carry the cross of Jesus up the hill to Golgatha. Cyrene was part of what is Libya today, a North African province of the Roman Empire. Some historians speculate that Simon was black, or of mixed race. The fact that the soldiers "compelled" him to carry the cross may be the reason. I wonder about this speculation. What difference would it make if Simon were black, mixed race, or white? By carrying the cross, Simon performed a great service to Jesus, doing so at a time when none of the disciples seem to be around to help. I would be proud to call Simon my brother.

Our prayer for this week begins with the statement, "Lord Jesus Christ, did I know how, I would break my heart with grief for You." That certainly expresses my feelings as I sit in this paradise called Serendipity. There was no justice at this trial, nor judgement from these judges. It was all a mockery. I read from John Caputo these lines about justice.

   The name of God is the name of justice, and justice is not a thought but a deed, and its truth
   is attained only in doing the truth, in making justice happen in truth.

After meditating on the passage from Matthew's Gospel, these words from Caputo, as beautiful as they are, ring hollow. My heart aches for Jesus. No truth was done on that day so long ago.

March 27

Repeat Matthew 27:26–32

MAGGIE AND I came down very early this morning, walking out into an unseasonably warm morning under a very clear sky. I tried without success to identify the stars, which were so bright they seemed to light the garden. The waves breaking on the beach were particularly loud, drowning out the sound of the fountains. As usual, Maggie searched for lizards as I prayed on the bench.

Reflecting on the passages from Matthew's Gospel leaves me deep in sorrow. The story of Jesus's trial, persecution, and death is one that I have known all my life, yet it continues to shock me. In fact, the depth of sorrow that I feel today is much greater than ever before. I have read each passage more carefully, and more often. I have allowed the words to mature in my thoughts, forcing me to better understand their full implication. The only solace comes from my knowledge that Easter is less than two weeks away. I know how the story ends.

Rumi captures this hopeful thought very well.

> Sorrow prepares you for joy. It violently sweeps everything out of your house, so that new joy can find space to enter. It shakes the yellow leaves from the bough of your heart, so that fresh, green leaves can grow in their place. It pulls up the rotten roots, so that new roots hidden beneath have room to grow. Whatever sorrow shakes from your heart, far better things will take their place.

The painful absurdity of such an unjust and unwarranted death is preparation for the resurrection. Joy will out in the end.

March 28

Matthew 27:33–38

³³ And when they came to a place called Golgotha (which means Place of a Skull), ³⁴ they offered him wine to drink, mixed with gall; but when he tasted it, he would not drink it. ³⁵ And when they had crucified him, they divided his clothes among themselves by casting lots; ³⁶ then they sat down there and kept watch over him. ³⁷ Over his head they put the charge against him, which read, "This is Jesus, the King of the Jews."

³⁸ Then two bandits were crucified with him, one on his right and one on his left.

THEN IT WAS done. Verse 35 states "they had crucified him" almost casually, like an afterthought. My anguish in anticipation of the event requires more than this.

I fantasized being at that place called Golgotha. The soldiers stripped Jesus of his clothes, exposing the bruises and lacerations from His multiple beatings. I saw them mix the bitter gall with their wine, then offer the foul drink to Jesus. I watched them nail Jesus's hands and feet to the cross. I watched them tilt the cross up so that it fell into the hole they had dug. The soldiers were hot and sweating, obviously exhausted from the hateful effort.

The crucifixion was not casual. It was nothing like an afterthought. It took time and hard work. Every second of the process was painful for me to watch, even in a fantasy. It was excruciatingly painful for Jesus to experience. The sorrow I felt after living through the farce of a trial was nothing like the grief produced by the crucifixion itself.

How could Pilate and his soldiers do such odious things? Part of the answer is simply that they were the dominant power. Dominance breeds a strange kind of morality (or absence of morality). Might makes right. They did it because they could.

The Greek historian Thucydides famously stated that "right, as the world goes, is only in question between equals in power, while the strong do what they can and the weak suffer what they must." *The strong do what they can and the weak suffer what they must.* What the strong can do when they are dominant is simply anything they want to do!

Plato states this a little differently, saying that "justice is nothing else than the interest of the stronger." The only thing that matters in determining what is a just act is the relative power of the one performing the act. Everything else is conversation. It I can do it, it is right. My ability to do it, my strength relative to others, these are the only tests of right and wrong.

Dominance has not been good for Christianity. Much of the message of Jesus was lost when Constantine made Christianity the state religion. Caroline W. Casey's Coyote Network Radio Show is dedicated to a powerfully simple concept:

> Let a willingness to cooperate with everything emerge from the smoldering ruins of dominance.

I love that. Our world is slowly falling into ruin at the hands of one dominant power system after another. We will only emerge from those ruins together. Survival requires cooperation. This is my prayer for today.

March 29

Repeat Matthew 27:33–38

It was still very dark when we walked down to the bench. I was struck by how different the sounds seem to be in the darkness. Perhaps it is because there are so few sources of sound that early in the morning. When the sky lightens, more and different birds come out, someone begins to operate a piece of equipment on the golf course, and the distant sounds of cars on A1A begin to compete with the ocean.

James Finley, my friend and teacher, began his reflections on Meister Eckhart with a description of a mystic. A mystic, he said, is an ordinary man or woman who has been transformed by an experience, or series of experiences, into a *habitual state of non-dual consciousness of the unitive oneness of God and all of God's creation.* A mystic habitually appreciates that the presence we call God is infinitely giving itself away as the very presence of creation, including the very immediacy of ourselves. The norm of this mystical consciousness is love. And its goal is to habitually live by faith, manifested as love, and filled with hope.

Finley refers to those of us who occasionally experience this state of unitive consciousness as *momentary mystics.* I consider myself to be a momentary mystic for two reasons. First, I am determined to someday truly understand what Finley means in his definition of a mystic! And, second, because I occasionally, not habitually, experience the indescribable joy of that transformed state of unitive consciousness.

I listened to Finley teach about Meister Eckhart while I was walking yesterday. As a "momentary mystic," I listened attentively this morning for changes in the sound of God's creation, and looked more carefully at the brightening sky for a glimpse of unitive oneness. It was a truly beautiful morning, but, alas, I experienced no transformation.

While reflecting on the passage from Matthew's Gospel, I tried to understand the crucifixion through the non-dual lens of a mystic, conscious of oneness with God. Finley says "we are not God, but we are not other than God." This is non-dual thinking. Being one with Christ is a concept I embrace enthusiastically in the abstract. How can I be one with Him in His trial, persecution, and crucifixion?

These events all happened in time, in the same eternity in which I am now writing this journal. Golgatha is an actual place in the same infinity in which the library I am now sitting is a place. In the enormously large sense of time and space represented by eternity and infinity, unitive oneness is theoretically possible. I was present in the same space and time as all the rest of the universe at the moment of the Big Bang, and, with all the rest of the universe, I have been present ever since. Christ was there as well. We were clearly one at the point creation began. Teilhard taught that the goal of the Christ Project is unitive consciousness, in effect, a re-uniting of all that was united at the beginning.

The first year of the Living School includes a one-week gathering in Albuquerque, consisting of about twenty students and Father Rohr. The students in each "small group intensive" establish bonds of friendship that, in most cases, have lasted since we met, more than five years ago. Our small group, called the Double Pancakes, meets each year in Rome, Georgia, for a reunion retreat. Matt Mumber, an oncological radiologist and member of our group, built Many Streams Ranch, a retreat center for cancer survivors located in the beautiful hills outside of Rome. The name Double Pancakes comes from the story about the first pancake being a sacrifice to the fire. The Living School class of 2013 was the inaugural class of the Living School, and our small group intensive was the first small group to meet as part of the Living School program. We are meeting at Matt's retreat ranch for the third year in a row this coming weekend.

For most of the last year, Matt and Evan Miller, a Mennonite spiritual advisor and another one of our small group members, have been going through Jim Finley's teaching on Contemplative Healing. I often read Matt's postings to the group, invariably finding his prayers to be especially inspirational. Matt recently attempted to work through the logic of Finley's teaching on self-giving love, infinity, and eternity. He ended that reflection thusly:

> … [T]he mystic realizes God giving God-self away as everything, including our personal self.
> … and that this unity has infinitely existed and will infinitely exist.
> … and that the word God—no matter how we utter it, is both the representation of the deep being of God
> … and the action of God in this present moment … giving away, foundational existence
> … .and both being and action simultaneously …
> maybe these form … a pattern, with new emergence being the present moment kingdom of heaven? sitting with this and asking for the mystery to get me—to be eternally understood …

Matt, an emerging mystic himself, makes the confusion of Finley a little more confusing, but does so in a beautiful way. I will end my morning, sitting with these thoughts as I contemplate the last day in the life of Christ.

March 30

Matthew 27:39–47

39 Those who passed by derided him, shaking their heads 40 and saying, "You who would destroy the temple and build it in three days, save yourself! If you are the Son of God, come down from the cross." 41 In the same way the chief priests also, along with the scribes and elders, were mocking him, saying, 42 "He saved others; he cannot save himself. He is the King of Israel; let him come down from the cross now, and we will believe in him. 43 He trusts in God; let God deliver him now, if he wants to; for he said, 'I am God's Son.'" 44 The bandits who were crucified with him also taunted him in the same way.

The Death of Jesus

45 From noon on, darkness came over the whole land until three in the afternoon. 46 And about three o'clock Jesus cried with a loud voice, "Eli, Eli, lema sabachthani?" that is, "My God, my God, why have you forsaken me?" 47 When some of the bystanders heard it, they said, "This man is calling for Elijah."

A FEW DAYS ago, when reflecting on the rapid change in the mood of the crowd following Jesus, from adoration to revulsion, I reached what seemed like an excellent understanding. The adoring crowd was simply a different group of people from the crowd that reviled Him. However, Matthew writes in today's passage that chief priests, scribes, and elders were among those "passing by" Christ on the cross. If this is so, then either my tidy solution to the crowd dilemma was wrong, or the bad crowd, the crowd that regularly followed mock trials and executions, included chief priests, scribes, and elders.

Sadly, I think my initial understanding is correct. I think that the corruption of dominance among the Jewish elite, particularly those friendly in any way with the occupation forces from Rome, was complete. Revolutionaries and Zealots were most often the targets of the trials and executions. It is likely that the chief priests and scribes would have come out to watch these political rebels die, if for no other reason, to prove that they, the Jewish elite, were not opposed to the Romans.

For this same reason, I can imagine the Pharisees leading the chorus of mockery, taunting Jesus, even as He was dying.

> He trusts in God; let God deliver him now, if he wants to; for he said, "I am God's Son."

Luke describes this scene with one significant difference, which is that only one of the two "bandits" taunted Jesus. The second criminal rebuked the first. Luke 23:40–43:

> But the other rebuked him, saying, "Do you not fear God, since you are under the same sentence of condemnation? And we indeed have been condemned justly, for we are getting what we deserve for our deeds, but this man has done nothing wrong." Then he said, "Jesus, remember me when you come into your kingdom." He replied, "Truly I tell you, today you will be with me in Paradise."

I put myself in the position of the "good bandit," fantasizing about the final twenty-four hours in Jesus's life. This prayer from Matt Mumber spoke to me in my fantasy.

> God, grant me the courage to trust that you are real, to listen to you and to feel you as you come to me in my life; and that the deepest part of me is you. Grant me the humility to align with you in all things, in every moment of life. Grant me the stamina to live with the unknown.

Matt is constantly challenging us to *align ourselves with God "in all things, in every moment in life."* That alignment requires a vast amount of courage, humility, and stamina.

March 31

Repeat Matthew 27:39–47

AT PRECISELY 3 p.m. on Good Friday, Christians all around the world pause to remember the moment Jesus died. For me, now in my converted state as a believing Catholic, the deep sadness of this moment is not lessened by the knowledge that the story ends differently. The Exercises have had an enormous impact on my experience of the Passion of Christ, this period from His entry into Jerusalem for the last time until His death on Good Friday. Each day involves another huge event in His life, and each of these events has become an important part of Christian worship: The Sanhedrin council, the cleansing of the temple, the anointment of Jesus, the Last Supper, the washing of the feet, the betrayal by Judas Iscariot, the denial by Peter, all followed by the arrest, trial, and, finally, the crucifixion of Jesus Christ.

It is actually quite simple. For the past several weeks, the guide to the Exercises has presented a passage from scripture describing one of these events, then asked that we reflect on that event for two days. Sometimes, the same event is presented again from the viewpoint of another of the Gospels. This has given me time to sit with Jesus and His disciples for several hours, often several days, reflecting on each event. I am saddened by the initial reading, but deepen the sadness a great deal by fantasizing about being a part of the event, engaging in conversation with other eyewitnesses. It is no surprise that I have been moved.

A group of us at our parish will perform a reenactment of the Stations of the Cross on Good Friday evening, two weeks from now. This will be our third year together. I feel somewhat odd today, reflecting for a second day on the death of Christ. At the same time, I am attempting, again, to memorize my lines as Caiaphas. It is a little discombobulating.

Today I will fly to Atlanta, then drive from there to Rome for the Double Pancake retreat. The men and women in this small group are some of the most spiritually enlightened people I have ever known. We will meet this afternoon at Many Streams Ranch. I will end the morning with anther prayer from Matt Mumber.

> Guide me to sincerely sit with you in silence, O God, such that my right hand does not know what my left hand is doing…

I am excited about seeing my friends. I am excited about sharing my faith in a group around whom I can be completely honest. I am excited about hearing their stories and knowing their truth.

April 1

Repeat and reflect on the week.

THE EXERCISE goal we have been given for the past two weeks has been the same,

> I ask God for sorrow with Jesus sorrowing, anguish with Jesus in anguish, tears and deep
> grief because of the great affliction Jesus endures for me.

William Faulkner famously said, "Given the choice between the experience of pain and nothing, I would choose pain." I suppose I am with Faulkner on this, but I have to be honest about my own experience. The anguish I have felt reading and reflecting on the trial and crucifixion of Jesus has been close to unbearable. The wonderful weather, the beauty of the garden, the joy of sharing my mornings with Maggie—all of these are overwhelmed by the grief of what Jesus endured. Why did this have to happen? 1 Corinthians 1:18:

> For the message about the cross is foolishness to those who are perishing, but to us who are
> being saved it is the power of God.

What was that message? Reflecting on this, it seems clear that different people heard different messages. Pilate, in spite of his vacillating behavior, must have seen the cross as a place where an innocent man had died. The Jewish priests, the Pharisees, and the Sadducees considered the cross as the way to eliminate a radical rabbi, who had challenged their authority. The political authorities saw the cross as the way one more political revolutionary was removed.

Mary must have been devastated, viewing the cross as the place where the Son of God died an undeserved death. The disciples lost a beloved friend on the cross. Their dreams of a new King of the Jews died on the cross as well.

My own understanding continues to evolve. I believe the *life* of Jesus provided a far more powerful message than His death. Serve the poor, feed the hungry, house the homeless, free the prisoner, and, in every conceivable way, care for those at the margins of life. Love trumps hate. Allow the wholeness of love to turn the world upside-down, a new life in Christ where the first will be last and the last will be first.

The upside-down Gospel might someday radically change the world. Even after more than two thousand years, however, the change is hardly complete. Some days, it feels as though it has not even begun. For most of that period, Christianity enjoyed (or suffered from) the immense power of the state.

I am sitting in my room at Many Streams Ranch, the retreat ranch outside Rome, Georgia, built by Matt Mumber and his wife fifteen years ago. Its purpose is to house retreats for cancer survivors, presumably those who had received treatment from Matt. Our retreat began last night in a powerful evening of reflection. Each of us named that part of our mask, our false self, that we would most like to discard. In my experience, much of the Living School teaching begins in a deep shadow of difficult concepts presented in dense passages from medieval scholars and mystics. I need light, not just to see what is written, but, more important, to understand the concepts. It is now clear to me that our love for each other in this small group of seekers is the source of that light.

Matt often reaches the place of understanding ahead of the rest of us, then invites us to sit with him in silence until we finally see. The group seems to be a perfect combination of very disparate talents, each person interjecting his or her special gift at precisely the right moment. I read this line about poetry from Adrienne Rich on the plane yesterday.

> Poetry can break open locked chambers of possibility, restore numbed zones to feeling, recharge desire…

We, the Double Pancakes, are engaged in a poetic dance of discovery. Together, we "open locked chambers of possibility and restore numbed zones to feeling." I will end this morning with another of Matt's asking prayers:

> Grant me the gift of being with my actions and reactions with a merciful nonjudgmental awareness, such that I may participate in the experience of life as un-manifested God manifesting itself.

We said goodnight to each other after sitting around a beautiful fire in the outside fireplace for three hours. We agreed to greet each other in the future with a variation of the Jesus *mudra* and the words, "What hump?" In the Mel Brooks movie, *The Young Frankenstein*, Igor responded to Dr. Frankenstein's offer of help with his hump back with "What hump?" Bill Ulweiling caused us to laugh uncontrollably by suggesting that we are occasionally so deluded that we believe our weaknesses or "masks" are invisible. It was one of those funny things about which it is later said, "You had to be there!"

CALENDAR WEEK TWENTY-NINE

April 2

Luke 23:33–43

³³ When they came to the place that is called The Skull, they crucified Jesus there with the criminals, one on his right and one on his left. [[³⁴ Then Jesus said, "Father, forgive them; for they do not know what they are doing."]] And they cast lots to divide his clothing. ³⁵ And the people stood by, watching; but the leaders scoffed at him, saying, "He saved others; let him save himself if he is the Messiah of God, his chosen one!" ³⁶ The soldiers also mocked him, coming up and offering him sour wine, ³⁷ and saying, "If you are the King of the Jews, save yourself!" ³⁸ There was also an inscription over him, "This is the King of the Jews."

³⁹ One of the criminals who were hanged there kept deriding him and saying, "Are you not the Messiah? Save yourself and us!" ⁴⁰ But the other rebuked him, saying, "Do you not fear God, since you are under the same sentence of condemnation? ⁴¹ And we indeed have been condemned justly, for we are getting what we deserve for our deeds, but this man has done nothing wrong." ⁴² Then he said, "Jesus, remember me when you come into your kingdom." ⁴³ He replied, "Truly I tell you, today you will be with me in Paradise."

THE DOUBLE Pancake retreat ended this morning, after another incredible conversation over another meal, this time discussing next year's reunion at breakfast. I often think to myself when these retreats end that I wish they could go on forever. In fact, however, part of what makes them so special is their brevity. We emptied ourselves honestly and completely from 5 p.m. on Friday afternoon until 9 a.m. Sunday morning, virtually non-stop. While I cannot speak for the others, I know that I slept both nights with the questions and conversations running through my mind. It is simply a wonderful experience with an amazing group of friends. What hump? Indeed.

I read the passage from Luke this morning, struggling to stay awake on the plane flying from Atlanta back to Jacksonville. It is Luke's version of the events described by Matthew in the readings last week. The Evangelist writing Luke's Gospel includes the famous statement by Jesus, "Father, forgive them; for they do not know what they are doing." Today I wondered just exactly to whom Jesus was referring when He uttered these well-known words.

Clearly, Jesus asked that His father forgive the soldiers driving the nails into His hands and feet. Presumably, He also asked that the Jewish religious leaders who ordered the crucifixion be forgiven. I read from a blog by an evangelical Christian that Jesus was also asking that God forgive mankind. The concept of substitutionary atonement is based on the belief that it is the sin of mankind that requires this sacrifice. Absent these sins of us humans, Jesus would not have had to die such a brutal death. I have already made it clear that I am not persuaded by the arguments for substitutionary atonement.

Jesus preached a Gospel of inclusion and forgiveness. His life, at least during the years of His ministry, was all about reaching out to the forgotten "other," truly loving our enemies. Reflecting on these final words of Jesus on the cross, I am deeply moved by the uncomplicated, straight forward understanding of His ultimate wish. Father, forgive them. He could have stopped there, without adding that the deeds were forgivable because the perpetrators did not know what they were doing. Forgiveness stands alone, without any need for qualifiers.

Sitting with the warm feelings of our little band very fresh in my mind, I found another prayer from Matt.

God, grant me the vision to see myself the way that you see me, and the courage to understand what is holding me back from living my life aligned with that beauty.

Christ sees me as a beautiful person. That alone is a powerful thought. Aligning myself with His vision of me is a commanding challenge. First, I have to see myself the way He sees me, something I can only achieve with His grant of a very special grace. And then I have to live the kind of life a beautiful person lives. What hump?

April 3

Repeat Luke 23:33–43

³⁹ One of the criminals who were hanged there kept deriding him and saying, "Are you not the Messiah? Save yourself and us!" ⁴⁰ But the other rebuked him, saying, "Do you not fear God, since you are under the same sentence of condemnation? ⁴¹ And we indeed have been condemned justly, for we are getting what we deserve for our deeds, but this man has done nothing wrong." ⁴² Then he said, "Jesus, remember me when you come into your kingdom." ⁴³ He replied, "Truly I tell you, today you will be with me in Paradise."

We came downstairs to sit in the garden under cloudy skies this morning. While the birds are out, it feels like all of creation is waiting for rain. I love the smell of the waiting air.

I read verses 39 to 43 of Luke 23 again and again. "Jesus, remember me when you come into your kingdom." Jesus replied, "Truly I tell you, today you will be with me in Paradise."

The criminal on the other side of Jesus had just mocked Jesus, saying, in effect, if you are so great, get us down from these crosses here and now. On the other hand, this criminal seems to have accepted the fact that he was about to die. He did not ask to be saved from death. Instead, having accepted that Jesus was the king of the Jews, this criminal asks to be remembered by Jesus when He comes into His kingdom.

Was the criminal referring to death? The answer to this seemingly simple question requires an understanding of Jewish views of life after death.

Jewish teaching on the afterlife changed during the so-called Second Temple period, which began with the end of the Babylonian exile in 515 BCE. While in Babylon, the Jews were exposed to Zoroastrianism, a Persian religion which may be as old as 1,500 BCE, but became the dominant religion in Persia in 600 BCE.

Three key elements of the religion seem to have been absorbed into Judaism during the exile in Babylon: Resurrection, Heaven, and Hell. These concepts are only found in the book of Daniel in the Hebrew Scriptures, which is said to have been written during the Babylonian Captivity, in the first half of the sixth century BCE. Daniel 12:1–3 is clear:

At that time Michael, the great prince, the protector of your people, shall arise. There shall be a time of anguish, such as has never occurred since nations first came into existence. But at that time your people shall be delivered, everyone who is found written in the book. Many of those who sleep in the dust of the earth shall awake, some to everlasting life, and some to shame and everlasting contempt. Those who are wise shall shine like the brightness of the sky, and those who lead many to righteousness, like the stars forever and ever.

These concepts were strongly supported by the Pharisees, whose very name was apparently derived from *parsi*, the name (and language) of the Persians. Sadducees, on the other hand, just as strongly held to the traditional Jewish beliefs that there was no afterlife, no Heaven, no Hell, and no Resurrection.

Both mainstream Jewish and Greek teaching about an afterlife conceived some shadowy place (Sheol for the Jews, Hades for the Greeks) where everyone went when they died. There was no distinction between good and bad, no place for reward or punishment. Neither Sheol or Hades was a desirable place, so death was to be delayed or avoided as long as possible. There was no resurrection or time of final judgement.

One rather odd footnote to my reflection on the meaning of this passage is my brief encounter with the Parsi faith, which is modern-day Zoroastrianism. While they are few in number, Parsis today live for the most part in Mumbai and Karachi. They are incredibly successful in business and finance, counting among their members the Tata and Mistry families in India. The Tata Group became well known in the west when they acquired the Jaguar and Land Rover automobile companies. I came into contact with them through Tata Power, the largest integrated electric power company in India, and one of the largest in the world. I did business with both Tata Power in India, and a smaller parsi family in Pakistan.

In the passage from Luke, the criminal asked to be remembered by Jesus when He comes into His kingdom. Frankly, I seriously doubt whether a common criminal in 33 CE would have known the subtleties of the Jewish faith, much less the variations introduced through Zoroastrianism. However, the Synoptic Gospels were probably written from around 60 CE to 70 CE, about the time of the tragic end to the Jewish Revolt. Paul, who wrote from 50 CE to 67 CE, had been a Pharisee. It seems only natural that Paul would have incorporated his understanding of life after death, Heaven, Hell, and Resurrection into his letters. The same understanding was clearly part of the early Christian teaching as described in the Gospels.

Jesus responded to the criminal's wish to be remembered with the suggestion that they would both be in a different place soon, which was a place called Paradise. Paradise, like the Garden of Eden, was a place (or state or condition) of delight, a place where everything is just, fair, and whole. This is certainly not Sheol. Nor was it Hell. Was Jesus suggesting that whatever crimes the criminal had committed would be forgiven, and he would join Jesus in this place of fairness and justice, presumably Heaven?

In my fantasy this morning, I put myself in the place of the criminal. My death is at hand. While I may not have known much about this man on the cross next to mine, I have witnessed enough just today to convince me that He is very special. Whether His kingdom is a physical place somewhere in the universe, or a state of mind, it is clear to me that I would rather be there than elsewhere. At a minimum, I want this prophet to remember me.

As I sit with this, I bring the Gospel story into my present understanding and belief. I want to be remembered by Christ. I want to be with Him in His kingdom, which I believe is a state of consciousness. I believe this state of oneness with Christ can be achieved in my life today, in this library. And I believe it is a wonderful place of fairness and justice.

I walked back down to the bench, stopping several times along the rill. Muslims believe rills like this, ribbons of water, will lead us to Paradise when we die. I prayed as I paused, seeking that paradise-like state of quiet and serenity. In my fantasy, not surprisingly, the rill, the garden on either side of the rill, the fountain from which the water flowed, and the pool at the end of the rill were all filled with my friends from the Double Pancake reunion. We were laughing and crying and sharing this delightful consciousness of each other and Christ.

Matt, as usual, provided words for our prayer.

> Grant us the presence to be filled with the beauty shared by all of creation such that we may deeply listen to and thereby acknowledge that reality.

April 4

John 19:25–30

²⁵ And that is what the soldiers did.

Meanwhile, standing near the cross of Jesus were his mother, and his mother's sister, Mary the wife of Clopas, and Mary Magdalene. ²⁶ When Jesus saw his mother and the disciple whom he loved standing beside her, he said to his mother, "Woman, here is your son." ²⁷ Then he said to the disciple, "Here is your mother." And from that hour the disciple took her into his own home.

²⁸ After this, when Jesus knew that all was now finished, he said (in order to fulfill the scripture), "I am thirsty." ²⁹ A jar full of sour wine was standing there. So they put a sponge full of the wine on a branch of hyssop and held it to his mouth. ³⁰ When Jesus had received the wine, he said, "It is finished." Then he bowed his head and gave up his spirit.

READING THE passage from John's Gospel brings up powerful images of women, underscoring the importance of females in the life and ministry of Jesus. From the Samaritan woman at the well to the anointing of Jesus by a woman in the final weeks of His life, it would be hard to consider this Gospel as anything other than gender neutral. Yet, following the Jewish tradition, the Church became an institution exclusively governed by men. Sad.

Sallie Ann and I visited Ephesus two years ago, celebrating Mass with Father Rohr in a chapel near the house traditionally known as the House of the Virgin Mary. Apparently, John, Jesus's beloved apostle, and Mary, the mother of Jesus, moved to Ephesus late in the first century. The Apostle Paul visited Ephesus during his second journey, spending several months there with Aquila and Priscilla in 52–53 BCE. Paul returned to Ephesus on his third journey, staying for as long as three years, during which he wrote his first letter to the Corinthians in 57 BCE. John lived in the Christian community in Ephesus in 64 CE, about the time Paul was killed in Rome. Traditionally, John traveled around Asia Minor for some time with Peter, was exiled to Patmos (where, it is believed, he wrote the book of Revelations), and finally returned to Ephesus to write the Gospel according to John in 95 CE. It is not clear when Mary died, or was "assumed into heaven."

What was clear when we were in Ephesus was that the house identified as the house of the Virgin Mary by a German nun in the 19th century was located a long way from the center of the city. Even for healthy, young, and middle-aged men and women, the long walk up that steep hill was challenging. The conclusion I reached then, one that I have had no reason to question since, is that Sister Catherine Emmerich, beatified by Pope John Paul II in 2004, had a nonetheless somewhat inaccurate vision. She missed the exact location of the house of Mary by what seemed like half a mile. Like so many of the miraculous teachings of the official church (which, in fairness, the tradition of Mary's house is not), pilgrimages have been organized for centuries to visit shrines and holy sites, not due to the precision or accuracy of the locations, but simply for the spiritual experience of the pilgrims.

I have decidedly mixed feelings about shrines and shrine pilgrimages. In my view, many of the shrines around the world come perilously close to "graven images," objects and traditions venerated and worshiped for all the wrong reasons. However, if the pilgrim or visitor encounters Christ in the course of the pilgrimage, what is wrong with that? After all, I encourage missionaries to open themselves to such an encounter while painting a house or chapel in the Dominican Republic. I believe there is a difference. When I talk about "encounter" and "community" to the missionaries, I am not basing that possibility on a made-up story or dubious vision.

My belief that Christ is present in and as all of creation is clearly faith based. There are no scientific facts that can prove this belief to be true. The science of the Big Bang, and what we have learned from quantum physics provide logical frameworks for that belief, but a leap of faith is required. So why am I troubled by the additional few steps of faith required to accept the miracles behind the pilgrimage shrines? As a Mormon missionary, I used to argue that the same faith that accepts the virgin birth of Jesus, or His resurrection after death, can just as easily accept a visit by Christ to America, or the presence of the Golden Tablets under a tree outside of Palmyra, New York.

The logical fallacy *reductio ad absurdum* states that something is false if the premises on which it is based will lead to absurd conclusions. Faith in God is often challenged on the grounds of this logical fallacy, especially when that faith is taken to the extremes of snake-handling Pentecostals (or Golden Tablets under trees!).

The logical defense against *reductio ad absurdum* is called *appeal to the extremes*, attempting to make a reasonable argument into an absurd one, by taking the argument to the extremes. I believe that faith in a power greater than me is completely reasonable. There can be no other sensible explanation for the universe that surrounds me. Does this faith in a higher power require that I believe in everything taught by any particular religion, whether that religion is Christian or Buddhist or Islam? And, if Christian, must I accept everything taught by the Magisterium in Rome? Must I go further, and accept the validity of every miraculous claim made down through the ages, including the veneration of shrines where these miracles allegedly took place?

For me, faith is an extremely personal matter. I respect the faith of people I have known throughout my life who believe in a variety of different religions. I respect people who believe in no religion. I respect those who profess no belief in anything not proven by science. I strongly reject the idea that being a Catholic requires that I accept everything about Catholicism. I believe it is a very personal matter just where the line is drawn with respect to what I fully accept, what I reject, and about which I am ambivalent.

Sallie Ann and I wrote prayers on little pieces of paper and threaded them into a wire fence next to the house of the Virgin Mary in Ephesus. I prayed sincerely. I felt the spirit of the place. The Mass in the little chapel was extraordinary. For an instant that morning, I was present to the Presence of Christ. It is not important to me that I would have had just as meaningful an experience at a shrine half a mile closer to the center of Ephesus, or one ever further away.

Paul wrote in Colossians, "There is only Christ: He is everything and He is in everything." Christ was with us in Ephesus, just as He is with us in the garden at Serendipity.

April 5

Repeat John 19:25–30

I FOCUSED on the second part of the passage from John's Gospel this morning.

When Jesus had received the wine, he said, "It is finished." Then he bowed his head and gave up his spirit.

Sitting with this on the bench caused me to sink into deep sadness. As I have reflected several times during the past few weeks, I know the end of this story! Jesus lives! Jesus will be walking and talking with His disciples again in three short days! Nonetheless, I grieve when I read about the trial, execution, and, now, death of this great man.

It is finished. The pain, suffering, humiliation, frustration, and sorrow that Christ experienced as Jesus was finally at end. Being human means all of that, but also joy, pleasure, pride, and deep love. Jesus experienced these as well. Christ is in all of it—the good and the bad, the joy and the pain. I believe Christ feels pain and frustration in the sins and stupidity of mankind. He felt it two thousand years ago, feels it now, and will feel it for as long as humans are human.

Our small group of Double Pancakes has been sharing pictures from the reunion these past two days. I am reminded of how present we were to each other, and how present Christ was in our discussions. Matt continues to be the emerging mystic in the group. He ended one of his reflections with this prayer.

…so for me, the living school has been an affirmation that what I seek is real… that the seeking of it most often feels like failure… and that the moments when my heart fills with an over-brimming ocean of oneness are a fleeting glimpse of what is real. And what is real is a limitless participation called love, and love is a good thing, and it is shared by all and can never run out and it has a positive purpose: [G]uidance. Love guides to transcend and include forever and ever—love guides in the form of my heart, my lectio practice, my teachers, friends, patients, my mistakes, pride, humility, actions and inactions, in knowledge and ignorance and unknowing. Love guides me in you because we are both here. I am thankful for love and am thankful for my teachers and teachings and I thank you. and I love you.

Once again, Matt finds the prayer that is in my heart, articulating it for me. It is good to walk and pray with giants.

April 6

John 19:31–42, Jesus' Side Is Pierced
31 Since it was the day of Preparation, the Jews did not want the bodies left on the cross during the sabbath, especially because that sabbath was a day of great solemnity. So they asked Pilate to have the legs of the crucified men broken and the bodies removed. 32 Then the soldiers came and broke the legs of the first and of the other who had been crucified with him. 33 But when they came to Jesus and saw that he was already dead, they did not break his legs. 34 Instead, one of the soldiers pierced his side with a spear, and at once blood and water came out. 35 (He who saw this has testified so that you also may believe. His testimony is true, and he knows that he tells the truth.) 36 These things occurred so that the scripture might be fulfilled, "None of his bones shall be broken." 37 And again another passage of scripture says, "They will look on the one whom they have pierced."
The Burial of Jesus
38 After these things, Joseph of Arimathea, who was a disciple of Jesus, though a secret one because of his fear of the Jews, asked Pilate to let him take away the body of Jesus. Pilate gave him permission; so he came and removed

his body. [39] *Nicodemus, who had at first come to Jesus by night, also came, bringing a mixture of myrrh and aloes, weighing about a hundred pounds.* [40] *They took the body of Jesus and wrapped it with the spices in linen cloths, according to the burial custom of the Jews.* [41] *Now there was a garden in the place where he was crucified, and in the garden there was a new tomb in which no one had ever been laid.* [42] *And so, because it was the Jewish day of Preparation, and the tomb was nearby, they laid Jesus there.*

THE SOLDIERS chose not to break the legs of Jesus in order to fulfill a prophecy, and, for the same reason, they chose to pierce his side with a spear. Perhaps in those days, and particularly for religious Jews, it was the historical style to emphasize the importance of an action by linking it to an earlier prophecy. To my modern, skeptical mind, the connection to earlier scriptural references is, at best, disconcerting.

The story of the soldiers coming to the site of the crucifixion on the day of Preparation is deeply troubling to me, not because it fulfills a prophecy, but because it is such a detailed description of atrocity. Breaking the legs of crucified men in order to honor the "solemnity of the sabbath" is simply disgusting, regardless of who these men were. Piercing the side of Jesus because "they saw that he was already dead" underscores the depravity of the age.

John's Gospel finally offers some respite to the heartbreaking story by describing the merciful actions of Joseph of Arimathea and Nicodemus. Jesus was wrapped in linen and spices (a hundred pounds of "myrrh and aloes"), then buried in a nearby garden tomb.

I will always remember visiting the Church of the Holy Sepulchre in Jerusalem more than thirty years ago with Sallie Ann. Our guide was a Palestinian, openly skeptical of the thousands of tourists visiting the various possible sites of the tomb of Jesus in and near Jerusalem. There are actually several "tombs of Jesus" inside the Church of the Holy Sepulchre. Our guide asked whether we wanted to visit the one with the shortest line, or the one he considered to be the most likely site of the actual burial!

Many Protestant churches believe another tomb, about a mile north of the Church of the Holy Sepulchre, is the actual tomb. Located near the Rockefeller Garden outside the Damascus Gate, it is known as the Garden Tomb of Jerusalem. Like so many shrines, the possible sites of various events in the life of Jesus are really only focal points for meditation and reflection.

In my fantasy this morning, I spent time talking to the two great men who cared for the body of Jesus after the crucifixion. What they did was not without risk. In the days and weeks that followed the death of Jesus, His followers were hunted down and punished. By so publicly caring for the body, treating it with the same traditional respect due Jews of particularly good standing, Joseph of Arimathea and Nicodemus distinguished themselves in ways that Peter did not. Yet they were humble about it. They talked easily about different times, times when they listened to Jesus preach or watched Him perform miracles. They talked about Him as a friend, not as the Son of Man or the Messiah.

The enormous effort to establish the Divinity of Jesus began within a very few years of His death. It continues to this day. For most Christians, this means accepting that "Jesus is God." Over the past five years, I have slowly, finally internalized the teaching of the Cosmic Christ. Jesus is not exactly God. He is more than that. Father Rohr addresses this in his meditation today.

> Jesus is instead a third something—the perfect union of "very God" with "very man." For the truly orthodox Christian, the Trinity must be "God," and Jesus can only be understood inside that Eternal Embrace. From within this loving relationship, the Christ came forth to draw us back (through the enfleshed Jesus) to where we all originally came from (Genesis

1:26, John 14:3). This is quite a different description of salvation—and, dare I say, the whole point! I wonder if "reincorporation" might not be a better word than salvation.

We have much less need to "prove" that Jesus is God (which of itself asks nothing transformative of us). Our deep need is to experience the same unitive mystery in ourselves and in everything else—"through him, with him, and in him," as we say in the Great Amen of the Eucharistic Prayer. The good news is that we also are part of the eternal divine embrace, now as the ongoing Body of Christ extended in space and time. We are the second coming of Christ!

For me, the operative phrase in this teaching is that "proving" the divinity of God is not transformative. It is not transformative to establish that the actions of another person are wrong. It is certainly not transformative to shame others. Transformation is a deeply personal, internal affair. Only if and when we open ourselves to His presence, becoming "egoless," is transformation possible. In the vulnerability of that defenseless condition, I believe the work of transformation can begin. It is only then that *kenosis*, truly self-emptying acts of love through service, can transform us, "reincorporate" us, into the oneness of the "divine embrace."

I asked God to grant me the grace to be humble at depth, to be radically vulnerable. Grant me the grace to be a friend of Christ today.

April 7

Repeat John 19:31–42

AS I REFLECTED on the respect shown to Jesus after His death, I sat for a long time thinking about my own death. What will I leave as a legacy? Many things crossed my mind, including, of course, Sister Parish and other things that have dominated my life in the past few years. The longer picture is not about me, but rather my posterity. How has my life effected the generations that will follow me? For some time, I looked for some great change I have made in the world, one that will last beyond my lifetime. It was a frustrating search. First, I am not sure what permanent changes I have made anywhere. Most of the results of my efforts are fleeting at best. Second, I could come up with nothing I have done that is even noticeable on a grand scale.

Not surprisingly, I finally realized that my posterity begins with my progeny. While I have done little that impacts the whole world, I have performed a major role in the lives of my daughters. It began, of course, when I married their mother and fathered them.

Now in my eighth decade on this planet, it is hard for me to accept that my relationship with my daughters is as puzzling and troubled as it is. By virtually any standard, I have not been much of a father. Normally, I qualify that statement by saying that I was a very poor father before I married Sallie Ann, or that I was not much of a father until my heart attacks in 2007. Sadly, I consider my performance to be an unqualified failure. Somehow, in spite of that, both of them are remarkable human beings.

Obviously, the most important thing shared by both girls is their mother, one of the strongest and most impressive women I have ever known. Phyllis was and is a remarkable person. The failure of our marriage had very little to do with her, or with anything that she did or failed to do. We were too young to get married, and I was far too interested in becoming successful in business to make marriage to anyone successful.

Melissa

Melissa was born on June 19, 1969 in Boise, Idaho. My memory of her first year is all positive, even though I had already begun to work obsessively. The house was great. The neighborhood was great. We had many good friends, several of whom were also beginning their families. I loved Boise Cascade, even accepting the transfers to Atlanta and Santa Monica with enthusiasm. I have to believe that Melissa's first year had all the right levels of love, caring, and security. I have early pictures of Melissa in Santa Monica, and many more at the house on Lookout Mountain. She is laughing in all of the pictures.

By the time Melissa entered pre-k and kindergarten, I was living in California. I remember visiting her at Graland Country Day School, where she attended elementary and middle school. I did move back to Denver for a year in 1973, allowing me to see the girls more frequently. However, I was clearly not the PTA kind of father. Matters were more than a little complicated by the fact that Phyllis re-married. Her new husband, Sidney Werkman, a child psychiatrist, was a very "hands-on" stepfather. He wanted the girls to call him "Daddy," referring to me as Bob or Daddy Bob. That was not good for me or for the girls. Honestly, however, I did not compete vigorously for my parental rights.

Melissa was extremely smart, and seemed to make friends easily. She was not terribly happy, but that did not seem to interfere with her success. When the time came to consider high school, Melissa wanted to follow in the tradition of her mother's family, which meant a boarding school in the East. She started the 10th grade at Andover, dropping out after the first semester. She came to Washington, DC, to live with Sallie Ann and me in the spring, attending Madeira for a semester. Neither of these very good private schools worked for Melissa. She moved back to Denver, finishing high school at East High School, an excellent, though very large, public school. One of the proudest moments of my life was listening to Melissa give the graduation speech in front of a massive audience, walking out in front of the podium and challenging parents and students alike to do good things.

The rest of Melissa's education sounds simply too good to be true. She finished Harvard College high in her class, taught at a high school in Greece for a year after graduation, then finished Harvard Law School on the *Law Review*, clerked for Guido Calabresi on the Second Circuit Court, and finally clerked for Justice John Paul Stevens on the Supreme Court. Throughout these amazing ten years, Melissa made and maintained lasting friendships with incredible people, most of whom are still in her life. She is now a tenured professor at the University of Colorado Law School.

Melissa married Kevin Traskos on June 2, 2001. Another big day in my life was walking her down the aisle at her wedding on a mountain west of Boulder, Colorado. She and Kevin have two amazing children. Talia was born on February 22, 2003, and Noah was born on April 11, 2005. Sadly, both Melissa and Kevin are as much workaholics as I was. Happily, they made the decision to be good parents in spite of that work ethic, and have made a serious success of it.

I asked Melissa what she could remember of major vacations or trips we made together.

> Big trips, of course, include New York and France. Both wonderful. I believe you took me to Hawaii with another family (the only thing I remember about it is being knocked over by

a huge wave and stung by a man o war. And the Easter egg hunt). I loved our time together in Greece and skiing with you in Zacopane.

Even though I knew in advance that Melissa's experience of me as a father could not have been very positive, I asked her to reflect on it.

> As you said in your email, here comes the tough part: I love you very much. I value the relationship we have now tremendously and I am so grateful for the grandfather you are to my children. They adore you. But I think the fact that you are asking these questions is sort of emblematic of our lifetime relationship. The number of times that you forgot my birthday is not small. That hurt. And the fact that you ask for it in this email hurts. We are very much, I think, creatures of the time that we were in.
>
> I often wonder what our relationship would be like if I had grown up with you. I think it would be very close, though I am also certain we would have fought like the strong-willed people we both are. The question of how you were as a person is one that is hard for me to answer because for so many years—most of my life—I only interacted with you for about 2 weeks a year. I remember you asking me at my law school graduation if I really wanted you to be one of those dads who made the obligatory weekly phone call. I guess I think it would have been good for us (though neither of is good at those conversations, maybe we should have trained ourselves to be).

There is very little about Melissa that does not make me very proud. Mostly, however, I am happy that much of her life seems to be happy. I know there have been tough times, and I know I was not there to help. However, she is incredibly resilient. Actually, I think we are resilient together. Our relationship has never been better than it is today. I can certainly imagine much worse alternatives!

Jennifer

My second daughter was born the year that my first entrepreneurial effort truly took off. Hart Associates had three low-income housing projects underway. I had become close friends with Buddy Tudor,

and had begun to travel even more than had been the case at Boise Cascade. Phyllis and I were not communicating very well, even to the point of not being able to discuss our difficulties. Her pregnancy with Jennifer was not accidental, but it was not carefully considered.

When Jennifer was born, March 17, 1971, I was in Louisiana, visiting Buddy. In fact, I remember dinner the night Jennifer was born. Buddy and his then wife, Jane Ann, and I were having dinner at their house in Pineville, talking about possible names. My recollection is that both Buddy and Jane Ann preferred Jennifer to any of the other names that Phyllis and I had been considering. That may be purely apocryphal.

My marriage with Phyllis was essentially over before Jennifer's first birthday. My memories of Jennifer as a little girl are all wrapped up in my memories of those very difficult years in both my personal and my business lives. More accurately, I remember very little "personal life." I was all business.

Jennifer was a strikingly attractive little girl. While I was not present to see her begin to speak, or begin to walk, or go to her first day of pre-kindergarten, my recollection is that she was happy. She remembers going to a "cute school in Park Hill," the neighborhood where we lived in Denver, and where Phyllis continued to live after we were separated. Jennifer remembers her time at that school as the only happy time of her youth.

In her brief recollection of early life in Denver, Jennifer believes that she had begun to feel out of place at St. Mary's Academy, one of the oldest and most respected kindergarten and elementary schools in Colorado. Jennifer remembers being a poor student. Perhaps for that reason, she moved to Graland, staying there until going to high school at Dublin.

Jennifer remembers going to Hawaii with me, and coming to our house in Chevy Chase, Maryland. Significantly, she recalls the formal living room, a room she was not allowed to enter! She remembers trips to the coal mine in West Virginia.

Most of Jennifer's recollections about her youth are unhappy. Graland was a very exclusive school, home to the children of Denver's finest families. Jennifer remembers taking diet pills in the fifth grade, and beginning to smoke in the seventh grade. One of her early memories is the visit from me when I learned from Phyllis that Jennifer had begun to smoke. She recalls feeling betrayed by her mother.

She had very few friends, and felt as if she were always being compared to her older (and more successful) sister. Sibling rivalry is difficult in the best of circumstances. Our divorce made it worse.

Jennifer writes that she was "confused about having a stepfather." I think that is an understatement. The story of Phyllis's second marriage is not a happy one, particularly for Jennifer. All of her doubts about herself were exacerbated by the confusion that I allowed to develop between her stepfather and me. Tragically, there are no "mulligans" in parenting.

When Sallie Ann and I were married in 1982, Jennifer and Melissa were among the bridesmaids. Jennifer was only ten years old, the youngest bridesmaid. She had a panic attack, almost choosing to go on strike just as the wedding began.

Sallie Ann made a serious effort to befriend the girls, hoping to establish with them the kind of relationship she routinely has with the young daughters and granddaughters of her friends. Those other relationships were perceived as competition for Melissa and Jennifer, leading them to believe they could never be as important to Sallie Ann and, by extension, to me, as the children of our other friends.

This competition was probably at its worst during the Spring Break of 1982, when Sallie Ann and I celebrated our honeymoon with our four children and the daughter of a good friend. Melissa and Jennifer were extremely unhappy with the level of apparent competition. Jennifer, whose birthday is four days earlier than Sallie Ann's, remembers that first "joint birthday" with Sallie Ann as the beginning of the end. Since then, Jennifer believes I have treated Sallie Ann's birthday as more important.

We took the girls on a very grand trip to Italy and England in the summer of 1982, resulting, among other things, in Jennifer's memory of being grounded in her room in Florence. She remembers the fancy hotels and dinners, but not fondly.

Phyllis decided it would be best for Jennifer to go to a boarding school for high school, leaving the unhappy experience of Graland behind. I am also certain that the fact that Melissa went to Andover to board was a factor. Jennifer competed with Melissa in everything. She continues to do so today. Dublin was an extremely expensive school (tuition and boarding today is $59,000 a year, more than

Andover and essentially the same as Harvard or Yale), one that was apparently well suited to a diverse student body. Part of the expense might be the effort to work with students with special needs. Jennifer writes:

> From September 1986 to June 1990 I went to Dublin School in New Hampshire for High School. High school was not easy. I struggled academically and had a very hard time making lasting friendships. At my graduation, you met my roommate Christine and the other people in the dorm.

After Dublin, Jennifer started college at Beloit College in Wisconsin, another expensive private school. She remembers it as one of the happiest times in her student life. She pledged a sorority and made good friends. Sadly, she had to leave due to complications with her jaw surgery.

Jennifer's jaw surgery was one of the most difficult and important decisions in her life. Phyllis and I were in violent disagreement about whether it was necessary. Jennifer recalls the decision as a choice between her mother and me, not just a choice about a medical procedure. The problem originated when Jennifer fell on the front step of her house when she was not even ten years old. The fall pushed one of her teeth into her jaw, and may have rearranged some of the bones in her face. Whether related to the fall or not, Jennifer developed temporomandibular joint (TMJ) problems. The first surgery in 1989, intended to solve the TMJ problem, dramatically changed her looks. And it failed to solve the problem of pain in her jaw.

After her second surgery in 1991, Jennifer transferred to the University of Colorado at Denver. She began a "re-enactment" phase, heavily involved in science fiction and fantasy. She calls it her nerd phase!

Only when Jennifer tried to describe how she felt about her early life did I learn about some of the difficulties. She writes:

> In the early 1990s I started bingeing and throwing up. As my relationship with myself deteriorated, my relationship with all the people in my life fell apart. I pushed people out of my life and then blamed them. I have recovered mostly (no more binging and purging.) I still push people away when I get scared or things aren't going my way. I still have body issues and self-esteem problems.
>
> In 1997, I came out as a lesbian and dated and eventually had a commitment ceremony with Lisa. It was a private affair and no one came. I pretty much forced her to do it. It was one of the things that was between us for the entire relationship.

I will never forget the phone call on Jennifer's birthday in 1997. I was walking on Ella Lee Lane, the street on which we lived in Houston, innocently wishing her a happy birthday. She rather casually announced that she had birthday news for me, which was her acceptance of her sexual orientation as a lesbian. I did not handle it well. Eventually, I not only met her partner, Lisa, but came to like her a great deal.

It was, therefore, a bit of a surprise to learn only five years later that she and Lisa were no longer partners, that she was no longer a lesbian, and that she had met and fallen in love with a man, Sean Love. They met through mutual friends at Western Carolina University, where Jennifer was earning a Master's Degree in History.

Jennifer is very well educated. She not only earned an undergraduate degree from the University of Colorado at Denver, but advanced degrees from Regis and Western Carolina. Applying this education in the employment world has proven very difficult.

Jennifer married Sean in 2006. While I was not a fan of Sean at the beginning, I have come to respect him as a father, and, more importantly, as a true soulmate for Jennifer. Their son, Parker, was born in 2010. He is somewhere on the autism scale, struggling with communication and connection. His parents are making well-informed decisions about Parker's education and care.

They lead a tough life with many problems, and not many friends. Jennifer and Melissa have a very troubled relationship, making family gatherings here in Ponte Vedra difficult at best. For all kinds of not great reasons, Sallie Ann and I do not visit them in Asheville. It made me sad to read Jennifer's final comment to me in her letter.

> I was angry a lot in my youth. I took that anger out on you and the people that I love. You were a good father but I was not always an appreciative daughter. I wanted to be smarter, a better athlete, prettier, and just more. When I could not be what I wanted to be, I took it out on others. I am sorry for the time we lost because I was angry. I think you met all my friends. I have not had a lot of them.

A better father would have helped Jennifer with all her issues, not least of which is that anger. What is done is done. I have no idea how much time I will have to be a better father to my daughters. I like to think I have begun to make "living amends," which is to say that I am living a different lifestyle today than I did for the first sixty years of my life. Every day gives me the chance to be a different grandfather to Parker, Talia, and Noah than I was a father to Jennifer and Melissa. There is no better way for me to show my daughters how much I love them.

It has been a very long morning. It has also been very painful to reflect on the difficult history of my fatherhood. However, returning to the initial question of my impact on posterity, on the difference I have made in the world, the answer is clear. My impact will be made by my daughters and by their children, and their children's children. That is what posterity is all about.

April 8

Read and reflect on the week.

THE READINGS this week have all been about the crucifixion and death of Jesus. Why did it happen? The answer that works for me is very simple. Jesus is the Christ become human. He showed through His life and His death that being human is inherently good, and that there is a good way to be human. In his book *The New Spiritual Exercises In the Spirit of Teilhard*, Louis Savary states this eloquently.

> Humans are the bearers of consciousness and free choice. Thus, we can endure unavoidable suffering with consciousness and hatred, or we can endure it with consciousness and love. When you are conscious of your suffering, you can take the energy of your suffering and direct it either into anger and resentment, or into compassion and healing. In His passion and death, Jesus teaches us how to suffer with consciousness and love. Jesus redirected the suffering energy during His passion toward service for others. Even in those moments of

unendurable pain, He never forgot His redemptive mission of reparation, forgiveness, and healing.

Teilhard teaches that everything that happens on Earth is happening in and as the Universal Christ. The passion of the Cosmic Christ is ongoing. This is the message of the cross. This is the living purpose of the life and death of Jesus.

There is, of course, an alternative. As I have reflected on the readings for the past two weeks, I have become aware of my strong aversion to the theory of substitutionary atonement. It is a concept deeply imbedded in Christian teaching, one that continues to prevail among most Catholics. Reading the Bible literally, there is a great deal of scriptural support for the idea that the death of Jesus was necessary to bear the penalty, and cancel the debt, of all mankind. Jesus died in the sinner's place, and on the sinner's behalf. The death of Jesus was necessary to satisfy the justice demands of an angry, but just God. Only through that ugly, vicious, terrible death could God ever forgive the rest of us sinners.

Father Rohr teaches that Jesus did not die to change the view of God about man. Rather, Jesus died to change the view of man about God. The fundamental problem with substitutionary atonement is the way it imagines God. God hated man because of a great mistake at the time of the creation. He required, even demanded, a violent death for atonement to be made. To me, this is patently ridiculous.

One of my Living School classmates sent me an article by Chuck Queen, a Baptist preacher. He writes,

> Substitutionary atonement reflects more of an ancient, primitive view of God than the view taught and embodied by Jesus of Nazareth. In the ancient world, sacrifice was demanded to placate the offended deity; to stay the deity's wrathful vengeance. Jesus imagined God as Abba—a loving, compassionate parent—seeking the best for God's children. The God of Jesus would have no need to save us from God's self.

Queen argues that the Christ hymn in Philippians 2:5–8, read correctly, states that "Jesus' death is not a payment for sin demanded by God, but is seen as the culmination of his life of obedience to God's will and cause in the world." Jesus's death was the ultimate act of kenosis, the self-giving love poured out for others.

> In bearing the sin—the hate, evil and animosity of the world—he exposed it and exhausted it, thus overcoming it. The resurrection served as God's vindication, God's "yes" to Jesus's sacrificial life and death … The God of Jesus, however, does not need to be propitiated. God's attitude toward God's children is love. Love does not need or require a sacrificial victim. Jesus did not have to die in order to satisfy some need in God or to pay off some debt owed to God. God is able to forgive freely.

The simple fact is that we humans crucified Jesus. He did not have to die in order to make atonement to God for sin. As Father Rohr says, we are the ones needing atonement, we are the ones needing to change, not God.

Savary argues that the writings of the Apostle Paul contain much of what Teilhard finally made clear in the twentieth century.

According to Saint Paul, it is quite legitimate theologically to interpret Jesus's passion and death primarily as a process of rebirth. For Paul, Christ's passion, death, and resurrection are like another baptism for Him, a moment of transformation from death to new life. It is a moment of radical change. He is transformed from being merely Jesus of Nazareth into Jesus Christ, the Risen Lord, a New Creation.

It is my belief that we are reborn every moment of every day. Our new birth is by choice, a choice to live outside and beyond ourselves, in service to others. Or a choice to deny the transformation of that moment, to stay enclosed in and controlled by our ego.

I want to end the day and this week with Teilhard's wonderful prayer to the Cosmic Christ in his Hymn to the Universe.

In the center of your breast I see nothing else than a furnace; and the more I gaze upon this burning hearth, the more it seems to me that, all round about, the contours of your Body are melting, that they are growing great beyond all measure, until I distinguish in you, no longer any other features than a world in flames.

The concept of dying in the flames of Christ, merging into His melting Body, is powerful beyond words. The Christ Project is oneness, unitive consciousness in, as, and with all of creation.

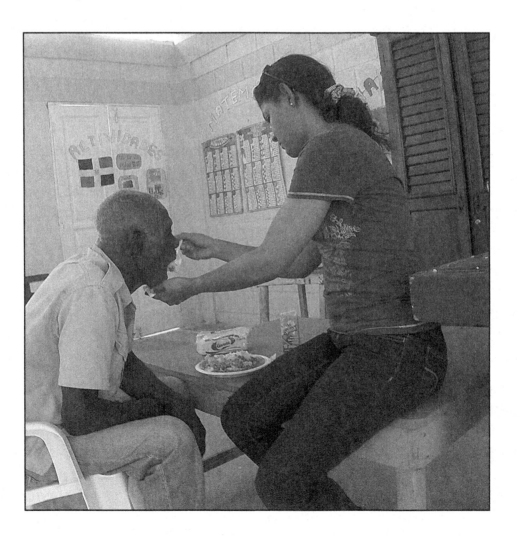

Calendar Week Thirty

April 9

Luke 23:56

Then they returned, and prepared spices and ointments. On the Sabbath they rested according to the commandment.

Today is Palm Sunday, the beginning of Easter Week. It is unseasonably cold. Even the bright morning sun seems unable to warm the garden.

What a strange mixture of celebration and suffering in the brief life of Jesus. Huge crowds greeted Jesus as He entered Jerusalem, cheering Him as the Son of Man, the Messiah. Similarly, palm parades will march through the streets of little towns like San Antonio de Guerra, where we celebrated Palm Sunday last year.

The festive atmosphere on Sunday turns very rapidly into one of the most somber and desolate weeks of the year. Traditionally, Wednesday is the day that Judas agrees to betray Jesus. Thursday is a celebration of the Last Supper, complete with a washing of the feet.

Jesus was arrested after that famous last dinner with His disciples. The farcical trial began late Thursday, and continued all through the night, ending with the crucifixion Friday afternoon. At least that is the way we celebrate it today. As I read and reflect on the story, it seems to me like the actual events must have occurred over a few days. The logistics of moving from one judicial venue to another, then back again, would certainly take at least that much time now.

The passage from Luke indicates that following the burial of Jesus in the tomb found by Joseph of Arimathea, everyone rested. It was the Sabbath, which begins at sundown on Friday. On that evening here in Ponte Vedra, our little troupe will present the Live Stations of the Cross, just as we have on Good Friday for the past three years.

Saturday, the Jewish Sabbath and day of rest, is actually very busy for the catechumens who have been preparing for baptism. Six years ago, this special Saturday was the day that I was baptized, confirmed, and received first communion. Sallie Ann and I were married in the church six years ago yesterday.

Easter Week, the last week of Lent, is also the last calendar week of Ignatian Week Three. Week Three began six calendar weeks ago with the story from Luke about the plot to kill Jesus. Each day for the next thirty-five days, we have read and reflected on passages from all four Gospels that tell the same story, beginning with the outlines of the plot and ending with the crucifixion. Our goal for this period has been a radical and empathetic understanding of the passionate suffering of Jesus.

> I want to feel sorrow at the wreckage, compassion with Jesus, and shame that He suffers because of our sins.

My sorrow derives from empathy for Jesus of Nazareth. My compassion for Jesus causes frustration that I was not there to assist Simon the Cyrene or Joseph of Arimathea when they helped Jesus and His family. My shame is a shame here and now, which springs from how my sin, and the sins of all humanity, cause the Christ to suffer in the world today. What we do (and what we do not do) for the least of our brothers and sisters, we do (or do not do) for Him.

I walked back down to the meditation bench to enjoy the mid-day sun, sitting with thoughts of my daughters. My reflections were filled with images of cute little girls, struggling teenagers, confident (and competent) young women, happy wives, extraordinary new mothers, and finally, very comfortable friends. Strangely, it is this friendship that surprises me most, especially after all the drama of the past forty years. For me, at least, deep friendship is both less frequent and more valuable each passing year. My relationships with Melissa and Jennifer are obviously different in many respects, but both have aged beautifully. When I reflect on love, conjuring up images that represent my growing understanding of eternal and infinite relationships, I find that I am looking at Melissa and Jennifer. I rest easy with this thought.

April 10

Reflect on the Passion

THE GARDEN this morning may have been more beautiful than it has been thus far this year. Maggie and I walked down later than usual. The sun had already warmed the day to a perfect spring temperature, and all of God's creatures that make the lagoon home were out and about. Finding tranquility in this environment was easy.

Reflecting on the Passion of Christ, however, is not a tranquil experience. The more time I spend in prayer, the more frequently I read the various Gospel descriptions of this horrible week, the more deeply I am effected by the story. Was Christ "persecuted for righteousness' sake"? As reported in Matthew 5:10, Jesus taught:

> Blessed are those who are persecuted for righteousness' sake, for theirs is the kingdom of heaven.

It has never occurred to me that He intended these words as a prediction of what He knew would ultimately happen to Him. Father Rohr introduced us to a wonderful Irish woman, Ruth Patterson, who was the first woman ordained as a Minister in the Presbyterian church in Ireland. She founded Restoration Ministries, an organization devoted to making peace between the Catholics and Protestants of North Ireland. She jokes about how painfully difficult it was for the first twenty years. Her impossible mission was clearly not succeeding. The peace that has come to Ireland has been achieved in no small part by "peace walls," brick and wire barriers that separate Catholic and Protestant neighborhoods. In August of 2016, the first of the forty-eight peace walls came down, initiating what is hoped will be the complete removal of the walls by 2023.

The insanity of this tragic divide between two ostensibly Christian communities is, for me, extremely hard to understand. It makes the difficulties between Muslims and Jews in Israel look hopeless. Frankly, there is little hope for Muslims and Christians anywhere that the relationship has deteriorated in the past several years.

Multi-generational feuds, those that originated years or even centuries ago, are very frustrating to me. Shia and Sunni Muslims, like Protestant and Catholic Christians, are fighting over differences that originated so long ago that most people cannot remember what happened or articulate the cause of the dispute. Yet they fight, doing so "for righteousness' sake."

Ruth Patterson reflected on the eighth Beatitude as follows:

We come to the holy ground of this eighth Beatitude, the one that perhaps is the most difficult to take on board. In fact, the temptation would be to say, "All the others, maybe yes, Lord, but not this!" It seems to be no accident that we reach this one in the season of Lent and Easter. Our doubts and questions fall into the vibrant, overwhelming silence filled with the presence of a God who is not remote but chose to be so near, knowing what it would cost him. This is the God who sweated blood in a garden and earnestly prayed that he would not have to be persecuted for righteousness' sake that far. This is the God who willingly 'climbed a hill' and found there, not acclamation but a cross. This is the God who not only submitted but actually embraced such a way, all for righteousness' sake, that is for the restoration of right relationships. This is the Blessed One.

And if we are his companions on the way, then we are called to enter the struggle against all those things that seek to damage or destroy *right relationships*. That is hard. Jesus never said "You're blessed when you are persecuted." To be so would be to encourage a masochism that has nothing to do with the Good News. Rather he said, "If your commitment to God provokes persecution, if you are living your belief out loud, no matter what the cost or pain, if you stand for the righteousness that is rooted in the very being of God, then blessed, blessed are you."

Two concepts stand out for me in this thoughtful piece. First, Ruth stresses the idea of "right relationships," something we should endure persecution to defend. The Quaker religion is based on the core doctrine of right relationships. Many Christians claim right relationships should take precedence over right doctrine. Pope Francis and other religious leaders have recently written very persuasive arguments for radically changing our economic and social systems to restore right relationships.

The second concept that Ruth articulates very well is the idea that Heaven is not a place. Rather, it is a "state of being where we have moved beyond our defensive/offensive ego into a *flow of relationship* that is characterized by a *mutuality of belovedness*." That state of being is achievable right here, right now. The challenge is to surrender our ego, allowing the flow to move around, in, and through every aspect of our lives. It means loving and accepting love, choosing love as the highest and best form of relating to ourselves and others.

How does this relate to the Passion of Christ? Reflecting on that on this perfect day, in this nearly perfect garden, in the safety and comfort of a retirement that is clearly working, I once again conclude that it was the life of Christ that changed the world, not His death. Granted, most of the religious teaching for the past two thousand years has focused on the claim that Jesus died for our sins. The Passion walks us through the painful trial and execution, bringing us closer to the experience. It also brings us closer to the life of Jesus, to His friendships, and to His humanity. Rather than focusing on the fraudulent trial, or the gratuitous brutality of both the treatment before the execution and the execution itself, we can focus on the loving acts of the woman who anointed Jesus, and of Simon and Joseph.

Matt Mumber suggested a prayer that works for me this morning.

Allow me today to enter into the flow of the unknown into the known that is the grace of God eternally being and becoming.

At the same time, God is both being and becoming. At the same time, and all time, the unknown is flowing into the known.

April 11

Reflect on the Passion

SALLIE ANN made lunch for the Bishop and some new parishioners yesterday. It was a perfect lunch, served at a perfect table, on a perfect day. It seemed almost out of place on the Monday of Holy Week. Thinking about the lunch last night, I tried to imagine where Jesus was on the Monday of the last week of His life.

Jesus rode into Jerusalem on a colt, cheered by the crowds, hailed as the Messiah, the Son of God. Each day of the following week is carefully documented in the Gospels. Both yesterday and today, Monday and Tuesday of that week, Jesus was spending the night in Bethany at the home of Lazarus, returning to the city each day to visit the temple.

I love the story in John's Gospel about Mary, the spiritual sister of Martha, anointing the feet of Jesus with expensive perfume, then wiping His feet with her hair. It is a powerful image of intimacy, humility, and close friendship.

> Six days before the Passover Jesus came to Bethany, the home of Lazarus, whom he had raised from the dead. There they gave a dinner for him. Martha served, and Lazarus was one of those at the table with him. Mary took a pound of costly perfume made of pure nard, anointed Jesus' feet, and wiped them with her hair. The house was filled with the fragrance of the perfume.

While Judas Iscariot has not yet been identified as the traitor, he is certainly denounced by the Evangelist in the next few verses of Chapter 12. Judas is playing the role played by several disciples in the same scene ending with the line about the poor. It is a slightly different message.

> But Judas Iscariot, one of his disciples (the one who was about to betray him), said, "Why was this perfume not sold for three hundred denarii and the money given to the poor?" (He said this not because he cared about the poor, but because he was a thief; he kept the common purse and used to steal what was put into it.) Jesus said, "Leave her alone. She bought it so that she might keep it for the day of my burial. You always have the poor with you, but you do not always have me."

This story is followed by an account of Jesus meeting with some Greeks. It is not clear whether this was on the Monday or the Tuesday of Holy Week.

> Now among those who went up to worship at the festival were some Greeks. They came to Philip, who was from Bethsaida in Galilee, and said to him, "Sir, we wish to see Jesus." Philip went and told Andrew; then Andrew and Philip went and told Jesus. Jesus answered them, "The hour has come for the Son of Man to be glorified. Very truly, I tell you, unless a grain of wheat falls into the earth and dies, it remains just a single grain; but if it dies, it bears much fruit."

The Evangelist then reports one of the most famous statements ever made by Jesus, one that underscores the messages of humility found in the Beatitudes. The first, "Blessed are the poor in heart," and the third, "Blessed are the meek," are actually less powerful than this statement in John's Gospel.

Those who love their life lose it, and those who hate their life in this world will keep it for eternal life. Whoever serves me must follow me, and where I am, there will my servant be also. Whoever serves me, the Father will honor.

Later in the passage from John's Gospel, Jesus once again makes one of the great statements about faith.

Jesus said to them, "The light is with you for a little longer. Walk while you have the light, so that the darkness may not overtake you. If you walk in the darkness, you do not know where you are going. While you have the light, believe in the light, so that you may become children of light."

Reflecting on this, I wondered whether John of the Cross based some of his *Dark Night of the Soul* on the concept of darkness contained in this Gospel passage from John the Evangelist. There is power in the line that we should believe in the light while we have the light. Obviously, the implicit message is that we will not always have that light.

My prayer this morning is that I will have the wisdom to see the light, the good sense to believe in it, and the courage to act accordingly.

April 12: Spy Wednesday

Mark 6:1–6, 16–18

Jesus said to his disciples: "Take care not to perform righteous deeds in order that people may see them; otherwise, you will have no recompense from your heavenly Father. When you give alms, do not blow a trumpet before you, as the hypocrites do in the synagogues and in the streets to win the praise of others. Amen, I say to you, they have received their reward. But when you give alms, do not let your left hand know what your right is doing, so that your almsgiving may be secret. And your Father who sees in secret will repay you.

"When you pray, do not be like the hypocrites, who love to stand and pray in the synagogues and on street corners so that others may see them. Amen, I say to you, they have received their reward.

But when you pray, go to your inner room, close the door, and pray to your Father in secret.

And your Father who sees in secret will repay you.

"When you fast, do not look gloomy like the hypocrites. They neglect their appearance, so that they may appear to others to be fasting. Amen, I say to you, they have received their reward. But when you fast, anoint your head and wash your face, so that you may not appear to be fasting, except to your Father who is hidden. And your Father who sees what is hidden will repay you."

SITTING WITH this reading in the garden, I realized that I have always assumed this passage was intended precisely for me. For too many years, I wanted my good deeds to be seen, acknowledged, and even rewarded by others. What others thought mattered as much or more to me as whether my actions were good or not.

Since the beginning of my current spiritual journey in 2007, I have attempted to control this desire for recognition. It is fair to say that most of the parishioners at Our Lady Star of the Sea are unaware of my role in the Sister Parish Ministry. In fact, many of the missionaries are not fully aware of why this white-haired old man is hanging around the mission projects and gatherings. Make no mistake, however, that when I am acknowledged at the reflection circles or the dinners, I beam with pride. It is very hard for me to be completely comfortable in my own skin, totally oblivious to the opinions of others.

Spy Wednesday. That is what this Wednesday was once called. Today is the day that Judas Iscariot made his deal with the chief priests. Jesus had been hinting about it all week.

The strange part of the story for me is that the chief priests needed someone to identify Jesus. It seems obvious to me that Jesus must have been very well known among the chief priests and scribes. Otherwise, why would they want to arrest and execute Him?

Personally, I believe that this underscores my argument that there were two quite different crowds. The "seekers," those who heard Jesus teach and preach, who witnessed Him perform miracles, obviously knew what He looked like. They would need no one to identify Him. The "hooligans," those who followed the trials and executions, might have heard of Jesus, but had almost certainly never seen Him or heard Him speak.

While I fully understand, and generally believe in the commandment to forgive others, I find very little forgiveness in my heart for Judas Iscariot. Some have argued that Judas was frustrated that Jesus was not founding a new Kingdom, replacing the Roman occupiers and their puppets. Even so, betrayal is stooping very low. In my business career, I regarded with suspicion and distaste any employee willing to betray a superior, regardless of the circumstances. Whistle blowers walk a fine line between simple treachery and courageous honesty.

Looking for a reason for the amount of thirty pieces of silver, I found a reference to this passage in Genesis 21:32:

> If the ox gores a male or female slave, the owner shall pay to the slaveowner thirty shekels of silver, and the ox shall be stoned.

The idea that Judas would betray Jesus for the price of a slave makes a deplorable act even worse. Then the ox is stoned. To say the least, the Hebrew Scriptures are challenging for me.

My prayer today is to act humbly and in private, eschewing public acclaim and recognition.

April 13, Maundy Thursday

Reflect on the Passion

JENNIFER, Sean, and Parker surprised me yesterday afternoon by arriving for an Easter visit. Jennifer had planned the surprise with Sallie Ann. For all kinds of reasons, seeing Jennifer and her family generated all manner of emotions. Having only recently received Jennifer's comments about her memory of her early life and my role in her childhood, I felt a high degree of guilt. When the opportunity arose, I talked to her about my regrets, apologizing for all the damage caused by my selfish climb up the ladder of worldly success. There is no way to "put the toothpaste back in the tube," but she has time now to make the second half of her life better than the first. My role continues to be a distant one, with little interest on the part of either of us to change things.

Parker is a different challenge altogether. Autism is not well understood, even after intense focus for the past two decades. I am particularly clumsy in my efforts to deal with Parker's struggle to connect, and with his living in what seems to be a completely separate universe. My guess is that he will live in this space for the rest of his life. There is no harm done to anyone, and he is increasingly able to act in a way that is safe to himself. Earlier episodes of "bolting" into traffic, or simply running away from his family, seem to be behind him. He eats poorly from a purist view of nutrition, but he manages to survive and stay relatively healthy. The fact that Sean does not work is actually a blessing for both Parker and Jennifer. He is the perfect "house husband" and full-time care giver.

When I returned from tennis this morning, I joined Jennifer and Sallie Ann for a strained conversation about Jennifer's life in North Carolina. "Walking on egg shells" is an apt description of these discussions. My normal reaction is to leave the room.

My effort this morning—to find enough silence and separation, to focus on the passion of Christ—has generally failed. So, my prayer is for humility, compassion, and surrender. I am not in control.

Tonight, Sallie Ann and I will have our feet washed in front of the parish. It is a very special opportunity to experience, at depth, the meaning of this worship-filled gesture. I imagine how the disciples must have felt when Jesus washed their feet. It is a deeply humbling experience.

I have returned to the Exercises tonight, following Mass. The foot washing celebration was extraordinary, as was the silent end of Mass. Five priests were involved in the ceremony, which ended when the Host was walked through the congregation, then installed in the Eucharistic Chapel. The priests walked out silently, followed by the whole congregation.

Father Keegan gave the homily, clearly describing the import of the Triduum, this three-day ceremony that begins with this Mass, the foot washing, and commemoration of the Last Supper. At three p.m. tomorrow, we will acknowledge the actual death of Christ with a very somber service, without the Eucharist. Traditionally, the church is silent from tomorrow afternoon until after midnight on Saturday. We will present a Live "Stations of the Cross" tomorrow night, which is not a part of the official Triduum program. The Easter Vigil Mass, beginning after dark on Saturday, celebrates the resurrection of Christ. The Easter Vigil is also the occasion when new catechumens will be baptized.

Reflecting on the significance of these various services, especially after a tense day with Jennifer and the rest of the family, I am most deeply moved by the import of the foot washing tonight. Father Keegan kissed my foot after washing it. This is humbling. I need this tonight.

April 14: Good Friday

The Passion in John 18:1–19,42

Jesus went out with his disciples across the Kidron valley to where there was a garden, into which he and his disciples entered. Judas his betrayer also knew the place, because Jesus had often met there with his disciples. So Judas got a band of soldiers and guards from the chief priests and the Pharisees and went there with lanterns, torches, and weapons. Jesus, knowing everything that was going to happen to him, went out and said to them, "Whom are you looking for?" They answered him, "Jesus the Nazorean." He said to them, "I AM." Judas his betrayer was also with them. When he said to them, "I AM, " they turned away and fell to the ground. So he again asked them, "Whom are you looking for?" They said, "Jesus the Nazorean." Jesus answered, "I told you that I AM. So if you are looking for me, let these men go."

This was to fulfill what he had said, "I have not lost any of those you gave me." Then Simon Peter, who had a sword, drew it, struck the high priest's slave, and cut off his right ear. The slave's name was Malchus. Jesus said to Peter, "Put your sword into its scabbard. Shall I not drink the cup that the Father gave me?" So the band of soldiers, the tribune, and the Jewish guards seized Jesus, bound him, and brought him to Annas first. He was the father-in-law of Caiaphas, who was high priest that year. It was Caiaphas who had counseled the Jews that it was better that one man should die rather than the people. Simon Peter and another disciple followed Jesus.

Now the other disciple was known to the high priest, and he entered the courtyard of the high priest with Jesus. But Peter stood at the gate outside. So the other disciple, the acquaintance of the high priest, went out and spoke to the gatekeeper and brought Peter in. Then the maid who was the gatekeeper said to Peter, "You are not one of this man's disciples, are you?" He said, "I am not."

Now the slaves and the guards were standing around a charcoal fire that they had made, because it was cold, and were warming themselves. Peter was also standing there keeping warm. The high priest questioned Jesus about his disciples and about his doctrine. Jesus answered him, "I have spoken publicly to the world. I have always taught in a synagogue or in the temple area where all the Jews gather, and in secret I have said nothing. Why ask me? Ask those who heard me what I said to them. They know what I said." When he had said this, one of the temple guards standing there struck Jesus and said, "Is this the way you answer the high priest?" Jesus answered him, "If I have spoken wrongly, testify to the wrong; but if I have spoken rightly, why do you strike me?" Then Annas sent him bound to Caiaphas the high priest. Now Simon Peter was standing there keeping warm.

And they said to him, "You are not one of his disciples, are you?" He denied it and said, "I am not." One of the slaves of the high priest, a relative of the one whose ear Peter had cut off, said, "Didn't I see you in the garden with him?" Again, Peter denied it. And immediately the cock crowed.

Then they brought Jesus from Caiaphas to the praetorium It was morning. And they themselves did not enter the praetorium, in order not to be defiled so that they could eat the Passover. So Pilate came out to them and said, "What charge do you bring against this man?" They answered and said to him, "If he were not a criminal, we would not have handed him over to you." At this, Pilate said to them, "Take him yourselves, and judge him according to your law." The Jews answered him, "We do not have the right to execute anyone," in order that the word of Jesus might be fulfilled that he said indicating the kind of death he would die. So Pilate went back into the praetorium and summoned Jesus and said to him, "Are you the King of the Jews?" Jesus answered, "Do you say this on your own or have others told you about me?" Pilate answered, "I am not a Jew, am I? Your own nation and the chief priests handed you over to me. What have you done?" Jesus answered, "My kingdom does not belong to this world. If my kingdom did belong to this world, my attendants would be fighting to keep me from being handed over to the Jews. But as it is, my kingdom is not here." So Pilate said to him, "Then you are a king?" Jesus answered, "You say I am a king. For this I was born and for this I came into the world, to testify to the truth. Everyone who belongs to the truth listens to my voice." Pilate said to him, "What is truth?"

When he had said this, he again went out to the Jews and said to them, "I find no guilt in him. But you have a custom that I release one prisoner to you at Passover. Do you want me to release to you the King of the Jews?" They cried out again, "Not this one but Barabbas!" Now Barabbas was a revolutionary.

Then Pilate took Jesus and had him scourged. And the soldiers wove a crown out of thorns and placed it on his head, and clothed him in a purple cloak, and they came to him and said, "Hail, King of the Jews!" And they struck him repeatedly. Once more Pilate went out and said to them, "Look, I am bringing him out to you, so that you may know that I find no guilt in him." So Jesus came out, wearing the crown of thorns and the purple cloak. And he said to them, "Behold, the man!" When the chief priests and the guards saw him they cried out, "Crucify him, crucify him!" Pilate said to them, "Take him yourselves and crucify him. I find no guilt in him." The Jews answered, "We have a law, and according to that law he ought to die, because he made himself the Son of God." Now when Pilate heard this statement, he became even more afraid, and went back into the praetorium and said to Jesus, "Where are you from?" Jesus did not answer him. So Pilate said to him, "Do you not speak to me? Do you not know that I have power to release you and I have power to crucify you?" Jesus answered him, "You would have no power over me if it had not been given to you from above. For this reason the one who handed me over to you has the greater sin." Consequently, Pilate tried to release him; but the Jews cried out, "If you release him, you are not a Friend of Caesar. Everyone who makes himself a king opposes Caesar."

When Pilate heard these words he brought Jesus out and seated him on the judge's bench in the place called Stone Pavement, in Hebrew, Gabbatha. It was preparation day for Passover, and it was about noon. And he said to the Jews, "Behold, your king!" They cried out, "Take him away, take him away! Crucify him!" Pilate said to them, "Shall I crucify your king?" The chief priests answered, "We have no king but Caesar." Then he handed him over to them to be crucified.

So they took Jesus, and, carrying the cross himself, he went out to what is called the Place of the Skull, in Hebrew, Golgotha. There they crucified him, and with him two others, one on either side, with Jesus in the middle. Pilate also had an inscription written and put on the cross. It read, "Jesus the Nazorean, the King of the Jews." Now many of the Jews read this inscription, because the place where Jesus was crucified was near the city; and it was written in Hebrew, Latin, and Greek. So the chief priests of the Jews said to Pilate, "Do not write 'The King of the Jews,' but that he said, 'I am the King of the Jews'." Pilate answered, "What I have written, I have written."

When the soldiers had crucified Jesus, they took his clothes and divided them into four shares, a share for each soldier. They also took his tunic, but the tunic was seamless, woven in one piece from the top down. So they said to one another, "Let's not tear it, but cast lots for it to see whose it will be, " in order that the passage of Scripture might be fulfilled that says: They divided my garments among them, and for my vesture they cast lots. This is what the soldiers did. Standing by the cross of Jesus were his mother and his mother's sister, Mary the wife of Clopas, and Mary of Magdala. When Jesus saw his mother and the disciple there whom he loved he said to his mother, "Woman, behold, your son." Then he said to the disciple, "Behold, your mother." And from that hour the disciple took her into his home. After this, aware that everything was now finished, in order that the Scripture might be fulfilled, Jesus said, "I thirst." There was a vessel filled with common wine. So they put a sponge soaked in wine on a sprig of hyssop and put it up to his mouth. When Jesus had taken the wine, he said, "It is finished." And bowing his head, he handed over the spirit.

Here all kneel and pause for a short time.

Now since it was preparation day, in order that the bodies might not remain on the cross on the sabbath, for the sabbath day of that week was a solemn one, the Jews asked Pilate that their legs be broken and that they be taken down. So the soldiers came and broke the legs of the first and then of the other one who was crucified with Jesus. But when they came to Jesus and saw that he was already dead, they did not break his legs, but one soldier thrust his lance into his side, and immediately blood and water flowed out. An eyewitness has testified, and his testimony is true; he knows that he is speaking the truth, so that you also may come to believe. For this happened so that the Scripture passage might be fulfilled: Not a bone of it will be broken And again another passage says: They will look upon him whom they have pierced.

After this, Joseph of Arimathea, secretly a disciple of Jesus for fear of the Jews, asked Pilate if he could remove the body of Jesus. And Pilate permitted it. So he came and took his body. Nicodemus, the one who had first come to him at night, also came bringing a mixture of myrrh and aloes weighing about one hundred pounds. They took the body of Jesus and bound it with burial cloths along with the spices, according to the Jewish burial custom. Now in the place where he had been crucified there was a garden, and in the garden a new tomb, in which no one had yet been buried. So they laid Jesus there because of the Jewish preparation day; for the tomb was close by.

FOR ME, THE account of the Passion in John's Gospel has a power that exceeds that of the accounts in the Synoptic Gospels. There are minor differences. The only one that I regret is the absence of the role of Simon the Cyrene, who carries the cross for Jesus in the Synoptic accounts, but is not present in John's Gospel. I find the two men, Simon and Joseph of Arimathea, extremely sympathetic, especially Joseph. When so many of Jesus's disciples, including even Peter, wanted nothing to do with Him during and after the trial, Joseph steps forward. He had apparently never disclosed the fact that he was a follower of Jesus.

After reading the story of the Passion in John's Gospel, from beginning to end, two or three times, Maggie and I walked down to the garden bench. A parade of egrets lined both banks of the lagoon. The sun was just coming up over the ocean. It was an amazing day, and an incredible place, to reflect on the Passion. Sitting on the bench amid all this profound display of creation, I went over my lines from the Passion play tonight. I play Caiaphas, not an attractive historical figure. He was not an impartial judge. He, and his father-in-law, Annas, had decided Jesus was guilty long before the so-called trial. In fact, Caiaphas clearly states (in the play, at least!) that he must act as both judge, prosecutor, and witness against Jesus.

Jesus answered one of the questions from Pilate about His being a King, saying, "My Kingdom does not belong to this world." Oddly, my doctrinal difference with many Christians has never been greater than it is during this profound Easter Week. For me, the Kingdom of Christ not only belongs to this world, it is the essence of this world. One of our teachers, Cynthia Bourgeault, recently wrote:

> The Kingdom of Heaven is "within you" (that is, here) and "at hand" (that is, now). It's not later, but lighter—some more subtle quality or dimension of experience accessible to you right in the moment. You don't die into it; you awaken into it.

The Kingdom of Heaven is really a *state of consciousness*; it is not a place you go to, but a place you *come from*. Sometimes, when working the practice of meditation extremely well, I can taste "nondual consciousness," when I feel absolutely connected to everything and everyone around me. Yes, we want to "go to Heaven" someday, presumably after we die. But what that is actually saying, is that we want to achieve unitive consciousness, we want to become one with God and all His creation. This is the fundamental teaching of Teilhard. For me, it is the essence of my faith. The Kingdom of Heaven, this state of oneness, is truly available to us right here, right now.

The April 10 passage from *God Calling*, a daily devotional, was read at one of my meetings this week. I loved the poetry, but the message, which speaks to an understanding of Heaven, is relevant to my reflection this morning.

> Obedience is one of the keys unlocking the door into my kingdom, so love and obey. No man can obey me implicitly without in time realizing my love, in his turn responding by love to that love, and then experiencing the joy won of the beloved, and the lover.
>
> The rough stone steps of obedience lead up to the mosaic of joy and love that floor my heaven. As one on earth who loves another says, "Where you are is home," so it is in relation with me. Where I am is my home—is heaven.

"The rough stone steps of obedience lead up to the mosaic of joy and love that floor my Heaven." This is beautiful poetry. Where God is, up those rough stone steps, is both His home and Heaven. Joining Him there, becoming one with the beloved, is what "going to Heaven" is all about.

> Heaven may be in a sordid slum or a palace, and I can make my home in the humblest heart. I can only dwell with the humble. Pride stands sentinel at the door of the heart to shut out the lowly, humble Christ.

"Pride stands sentinel at the door of the heart to shut out the lowly, humble Christ." Again, this is beautiful poetry. I can literally see pride standing at the door of my heart, blocking me from entering the very space where I can find Christ. He is that humble. He sets the example.

My prayer this morning is that I might achieve this state of oneness today, that I might hold on to it, savor it, and live it.

April 15: Holy Saturday, Easter Vigil

Reflect on the Passion

EASTER VIGIL arrived in the form of a nearly perfect day, beginning with tennis and a blueberry oatmeal from Starbucks. The spiritual hangover from the live Stations of the Cross last night persisted through a busy, but very moving morning at the St. Francis Soup Kitchen with Jennifer.

I finally have time to reflect on the weekend, a combination of traditional Catholic Easter Week activities and the emotional turmoil of a visit from my daughter. Both experiences forced me out of any peaceful stillness that might have been possible during long holiday weekends in the past.

I have played an active role in a Catholic service every day of this Triduum, and will attend one Mass and read at a second tomorrow. I have read a part of, or acted in the Passion four times, each time going deeper into the experience. Particularly last night during the live Stations, I listened to the stories of the maid servant of Caiaphas, the woman in the crowd in Jerusalem, and the soldiers who were part of the shameful beating and scourging of Jesus. Each of them caused me to vividly fantasize active participation in the scene or event. I noticed tears on the faces of both my fellow actors, and some of the people in the audience. I watched as our parishioners knelt, one after the other, to kiss the cross. Many of them were weeping when they stood up and walked in front of me. I read the parts of Judas and Pilate in the readings from two different Gospels. Each of these experiences took me further into a profound torment.

Between these extraordinary religious moments, I was jolted into the uncomfortable consciousness of a history of unhappy tension in my family. The wounds from four decades of unmet expectations and frustrated anticipation are still open in Jennifer and, sadly, in me. Sallie Ann plays an unfortunate role, mediating between and among the rest of us. Add to that Parker's autism, Sean's chronic health condition, and even Maggie vying for attention, and the result is quite a concoction.

Quite by accident, I read Jim Finley's reflections on shared loneliness. Evan Miller used them as a prelude to our Double Pancake retreat in Georgia.

> Next, in this moment, the person is all alone. He's all alone. This is solitude. He's all alone. Merton says in the hour of your death, you can get all the people in the room with you that you want. They can all climb up in the bed with you if you want, but you're dying alone. He says, all of us are that alone right now. And you'll never find true intimacy, by running away from that aloneness. And this person is alone. They're alone. And yet in being alone, they bear witness to the community that binds us all together as one. Because he's our brother. He's our brother. When we hug him, we do not hug one other than our self. We hug the one who reveals us to our self. And we're in this together. Together.

In our painful dysfunction, my family is a collection of individuals alone together. I know, it is extremely important that I focus this week on the Passion of Christ. The problems of my family amount to very little in comparison to that. Perhaps the message in the Passion is about surrender and forgiveness, both essential keys to making my time with family not just a bearable burden, but an opportunity for joy.

Paraphrasing *God Calling*, the rough stone steps of surrender open onto the acceptance that paves my heart space. Matt Mumber ended a recent reflection with this asking prayer:

> Grant me the eyes to see through the veil of illusion and know that God is ever present in all things without exclusion.

God is present in and as this universe. Every human being, along with every other created thing, that has ever been, is now, or ever will be, is included in that universe. Infinity, eternity, and cosmic oneness are very hard to see and understand through that veil of illusion.

We have reached the end of Ignatian Week Three. This ten-month journey with Ignatius Loyola enters its final month tomorrow.

IGNATIAN WEEK FOUR

CALENDAR WEEK THIRTY-ONE

I ask God for the gift to feel glad and to rejoice intensely because Jesus Christ rises in exultation and in great power and glory.

Praise to You, Lord Jesus Christ, King of eternal glory! Alleluia! Praise to You, triumphing over death, rising again to share Your triumph! Alleluia! Praise to You, sending out Your friends to share Your labour and Your eternal life! Alleluia! Alleluia!

April 16: Easter Sunday

After he arose, the Lord appeared first to his Mother; this is contained in the Scripture saying that he appeared to many. For, although this event is not mentioned explicitly, Scripture is our source of this definite information.

So sacred is the reunion of the Risen Christ with His Mother, that the Evangelists are silent on the subject. Following the example of their reticence, I will not attempt to reconstruct this scene, but ask the Lord through his Holy Spirit to tell me about it.

I humbly ask to be allowed to join my voice with the great chorus of Christ's Kingdom in heaven and on earth as together we sing:

QUEEN OF HEAVEN REJOICE ALLELUIA! You are more glorious than Judith who cried aloud to the people: "Open the gates! God is on our side. Open the gates! His power yet lives in Israel.: (Judith 13:13) Judith was acclaimed by her nation: "Thou art the boast of Jerusalem, the joy of Israel, the pride of our people." (Judith 15:10) Much more, 0 Queen of Heaven, art thou the boast of all nations, the joy, and the pride of all peoples, of heaven and of earth.

"BECAUSE THE SON WHOM IT WAS YOUR PRIVILEGE THE BEAR, ALLELUIA" Rejoice, because Christ, whom you first bore in your mind by your obedience and humility, and whom you were found worthy to bear in your womb, HAS RISEN AS HE SAID, ALLELUIA. As he speaks, so is it done. Long ago God had spoken: "Let there be light; and the light began." (Genesis 1:3) Again God speaks, and in that moment of divine command, the Son of Justice rises in his glory. PRAY TO GOD FOR US. Pray for us indeed to God, 0 Queen of heaven.

I make my colloquy, asking for the prayers of Heaven's Queen, that being transferred into the kingdom of her Divine Son, I may be made worthy to contemplate the Divine Glory forever. The Risen Lord Goes to His Mother. St. Inigo de Loyola wrote in his book of the Exercises:

> *The Resurrection of Christ our Lord? The First Apparition: First Point. He appeared to the Virgin Mary. Though this is not mentioned explicitly in the Scripture it must be considered as stated when Scripture says that He appeared to many others. For Scripture supposes that we have understanding, as it is written, 'Are you also without understanding?'"*

Remember, after asking the Lord to make you aware in His presence and offering to Him your time and yourself, where this fits into salvation history. Jesus had died on the cross and His Spirit had gone down among the dead to declare the great Good News that they will rise on the day the Father has appointed. Then His Spirit returns to the tomb and inspirits His cold, battered flesh. Straightway, He goes to his mother, the Lady Mary.

Imagine His coming to her. Stay to hear what they say, to see what they do, and to let them share with you what they experienced together. Consider, then, that Jesus Christ is God and mighty Lord. How did He manifest His divinity to His mother? Consider, too, how He consoled His mother after her sufferings. Then talk with Jesus or His mother, or with the Father. End with the Our Father.

THE EASTER Sunday celebration began at the 9 a.m. Mass with the family, which continued the uncomfortable combination of joy and tension that has characterized this Easter visit from Jennifer and her family. Sean and Parker did not come to Mass. Jennifer sat next to me, but seemed to be a little out of sorts, perhaps due to her being excluded from the Eucharist, perhaps only due to the frequent standing, kneeling, sitting, over and over again. Or maybe it was all in my mind. Perhaps, she was not ill at ease at all. Perhaps, I entered the church with the baggage of unresolved family tension, refusing to check it at the door, or to allow the music, the prayers, or any other part of the celebration to break through my mood.

What is really going on? I am actually quite proud of Parker, even when he "acts out." Thus far, that has only meant some loud six-year-old behavior, nothing "autistic" about it. Sean is simply a quiet supporter in the background.

It comes back to Jennifer or, more accurately, Jennifer and me. Guilt is such a worthless emotion, or it is worthless to ruminate on guilt over actions long past and far beyond control. The Serenity Prayer comes to mind. God, grant me the grace of serenity to accept what cannot be changed. Allow me to surrender to what is, to embrace the Christ in this moment and in this relationship and, especially, in this person.

Easter Sunday is such a huge day at the hundreds of Christian churches that are sprinkled around North Florida. The county sheriff controls the traffic along A1A, stopping cars to allow access to people arriving and leaving the numerous Easter services. Our Lady Star of the Sea is no exception. More than 1,500 people attend each of the morning Masses on Easter Sunday, three times the normal Sunday. I have to admit that I love the excitement and extra attention paid by everyone involved in making the Easter services special. Thinking about the process of celebrating this special Sunday is not a substitute for reflecting on its substance. In fact, most of the distinct features of the celebration are intended to remind us of one or another aspect of the events that occurred two thousand years ago.

I imagined myself walking with Mary and John, talking about the steps we would soon have to take in the face of anger and suspicion from the authorities. The crucifixion of Jesus would not end the effort to stamp out the movement that He started. Our first step would be to join the other followers in the underground network that provided hiding places during the day and passage out of Jerusalem after dark.

It is not entirely clear whether Jesus appeared to His disciples in Jerusalem or not. Luke's Gospel clearly states that Jesus appeared to them in Jerusalem and, further, instructed them to stay in Jerusalem until they were "clothed from on high." We do know that two disciples were walking on the road to Emmaus, a community only ten or twelve miles out of Jerusalem. Some accounts of the Great Commission seem to have occurred in the Galilee, a walking distance of about four days. My guess is that Mary and John were helped by others in the community to leave Jerusalem as soon as they could safely do so.

As I sat with this image, I was clearly afraid. To begin with, I was struggling with the whole concept of resurrection. In the Jewish tradition, bodily resurrection was neither possible nor particularly desirable. Paul's letters focus less on the bodily nature of resurrection than do the Gospels, written more than twenty years later. I have read that this reflects the growing distance from traditional Jewish thought. I know that bodily resurrection is church dogma, meaning that belief in it is a "required" part of my status as a Catholic. In fact, part of the Easter morning service was a repetition of our baptismal vows, which include a statement about bodily resurrection. So, I am afraid that my failure as a dogmatically pure Catholic will be obvious to everyone, including, especially, the risen Christ!

I am afraid for Mary, John, and myself that we will be discovered by the authorities. While Jerusalem is a large city, with numerous groups of dissidents, Jesus attracted undue attention. Too many people know that Mary is His mother, and John, His beloved disciple.

I am afraid of the uncertainty about the future. We have never lived anywhere other than Israel, albeit most of the time in the Galilee. It is no safer there than it is here. We know that we must keep moving, and it is not clear where we will be able to stay.

Fear is an unpleasant, but highly effective, source of motivation. This morning, fear helped bond me to Mary and John, and, through them, to Jesus. I sat with both the fear and the energy with which this fear filled me. I feel extremely close to them.

April 17

Repeat the reflection from April 16

ONCE AGAIN today, I am reflecting on my new friends, Mary and John. We have lived and suffered together through the arrest, trial, and crucifixion of Jesus. Every part of that experience was unbearable. Taken together, however, I am amazed that we were able to hold ourselves together through it all, especially filled with fear that the authorities would arrest us next.

After all that, with every fiber of our being stretched thin by the emotional energy of mourning His death, combined with fearing for our lives, Jesus walked into the room to bless us and re-affirm His love. His very presence challenged all that we thought about death. Consider the passage in 1 Corinthians 15:55–57.

> "Where, O death, is your victory?
> Where, O death, is your sting?"
> The sting of death is sin, and the power of sin is the law.
> But thanks be to God, who gives us
> the victory through our Lord Jesus Christ.

Romans 6:9 echoes this victory of Christ over death.

> We know that Christ, being raised from the dead, will never die again;
> death no longer has dominion over him.

I cannot make the moments of awakening happen, but I can assume the stance that offers the least resistance to being overtaken by the graced event of awakening.

April 18

Mark 16:1–11, The Resurrection of Jesus

¹ When the sabbath was over, Mary Magdalene, and Mary the mother of James, and Salome bought spices, so that they might go and anoint him. ² And very early on the first day of the week, when the sun had risen, they went to the tomb. ³ They had been saying to one another, "Who will roll away the stone for us from the entrance to the tomb?" ⁴ When they looked up, they saw that the stone, which was very large, had already been rolled back. ⁵ As they entered the tomb, they saw a young man, dressed in a white robe, sitting on the right side; and they were alarmed. ⁶ But he said to them, "Do not be alarmed; you are looking for Jesus of Nazareth, who was crucified. He has been raised; he is not here. Look, there is the place they laid him. ⁷ But go, tell his disciples and Peter that he is going ahead of you to Galilee; there you will see him, just as he told you." ⁸ So they went out and fled from the tomb, for terror and amazement had seized them; and they said nothing to anyone, for they were afraid.

[[And all that had been commanded them they told briefly to those around Peter. And afterward Jesus himself sent out through them, from east to west, the sacred and imperishable proclamation of eternal salvation.]]

Jesus Appears to Mary Magdalene

⁹ [[Now after he rose early on the first day of the week, he appeared first to Mary Magdalene, from whom he had cast out seven demons. ¹⁰ She went out and told those who had been with him, while they were mourning and weeping. ¹¹ But when they heard that he was alive and had been seen by her, they would not believe it.

THE PASSAGES this week are all accounts of the resurrection, appropriately shifting the focus from the trial and crucifixion to the big event. For many Christians, the core message of the Gospel of Jesus Christ is His resurrection. Without the resurrection, they argue, the story of Jesus would simply be the account of a dynamic prophet seeking to reform traditional Judaism. Preeminent New Testament scholar and one of my favorite authors, N.T. Wright, puts it this way.

> The resurrection completes the inauguration of God's kingdom… It is the decisive event demonstrating that God's kingdom really has been launched on earth as it is in heaven.

For me, the resurrection represents the springing forth of consciousness, a new life of understanding, coming out of the darkness into the full light of a glorious creation. The death that precedes resurrection is the death of the false self, which may not occur until the moment of our actual physical death. However common that is, however, it is a shame. Perhaps our earthly life is only a nano-second in universal time, but it is nonetheless what we have, right here and right now. Living the rest of our life in the light of the resurrection is a great alternative to staying numbly in the darkness of doubt.

Bodily resurrection remains one of those elements of traditional faith that I have chosen to live without. In fact, I am agnostic on the issue. I believe that our ultimate goal is unitive consciousness with God and all of His creation. That consciousness is not dependent on a physical body, whether whole or impaired, young or old, resurrected or still in a state of mortal death.

Raymond Brown, perhaps the greatest biblical scholar of the modern period, does believe in the bodily resurrection of Jesus Christ, but urges us not to become obsessed with the nature of that bodily return from death.

> Jesus' risen body was no longer a body as we know bodies, bound by the dimensions of space and time. It is best to follow Paul's description [in 1 Corinthians 15] of risen bodies

as spiritual, not natural or physical (psychos); he can even imply that these bodies are no longer flesh and blood (1 Corinthians 15:50). Small wonder he speaks of a mystery!

Brown makes an interesting observation about the importance of the various miracles performed by Jesus. Feeding the multitude bread and fish was an interesting sign of His status, but this food for the body was actually quite unimportant. The people who ate the bread and fish will be hungry tomorrow. If, however, the people partake of the important "food" offered by Jesus, which was food for the soul, they will never hunger. Likewise, giving sight to the blind man allows him to see what the rest of his fellows see, which is actually not very much. Jesus taught a radically different kind of "seeing," the importance of which vastly exceeds mere human vision. Lazarus was undoubtedly happy to be given a few more months or years of life, but that is a very insignificant gift when compared to the eternal life which Christ offered to everyone. I love this perceptive understanding of the contrast between "bible story miracles" on one hand, and the genuine Gospel miracles available from faith.

Sitting with the passage from Mark, I thought long and hard about the meaning of this week after Easter. Christ is risen! The painful, ugly story of an unfair trial and an inhumane execution end with the hope and joy of Christ alive in and as our lives. N.T. Wright expressed this beautifully.

> Easter was when Hope in person surprised the whole world by coming forward from the future into the present.

April 19

Repeat Mark 16:1–11

POPE FRANCIS "tweeted" this message yesterday:

> Today is the celebration of our hope, the celebration of this truth: Nothing and no one will ever be able to separate us from God's love.

"Nothing and no one will ever be able to separate us from God's love." The simple, but profound concept of grace is one of the hardest elements of my faith for me to fully embrace. God loves us regardless of what we think, say, and do. Note, however, that what we think, say, and do can prevent us from *experiencing* His love. These things can act as obstacles to all manner of great experiences, all of which require only that we surrender.

When our Double Pancakes met in Rome, Georgia, I lamented the fact that most of our teachers were either dead or quite old. It is not that there is anything wrong with learning from great men and women whose teaching survives in books. However, there is so much that we learn from actually living with and listening to Father Rohr, Uncle Finley, and the numerous other elders who have helped to shape our lives. Where will the next wisdom generation come from? Who are the contemporary mystics?

Increasingly, I believe Matt Mumber is one of those mystics. His presence seemed special to me five years ago when we first met. I am repeatedly moved by his observations on the teaching, both of the medieval mystics and of the great men and women we have been blessed to know through the Living School. This morning, Matt commented on one of Jim Finley's lectures on healing.

…so the practice is not just about my private enlightenment or salvation, it is about heal‑
ing, and healing is a difficult situation for which it is important to be trained and ready
in survival methods that are different from the usual ego survival agenda. the trained
firefighter goes into the burning building because that is his elected responsibility…the
trained healer goes into the world with the same level of danger that is exposure to a world
of suffering…we need to know how to get in, how to stay present to suffering, and how to
take care of ourselves such that the suffering does not overwhelm us, and in channeling
grace, allows for the fires of suffering to be quenched in some way… maybe not the actual
fires but the dangerous part… freedom from the tyranny of the fires of suffering even in
the presence of the flames of suffering…

Matt is a radiologist, treating terminal cancer patients. Healing is his calling. Surviving the "tyr‑
anny of the fires of suffering" is an absolute necessity in his life.

Jesus Christ lived, died, and lived again to teach us that the flames of suffering make us stronger. My
friend Charlie Hoskins told me yesterday that his favorite golf prayer was, "God, give me the strength
to hit it easy." It is a prayer for life as well as golf.

April 20

Luke 24:9–12, 34
*⁹ and returning from the tomb, they told all this to the eleven and to all the rest. ¹⁰ Now it was Mary Magdalene,
Joanna, Mary the mother of James, and the other women with them who told this to the apostles. ¹¹ But these words
seemed to them an idle tale, and they did not believe them. ¹² But Peter got up and ran to the tomb; stooping and
looking in, he saw the linen cloths by themselves; then he went home, amazed at what had happened.*
³⁴ They were saying, "The Lord has risen indeed, and he has appeared to Simon!"

READING THROUGH this passage again this morning, I am struck with how obtuse the Apostles were.
Not only did they seem to completely disappear at the time of the trial and execution, they hid as much
from the risen Christ as they did from the authorities. It is hard not to wonder at the deep faith that
developed among the followers of Jesus in the second half of the first century through the end of the
second century (before the faith was endorsed by the state), compared with the doubt and cowardice
of those who had been in His personal presence so often. Perhaps it is the sad fact that the Apostles
would not believe what the three women told them, but did accept the word of Simon Peter. While the
Evangelists were not as misogynist as the later hierarchy of the Church, it is possible. Perhaps it was the
fact that it was Mary Magdalene, Mary, the mother of James, and other women, not Mary, the mother
of Jesus. Whatever the reason, "the eleven and all the rest" come across rather poorly in this passage.

Reflecting on my reaction to this passage, I considered how often I question scripture. Implicitly, my
questions are also aimed at those who wrote, transcribed, translated, and recorded these documents
that have become Canon. Thomas Keating, the great contemplative pioneer responsible for introducing
Centering Prayer, commented on the work of the Bishops and Cardinals gathered in the mid-sixties to
look again at various doctrinal issues that had been un-resolved for centuries.

…[We] believe, following the teaching of Vatican II, that the Spirit is working in them also.
That means that the Word of God is manifesting itself in them…and is guiding them in

other ways that can become a source of grace for them. The fact that the Incarnation took place means that Christ is in relationship to every human being. Everybody is religious just by becoming born and, by that very fact, is in relationship with God. You don't have to search for it—you are already in relationship to the Source of all. We already are what we most want to be, but that state is unconscious to us....

The Second Ecumenical Council was a gathering of serious men (sadly, only very few women) in a relationship with Christ. Just like the evangelists two thousand years earlier, these men were of serious purpose, doing their best to leave behind an accurate record of the teachings and acts of Jesus. Whatever the reason, the Apostles were initially dubious about one of the central teachings of Jesus—His return three days after His death. The witness of Simon Peter assuaged some of the doubts on this Sunday afternoon so long ago, but Christ would face numerous further questions about the reality of the resurrection.

I imagined myself in that upper room, waiting for a message of some kind as to what we were meant to do next. Waiting in Jerusalem was dangerous, whereas traveling presented its own kinds of danger. Waiting in the company of the others felt better than the prospect of walking the dusty roads alone. While it cannot be said that I chose not to believe what the women reported from the grave, it was reassuring to hear Simon Peter say the same thing.

There appears to be a little confusion in the scriptural accounts in the period immediately following the discovery of the empty tomb. Matthew states that Jesus appeared to the Apostles in Galilee. Mark and Luke say that the appearance to the Apostles occurred in Jerusalem. Verse 34 in Luke, which is part of the reading today, states that the risen Christ had been seen by Simon. As I read the account, Simon only saw the empty tomb, not the risen Christ. Presumably, Christ did appear to Simon Peter at the same time that He appeared to the other Apostles, whether that was in Galilee or Jerusalem.

Further, Christ apparently appeared to two disciples, Cleopas and another, on the road to Emmaus, before appearing to the Apostles. In my fantasy, I followed the account of Luke, first discovering the empty tomb with the women, then joining the two men on the walk to Emmaus. I sat with this fantasy for two extended periods today.

Christ has risen indeed! Teilhard once said that "Matter is simply spirit moving slowly enough that we can see it." Christ slowed down for a few moments, allowing people to see Him again after His death. He continues to do so today, often taking the form of a new baby, whose smile gives away the Holy presence within, or a flight of birds, whose precision is key to a profound sense of order and peace in the universe. I pray silently, asking for the spirits of my friends and teachers to slowly move in and out of my life more often.

April 21

Repeat Luke 24:9–12, 34

THERE ARE few words that can describe the beauty of this spring day in Ponte Vedra Beach, sitting on a bench in the meditation garden. God is present here. The radical "panentheism" of Meister Eckhart is obvious. "All in God, God in all." God is transcendent, beyond all, and, at the same time, fully immanent, within all.

Sitting in this little corner of Creation, I find it impossible to conceive of a God somewhere up in the Heavens, who occasionally intervenes here on earth, especially when the right combination of prayer and obeisance compels Him to do so. And it is equally impossible to revert to the ancient belief system based on all things being God. Panentheism, God in all things, is the only way for me to understand the concept of grace. God is present in, to, and as all of creation. He requires no invitation. There are no conditions on His presence, or His love and forgiveness.

Sitting with this understanding, talking quietly to God about what He has done in my life and how much I owe everything to Him, I am overwhelmed by joy. There is no other way to describe it.

Sister Ilia Delio sent this Easter message to the contemplative community:

> Easter is the sacrament of a new consciousness, a new awareness of belonging to God, creation, and to one another. Resurrected life is transcendent life, breaking through our partial selves into a new wholeness of belonging. Christians are meant to be 'Easter people,' those who live with a new consciousness of belonging to a new whole, a new cosmos, where God is center. For Teilhard [de Chardin] and [Beatrice] Bruteau, it is this new consciousness that should render us 'evolvers,' participants in the awesome process of Christogenesis, birthing Christ by nurturing the love of God within us and among us. …

"Easter people" live in and with a new consciousness. This morning, more than ever, I feel like an "Easter person."

April 22

Read and reflect on the week.

WE HELD A party for Ability Housing here at Serendipity last night. Most of the seventy-five guests work "in the vineyard" of fighting homelessness and poverty. Ability Housing provides housing for homeless people, all of whom require a wide variety of services, ranging from addiction treatment to mental health care. Following the principle of "Housing First," Ability Housing partners with Sulzbacher Center, Gateway Community Services, and various city organizations. The purpose of the party was to bring the board and staff of Ability Housing together with the leadership of the various partner organizations in the Jacksonville area. It was a successful evening all around.

For the past week, our Living School teacher, Cynthia Bourgeault, has been writing about the Beatitudes from the perspective of non-dual contemplation. I find her summary statement to be profound.

> In these eight familiar sayings, we can now see that Jesus is talking about a radical transformation of consciousness, embraced through an attitude of inner receptivity; a willingness to enter the flow; a commitment to domesticate those violent animal programs within us; and above all, a passionate desire to unify the heart.

Transformed consciousness, an "inner receptivity," entering "the flow," and taming the "violent animal programs within us"—these are all wonderful ways to view the deeper message behind the already powerful messages of the Beatitudes. My favorite, however, is the suggestion that Jesus was talking, above all, about a "passionate desire to unify the heart."

Sadly, life presents us with what seems like an endless supply of opportunities for dualism—separating rights and wrongs, ourselves from others, our tribe from their tribe, and our true self from our false self. The goal of non-dual consciousness begins with a united heart. Oneness is not sameness. Uniting the heart does not require that we embrace the false self. It does, however, require that we forgive our imperfect true self.

Sitting with that concept, I considered all the ways that I have acted to create disunity in my heart. I have made so many mistakes, hurt so many people, and done so much damage. How can I ever be forgiven? How can I ever "unify my heart"? The simple answer is that I cannot. I can't, He can. I have to surrender to that fundamental fact. With my complete surrender, God's grace works quickly. What has been hard for me to learn is that it is not a one-time surrender. My ego constantly tries to take charge, asserting itself in competition with grace. I learn the lesson again each day, often several times during the day. The amazing thing is amazing grace! It is always present, always free, always unearned.

God, grant me the strength to hit it easy.

Calendar Week Thirty-Two

I ask God for the gift to feel glad and to rejoice intensely, sharing the joy and exultation of my Lord Jesus Christ.

You did a marvel, Lord Jesus Christ, and make me feel beside myself in surprise. My spirit glistens with Your rising. I smile and smile with you, I'm drowning in the laughter of Your friends. You have won, Lord, we know You have won! You have defeated all the worst that we could do, each alone and all together. You crushed the power of darkness and of death to walk peacefully again in our flesh, now and forever. Send me to console those around me who hurt. Come, and send our friends into this daily world to labor full of hope for the Reign of God.

April 23

John 20:19–23, Jesus Appears to the Disciples
[19] When it was evening on that day, the first day of the week, and the doors of the house where the disciples had met were locked for fear of the Jews, Jesus came and stood among them and said, "Peace be with you." [20] After he said this, he showed them his hands and his side. Then the disciples rejoiced when they saw the Lord. [21] Jesus said to them again, "Peace be with you. As the Father has sent me, so I send you." [22] When he had said this, he breathed on them and said to them, "Receive the Holy Spirit. [23] If you forgive the sins of any, they are forgiven them; if you retain the sins of any, they are retained."

Jesus appeared to a group of His disciples on Sunday, the third day after His death, and again, one week later, presumably in the same house. The difference between the two visits was the presence of Thomas for the second. In both cases, the primary purpose seems to have been to "prove" His resurrection. Allowing the disciples to see His hands and side and, in the second visit, instructing Thomas to actually put his fingers into the holes in Jesus's hands, and thrust his hand into the wound in Jesus's side—all of these were designed to demonstrate the reality of the bodily resurrection of Jesus. Twice, Jesus said to them, "Peace be with you."

My good friend, Father Frank, wrote about faith in his blog today. As I reflect on the appearances of Jesus reported by the Evangelists, it strikes me that it is all about faith. As often as Jesus had spoken to His disciples during His ministry, often performing miracles, they still doubted. Not just Thomas, who famously doubted, and Peter, who denied, but all the disciples, who were mysteriously absent from the trial and crucifixion, apparently lacked faith. It is incredible to me that so many people over the centuries have demonstrated such amazing faith *without* the opportunity to meet and touch the risen Christ.

That says a great deal about the power of grace. As Father Frank points out, "We can believe in God because God takes the initiative to connect with us." God is the aggressor in our dance of love with Him. Our role is to surrender to His love. We let Him act in, on, and through us. We never cause or make Him do anything.

On this Divine Mercy Sunday, I am particularly moved by the soft power of this ever-present grace. I feel gently overcome by a quiet influence I cannot ignore or escape. Even in my most selfish, egoistic moments, when I least want to consider the role of faith in my life, I am reminded by tender signs of His presence. He is the aggressor in a most unassertive way.

April 24

Repeat John 20:19–23

THIS MORNING, still feeling the gentle power of God's advancing love, I sat on the bench with Maggie, overwhelmed by the presence of so much creation around us. The ocean waves were breaking loudly on the beach, numerous species of birds were making their morning cries, the garden emerged green and beautiful from the darkness. When I returned to the library, I read the Canticle of the Sun, written by Saint Francis almost a thousand years ago.

Most High, all-powerful, all-good Lord, All praise is Yours, all glory, all honour and all blessings.

To you alone, Most High, do they belong, and no mortal lips are worthy to pronounce Your Name.

Praised be You my Lord with all Your creatures, especially Sir Brother Sun, Who is the day through whom You give us light.
And he is beautiful and radiant with great splendour,
Of You Most High, he bears the likeness.

Praised be You, my Lord, through Sister Moon and the stars,
In the heavens you have made them bright, precious and fair.

Praised be You, my Lord, through Brothers Wind and Air,
And fair and stormy, all weather's moods, by which You cherish all that You have made.

Praised be You my Lord through Sister Water,
So useful, humble, precious and pure.

Praised be You my Lord through Brother Fire, through whom You light the night and he is beautiful and playful and robust and strong.

Praised be You my Lord through our Sister, Mother Earth
who sustains and governs us, producing varied fruits with coloured flowers and herbs.
Praise be You my Lord through those who grant pardon for love of You and bear sickness and trial.
Blessed are those who endure in peace, By You Most High, they will be crowned.
Praised be You, my Lord through Sister Death, from whom no-one living can escape. Woe to those who die in mortal sin! Blessed are they She finds doing Your Will.

No second death can do them harm. Praise and bless my Lord and give Him thanks, And serve Him with great humility.

Saint Francis broke new ground when he lived what he believed. I sit with the concepts of my very large and wonderful family: Brother Sun, Sister Moon, Brothers Wind and Air, Sister Water, and Brother Fire. All of us children of Mother Earth (also a sister!), and all of us subject to Sister Death. What a family! The cool part is spending time with this whole family every morning.

In the last line of the canticle, Francis refers to a second death for those who do God's will, a death that can do them no harm. Reflecting on that, I am once again struck by the importance of an initial death of ego, a death of the false self. Spiritual growth requires the new birth that follows this death. Father Rohr teaches that transformation can result from deep love as well as deep suffering. I tend towards the view that suffering alone, suffering to the point of ego death, leads to true transformation.

Verse 22 of the passage from John's Chapter 20 is worthy of repeated reflection. The Holy Spirit is described as the breath of Christ.

> When he had said this, he breathed on them and said to them, "Receive the Holy Spirit."
> Brother Air, breathes on me each day as the Holy Spirit, making life not just possible, but abundant. Halleluiah!

April 25

The Contemplation for Learning to Love like God
Parts 1and 2
Remember two things about love: First, love is act, not talk; it shows itself in the deed done, not simply in words spoken. Second, love works itself out in mutual sharing, so that the lover always gives to and receives from the beloved—everything: gifts, money, convictions, honors, position.

I begin by asking the Lord God to let me become aware of myself in the divine presence, and I offer myself to God. Then I use my fantasy. I imagine that I am standing before the throne of God, and all around me I see saints and martyrs, angels and powers and dominions. They all smile at me and seem to recommend me to God the Lord. Then I ask God for what I want right now. I want to have an intimate understanding of myself and my life as gift, and all my world as gift, so that I will be incandescent with gratitude, and then go beyond that to love the Giver of all this, who loves me vastly in deed and in sharing.

FIRST PART
I run through my mind all the splendors of the created world. I wonder at the vast plains and mountains and the tiny wild flower. I let my mind run among the stars and planets, and then delve into the tiniest atom with its elegant particles and forces. I remember that God has created and does create all humankind, and that God has redeemed and does redeem all peoples. And I remember how much God gives me in all this.

I consider this, and ponder it, letting my heart go out to God. The Lord has done much for me. He lavishes on me life, light, understanding, desiring, free choice, and the summons to love and to be loved. Most astonishing of all, God plainly wants to and does communicate God's Self to me.

Then I think about my own case, about my own life history and my own self. I am being created by this great Lord to live and function according to gifts coming from God's Self. How am I to love in return? What makes sense except to do as God does, to give as God gives? What would be right except to offer all that I am and all that I have?

So I say the prayer below, putting my whole mind and strength into the offering and the petition.

Accept, 0 Lord, and treat as Your own my liberty, my understanding, my memory—all of my decisions and my freedom to choose. All that I am and all that I have You gave and give to start; now I turn and return all to You, looking to find Your hopes and will in all. Keep giving me Your holy love, hold on me Your life-giving gaze, and I neither need not want anything else.

At the end of each time of prayer that I spend in this Contemplation, I reflect a moment and then speak with God my Lord. And end with the Our Father.

SECOND PART

I look at all the varieties of creatures on the earth and in space and let it come home to me that God continues creating them and dwells within them. Through eons and eons, God faithfully stayed present to each kind of living thing, energizing by the divine presence through all the centuries the genetic codes that opened each phylum to its proper evolution. At this very moment, God gives each order and kind of creature what God can give it: To rocks, weight and solidness and presence. To plants, affinity for light and an inward impulse to grow and to mature authentically according to its kind. To animals, sight and smell and feeling, and the enormous range of impulses and instincts that move herds to migrate and butterflies to sip nectar from flowers. All of that God sustains.

Then I consider and ponder this, That God remains present at every moment to every creature. God stays there always, sustaining existence and life and reflection. God at the core of the core of all creation flames the creative love of God, summoning out of chaos and nothingness all that exists and lives and comprehends.

Finally, I think about my own case. I turn to myself and ask what this means to me? God present at my conception. God present at my birth and my growth into infancy. God faithful to me as I came to the use of reason and to freedom. God loyal to me who committed myself to be a soldier of Christ, and through my other permanent commitments. All along, the energies of God rising through mine, through digestion and gesture and muscle growth and seeing and interpreting. God the ground of my being. God the core of myself.

So, I wonder what I ought to do and offer to God, now. And I say with all my heart the prayer below:

Accept, 0 Lord, and treat as Your own my liberty, my understanding, my memory all of my decisions and my freedom to choose. All that I am and all that I have You gave and give to start; now I turn and return all to You, looking to find Your hopes and will in all. Keep giving me Your holy love, hold on me Your life giving-gaze, and I neither need not want anything else.

At the end of each time of prayer that I spend in this Contemplation, I reflect a moment and then speak with God my Lord. And end with the Our Father.

WHEN I PREPARED the framework for these Exercises last September, I printed out this contemplation for Learning to Love like God. I have read it at least once a week for the past seven and a half months. As I sat with it this morning, I listened to a most incredible rendition of one of my favorite songs, the Leonard Cohen classic, "Hallelujah." This version, written by Kelley Mooney, adapts the Cohen music to lyrics adapted for Easter.

> A crown of thorns placed on His head, He knew that He would soon be dead.
> He said did you forget me Father did you?
> They nailed Him to a wooden cross, Soon all the world would feel the loss
> Of Christ the King before His Hallelujah.
>
> He hung His head and prepared to die Then lifted His face up to the sky
> Said I am coming home now Father to you.
> A reed which held His final sip Was gently lifted to his lips
> He drank His last and gave His soul to glory.

The soldier who had used his sword To pierce the body of our Lord
Said truly this was Jesus Christ our Savior
He looked with fear upon his sword Then turned to face his Christ and Lord.
Fell to his knees crying Hallelujah.

Took from his head the thorny crown And wrapped him in a linen gown
And laid him down to rest inside the tomb.
The holes in his hands, his feet and side Now in our hearts we know he died
To save us from ourselves oh hallelujah

Three days went by again they came To move the stone to bless the slain
With oil and spice anointing hallelujah.
But as they went to move the stone They saw that they were not alone
But Jesus Christ has risen Hallelujah

Listening to this song over and over again, reflecting on all that we have commemorated over the past month, I am overcome.

After a long time, I returned to the contemplation on learning to love like God. The first and second parts go together well. The first deals with the inorganic world of stars, planets, atoms, and particles. The second moves from the inorganic to the organic, asking that we reflect on the incalculable number of varieties of creatures that God continues to create and dwell within. God "energized... through genetic codes that opened each phylum to its proper evolution." The contemplation ends with the thought that every inorganic and organic creature has exactly the right properties and characteristics, ideally equipping that creature to perform precisely the role in creation for which it was created. For all of these creatures, a significant part of the role is *adaptation*, which means that an expanding universe, changing ever so slowly as it expands, will require minute changes in each and every creature. Part of each creature's perfection is its ability to adapt.

If I view God as love, and creation as His first and greatest act of love, and evolution as the form His love takes, then learning to love like God means that I must recognize how perfectly I have been created. Like all other creatures, human perfection includes both the requirement and the ability to adapt. Unlike other creatures, however, we humans, being sapient, have the ability to know that we know, and to reason on the basis of that knowledge. I believe all sentient beings can love like God, often achieving a much higher level of non-judgmental, unconditional love than humans.

Thomas Berry speaks powerfully about the relationship between and among God's creatures.

The universe is a communion of subjects, not a collection of objects. As we recover our awareness of the universe as a communion of subjects, a new interior experience awakens within the human. The barriers disappear. An enlargement of soul takes place. The excitement evoked by natural phenomena is renewed. Dawn and sunset are once again transforming experiences, as are the sights, sounds, scents, tastes, and feel of the natural world about us—the surging sea, the sound of the wind, the brooding forests.

Tragically, modern man has largely lost his ability to view the universe as anything other than objects. On a personal level, I have sometimes struggled to shift my view of people *from objects*, temporarily necessary to a deal or project, *to subjects*, with views, interests, and roles just as important as mine. Employees, partners, customers, and communities are stakeholders in the transaction. On those occasions where I have engaged with these various groups as equal participants, not only have the projects been better, but everyone involved has found some level of joy in the process.

Berry raises this discussion from the individual transaction level to one of planetary significance.

> The devastation of the planet can be seen as a direct consequence of the loss of this capacity for human presence to and reciprocity with the nonhuman world. This reached its most decisive moment in the seventeenth-century proposal of René Descartes that the universe is composed simply of "mind and mechanism." In this single stroke, he devitalized the planet and all its living creatures, with the exception of the human.

How does God love? He loves each of His creatures as subjects, inviting each of us to join Him in the dance of life. Berry describes a world where "Every being exists in intimate relation with other beings and in a constant exchange of gifts with each other." God relates to all of His creatures as "thou," never "it." Relating to the world in this mutually respectful way requires a significantly higher level of consciousness than most of us ever achieve.

Many great teachers, particularly the mystics, recognized the potential humans have to grow increasingly conscious, some ultimately even reaching non-duality or unitive consciousness. Many individuals occasionally achieve *states* of this unitive consciousness. A much smaller number live at least part of their lives at the *stage* of non-dual consciousness. Teilhard goes further, teaching that the human race is collectively progressing toward unitive consciousness. I am not overly optimistic.

Robert Heinlein famously said, "The capacity of the human mind for swallowing *nonsense* and spewing it forth in violent and repressive action has never yet been plumbed." My thesis advisor at Harvard, Samuel P. Huntington, had a similarly dim view of man's progress. He argued that a great deal of human history is the story of men inventing increasingly effective technology to kill other men in large numbers.

> The West won the world not by the superiority of its ideas or values or religion (to which few members of other civilizations were converted) but rather by its superiority in applying organized violence. Westerners often forget this fact; non-Westerners never do.

When Professor Huntington first wrote *Clash of Civilizations*, I was very much opposed to its thesis about the inevitability of conflict between Judeo-Christianity and Islam. I wanted the future to be more inclusive. I still want that, but am growing despondent with the recent global retreat into nationalism, and to the erection of higher barriers between people and cultures.

This does not strike me as loving like God loves. God's love represents exactly the opposite process to that of "swallowing nonsense and spewing violence." As I sit with this depressing contrast, I pray the Our Father. "Thy will be done on earth as it is in Heaven." I believe to the depth of my soul that God's will is not violence, hatred, and exclusion. Father John convinced me to become Catholic with the words inclusion and forgiveness. They remain the two most important words in my faith.

April 26

The Contemplation for Learning to Love like God

   Parts 3 and 4

   Remember two things about love: First, love is act, not talk; it shows itself in the deed done, not simply in words spoken. Second, love works itself out in mutual sharing, so that the lover always gives to and receives from the beloved—everything: gifts, money, convictions, honors, position.

   I begin by asking the Lord God to let me become aware of myself in the divine presence, and I offer myself to God. Then I use my fantasy. I imagine that I am standing before the throne of God, and all around me I see saints and martyrs, angels and powers and dominions. They all smile at me and seem to recommend me to God the Lord. Then I ask God for what I want right now. I want to have an intimate understanding of myself and my life as gift, and all my world as gift, so that I will be incandescent with gratitude, and then go beyond that to love the Giver of all this, who loves me vastly in deed and in sharing.

   THIRD PART

   I consider that God—to use Saint Peter's words—works busily in all creation. I use a metaphor here, of course, but I can see that God attends to each and every creature and keeps shaping instincts and consciences and raising the energies that form our weather and our interactions, then I make a lot of sense when I say that God works busily. I let my mind run through all created things: the far reaches of space, our own galaxy, the globe of the earth, imagining how God labors to keep their magnificent order and functioning. Then I enter into living things, perhaps individual birds or animals and individual persons, imagining how God keeps nerves crackling and bone marrow producing blood, and the like. I might consider a tiny little bug or flower, and imagine how many other living and non-living things conspired to bring it to life and sustain it.

   I consider this and ponder it, letting my heart go out to God. How great God is! How full of life, and how eager to have others exist, particularly other rational creatures. God labors and hopes and keeps sustaining us even when we destroy. Then I think about my own case, about my own life history and my own self. How did God have to labor to keep me alive? to keep me growing and learning and believing and hoping? Were there no times when I realized that God was working in me? for me? So I say the prayer below, putting my whole mind and strength into the offering and the petition.

   Accept, 0 Lord, and treat as Your own my liberty, my understanding, my memory—all of my decisions and my freedom to choose. All that I am and all that I have You gave and give to start; now I turn and return all to You, looking to find Your hopes and will in all. Keep giving me Your holy love, hold on me Your life-giving gaze, and I neither need nor want anything else.

   At the end of each time of prayer, I reflect a moment and then speak with God my Lord ending with the Our Father.

   FOURTH PART

   I consider that all the good that I see and know comes to be as a share in the divine good. That is, all power echoes the divine power whose action elicited it from chaos. All beauty mirrors the divine beauty and comes from it in the first place the way an image in a mirror comes from the origin. All holiness on earth is the fragrance of God present in and with all of us. And so through justice, goodness, mercy, understanding, compassion.

   Then I consider this, and ponder it, letting my heart go out to God who pours out His own Self and all His infinity of gifts. And I think about my own case, about how my own gifts are a share, an effulgence, of God my Creator and Lord. I am like a mirror reflecting the sun. I am like a leaf's chlorophyll, moving excitedly and warmly with the sun's excited and warm light. All that I am and all that I have are a participation in God.

   So I say the prayer below, putting my whole mind and strength into the offering and the petition:

Accept, 0 Lord, and treat as Your own, my liberty, my understanding, my memory, all of my decisions and my freedom to choose. All that I am and all that I have You gave and give to start; now I turn and return all to You, looking to find Your hopes and will in all. Keep giving me Your holy love, hold on my Your life-giving gaze, and I neither need not want anything else.

At the end of each time of prayer that I spend in this Contemplation, I reflect a moment and then speak with God my Lord. And end with the Our Father.

THE FIRST part of this contemplation dealt with the inorganic world, and the second part with the organic world. In these final parts, the third and fourth, the contemplation focuses on God's continuing providential role, and the extent to which the result of His efforts mirrors its divine origin.

It was Teilhard who finally resolved my personal difficulty understanding and accepting the concept of a provident God. I questioned the constant reference many believers make to God's direct role in everything, even the smallest event in a person's life. I rebel against statements like, "There are no accidents," "God intended for me to meet this person on this day," or "Everything has a purpose." These statements reflect an understanding of divine control similar to what Mormons refer to as foreordination, and other religions call predestination.

These comments continue to trouble me today, but I now better understand the incredible power of evolution, combined with the collective role of individual free choice, in the universe. Seven billion humans are freely making choices every second of every day, the combined impact of which constantly changes everything. The global direction of this change is toward higher consciousness, with the ultimate goal of non-dual, conscious unity of God and all creation.

Another way of saying this is that God momently creates all of creation, following His rules of adaptation to the environment and free choice. He *wills* that what started out good get better. The universe, all of which existed at the moment of the big bang, was good, even though it was then only inchoate energy. The universe "got better" and is getting better over billions of years, moving from energy to gaseous matter, to solid inorganic matter, and, finally, to living, organic beings. In the context of the time scale of God's creative process, mankind is the last letter of the last word on the last page of a massive book. And every additional being represents a movement of creation toward better adaptation to the environment, including increasing consciousness of itself.

Note that I am using "better" to describe greater complexity and greater consciousness. Evolution, even on the massive scale of infinity and eternity, is not always smooth. There are five known periods of mass extinction in the history of Earth, all of which pre-dated the appearance of sapient mankind. Some environmentalists, including Berry, argue that our irresponsible actions since the beginning of the industrial revolution, with its highly capitalistic world order, are leading to a sixth mass extinction. This hardly seems to me to be a better universe, even though it is more complex. Science deniers do not strike me as particularly conscious of the universe around them.

Meister Eckhart opened my eyes to the wonderful relationship between man and God, expressed extremely well in the fourth part of today's contemplation on learning to love like God.

All beauty mirrors the divine beauty and comes from it in the first place the way an image in a mirror comes from the origin. All holiness on earth is the fragrance of God present in and with all of us. And so through justice, goodness, mercy, understanding, compassion.

God created man in His image, doing so according to the rules of His evolutionary system. He continues to create us in His image, an image of "justice, goodness, mercy, understanding, compassion," and beauty.

Eckhart wrote that man, among all creatures, is most like God.

> This similarity between God and man surpasses that between God and the other creatures, because man, on account of his intellect, is spiritually an image of the divine essence, whereas the rest of creation reflects not the essence of the deity, but only ideas that exist in him.

Eckhart taught that a saint becomes a pure mirror, in and through which God is reflected. Note that the mirror takes its reflected being solely from the object it reflects. It is not the saint that is divine. It is God that is divine, reflected by the saint only as and to the extent that the saint achieves the essence of what Eckhart called a "poor man."

> A poor man is one who wants nothing, knows nothing, and has nothing.

In short, a poor man has emptied himself of all ego. Only by completely emptying oneself is it possible to be filled with "justice, goodness, mercy, understanding, compassion, and beauty."

There is more to this issue of man's relationship with God, and with all the rest of His creation. As Berry writes, "the universe is composed of subjects to be communed with, not of objects to be exploited."

Tragically, several factors have combined over the past several hundred years to result in a reality far different from one that is conducive to loving like God. Quoting Berry again,

> The human is seen as the supreme reality. Every other being is available for exploitation. The supreme law of economics calls for taking as much as possible of the Earth's resources to be processed, passed through the consumer economy as quickly as possible, and then deposited as residue on the waste heap. The nonhuman world becomes property to be used by the human.

The task of reversing this situation, of returning the relationship between and among God and His creatures to one consistent with God's love is enormous. Time is of the essence, even in the long view of very gradual evolutionary change.

> The primary community is not the human community, it is the Earth community. Our primary obligations and allegiances are to this larger community....If the Earth is only a background or a collection of resources for the human, then the devastation presently taking place will continue.

My prayer this morning is that I can become an agent of change, helping to establish (or re-establish) the supremacy of the Earth community over the human community. I pray that I will view and treat all of God's creation as subjects, not objects. I pray that I can empty myself, particularly now, as I come to the end of the Exercises. Just as I believe that God creates me momently, I believe that the state of my *kenosis*, the "self-emptying" of my own will such that I become entirely receptive to God's divine will, is constantly in flux. Prayer, meditation, contemplation, and service—especially service—are the tools that seem to remove the greatest number of obstacles to achieving a true state of "self-emptiness." The very good news is that the smallest, most fleeting experience of joy, the joy that results from this emptying out of self, is enough. Just that—enough. The end of all wanting, striving, and seeking. Enough.

April 27

Luke 24:13–35, The Walk to Emmaus

¹³ Now on that same day two of them were going to a village called Emmaus, about seven miles from Jerusalem, ¹⁴ and talking with each other about all these things that had happened. ¹⁵ While they were talking and discussing, Jesus himself came near and went with them, ¹⁶ but their eyes were kept from recognizing him. ¹⁷ And he said to them, "What are you discussing with each other while you walk along?" They stood still, looking sad. ¹⁸ Then one of them, whose name was Cleopas, answered him, "Are you the only stranger in Jerusalem who does not know the things that have taken place there in these days?" ¹⁹ He asked them, "What things?" They replied, "The things about Jesus of Nazareth, who was a prophet mighty in deed and word before God and all the people, ²⁰ and how our chief priests and leaders handed him over to be condemned to death and crucified him. ²¹ But we had hoped that he was the one to redeem Israel. Yes, and besides all this, it is now the third day since these things took place. ²² Moreover, some women of our group astounded us. They were at the tomb early this morning, ²³ and when they did not find his body there, they came back and told us that they had indeed seen a vision of angels who said that he was alive. ²⁴ Some of those who were with us went to the tomb and found it just as the women had said; but they did not see him." ²⁵ Then he said to them, "Oh, how foolish you are, and how slow of heart to believe all that the prophets have declared! ²⁶ Was it not necessary that the Messiah should suffer these things and then enter into his glory?" ²⁷ Then beginning with Moses and all the prophets, he interpreted to them the things about himself in all the scriptures.

²⁸ As they came near the village to which they were going, he walked ahead as if he were going on. ²⁹ But they urged him strongly, saying, "Stay with us, because it is almost evening and the day is now nearly over." So he went in to stay with them. ³⁰ When he was at the table with them, he took bread, blessed and broke it, and gave it to them. ³¹ Then their eyes were opened, and they recognized him; and he vanished from their sight. ³² They said to each other, "Were not our hearts burning within us while he was talking to us on the road, while he was opening the scriptures to us?" ³³ That same hour they got up and returned to Jerusalem; and they found the eleven and their companions gathered together. ³⁴ They were saying, "The Lord has risen indeed, and he has appeared to Simon!" ³⁵ Then they told what had happened on the road, and how he had been made known to them in the breaking of the bread.

SEVERAL TIMES over the past five years, I have entered into the fantasy of walking with the two disciples on the road to Emmaus. Each time, I joined with others from my parish, singing over and over again, "Were not our hearts burning within us? Were not our hearts burning with fire?"

It is an extremely powerful fantasy. As I sat in the chilly morning air in the garden, I started singing those verses, then walked along the lagoon as I quietly mouthed the words. The concepts of fire, flame, and burning frequently come up in reference to the Holy Spirit, the Divine Presence. John the Baptist proclaimed that Jesus would "baptize with the Holy Spirit and fire." One of my favorite statements from Teilhard involves fire.

Someday, after mastering the winds, the waves, the tides and gravity, we shall harness for God the energies of love, and then, for a second time in the history of the world, man will have discovered fire.

Even, or especially, Rumi frequently used the concept of fire for emphasis: "Set your life on fire. Seek those who fan your flames." One verse from Rumi could have been used on that walk to Emmaus: "My head is bursting with the joy of the unknown. My heart is expanding a thousand-fold."

What is it about this story that evokes such passion? I believe one part of the answer lies in the idea of "the unknown." Christ walked and talked with Cleopas and his friend, then joined them at the dinner table, all the while not disclosing who He was. At the moment when they recognized Him, I can imagine all manner of emotions, from temporary fear to indescribable joy. A bursting head and expanding heart seem to be appropriate reactions. Rumi again:

In each moment the fire rages, it will burn away a hundred veils. And carry you a thousand steps toward your goal.

Further reflecting on this story, I like the idea that there were two disciples walking on that road. While Paul's lone conversion on the road to Damascus is far more famous, my preference would be to have a friend with me, confirming what I experience and sharing the joy with me. Community is extremely important at times of peak emotional experiences.

Oddly, the only other Gospel reference to the story appears in Mark 16:12–13. It is very simple.

After this he appeared in another form to two of them, as they were walking into the country. And they went back and told the rest, but they did not believe them.

The Apostle Paul is adamant about the fundamental importance of the resurrection. He writes in 1 Corinthians 15:14:

…and if Christ has not been raised, then our proclamation has been in vain and your faith has been in vain.

My strong belief in the Cosmic Christ makes bodily resurrection unimportant, just as it makes continued life in a different form obvious. There will be life after death, just as there was life before birth. Like Christ, we humans, along with every other creature in the universe, organic and inorganic, were present at the moment of the Big Bang. Obviously, we existed in a radically different form than that in which we exist today. Human kind in its present form has only existed for a few thousand years, hardly a blink in the 14.7 billion years since that Big Bang.

My understanding of the full implications of the Cosmic Christ is not at all unlike seeing the risen Christ in person. Christ is here, now. Christ is in every person. Christ is in every one of His creatures, organic and inorganic. Christ is present in actions as well as things. Fully living with this knowledge is very powerful. Reflecting on it this morning, I am filled with indescribable joy.

April 28

Repeat Luke 24:13–35

THERE IS A wedding at Serendipity tomorrow. The daughter of our good friends will be married in the garden in front of 150 friends and family members. In my new capacity as a Notary Public, I am officiating. Tradesmen and gardeners have been here all week, making sure that house and garden are at their best for the event. All the newness, excitement, glory, and joy of Easter have returned with emphasis!

It is odd, then, that I spend this early dawn sitting in the meditation corner of the garden, contemplating the significance of the Cross. The contrast of great joy and great suffering is extraordinary. It is as though each further deepens the significance of the other. There is simply no way of sitting with the intensity of the suffering exemplified by the Cross without seeing the equally intense meaning of the risen Christ, the Cosmic Christ.

For two thousand years, Christians throughout the world have been worshiping what Father Rohr describes as the "central Christian image of a naked, bleeding, suffering man." He goes on. "Christians strangely worship a suffering God, largely without realizing it; and Christian mystics even say that there is *only one cosmic suffering, and we all share in it.*"

Joy and suffering are about as dualistic as it is possible to be, with each at the extreme end of a scale. Meditating about the two of them together, however, I imagine a tuning fork, beginning with a slow vibration, moving from one radical note to another. As the speed of the vibration increases, however, the difference between the two sounds resolves itself into a single resonance. My musical ignorance might be painfully evident at this point, but the message is clear to me. Father Rohr said it differently this morning.

> If you gaze upon the mystery of the cross long enough, your dualistic mind breaks down, and you become slow to call things totally good or totally bad… The genius of Jesus' ministry is his revelation that God uses tragedy, suffering, pain, betrayal, and death itself, not to wound you but in fact to bring you to God. There are no dead ends. Everything can be transmuted and everything can be used. On the cross, in dramatic theater, God took the worst thing, the killing of God, and made it into the best thing—the redemption of the world!

I like the Swedish saying, "Shared joy is a double joy, shared sorrow is half a sorrow." Expand that idea to the universe. I sat with this thought for a long time this morning, looking from the meditation garden out at the lawn where the crowd will sit while watching the wedding tomorrow. In this place, on this morning, there is simply too much joy to allow lengthy reflection on suffering. Thank God for that.

April 29

Read and reflect on the contemplation to love like God.

HERE I AM in the garden, now furnished with seating for 150 guests, ready for the reception after the ceremony, with food stations and bars. Nonetheless, the images of Christ suffering remain foremost in my mind. Gradually, the image of suffering morphed into an image of love. God loves through His suffering, not in spite of it.

Father Rohr, again:

> Sooner or later, life is going to lead you (as it did Jesus) into the belly of the whale, into a place where you can't fix, control, explain, or understand (usually very concrete and personal; it cannot be merely theoretical). That's where transformation most easily and deeply happens. That's when you're uniquely in the hands of God because you cannot "handle" it yourself.
>
> Suffering is the only thing strong enough to destabilize the imperial ego. It has to be led to the edge of its own resources, so it learns to call upon its Deepest Source. Some might call this the God Self, the True Self, the Christ Self, the Buddha Self, or just the soul. Life at this point is indestructible! In short, you must discover or "save" your own soul, and nothing else can compare with this discovery.

I have found myself "in the belly of the whale" on a few occasions in my life. For me, it was not just a deep depression. It was that, combined with a desperate feeling of helplessness; a growing suffocation from which there was no escape.

The suffocation felt like what I imagine water-boarding would feel like. Just as I would catch my breath, more water would rush in, washing away both air and the hope for air. Time stood still. More accurately, time ceased to measure the passage of events or feelings. Everything seemed to be endlessly instantaneous.

Moments of relief from the torment felt like being born again after death, but not a birth of joy. Rather, it was being born into a new identity, not recognizable, not comfortable. Particularly for me, my old identity—the outer shell of my life container—was all about *what I did*, not who I was, or what I believed in, or what made my life important. I would briefly come out of the belly of the whale without moorings, unable to rely upon the usual tools and mechanisms, facades and "dramatic roles" that had theretofore helped me find at least superficial balance.

In the period of my deep depression from the winter of 2005 through the summer of 2007, I vividly and painfully remember a few brief efforts of near sanity. In a panic, I would rush to find another deal, to raise financing, or start another new company. Then the torment would begin again, like wading out into a deep lake, going deeper and deeper, until I could no longer feel the bottom. Once again, I lost all control, all will, and all hope.

When the suffering could get no worse, I finally surrendered. I allowed the presence of God to force its way into my consciousness, not so much by doing anything, but by conceding that I had nothing more to try, no more tricks up my sleeve, no more willingness to pretend. Somewhere in those moments of complete surrender, I recognized God's love. Then slowly, in fits and starts, I learned some early lessons in how to love like God.

Remembering that today, reflecting on both the hopeless anguish and the exquisite joy of the climb up and out of the belly of the whale, I look out on the wedding garden. Wedding music is playing softly throughout the house and garden. The birds are playing in the sky and along the lagoon. Bridesmaids are having their hair done. The caterer is setting up. The joy is so rich and abundant that my solitary journey into the pain of my past is forced to an early end. I join the rest of this happy party, savoring every moment and movement in anticipation of the big event this afternoon.

CALENDAR WEEK THIRTY-THREE

I ask God for the gift to feel very glad and to rejoice intensely, sharing in the delight and joy that Jesus Christ felt in rising from the dead and returning to console His friends.

April 30

John 20:24–29, Jesus and Thomas
²⁴ But Thomas (who was called the Twin), one of the twelve, was not with them when Jesus came. ²⁵ So the other disciples told him, "We have seen the Lord." But he said to them, "Unless I see the mark of the nails in his hands, and put my finger in the mark of the nails and my hand in his side, I will not believe."
²⁶ A week later his disciples were again in the house, and Thomas was with them. Although the doors were shut, Jesus came and stood among them and said, "Peace be with you." ²⁷ Then he said to Thomas, "Put your finger here and see my hands. Reach out your hand and put it in my side. Do not doubt but believe." ²⁸ Thomas answered him, "My Lord and my God!" ²⁹ Jesus said to him, "Have you believed because you have seen me? Blessed are those who have not seen and yet have come to believe."

THE BEAUTIFUL sounds of silence greeted me in the garden this morning, as dawn broke on the scene of a most amazing wedding. Empty chairs in the lower lawn, empty tables where the bars had been and the diners sat, crates with plates and glasses, piles of linens, and the cabling for the sound system—all witness to extremely loud music, a prodigious amount of drinking, and a remarkable combination of dancing styles that combined the New York club scene with some country rock and roll. I walked from the meditation bench to the platform, still in place at the center of the wooden walkway along the lagoon.

It was on this platform that I officiated my first wedding, almost certainly my last as well. I read poetry from Rumi, Pablo Neruda, John O'Donohue, and e.e. cummings, adding my own bits about how the wedding ceremony invites all of us to come together as one. It was a very special experience for me, bringing me close to tears as the beautiful couple read the vows they had each written for themselves.

The line from the reading today that most captured my attention was the classic ending of verse 28:

> Blessed are those who have not seen and yet have come to believe.

With the very significant exception of the mystics, every believer since Paul met the risen Christ on the road to Damascus is a believer who has come to believe without seeing. This is truly extraordinary. After two thousand years, which comprise, *inter alia*, the Dark Ages, the Black Death, the Enlightenment, several conquering armies presiding over the rise and fall of several empires, and two brutal world wars—after all that, close to a third of the world's population profess to believe in Jesus Christ. Blessed are they.

Father Rohr, whose daily meditations tend to follow the liturgical year in much the same way as these Exercises, describes the healing ministry of Jesus as one with three possible meanings. In one possible sense, His ministry was that of the Passover Lamb, a sacrificial metaphor that is often erroneously characterized as substitutionary atonement. In a second conceivable sense, Christ lived, died, and was resurrected in order to show us that we will rise up, just as He rose up, defeating death, particularly the death of the false self.

A third possibility is that the trial and execution of Jesus provided us with a classic example of scapegoating. The political and religious leaders of Israel at that time were both afraid and, in many ways, evil. Rather than confronting their shortcomings in an honestly introspective way, these morally corrupt people sought, and found, a scapegoat. In effect, they were saying to the people of Israel, "You are not happy with the way we govern, so take Jesus." In Father Rohr's words:

> If your ego is still in charge, you will find a "disposable" person or group on which to project your problems. People who haven't come to at least a minimal awareness of their own dark side will always find someone else to hate or fear. Hatred holds a group together much more quickly and easily than love and inclusivity, I am sorry to say. Something has to be sacrificed. Blood has to be shed. Someone has to be blamed, attacked, tortured, imprisoned, or killed. Sacrificial systems create religions and governments of exclusion and violence. Yet Jesus taught and modeled inclusivity and forgiveness!

Sitting with this, I consider the numerous times in my life and experience where I chose to blame another rather than be accountable myself. It is seldom sufficient for me to simply point the finger at someone else for something I have done, or not done. I gather support for my position, lobbying as many people as I can to join me in the false placement of blame.

Forgiveness and inclusion continue to be the essential elements of my faith. Forgiveness cannot be one-sided. I forgive as I ask to be forgiven, and I can only ask to be forgiven when I have been fully and honestly accountable for my actions. Scapegoating, in full or in part, seeks to shift all or a share of the responsibility to another. That, of course, leads to exclusion on the basis of hatred or fear. As I reflect on it, exclusion, like forgiveness, is not one-sided. When I exclude the Other, I invariably exclude myself. I violate the fundamental covenant of honest accountability that is the basis for belonging.

Yesterday was all about inclusion, about becoming one in a marriage, a family, and a community of love. I opened the wedding ceremony with these words from Rumi:

> The minute I heard my first love story
> I started looking for you,
> Not knowing how blind that was.
> Lovers don't finally meet somewhere.
> They're in each other all along.

Addressing my comments to both the assembled guests and the wedding couple, I asked that they look around at the sky, the garden, the lagoon, and the other guests. I asked that they savor the sounds of the string quartet, the lagoon birds, and the ocean waves. "This little piece of creation is whispering to each of you privately, and, at the same time, shouting for everyone to hear—come, *be one with us*. With Rumi, we know that we have been here, in this oneness, all along."

May 1

Repeat John 20:24–29

EVEN THOUGH the wedding was officially over at 10 p.m. Saturday night, and the last wedding guests left yesterday, Serendipity is only now beginning to get back to its normal serenity. The equipment rental company will pick up the chairs, tables, and eating utensils sometime today. We will clean the guest house and the guest rooms in the main house. Most of the leftover food will be given away. The sounds of dance music have already been replaced with baroque trumpets.

Maggie is still in the kennel, leaving me alone in the meditation garden. Not really. Even in the darkness of early dawn, the numinous sounds of God's creation are loudly proclaiming that we are never alone. The magic of the awakening universe, repeated gloriously each day, once again confirms Rumi's statement that God, the ultimate lover in the world, has been here all along.

The prayer for this week is that I share in the gifts of delight and joy that Jesus Christ felt in rising from the dead and returning to console His friends. Imagine the love required for Jesus, who had just been brutally murdered by His own people, to offer consolation to His friends. Imagine that He is filled with delight and joy! This is the message of eternal life, that there is no valid reason to fear death. There is a reason to feel delight and joy from both what seems good, and what seems bad. That is the message of the cross.

Father Rohr touched on this in his meditation last week.

> Those who agree to carry and love what God loves, which is both the good and the bad of human history, and to pay the price for its reconciliation within themselves—these are the followers of Jesus—the leaven, the salt, the remnant, the mustard seed that God can use to transform the world. The cross is a very dramatic image of what it takes to be a usable one for God.

Being a "usable one for God" is a powerful aspirational goal. Today, May Day, International Workers' Day, is a day to celebrate labor, especially organized labor. One of my most important mentors was Lane Kirkland, long-time head of the AFL-CIO. I miss him and the robust support he provided the trade union movement. Sadly, the near demise of organized labor in the United States, something vigorously promoted by the Republican Party for the last half century, was well underway when Lane ascended to the top job. He could do little to arrest the decline. While he never wore his religion on his sleeve, Lane was very much a "usable one for God," working tirelessly for justice around the world.

This year, May Day protests have been organized in many cities, focusing primarily on the issue of the government's position on immigrants. Whether it is the infamous wall along the southern border, the travel ban on Muslims, or the current increased level of deportation, immigration policy has been about as bad as we all expected. All that can be said now is that elections have consequences.

May 2

Repeat the Contemplation for Learning to Love like God, Parts 1and 2

I SPENT THE morning reflecting on learning to love like God, repeatedly walking down to the meditation garden, then back up along the rill to the library. The time and space were simply exploding with God's creation. Birds, lizards, insects, plants of every description, clouds, sun, and sky were all clamoring for attention. The odd thing was that the longer I sat in silence, the more the cacophony of assorted sights, sounds, and movements began to come together in a regular pattern, a happy rhythm, an elegant symphonic celebration of the day! I accepted the invitation to sing and dance as I walked back and forth along the rill. It was a glorious morning!

Father Thomas Berry was a powerful voice promoting God's creation. The Great Work that he called for requires a massive shift in the way mankind views themselves and the planet. For all kinds of tragic reasons, we consider ourselves primary, and view the rest of creation as subordinate to us. In fact, the victors in the global competition for power, prestige, and possessions *consider all the other humans as subordinate.*

Father Berry writes that "the Earth is primary and that humans are derivative. The primacy of the Earth community applies to every mode of human activity: Economics, education, law, medicine, and religion. The human is a subsystem of the Earth system." He exhorts us to make the enormous shift in thought and action that would put the Earth first, as it was before the Industrial and Technological revolutions. He believes the Cenozoic Era is coming to an end, either in the normal course of evolutionary change, or as a result of our misuse and abuse of the planet. Father Berry wants us to replace the Cenozoic Era with a new "Ecozoic Era."

Father Berry was present in the garden this morning, singing with me, and pushing me to dance with greater abandon. He knew how to love like God. There can be no better way to express this love than to join in the Great Work of saving this planet. It is an awesome challenge. As he writes:

> [It] would involve celebrating the primordial moment of emergence of the universe. Any sense of the sacred, any restraint in favor of maintaining the inner coherence and resplendence of the natural world, is considered an expression of an unendurable romanticism. This new, emergent phase of Earth history can be defined as that period when humans would be present to the Earth in a mutually enhancing manner.

The simple fact is that we are already connected to everything in the universe. I believe this is true in a scientific, factual way, not just the spiritual way that I celebrate each day with these Exercises. Again, Father Berry left us with an eloquent description of what *already exists.*

> The universe constitutes a single multiform sequential celebratory event. Every being in the universe is intimately present to, and is influencing, every other being in the universe. Every being contributes to the magnificence of the whole. The universe is the only text without a context. Every particular mode of being is universe-referent, and its meaning is established only within this comprehensive setting. That is the fascination, the mystery, the immeasurable depth of the universe into which we are plunged with each of our experiences of the world about us.

God's love is here now. Engaging in the Great Work of saving the planet is precisely loving the way God loves. In *Laudato Si*, Pope Francis exhorted us to make the fundamental changes in our economic system that would lead to a radically different treatment of the planet, and all the other creatures that share this planet with us. Father Berry describes the work to be done as a global transformation.

> The transformation required is a transformation from an anthropocentric norm of reality and value to a biocentric or geocentric norm in all our activities. The Earth is primary, the human is derivative.

As I sat with the enormity of the challenge put to us by Father Berry and Pope Francis, I began to sink into despair. This wonderful garden exists in all its glory in a ridiculously rich ghetto. The huge majority of the uniformly white, upper-class, comfortable Republicans that surround me (many of them are my very close friends) believe that climate change is a hoax. They may not articulate their use of God's creation in the same way that Father Berry did, but their actions clearly exemplify that view.

I am not writing this from any position of moral superiority. Most of my career involved the use of hydrocarbons, beginning with coal and then adding heavy fuel oil and natural gas. My actions were based solely on the profit motive at the core of orthodox capitalism. While I would give occasional speeches about the need to put the cost of reclaiming closed mines into the price of coal, I knew at the time that my words fell on deaf ears. I spoke more often about the inequality that resulted from globalization, but offered few alternatives.

Loving like God requires actions, not words. The good work of the Sister Parish Ministry will never fully compensate for the decades of indifference. However, it is a good beginning.

May 3

Repeat the Contemplation for Learning to Love like God, Parts 3 and 4

SITTING ON the bench in the pre-dawn darkness, shivering in the cold air, I was again overwhelmed by God's creation. As usual, the whole community was present in all its glory. Today, however, I noticed another dimension of His creation, one that must have been here all along. The garden was filled with memories. That sounds so obvious, but there was a quality to it this morning that greatly enhanced my meditation experience.

The wedding party was very prominent, of course, dancing, laughing, and tearing up in joy. My granddaughters, Alexis, Alison, and Talia, were doing hand stands and back flips on the lawn. Father Tom, the priest who baptized me in Houston, was sitting on the bench on the pier, dozing while "praying" during his visit. My grandson, Noah, was fishing in the lagoon. Parker was playing with his toy cars, much as Tyler had done so many years ago. And Maggie, of course Maggie, was present in every one of these memories, along with her sister Annie.

I realized that the world with which I am gradually becoming one is a world populated with not just the nearly seven billion alive today, but with all of those who have come before. The surprise realization for me this morning is that the notion of "those who have come before" includes much more than the men and women (and other creatures of God) who once lived and are now dead. It includes all of the people who were here yesterday and the day before, who are alive today in a different garden in a different town. All of the instants in time that make up eternity are ever present. There is no past or future. There is only now. And everything that is, everything that exists, does so in all the places and all the times that they have ever been, or will ever be, simultaneously. That is the great mystery of eternity and infinity.

When I become fully present to the Divine, I am at the same time fully present to all of these people and events whenever and wherever they occurred, or will occur. Here and now is an enormous time and place!

There is a message in this about how to love like God. So much of the religion I learned about as a young person, before going to Germany as a missionary, and so much of what I taught while on that mission, focused on life after death. The here and now was, at best, a proving ground, serving the primary purpose of determining what would happen to us when we died. While we occasionally referred to the "presence of God in our lives," my best recollection is that He was only here as an occasional visitor.

The almost tangible presence of all of creation—past, present, and future—in the garden this morning served as a powerful reminder that the here and now is the whole deal. It is here that I encounter Christ. It is now that His presence can transform me. Or not. The choice is mine. It is a choice I must make moment by moment.

The crucifixion and resurrection of Jesus, represented by the cross, shows me that I must be accountable for my thoughts, words, and deeds. I cannot blame others, or project the pain elsewhere. I cannot live in denial. He did not play the victim card, nor did He ask us to revenge His unjust treatment. He asks only that we love the way He loves. The two words—inclusion and forgiveness—come back into my meditation space like a large, blinking neon sign. That is how God loves. He includes all. He forgives all.

Father Rohr said it perfectly this morning.

> Jesus is the forgiving victim, which really is the only hope of our world, because most of us sooner or later will be victimized on some level. It is the familiar story line of an unjust and often cruel humanity. *The cross is a healing message about the violence of humanity, and we tragically turned it into the violence of God, who we thought needed "a sacrifice" to love us.* An utterly new attitude (Spirit) has been released in history; it's a spirit of love, compassion, and forgiveness. As Jesus prayed on the cross, "Father, forgive them, they know not what they do."

May 4

John 21:1–17, Jesus Appears to Seven Disciples

After these things Jesus showed himself again to the disciples by the Sea of Tiberias; and he showed himself in this way. ² Gathered there together were Simon Peter, Thomas called the Twin, Nathanael of Cana in Galilee, the sons of Zebedee, and two others of his disciples. ³ Simon Peter said to them, "I am going fishing." They said to him, "We will go with you." They went out and got into the boat, but that night they caught nothing.

⁴ Just after daybreak, Jesus stood on the beach; but the disciples did not know that it was Jesus. ⁵ Jesus said to them, "Children, you have no fish, have you?" They answered him, "No." ⁶ He said to them, "Cast the net to the right side of the boat, and you will find some." So they cast it, and now they were not able to haul it in because there were so many fish. ⁷ That disciple whom Jesus loved said to Peter, "It is the Lord!" When Simon Peter heard that it was the Lord, he put on some clothes, for he was naked, and jumped into the sea. ⁸ But the other disciples came in the boat, dragging the net full of fish, for they were not far from the land, only about a hundred yards off.

⁹ When they had gone ashore, they saw a charcoal fire there, with fish on it, and bread. ¹⁰ Jesus said to them, "Bring some of the fish that you have just caught." ¹¹ So Simon Peter went aboard and hauled the net ashore, full of large fish, a hundred fifty-three of them; and though there were so many, the net was not torn. ¹² Jesus said to them, "Come and have breakfast." Now none of the disciples dared to ask him, "Who are you?" because they knew it was the Lord. ¹³ Jesus came and took the bread and gave it to them, and did the same with the fish. ¹⁴ This was now the third time that Jesus appeared to the disciples after he was raised from the dead.

Jesus and Peter

¹⁵ When they had finished breakfast, Jesus said to Simon Peter, "Simon son of John, do you love me more than these?" He said to him, "Yes, Lord; you know that I love you." Jesus said to him, "Feed my lambs." ¹⁶ A second time he said to him, "Simon son of John, do you love me?" He said to him, "Yes, Lord; you know that I love you." Jesus said to him, "Tend my sheep." ¹⁷ He said to him the third time, "Simon son of John, do you love me?" Peter felt hurt because he said to him the third time, "Do you love me?" And he said to him, "Lord, you know everything; you know that I love you." Jesus said to him, "Feed my sheep.

THIS IS A wonderful story for several reasons. I love it that Jesus joined the disciples as they were fishing. Somehow, I suspect these men loved to fish, even though it was also the way they fed their families and made a living. And I suspect Jesus loved to fish. I like to think so.

After instructing the disciples where to fish for the greatest success, he used that success to make the extremely important point that service—"feed my lambs, tend my sheep, feed my sheep"—is the best way to show love. It is a perfect scripture for this week, as we meditate each day in learning to love like God.

There can be no other conclusion than that the best way to love God is to love His creation, all of it. I have been reading Thomas Berry this week, along with information from the Catholic Climate Covenant. Annie Leonard, a devotee of Berry, and a fierce advocate for the environment, was recently interviewed by *The Guardian*. In her words:

> In many ways we have created for ourselves a culture of overconsumption and waste, a culture in which we value persons and things only to the degree that they are useful for us in the present moment, afterwards discarding them as if they have no value, a culture which Pope Francis fittingly calls the "throwaway culture." Unfortunately, there is still a lot of ignorance about the situation and the extent of the damaging effects of our overconsumption and waste. And there is still a lot of resistance to change, even among many Christians, unfortunately. This is why Pope St. John Paul II, Pope Benedict XVI, and Pope Francis more recently and in a magnified way, have called the Church, and the world, to an "ecological conversion."

I sat with these words for a long time in the meditation garden this morning. While I could not help but be overcome with the natural beauty and wonder of place that enveloped me, I also reflected on the "throwaway culture" represented by the golf course. Each day, a huge amount of manpower, water, fertilizer, and petroleum-fueled equipment is used to manicure the fairways and greens of just this one golf course, one of eleven golf courses in this town with a population of 36,000. Think about that.

Sadly, I do not need to leave my library to see overconsumption and waste. Working at a computer today exposes me to as much shopping temptation as walking through every specialty store in every city in the world, each offering precisely what I express even the smallest interest in having. Not only is everything available, it is obtainable instantly, and can be paid for painlessly with a credit card, and shipped overnight right to my door. I take a tiny amount of solace from the fact that I return most of what I buy, but imagine the waste of human effort and natural resources required for the returns! My full-throated participation in the consumer society is *not* loving like God loves!

Last Saturday, April 29, was the Feast Day for St. Catherine of Siena, a medieval mystic and spiritual reformer. She lived only thirty-three years, from 1347 to 1380. It is almost inconceivable how much adversity she faced in her short life.

The Black Death, an insidious plague caused by rat-borne fleas, killed as many as 200 million worldwide. More than sixty percent of Europe's population was taken by the plague, which meant that several whole towns and regions were wiped out completely. It would take Europe three hundred years to reach its pre-plague level of population. These are staggering statistics!

St. Catherine was born into a thriving metropolis with a population in 1340 of close to 35,000 souls. By the time of her birth in 1347, one year after the plague hit, Siena had been reduced to a population of only 12,000! It would be mid-20th century before the city reached its 1340 population again. I can only imagine what it must have been like. Families were decimated, with many of the lone survivors ill or incapacitated for the rest of their lives. St. Catherine could never have known what it was like to live in a functional city.

Nonetheless, St. Catherine of Siena became a Doctor of the Church, a Patron Saint of both Italy and Europe. She famously said,

The soul is in God and God in the soul, just as the fish is in the sea and the sea in the fish.

The advice St. Catherine provides for this week of the Exercises is simple and direct.

God requires nothing else of us except that we show our neighbors the love we have for God.

"Feed my lambs, tend my sheep, feed my sheep." My prayer today is very simple. Grant me the grace to love like God.

May 5

Repeat John 21:1–17

IT RAINED hard during the night, leaving debris along the rill and in the meditation garden. The bench was wet, but would dry quickly in the sun, which was just coming up in a cloudless sky.

Sitting again this morning with the passages from John about Jesus fishing with His disciples, I read through the sermon by Ruth Patterson on the Beatitudes. If someone were to ask that I reduce how Jesus instructed us to love like God to a single word, I would simply say, the Beatitudes. I often lament that our Nicene Creed is missing this hugely important part of the core of our faith. The Beatitudes express my belief far better than anything in either the Nicene or the Apostles' Creed.

Reverend Patterson reminded me of Matthew 5:13:

You are the salt of the earth; but if salt has lost its taste, how can its saltiness be restored? It is no longer good for anything, but is thrown out and trampled under foot.

The US Council of Catholic Bishops has been promoting Communities of Salt and Light, a movement designed to re-invigorate Catholic Social Teaching in the parishes throughout the United States. I spent three frustrating years as the Chairman of the Diocesan Justice and Peace Commission here in the Diocese of St. Augustine. There was virtually no support for Justice and Peace from the fifty-two Pastors in the Diocese. Catholic Social Teaching has been reduced to two issues—anti-abortion and anti-homosexuals. This has been very painful for me. I resigned from the Commission two years ago.

In fact, I find it almost bizarre how little I think about it today. Sister Parish has become a vehicle for me to express my faith, allowing me to essentially ignore the political and social attitudes of other Catholics in North Florida. Among other things, close to a thousand of my fellow parishioners have joined me in the mission work of Sister Parish. A very large majority of them voted for Donald Trump, and passionately support his policies. At heart, however, every one of them believes in the messages contained in the Beatitudes. They teach their children that loving the people at the margin is the best way to love God. I have learned that these good people are the salt and light Jesus was talking about in Matthew's Gospel. Reverend Patterson puts it this way:

> The function of salt is to bring zest, life, taste. Our calling as friends of Jesus is to bring a whole new dimension to living. Sadly, a blandness and lack of vitality characterizes much of the so-called witness of today's church, certainly in the West. Paradoxically, in places where it is extremely difficult to be Christian, we find courageous, vibrant communities of resurrection, signs of outrageous hope for a weary, warring, anguished world. Here is precious salt, bringing out the full flavour of what it means to be citizens of the kingdom. It is possible for all of us—even here where we are right now. We may feel very small, as if our stance or our 'witness' couldn't make a difference. *But history is peopled with such 'little ones' who changed its course.* The biggest 'little one' is Jesus himself and, after him, a long line of followers.

I am humbled by the service of my fellow missionaries, all of whom are "little ones." Our Ministry may make precious little difference in the universe, but it makes all the difference in the world in the lives of the people who serve and are served. "Feed my lambs, tend my sheep, feed my sheep."

May 6

Read and reflect on the Contemplation of learning to love like God.

As I REFLEcted on the readings of this week, I read these verses from Hildegard of Bingen.

> The marvels of God are not brought forth from one's self.
> Rather, it is more like a chord, a sound that is played.
> The tone does not come out of the chord itself, but rather,
> through the touch of the Musician.
> I am, of course, the lyre and harp of God's kindness.

Loving like God loves is all about surrender, allowing God to make the music by touching the chords. We are but instruments in His hands.

CALENDAR WEEK THIRTY-FOUR

I ask God our Lord to fill me with tremendous gratefulness, so that when I see how everything and my own self are gift, I may want to return thanks and praise and service to the One who gives and shares with such total generosity.

May 7

Matthew 28:16–20, The Commissioning of the Disciples
[16] Now the eleven disciples went to Galilee, to the mountain to which Jesus had directed them. [17] When they saw him, they worshiped him; but some doubted. [18] And Jesus came and said to them, "All authority in heaven and on earth has been given to me. [19] Go therefore and make disciples of all nations, baptizing them in the name of the Father and of the Son and of the Holy Spirit, [20] and teaching them to obey everything that I have commanded you. And remember, I am with you always, to the end of the age."

TWO OF SALLIE Ann's friends from Houston have been house guests this weekend. Sitting in the garden with Maggie this morning, I reflected on hospitality. I believe it is an obvious extension of my two essential words of faith, *inclusion*, and *forgiveness*. Serendipity, our house, has been an extraordinary blessing for us, primarily because it allows us to practice hospitality. Sallie Ann is the perfect hostess, thinking of everything from fresh flowers by the beds to special soap in the bathrooms.

I listened today to Neil deGrasse Tyson, the popular head of the Hayden planetarium in New York, talk about his new book, *Astrophysics for People in a Hurry*. He explained that the basic elements that make up the Earth and all its inhabitants, are the same elements that make up everything else in the universe. Sitting with that simple, yet profound, statement leads me straight back to my core belief in *oneness*. From the moment of the Big Bang, we have been one with the universe, remaining one for all these more than fourteen billion years, and destined to be one forever. One of the classic Tyson statements is, "The good thing about science is that it's true whether or not you believe in it."

Father Rohr likes to say that something that is true anywhere is true everywhere. That is the nature of truth. I go back to my effort to sort out my beliefs, accurately negotiating the narrow path between myth and reality. Almost by definition, matters of faith are not scientific, nor can they be scientifically proven.

Faith is really not required for scientifically provable matters. The bizarre thing about much of the current political debate is that the two sides of many issues claim conflicting science. This simply cannot be the case. One or the other of the two sides is wrong. Climate science, life science, and even (or especially) econometric science cannot be based on separate, conflicting facts. The science may end before we understand what specifically *causes* certain facts, or what the *ultimate impact* of those facts will be in the future. The facts themselves, however, cannot be in dispute.

Yet they are. Each side now accuses the other of "fake news," of intentionally putting out false information. Sadly, there is a great deal of this fake news in cyber space, that vast world of electronically accessible data that is increasingly relied upon by all of us to inform our decisions. The traditional "fact checkers" have lost credibility. The once rock-solid sources of information are no longer trusted. It is impossible to make sound decisions when institutions like the Census Bureau and the Labor Department require faith.

As I reflect on this, however, it occurs to me that the faith community has traditionally been at odds with the community of science. Virtually every major advance in human knowledge was initially questioned by the Church. The early scientists were condemned. Galileo is the poster child of this conflict. In spite of the important role played by the Catholic Church in supporting education, learning, and science, it is my sense today that much of what I consider to be scientifically established fact is simply not accepted in my parish.

When sending them out to all the nations, Jesus said to His disciples, "And remember, I am with you always, to the end of the age." I love this. Eternity is a very long time. Christ will be with us, and we will be with Him, for all of that time, "until the end of the age."

Tyson famously said, "We are part of this universe; we are in this universe, but perhaps more important than both of those facts, is that the universe is in us." Infinity, very much like eternity, is a very big place. As hard as it is to fathom, we are in it, and it is in us. Ponder that.

May 8

Repeat Matthew 28:16–20

MY MEDITATION this morning was wistful, filled with mixed feelings about coming to the end of the Exercises this second time. On one hand, I feel very peaceful, filled with both the knowledge that I have been very faithful to the rhythm of Ignatius, and, at the same time, that I have allowed myself to venture into a variety of "faith detours." Both the steady rhythm and the chase down rabbit holes have brought a sense of quiet depth to my faith.

On the other hand, some of the questions I have asked seem like open wounds. I wonder if my "enlightened" faith is little more than relativistic mishmash. I have long believed that deep faith allows everything to be questioned. When the answers to those questions are unclear, we have a simple choice: Believe or reject. This is too dualistic. Perhaps the right answer is that there is no answer. Perhaps the simple solution is to live with the paradox, to be satisfied with mystery.

Much of what I have written in this journal feels like little more than a plaintive cry for attention from my false self, like a final shout out from the exterior of my life container. The very idea that I would make such a cry raises questions about both with what, and how much, I have filled my container.

I force myself to consider Jesus talking to me about what I should do next. Yes, I am to "make disciples of all nations." I believe He wants me to do that by my actions, not by my words. The last day of the Exercises is May 20. I leave for the Dominican Republic May 30.

It is said that when faith and hope fail, as they sometimes do, we must try charity, which is love in action. As the Nike advertisement goes, *just do it*. Don't spend a lot of time speculating, just act, allowing God to show us why. Or not.

May 9

Repeat the Contemplation for Learning to Love like God, Parts 1 and 2

REFLECTING on the Scriptural passages and readings this week, I returned to my friend, Reverend Ruth Patterson.

> "No one lights a lamp and then puts it under a basket," says Jesus. "No—a lamp is placed on a stand where it can give light to everyone." We are challenged to be such lights, in fact

to be so visible, so public that we are like a city on a hill that just cannot be hidden. This is what happened to the friends of Jesus at Pentecost. They were set on fire with a whole new energy and power to show Jesus to the world. They were so effective that they were accused of turning the world upside-down. Sometimes we may feel as if the light has gone out and that nothing can hold back the dark that seems to be creeping over the world. It only takes a pinprick of light to change everything. A single candle flame is all it takes to let the darkness know it cannot win. And as we begin again, as we allow the tiny candle of our life to bravely burn for all to see, then the promise is that everyone will pour out their praise to God, will acknowledge him. And isn't that the nub of it all? *Isn't that why we began this journey in the first place?* Alleluia!

Ruth presents a formidable challenge. She worked for two decades in Belfast, Ireland, the heart of the "troubles," which is the understated way the brutal war between Catholics and Protestants was described. Over and over again, it must have seemed to her as though "the light had gone out and that nothing could hold back the dark." In my darkest moments, I have never had to face anything like that.

Nor have my troubles come remotely close to what the early disciples of Jesus faced. I suspect some of the disciples would have had a little trouble simply understanding the good news of the upside-down teaching of Jesus. His ability to weave Scripture together with experience comes through in the Bible stories two thousand years later! Seminarians and new priests spend months, even years, perfecting their homilies. Some are never capable of consistently teaching in a way that inspires, or even keeps the congregation fully awake!

Add to the normal difficulty of preparing and delivering homilies, the extraordinary physical danger the early disciples faced every day. It is very hard to imagine they could meet large groups of potential disciples, particularly in the open.

In Acts 2:41, the author, presumably Luke, reports that three thousand people were baptized in a single day. This must be a bit hyperbolic. It is generally accepted as fact that Paul's audiences for his epistles were groups of only thirty to forty people. Moreover, the Apostles were most likely in Jerusalem on Pentecost, very likely gathered in the same upper room where they celebrated the Last Supper. It is hard to believe three thousand people could fit anywhere in the old town of Jerusalem, much less in one room.

There is no need to exaggerate. Jesus charged His Apostles to spread the word, promising that He would be with them always. They did so, facing danger and difficulty everywhere they went. At the end of each Mass, we are charged with the same duty, to go out and spread the Gospel, by word and by deed. We do so in complete safety and comfort. The challenge for most of us today is to take the light out from under the basket, to let it shine for all to see.

May 10

Repeat the Contemplation for Learning to Love like God, Parts 3 and 4

FATHER FRANK joined me for lunch yesterday. At my request, he had read an earlier draft of my journal, looking for obvious bits of blatant heresy. The lunch was prompted by an email Father Frank sent me after his initial reading. One paragraph deeply unsettled me, for obvious reasons.

You've asked me to alert you to possible heresy. I believe you skirt the issue when you speculate whether or not Jesus might have had a family (and Mary more children), but I think you were simply saying that it would not make a difference in your conviction of faith. However, when you later state that Jesus and God are not one, even covering yourself with a Rohrian mantle doesn't get you off the hook. It's the height of heresy.

When I first joined the Arrupe Advisory Board of the Woodstock Theological Center, I was not a Catholic. I was not even certain that my faith journey would result in a decision to affiliate with any organized religion, especially Catholicism. I explained to both Gap LoBiondo, the Director of the Center, and Vince Wolfington, its Chairman, that I struggled with deep faith questions every day. Nonetheless, they vigorously rejected my reservations about serving, arguing that only by raising questions could we find answers. Father John, my pastor and mentor in Houston, encouraged the doubts, frequently stating that the Catholic Church needs all new members, but particularly those who regularly challenge accepted doctrines and beliefs.

Almost three year after I joined that Arrupe Advisory Board, I completed RCIA and was baptized, becoming a Catholic. In the weeks leading up to my baptism, I studied and agreed to the "three scrutinies." Stated briefly, I swore to God and my parish my belief that sin and evil are real. They are part of our lives. Their power is strong. Salvation is also real. Christ's power to save, protect, and strengthen us is stronger. Sin is only recognized in the light of grace. God's grace is always first.

Shortly thereafter, I professed my faith by giving an affirmative answer to each of these questions.

Do you reject Satan? And all his works? And all his empty promises? Do you believe in God, the Father Almighty, creator of *heaven* and earth? Do you believe in *Jesus* Christ, his only Son, our Lord, who was born of the Virgin *Mary* was crucified, died, and was buried, rose from the dead, and is now seated at the *right* hand of the Father? Do you believe in the Holy Spirit, the holy *Catholic* Church, the communion of saints, the forgiveness of sins, the resurrection of the body, and *life* everlasting?

Approximately three hundred times since my baptism on April 3, 2010, I have repeated the Nicene Creed, essentially professing each time that I continued to believe what I swore to at my baptism. Yet, throughout these past ten months, I have filled this journal with questions and doubts about the official doctrines of the Catholic Church, and just about every single article of that faith.

This certainly sounds heretical to me! I take some small comfort from the traditional story that Saint Francis asked two questions over and over again, every day, "Who are You, God? And who am I?" While I am certainly no saint, particularly not Francis, I do believe that good questions make for better faith. I have worked to understand and accept a great deal of what Father Rohr calls the alternative orthodoxy. It is well-grounded in both Scripture and Tradition. Importantly, it has been confirmed by the personal experiences of countless mystics, down through the ages and today.

Nonetheless, I will read what I have written with a very careful eye. I am not sure exactly where Father Frank found that I did not believe that the Father and the Son were one. Given the extraordinary confusion that has forever surrounded the Trinity, it would not surprise me in the least to find at least one instance where I have referred to God the Father and Jesus the Son as separate beings. Setting the record straight, once again, I want to be clear that I believe in a relational God. The elements or components of that God are able to relate precisely because there are at least two parts. While I have no problem whatsoever with the possibility that there are three parts, I believe a relational God could quite comfortably exist in two parts or any number of parts. The key is not the number of parts that are relating to each other in and through love. The key is the love. The key is the act of relating.

As Rumi puts it,

Love is the bridge between you and everything.

Which brings me all the way from lunch with Father Frank to the reading for today, which is to once again reflect on learning to love like God. What strikes me as the most important aspect of God's love is the very nature of God, which is active. God is not a person, with certain static characteristics. If He were a person, He would be an extremely active person, and the core of His nature would be the activity.

Learning to love like God is learning to dance with complete abandon. It is surrendering ego so completely that nothing exists outside the dance. It does not matter what we look like while dancing this Divine Dance.

It is a dance of love. The greatest "dance moves" involve giving everything away in service. The goal of the dance is to get everyone on the floor, flowing in and flowing out. One does not have to hear to feel the music, or have legs to make the intricate movements, or a voice to express the deepest thoughts.

Everyone can join the dance. No one has so little that they cannot give to the dance. No one has so much that they cannot receive from the dance.

The dance is not a slow dance, swaying to the steady rhythm of gentle music. Rather, it is a fast waltz, or a fox trot, or swing. Like a line dance, the Divine Dance can be done in large numbers.

I end this morning in movement, dancing in delight to the sounds, sights, and rhythm of faith. In my experience, the only way I could learn a new dance step was to do it. I think the Divine Dance is like that. How do we learn to love like God? We start by loving.

May 11

Acts 1:3

After his suffering he presented himself alive to them by many convincing proofs, appearing to them during forty days and speaking about the kingdom of God.

I Corinthians 15:6–8

⁶ Then he appeared to more than five hundred brothers and sisters at one time, most of whom are still alive, though some have died. ⁷ Then he appeared to James, then to all the apostles. ⁸ Last of all, as to one untimely born, he appeared also to me.

POPE FRANCIS recently addressed the Pontifical Campano Seminary of Posillipo, the only seminary in Italy run by the Jesuits. I read about his remarks in *America Magazine*, the weekly Jesuit publication. Among other things, the Pope praised the group for the efforts they have made to bring the education of young Jesuits together with the vocational training of the dioceses. I was particularly pleased to see the Pope specifically mention the value of the Spiritual Exercises in this "exercise in communion." He said the Exercises, as a "pure point of reference," mediate the directions that come from the Magisterium of the Church. While recognizing the obvious bias of his Jesuit background, I was still intrigued with the idea that the Pope considered Magisterial edicts to need mediation, much less, from the Jesuits!

The Pope admonished the seminarians to take advantage of what he called "Ignatian style." He discussed three elements of that style, all of which remind me so much of the years that I spent on the Woodstock board. The account of the Pope's meeting at the Seminary in Rome sounded to me like a short seminar in learning to love like God.

Jesuit style, according to the Pope, is based first and foremost on a *personal friendship with Jesus Christ*, a friendship hinging on a dialogue of love. The friendship begins with *seeing* Christ, and coming to a full knowledge of Christ through self-knowledge. I often talk to new missionaries about the possibility of encountering Christ in the Other, but only as and to the extent that we come to terms with the Christ in us.

The second element of Jesuit style, not surprisingly, is *discernment*. God's voice is not easy to hear in the cacophony of so many voices surrounding us in daily life. The Pope described this noise as thunder in our ears and hearts. However difficult it may be, discernment requires that we listen in an environment of truth, beginning with telling the truth to ourselves. Doing that, of course, requires that we know the truth about ourselves, not getting lost in affections and fears. Somewhat surprising to me, the Pope warned against allowing rigid norms to limit the genuine sound from getting through.

Finally, Pope Francis argued that Jesuit style requires that we seek first *the Kingdom of God*, and the justice on which it is based. He urges us to cultivate what he calls "holy restlessness," something that broadens the soul and makes it more capable of receiving the love of God.

Paul writes in his first letter to the Corinthians, part of our reading today, that Christ appeared to more than five hundred people at one time. As usual, I struggle with Biblical accounts of large numbers of people gathering to hear Jesus. The point Paul was making was that the resurrected Jesus appeared to a lot of people. I cannot imagine more than a handful of believers daring to gather in one place in the dangerous period following the crucifixion. And, here, as in so many other situations, the truth of their witness is not made greater by their number.

Christ appeared bodily after His death and resurrection. That is the primary message for the readings this week, including the two passages today. Most Christians would say that the resurrection of Jesus is the central truth of the Christian faith. Without it, there is no such thing as the Christian faith. I do not agree. Christ existed at the beginning. He was there before the Big Bang. I believe the birth of Christ was the main event. It was then that God became man, "emptied himself, taking the form of a slave, being born in human likeness. And being found in human form, he humbled himself." The resurrection of Jesus is certainly important, but I cannot imagine it was the first resurrection. I believe all men and women, from the very first human to walk the earth, were resurrected after they died, along with every other creature in God's glorious creation.

Paul was presumably part of the Sanhedrin either at the time of the crucifixion or very shortly thereafter. He consented to the killing of Stephen. He took his famous trip to Damascus in either 32 CE or 36 CE, depending upon the exact date of the crucifixion. He actively worked in the nascent Christian community for the rest of his life. While he had never seen, or heard, Jesus while He was alive, Paul knew and worked with many disciples, including several of the Apostles, all of whom had been with Jesus throughout His ministry. Paul did meet the risen Christ on that Damascene journey, becoming at that moment another eyewitness.

I have recently read an interesting account of Paul's meeting in Jerusalem with Peter and James. Using Paul's account of that meeting in his letter to the Galatians, scholars have calculated that the three of them met as early as 35 CE, three years after the crucifixion! By then, the critical elements of the Christian creed—Christ died for our sins, was buried, and rose again on the third day—were apparently in place. All three of the key figures who met in Jerusalem so soon after the crucifixion—Paul, Peter, and James—had seen the risen Christ. They, along with other eyewitnesses, incorporated what they had seen in a creed very early in the history of the faith. This is powerful testimony.

To be sure, all of the "historical evidence" of these credal statements comes from accounts written by believers. Nonetheless, I sat with the readings, running through the first part of the creed I recite at every Mass, over and over again.

> I believe in one God, the Father almighty, maker of heaven and earth, of all things visible and invisible. I believe in one Lord Jesus Christ, the Only Begotten Son of God, born of the Father before all ages. God from God, Light from Light, true God from true God, begotten, not made, consubstantial with the Father; through him all things were made. For us men and for our salvation he came down from heaven, and by the Holy Spirit was incarnate of the Virgin Mary, and became man. For our sake he was crucified under Pontius Pilate, he suffered death and was buried, and rose again on the third day in accordance with the Scriptures. He ascended into heaven and is seated at the right hand of the Father. He will come again in glory to judge the living and the dead and his kingdom will have no end.

I sit for a while with the idea that these fundamental concepts were largely in place within two or three years of Jesus's death, two thousand years ago. During these two millennia, hundreds of thousands of men and women have preached, taught, and written about the key elements of this creed. Some, the Doctors and Fathers of the Church, the mystics, and the great theologians, have expanded on the creed, adding depth and richness to its meaning. Sadly, more than a few of the leaders of the Church have taken the creed in the tribal direction of exclusion.

In virtually every age, however, specifically including the present age, thousands of men and women have been deeply moved by these words, and have anchored their lives in these beliefs. I am one of those people. My whole life has benefited from this rich history. My faith benefits from all the experience, research, contemplation, prayer, and mystical revelation of all those who have gone before. I have been blessed, especially in the last five years, to spend time in the company of many extraordinary people, whose lives have been dedicated to this creed.

I ended the morning on my knees in the library, looking at the Rublev icon, quietly praying the Our Father. I am in awe as I consider the long tradition of this faith. I am deeply grateful to the countless men and women down through history, whose experience, teaching, and writing form the foundation of my faith.

May 12

Repeat Acts 1:3

Scholars believe the account in Acts of the risen Christ's appearance was written in the period 80 CE to 90 CE. Most of the eyewitnesses were dead. Acts is considered the second of a two-part writing effort, the first of which is the Gospel of Luke. If Luke is indeed the name of the author, it is likely that it was the same Luke who traveled with Paul, as mentioned in Colossians. While Paul saw the risen Christ on the road to Damascus, his companion, Luke, was not an eyewitness, though he obviously knew and worked with several people who had been with Jesus throughout His ministry.

As I sat with these passages again today, I put myself in Luke's place, first traveling with Paul, then, almost twenty years later, putting his account of both the Gospel and the early activities of the Apostles, in writing. In my fantasy, I kept bits and scraps of papyrus, each containing snippets of conversation I had written down over the years. When I finally had the time to write, I first organized both my own recollections, and copies of other accounts. I had an early draft of what historians now call the Q document, and a copy of the Gospel written by John Mark, Peter's longtime companion and interpreter. I also had copies of several of the letters Paul wrote to the small groups of Christians he visited during his travels. Sadly, Paul was reportedly killed in Rome many years before all the rest of us were driven out of Jerusalem by the Romans. I miss him very much, and hope that I can write an accurate and helpful account of his activities during those very early years following the crucifixion.

Sitting this morning on the bench in the garden on a beautifully sunny Florida morning, it was hard to imagine the circumstances and surroundings of a lonely Christian scribe two thousand years ago. Just finding a dry, safe place to keep my drafts together was painfully difficult. My own personal safety was constantly in jeopardy. I hear accounts of various Apostles being killed, and Christians throughout the empire being persecuted. It is hard to know what is true, but caution is obviously advised.

I ended my fantasy thinking about how hard it is to write today, with computers, search engines, quiet places, complete personal safety, and many willing editors and contributors. I compare this with the situation faced each day by Luke. Yet he managed to produce two books of Scripture, each providing invaluable support for two thousand years! I am humbled.

May 13

Reflect further on how Christ appeared to others.

WE HAVE READ this week about Christ appearing to various people after His death and resurrection. My primary thought this morning is the straight forward question, how has Christ appeared to me? Sitting here now, in the library, listening to the quiet rhythm of Maggie sleeping, Christ is present. He was present in the garden earlier this morning. He has been present every day for the past two hundred and thirty-seven days, since I began the Exercises. How has He appeared to me?

Reflecting on this, I consider how often I have felt His presence, gently nudging me to ask questions in a slightly different way, or consider nuances that add depth to my understanding. I regularly feel His presence when I formulate questions. More often, I know that it is only due to His urging that I embrace the paradox of conflicting answers.

Christ is often most present to me when I feel most alone. Fortunately, my efforts to hide from Him through isolation work less well as I grow older. It is as though my life container conceals less each year. I like the idea that just as God enters me through the cracks in my shell, He shines through those cracks, allowing others to see His influence in, and on, my life.

I consider the various forms that Christ has taken in His frequent appearances. He is present in each and every one of His creatures, those, like Maggie, who I believe I know so well, and others, like the birds and lizards, who express the Christ in them in ways that I only imprecisely understand.

Then I think about the times when, by God's grace, I have been able to see the Christ in the people in my life. The villagers in the Dominican Republic, especially the very young and the very old, do a very poor job of hiding Christ. Volunteers and missionaries virtually glow with His presence, especially when they are laughing or crying. Both happen with amazing regularity. I contemplate the people closest to me, humbled by their persistent love and acceptance. Christ speaks to me when I please them, and when I fail them.

Looking around the library, I am simply overwhelmed by the presence of Christ in the long, rich tradition of great teachers, whose books line the shelves all around me. I have no idea where to start. I can open any book on any shelf to any page, finding in the words on that page wisdom beyond description. Drinking from a fire hose! Christ was with these great men and women when they lived and taught and wrote. He was with the scribes and translators and teachers who made this wisdom available to posterity. He is present today as I struggle to understand His message.

In all of these ways and many more, Christ has appeared to me often. He continues to be present in my life. He challenges me to surrender to His presence, to simply say yes. He reminds me that I can only return His love by loving others.

Calendar Week Thirty-Five

I beg the Lord God for the gift of living the joy of Christ Risen. I ask the gift to live grateful for all that is in my life world, my life, and myself. And I ask for the great gift of bringing the Good News to others, in many forms.

May 14

Acts 1:1–12, The Promise of the Holy Spirit
[1] In the first book, Theophilus, I wrote about all that Jesus did and taught from the beginning [2] until the day when he was taken up to heaven, after giving instructions through the Holy Spirit to the apostles whom he had chosen. [3] After his suffering he presented himself alive to them by many convincing proofs, appearing to them during forty days and speaking about the kingdom of God. [4] While staying with them, he ordered them not to leave Jerusalem, but to wait there for the promise of the Father. "This," he said, "is what you have heard from me; [5] for John baptized with water, but you will be baptized with the Holy Spirit not many days from now."
The Ascension of Jesus
[6] So when they had come together, they asked him, "Lord, is this the time when you will restore the kingdom to Israel?" [7] He replied, "It is not for you to know the times or periods that the Father has set by his own authority. [8] But you will receive power when the Holy Spirit has come upon you; and you will be my witnesses in Jerusalem, in all Judea and Samaria, and to the ends of the earth." [9] When he had said this, as they were watching, he was lifted up, and a cloud took him out of their sight. [10] While he was going and they were gazing up toward heaven, suddenly two men in white robes stood by them. [11] They said, "Men of Galilee, why do you stand looking up toward heaven? This Jesus, who has been taken up from you into heaven, will come in the same way as you saw him go into heaven."
Matthias Chosen to Replace Judas
[12] Then they returned to Jerusalem from the mount called Olivet, which is near Jerusalem, a sabbath day's journey away.

Reading this again this morning, I was particularly struck by the admonition of the two men in white robes. *"Why do you stand looking up toward heaven?"* As I begin this final week of the Exercises, I make a quiet promise to myself not to stand around, looking up to Heaven for accolades. God loves by serving. He has made it crystal clear that I must do likewise.

More than that, He has offered His presence as a constant source of support and assistance. *"You will receive power when the Holy Spirit has come upon you."* It is said that God never asks us to do what He does not empower us to do.

Hildegard of Bingen offered this simple prayer:

> May the Holy Spirit enkindle you with the fire of His Love so that you may persevere, unfailingly, in the love of His service.

Jim Finley often says that God continually sends us gentle reminders of His presence. It might be a flock of birds flying in perfect formation, or simply the smile on a child's face. When we least expect it, a subtle cue tells us to carry on, to persevere in our efforts to please Him through service.

I talked to Daniel yesterday, interrupting him at a Mother's Day celebration. Mother's Day is taken very seriously in the Dominican Republic, with festivities each day of the long weekend. The Dominican Sister Parish team has almost finished building what we call the "duplex" in Caoba. Two dilapidated houses, each occupied by a single woman, blocked the entrance to our new chapel. Both women enthusiastically agreed to move into new houses, separated by a common block wall. After their move, the old houses will be demolished, allowing us to build a "garden entrance" in front of the chapel, with landscaping and benches.

I am flying down to Santo Domingo with Gabby Castello right after Memorial Day. Gabby will spend two months in and around Guerra, staying with the Torres family. We have fixed some ambitious goals for her extended stay, including a training program for grandmothers in the five villages where we are now working.

I reflected on the idea of the Holy Spirit "enkindling Gabby with the fire of His Love" during these months in Guerra. It is clear in my mind that she will teach, lead, inspire, and bring joy to everyone she meets. I say that because I have that much faith in Gabby. But there is more.

> But you will receive power when the Holy Spirit has come upon you; and you will be my witnesses … to the ends of the earth.

I know that I am not ordained to "send out" any missionaries, or endow them with any power. But I deeply believe that Gabby, along with all the other Sister Parish missionaries, whether they stay an extended time or only a weekend, are witnesses to the essential good news of the Gospel. I am equally certain that they will not be alone in their efforts. All is in all, and all is in God, and God is in all. Feed the poor. Heal the sick. Comfort the lonely. Spread the joy!

May 15

Luke 24:50–53, The Ascension of Jesus
⁵⁰ Then he led them out as far as Bethany, and, lifting up his hands, he blessed them. ⁵¹ While he was blessing them, he withdrew from them and was carried up into heaven. ⁵² And they worshiped him, and returned to Jerusalem with great joy; ⁵³ and they were continually in the temple blessing God.

Reading this passage from Luke today, I was initially struck by how odd it seemed that the Apostles could return to Jerusalem from Bethany to continually go to the temple. I have always assumed that the followers of Christ were in grave danger in the weeks and months after the crucifixion, especially in Jerusalem, and, most especially, in the temple.

There is a classic picture of the Ascension, which shows the Apostles looking on as only the feet of Jesus are visible below the clouds. I sat with this mental picture, marveling at the power of language and imagination. The contrast between burying the body below ground, while the soul ascends up into Heaven, is reflected in the dualism of the theology. Ascent is better than descent. Soul is better than body. Heaven is better than Hell.

It is only natural that I have begun to reflect on the past thirty-five weeks, looking for the themes that have made a lasting impression. Very high on that list is the concept of *ascent through descent*, followed closely by *transcend and include*.

It is obvious why a society that buries its dead considers down rather less attractive than up! We worship a "Higher Power." We try to avoid "bottoms." We *sink* into despair, and *raise* our voices in adoration. Yet every transforming spiritual experience in my life has been the result of descent, of hitting a bottom, of being lost in darkness. There have been many high points of exquisite joy, but my experience is that these great highs have not been life-changing. *Metanoia, transformational change* has come from suffering. Moreover, the transformation has been greatest when my suffering has been deepest; when I have been most vulnerable. My greatest ascent has been the result of my deepest descent.

On most occasions, I have endeavored to "put my troubles behind me," to forget the bad and focus on the good. Again, this seems obviously better than relishing my depression or wallowing in self-pity. Somewhat counter intuitively, however, my experience has been that the transformation is more complete when I hold on to the bottom; when I transcend it, but include it in my "better life." This is something more than simply remembering the lessons I learned from the bad experience, or holding on to the pain.

It requires a shift in consciousness to at least a minimal level of non-duality. I have to truly see that the dark, or down, or bad is certainly not *all dark, all down, or all bad*. More than that, the *negative* played an essential role in defining and allowing the *positive*. Transformation requires that I honor, and hold onto the descent, celebrate the darkness, see Christ in the Cross. This is extremely hard for me to do.

Sitting with these two concepts—*ascent through descent* and *transcend and include*—I look around me at the glory of my tiny corner of the universe. Here in the garden there is no darkness, pain, suffering, or sin. I imagine the different places I have been in life, where virtually every aspect of my environment was dark, sin-filled suffering. By including that past in my present, I feel an overwhelming sense of gratitude. What amazing grace! How sweet these sounds! How great my joy!

May 16

Acts 2:1–4, The Coming of the Holy Spirit
  ¹ When the day of Pentecost had come, they were all together in one place. ² And suddenly from heaven there came a sound like the rush of a violent wind, and it filled the entire house where they were sitting. ³ Divided tongues, as of fire, appeared among them, and a tongue rested on each of them. ⁴ All of them were filled with the Holy Spirit and began to speak in other languages, as the Spirit gave them ability.

AS I SAT WITH this passage from Acts, I struggled with the image of a tongue resting on me, giving me the power to speak in a foreign language. I have been blessed (or forced!) to learn to speak four different foreign languages on a conversational level. I am certain that many of the people who have listened to me carry on in any one of those languages would suggest that the tongue from Acts was stuck in my teeth! One of my good friends, a nun from Futuro Vivo, says that my Spanish hurts her ears.

Actually, I take very seriously the concept of the Holy Spirit helping us to speak foreign languages. Fifty years ago, I learned to speak passable German in a matter of weeks, and was conversing at a relatively sophisticated level in the first three months. I believed at the time that my prayers and meditation were partly responsible for the success of my language efforts. Reflecting on this for a moment, several thoughts occur to me.

First, no particular religion has the exclusive right to assistance from the Divine. I have not been a member of the Mormon Church since 1965. I owe no allegiance to them, rather, I have only recently dropped my resentment against the Mormons. Nonetheless, I continue to believe that Christ participated with me and my companions in the West German mission field. I believe He counseled me in my pastoral duties, using me as a vehicle through whom He could aid the sick and comfort those in distress. I believe I had divine assistance in learning German, dealing with my own loneliness as a new missionary, and serving as a leader in the mission.

Second, my experience in Germany did not feel like a tongue of fire, nor did I sense the active presence of Christ or the Holy Spirit. I did pray each day, asking for help. I believe the simple act of "hitting my knees," humbly requesting assistance, made a real difference. It focused my mind and energy on whatever it is for which I needed assistance. The form of the divine intervention may have been simply an increased focus, or higher level of energy. In other words, I have developed ways to rationalize my experience with God. I can describe it to skeptical secularists in a way that allows me to avoid being discounted as a "religious nut."

Matthew 6:6 suggests that we not parade our spirituality in public.

> But whenever you pray, go into your room and shut the door and pray to your Father who is in secret; and your Father who sees in secret will reward you.

While I take some comfort in this passage, I believe I have often been guilty of "hiding my light under a basket." There is a fine line between praying in secret and denying Christ. I have no interest in making my faith a public spectacle. I certainly want to avoid the kind of proselytizing I did in Germany. However, I am increasingly comfortable with people knowing that my faith matters a great deal to me.

In one sense, Sister Parish is a community development program, with projects and activities that could be done by the Peace Corps or any other secular organization. But Sister Parish is also Christ centered. We pray a lot, almost always in public. We talk about *encounter* a lot. We openly express our love, for each other, for the villagers, and for Christ. We hug a lot.

I ended my morning on my knees in front of the Rublev icon, focusing again on the concept of the Divine Dance. Faith is an active thing. It involves a constant flow of love between and among the members of the Trinity, between and among our families and close friends, between and among the community that is the Body of Christ. The single most powerful message of the past eight months is *oneness, the unity of Christ and all His creation.* Once again, like almost every day since I began the Exercises last September, I humbly, joyfully, and gratefully dance out of the library, down the rill, and into this glorious day.

May 17

Acts 2:5–36

⁵ Now there were devout Jews from every nation under heaven living in Jerusalem. ⁶ And at this sound the crowd gathered and was bewildered, because each one heard them speaking in the native language of each. ⁷ Amazed and astonished, they asked, "Are not all these who are speaking Galileans? ⁸ And how is it that we hear, each of us, in our own native language? ⁹ Parthians, Medes, Elamites, and residents of Mesopotamia, Judea and Cappadocia, Pontus and Asia, ¹⁰ Phrygia and Pamphylia, Egypt and the parts of Libya belonging to Cyrene, and visitors from Rome, both Jews and proselytes, ¹¹ Cretans and Arabs—in our own languages we hear them speaking about God's deeds of power." ¹² All were amazed and perplexed, saying to one another, "What does this mean?" ¹³ But others sneered and said, "They are filled with new wine."

Peter Addresses the Crowd

¹⁴ But Peter, standing with the eleven, raised his voice and addressed them, "Men of Judea and all who live in Jerusalem, let this be known to you, and listen to what I say. ¹⁵ Indeed, these are not drunk, as you suppose, for it is only nine o'clock in the morning. ¹⁶ No, this is what was spoken through the prophet Joel:

[17] 'In the last days it will be, God declares, that I will pour out my Spirit upon all flesh, and your sons and your daughters shall prophesy, and your young men shall see visions, and your old men shall dream dreams. [18] Even upon my slaves, both men and women, in those days I will pour out my Spirit; and they shall prophesy. [19] And I will show portents in the heaven above and signs on the earth below, blood, and fire, and smoky mist. [20] The sun shall be turned to darkness and the moon to blood, before the coming of the Lord's great and glorious day. [21] Then everyone who calls on the name of the Lord shall be saved.' [22] "You that are Israelites, listen to what I have to say: Jesus of Nazareth, a man attested to you by God with deeds of power, wonders, and signs that God did through him among you, as you yourselves know— [23] this man, handed over to you according to the definite plan and foreknowledge of God, you crucified and killed by the hands of those outside the law. [24] But God raised him up, having freed him from death, because it was impossible for him to be held in its power. [25] For David says concerning him,

I saw the Lord always before me, for he is at my right hand so that I will not be shaken; [26] therefore my heart was glad, and my tongue rejoiced; moreover, my flesh will live in hope. [27] For you will not abandon my soul to Hades, or let your Holy One experience corruption. [28] You have made known to me the ways of life; you will make me full of gladness with your presence.'

[29] "Fellow Israelites, I may say to you confidently of our ancestor David that he both died and was buried, and his tomb is with us to this day. [30] Since he was a prophet, he knew that God had sworn with an oath to him that he would put one of his descendants on his throne. [31] Foreseeing this, David spoke of the resurrection of the Messiah, saying,

'He was not abandoned to Hades, nor did his flesh experience corruption.'

[32] This Jesus God raised up, and of that all of us are witnesses. [33] Being therefore exalted at the right hand of God, and having received from the Father the promise of the Holy Spirit, he has poured out this that you both see and hear. [34] For David did not ascend into the heavens, but he himself says,

'The Lord said to my Lord, sit at my right hand, [35] until I make your enemies your footstool.'"

[36] Therefore let the entire house of Israel know with certainty that God has made him both Lord and Messiah, this Jesus whom you crucified."

SPRING IS in full glory here in Ponte Vedra Beach. Unlike later in the summer, the breeze blowing up the lagoon this morning is cool. Sitting in the garden, under the cloudless sky, next to the glistening water, is simply delightful. At these moments, surrounded by His creation, basking in His abundant blessings, I feel Christ in me, and all around me.

Uncle Jim Finley says that we should "find that act, which, when you give yourself over to it with your whole heart, it takes you to the deeper place." For me, that act is sitting in the meditation garden. It is walking from the library along the rill. It is listening with intention to the sounds of creation— the birds, the waves, the rustling in the bushes as Maggie searches for lizards. These acts take me to a deeper place, one where I am present to His Presence, attuned to His voice, quiet in His peace.

In only three days, the Exercises will end. What an extraordinary blessing to go out this way, overflowing with this powerful sense of being loved. Verse 26 of the passage from Acts speaks to me today.

...my heart was glad, and my tongue rejoiced; moreover, my flesh will live in hope...

Luke talks about God "pouring" the Holy Spirit out to us. Reflecting on that image, I remember Meister Eckhart writing about *bullitio*, literally the "boiling" of the inner life of the Trinity, which become *ebullition*, the "boiling over" of God's love into the love of all creation. As God pours out His love for me, a love that is so great that it continuously boils over in God, I am filled beyond my capacity. His love lights a fire in me, it "boils" in me. It demands that I allow it to boil over, then pour it out to others. This is a powerful image. I become ebullient!

Paul touches on the same concept in his first letter to the Thessalonians, chapter 3, verse 12:

> May the Lord make your love increase and overflow for each other and for everyone else,
> just as ours does for you.

God's love may be gentle and peaceful. But it is absolutely not passive, nor does it invite, or even allow, passivity in us. He "gently demands" that we be transformed by His love, then pass it on to others through service.

Another one of my favorite lines in this passage from Acts continues to speak to me:

> …your young men shall see visions, and your old men shall dream dreams…

I was a visionary young man. I longed for a better world, one I envisioned with greater equality, no war, and no poverty. I spent much of my life working toward that vision, but with extremely little success. I think I was moving too fast, taking very little time to experience at depth the world around me. Sitting in the garden each morning, I now "smell the flowers," realizing as I do so that it is not something I have done much in the past.

Now, as an old man, I dream dreams that are less ambitious. Pope Francis said this very morning in Rome that "Our God is a dreamer, who dreams of the transformation of the world." I love that. Sadly, I suspect I will leave this world in roughly the same shape as I found it, or worse.

I dream a lot about God. I see a great deal of unity in the tiny part of the world where I live, but it is largely unity in the absence of diversity. It is not a community united by love. I often dream about Sister Parish. In those dreams, God's love is pouring out over people from very different backgrounds and with radically unequal resources. His love unites them nonetheless. I am caught up in the harmonious union of that dream.

Occasionally, I realize that I am not dreaming. I am sitting in the circle under the cross at the retreat center. Or I am taking food to the elderly in Mamey. Or I am painting the wall of a new house or chapel. Christ is tangibly present. The oneness is not a dream. His love has united us with Him, with each other, and with His creation.

In the same speech this morning, the Pope said that the joy of Christ does not come "in dribs and drabs with an eyedropper, but as a waterfall that will envelop one's whole life." Eckhart would have loved this Pope! I end the morning drowning in a waterfall of joy.

May 18

Repeat The Contemplation for Learning to Love like God

GOD WANTS us to love Him and all of His creation. He wants us to love the way He loves. Unconditionally. Universally. Radically. Intently.

That sounds like such a tall order, but if we can get past our ego, it is entirely achievable. It is the ego that places conditions on love; that limits love to certain specifics; that loves superficially, or loves casually.

Eckhart famously said,

To be full of things is to be empty of God. To be empty of things is to be full of God.

John of the Cross said the way to that love is *nada*, nothing. "If a man wishes to be sure of the road he's traveling on, then he must close his eyes and travel in the dark." In his iconic map of Mt. Carmel, John offers poetic guidance along the sides of the path up the mountain.

To come to savour all, seek to find savour in nothing;
To come to possess all, seek possession in nothing,
To come to be all, seek in all to be nothing....
To come to what you know not, you must go by way where you know not,
To come to what you are not, you must go by a way where you are not.

We are asked again today to contemplate learning how to love like God. Reflecting on these past eight months, it occurs to me that this task, learning to love like God, is the primary purpose of the Exercises. Ignatius was so transformed by his conversion that he completely changed his life, dedicating his remaining thirty-three years to God. I am reasonably certain that Ignatius would never say that he had learned completely how to love like God. Rather, I think he would say that he devoted his life to that project—learning to love like God. I suspect he was still learning the day that he died.

To some extent, the whole idea of Spiritual Exercises flies in the face of the advice from John of the Cross. John exhorted us to nothing. Are the Exercises not doing something, seeking something, finding something? This morning, my answer to that is that the Exercises provide a path only to *the beginning point of the journey to nothing.*

Daily prayer, meditation, reflection, and contemplation prepare us "to come to what we know not, going by way where we know not." If I have succeeded in these Exercises, I am now well prepared to commence the journey. I know that I don't know.

Of course, this is not totally the case. I know that God loves me, which leads to the obvious conclusion that I must be lovable. I know that He has commanded me to love Him, and His creation, in return. I know that serving Him is loving Him. I know that I cannot "bank" miles on this journey. My love for Him and His creation yesterday is simply that, yesterday. I begin my love anew each moment, and my love lasts only for as long as I continue to love.

Reflecting on how much I know in my "unknowing," I feel good about next steps. God never asks us to do what he does not empower us to do.

I walked back down to the meditation bench. Nostalgic would be a good description of how I feel. The beauty of this place, the layer upon layer of wonderful memories, the immediacy of Christ's presence, the love that enfolds me, and the love that is evoked from me by this place and all that it represents—all of this fills me to overflowing. This morning, again, I am truly ebullient!

May 19

Ephesians 4:7–16
[7] But each of us was given grace according to the measure of Christ's gift. [8] Therefore it is said,
"When he ascended on high he made captivity itself a captive; he gave gifts to his people."

⁹ (When it says, "He ascended," what does it mean but that he had also descended into the lower parts of the earth? ¹⁰ He who descended is the same one who ascended far above all the heavens, so that he might fill all things.) ¹¹ The gifts he gave were that some would be apostles, some prophets, some evangelists, some pastors and teachers, ¹² to equip the saints for the work of ministry, for building up the body of Christ, ¹³ until all of us come to the unity of the faith and of the knowledge of the Son of God, to maturity, to the measure of the full stature of Christ. ¹⁴ We must no longer be children, tossed to and fro and blown about by every wind of doctrine, by people's trickery, by their craftiness in deceitful scheming. ¹⁵ But speaking the truth in love, we must grow up in every way into him who is the head, into Christ, ¹⁶ from whom the whole body, joined and knit together by every ligament with which it is equipped, as each part is working properly, promotes the body's growth in building itself up in love.

REFLECTING on this passage from Ephesians this morning, I thought about the idea of the universe evolving through stages of consciousness. I wrote about it in the first few weeks of the Exercises last fall. Look at verses 14 and 15.

> We must no longer be children…but speaking the truth in love, we must grow up in every way into him who is the head, into Christ.

Teilhard, Father Rohr, Ken Wilbur, and many of the mystics down through the ages have been teaching us about growing up, evolving through the stages of consciousness. The goal of evolution, both of the universe and of each of us as individual parts of that universe, is to grow into unity with Christ. And we must do so by "speaking the truth in love"! This is a powerful message.

Over the past five years, all of my teachers, both those I have met and listened to in person, and those I have only met in books, have accepted as fundamental the idea that *God is love*. God loves us and all of His creation. "God so loves the world that He gave His one and only Son."

Julian of Norwich wrote that because we have been loved in God's mind "from without beginning…our life is everlasting." She wrote that she had learned from her "shewings" that love was the meaning of all Christ's revelations.

How casually I say that God is love, or Christ is love. The words are simple. The concept is overwhelming. God loves me into being me, right here, right now. His love makes this garden and all the life in it. His love makes my enemies, along with my friends. His love sets out the rules of engagement for my life.

May 20

Romans 8:8–27

⁸ and those who are in the flesh cannot please God.

⁹ But you are not in the flesh; you are in the Spirit, since the Spirit of God dwells in you. Anyone who does not have the Spirit of Christ does not belong to him. ¹⁰ But if Christ is in you, though the body is dead because of sin, the Spirit is life because of righteousness. ¹¹ If the Spirit of him who raised Jesus from the dead dwells in you, he who raised Christ from the dead will give life to your mortal bodies also through his Spirit that dwells in you.

¹² So then, brothers and sisters, we are debtors, not to the flesh, to live according to the flesh— ¹³ for if you live according to the flesh, you will die; but if by the Spirit you put to death the deeds of the body, you will live. ¹⁴ For all who are led by the Spirit of God are children of God. ¹⁵ For you did not receive a spirit of slavery to fall back into fear, but you have received a spirit of adoption. When we cry, "Abba! Father!" ¹⁶ it is that very Spirit bearing witness with our spirit that we are children of God, [17] *and if children, then heirs, heirs of God and joint heirs with Christ—if, in fact, we suffer with him so that we may also be glorified with him.*

Future Glory

[18] *I consider that the sufferings of this present time are not worth comparing with the glory about to be revealed to us.* [19] *For the creation waits with eager longing for the revealing of the children of God;* [20] *for the creation was subjected to futility, not of its own will but by the will of the one who subjected it, in hope* [21] *that the creation itself will be set free from its bondage to decay and will obtain the freedom of the glory of the children of God.* [22] *We know that the whole creation has been groaning in labor pains until now;* [23] *and not only the creation, but we ourselves, who have the first fruits of the Spirit, groan inwardly while we wait for adoption, the redemption of our bodies.* [24] *For in hope we were saved. Now hope that is seen is not hope. For who hopes for what is seen?* [25] *But if we hope for what we do not see, we wait for it with patience.*

[26] *Likewise the Spirit helps us in our weakness; for we do not know how to pray as we ought, but that very Spirit intercede with sighs too deep for words.* [27] *And God, who searches the heart, knows what is the mind of the Spirit, because the Spirit intercedes for the saints according to the will of God.*

I REALIZED this morning that it was five years ago today that Sallie Ann and I met Father Rohr in Assisi, Italy. What an incredible coincidence! Little did I know how much that meeting would change my life. I am deeply grateful to Father Rohr for all that he has done—and caused to be done—in and for my life, my faith, and my joy.

Maggie and I walked down to the meditation garden slowly this morning, savoring the knowledge that this is the last day of the Exercises. Of course, the fountain, the rill, and the garden will be here tomorrow, along with all the rest of this spectacular universe. Each morning for the past two hundred and forty-four days we have communed with God surrounded by, and filled with, His creation! I hope and intend that I will continue to meditate, pray, and reflect. I readily admit, however, that the Exercises have provided a discipline that will not easily be replaced. I will miss the discipline.

I read through the passage from Paul's letter to the Romans last night, and again this morning. Generally, this passage captures the essence of my faith. I believe the "Spirit dwells within" me, and all of God's creatures.

Typically, however, Paul adds a bit of exclusivity, which produces my customary negative reaction. For example, the line, "Anyone who does not have the Spirit of Christ does not belong to him.," is, for me, unnecessary. I believe the Spirit of Christ is in all of creation; that everyone "has the spirit of Christ" and, therefore, everyone and everything belongs to Him. I do not believe there is a place called Heaven where only the select few will go. Nor do I accept the concept of a place called Hell for all the rest.

Catherine of Siena said that:

The path to heaven lies through heaven, and all the way to heaven is heaven.

I believe this is just as true for the path to Hell. We choose the path we take, toward Heaven or toward Hell. The path to Heaven runs toward God. The path to Hell runs away from God. Until or unless we change directions, we are in Heaven or Hell from the first step. Changing directions requires a fundamental change in our thoughts, words, and deeds.

Significantly, both Heaven and Hell are right here, right now. They are not places or states of mind that await us at our death, nor are the choices we make permanent. Also, applying this logic, I can be moving away from God all my life, but the instant I turn around toward God, I enter Heaven, even if only for that instant.

As it is often said, just as God creates us momently with His love, we make the decision momently whether to be in Heaven or Hell. Years of choosing Heaven can be wiped out in a nanosecond when we make the wrong choice, just as a long career in Hell can be ended immediately.

Reflecting on this, I fear it makes life seem very tenuous and uncertain. A life repeatedly shifting back and forth between Heaven and Hell seems far from peaceful. In truth, a life characterized by repeated decisions to separate ourselves from God is not peaceful. Perversely, I can imagine there is a certain amount of stability in a continuous life of sin, though it is certainly not peace.

This morning, I choose God. In fact, I am experiencing a run of good choices. While I do not believe that I can create a credit balance of good choices, I do think there is such a thing as momentum. Whichever way I am going, away from God or toward God, my momentum acts as a support for my present choice; as resistance to a different choice. In other words, if I have regularly been making poor choices, a single good choice will not abruptly change the direction of my life. The momentum of all the poor choices will act to resist change. Likewise, a single poor choice will face a certain amount of resistance from positive momentum.

The momentum in my life today is toward God. There are many reasons for that. The past eight months of these Exercises have deepened my commitment to grow closer to oneness with God, both intellectually and spiritually. Sallie Ann is a powerful source of support for the good choices that created that momentum.

The Living School launched me on an amazing intellectual journey. I have read and studied the teaching and writing of some incredible men and women, whose work over the past two thousand years has shed light on every aspect of our existence and its purpose. Each day, I read or listen to something new. Each day, I revisit one or more of the great mystics of the past. And every day I am renewed by the experience. My head space is filled with much more than I can recall!

The Sister Parish Ministry introduced me to the deep encounter of service. Each day that I meet and hear the story of another new person, my heart is fed. Sometimes, it is a missionary from Ponte Vedra Beach, or a volunteer from one of the parishes in the Dominican Republic. Very often, it is one of the villagers in Mamey, or a resident of Hogar San Jose, or a visitor at the St. Francis Soup Kitchen.

Service is about authentic encounter at depth; about going beyond the superficial to discover and share the essence of the other. Sister Parish allows and facilitates these encounters. Service fills my heart space to overflowing.

My heart also grows each time I encounter some aspect of myself that had theretofore been hidden or unnoticed. I grow when I laugh deeply. I grow when I weep.

What is really going on in all of these encounters is complete surrender to the Cosmic Christ. The joy in the encounters is Christ. The love that envelops me, that reaches into my soul and calls out the best in me, is Christ. Christ is present in the smiles on the faces of the children and in the tears on the cheeks of the elderly. Christ worships in the chapels we build. Christ lives in the houses we build. The ultimate encounter is Christ.

ABOUT THE AUTHOR

BOB HART co-founded and chairs the Sister Parish Ministry of Our Lady Star of the Sea Catholic Church, a program of spiritual growth and discovery, which works through service to communities of Haitian migrant workers in the Dominican Republic. He is on the board of Ability Housing and the Jacksonville World Affairs Council. He retired in 2007 from a thirty-year energy career that began in the coalfields of West Virginia and extended to the electric power industries of more than thirty countries throughout Eastern Europe, Africa, Asia, and Latin America. Mr. Hart holds an AB, magna cum laude, from Harvard University.

CPSIA information can be obtained
at www.ICGtesting.com
Printed in the USA
BVOW04*2012080817

491515BV00002B/2/P